Advances in Infrared and Raman Spectroscopy

VOLUME 5

Advances in Infrared and Raman Spectroscopy

Edited by R. J. H. Clark and R. E. Hester

Contents of Previous Volumes

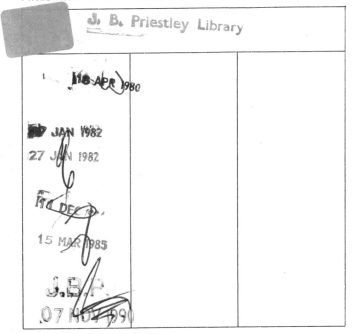

Advances in Infrared and Raman Spectroscopy

VOLUME 5

Edited by

R. J. H. CLARK
University College, London

R. E. HESTER
University of York

London · Philadelphia · Rheine

Heyden & Son Ltd., Spectrum House, Hillview Gardens, London NW4 2JQ
Heyden & Son Inc., 247 South 41st Street, Philadelphia, PA 19104, U.S.A.
Heyden & Son GmbH, Münsterstrasse 22, 4440 Rheine, Germany

ISBN 0 85501 185 8

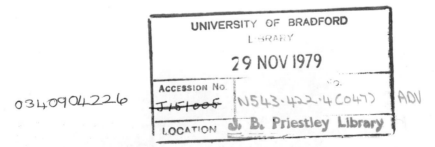

Set by Eta Services (Typesetters) Ltd., Beccles, Suffolk.
Printed litho and bound in Great Britain
by W & J Mackay Ltd, Chatham.

CONTENTS

CHAPTER 1: High Resolution Infrared Spectroscopy with Tunable
Lasers—
Robin S. McDowell

CHAPTER 2: The Vibrational Spectra of Carbon Monoxide
Chemisorbed on the Surfaces of Metal Calalysts—
A Suggested Scheme of Interpretation—
N. Sheppard and T. T. Nguyen

CHAPTER 3: The Vibrational Spectroscopy of Water—
         James R. Scherer

CHAPTER 4: Resonance Raman Spectroscopy of Nucleic Acids—
         Yoshifumi Nishimura, Akiko Y. Hirakawa and
         Masamichi Tsuboi

CHAPTER 5: Recent Advances in Microwave Spectroscopy—
         J. Sheridan

LIST OF CONTRIBUTORS

B. N. CYVIN, Division of Physical Chemistry, The University of Trondheim, N-7034 Trondheim-NTH, Norway (p. 322).

S. J. CYVIN, Division of Physical Chemistry, The University of Trondheim, N-7034 Trondheim-NTH, Norway (p. 322).

A. Y. HIRAKAWA, Faculty of Pharmaceutical Sciences, University of Tokyo, Hongo, Bunkyo-ku, Tokyo, Japan (p. 217).

R. S. MCDOWELL, University of California, Los Alamos Scientific Laboratory, Los Alamos, New Mexico 87545, U.S.A. (p. 1).

T. T. NGUYEN, School of Chemical Sciences, University of East Anglia, Norwich NR4 7TJ, U.K. (p. 67).

Y. NISHIMURA, Faculty of Pharmaceutical Sciences, University of Tokyo, Hongo, Bunkyo-ku, Tokyo, Japan (p. 217).

J. R. SCHERER, Western Regional Research Center, Science and Education Administration, U.S. Department of Agriculture, Berkeley, California 94710, U.S.A. (p. 149).

N. SHEPPARD, F.R.S., School of Chemical Sciences, University of East Anglia, Norwich NR4 7TJ, U.K. (p. 67).

J. SHERIDAN, School of Physical and Molecular Sciences, University College of North Wales, Bangor, U.K. (p. 276).

M. TSUBOI, Faculty of Pharmaceutical Sciences, University of Tokyo, Hongo, Bunkyo-ku, Tokyo, Japan (p. 217).

J. C. WHITMER, Department of Chemistry, Western Washington State University, Bellingham, Washington 98225, U.S.A. (p. 322).

PREFACE TO VOLUME 1

There are few areas of science which have not already benefited from the application of infrared spectroscopic methods, and progress in this field remains vigorous. Closely related information on chemical and biological materials and systems is obtainable from Raman spectroscopy, though there are also many important differences between the types of information yielded and the types of materials and systems best suited to study by each technique. The close relationship between these two sets of spectroscopic techniques is explicitly recognized in this Series. Advances in Infrared and Raman Spectroscopy contains critical review articles, both fundamental and applied, mainly within the title areas; however, we shall extend the coverage into closely related areas by giving some space to such topics as neutron inelastic scattering or vibronic fluorescence spectroscopy. Thus the Series will be firmly technique orientated. Inasmuch as these techniques have such wide ranging applicability throughout science and engineering, however, the coverage in terms of topics will be wide. Already in the first volume we have articles ranging from the fundamental theory of infrared band intensities through the development of computer-controlled spectrometer systems to applications in biology. This integration of theory and practice, and the bringing together of different areas of academic and industrial science and technology, constitute major objectives of the Series.

The reviews will be in those subjects in which most progress is deemed to have been made in recent years, or is expected to be made in the near future. The Series will appeal to research scientists and technologists as well as to graduate students and teachers of advanced courses. The Series is intended to be of wide general interest both within and beyond the fields of chemistry, physics and biology.

The problem of nomenclature in a truly international Series has to be acknowledged. We have adopted a compromise solution of permitting the use of either English or American spelling (depending on the origin of the review article) and have recommended the use of SI Units. A table on the international system of units is given on p. xv for reference purposes.

R. J. H. CLARK
R. E. HESTER

PREFACE

The present volume continues the policy established by the Editors for earlier Volumes of this Series of commissioning critical review articles in both fundamental and applied aspects of infrared and Raman spectroscopy, as well as in topics closely allied to these. The Volume opens with an authoritative and timely survey of the progress which has been made in the development and application of tunable infrared lasers since the first such device was realized about a decade ago. An illustration of the resolving power provided is given by the v_3 stretching fundamental of SF_6. Within this single band approximately 10 000 vibration–rotation transitions now have been observed and assigned through the technique of sub-Doppler saturation spectroscopy. The relative merits and performance characteristics of the various laser sources are discussed and an extensive survey of the experimental techniques for their use in high resolution spectroscopy, including applications to atmospheric studies and pollution monitoring, is presented with great clarity and breadth of detail. The ever-current topic of chemisorption at catalytically active metal surfaces is examined in the second chapter, the adsorption of carbon monoxide providing a focus for an in-depth discussion of mechanisms. A scheme for the interpretation of vibrational spectra is proposed, following a comprehensive review of results for CO on a wide variety of metal surfaces. In Chapter 3 an expert examination is made of the controversy regarding the interpretation of vibrational spectra of liquid water in terms of its structure. Previous over-ambitious interpretations are criticized and the extensive data are re-evaluated in arriving at a final set of structural conclusions. The molecular biology content of this Series is expanded in the next chapter. This is devoted to the relatively new field of resonance Raman studies of nucleic acids. The technique is seen to provide a sensitive probe for characterizing the structures of these important biopolymers. The wealth of detail which is presented on the vibrational modes of the component base residues will be found invaluable by others working in this area. Chapter 5 contains a review of recent advances in microwave spectroscopy. The information presented on molecular structures and energetics bears closely upon problems which are of interest to vibrational spectroscopists. Mean amplitudes of vibration for organic molecules are reviewed in the final chapter. This includes an outline of the theory and a discussion of the implications of mean amplitudes as well as a survey of available data.

As with earlier Volumes, we have favoured IUPAC nomenclature and the use of SI units. To aid the reader, a table of SI units and conversion factors from the units of other systems to SI units is included on pages xv–xvii.

May 1978   R. J. H. CLARK
                                                           R. E. HESTER

THE INTERNATIONAL SYSTEM OF UNITS (SI)

Physical quantity	Name of unit	Symbol for unit

SI Base Units

length	metre	m
mass	kilogram	kg
time	second	s
electric current	ampere	A
thermodynamic temperature	kelvin	K
amount of substance	mole	mol

SI Supplementary Units

plane angle	radian	rad
solid angle	steradian	sr

SI Derived Units having Special Names and Symbols

energy	joule	$J = m^2\,kg\,s^{-2}$
force	newton	$N = m\,kg\,s^{-2} = J\,m^{-1}$
pressure	pascal	$Pa = m^{-1}\,kg\,s^{-2} = N\,m^{-2} = J\,m^{-3}$
power	watt	$W = m^2\,kg\,s^{-3} = J\,s^{-1}$
electric charge	coulomb	$C = s\,A$
electric potential difference	volt	$V = m^2\,kg\,s^{-3}\,A^{-1} = J\,A^{-1}\,s^{-1}$
electric resistance	ohm	$\Omega = m^2\,kg\,s^{-3}\,A^{-2} = V\,A^{-1}$
electric conductance	siemens	$S = m^{-2}\,kg^{-1}\,s^3\,A^2 = \Omega^{-1}$
electric capacitance	farad	$F = m^{-2}\,kg^{-1}\,s^4\,A^2 = C\,V^{-1}$
magnetic flux	weber	$Wb = m^2\,kg\,s^{-2}\,A^{-1} = V\,s$
inductance	henry	$H = m^2\,kg\,s^{-2}\,A^{-2} = V\,s\,A^{-1}$
magnetic flux density	tesla	$T = kg\,s^{-2}\,A^{-1} = V\,s\,m^{-2}$
frequency	hertz	$Hz = s^{-1}$

SOME NON-SI UNITS

Physical quantity	Name of unit	Symbol and definition

Decimal Multiples of SI Units, Some having Special Names and Symbols

length	ångström	$\text{Å} = 10^{-10}$ m $= 0.1$ nm $= 100$ pm
length	micron	$\mu\text{m} = 10^{-6}$ m
area	are	$a = 100$ m^2
area	barn	$b = 10^{-28}$ m^2
volume	litre	$l = 10^{-3}$ m$^3 = $ dm^3 $= 10^3$ cm^3
energy	erg	$\text{erg} = 10^{-7}$ J
force	dyne	$\text{dyn} = 10^{-5}$ N
force constant	dyne per centimetre	$\text{dyn cm}^{-1} = 10^{-3}$ N m^{-1}
force constant	millidyne per ångström	$\text{mdyn Å}^{-1} = 10^2$ N m^{-1}
force constant	attojoule per ångström squared	$\text{aJ Å}^{-2} = 10^2$ N m^{-1}
pressure	bar	$\text{bar} = 10^5$ Pa
concentration	—	$M = 10^3$ mol m^{-3} $= $ mol dm^{-3}

Units Defined Exactly in Terms of SI Units

length	inch	in $= 0.0254$ m
mass	pound	lb $= 0.453\ 592\ 27$ kg
force	kilogram-force	kgf $= 9.806\ 65$ N
pressure	standard atmosphere	atm $= 101\ 325$ Pa
pressure	torr	Torr $= 1$ mmHg $= (101\ 325/760)$ Pa
energy	kilowatt hour	kW h $= 3.6 \times 10^6$ J
energy	thermochemical calorie	$\text{cal}_{\text{th}} = 4.184$ J
thermodynamic temperature	degree Celsius[a]	$^\circ\text{C} = \text{K}$

[a]Celsius or "Centigrade" temperature θ_C is defined in terms of the thermodynamic temperature T by the relation $\theta_C/^\circ\text{C} = T/\text{K} - 273.15$.

OTHER RELATIONS

1. The physical quantity, the wavenumber (units cm^{-1}), is related to frequency as follows:

$$cm^{-1} \approx (2.998 \times 10^{10})^{-1} \, s^{-1}$$

2. The physical quantity, the molar decadic absorption coefficient (symbol ϵ) has the SI units $m^2 \, mol^{-1}$. The relation between the usual non-SI and SI units is as follows:

$$M^{-1} \, cm^{-1} = 1 \, mol^{-1} \, cm^{-1} = 10^{-1} \, m^2 \, mol^{-1}$$

3. It appears that for many years to come a knowledge of the 'electromagnetic CGS' unit system will be a necessity for workers in various fields of spectroscopy, but for practical purposes it is usually sufficient to note that for magnetic flux density, 1 gauss (G) corresponds to 10^{-4} T and for electric dipole moment, 1 debye (D) corresponds to approximately 3.3356×10^{-30} C m.

The SI Prefixes

Fraction	Prefix	Symbol	Multiple	Prefix	Symbol
10^{-1}	deci	d	10^1	deca	da
10^{-2}	centi	c	10^2	hecto	h
10^{-3}	milli	m	10^3	kilo	k
10^{-6}	micro	μ	10^6	mega	M
10^{-9}	nano	n	10^9	giga	G
10^{-12}	pico	p	10^{12}	tera	T
10^{-15}	femto	f	10^{15}	peta	P
10^{-18}	atto	a	10^{18}	exa	E

Chapter 1

HIGH RESOLUTION INFRARED SPECTROSCOPY WITH TUNABLE LASERS†

Robin S. McDowell

University of California, Los Alamos Scientific Laboratory,
Los Alamos, New Mexico 87545, U.S.A.

1 INTRODUCTION

About a decade ago it first became possible to obtain very high resolution spectra in the infrared region by using tunable narrow-linewidth laser sources. Since then the literature in this field has grown so rapidly that any review short of a full-length book must necessarily be limited in scope. The present approach will be to introduce the spectroscopist who is familiar with the traditional grating and interferometric instruments to the different tunable infrared sources available and the types of spectroscopic information they have been yielding over the past few years. The emphasis will be on Doppler-limited linear absorption spectroscopy, but such exciting and powerful techniques as sub-Doppler saturation spectroscopy and double-resonance methods will be covered briefly insofar as they use broadly tunable sources (as opposed to molecular-gas-laser sources that operate on one or more individual lines). Several useful reviews on infrared laser spectroscopy have appeared recently,[1-8] and the reader who is seriously interested in this field is encouraged to consult these; other reviews on individual topics will be cited in the appropriate sections.

For the purposes of this review 'infrared' is taken to mean the region between 2 and 200 μm, and 'high resolution' to mean a resolving power capable of accurately following the Doppler contours of small molecules at room temperature, which is to say resolutions of at least 10^{-3}–10^{-4} cm^{-1}. *Temporal* resolution will not be considered here, but it should be mentioned that picosecond spectroscopy employing laser pulses with durations of 10^{-12} s or less is an increasingly important tool for the investigation of relaxation processes, radiationless transitions, and other short-lived phenomena.[6,9,10]

† This work was supported by the United States Department of Energy.

1

The impact of laser spectroscopy can be appreciated from Fig. 1, which shows a thoroughly studied infrared absorption band, the v_3 stretching fundamental of SF_6 at 10.55 μm, at four different stages of resolution. The first reported spectrum, obtained in 1934 with a prism spectrometer,[11] showed only a featureless absorption; this was true also of several other spectra published over the next 30 years. In 1969 Brunet and Perez[12] recorded the band at a resolution

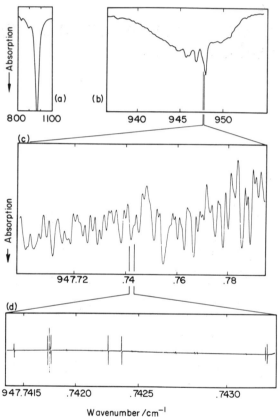

Wavenumber /cm⁻¹

Fig. 1. The infrared-active stretching fundamental v_3 of SF_6 at 300 K, as it appears with increasing resolving power. (a) Early prism spectrum (Eucken and Ahrens, Ref. 11). The band appears to be at 965 cm⁻¹ because of poor frequency calibration. (b) Spectrum obtained with a Girard 'grille' grating spectrometer at 0.07 cm⁻¹ resolution (Brunet and Perez, Ref. 12). (c) Doppler-limited spectrum of a portion of the Q branch, recorded using a tunable semiconductor diode laser at a resolution of 3×10^{-6} cm⁻¹ (Hinkley, 1970; cf. McDowell et al., Ref. 13). The Doppler linewidth at 300 K is 9.7×10^{-4} cm⁻¹ (f.w.h.m.). (d) Sub-Doppler saturation spectrum recorded (in the derivative mode) inside the gain profile of the $P(16)$ line of a CO_2 laser; effective resolution better than 10⁻⁶ cm⁻¹ (Clairon and Henry, Ref. 14). About 10⁴ such scans would be required to cover this one band completely. All of the lines shown in (c) and (d) have been identified; the center line of the triplet at 947.7417 cm⁻¹ in (d) is v_3 $Q(38)$ E^0 (McDowell et al., Ref. 13; Loëte et al., Ref. 15).

of 0.07 cm^{-1}, which represents about the best that most grating spectrometers can do; the P,Q,R-branch contour and some additional Q branches due to hot bands were resolved, but no individual rotational lines were seen. Within a year Hinkley had used a tunable diode laser to record portions of the band at Doppler-limited resolution, revealing for the first time a dense vibration-rotation structure that has taken some years to unravel.[13] At about the same time saturation techniques (Section 6) were being used to obtain sub-Doppler spectra of small regions near the CO_2 laser lines; a recent example[14] of such a scan is shown in Fig 1(d). Portions of this spectrum have been recorded at a scale expansion such that some 50 miles of chart paper would be required to cover the whole v_3 band! Approximately 10 000 vibration–rotation transitions have now been observed in this one fundamental band, and all have been assigned. Clearly, the capability of achieving effective resolving powers of this order presents both new opportunities and new challenges to vibrational spectroscopists.

The tunable infrared laser sources that are presently available will be described in Section 2 of this review. This is a rapidly expanding field and the limits of resolution and power are being constantly extended, so this section will include accounts of some sources that have not yet demonstrated a high-resolution capability but that may yet be developed to this stage. Experimental techniques employing these devices will be considered in Section 3, including discussions of calibration problems and of some ·special techniques such as source modulation and specialized detection methods. Section 4 will review the spectroscopic results that have been obtained in band analysis, rotational fine structure, studies of line shapes and widths, and measurements of line and band intensities. Sections 5 and 6 will include brief discussions of tunable lasers in double resonance and saturation spectroscopy, and we will conclude with some examples of analytical applications in Section 7.

2 GENERATION OF TUNABLE MONOCHROMATIC INFRARED RADIATION

Over the last decade a vast literature has developed on tunable lasers. We will not review in detail the various devices that have been developed, but instead will attempt to give a general idea of the types of sources available and the levels of performance that can be expected from them. Most of the known tunable lasers operate in at least some portion of the 2–200 μm wavelength region of interest here; but organic dye lasers,[2,4,7,16−18] for example, are not included.

Table 1 presents one of several possible classifications of the tunable infrared lasers that have been described up to mid-1977, together with indications of their demonstrated spectral coverage, resolution, and power levels. Here 'continuous coverage' means that available in a single scan; a given device may cover a much larger frequency range, but with interruptions due to mode hopping or the

TABLE 1
Generation of tunable monochromatic infrared radiation

Device[a]	Spectral coverage overall/ μm	continuous/ cm^{-1}	Highest reported resolution/ cm^{-1}	Approximate power/W[b] c.w.	pulsed
*Semiconductor diode lasers	0.4–34	2	2×10^{-6}	$10^{-3}(0.3)$	$10(10^2)$
Gas lasers:					
*High-pressure gas lasers	9.1–12.5	10	$<3 \times 10^{-6}$	1	$10^6(3 \times 10^7)$
*Zeeman-tuned gas lasers	0.63–9^c	5	1×10^{-3}	10^{-3}	. . .
Raman scattering processes:					
*Spin-flip Raman lasers	~3.0	15	?	. . .	~10^2
	5.0–6.5	50	1×10^{-6}	1(3)	$10^2(10^4)$
	9.0–16.8	100	3×10^{-5}	. . .	$10^2(10^3)$
	87–100	15	~6	. . .	4×10^{-4}
Polariton lasers	16–20, 40–710	200	<0.5	. . .	$10(10^3)$
Raman frequency-shifting	0.7–15	1000	0.2	. . .	$10^4(10^8)$
Optical parametric oscillators	0.4–16.5	3000	$<1 \times 10^{-3}$	$10^{-3}(0.03)$	$10^2(10^7)$
Non-linear optical-mixing techniques:					
*Difference frequency generation	2.2–24.3	5	2×10^{-5}	10^{-6}	$0.1(10^4)$
	52–8300	150	3×10^{-6}	10^{-7}	$10^{-2}(0.2)$
*Infrared-microwave mixing	3.4	$<10^{-5}$	2×10^{-10}	?	. . .
	9–11	0.5	3×10^{-5}	$10^{-5}(10^{-3})$	. . .
Four-wave parametric mixing	2–31		0.07	. . .	$10^{-3}(3 \times 10^5)$
Miscellaneous lasers:					
Color-center lasers	0.88–3.3	500	10^{-6}?	$10^{-2}(0.1)$	. . .
Free-electron laser	3.4	?	7	. . .	10^4

  ^{a} Asterisks indicate devices that have actually been used for high resolution spectroscopy experiments.

  ^{b} Typical and (maximum).

  ^{c} Tunable only near discrete laser lines in this region.

necessity of changing optical components. Also, the 'best resolutions' listed here were measured under ideal conditions, and may normally be an order of magnitude or so poorer. It should be emphasized that both resolution and output power depend upon details of construction and operation, and may vary greatly with wavelength and operating conditions. Furthermore, high-power pulsed operation, which may be useful for photochemistry experiments, is generally not compatible with the high resolution c.w. operation that is desirable for spectroscopy. Many trade-offs are possible, and Table 1 is intended only to suggest the characteristics of the different devices.

2.1   Semiconductor Diode Lasers

Tunable semiconductor diode lasers (SDLs) have been used for most of the high resolution infrared spectroscopy that has been reported to date. They are about the least expensive and simplest to operate of any of the infrared laser systems, offer narrow linewidths and good frequency stability at modest power levels, and are widely tunable. They do require cryogenic cooling and suffer from uncontrollable mode qualities and a tendency to long-term degradation of performance (probably due to contact effects rather than to any inherent properties), but these disadvantages are no more formidable than those of most other tunable infrared devices. Several recent review articles are available that emphasize various aspects and applications of SDLs,[4,5,7,19-22] and the reader is referred to these for more detailed discussions than can be offered here.

The operation of SDLs can be sketched as follows. In an *intrinsic* semiconductor at low temperatures, all electrons are in the valence band (i.e. they participate in the chemical bonding of the crystal). An external electric field will raise some of these electrons to the conduction band, at which energies they are free to move about the crystal lattice, and will create corresponding holes in the valence band. The holes will migrate to the highest energy levels in the valence band; similarly, the electrons will migrate to the lowest energy levels in the conduction band, from which they can transfer to the valence band, recombine with a hole, and in the process emit a photon with a wavelength corresponding approximately to the semiconductor energy bandgap. *Extrinsic* semiconductors, such as are used for lasers, are doped with atoms that can accept an extra electron from, or donate one to, the crystal; the semiconductor is said to be *p*-type or *n*-type according to whether there is an excess of acceptor or donor atoms, respectively. When current is applied across a *p–n*-junction in a diode, electrons (from the *n*-type material) and holes (from the *p*-type material) are simultaneously injected into the junction region and their recombination creates photons. Each of these photons can induce further recombination, resulting in additional emitted photons, and laser action can result if the active region is contained in an optical resonator, such as can be furnished by the polished end faces of the semiconductor crystal. There is a threshold value for the current, typically a few hundred mA, above which the laser action dominates the combined losses due to spontaneous emission, absorption by free carriers, and penetration of light outside the active region.

Diodes have been designed to emit from visible frequencies throughout most of the infrared. The most useful for infrared spectroscopy in the 3–30 μm region are the lead–salt IV–VI pseudo-binary compounds such as $Pb_{1-x}Sn_xTe$. These materials offer the advantage that the bandgaps can be controlled by adjusting the chemical composition. This permits control over the spontaneous emission frequency v_s, which depends upon the bandgap; v_s is approximately a linear function of the alloy composition factor x:

$$v_s \approx v_0 + \delta x. \tag{1}$$

Values of v_0 and δ for the most important of these compounds are given in Table 2, taken from Hinkley *et al.*[5]

TABLE 2
Composition parameters for lead-salt semiconductor diode lasers[5]

Material	$\bar{\nu}_0/\text{cm}^{-1}$	δ/cm^{-1}	Composition range	Wavenumber range/cm^{-1}
$Pb_{1-x}Sn_xTe$	1540	-3837	$0 \leqslant x \leqslant 0.32$	312–1540
$Pb_{1-x}Ge_xTe$	1540	14 600	$0 \leqslant x \leqslant 0.05$	1540–2270
$Pb_{1-x}Sn_xSe$	1190	-8780	$0 \leqslant x \leqslant 0.10$	312–1190
	(-819)	5952	$0.19 \leqslant x \leqslant 0.40$	312–1562
$PbS_{1-x}Se_x$	2295	-1105	$0 \leqslant x \leqslant 1$	1190–2295
$Pb_{1-x}Cd_xS$	2295	29 396	$0 \leqslant x \leqslant 0.058$	2295–4000

The semiconductors are usually grown by crystallization from the vapor using a closed-tube growth technique. The *p–n* junction is created by diffusion, and the crystals are then cleaved into rectangular parallelopipeds with typical dimensions 0.5–1.0 mm long and 0.2 × 0.3 mm in cross-section (Fig. 2).[23] The end faces, which form the Fabry–Perot cavity, are polished, the side faces are etched to reduce their reflectance, and the faces parallel to the *p–n* junction are electroplated to provide ohmic contacts. The lower of these faces is bonded to an electrically grounded copper base that acts as a heat sink and is cryogenically cooled during operation, and the forward bias current that causes laser emission is introduced through a copper lead attached to the upper face. Several variations in this basic technique can greatly improve the performance. For example, diodes in which the *p–n* junction extends across the entire width of the crystal often operate in parasitic bounce modes with resulting poor beam patterns and low efficiency. This can be avoided by a 'stripe' geometry,[20,24] in which a

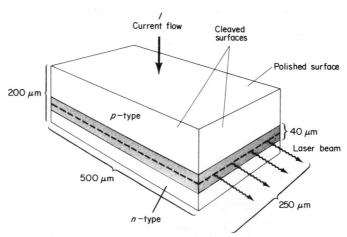

Fig. 2. Diagram of a typical lead–salt semiconductor diode laser. The dashed line shows the position of the *p–n* junction; the radiation is emitted from an area 40 × 250 μm (Steinfeld, Ref. 23).

p-type substrate is coated with an SiO_2 diffusion mask containing a single, central, lengthwise opening 20–100 μm wide; the n region is deposited on this and diffusion into the substrate and consequent p–n junction formation occurs only in this stripe region. The bounce modes are suppressed by the lossy oxide along the sides of the active region, and the diode operates principally in a single fundamental spatial mode, although some other weaker modes will usually lase also, especially at higher injection currents. If both the injected carriers and the emitted photons can be further confined to the active region in the other direction, the threshold current can be greatly reduced. This is accomplished in *heterostructure* diodes by bounding the active region with epitaxially grown regions of wider energy gap and different refractive index, as for example by evaporating layers of n-type PbTe on a p-type $Pb_{1-x}Sn_xTe$ substrate. Double-heterostructure stripe-geometry diodes fabricated by means of liquid-phase epitaxy have operated c.w. in the infrared at 80 K, and have been tuned from 10.5 μm at 12 K to <8.2 μm at 80 K.[25] Walpole et al.[26] have recently fabricated $Pb_{0.78}Sn_{0.22}Te$ diodes by molecular-beam epitaxy that operate c.w. to 114 K, with temperature tuning from 8.54 to 15.9 μm, a range of 540 cm^{-1}. Pulsed operation at 5.5 μm has been achieved at temperatures up to 230 K.[27] A new method of forming simple heterojunctions without epitaxial growth steps is compositional interdiffusion;[28] diodes produced by this technique have operated c.w. at 100 K with a tunability of 300 cm^{-1}.[29] Frequency selectivity can be improved by fabricating a grating in the surface of the active region using photoresist and etching techniques. Such *distributed feedback* (DFB) lasers have low threshold currents, will operate in a single mode for large variations in temperature and current, and can be continuously tuned up to seven cm^{-1}. DFB lasers made from $Pb_{1-x}Sn_xTe$ with double-heterostructure stripe-geometry have recently been reported to be operating at 740–750[30] and 795–810[31] cm^{-1}.

The tuning characteristics of semiconductor diode (and other) lasers have been considered in detail by Calawa,[20] Hinkley et al.[5] and Melngailis and Mooradian.[21] Their discussions can be summarized as follows. The spontaneous emission frequency v_s of an SDL is given by eqn. (1), and typically will have a width of 5–50 cm^{-1}. It may be tuned by changing the bandgap energy by altering the temperature of the semiconductor, or by applying pressure or a magnetic field. Within the spontaneous-emission gain profile, narrow-line emission is produced by multiple reflection and amplification between the end faces of the crystal, which will occur at a wavelength determined approximately by the Fabry–Perot equation of the optical cavity,

$$m\lambda_m = 2nl,\qquad(2)$$

where n is the index of refraction of the semiconductor material, l is the cavity length, and m is the number of half-wavelengths in the cavity. The tuning techniques mentioned will affect the index of refraction n (and pressure will also change the cavity length); if it were possible to make the cavity tuning rate and the laser tuning rate equal, then continuous tuning would be possible across the entire spontaneous-emission tuning range. In practice, all tuning methods shift v_s relative to the mode frequency spectrum of the cavity, so mode hopping occurs: continuous tuning ranges of a few cm^{-1} will be separated by somewhat smaller gaps representing discontinuous shifts to adjacent cavity modes.

Temperature tuning of an SDL is typically about 0.5 cm^{-1} K^{-1}, but changing the overall temperature is not a practical method of fine-tuning the output. In most devices the temperature is effectively changed by current tuning: since semiconductors have relatively poor thermal conductivity, the I^2R dissipation of the injection current raises the temperature in the junction region. This increases the energy gap and hence the emitted frequency, and also changes the effective cavity length through the index of refraction. Current tuning rates are typically 1 to 30 cm^{-1} A^{-1}, with continuous coverage of 1 to 3 cm^{-1} in a single mode; an example of a current tuning curve is shown in Fig. 3. For magnetic field tuning[32] and pressure tuning [33] the values are approximately 0.03–0.2 cm^{-1} (kG)$^{-1}$ and 5 to 20 cm^{-1} (kbar)$^{-1}$, respectively. Pressure tuning is capable of providing a broad frequency output; thus Besson et al.[33] have tuned a PbSe laser from 7.5 to 22.3 μm with hydrostatic pressures of up to 14 kbar.

Despite the general convenience of current tuning, it can not be the sole tuning mechanism if one is to avoid the incomplete wavelength coverage that results

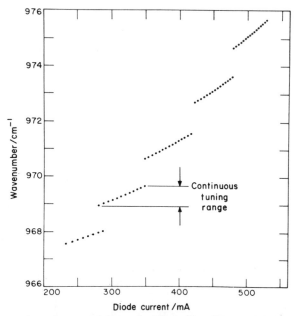

Fig. 3. Current-tuning characteristics of a Pb$_{0.88}$Sn$_{0.12}$Te semiconductor diode laser operating c.w. in a liquid-helium-cooled Dewar. The tuning is continuous within each of the five modes; the points indicate the transmission maxima of a germanium etalon (free spectral range 0.0652 cm^{-1}) used for calibration (Hinkley et al., Ref. 5).

from mode hopping. Most systems now use current for the fine tuning during a scan, with coarse tuning and mode selection provided by controlling either the temperature or the magnetic field. Closed-cycle variable-temperature coolers are used in the first case, but stringent demands are placed on their temperature stability, because maintaining a linewidth of $ca.$ 10^{-4} cm^{-1} requires temperature control to within a small fraction of a mK. This difficulty can be avoided by mounting the diode on a fixed-temperature helium Dewar and using magnetic fields for coarse tuning.[34,35] With such techniques single diodes can be tuned almost continuously over spans of 100 cm^{-1} or more.

Hinkley and Freed [36] studied the line shape of a $Pb_{0.88}Sn_{0.12}Te$ laser and observed Lorentzian linewidths as narrow as 54 kHz $= 1.8 \times 10^{-6}$ cm^{-1} by heterodyning the laser output against a stabilized CO_2 laser operating on a single line; the linewidth was found to vary inversely with power. Typical output powers of SDLs are of the order of microwatts c.w. Because of the small gain region, diffraction effects result in large beam divergence ($\approx f/1$), and focusing optics are required.

Laser action in III–V compounds ($In_xGa_{1-x}As$, $InAs_{1-x}P_x$, $InAs_{1-x}Sb_x$) has been observed between 1 and 3.2 μm, but these have not received the same development attention as have the lead–salt diodes. Melngailis and Mooradian[21] have discussed these and other less-used diode laser materials. While most SDLs have been injection pumped, Pine and Menyuk[37] have optically pumped InSb with CO, Nd:YAG, and GaAs lasers to obtain output at 5.3 μm. The frequencies of the individual laser modes are almost independent of magnetic field, so tuning was accomplished by changing the current of the GaAs pump laser to change the InSb temperature. This paper[37] includes references to other optical and electron-beam pumping experiments with InSb.

2.2 Gas Lasers

The most widely used molecular gas lasers are those employing transitions in CO (5.0–8.2 μm) and CO_2 (9.1–11.3 μm).[38] These oscillate in discrete vibration–rotation lines and thus are step-tunable since, with proper operation, output can be obtained on any single line. Any laser can, of course, be continuously tuned within its gain profile but, at the low pressures normally used in gas lasers, this is determined by the Doppler width of the vibration–rotation transitions, and so the tuning range is limited to a span of about ± 0.005 cm^{-1} near each CO transition and about ± 0.002 cm^{-1} near each CO_2 transition. The same is true of the more randomly distributed lines of atomic gas lasers; the gain profile of the 3.39-μm He–Ne laser line, for example, permits tuning over ± 0.01 cm^{-1}.

These ranges are too limited for general spectroscopic purposes, although it should be emphasized that very useful spectroscopy can be carried out even within such narrow frequency limits. Gas lasers have the output powers necessary to saturate molecular transitions, thus allowing the observation of Lamb dip and other saturation effects in which the resolution is no longer limited by the Doppler width of the absorbing molecules (Section 6). Trace (d) of Fig. 1 is an example of the sort of spectral detail that can be recovered from a scan covering only 0.0018 cm^{-1}.

In attempting to increase the tuning ranges of gas lasers, two techniques have proved useful: operating at higher pressures to broaden the gain profiles of the lines and, for atomic gas lasers, tuning by means of the Zeeman effect.

2.2.1 High pressure gas lasers[5,7]

The self-broadening coefficient for CO_2 is about 0.19 cm^{-1} atm^{-1} or 7.6 MHz Torr^{-1}[39,40] (at higher temperatures and in the gas mixtures typically used in CO_2 lasers the effective broadening coefficient will be reduced somewhat from this value). Since the CO_2 Doppler width at 300 K is approximately 50 MHz, collisional broadening will dominate the lineshape for operating pressures greater than about 10 Torr. For most gas lasers, the electron temperature, and hence the characteristics of the discharge, are determined by the product of the pressure and the discharge tube diameter, so by going to small-diameter tubes one can increase the pressure and still obtain high-gain performance. These arguments led to the development of the waveguide CO_2 laser,[41-43] in which the discharge is contained in a hollow dielectric waveguide with an inside diameter of a millimetre or less. These have been operated at pressures of 50 Torr to 1 atm and provide tuning ranges of up to 0.1 cm^{-1} and powers of a few watts c.w. In a heterodyne experiment, Abrams[43] measured an output linewidth of <100 kHz $= 3 \times 10^{-6}$ cm^{-1} for such a laser.

Since the individual vibration–rotation lines of CO_2 are separated by 1 to 2 cm^{-1}, pressures of about 10 atm are necessary to provide adequate overlap for continuous tuning; somewhat lower pressures will suffice if isotopic mixtures of CO_2 are used to increase the number of lines. Unfortunately, it is difficult to obtain population inversion and gain in this pressure regime, and when laser action can be achieved the linewidths tend to be of the order of a few tenths of a cm^{-1}. The mechanisms that have been used to operate multi-atmospheric CO_2 lasers include transverse electrical excitation provided by a discharge between a solid anode and a multiple-pin cathode (the transversely-excited atmospheric, or TEA, laser),[44] and preionization of the gas either by optical pumping[45] or with high-energy electron beams. Electron-beam-controlled lasers seem to be the most promising for spectroscopic use; several systems have been reported that offer wide tuning ranges, output powers of the order of megawatts, and reasonably narrow linewidths. Bagratashvili et al.[46] have described a CO_2 laser with a tuning range of 45 cm^{-1} and linewidth of 0.05 cm^{-1} that they have used in resonance excitation experiments. Harris et al.[47] used intracavity etalons to obtain line narrowing and continuous tuning in the 9.2 to 10.7 μm region in a 15 atm CO_2 laser. They found an overall tuning range of 70 cm^{-1} and a linewidth of 0.03 cm^{-1}, which represents the best resolution yet reported for a multi-atmosphere discharge. This system was recently operated between 9.1 and

12.5 μm (with some gaps) by choosing among the lasing gases $^{12}CO_2$, $^{13}CO_2$, N_2O, $^{12}CS_2$, and $^{13}CS_2$.[48]

2.2.2 Zeeman-tuned atomic gas (ZTG) lasers[5,7]

He–Ne and He–Xe lasers can be tuned by as much as ± 3.5 cm^{-1}[49,50] about each transition by means of the Zeeman effect; this technique was in fact the basis of the first frequency-tuned lasers in the early 1960s. In the presence of an axial magnetic field, the Zeeman interaction between the field and the magnetic moment of the atoms causes a splitting of the laser output into two components of higher and lower frequencies and opposite circular polarizations. Either one of these can be selected with a quarter-wave plate and a polarizer, resulting in a laser output of frequency

$$\omega_L = \omega_0 \pm g\mu_B B/h,$$

or

$$\omega_L = \omega_0 \pm 1.40\, gB, \tag{3}$$

with ω in MHz and B in gauss units, where ω_0 is the laser frequency at zero field, μ_B is the Bohr magneton, B is the field strength, and g is the effective Landé factor (i.e. the g-value averaged between the upper and lower states of the transition).

The transitions that have been most used for infrared spectroscopy are 5s–4p of neon (2948 cm^{-1}) and 5d–6p of xenon (2851 cm^{-1}), both of which have effective gs of about 1.1, resulting in tuning rates of approximately 1.5 MHz G^{-1}. But while the magnetic field determines the spontaneous emission frequency, it of course has little effect on the laser mode frequency itself; the output will thus consist of a series of discrete cavity-mode frequencies, resulting in a more complex tuning behavior.[5,51–53] By selecting a single axial cavity mode with an intracavity etalon, a single frequency output can be obtained that is tunable over a range of 0.2 to 7 cm^{-1}.

ZTG lasers are thus limited to narrow tuning ranges near atomic gas laser transitions; they are also rather complex to operate and have resolutions of only *ca.* 10^{-3} cm^{-1}.[54] These factors combine to make them of rather limited applicability in laser spectroscopy, but they have nonetheless yielded useful information on several molecules. A stimulus to the use of the He–Ne laser has been the almost exact coincidence between its transition at 2947.90 cm^{-1} and a vibration–rotation line (an F component of $P(7)$ at 2947.912 cm^{-1}) of the CH$_4$ stretching fundamental ν_3;[55,56] the He–Ne laser has been frequency-stabilized using this line and has also been used to study its hyperfine structure (Section 6).

2.3 Raman Scattering Processes

2.3.1 Spin-flip Raman (SFR) lasers

In this very useful class of tunable sources, a fixed-frequency pump laser beam is inelastically scattered, by the stimulated Raman effect, from conduction electrons in a semiconductor crystal that is subjected to a homogeneous magnetic field. The first SFR laser was reported in 1970 by Patel and Shaw,[57] and the process has since been the subject of numerous reviews.[2,4,7,58–65]

The electrons in the conduction band of a semiconductor are quantized into Landau levels; in a magnetic field, each Landau level is split into two sublevels with electron spins oriented parallel and antiparallel to the field. The energy separation between these sublevels is $|g|\mu_B B$, where μ_B is the Bohr magneton, B is the applied field strength, and $|g|$ is the effective gyromagnetic ratio of the conduction electrons in the crystal, which will be very different from the free-electron value of 2.002. Coherent pump-radiation illuminating such a semiconductor will interact with the electrons, causing transitions in which their spin state is reversed or 'flipped' relative to the magnetic field. If the semiconductor crystal is designed as an optical resonator, then at sufficiently high pump power the stimulated emission will exceed losses and oscillation will occur. The frequency of the resulting laser light is given by

$$\omega_{SFR} \approx \omega_p - n|g|\mu_B B/hc$$
$$\approx \omega_p - 0.047\, n|g|B, \tag{4}$$

where ω_p is the wavenumber of the pump beam (in cm^{-1}), B is in kG and $n = 1, 2, \ldots$ for the first, second, ... Stokes lines and $n = -1$ for the first anti-Stokes line (this equation is only approximate because $|g|$ depends to some extent upon the magnetic field, electron concentration, temperature, and cavity parameters). Thus the output frequency is a function of the magnetic field and can be easily tuned. The process has a large Raman scattering cross-section, which can be further increased by resonant enhancement if the pump frequency is near that of the semiconductor bandgap, resulting in high efficiencies.

The magnetic field strength at which SFR lasing will occur is subject to certain limits that depend upon the number of charge carriers in the semiconductor crystal. For InSb, the most widely used scattering medium for SFR, the minimum field is about 20 kG for a carrier concentration of $ca.$ 10^{16} electrons cm^{-3}. If the carrier concentration is reduced to $ca.$ 10^{15} electrons cm^{-3}, the minimum field is only 0.4 kG. but the power output is correspondingly reduced. The optimum carrier concentration for maximizing the SFR power in InSb is 1.3×10^{16} electrons cm^{-3}, which requires operation at fields of at least 23 kG.[60] There is also an upper limit to the useful magnetic field strength, above which the Raman gain falls below the losses due to reflection and free-carrier absorption, and simulated scattering ceases.

With this introduction we can consider the properties of an InSb SFR laser. Pertinent operating parameters, together with those of some other useful semiconductor materials, are summarized in Table 3. A typical experimental arrangement[66] is shown in Fig. 4. The InSb crystal has polished plane-parallel surfaces to form the optical cavity, and is cooled to cryogenic temperatures both to minimize the thermal population of the upper spin level and to remove the

TABLE 3
Narrow-gap semiconductors used in infrared spin-flip Raman lasers

Material	$\|g\|^a$	Typical tuning rates for first Stokes line/cm^{-1} kG^{-1}	Band gap at 0 K/μm	Useful spectral range/μm
InAs	≈ 15	~ 0.6	3.0	3–5.3
InSb	≈ 53	1.6–2.5^a	5.3	$\geqslant 5$
Hg$_{1-x}$Cd$_x$Te ($x = 0.23$)	≈ 80	3.4–3.8^a	9.4	≈ 10

^{a} Zero-field limit at helium temperatures.

heat deposited by the pump beam. According to eqn. (4), with a tuning rate of *ca.* 2 cm^{-1} kG^{-1} (Table 3), a spectral range of *ca.* 150 cm^{-1} is available in either the Stokes or anti-Stokes lines for magnetic fields of 25 to 100 kG, which represent typical operating conditions using a superconducting magnet. Pulsed output powers are of the order of 1 kW in the first Stokes, tens of watts in the first anti-Stokes, and a few watts in the second Stokes lines. The tuning curves[67] for these three lines are shown in Fig. 5; note that they have a slight curvature due to a decrease in the effective value of $|g|$ at higher fields. InSb SFR lasers have been operated with pump beams near 9–10 μm (CO$_2$ laser) and 5 μm (CO or frequency-doubled CO$_2$ lasers); in the latter case the pump wavelength is close to the band gap, giving the advantages of resonant enhancement as discussed above (and only for 5 μm pumping has c.w. operation been demonstrated).[68-70] The output thus covers the spectral regions 5.0 to 6.5 μm and

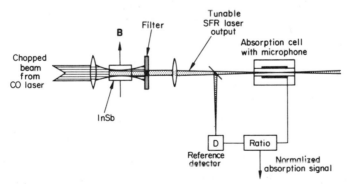

Fig. 4. Typical experimental arrangement for infrared spectroscopy using a spin-flip Raman source. Pump radiation from a CO laser is focused into a $2 \times 2 \times 4$ mm InSb crystal contained in a magnetic field at cryogenic temperatures; a dielectric-coated filter rejects the unused emerging pump beam and allows the collinear SFR radiation to pass to the detector. In this case optoacoustic detection (Section 3.2.1) is used with ratio recording (Kreuzer and Patel, Ref. 66).

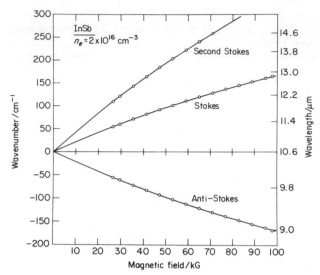

Fig. 5. Tuning curves for the first and second Stokes and first anti-Stokes components of the stimulated SFR radiation from an InSb crystal with the carrier concentration indicated. The pump was a high pressure CO_2 laser at 10.6 μm, and the SFR components tune over the ranges 9.0 to 10.0 and 11.3 to 14.6 μm for magnetic fields of approximately 25 to 100 kG (Aggarwal *et al.*, Ref. 67).

9.0 to about 14 μm; the latter limit has been extended to 16.8 μm by Patel *et al.*,[71] who pumped with an ammonia laser line at 780 cm^{-1} (12.8 μm).

The above wavelengths, produced by scattering in InSb, account for most of the infrared SFR work reported to date, but some other semiconductor materials (Table 3) show promise for future developments in these and other spectral regions. Sattler *et al.*[72] have scattered 9.5 μm CO_2 laser radiation from $Hg_{0.77}Cd_{0.23}Te$ and obtained first-Stokes output, tunable from 9.66 to 10.18 μm. Because of its large g-factor, this material has the largest tuning rate yet observed, and with its bandgap at 9.4 μm it offers the advantages of resonant enhancement in the 10 μm region with CO_2 pumping.[73] Eng *et al.*[74] have pumped InAs with an HF laser ($\omega_p = 3385$ cm^{-1}); the output at *ca.* 3340 cm^{-1} was tunable over about 15 cm^{-1} with kilowatt power; again there is near-resonance between the bandgap and the pump wavelength. In the far infrared, Shaw[75] has observed emission near 100 μm from an InSb SFR laser, confirming a prediction by Shen.[76] This radiation arises from polariton scattering, as will be discussed in Section 2.3.2, except that in this case the polariton is excited by the electronic spin-flip transition.

The linewidths and mode patterns of SFR lasers have been the objects of several studies.[4,63,70,77–79] In general, the spectral width of the output is strongly affected by the tuning properties of the cavity and the free carrier concentration, and can vary from a nearly continuous tunable 'broadband'

(≈ 0.01 cm^{-1}) output with high power, to a lower power signal with much better resolution and continuous tuning over only a single cavity mode, similar to semiconductor diode lasers. For c.w. operation, the limiting linewidth is given by the Schawlow–Townes formula, and is of the order of 1 to 100 Hz or 10^{-9} to 10^{-10} cm^{-1}.[77] In practice this limit is never achieved because of instabilities in the magnetic field, the gain linewidth of the pump laser, local temperature variations in the semiconductor, and inhomogeneous broadening caused by the non-parabolic nature of the semiconductor conduction band. Patel [77] measured a linewidth of 3×10^{-8} cm^{-1} but this was increased by short-term frequency jitter to an effective value of 1×10^{-6} cm^{-1}. Brueck and Mooradian[70] have maintained a spectral width of 10^{-6} cm^{-1} for periods of several minutes by using frequency-locking techniques. For pulsed operation the linewidth is limited by the uncertainty principle to values of the order of 10^{-4} to 10^{-5} cm^{-1}.[60]

Spin-flip Raman lasers offer reasonably high power, narrow linewidths, and good mode quality. Most systems require the complication of a superconducting magnet, but Patel[80] has used InSb with a carrier concentration of only 10^{15} electron cm^{-3} and a threshold of 400 G, thus allowing operation with a small electromagnet (fields <20 kG). Guerra et al.[81] went even further, using a 1.5 kG permanent magnet with tapered pole pieces to provide a field gradient; the output was tuned by moving the magnet relative to the InSb and by adjusting the current in a pair of Helmholtz modulation coils that provided a fine-tuning capability of ± 135 G (about ± 0.3 cm^{-1}). This provides greater stability than can be obtained with a superconducting magnet, in addition to being cheaper and easier to operate. The principal drawback to SFR lasers at present is their limited spectral range, which does not extend beyond about ± 150 cm^{-1} from a strong pump line.

Doppler-limited spectra obtained with SFR lasers will be tabulated and discussed in Section 4. Mention might be made of some SFR spectra that do not fit the present definition of high resolution, but which are comparable to, or better than, that provided by most grating spectrometers: H_2O from 1780 to 1850 cm^{-1},[82,83] NH_3 from 846 to 874 cm^{-1},[58,84,85] and UF_6 from 630 to 680 cm^{-1}.[71] A particularly good review, with several examples of spectroscopic applications, is that of Butcher et al.[63]

2.3.2 Polariton lasers[2,4]

In polar crystals, photons and transverse-optical phonons with nearly the same energy and wave vector are strongly coupled, forming a long-wavelength excitation of mixed electromagnetic and mechanical character that is called a polariton.[86,87] When radiation is Raman-scattered from such a crystal, the momentum of the polariton created in the scattering process is the difference between the momenta of the incident and scattered (Stokes) photons, and thus is determined by the angle between the pump and Stokes radiation. The process can be considered as stimulated Raman scattering from the polariton, or alternatively as a parametric oscillation (Section 2.4) in which the signal and idler waves are identified with the Stokes and polariton frequencies, respectively.

Polariton scattering was the subject of intensive study about a decade ago, but little has been done recently to develop it as a source of tunable infrared radiation. For this purpose it has the advantages of room-temperature operation and simple angular tuning without requiring a tunable pump source, but sufficiently narrow linewidths for high resolution spectroscopy have yet to be demonstrated. The tunable infrared work reported to date has used $LiNbO_3$ as the non-linear crystal. In a typical arrangement, the crystal is placed between resonator mirrors, forming an interferometer that determines the direction of the stimulated Stokes beam; pump radiation from a ruby laser is introduced into the crystal at a small angle that can be varied between 0° and 5° to tune the Stokes and output frequencies simultaneously. Scattering from the long-wavelength side of the low-frequency A_1 polariton mode (248 cm^{-1}) in $LiNbO_3$ generates wavelengths from 40 to 238 μm.[88-90] Shorter wavelengths (16 to 20 μm) are similarly obtained by scattering from the 628 cm^{-1} polariton mode.[88] Recently Piestrup et al.[91] have used an Nd:YAG pump to achieve 10 to 100 W of output tunable from 150 to 710 μm.

2.3.3 Raman frequency shifting

In spin-flip and polariton lasers, a fixed input frequency is tuned by means of a non-linear Raman medium. An alternative method is to transform a tunable source into a different spectral region by a Raman process having a fixed frequency shift. Hydrogen gas is attractive for this purpose because it has a large vibrational Raman shift (4155 cm^{-1}) and high Raman gain, and is transparent throughout the visible and infrared. Thus a dye laser tunable from 540 to 700 nm and scattered from hydrogen will produce tunable infrared radiation of wavelengths 0.7 to 1.0, 1.0 to 1.7, and 1.6 to 5.5 μm from the first through third Stokes lines, respectively; the fourth Stokes line will cover the remainder of the infrared and microwave regions.

In 1972 Schmidt and Appt[92] reported infrared radiation at 1.2 μm from the first Stokes line of an 800 nm dye laser scattered by hydrogen; this system has since generated 0.75–1.5 μm radiation at kilowatt powers.[2] Frey and Pradère[93-95] used an amplified dye laser tunable from 710 nm to 1.09 μm and obtained first and second Stokes output from 1.03 to 7.7 μm, with megawatts in the first Stokes line.

Stimulated electronic Raman scattering of tunable dye-laser radiation from potassium,[96] cesium,[97] and barium[98] vapors has also been reported. Cotter et al.[97] used three different Raman transitions in cesium to obtain infrared output in the regions 2.5 to 4.8, 5.7 to 8.7, and 11.7 to 15 μm with peak powers of 2–25 kW. In a different experiment,[96] they scattered nitrogen-pumped dye-laser radiation (404 nm) from potassium vapor and achieved tunability between 2.56 and 3.5 μm. They used this system to record a spectrum of the $v_1 + v_3$ band of CO_2 (3715 cm^{-1}) at 0.4 cm^{-1} resolution, which does not qualify as a high resolution scan but illustrates the promise of this technique. In another variation, Ambartsumyan et al.[99] used liquid pyridine ($\tilde{\nu} = 990$ cm^{-1}) to scatter narrowly tunable Nd:glass laser output at 1.06 μm and reported megawatt power in the first Stokes line between 8406 and 8434 cm^{-1}, which they used to pump the second harmonic of HCl in a laser excitation experiment.

Raman frequency shifting is relatively simple and broadly tunable, but the best linewidth reported to date is about 0.2 cm^{-1}. Because of the very high output power that can be achieved, this technique currently seems more attractive for photochemistry than for spectroscopy.

2.4 Optical Parametric Oscillators (OPOs)

Parametric oscillation can be regarded as a special case of the non-linear mixing of two different input frequencies discussed in Section 2.5. Mixing can result from the interaction of a single high-power driving frequency with the electric fields of the random spontaneous photon noise in a parametric medium. The result is an optical parametric oscillator, in which a pump photon of frequency ω_p is converted by the non-linearity of the electric polarization into photons of two different frequencies, designated as the signal and idler (usually identified with the shorter- and longer-wavelength outputs, respectively):

$$\omega_p = \omega_s + \omega_i. \tag{5}$$

The mixing crystal is placed in an optical cavity to provide the feedback necessary to maintain oscillation, and thus only those signal and idler waves are amplified for which the wave vectors are nearly phase-matched. In the collinear case, this requires

$$n_p\omega_p = n_s\omega_s + n_i\omega_i, \tag{6}$$

where the ns are the indices of refraction of the medium at the different frequencies. The system can be tuned by varying the refractive indices (for example, by changing the temperature or applying pressure or an electric field to the crystal), or (most conveniently) by changing its orientation. Since there are cavity losses in the process, there is a threshold power for oscillation that depends upon the nature of the optical resonator. Lowest thresholds are obtained when the cavity is resonant for both the signal and idler (doubly-resonant oscillator), but this results in poor frequency stability and in tuning difficulties because of the additional constraint imposed on the phase matching. Singly-resonant oscillators, in which the cavity is resonant for either the signal or idler, are more stable and more conveniently tunable, but require a greater pump power to reach threshold. The reader is referred to several excellent review articles for further details of OPOs.[2,4,100-104]

A typical tuning curve for an OPO is shown in Fig. 6. In this work[105] the non-linear crystal was LiNbO$_3$ and its refractive index was varied by changing its temperature, but similar curves are obtained for angle tuning. The wavelength of degeneracy corresponds to the point at which the signal and idler frequencies are equal, and thus to twice the wavelength of the pump, which in this case was an Nd:YAG laser emitting at 1.06 μm.

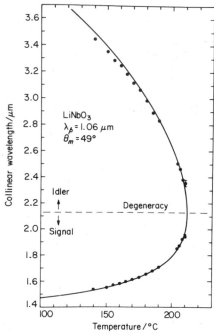

Fig. 6. Temperature tuning curve for optical parametric oscillation in LiNbO₃. The solid line is calculated from the index of refraction of LiNbO₃, assuming an Nd:YAG laser pump source ($\lambda_p = 1.064$ μm) and a phase-matching angle of 49° between the pump beam and the optic axis of the crystal. The experimental points are measured wavelengths of parametric fluorescence (Pearson *et al.*, Ref. 105).

Optical parametric oscillation has been observed in about ten different crystals, with tunable output from 0.4 to almost 17 μm. The long-wavelength limit is now 16.5 μm, achieved by pumping CdSe with an HF laser.[106] Optical parametric oscillators offer the advantage of very wide tuning ranges (though several different mirror combinations may be necessary to achieve this) and high pulsed power; c.w. operation has so far proved to be difficult, for the output tends to consist of high-frequency spikes. These devices have demonstrated their usefulness as Raman sources, in photochemistry experiments, and as sources for difference-frequency mixing (Section 2.5.1).[4,103] Typical linewidths, however, are of the order of 0.1 to 1 cm⁻¹, and may be larger near the region of degeneracy; this has limited their usefulness in high-resolution spectroscopy. A few exceptions may be noted: Pinard and Young [107] used as a mode selector an optical interferometer mode-matched to the cavity, and achieved a linewidth of 10^{-3} cm^{-1} near 2.5 μm; they scanned a rotational line in the 2.5 μm HF fundamental with this instrument and resolved the Doppler linewidth (≈ 0.01 cm^{-1} at 300 K). More recently Hordvik and Sackett[108] have modified a commercial Chromatix OPO to obtain stable, single-mode output, and reported a resulting linewidth of 10^{-3} cm^{-1} or less and an equivalent long-term frequency stability.

2.5 Non-linear Optical Mixing Techniques

In this section we discuss processes in which two different input frequencies, at least one of which is tunable, are mixed in a non-linear medium.

2.5.1 Sum- and difference-frequency generation[2]

Frequency mixing in solids is a second-order non-linear process. If two intense coherent electromagnetic waves of frequencies ω_1 and ω_2 are combined in a suitable crystal, the induced dielectric polarization will emit sum and difference frequencies

$$\omega_3 = |\omega_1 \pm \omega_2|. \tag{7}$$

If one or both of the input lines is tunable, the output will be correspondingly tunable and will have a spectral width equal to the sum of the widths of the input frequencies. To obtain a reasonably high conversion efficiency, the fundamental and generated waves must propagate with equal phase velocity in the non-linear crystal, so phase matching of the wave propagation vectors is critical to the process. Tuning is accomplished by varying ω_1 and/or ω_2, while simultaneously ensuring that the phase-matching condition is satisfied by changing either the orientation or temperature of the mixing crystal.

Frequency mixing is a useful method for extending the tunability of a primary laser into other spectral regions, and a variety of mixing processes has been reported. Some of the more important (or promising) of these for infrared generation are listed in Table 4. Most of these are difference-frequency techniques; sum-frequency mixing, which generates wavelengths shorter than those of either primary laser, are more often used to obtain ultraviolet output,[2] although Pidgeon et al.[115] have summed CO_2 radiation at 10.6 μm with the output of a CO_2-pumped spin-flip Raman laser to achieve emission at 1725 to 1830 cm^{-1}.

A difference-frequency spectrometer that has demonstrated a useful high resolution capability between 2 and 4 μm has been constructed by Pine.[109,110] A schematic of this instrument is shown in Fig. 7. The input is provided by a fixed-frequency argon-ion laser (output typically 100 mW in the 515 and 488 nm lines) and an argon-laser-pumped tunable dye laser that yields 50 mW in the rhodamine 6G band (560 to 620 nm). These two visible frequencies are combined collinearly by the dichroic mirror M_1 and focused by the lens L_1 into the

$LiNbO_3$ non-linear crystal, which is contained in an oven so that phase-matching can be satisfied by temperature tuning. The emerging infrared radiation is divided by the germanium beamsplitter BS_6 into sample and reference beams and the sample/reference ratio is displayed on a strip-chart recorder. Phase-sensitive detection is used, with the beams chopped at 800 Hz by the tuning fork TF. Continuous scans can cover up to 5 cm^{-1}. The resolution is primarily limited by the frequency jitter of the dye laser; with special modifications this was reduced to *ca.* 3 MHz $(1 \times 10^{-4}$ cm$^{-1})$. Frequency reproducibility is 6×10^{-5} cm^{-1}, achieved by a scan-delay tracking scheme performed by the scan calibration interferometer.[110]

Difference-frequency generation has now covered the near- and mid-infrared regions from 2.2 to 24 μm. In addition, far-infrared radiation continuously tunable from 52 μm to 5 mm has been obtained by mixing two different dye-laser

TABLE 4
Some examples of difference-frequency generation of tunable infrared radiation

Pump[a]	Non-linear material	Coverage/ μm	Resolution/ cm^{-1}	Approx. power/W	Mode[b]	References
(Ar+)/dye	$LiNbO_3$	2.2–4.2	5×10^{-4}	10^{-6}	c.w.	(109,110)
(Nd:YAG)/dye	$LiIO_3$	2.8–3.4		0.08	p	(111)
(ruby)/dye	proustite[c]	3.20–6.47	8	100–2000	p	(112,113)
(ruby)/dye	$AgGaS_2$	4.6–12		0.2	p	(114)
(CO_2)/SFR[d]	Te	5.47–5.79	≈ 0.2	3	p	(115)
dye/dye	$AgGaS_2$	5.5–18.3		4	p	(116)
dye/dye	proustite	5.82–7.25		50	p	(113)
(Nd:YAG)/OPO	$AgGaSe_2$	7–15	2		p	(117)
OPO signal/idler	proustite	7.8–11.9	≈ 0.1	2×10^{-4}	p	(118)
dye/dye	$AgGaS_2$	8.7–11.6	≈ 9	10^{-4}	p	(119)
OPO signal/idler	CdSe	9.4–24.3		0.1–10	p	(120)
(ruby)/dye	proustite	10.1–12.7	<0.1	0.1	p	(121)
dye/dye	proustite	11–23		0.2–20	p	(122)
dual-freq. dye	ZnO	52–?		0.014	p	(123)
dual-freq. dye	$LiNbO_3$	63–500		10^{-3}–0.2	p	(123)
(CO_2)/(CO_2)[e]	GaAs	70–1000	$<3 \times 10^{-6}$	10^{-7}	c.w.	(124)
(CO_2)/(CO_2)[e]	GaAs	70–2000		0.02	p	(125)
(CO_2)/SFR	InSb	93–100	≈ 0.2	2×10^{-6}	p	(126)
(CO_2)/(CO_2)[e]	$ZnGeP_2$	93–145	$\approx 10^{-3}$	2×10^{-6}	p	(127)
dye/dye	$LiNbO_3$	200–5000		0.002	p	(128)
(ruby)/ruby	$LiNbO_3$	1230–8300	≈ 0.04	10^{-3}–0.02	p	(129)

[a] Fixed-frequency pump lasers in parentheses; SFR = spin-flip Raman laser, OPO = optical parametric oscillator.
[b] C.w. or pulsed.
[c] Proustite = Ag_3AsS_3.
[d] Sum-frequency generation.
[e] Step-tunable.

frequencies in $LiNbO_3$,[123,128] and by mixing the pump and Stokes beams of a spin-flip Raman laser in InSb.[126] Far-infrared output can also be generated by a mixing different CO_2 laser lines;[124,125,127] this provides a step-tunable source, but the frequency spacing can be as little as 0.01 cm^{-1} with proper choice of input lines,[125] so a continuously-tunable high resolution far-i.r. source should be possible if CO_2 laser mixing is combined with one of the processes discussed in Section 2.2. This spectral region has always been very difficult experimentally, and tunable laser sources offer the promise of finally being able to bridge satisfactorily the gap between the infrared and microwave regions.

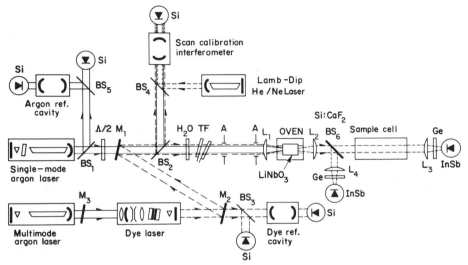

Fig. 7. Schematic diagram of a difference-frequency spectrometer (Pine, Ref. 110).

2.5.2　Infrared-microwave mixing

This also involves sum/difference-frequency generation by non-linear methods, but the techniques are different from those in the preceding section. Here the tunable frequency is provided by a millimeter-wave klystron that modulates a fixed-frequency laser. The output consists of the laser carrier signal plus side-bands offset by the klystron frequency; these sidebands have the spectral purity of the laser but are tunable by as much as 16 GHz (0.5 cm^{-1}).[130,131] This is essentially a frequency-measuring device, and since the laser frequency is known and that of the klystron can be measured, extreme frequency precision is possible without any other calibration. The output has a very narrow linewidth and high stability. On the other hand, the mixing efficiency is generally low, resulting in output powers of the order of microwatts per sideband, and the tuning range is, of course, limited.

Most systems reported to date have used stabilized CO_2 lasers for the fixed frequency at 9 to 11 μm. Corcoran *et al.*[132–134] mixed this with the output of a 54 GHz klystron in a GaAs-loaded waveguide outside the laser cavity, then separated the sidebands from the carrier signal with a grating. Frequency stability was of the order of 1 MHz.[134] Bonek and Korecky[135] achieved an output of better than 10^{-4} W in each sideband per watt of driving power by using intracavity modulation from the transverse electro-optical effect in a GaAs crystal. The crystal becomes birefringent under the influence of the modulating field, so the sideband frequencies have a polarization orthogonal to that of the carrier beam, and can be coupled out of the cavity by partial reflection at the Brewster-angle window of the CO_2 laser.

Recently a He–Ne laser has been modulated by a radio-frequency oscillator, resulting in a narrowly tunable laser at 3.39 μm.[136] The tunable output was measured against that of a stabilized reference laser, allowing precise frequency measurements, and the claimed linewidth of 7 Hz (2×10^{-10} cm^{-1}!) represents the best resolution yet reported for any tunable infrared source. It should be possible to use such a system with a CO_2 laser in the 9 to 11 μm region.

2.5.3 Four-wave parametric mixing[2,7]

Four-wave parametric conversion is a third-order process, and so does not require an anisotropic mixing medium as do the second-order mixing techniques described above. Such conversion can be enhanced by resonance effects to the point where it is competitive with second-order processes. For the infrared, it is difference-frequency mixing that is of interest: three coherent electromagnetic waves beat together to generate a polarization that coherently emits infrared radiation of frequency

$$\omega_{i.r.} = \omega_1 - \omega_2 - \omega_3. \tag{8}$$

Three different input frequencies could be employed, but in all the systems reported to date only two are used, with ω_2 provided by stimulated Raman scattering generated by the pump beam ω_1; this modification ('coherent Raman mixing') is not only simpler but also automatically ensures the desired resonant enhancement. The tunable input ω_3 can be thought of as being coherently scattered from the Raman polarization induced by ω_1, thus generating the infrared frequency $\omega_{i.r.}$. Since the mixing medium can be isotropic, atomic or molecular vapors can be used; these offer the advantages of high damage threshold, broad infrared transmission range, and high optical quality compared with crystals.

Sorokin et al.[137,138] first used this process in mixing the output of two dye lasers in alkali metal vapors. The pump laser ω_1 was tuned near the resonance lines corresponding to the $(n+1)p \rightarrow ns$ transitions to stimulate the Raman (Stokes) emission of ω_2. An orthogonally polarized dye laser beam was collinearly combined with this by a Glan prism to provide the tunable input ω_3, and the combined beams were focused into a heat-pipe oven containing the metal vapor. A monochromator selected the desired frequency output $\omega_{i.r.}$. Phase matching was accomplished by adjusting the frequency of the pump beam ω_1, or more generally by adding a second alkali metal vapor to change the anomalous dispersion of the mixing medium. This device has been tuned from 2 to 31 μm and, in principle, could be extended out to 500 μm with the proper combinations of metal vapors. Four-wave mixing in potassium vapor has yielded 3 W of peak output power at 2.4 μm.[139]

Hydrogen can also be used for mixing,[140,141] and has the advantage of allowing room-temperature operation. Byer[141] proposed mixing an Nd:YAG pump ($\omega_1 = 1.06$ μm) and the tunable output of an optical parametric oscillator in hydrogen to reach a wavelength of 70 μm; this system has so far been demonstrated between 3.5 and 13 μm.[142] Kilowatt powers with a linewidth of 0.07 cm^{-1} at 16 μm have been obtained by mixing a tunable dye laser with a ruby laser in hydrogen;[143] this wavelength corresponds to the strongest fundamental of UF_6[144] and thus is of interest for possible uranium isotope separation.

All of these systems are pulsed. They offer broad, smooth tuning ranges but suffer from low power and rather complex operating requirements. To date none has demonstrated a linewidth that would make it useful for high resolution spectroscopy, but if the predicted linewidth of 10^{-5} cm^{-1}[7] can be achieved, four-wave mixing processes will become more widely used.

As with difference-frequency generation (Section 2.5.1), discrete laser lines can be combined in a four-wave process to yield step-tunable output. Lee *et al.*[145] have thus mixed CO_2 lines in germanium, and observed many individual lines in the 8.6 μm region (about 10 per cm^{-1}), with pulsed output powers to 300 kW.

2.6　Miscellaneous Lasers

Two other devices that have not yet been used for high resolution spectroscopy but that offer promise for the future are the color-center laser and the free electron laser.

When certain types of *F*-like color centres in alkali halide crystals are pumped in the visible, they quickly relax into a new excited-state configuration that allows luminescent emission in the near infrared. Laser action in such systems was first demonstrated by Mollenauer and Olson.[146,147] The output can be tuned with an external grating[146,148] or by rotation of a birefringent plate inside the cavity;[146,147] wavelengths of 0.88[148,149] to 3.3[147] μm have been covered to date, and a single-mode linewidth of 10^{-6} cm^{-1} has been estimated.[150]

The first operation of a laser based on stimulated radiation by free electrons was reported in 1977.[151,152] A 43 MeV bunched electron beam from a linear accelerator was fired along the axis of a spatially periodic transverse magnetic field produced by a superconducting helix, and the emitted bremsstrahlung radiation was amplified between a pair of resonator mirrors. The output wavelength (3.4 μm in these first experiments) should be tunable from the infrared to the ultraviolet by varying the beam energy. If the reported oscillator linewidth of 7 cm^{-1} can be narrowed, as seems probable, this device may provide a useful high-power broadly tunable source, but it is not likely to be found soon in many laboratories.

3   LINEAR ABSORPTION SPECTROSCOPY: EXPERIMENTAL TECHNIQUES

3.1   Typical Experimental Arrangement

The experimental arrangement used will depend in part upon the tunable source employed, and for some of the lasers discussed in Section 2 special techniques are necessary. We will discuss here the components of a typical tunable-diode laser spectrometer that illustrates the general principles involved, and then mention briefly some of the modifications that may be necessary in special cases.

While complete laser-diode spectrometers are now available commercially, most work is still being done with systems assembled from components. An arrangement that has proved satisfactory over the last several years at Los Alamos is illustrated in Fig. 8. The diode may be mounted either in a variable-temperature closed-cycle cooler or at the center of a superconducting magnet contained in a liquid-helium cryostat, depending upon whether mode selection by temperature or magnetic-field tuning is most convenient (Section 2.1). During a spectral scan the diode is current-tuned by the output of a ramp generator. The laser emission is collected by an $f/3$ zinc selenide lens and focused on the entrance slit of a 1 m grating monochromator. The function of the mono-chromator is simply to filter out unwanted modes, and it is usually operated

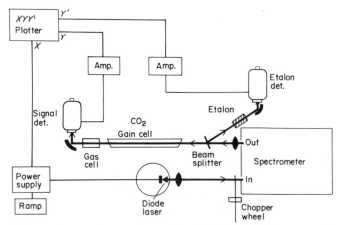

Fig. 8. Typical experimental arrangement for infrared spectroscopy using a tunable semiconductor diode laser.

with wide slits so that its transmission is nearly constant over the desired tuning range, but with narrowed slits it can be used to provide a coarse frequency calibration. A 700 Hz mechanical chopper immediately in front of the entrance slit modulates the beam for synchronous detection by a lock-in amplifier. At the exit slit of the monochromator the beam is collimated by a second ZnSe lens and then divided by a germanium beamsplitter into sample and calibration beams; each of these is focused by a parabolic mirror onto a Cu-doped germanium detector. The sample and calibration signals are recorded simultaneously on a two-pen XYY' recorder, with the current ramp driving the X axis. Frequency calibration is provided by the etalon and gain cell, which will be discussed in Sections 3.2 and 3.3.

Although it records a separate calibration signal, the arrangement of Fig. 8 is not a true double-beam spectrometer in the usual sense of having a reference signal to compensate for atmospheric absorption and changes in source output. This is not usually a major problem in laser spectroscopy, for normally only a small spectral interval is recorded in a given scan and atmospheric absorptions can be easily recognized by their pressure-broadened contours. Background compensation is always a convenience, however, and ratio-recording tunable-laser spectrometers have been constructed (for example, the SFR arrangement of Fig. 4 and the difference-frequency spectrometer of Fig. 7). With some sources double-beam operation may even be a necessity: for example, in using a Zeeman-tuned He–Xe laser source at 3.5 μm, Kasuya[50] observed a strong power modulation with a period of 150 MHz (caused by cavity-mode resonances) that largely obscured the spectral features being studied; this background was eliminated by using a ratio-recording technique.

3.2 Absolute Frequency Calibration

It has been mentioned that infrared-microwave mixing constitutes a frequency-measuring technique in itself (Section 2.5.2). For all other tunable lasers, however, the output frequency can be calculated only approximately from the tuning parameter(s), and some method of calibration is necessary. This problem can be considered in two parts: (a) the establishment of absolute frequency standards; and (b) the calibration of the laser tuning rate relative to these standards, which will be discussed in Section 3.3.

With sources capable of providing Doppler-limited resolution of gaseous molecules, the calibration of absorption line positions with commensurate accuracy becomes a significant problem. Ideally, one would like to be able to measure the frequency of an absorption feature to within a small fraction of its Doppler width, or with an accuracy of 10^{-4} to 10^{-5} cm^{-1}. Unfortunately, this goal can not be reached at present except in certain rather special circumstances.

The simplest procedure is to use a monochromator or interferometer to measure the laser frequency. This is particularly straightforward if a monochromator is already part of the experimental apparatus, as in the diode laser experiment of Fig. 8. However, this can provide an accuracy of only about ± 0.01 cm^{-1}, at best: sufficient to identify an absorption feature but of little use if a band analysis is to be undertaken.

／A better procedure is to calibrate against a simple gaseous molecule contained in an absorption cell at low pressure. The best comprehensive source of critically evaluated line positions is the IUPAC tabulation,[153] which lists frequencies with an absolute accuracy of from 5×10^{-3} to 10^{-4} cm^{-1}, depending upon the molecule, over the region 1–4350 cm^{-1}. These lines are intended for users of grating spectrometers, and are often not spaced as closely as would be desirable for laser spectroscopy, but in some cases additional line frequencies are given in the original papers from which the IUPAC tables were compiled. Thus Rao[154] has measured some 900 lines of NH$_3$ between 7.7 and 15 μm with an accuracy of better than ± 0.005 cm^{-1}, but only about 160 of these are included in Ref. (153); in certain regions these additional lines might be useful.

There are other molecular absorption frequencies with accuracies comparable to or better than those in the IUPAC compilation, but these must be evaluated on an individual basis. Recently Knoll et al.[155] have used the best available molecular constants to calculate transition frequencies in the ν_2 bands of CO$_2$ (622 to 717 cm^{-1}) and HCN (564 to 858 cm^{-1}). They then measured HCN $P(15)$ relative to the adjacent CO$_2$ $Q(14)$ and $Q(16)$ lines as shown in Fig. 9, and found agreement to within 0.0008 cm^{-1}, so their frequencies can be used with some confidence in the 14 to 16 μm region. (It should be noted that the CO$_2$ Q branch is not tabulated in Ref. (153), since it cannot be adequately resolved with grating spectrometers. Furthermore, while the calculated frequencies of the CO$_2$ P- and R-branch lines agree well with the IUPAC tables (an r.m.s. difference of 0.001 cm^{-1} between 640 and 717 cm^{-1}, and slightly greater at lower frequencies), there are discrepancies between the two sets of HCN values that reach 0.03 cm^{-1} at 800 cm^{-1}). Several authors have selected calibration lines from one of the several available compilations of atmospheric absorption features such as those of CO$_2$[156,157] but we have found that these contain lines of varying dependability; in particular, the calculated positions of the less-common isotopic species tend to be in poor agreement with measurements made using tunable lasers.

One can anticipate that in the next few years there will be further attempts to check and improve upon the accuracy of molecular absorption standards, and also to select new molecules that have more closely-spaced absorption features than is necessary or desirable for grating calibration. Thus C$_2$H$_4$, which has a compact asymmetric-rotor-type rotational structure, has been suggested as a calibrating gas near 10.5 μm,[158] and OCS near 5.3 μm.[159] SF$_6$ is another gas with possibilities between 942 and 952 cm^{-1}; it will be discussed in more detail in Section 4.1. Obviously any such molecule with dense rotational structure will cover only a small spectral region, and the measurement of enough line positions to cover thoroughly the infrared region will not be quickly accomplished.

The best-known molecular frequencies are of course those belonging to laser transitions that have been measured, by frequency-mixing techniques, relative to the cesium-beam primary frequency standard. In the regions where these are available, they provide calibration frequencies of exceptional accuracy. Thus Petersen *et al.*[160] have used a frequency synthesis chain[161] to measure the

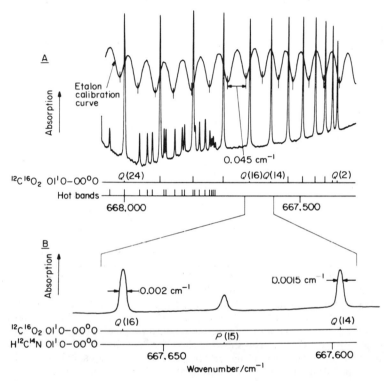

Fig. 9. Diode laser spectra of (A) the $CO_2 \nu_2 Q$ branch at 667 cm⁻¹, recorded together with etalon fringes to calibrate the diode tuning rate; and (B) a CO_2–HCN mixture, showing the position of HCN $\nu_2 P(15)$ relative to two nearby $CO_2 Q$-branch lines (Knoll *et al.*, Ref. 155).

lines in the $00^00 1$–$[10^00, 02^00]_{I,II}$ CO_2 laser bands (903–1099 cm⁻¹) with an absolute uncertainty of about 25 kHz in frequency or 4×10^{-6} cm⁻¹ in wavenumber. A convenient way to introduce these lines into the spectrum is to insert a high-voltage CO_2 gain cell into the sample beam, as shown in Fig. 8. When the diode is tuned through a frequency corresponding to a CO_2 laser transition, there is a sharp increase in the detected signal due to gain in the electrically pumped CO_2 gas. This provides an accurate frequency marker, as shown in Fig. 10.

The main drawback to the use of CO_2 gain lines is that those in the $00^01-[10^00,02^00]_{I,II}$ transitions are separated by 0.8 to 2.3 cm^{-1}, which in some cases may be inconveniently large. There are several ways to increase the line density. An obvious solution is to use isotopic species of CO_2 (though this may become expensive in a flow-type gain cell). Wavenumbers accurate to better than 10^{-4} cm^{-1} have been reported for $^{13}C^{16}O_2$,[162] $^{12}C^{18}O_2$,[162,163] and $^{13}C^{18}O_2$,[162] and measurements of other isotopic species are under way.[164]

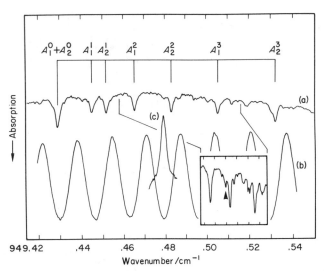

Fig. 10. The $P(46)$ manifold of $^{192}OsO_4$ recorded with a tunable semiconductor diode laser. (a) Approximately 0.17 Torr $^{192}OsO_4$ in a 10 cm cell at 257 K; (b) simultaneous recording of a germanium etalon with a free spectral range of 0.016533 cm^{-1}; (c) signal from a high-voltage CO_2 gain cell showing the CO_2 $P(14)$ line at 949.479313 cm^{-1}. The inset, recorded at a somewhat higher temperature, illustrates better the hot-band structure, including (arrow) the transition at $+1.5$ MHz from the CO_2 laser line.

Another technique is to use higher-level CO_2 laser transitions (sequence bands) which appear weakly in a normal gain cell but can be enhanced relative to the usual $00^01-[10^00,02^00]$ lines by increasing the pressure and discharge current.[165,166] Siemsen et al.[165,167,168] reported lines of the $00^02-[10^01,02^01]_{I,II}$ and $00^03-[10^02,02^02]_I$ sequences in the 899–995 and 1001–1096 cm^{-1} regions, while Monchalin et al.[169] have used an interferometer to measure the $01^11-[11^10,03^10]_I$ P branch (890–916 cm^{-1}) with an accuracy of 10^{-5} cm^{-1}. Further measurements on these and other upper-level sequences are in progress.[165,170]

Accurate measurements of the CO laser lines have been made by heterodyne methods, comparing them with the second harmonics of the CO_2 frequencies.[171-173] Some two dozen NO lines between 1810 and 2000 cm^{-1} are nearly coincident with CO transitions and have been measured relative to the latter with accuracies of 10^{-4} cm^{-1},[174] and 11 NH$_3$ lines that overlap the CO$_2$ laser have been measured with equivalent accuracy between 887 and 972 cm^{-1} [175] Other transitions that are known precisely enough to be considered as standards for infrared laser spectroscopy are those of CH$_4$ at 3.39 μm,[161,176,177] H$_2$O at 28.0 and 78.4 μm,[178] CH$_3$OH at 70.5 and 96.5 μm,[179] and numerous lines of HCN,[178,180] CH$_3$OH,[179] CH$_3$NH$_2$,[179] and N$_2$H$_4$[179] lasers beyond 100 μm.

3.3 Calibration of Laser Tuning Rate

If a gas sample is examined at a pressure low enough to ensure negligible collision broadening (less than 0.1 to 1 Torr, depending upon the molecule), the width of an absorption feature can serve for an internal calibration of tuning rate. For a molecule of molecular weight M[a.m.u.] at temperature T[K], the full Doppler width at half-maximum absorption for a line of wavenumber $\tilde{v}$[cm^{-1}] is[181]

$$\Delta\tilde{v} = \frac{2\tilde{v}}{c}\left[\frac{2kT\ln2}{Mu}\right]^{1/2} = 7.1623 \times 10^{-7}\,\tilde{v}\left[\frac{T}{M}\right]^{1/2} \tag{9}$$

where u is the atomic mass unit (1.6606×10^{-24} g).

As will be discussed in Section 4.3, the agreement between linewidths calculated from eqn. (9) and those measured at low pressures is quite good. Of course, one must be certain that the line in question has no fine structure that would affect its measured contour. Doppler linewidths have been used to calibrate the tuning rate of semiconductor diode lasers as functions of current[182] and magnetic field.[32] The method can be extended to higher sample pressures, where pressure broadening becomes important, if the broadening coefficient of the gas is accurately known.[183]

A more generally useful calibration technique is to monitor the laser emission with a Fabry–Perot interferometer. Solid germanium etalons are particularly convenient for this purpose and have been used extensively in infrared laser spectroscopy. Figure 8 shows how interference fringes from an etalon can be recorded with the spectrum; some such method of simultaneous recording is essential, for non-linearities in the laser tuning rate may not be reproducible from one scan to the next. Examples of etalon traces are shown in Figs 9 and 10. The spacing of the interference fringes (i.e. the free spectral range of the etalon) is given by

$$\Delta\tilde{v} = 1/2h[n - \lambda(dn/d\lambda)] \tag{10}$$

for radiation at normal incidence, where h is the etalon length and n is the index of refraction of germanium at the wavelength of measurement λ. The best available values of n and $dn/d\lambda$ are probably those obtained from Herzberger and Salzberg's[184] equation:

$$n = 3.99931 + 0.391707L + 0.163492L^2 - 6.0 \times 10^{-6}\lambda^2 + 5.3 \times 10^{-8}\lambda^4, \quad (11)$$

where $L = 1/(\lambda^2 - 0.028)$ and λ is in μm. This reproduces Salzberg and Villa's[185] measurements on single-crystal germanium to within ± 0.0003 between 4 and 13 μm. Equation (11) cannot be used beyond 13 μm; for the region 13 to 16 μm the earlier measurements of n by Salzberg and Villa [186] can be used directly, but should probably be increased by 0.0005 to bring them into agreement with the remeasured values.[185] Since germanium has become so important in tunable laser spectroscopy, a new and more precise determination of its refractive index as a function of wavelength would be desirable.

Calibration with etalons is not without its difficulties. In particular, small changes in the angle of incidence of the laser beam on the etalon, such as can be expected if a non-scanning monochromator is used for mode selection in an arrangement such as that of Fig. 8, can affect the apparent fringe spacing. This problem has been considered by Flicker et al.[187] It can be overcome by ensuring that during each spectral scan the monochromator grating drive is advanced at a rate that keeps the image of the source motionless at the exit slit; or, alternatively, by using a double monochromator with zero dispersion. With sufficient care, etalons can provide frequencies accurate to within 10^{-3} to 10^{-4} cm^{-1} near a calibration line.

Air-spaced etalons have also been used to calibrate tuning rate,[109] and have the advantage that they, unlike germanium, can be used beyond 17 μm. The low index of refraction, however, requires a much greater physical length to achieve a reasonably small fringe spacing, and means that such etalons are more susceptible to angle-of-incidence problems.[187]

The most accurate calibration can be achieved by optical heterodyne methods,[162,188] in which a spectrum analyzer is used to measure the beat frequency between the tunable laser and a known frequency such as that of a gas laser (cf. Section 3.5.2). Heterodyne calibration has not been widely used because it requires both the availability of nearby calibration lines and a somewhat more sophisticated level of instrumentation, including a wide-bandwidth infrared detector. Spears and Freed[189] have demonstrated that HgCdTe varactor photodiodes can detect beat frequencies as high as 61 GHz (2.0 cm^{-1}), and a 54 GHz beat-note has been observed in an InSb hot-carrier diode mixer;[190] these advances will significantly increase the applications of heterodyne techniques. Examples of heterodyne calibration against CO_2 laser lines can be found in Hinkley's tunable diode spectra of SF_6[191] and in Abrams' study of the contour of the CO_2 P(20) laser transition using a high pressure CO_2 source.[40]

3.4   Laser Modulation

The high powers available from tunable lasers allow the use of wide synchronous detection bandwidths without any serious degradation of the signal-to-noise ratio. This makes practicable fast-scanning techniques, in which the laser mode is rapidly swept and the detected signal is displayed directly upon an oscilloscope. With semiconductor diode lasers, this is accomplished by superimposing a sawtooth ramp upon a steady injection current, the latter serving to maintain the start of the frequency sweep at the desired position. Thus Hanson,[192] in studying the transient spectrum of shock-heated CO, scanned at a tuning rate of 10^3 cm^{-1} s^{-1} to record the full 0.05 cm^{-1} width of individual absorption lines in 50 μs. In the difference-frequency spectrometer shown in Fig. 7,[110] the cavity mirror that controls the output of the dye laser can be piezoelectrically tuned at speeds that provide a coverage of 0.1 cm^{-1} in 10 ms. These scanning rates can certainly be improved, and will find applications to studies of the kinetics of fast reactions.

The ease with which some types of tunable lasers can be frequency-modulated provides alternatives to the conventional scheme of amplitude modulation by a mechanical chopper.[5] Thus if a small sinusoidal current is superimposed on the injection current of a semiconductor diode, the signal synchronously detected at the modulation frequency will be the first derivative of the transmission spectrum, like that shown in Fig. 1(d); similarly, the second derivative can be detected at the first harmonic of the modulation frequency. Frequency modulation eliminates the need for a mechanical chopper and also makes mode filtering unnecessary, since only the mode absorbed by the sample will produce a derivative signal. The resulting simplification in the experimental arrangement is particularly attractive in applications such as pollution monitoring, where portability of equipment is more important than it is for laboratory uses. The derivative signals offer the additional advantage of tending to emphasize weak spectral features. Examples of derivative spectra obtained by frequency-modulated diode lasers have been published by Hinkley,[5,193] Antcliffe and Wrobel,[194] and others in papers cited in Section 4.1. Patel[60] has obtained derivative spectra with a spin-flip Raman laser by applying a small alternating-current magnetic field to the InSb crystal by means of air-core modulation coils mounted inside the main magnet.

Another type of modulation that may be useful in pollution monitoring and other analytical techniques is to use a square-wave excitation so the laser alternately tunes from an absorption line center to an adjacent region of no absorption. If the laser is mechanically chopped at a second frequency and detected with a second lock-in amplifier, then the ratio of the detected signals can give the fractional absorption of the monitored gas directly.[195] Square-wave modulation of Pb$_1$ $_x$Sn$_x$Te diodes at 10.3 μm has been studied by Antcliffe and Parker[19] as a method of achieving very short ($\ll 50$ μs) scan times for narrow spectral regions.

3.5 Special Detection Methods

We discuss here some detection techniques that are particularly suited to use with tunable laser sources, although they are not limited to such applications.

3.5.1 Optoacoustic detection

In this technique the gas under study acts, in effect, as its own detector: the absorbed infrared radiation excites the molecules to higher vibration–rotation levels which then relax, on microsecond time scales, by non-radiative processes that heat the gas. The incident radiation is chopped at acoustic frequencies, and the resulting periodic pressure fluctuations in the sample are detected by a sensitive pressure transducer or microphone and a lock-in amplifier. This device, called a 'spectrophone', is capable of high sensitivity for weak absorptions, since absorbed power is measured directly, and not as the difference between incident and transmitted radiation as in conventional detection. The signal is linear over a wide dynamic range, and the need for cooled detectors is eliminated, which may be an advantage in portable systems.

Optoacoustic detection was discovered as early as 1881 (see the review by Delany[196]) and was commercially developed for non-dispersive gas analyzers in the 1940s. New interest was stimulated by the development of lasers, because in an optoacoustic system the detected signal is proportional to the absorption in the gas and the intensity of the source, and thus the sensitivity improves with more powerful sources, which is not true of conventional absorption spectroscopy. Kreuzer[197] has considered in detail the applications of optoacoustic detection with laser (as opposed to thermal) sources. Since then there have been significant improvements in the technology,[198,199] most notably by the design of a resonant acoustic chamber so that the pressure fluctuations contribute to the formation of a standing acoustic wave with a pressure greater than can be induced in any single cycle, and further by modulating the beam at a frequency that coincides with one of the natural resonant frequencies of the chamber. Laser sources operating at milliwatt power levels offer the possibility of detecting molecular species at concentrations of less than 1 part in 10^9 with such techniques.[198]

Optoacoustic detection has been widely used for detection of pollutants and other vapors in low concentrations with fixed-frequency molecular gas lasers,[200–202] spin-flip Raman lasers,[61,63,66] and tunable waveguide CO_2 lasers.[40] Figure 4 shows such a detector in a spin-flip Raman laser spectrometer.[66]

3.5.2 Heterodyne detection

The use of heterodyne methods in frequency calibration was discussed briefly in Section 3.3. Optical heterodyning is also a useful method of detecting weak signals, particularly those that originate from remote thermal sources such as are of interest in pollution monitoring and in atmospheric and astrophysical studies. It provides significantly higher sensitivities than can be obtained with background-limited incoherent detection. Heterodyne detection is common in astronomy, and detailed analyses of its sensitivity and other characteristics have been made from the point of view of astrophysical applications.[203–206]

A typical experimental arrangement is shown in Fig. 11.[207] The incident radiation is mixed with the output of a coherent local oscillator (LO; here a tunable diode laser) in a high-speed wide-band infrared detector, generating a difference frequency called the intermediate frequency, or IF. The spectral characteristics of the source are preserved in the IF, but the frequency is shifted into the radiofrequency region where radio detection techniques can be used. With a fixed-frequency LO, the spectral analysis is performed by a multichannel RF filter bank, with the channel width determining the resolution. The tuning

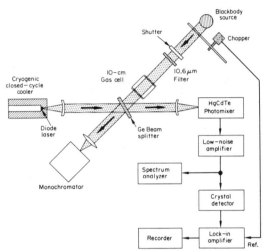

Fig. 11. Experimental arrangement for heterodyne radiometry using a tunable semiconductor diode laser as the local oscillator. The monochromator was used to examine the mode structure of the laser and for approximate wavelength calibration; the spectrum analyzer monitored the IF noise from the preamplifier (Ku and Spears, Ref. 207).

range is limited by the IF bandwidth of the mixer; the HgCdTe photodiodes used in the infrared typically have 1 to 2 GHz bandwidths, yielding a spectrum in the region $\pm(0.03 \text{ to } 0.07)$ cm^{-1} around the LO frequency.

Since the mixing signal increases with the power of the local oscillator, the limiting sensitivity is reached when the LO power is such that its fluctuations are the chief noise source; this requires power levels of the order of milliwatts c.w. in the infrared region, which are readily available from fixed-frequency gas lasers and from some types of tunable lasers (Table 1). The resolution of a heterodyne spectrometer is theoretically limited only by the long-term frequency stability of the laser which, for a stabilized gas laser, can be 10 kHz $= 3 \times 10^{-7}$ cm^{-1}. The general requirements for lasers as local oscillators have been reviewed by Wiesendanger.[208]

Heterodyne detection using fixed-frequency CO_2 LO lasers has found applications in laboratory absorption measurements on pollutant molecules,[209] in the measurement of NH_3 line positions,[175] in terrestrial atmospheric studies,[210,211] and in observations of CO_2 in the atmospheres of Mars and Venus.[212–216] However, except for CO and CO_2 lines and occasional accidental coincidences of these with absorption features of other molecules,[217,218] this method is of limited applicability. Hinkley and Kelley[219] first suggested using a tunable semiconductor diode laser as the local oscillator to increase the spectral range of the technique, and in 1975 Mumma *et al.*[220] reported the use of such a system near 8.5 μm for laboratory measurements on N_2O and to detect thermal emission from the moon and Mars at a resolution of 8×10^{-4} cm^{-1}. Semiconductor diode laser heterodyning has also been used to obtain the spectrum of atmospheric ozone,[221] and an improved system with order-of-magnitude better signal-to-noise performance has recently been reported by Ku and Spears.[207] This tunes from 920 to 980 cm^{-1}, though with a resolution at present of only *ca.* 0.02 cm^{-1}. Menzies [222] has used heterodyne detection with a CO_2 waveguide laser for ozone spectroscopy.

3.6 Techniques for Reducing the Linewidth of Gases

In a linear absorption experiment using the laser sources which we have discussed, the effective resolution is limited by the Doppler linewidth of the absorbing gas, eqn. (9), and to some extent also by the collisional linewidth,

$$\Delta\tilde{\nu} = \frac{4NQ}{c}\left[\frac{2kT}{\pi Mu}\right]^{1/2} = 9.71 \times 10^{-7} NQ \left[\frac{T}{M}\right]^{1/2}, \qquad (12)$$

where N is the number of molecules per cm^{-3} and Q is their collisional cross-section (typically $\approx 10^{-14}$ cm^2). It is obviously desirable to reduce this width, if possible, to recover the maximum amount of spectral information. One can sometimes accomplish this by lowering the sample temperature (which also has the advantage of suppressing hot-band structure), but in most cases only a modest improvement can be effected in this way before the vapor pressure becomes too low to generate a useful absorption signal in reasonable path lengths. There are, however, molecular beam techniques[223] that can almost completely eliminate inhomogenous broadening. Under such conditions collisions are virtually absent, and if the laser and molecular beams are orthogonal the Doppler width will be determined by the beam divergence, which can be made quite small.

Chu and Oka[224] used capillary tubes to produce collimated effusive beams of NH_3 and CH_3F. The tubes were 2 mm long with inside diameters of 5 μm and were arranged in bundles to provide a sufficient optical path length; Doppler width reduction by a factor of 35 was observed in Stark-modulation spectra. Pine and Nill[225] have constructed a similar system for spectroscopy of NO and CO. In both cases the reduction in the linewidth was limited by the beam divergence, which Pine and Nill[225] measured to be about 10°. There is, of course, no cooling of the gas in this technique.

A different approach is to cool the molecules dynamically by supersonic adiabatic expansion of the gas through a nozzle. The usefulness of such non-equilibrium cooling has been recognized for some years;[226,227] it has been used to study condensation products such as dimers[226] and van der Waals molecules,[227,228] but it is also applicable to the study of monomeric molecules at very low rotational and vibrational temperatures, despite extremely high supersaturation ratios. The lowest temperatures are attained from the expansion of light, inert, monatomic gases; a heavier polyatomic molecule seeded into such a gas will be aerodynamically accelerated to the carrier-gas velocity and thus will be cooled to nearly the same extent. Several such experiments using tunable diode lasers have recently been reported. Gough et al.[229] examined a free jet expansion beam of CO and measured line narrowing from 150 MHz at 300 K to ca. 20 MHz (7×10^{-4} cm^{-1}); again beam divergence was the limiting factor. In this experiment a single beam expanding from a 40 μm-diameter orifice was chopped and directed on to a doped-silicon cryogenic bolometer, which detected directly the power absorbed by the molecules from an orthogonal intersecting laser beam. Travis et al.[230] used a converging nozzle followed by free-jet expansion to study several molecular species; observation of the jet was made far enough downstream so that gas-dynamic expansion was complete and the molecules were in a condition of uniform supersonic flow. From the relative intensities of the rotational lines, rotational temperatures of 32 K in pure CO_2 and 18 K in a 10:1 He:CO_2 mixture were estimated; the vibrational temperature, however, was >250 K, indicating negligible vibrational relaxation. In SF_6, WF_6, and UF_6, both vibrational and rotational temperatures were of the order of 30 K. Similar spectroscopy of UF_6 has been carried out at Los Alamos,[231] but using a two-dimensional converging–diverging contoured nozzle with a slit throat to control the expansion.

3.7 Intraresonator Absorption

It has been known for some years that the sensitivity of detecting very weak absorptions can be increased by factors of the order of 10^5 by placing the absorber inside the resonator cavity of a multimode laser having a wide gain profile.[6,232] The absorption results in a redistribution of the emitted modes by selectively quenching those that fall within the contours of the absorption lines and thereby suffer higher losses.

This method has been used in the visible and near infrared with Nd:glass and dye lasers, but tunable lasers in the infrared proper are less easily adapted to such use, and it is, of course, out of the question for conventional diode and spin-flip Raman systems in which the inside of the optical cavity is inaccessible. Dutta et al.[233] have operated a c.w. CO-pumped SFR laser in an external cavity to permit use of an intracavity cell, and obtained a 10-fold enhancement of absorption. Brunner and Paul[232] made a theoretical investigation of intraresonator absorption in a multimode optical parametric oscillator, and concluded that mode competition can lead to enhancement factors of 10^8; to date there has been no experimental confirmation. In a double-resonance experiment, Oka et al.[234] have applied a radiofrequency field to CH_3I in a CO_2-laser cavity to observe the nuclear quadrupole spectrum.

4 LINEAR ABSORPTION SPECTROSCOPY: RESULTS

Molecules whose linear absorption spectra have been studied to date using tunable infrared sources are listed in Table 5, which summarizes the types of laser used, frequency ranges covered, calibration techniques employed, reported results, and references to the original work. In the course of tunable laser development, scans of common molecules have frequently been used to illustrate a device's capabilities; such references have been included only when they have yielded some useful spectral information on the molecules studied. In Sections 4.1 through 4.4 we will discuss in more detail the results obtained from the analyses of these data.

4.1 Band Analysis

The full analysis of a spectrum obtained with a tunable laser may present certain problems that do not exist with dispersive-spectrometer or interferometer data. A good illustration of this is the fact that the high resolution diode scans of SF_6 published by Hinkley in 1970[191,219] waited six years for a successful assignment and analysis. The major problem has been the limited tuning ranges typical of diode lasers, gas lasers, and infrared-microwave mixing techniques. These methods are very useful in studying single absorption lines, as will be discussed in Sections 4.2 through 4.4, but they have been less suitable for recording full vibration–rotation bands. Even with difference-frequency spectrometers and spin-flip Raman systems there are, as we have seen, limitations to the narrow-linewidth tuning ranges. The difficulties encountered in attempting to piece together numerous scans of different and often discontinuous spectral regions have been discussed by Montgomery and Hill,[158] and are poignantly familiar to anyone with much experience in laser spectroscopy. Fortunately, the temperature- and magnetic-tuning techniques discussed in Section 2.1 have helped to overcome these problems with diodes, and spectra with continuous wide-frequency coverage have been reported more frequently lately.

Scanning limitations have thus largely determined what types of band analyses have been attempted with tunable laser data. Q branches have been popular because they are compact and can be covered with relatively small tuning ranges, and even for light molecules Q branches are often unresolvable with conventional instrumentation. Figure 12 shows a Q branch of C_3O_2 with rather unusual characteristics. C_3O_2 has a low frequency, highly anharmonic bending mode, v_7, at about 18 cm^{-1}, and thus exhibits badly overlapping hot bands that have only begun to be disentangled with diode laser spectra.[260] The branch illustrated originates in the transition from v_7 to $v_2 + 2v_7$ at 840.0 cm^{-1}. The lower level is a Π_u state with vibrational angular momentum $l = 1$ and large l-type doubling, while the upper state is Δ_g with $l = 2$ and no first-order l-doubling.

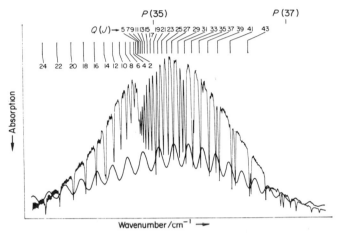

Fig. 12. The spectrum of C_3O_2 between 839.75 and 840.4 cm^{-1}, showing the $v_2 + 2v_7^2 - v_7^1$ Q branches, taken with a semiconductor diode laser in an 8.5 kG magnetic field. In the etalon trace at the bottom the fringes have a spacing of 0.03296 cm^{-1}. The $P(J)$ lines are from the $v_2 + 2v_7^0 - v_7^{1c}$ hot band (Weber *et al.*, Ref. 260).

B' for the upper state happens to fall between the B'' values for the odd and even J levels of the lower state, which differ by the l-doubling constant q. The result is a double Q branch with the odd Js of $v_2 + 2v_7^{2c} - v_7^{1d}$ progressing to higher frequencies and the even Js of $v_2 + 2v_7^{2d} - v_7^{1c}$ to lower frequencies. From the analysis of the spectrum, Weber *et al.*[260] were able to determine q, ΔB, ΔD, and ΔH, the last constant in this case representing the onset of perturbations in the high-J transitions.

Examples of wideband spectra covering P, Q, and R branches that have led to full band analyses can be found by reference to Table 5. Several of these molecules are spherical tops (i.e. they have tetrahedral or octahedral symmetry); these have characteristic vibration–rotation structures in which the individual J-levels are split by tensor terms in the Hamiltonian. While spherical tops with small moments of inertia, such as CH_4, have been adequately resolved with grating instruments, heavier molecules of this type were intractable without the resolution provided by tunable laser sources. Some of these compounds have become important in non-linear optics and laser isotope separation experiments,

TABLE 5
Linear absorption spectra obtained using tunable narrow-linewidth infrared laser sources

Molecule	Band	Laser[a]	Frequency range/cm^{-1}	Absolute frequency[b]	Tuning rate[c]	Results[d]	Special techniques used[e]	References
CH$_4$	$\nu_3, P(7)$	ZTG	2947.7–2948.0	L	I	C,W(p)		(51,235)
	$\nu_3, P(7)$	ZTG	2947.75–2948.05	L		C,W(p)		(53,236)
	$\nu_3, P(7)$	ZTG	2947.75–2948.02	L			S	(237)
	$\nu_3, P(7)$	ZTG	2947.87–2947.91	L	C	S,W		(54)
	ν_3	DFS	2916–3132	A	I	A,F(t),I		(109,110,238)
	ν_4	ZTG	1287–1337(portions)	L	I			(52)
	ν_4	SDL	1300–1340	A	E	A,B,F(t)		(239)
C$_2$H$_4$	ν_7, Q	SDL	949.18–949.26	M		S	D	(219)
	ν_7	SDL	947.1–951.9	A,M				(158)
	ν_7	SDL	1030.4–1031.3		E			(29)
	$\nu_7 + \nu_8, P$	SFR	1877–1884			A,B		(240)
C$_2$H$_6$	ν_9, Q	SDL	806–846	A	E	A,B		(241)
CH$_3$F	$\nu_1, P(6-8)$	ZTG	2850.6–2853.0	L	C	A		(50,242)
	ν_3, Q	SDL	1005–1100		E	A		(243)
^{13}CH$_3$F	$\nu_3, R(4)$	CTG	1035.5			W	F	(224)
CH$_3$I	ν_1	ZTG	2848.7–2849.7	L			D,S,W	(50)
CH$_2$O	ν_1/ν_4	SDL	2802–2803	L	C		D	(244)
	ν_4	ZTG	2850.43–2850.83	L	M	A,B,C,F(s,k),W(p)	F	(53,236,245)
	ν_4	ZTG	2848.2–2853.0	L	C		S	(50)
CHDO	ν_1	ZTG	2850.43–2850.83	L	M	A,B,F(s,k)	D	(245)
C$_3$H$_2$O	ν_6	SDL	942.8, 952.3	M	M	W(p)		(246)
CF$_4$	ν_4	SDL	602–654	A	E	A,B,F(t),I	F	(247,248)
CO	1–0, $P(10,11)$	SDL	2077.0, 2099.0		E	C,S,W		(192,195)
	1–0, $P(7,9)$	SDL	2107.4, 2115.6	A	C,D	C,S,W		(32,249)
	1–0, $P(1-8)$	SDL	2110–2140			S,W	D	(250)
	1–0, $R(23)$	SDL	2227.6		E	S		(251)

Molecule	Band	Laser[a]	Frequency range/cm^{-1}	Calibration — Absolute frequency[b]	Calibration — Tuning rate[c]	Results[d]	Special techniques used[e]	References
CO_2	ν_2, Q	SDL	667.3–668.1	A	E	S		(155)
	ν_2, Q	SDL	667.3–667.7				W	(230)
	ν_2, Q, R	SDL	667.3–669.0	A	A	A,S,W(p)		(252,253)
	$2\nu_2 - \nu_2, Q$	SDL	617.8–618.1	M	E	A,B		(254)
	ν_3	SDL	2305.1–2306.3		E	A,W		(255)
	$\nu_3 - \nu_1, P(18)$	IMM	945.975–945.985	L	F	W(p)		(134)
	$\nu_3 - \nu_1, P(20)$	HPG	944.2		H	C,W(p)	O	(40)
$^{13}CO_2$	ν_2, Q	SDL	648.4–649.3	A	E	A,B		(256)
	$\nu_3, P(46)$	SDL	2241.5		E	S		(251)
	$\nu_1 - \nu_2, Q$	SDL	617	A	E	A,B		(251)
$^{14}CO_2$	ν_3	SDL	2203–2245	A	E	C,S,W		(258)
CO_2 isotopes	ν_3	SDL	2330			S		
C_3O_2	ν_4	SDL	1565–1612	A	E	A,B		(259)
	$\nu_2 + \nu_7, Q$	SDL	819–850	A,I	E	A,B		(260)
COS	$\nu_1 + 2\nu_2$	SFR	1876–1896	A,T	E,H	A,B,W(p)	O,P	(63,64)
	$\nu_1 + 2\nu_2$	SFR	1852–1914	A	C	A,B,I	P	(159)
	$\nu_1 + 2\nu_2$	SFR	1875–1882	A	C	A	I	(233)
$^{35}ClO, ^{37}ClO$	$1-0$	SDL	840–870	A,M	E	A,B,F(Λ),I,S	D	(261)
DBr	$1-0, R(4)$	SFR	1879–1881			I	P	(64,262)
HCN	$\nu_2, P(15)$	SDL	667.6	A	E	W		(155)
H_2O	ν_2	SFR	1885.0–1885.5	L	H	C,P,S,W(p)		(77)
	ν_2	SDL	1860–1970	A,L,M	D,E,H	S		(183,263–266)
	ν_2	SFR	1889.55–1889.61					(267)
	ν_2	SFR	1884.6, 1889.6	I		W(p)	O	(268)
$H_2O, H_2^{18}O$	ν_3	DFS	3839.1–3840.3		I	A,C,W		(109)

TABLE 5—*continued*

Molecule	Band	Laser[a]	Frequency range/cm^{-1}	Calibration Absolute frequency[b]	Calibration Tuning rate[c]	Results[d]	Special techniques used[e]	References
NH$_3$	ν_1,Q	DFS	3331.3–3332.5		I	A,C,W		(109)
	$\nu_2,aQ(8,7)$	CTG	927.7	L		W	D,S,W	(224)
	$\nu_2,sP(1,0)$	SDL	948.2–948.3	M		W		(219)
	$\nu_2,sQ(5,K)$	SDL	966.0–966.9	M		A	F	(19)
	$\nu_2,sR(5,K)$	SDL	1084.4–1084.8	L	E	A,S,W(p)		(29)
	ν_4	SDL	1545–1595		E	A,F(i),S	S	(269)
ND$_3$	ν_3	ZTG	2851.7–2853.3	L	C		D	(50)
NO	1–0	SFR	1835–1890	A,T	E,H	A,F(λ,n),S,W(p)	O,P	(63,64,262,270)
	1–0,P	SFR	1810–1825			A,S		(66)
	1–0,Q	SDL	1876–1880	M	D	F(λ,n),S		(32,182)
	1–0,Q	SDL	1875.2–1876.2			A,F(λ)	F	(37)
	1–0,$Q_{3/2}$	SFR	1874.2–1875.2	A	C	A	I	(233)
	1–0,$R(1/2)_{1/2}$	SDL	1881.15–1881.19	M		F(λ),S,W		(271)
	1–0,$R(15/2)$	SDL	1903.1–1903.7		E	F(λ),S,W	D,Z	(272)
	1–0,$R(15/2)$	SDL	1903		E	F(λ)	D,W	(225)
N$_2$O	$\nu_1+\nu_3$	DFS	3480.9–3482.0	T	I	A,F(λ),W	F	(109)
	$\nu_2+\nu_3,Q$	DFS	2796.9–2798.3	T	I	A,B		(110)
O$_3$	ν_3	SDL	1010.9–1011.8		H		H	(221)
OsO$_4$	ν_3	SDL	944–968	A,L	E	A,B,F(t),S		(273–275)
SF$_6$	ν_3	SDL	940–951	L,M	H			(191,219)
	ν_3	SDL	942–952	A,L	E,H	A,B,F(o)		(13,247,273,276–8)
	ν_3,P	HPG	944.19–944.20	L				(279)
	ν_3,P	IMM	944.6–944.8	L	H			(131)
	ν_4,Q	SDL	615		E		W	(230)

Molecule	Band	Laser[a]	Frequency range/cm⁻¹	Calibration Absolute frequency[b]	Tuning rate[c]	Results[d]	Special techniques used[e]	References
SO₂	ν_1	SDL	1128–1132	M		W(p)	D	(194)
	ν_1	SDL	1115–1158	A		A,C,S,W(p)		(350)
	ν_1,R	SDL	1176–1266	A,M	A	W(p)	F	(35)
	ν_3	SDL	1350–1356	A	E	C,W	M	(280)
	$\nu_1+\nu_3$	DFS	2463–2526	A	I	A,B		(281)
SbH₃	$\nu_1/\nu_3,Q$	SFR	1872	A,T	E			(63,64)
UF₆	ν_3	SDL	625–630			A,B,F(o)	W	(230)
	ν_3	SDL	624–630	A	E	A,B,I,F(o),S	F,W	(231)
WF₆	ν_3,Q	SDL	713.0–714.0	A		I	W	(230)

[a] CTG = cavity-tuned gas laser, DFS = difference-frequency spectrometer, HPG = high-pressure gas laser, IMM = infrared-microwave mixing, SDL = semiconductor diode laser, SFR = spin-flip Raman laser, ZTG = Zeeman-tuned gas laser.

[b] A = absorption lines of gases, I = interferometer, L = gas laser frequencies, M = monochromator, T = laser tuning curve.

[c] A = absorption lines of gases, C = calculated from laser tuning parameters, D = Doppler width of known lines, E = etalon, F = direct frequency measurements, H = heterodyne techniques, I = interferometer, M = laser mode separation.

[d] A = assignments; B = band analysis and molecular constants; C = line contour and shape studies; F = fine structure, including (i) = inversion doubling, (k) = K-type doubling, (Λ) = Λ-doubling, (n) = nuclear hyperfine structure, (o,t) = octahedral and tetrahedral splitting in spherical tops, (s) = Stark splitting; I = linewidths; P = pressure shift coefficients; S = line strengths, absorption coefficients, and intensity measurements; W = linewidths, including (p) = pressure-broadening coefficients; no entry indicates that the spectrum is illustrated but that no analysis was made.

[e] D = derivative spectra, F = fast-scan techniques, H = heterodyne detection, I = intracavity absorption, M = matrix isolation spectra, O = optoacoustic detection, P = pulsed laser operation, S = Stark modulation, W = linewidth reduction by beam or nozzle techniques, Z = Zeeman spectra.

and since tunable lasers have furnished such detailed spectra of their vibration–rotation transitions and have been successfully analyzed, it seems appropriate to discuss briefly these results.

The theory of the band structure of spherical tops was developed in the early 1960s by Moret-Bailly[282,283] and Hecht[284] and was applied to the infrared absorption spectra of CH_4 and its analogues. Their results for the transition frequencies in the P, Q, and R branches can be approximated as[285]

$$v_{P,R}(J,p) = m+nM+pM^2+qM^3+ \ldots +(g-hM+kM^2+ \ldots)\bar{F}(4)$$
$$v_Q(J,p) = m+vJ(J+1)+wJ^2(J+1)^2+ \ldots +[-2g+uJ(J+1)+ \ldots]\bar{F}(4) \quad (13)$$

with off-diagonal terms in the Hamiltonian neglected. Here $M = [-J,(J+1)]$ for $[P,R]$-branch transitions, p designates the sublevel (classified according to its tetrahedral or octahedral symmetry), and $\bar{F}(4)$ is the product of a symmetry-adapted fourth-rank tensor operator times a J-dependent factor. The first terms in these equations will be recognized as the usual scalar expressions for the manifold frequencies, where m is the band origin, $n \approx B_v+B_0-2(B\zeta)_i$, $p \approx v \approx B_v-B_0$, etc. The second or tensor portions describe the splitting of the individual J-manifolds into their various symmetry-allowed component levels. Values of $\bar{F}(4)$ for all (J,p) levels up to $J = 100$ have recently been tabulated by Krohn.[286] An example of the splitting patterns of high-J manifolds is provided by the CF_4 spectrum in Fig. 13.[247] Such patterns have been explained by Harter and Patterson[287,288] on the basis of quantization

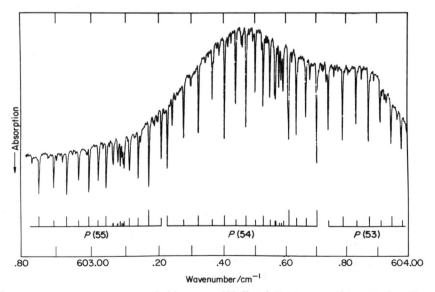

Fig. 13. Spectrum of CF_4 recorded between 602.8 and 604.0 cm^{-1} with a semiconductor diode laser, showing resolved, high-J, P-branch manifolds (McDowell, Ref. 247).

of the total angular momentum J about the three-fold and four-fold symmetry axes of the molecule.

For methane-type molecules, with small moments of inertia, observed transitions are limited to J values of 15 or so. There was no need to consider higher angular momentum states because the bands of heavier molecules that exhibit high-J transitions simply could not be adequately resolved before the development of tunable laser spectroscopy. Now that this capability is available, additional interest in spherical tops has been stimulated by the fact that two important non-linear absorbers of 10.5 μm CO_2 laser radiation, SF_6 and OsO_4, belong to this class.

The most thoroughly studied absorption at 10.5 μm is the v_3 fundamental of SF_6 shown in Fig. 1. A wide variety of non-linear optics experiments (saturation, self-induced transparency, optical nutation, photon echoes, etc.) have been carried out using this molecule; a bibliography covering such work is available,[273] as is one on photodissociation and laser isotope experiments on SF_6.[274] Since these effects have been observed with specific CO_2 laser lines, it became important to identify the SF_6 transitions involved. Heterodyne-calibrated, Doppler-limited SF_6 spectra near the CO_2 $P(14)$ to $P(22)$ laser frequencies were obtained by Hinkley in 1970 using semiconductor diodes,[191,219] Fig. 1(c); they revealed a complex vibration–rotation structure with a high line density, caused by the overlapping of individual manifolds such as the ones shown in Fig. 13. Because of the small fraction ($\approx 2\%$) of the v_3 band covered in these measurements, however, it was not possible to assign the individual transitions.

In 1975 Aldridge et al.[276] at Los Alamos first obtained diode spectra that were nearly continuous over much of the band, and concurrently Cantrell and Galbraith[289] derived the nuclear-spin statistical weights for octahedral XY_6 molecules, which are 2,10,8,6,6 for sublevels of $p = A_1, A_2, E, F_1, F_2$ symmetry if the Y-nuclei have spins $I = 1/2$. These advances allowed most of the rotational structure in Hinkley's spectra to be assigned.[13,277,278] Thus the strong absorption of SF_6 that almost coincides with CO_2 $P(16)$ (947.741978 cm^{-1}[160]) in Fig. 1(c) is identified as $Q(38)$ $F_1^0 + E^0 + F_2^0$; its triplet nature, unresolved in the Doppler-limited spectrum, is clearly shown in the saturation spectrum of Fig. 1(d).[14] The splitting between E^0 and each of the F^0 lines is 500 kHz or 1.7×10^{-5} cm^{-1}. Figure 14 shows an example of the high-J assignments near CO_2 $P(12)$.[278] Some 10 000 transitions have thus been identified between 942 and 952 cm^{-1}. With these detailed assignments available, it was possible to identify the absorptions in a series of very high resolution saturation spectra, such as that of Fig. 1(d), observed by Clairon and Henry[14] and measured with an accuracy of ± 30 kHz (10^{-6} cm^{-1}) in absolute frequency. Equations (13) were then fitted to these line positions with off-diagonal terms in the Hamiltonian included, resulting in a determination of the molecular constants of this band to very high precision.[15] The v_3 band origin, for example, is $m = (947.9765759 \pm 0.0000043)$ cm^{-1}; the uncertainty of 4.5 parts in 10^9 is about that of the currently accepted value of the velocity of light! Such results were beyond the reach of infrared techniques until the development of laser spectroscopy. The application of the assignments to the interpretation of self-induced transparency and photon-echo-polarization experiments on SF_6 is discussed in Refs (273, 274, 278).

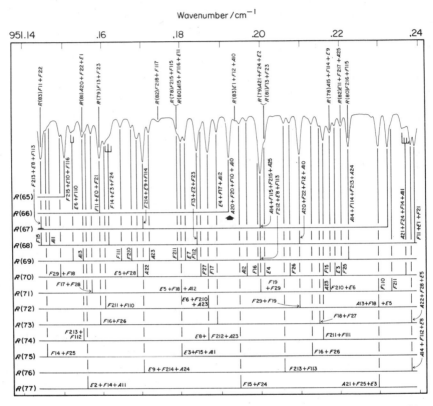

Fig. 14. The absorption spectrum of SF_6 at 140 K between 951.14 and 951.24 cm⁻¹ with the transitions identified. To reduce crowding, the octahedral quantum numbers are all written on one line; thus $E8 + F212 + A23$ is to be read as $E^8 + F_2^{12} + A_2^3$. The arrow indicates the position of the CO_2 P(12) laser line at 951.192262 cm⁻¹ (McDowell *et al.*, Ref. 278).

Figure 10 shows a *P*-branch manifold of the stretching fundamental v_3 of OsO_4, which is also nearly coincident with a CO_2 laser line. Because of the zero nuclear spin of the oxygen ligands, only sublevels of $p = A_1$ or A_2 symmetry exist; since, on the average, only 20% of spherical-top rotational levels have these symmetries, a considerable simplification of the spectrum results for tetroxide molecules. A full analysis of this band is now complete and will be published shortly.[275]

4.2   Rotational Fine Structure

The narrow linewidths of tunable laser sources have made it possible to study in the infrared region details of rotational fine structure that could previously be resolved only with microwave techniques. An excellent example is provided by Λ-doubling in such molecules as nitric oxide. NO is the only stable diatomic molecule with an unpaired π electron in its electronic ground state; it thus has a total electron spin $S = 1/2$ and a net electronic orbital angular momentum $\mathbf{L}$ whose projection on the internuclear axis is $\Lambda = 1$. The resulting ground state configuration, $^2\Pi$, is split into its two components ($^2\Pi_{1/2}$ and $^2\Pi_{3/2}$) by spin-orbit interaction: the projection of S on the molecular axis, $\Sigma = \pm 1/2$, can be parallel or opposed to Λ, and these two alignments have resultant total electronic angular momenta about the axis of $\Omega = \Lambda + \Sigma = 1/2$ and $3/2$, respectively. Each J-transition in the vibrational fundamental $[^2\Pi_\Omega(v = 1,J') - {}^2\Pi_\Omega(v = 0,J)$, $J = \Omega, \Omega + 1, \ldots]$ near 5.3 μm will have two components corresponding to these two values of Ω.

Nill et al.[272] first observed the Λ-doubling of $R(15/2)_{1/2}$ in 1972, in a Doppler-limited diode spectrum. The two components were split by 318 MHz = 0.0106 cm^{-1}; the $R(15/2)_{3/2}$ line, on the other hand, has a calculated splitting of only 28 MHz that could not be resolved because of the 127-MHz Doppler linewidth at 300 K. Λ-doubling in NO has since been observed at many different lines in the vibrational fundamental, using both diode[37,182,271] and spin-flip Raman[63,81] lasers, and magnetic rotation[290] as well as standard absorption techniques. Figure 15 shows the $Q(1/2)_{1/2}$ transition as recorded by Blum et al.[182] with a diode, with the Λ-doubling represented by the gross splitting Δ_2; the additional structure will be discussed below. The two main components are separated by 843 MHz, compared with a value of 838 MHz calculated from the known microwave constants of NO. Recently Pine and Nill[225] have obtained sub-Doppler derivative spectra using the collimated beam technique (Section 3.6) in which the 28 MHz splitting of $R(15/2)_{3/2}$ is clearly resolved. In the free radical ClO, Menzies et al.[261] observed a Λ-doubling of ca. 700 MHz in the $^2\Pi_{1/2}$ states; again the $^2\Pi_{3/2}$ doubling is too small to be resolved in Doppler-limited spectra.

In Π, Δ, $\ldots$ vibrational levels of linear polyatomic molecules there is an analogous effect arising from the vibrational angular momentum $\mathbf{l}$ and known as l-type doubling. Such a splitting has been observed in the 11^11-01^10 hot band of N_2O at 2.87 μm; it amounted to 0.030 cm^{-1} for the $R(9)$ and $R(10)$ transitions.[109] Manifold splittings due to the vibrational angular momentum in spherical top molecules have been illustrated in Section 4.1.

The additional structure observed in Fig. 15 arises from nuclear hyperfine splitting.[182] The molecular angular momentum J is coupled to the nuclear spin ($I = 1$) of the ^{14}N nucleus by the electron magnetic moment, resulting in a total angular momentum $F = I+J, I+J-1, \ldots, |I-J|$. The energy levels and hyperfine transitions for one component of the Λ doublet are shown in the figure; there are thus eight components in $Q(1/2)_{1/2}$ that fall into four nearly degenerate pairs. The structure calculated using microwave values for the Λ-doubling and magnetic hyperfine coupling constants is shown at the bottom of Fig. 15, and agrees well with the observed spectrum. This splitting has also been resolved in NO with a spin-flip Raman source.[63] Hyperfine structure in CH_4 at 3.39 μm has been observed using an He–Ne laser by means of saturation spectroscopy (Section 6).

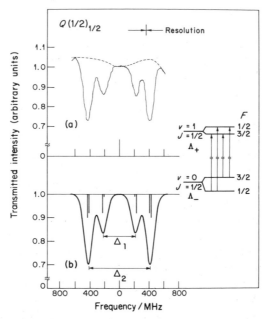

Fig. 15. The $Q(1/2)_{1/2}$ transition in the vibrational fundamental of NO at 1876.1 cm^{-1}, as (a) observed using a semiconductor diode laser, and (b) calculated from microwave parameters and an assumed Gaussian lineshape (Blum *et al.*, Ref. 182).

Another type of rotational fine structure is inversion doubling in non-planar molecules. In $v_3 = 1$ of NH_3 this amounts to about 36 cm^{-1}; the doubling of this band at 10.5 μm can be resolved even with prism instruments and has been understood for some years.[291] Weber *et al.*[269] have measured the splittings in the v_4 fundamental with a diode laser and have compared them with microwave values; in $v_4 = 1$ the inversion doubling is ≈ 1 cm^{-1}. In heavier pyramidal molecules, particularly for vibrational states that do not tend to excite the inversion directly as does v_3 of NH_3, this effect will be observable only with the resolution provided by tunable laser sources.

Stark and Zeeman spectroscopy, in which the molecule under study interacts with an external electric or magnetic field, respectively, are useful methods for resolving rotational levels that are degenerate in the absence of an applied field.

Those studies in which Stark or Zeeman splittings have been resolved using tunable laser sources are indicated in Table 5; the reader is referred to Hinkley et al.[5] and Querry[7] for further discussions.

4.3 Lineshape and Linewidth Studies[292]

Even when grating spectrometers or interferometers can resolve individual vibration–rotation lines, they fall far short of being able to reveal the details of the line contours. Thus at 300 K the full Doppler width of a 10 μm transition is only 0.002 cm^{-1} for a molecule of mass 38 a.m.u. (eqn. (9)), and a resolution much less than this would be required to show the contour accurately. Here laser spectroscopy offers an advantage that was exploited soon after the development of tunable sources.

The Doppler linewidths observed at very low pressures were discussed in Section 3.3 as providing known frequency intervals useful in calibrating the laser tuning rate. Examples of Doppler-limited spectra are those of SF_6 in Figs 1(c) and 14. A particularly good example is the H_2O line[293] to be discussed in Section 6 (Fig. 18); its measured full width at half-maximum absorption is 167 MHz, compared with 166 MHz calculated from eqn. (9). It is well known that in the Doppler-broadening pressure regime the lineshapes are Gaussian;[294] a careful study of the low-pressure contour of $P(7)$ of CO at 2115.6 cm^{-1} indicates that the theoretical Gaussian shape is an excellent fit to the observed line.[5]

When the pressure is great enough for pressure (collisional) broadening to dominate, the lineshape is Lorentzian;[294] this shape has been confirmed for water vapor lines near 5 μm by Eng et al.[264] Pressure-broadening coefficients, both for self-broadening and foreign gas broadening, have been measured for many of the molecules listed in Table 5. There is typically a linear relation between the pressure and linewidth in the collision-dominated regime, with coefficients in the range 0.01 to 1 cm^{-1} atm^{-1}. Thus for the $aQ(9,3)$ transition in NH_3 at 939.2 cm^{-1}, Hinkley[5] has measured a Doppler linewidth of 0.0028 cm^{-1} below ca. 4 Torr; above this pressure the width increases with pressure at the rate of 0.63 cm^{-1} atm^{-1} for self-broadening and 0.16 cm^{-1} atm^{-1} for broadening by air. The air-broadening coefficients of several 5 μm water-vapor lines have been measured by Eng et al.[264,265] and fall between 0.014 and 0.18 cm^{-1} atm^{-1}. The values for low-J lines are in reasonable agreement with those calculated from accepted line-broadening theory, but for $J \geqslant 12$ the observed widths are much narrower than they are calculated to be.

In the pressure regime intermediate between Doppler and collisional broadening, lineshapes are represented by the convolution of Gaussian and Lorentzian shapes (Voight profile).[294] Hansen et al.[195] have obtained a good fit to a CO line observed in combustion gases using such a contour with an adjustable Voight parameter a, which is $(\ln 2)^{1/2}$ times the ratio of the collision-broadened and Doppler-broadened linewidths. From the best-fit value of

$a = 2.47$ and the known Doppler width at the temperature of observation (2066 K), they were able to estimate a pressure-broadening coefficient of $0.0995 \text{ cm}^{-1} \text{ atm}^{-1}$.

While increasing the pressure normally broadens the line contours, Dicke[292,295] has shown that the opposite effect can be observed under conditions in which the mean free path for velocity-changing collisions is both shorter than the mean free path for line-broadening collisions and much less than the wavelength of the probe radiation.[5] Such Dicke narrowing has been observed in the infrared by Eng et al.[183] for high J-transitions in water vapor. For the line at 1879.0 cm^{-1}, which consists of the degenerate transitions $16_{0,16} \leftarrow 15_{1,15}$ and $16_{1,16} \leftarrow 15_{0,15}$, they measured a full width at half-maximum of 170 MHz at 2.0 Torr (calculated Doppler width 165 MHz); with the addition of 82 Torr of xenon this decreased to 115 MHz, and then began to increase at higher pressures.

Investigations of the gain lineshapes of laser lines were first carried out by Blum et al.,[296] using a tunable diode to probe a CO laser line at 5.3 μm. They were able to determine directly the temperature of the lasing gas for the first time from the observed Doppler widths. Corcoran et al.[134] used their infrared-microwave mixing spectrometer (Section 2.5.2) to scan the gain line profile of CO_2 $P(18)$ under different conditions of temperature and pressure.

4.4   Line Intensity and Band Strength Measurements

For pollutant molecules or those of interest in atmospheric studies, quantitative determination of line intensities is particularly important. Molecules for which these measurements are available are indicated in Table 5; further reference is made to the works cited in Section 7.2.

It is well known that a vibrational transition dipole moment can be obtained either from the strength of an individual gas-phase vibration–rotation line or from the total band strength.[294] Determination of the latter quantity is plagued by several significant experimental difficulties, of which the most important arise from the finite resolving power of the spectrometer; these have hindered progress in this area.[294,297,298] Now that the contours of individual lines can be completely resolved, it appears that line-strength measurements may offer the most accurate method of determining band-intensity parameters.

Recently Fox and Person[299] have derived the expression relating the total band strength of spherical-top molecules to individual line strengths and have reviewed the available data. There are only a few cases in which the two approaches can be compared, but in these the agreement is satisfactory. Most of the line intensity measurements were made with grating spectrometers on light tetrahedral molecules such as CH_4 and GeH_4, but Fox and Person were able to determine a transition moment of 0.11 D ($1D \equiv 3.3356 \times 10^{-30}$ C m) for ν_4 of SF_6 from unpublished diode spectra obtained at Los Alamos;[300] this is within 10% of the value obtained from Schatz and Hornig's band intensity measurements using a prism spectrometer.[301] Fox[302] has since used such results to calculate the strengths of the v_3 transitions that fall near the CO_2 laser lines, and found reasonable agreement with the available experimental values. For this particular band, the experimental data consist not only of line strengths measured from high resolution diode spectra, but also of estimates of the transition dipole obtained from non-linear effects such as saturation data, optical nutation, and self-induced transparency. These results are not always in close agreement, and there is not yet a final estimate available for the v_3 transition moment, though it falls near 0.4 D.

It seems clear that line strength measurements, which are the most direct methods of obtaining band strength and transition-moment information, will become more important in such studies over the next few years.

5   DOUBLE RESONANCE SPECTROSCOPY

In double resonance spectroscopy (DRS), two different frequencies are used simultaneously to excite and probe a set of molecular energy levels. It is a useful technique for both the analysis of complex spectra and the study of relaxation processes of specific molecular energy levels.[303,304]

Most such spectroscopy to date has used a fixed-frequency infrared pump together with a microwave spectrometer or a fixed-frequency infrared probe, and thus does not fall within the subject of this review. In infrared-microwave DRS the molecules are excited by fixed (or line-tunable) infrared frequencies and the ensuing population changes are monitored by microwave absorption; references to recent theoretical and experimental work in this area are given by Shimoda.[304,305] Infrared–infrared double resonance using CO_2 laser lines for both pump and probe have been reported on CO_2,[306] SF_6,[307–312] BCl_3,[309,312,313] and other molecules that absorb in the 9 to 11 μm region. These experiments have yielded interesting results on the nature of higher vibrational levels and on V–V and V–T energy transfer processes, especially as they apply to multiphoton absorption and laser isotope separation. Steinfeld et al.,[308,310] for example, were thus able to map the absorption curve of the $2v_3$–v_3 transition in SF_6, but only at the resolution of 1.8 cm^{-1} provided by the CO_2 line spacing in this region.

In an important recent experiment, Moulton et al.[314] have detected transient DR phenomena using a tunable laser for the first time. The beams from a low-power semiconductor diode laser and a high-power (≈ 1 kW cm^{-2}) Q-switched CO_2 laser were crossed within a low-pressure cell of SF_6. The probe beam was chopped at 400 Hz and detected by a system with a < 100 ns response time; this component was processed by a lock-in amplifier to give the usual absorption spectrum of the sample. The pump laser was synchronized to go on as the chopper opened, so a fast component, coincident with the pump pulse, appeared under double-resonance conditions; this was recovered by a boxcar integrator to give a signal proportional to the transient *change* in transmission caused by the pump laser.

Four different processes, illustrated schematically in Fig. 16, were observed in v_3 of SF_6. (The pump field, of amplitude E, induces a level splitting by the Rabi frequency $\mu E/\hbar$, where μ is the transition dipole moment. These split levels are indicated by dashed lines; they were not resolved in the experiments of Moulton *et al.* and were apparently smeared out by Doppler broadening.) In the induced

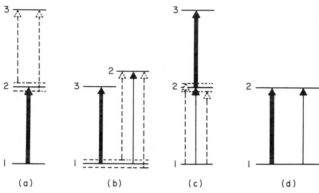

Fig. 16. Excitation diagrams for four processes observed in double-resonance experiments. Thick arrows represent the pump radiation, thin arrows the probe radiation. The Rabi-split levels and their associated transitions are indicated by dashed lines and arrows (Moulton *et al.*, Ref. 314).

transient-absorption process of Fig. 16(a), the pump beam populates level 2 and the probe detects a transition from that level to a higher excited level. An example of the DR signal is shown in Fig. 17(a); it represents the direct observation of a $2v_3 - v_3$ transition, and of course does not coincide with any feature of the ground-state spectrum shown at the bottom of Fig. 17(a). In (b) and (c), also three-level processes, the effect of the pump pulse is to induce transmission at the frequency of the transition from the ground state (level 1) to level 2. Finally, (d) illustrates induced transmission signals from a two-level process in which the probe frequency is tuned through the pump frequency ('hole burning'). The probe absorption is bleached at frequencies out to a few Doppler widths from the pump, which excites several different $2 \leftarrow 1$ transitions because of power broadening.

The type (a) signal in Fig. 17 represents the first high resolution observation of a $2v_3 - v_3$ transition in SF_6. Such sampling of upper-stage levels should yield significant information about the mechanism of multiphoton absorption and dissociation. Perturbations in the ground-state spectrum (processes b, c, d) have been useful in making high-J assignments for SF_6.[278] In addition, Moulton *et al.*[314] were able to study relaxation behavior at fixed probe frequencies using a transient digitizer and signal averaging system, and obtained estimates for collisional decay times in the ground and excited states. Clearly, transient double-resonance spectroscopy is a technique of great promise.

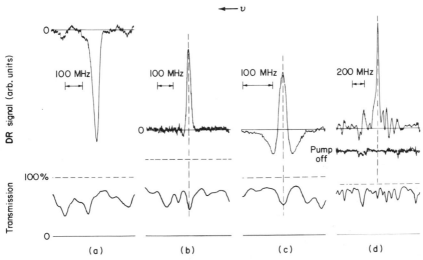

Fig. 17. Transient double resonance signals in SF_6 corresponding to the four processes of Fig. 16, with simultaneously-recorded absorption spectra shown below. The CO_2 pump lines were $P(18)$, $P(16)$, $P(22)$, and $P(12)$ in (a)–(d), respectively, and the main DR peaks are at 944.91, 945.69, 943.59, and 951.19 cm^{-1}, respectively. The absorption spectrum in (d) corresponds to the central region of Fig. 14, except that here the temperature was 300 K and the higher-J transitions appear stronger (note also that the frequency increases in the opposite direction in this figure) (Moulton et al., Ref. 314).

6 SATURATION SPECTROSCOPY

In linear absorption spectroscopy 'natural' linewidths (i.e. the linewidths characteristic of the radiative lifetimes of the transitions) are always obscured by Doppler broadening. One method of reducing this effect is by the use of the molecular beam methods discussed in Section 3.6. Another is by the techniques of non-linear spectroscopy using intense optical fields.[6,223,315–321] We will discuss here only the simplest non-linear effect, saturation spectroscopy.

A Doppler-broadened line in a gas sample is actually the superposition of numerous individual absorptions due to molecules having different thermal velocities; this process is thus termed 'inhomogeneous broadening'. Each of these lines has a 'homogeneous' width that is the natural (radiative-lifetime) linewidth (typically of the order of some kHz in the infrared), modified by broadening due to collisions, the effect of the molecular transit time through the beam, and power broadening by the field. A coherent light wave will interact with only those molecules whose Doppler shift exactly compensates the detuning of the source frequency from the transition frequency. If the incident wave is strong enough to saturate the absorption (i.e. to raise an appreciable fraction of the molecules to an excited state), a hole will form in the Doppler distribution of the ground-state molecules due to their removal by the saturating beam (cf. the 'hole-burning' process of Fig. 16(d)).

Consider now the following experiment: a powerful, tunable monochromatic source illuminates a gas cell that has a partially reflecting mirror at the far end, so that part of the beam is reflected back through the cell as a probe wave. Since the saturating and probe waves have the same frequency but opposite directions, the probe will interact with only molecules whose velocity is of opposite sign from that of the molecules with which the saturating beam interacted. If the source is now tuned to coincide with the transition frequency v_0, then the probe wave will sample molecules which have already had their ground-state populations depleted by the saturating wave. The probe wave absorption then has a sharp resonance minimum at exactly the center v_0 of the Doppler-broadened line. Resonances of this type are called 'Lamb dips' after W. E. Lamb, who predicted a similar dip in the tuning characteristics of a gas laser in 1964;[322] in an absorption experiment such as described here, the resonance is more properly called an inverted Lamb dip.

As an example we may cite an experiment performed by Patel[293] using a CO-pumped InSb spin-flip Raman laser. To avoid power broadening, the usual 1 W output was attenuated to $ca.$ 10 mW in a 2 cm diameter beam. The probe wave making the second traversal of the cell was incident on a detector whose signal was ratioed against that of a reference detector which monitored the beam entering the cell. The results for a water vapor transition at 1889.58 cm^{-1} are shown in Fig. 18. The absorption feature was discussed in Section 4.3, and shown there to have the width predicted for a Doppler-broadened line. In addition, a Lamb dip appears at the line center with a width of about 200 kHz $= 7 \times 10^{-6}$ cm^{-1}. Patel estimated that under the conditions of this experiment the homogeneous broadening of the absorption line should be about 100 kHz; the remainder of the observed width is due to frequency instabilities of the pump laser.

The observation of non-linear responses requires power densities of the order of 10 mW cm^{-2}, and the size of the effect scales directly with this quantity; furthermore, the laser linewidth must be narrower than the homogeneous width of the transition to resolve all the fine structure that might be hidden by inhomogeneous broadening. This places stringent requirements on the power and frequency stability of the laser source, and in fact Patel's experiment described above is the only case yet reported of a widely tunable laser being used for saturation spectroscopy. There are, however, scores of examples of the use of narrowly tunable gas lasers to study either the laser transitions themselves or absorption lines of other molecules that are accidentally in near coincidence with the laser lines. Since this is somewhat outside the main subject of this review, the reader is referred to the articles cited earlier for further details;[6,223,315—321] here we will just take note of some of the more interesting of these results.

The near coincidence of the 3.39 μm He–Ne laser line with a vibration-rotation transition of CH_4 was noted in Section 2.2.2. This line has been thoroughly studied using non-linear techniques.[56,136,323—327] In their most recent work, Hall and Bordé[328] have pushed the resolution of the Lamb dip in methane to 1 kHz (resolving power 8×10^{10}) and were able to observe a line splitting of 2.15 kHz due to the radiative recoil of the molecules that emit or absorb infrared photons. Other organic molecules have C—H stretching fundamentals in this region, and saturation spectra of CH_3X (X = F, Cl, Br, or I), CH_3OH, and C_2H_6 have been discussed by Hall and Magyar.[327]

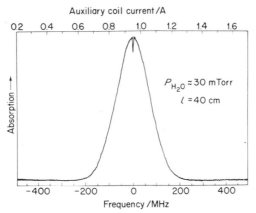

Fig. 18. Lamb dip superimposed on the $\nu_2(6_{4,3} \leftarrow 5_{3,2})$ transition of H_2O at 1889.58 cm^{-1}. Recorded with a CO-pumped spin-flip Raman laser with a primary magnetic field of 1.17 kG and fine-tuned with the current in an auxiliary trimmer coil mounted inside the magnet (Patel, Ref. 293).

In the 9 to 11 μm region, CO_2 lasers have been used for saturation spectroscopy of several molecules. In connection with the non-linear optical results that were being obtained by pumping SF_6 with CO_2 laser radiation, and with the search for resonances against which the laser could be stabilized, saturation spectra of SF_6 were reported in 1969.[329—333] A recent high resolution saturation spectrum of SF_6 obtained by Clairon and Henry[14] is shown in Fig. 1(d), and was discussed in Section 4.1. An expanded scan of the triplet at 947.7417 cm^{-1} was recently published by Ouhayoun and Bordé;[334] they used these lines to stabilize a CO_2 laser to within 3 parts in 10^{13}. Kompanets, Letokhov, et al.[335—337] have reported the saturation spectra of several isotopic species of OsO_4 within ± 15 MHz of the CO_2 laser lines. The strongest absorption they observed, in $^{192}OsO_4$, is at $+1.5$ MHz from CO_2 P(14), and they have proposed using this resonance for the stabilization of the CO_2 laser. As shown in Fig. 10, this is a hot-band transition whose identity has not yet been established. Perhaps their most interesting observation was a hyperfine splitting of the individual lines in $^{189}OsO_4$ into doublets with components separated by about 500 kHz, caused by the quadrupole moment of the ^{189}Os nucleus.[336]

Some other non-linear techniques such as two-photon and trapped-particle spectroscopy are capable of even higher resolutions because they are not limited by transit broadening or geometric effects.[6,317] The entire field of non-linear spectroscopy in the infrared will expand rapidly as ways are found to increase the power of broadly tunable laser sources.

7 APPLICATIONS

Obviously the capability of yielding Doppler-limited vibration–rotation spectra makes tunable laser spectroscopy a potentially powerful method for the analysis of gaseous species. The current interest in pollutant gases and in photochemical processes in the atmosphere has provided a strong impetus to such applications, and these will be discussed in Section 7.2. First we will treat briefly some interesting analytical techniques for laboratory samples that employ tunable laser sources.

7.1 Laboratory Analytical Techniques

High resolution spectroscopy offers an attractive method for isotope analysis that may under some conditions have advantages in simplicity and speed of operation over mass spectrometry. Wahlen et al.[251] have used semiconductor diode lasers to obtain absorption coefficients and line intensities of $^{13}CO_2$ and $^{14}CO_2$ at 4.5 μm; their results indicate a detection limit of ca. 6×10^8 cm^{-3} in a 60 m multipass cell at 13 Torr pressure; this corresponds to 3.5 picoCurie cm^{-3} and compares favorably with the level of activity used in biological labelling and tracer experiments. Such techniques may be useful also for isotope analyses in geophysical and geochemical studies.[258]

Hanson[192,195] has recently demonstrated the usefulness of diode spectra in the analysis of high-temperature gases. In a shock-tube experiment[192] he used fast-scan techniques to determine the strength and collisional broadening coefficient of a CO line in a CO–H_2–Ar mixture that was shock-heated to 3340 K. Similar data have been obtained for CO in the post-flame region of a flat-flame burner; from such spectra one can determine the concentrations of various combustion gases and their temperatures.[195]

7.2 Atmospheric Studies and Pollution Monitoring

Studies of natural atmospheric constituents and pollutant molecules share the same techniques and are conveniently treated together. Indeed, they may even share the same molecules; an example is CO_2, which has a permanent abundance of about 0.033 % but which may have great spatial and temporal variations due to local sources and sinks, both natural and man-made; furthermore, this average concentration is undergoing a secular increase of the order of a few percent per decade from the combustion of fossil fuels. Several useful reviews of these topics have appeared recently.[338-340]

We consider first absorption by the natural or unpolluted atmosphere. Ideally, for atmospheric modelling and problems of transmission and radiative transfer, one would like to know the frequency, intensity, lineshape, broadening coefficients, and pressure-shift coefficients for every line in every infrared-active vibration–rotation band of the various constituent molecules.[266,341] This list would include, in approximate order of their abundances at sea level, H_2O, CO_2, CH_4, CO, O_3, N_2O, NO, NO_2, NH_3, CH_2O, HNO_3, H_2S, SO_2, and HCl, which have volume concentrations from up to a few percent for water to ca. $10^{-7}\%$ for HCl.[266] Clearly all this information will not be assembled soon. Table 5 shows, however, that at least preliminary high resolution data exist for nearly all of these molecules, so a start is being made. Methods of atmospheric monitoring and the laboratory measurements needed to support them were discussed by the various Working Committees at the 1975 NATO Conference on Laser Spectroscopy of the Atmosphere.[341-343] An extensive bibliography on spectra of minor atmospheric constituents has been compiled by Laulainen;[344] it contains references up to 1971 and thus is mainly limited to classical spectroscopic methods. Kelley et al.[266] have reviewed the infrared absorption characteristics of the natural atmosphere, both for fixed-frequency gas lasers (CO, CO_2, or DF) and for tunable lasers.

In a series of papers that demonstrate the usefulness of laser sources for the monitoring of trace atmospheric constituents, Patel and co-workers[267,345,346] have measured NO and H_2O concentrations in the stratosphere using a balloon-borne CO-pumped spin-flip Raman laser at altitudes of 28 km. The apparatus was similar to that of Fig. 4, using an optoacoustic detector, and had a sensitivity of about 10^8 molecules cm^{-3}, corresponding to a mixing ratio of ca. 0.2 p.p.b. (parts per billion, i.e. parts in 10^9) at that altitude. They found that the NO concentration rose from $<10^8$ molecules cm^{-3} before sunrise to ca. 2×10^9 molecules cm^{-3} (ca. 3.8 p.p.b.) during the day as NO was produced by the ultraviolet irradiation of NO_2. Shortly after sunset the NO disappeared, reflecting the recombination reaction $NO + O_3 \rightarrow NO_2 + O_2$. These measurements confirmed the role of NO in the important ozone balance of the stratosphere.

There are several different ways in which tunable lasers can be used in pollution measurements: (1) point sampling at reduced pressure, in which a sample is taken from the ambient air and examined in an absorption cell; (2) long-path resonant absorption; (3) single-ended remote sensing, in which the laser beam is returned by a distant reflector or by backscatter from the surroundings; (4) heterodyne detection (Section 3.5.2) of hot sources such as smokestack plumes. These have been considered in detail in several recent reviews to which the reader is referred.[5,193,219,338-340] Many of the studies of such molecules as C_2H_4,

NO, N_2O, O_3, SO_2, or the halocarbons cited in Table 5, were initiated to evaluate the applicability of laser sources in pollution measurements, and these references should also be consulted. Here we will consider only a few of the most recent papers on pollutant molecules.

Henningsen et al.[347] have described a single-ended system in which the output of a pulsed optical parametric oscillator is reflected by topological backscatter and collected by an 8 inch $f/15$ Cassegrain telescope. The return beam from foliage 107 m from the source yielded a spectrum of the 2–0 band of CO with a signal-to-noise ratio of 27. They estimate that kilometer ranges and sensitivities of a few p.p.b. could be achieved by operating on the vibrational fundamental.

Ku et al.[250] have monitored CO concentrations using a frequency-modulated $PbS_{0.82}Se_{0.18}$ diode at 4.7 μm, with the beam returned by a remote retro-reflector. The minimum detectable CO concentration over a 0.6 km path was 5 p.p.b., and they were able to observe both individual automobile exhausts and the collective effects of commuter traffic over several hours of unattended operation. Recently this system has been extended with the installation of a widely tunable quaternary $(PbSe)_{1-x}(SnTe)_x$ diode laser fabricated by compositional inter-diffusion and mounted in a variable-temperature closed-cycle refrigerator.[29] This laser can be tuned to cover any molecule that absorbs in the 9 to 12 μm atmospheric window, and results were obtained for NH_3, O_3, C_2H_4, vinyl chloride, and two Freons.

Reid et al.[348] have constructed a diode laser absorption spectrometer that uses a multipass White cell and modulated diode drive current with detection at the second harmonic. They were able to detect a weak absorber such as SO_2 at the 1 p.p.b. level and stronger absorbers at a few parts in 10^{12}. Laboratory experiments have established the feasibility of using diodes to monitor ClO, whose stratospheric concentration is a measure of the extent of O_3 destruction due to halocarbons.[261,349] These data led to the design of a balloon-borne heterodyne radiometer for stratospheric ClO measurement, scheduled to be launched in the autumn of 1977.[349]

In a novel application of atmospheric monitoring, Eng and Max[351] have proposed using diode lasers for mineral prospecting, by detecting surface gases associated with metallic ore deposits. In initial laboratory experiments they found SO_2 concentrations of ca. 10 p.p.m. above rocks containing pyrites (FeS_2) and other sulphides.

These examples are only a sampling of the atmospheric studies now under way, and we may expect a large effort in this field to develop over the next few years.

REFERENCES

(1) V. J. Corcoran, *Appl. Spectrosc. Rev.* 7, 215 (1973).
(2) J. Kuhl and W. Schmidt, *Appl. Phys.* 3, 251 (1974).

(3) K. W. Nill, *Opt. Eng.* **13**, 516 (1974).
(4) M. J. Colles and C. R. Pidgeon, *Rep. Prog. Phys.* **38**, 329 (1975).
(5) E. D. Hinkley, K. W. Nill and F. A. Blum, in *Laser Spectroscopy of Atoms and Molecules* (H. Walther, ed.), Springer-Verlag, Berlin, 1976, p. 125.
(6) V. S. Letokhov, *Sov. Phys. Usp.* (*Engl. Transl.*) **19**, 109 (1976).
(7) M. R. Querry, in *Methods of Experimental Physics*, Vol. 13, part B (D. Williams, ed.), Academic Press, New York, 1976, p. 273.
(8) J. K. Burdett and M. Poliakoff, *Chem. Soc. Rev.* **3**, 293 (1974).
(9) M. S. Pesin and I. L. Fabelinskii, *Sov. Phys. Usp.* (*Engl. Transl.*) **19**, 844 (1976).
(10) S. L. Shapiro, ed., *Ultrashort Light Pulses: Picosecond Techniques and Applications*, Springer-Verlag, Berlin, 1977.
(11) A. Eucken and H. Ahrens, *Z. Phys. Chem. Abt. B* **26**, 297 (1934).
(12) H. Brunet and M. Perez, *J. Mol. Spectrosc.* **29**, 472 (1969).
(13) R. S. McDowell, H. W. Galbraith, C. D. Cantrell, N. G. Nereson and E. D. Hinkley, *J. Mol. Spectrosc.* **68**, 288 (1977).
(14) A. Clairon and L. Henry, *C. R. Hebd. Seances Acad. Sci., Ser. B*, to be published.
(15) M. Loëte, A. Clairon, A. Frichet, R. S. McDowell, H. W. Galbraith, J.-C. Hilico, J. Moret-Bailly and L. Henry, *C. R. Hebd. Seances Acad. Sci., Ser. B* **285**, 175 (1977).
(16) A. Dienes, in *Laser Applications to Optics and Spectroscopy* (S. Jacobs, M. Sargent, J. F. Scott and M. O. Scully, eds.), Addison-Wesley, Reading, Mass., 1975, p. 53.
(17) F. P. Schäfer, ed., *Dye Lasers*, 2nd ed., Springer-Verlag, Berlin, 1977.
(18) F. P. Schäfer, in *Laser Handbook*, Vol. 1 (F. T. Arecchi and E. O. Schulz-DuBois, eds.), North-Holland, Amsterdam, 1972, p. 369.
(19) G. A. Antcliffe and S. G. Parker, *J. Appl. Phys.* **44**, 4145 (1973).
(20) A. R. Calawa, *J. Lumin.* **7**, 477 (1973).
(21) I. Melngailis and A. Mooradian, in *Laser Applications to Optics and Spectroscopy* (S. Jacobs, M. Sargent, J. F. Scott and M. O. Scully, eds.), Addison-Wesley, Reading, Mass., 1975, p. 1.
(22) H. Kressel, in *Laser Handbook* (F. T. Arecchi and E. O. Schulz-DuBois, eds.), North-Holland, Amsterdam, 1972, p. 441.
(23) J. I. Steinfeld, *Molecules and Radiation: An Introduction to Modern Molecular Spectroscopy*, Harper and Row, New York, 1974.
(24) R. W. Ralston, I. Melngailis, A. R. Calawa and W. T. Lindley, *IEEEJ. Quantum Electron.* **QE-9**, 350 (1973).
(25) S. H. Groves, K. W. Nill, and A. J. Strauss, *Appl. Phys. Lett.* **25**, 331 (1974).
(26) J. N. Walpole, A. R. Calawa, T. C. Harman and S. H. Groves, *Appl. Phys. Lett.* **28**, 552 (1976).
(27) H. Preier, M. Bleicher, W. Riedel, H. Pfeiffer and H. Maier, *Appl. Phys.* **12**, 277 (1977).
(28) K. J. Linden, K. W. Nill and J. F. Butler, *IEEE J. Quantum Electron.* **QE-13**, 720 (1977).
(29) E. D. Hinkley, R. T. Ku, K. W. Nill and J. F. Butler, *Appl. Opt.* **15**, 1653 (1976).
(30) J. N. Walpole, A. R. Calawa, S. R. Chinn, S. H. Groves and T. C. Harman, *Appl. Phys. Lett.* **29**, 307 (1976).
(31) J. N. Walpole, A. R. Calawa, S. R. Chinn, S. H. Groves and T. C. Harman, *Appl. Phys. Lett.* **30**, 524 (1977).
(32) K. W. Nill, F. A. Blum, A. R. Calawa and T. C. Harman, *Appl. Phys. Lett.* **21**, 132 (1972).
(33) J. M. Besson, W. Paul and A. R. Calawa, *Phys. Rev.* **173**, 699 (1968).
(34) H. Flicker and N. Nereson, *IEEE J. Quantum Electron.* **QE-12**, 326 (1976).

(35) F. Allario, C. H. Bair and J. F. Butler, *IEEE J. Quantum Electron.* **QE-11**, 205 (1975).
(36) E. D. Hinkley and C. Freed, *Phys. Rev. Lett.* **23**, 277 (1969).
(37) A. S. Pine and N. Menyuk, *Appl. Phys. Lett.* **26**, 231 (1975).
(38) W. W. Duley, CO_2 *Lasers: Effects and Applications*, Academic Press, New York, 1976.
(39) E. Arié, N. Lacome and C. Rossetti, *Can. J. Phys.* **50**, 1800 (1972).
(40) R. L. Abrams, *Appl. Phys. Lett.* **25**, 609 (1974).
(41) R. L. Abrams and W. B. Bridges, *IEEE J. Quantum Electron.* **QE-9**, 940 (1973).
(42) P. W. Smith, in *Laser Spectroscopy* (R. G. Brewer and A. Mooradian, eds.), Plenum Press, New York, 1974, p. 247.
(43) R. L. Abrams, *ibid.*, p. 263.
(44) A. J. Beaulieu, *Appl. Phys. Lett.* **16**, 504 (1970).
(45) A. J. Alcock, K. Leopold and M. C. Richardson, *Appl. Phys. Lett.* **23**, 562 (1973).
(46) V. N. Bagratashvili, I. N. Knyazev, V. S. Letokhov and V. V. Lobko, *Opt. Commun.* **14**, 426 (1975).
(47) N. W. Harris, F. O'Neill and W. T. Whitney, *Opt. Commun.* **16**, 57 (1976).
(48) F. O'Neill and W. T. Whitney, *Appl. Phys. Lett.* **31**, 270 (1977).
(49) T. Kasuya, *Appl. Phys.* **2**, 339 (1973).
(50) T. Kasuya, *Appl. Phys.* **3**, 223 (1974).
(51) H. J. Gerritsen and M. E. Heller, *Appl. Opt. Suppl.*, **2**, 73 (1965).
(52) H. Brunet, *IEEE J. Quantum Electron.* **QE-2**, 382 (1966).
(53) K. Sakurai and K. Shimoda, *Jpn. J. Appl. Phys.* **5**, 938 (1966).
(54) B. A. Antipov, V. E. Zuev, P. D. Pyrsikova and V. A. Sapozhnikova, *Opt. Spectrosc. (U.S.S.R.)* **31**, 488 (1971).
(55) A. Brillet, P. Cerez, S. Hajdukovic and F. Hartmann, *Opt. Commun.* **17**, 336 (1976).
(56) Ch. Bordé and J. L. Hall, in *Laser Spectroscopy* (R. G. Brewer and A. Mooradian, eds.), Plenum Press, New York, 1974, p.125.
(57) C. K. N. Patel and E. D. Shaw, *Phys. Rev. Lett.* **24**, 451 (1970).
(58) C. K. N. Patel and E. D. Shaw, *Phys. Rev. B* **3**, 1279 (1971).
(59) R. B. Dennis, C. R. Pidgeon, S. D. Smith, B. S. Wherrett and R. A. Wood, *Proc. R. Soc. London, Ser. A* **331**, 203 (1972).
(60) C. K. N. Patel, in *Coherence and Quantum Optics* (L. Mandel and E. Wolf, eds.), Plenum Press, New York, 1973, p. 567.
(61) C. K. N. Patel, in *Laser Spectroscopy* (R. G. Brewer and A. Mooradian, eds.), Plenum Press, New York, 1974, p. 471.
(62) J. F. Scott, in *Laser Applications to Optics and Spectroscopy* (S. Jacobs, M. Sargent, J. F. Scott and M. O. Scully, eds.), Addison-Wesley, Reading, Mass., 1975, p. 123.
(63) R. J. Butcher, R. B. Dennis and S. D. Smith, *Proc. R. Soc. London Ser. A* **344**, 541 (1975).
(64) S. D. Smith, in *Very High Resolution Spectroscopy* (R. A. Smith, ed.), Academic Press, London, 1976, p. 13.
(65) R. L. Aggarwal, *Physica B (Amserdam)* **89**, 218 (1977).
(66) L. B. Kreuzer and C. K. N. Patel, *Science* **173**, 45 (1971).
(67) R. L. Aggarwal, B. Lax, C. E. Chase, C. R. Pidgeon, D. Limbert and F. Brown, *Appl. Phys. Lett.* **18**, 383 (1971).
(68) A. Mooradian, S. R. J. Brueck and F. A. Blum, *Appl. Phys. Lett.* **17**, 481 (1970).
(69) S. R. J. Brueck and A. Mooradian, *Appl. Phys. Lett.* **18**, 229 (1971).
(70) S. R. Brueck and A. Mooradian, *IEEE J. Quantum Electron.* **QE-10**, 634 (1974).
(71) C. K. N. Patel, T. Y. Chang and V. T. Nguyen, *Appl. Phys. Lett.* **28**, 603 (1976).
(72) J. P. Sattler, B. A. Weber and J. Nemarich, *Appl. Phys. Lett.* **25**, 491 (1974).

(73) P. Norton and P. W. Kruse, *Opt. Commun.* **22**, 147 (1977).
(74) R. S. Eng, A. Mooradian and H. R. Fetterman, *Appl. Phys. Lett.* **25**, 453 (1974).
(75) E. D. Shaw, *Opt. Commun.* **18**, 16 (1976).
(76) Y. R. Shen, *Appl. Phys. Lett.* **23**, 516 (1973).
(77) C. K. N. Patel, *Phys. Rev. Lett.* **28**, 649 (1972).
(78) J. F. Scott, T. C. Damen and P. A. Fleury, *Phys. Rev. B* **6**, 3856 (1972).
(79) M. J. Colles, R. B. Dennis, J. W. Smith and J. S. Webb, *Opt. Commun.* **10**, 145 (1974).
(80) C. K. N. Patel, *Appl. Phys. Lett.* **19**, 400 (1971).
(81) M. A. Guerra, S. R. J. Brueck and A. Mooradian, *IEEE J. Quantum Electron.* **QE-9**, 1157 (1973).
(82) R. L. Allwood, R. B. Dennis, R. G. Mellish, S. D. Smith, B. S. Wherrett and R. A. Wood, *J. Phys. C* **4**, L126 (1971).
(83) R. G. Mellish, R. B. Dennis and R. L. Allwood, *Opt. Commun.* **4**, 249 (1971).
(84) C. K. N. Patel, E. D. Shaw and R. J. Kerl, *Phys. Rev. Lett.* **25**, 8 (1970).
(85) R. V. Ambartsumyan, V. S. Dolzhikov, Yu. I. Milin'chuk, E. L. Mikhailov and N. V. Chekalin, *Sov. J. Quantum Electron.* (*Engl. Transl.*) **5**, 938 (1975).
(86) J. F. Scott, *Am. J. Phys.* **39**, 1360 (1971).
(87) R. Claus, *Phys. Status Solidi B* **50**, 11 (1972).
(88) J. Gelbwachs, R. H. Pantell, H. E. Puthoff and J. M. Yarborough, *Appl. Phys. Lett.* **14**, 258 (1969).
(89) J. M. Yarborough, S. S. Sussman, H. E. Puthoff, R. H. Pantell and B. C. Johnson, *Appl. Phys. Lett.* **15**, 102 (1969).
(90) B. C. Johnson, H. E. Puthoff, J. SooHoo and S. S. Sussman, *Appl. Phys. Lett.* **18**, 181 (1971).
(91) M. A. Piestrup, R. N. Fleming and R. H. Pantell, *Appl. Phys. Lett.* **26**, 418 (1975).
(92) W. Schmidt and W. Appt, *Z. Naturforsch. Teil A* **27**, 1373 (1972).
(93) R. Frey and F. Pradère, *Opt. Commun.* **12**, 98 (1974).
(94) R. Frey and F. Pradère, *Infrared Phys.* **16**, 117 (1976).
(95) M. Bierry, R. Frey and F. Pradère, *Rev. Sci. Instrum.* **48**, 733 (1977).
(96) D. Cotter, D. C. Hanna, P. A. Kärkkäinen and R. Wyatt, *Opt. Commun.* **15**, 143 (1975).
(97) D. Cotter, D. C. Hanna and R. Wyatt, *Opt. Commun.* **16**, 256 (1976).
(98) J. L. Carlsten and P. C. Dunn, *Opt. Commun.* **14**, 8 (1975).
(99) R. V. Ambartsumyan, V. M. Apatin and V. S. Letokhov, *JETP Lett.* (*Engl. Transl.*) **15**, 237 (1972).
(100) S. E. Harris, *Proc. IEEE* **57**, 2096 (1969).
(101) R. G. Smith, in *Laser Handbook* (F. T. Arecchi and E. O. Schulz-DuBois, eds.), North-Holland, Amsterdam, 1972, p. 837.
(102) R. L. Byer, in *Quantum Electronics: A Treatise* (H. Rabin and C. L. Tang, eds.), Vol. I, part B, Academic Press, New York, 1975, p. 587.
(103) R. Fischer and L. A. Kulevskii, *Sov. J. Quantum Electron.* (*Engl. Transl.*) **7**, 135 (1977).
(104) R. L. Byer and R. L. Herbst, in *Non-Linear Infrared Generation* (Y.-R. Shen, ed.), Springer-Verlag, Berlin, 1977, p. 81.
(105) J. E. Pearson, A. Yariv and U. Ganiel, *Appl. Opt.* **12**, 1165 (1973).
(106) S. Rockwood, in *Tunable Lasers and Applications* (A. Mooradian, T. Jaeger and P. Stokseth, eds.), Springer-Verlag, Berlin, 1976, p. 140.
(107) J. Pinard and J. F. Young, *Opt. Commun.* **4**, 425 (1972).
(108) A. Hordvik and P. B. Sackett, *Appl. Opt.* **13**, 1060 (1974).
(109) A. S. Pine, *J. Opt. Soc. Am.* **64**, 1683 (1974).
(110) A. S. Pine, in *Laser Spectroscopy III* (J. L. Hall and J. L. Carlsten, eds.), Springer-Verlag, Berlin, 1977, p. 376.

(111) H. Tashiro and T. Yajima, *Opt. Commun.* **12**, 129 (1974).
(112) C. D. Decker and F. K. Tittel, *Appl. Phys. Lett.* **22**, 411 (1973).
(113) C. D. Decker and F. K. Tittel, *Opt. Commun.* **8**, 244 (1973).
(114) D. C. Hanna, V. V. Rampal and R. C. Smith, *Opt. Commun.* **8**, 151 (1973).
(115) C. R. Pidgeon, B. Lax, R. L. Aggarwal, C. E. Chase and F. Brown, *Appl. Phys. Lett.* **19**, 333 (1971).
(116) R. J. Seymour and F. Zernike, *Appl. Phys. Lett.* **29**, 705 (1976).
(117) R. L. Byer, M. M. Choy, R. L. Herbst, D. S. Chemla and R. S. Feigelson, *Appl. Phys. Lett.* **24**, 65 (1974).
(118) G. C. Bhar, D. C. Hanna, B. Luther-Davies and R. C. Smith, *Opt. Commun.* **6**, 323 (1972).
(119) D. C. Hanna, V. V. Rampal and R. C. Smith, *IEEE J. Quantum Electron.* **QE-10**, 461 (1974).
(120) D. C. Hanna, B. Luther-Davies, R. C. Smith and R. Wyatt, *Appl. Phys. Lett.* **25**, 142 (1974).
(121) D. C. Hanna, R. C. Smith and C. R. Stanley, *Opt. Commun.* **4**, 300 (1971).
(122) L. O. Hocker and C. F. Dewey, *Appl. Phys.* **11**, 137 (1976).
(123) K. H. Yang, J. R. Morris, P. L. Richards and Y. R. Shen, *Appl. Phys. Lett.* **23**, 669 (1973).
(124) R. L. Aggarwal, B. Lax, H. R. Fetterman, P. E. Tannenwald and B. J. Clifton, *J. Appl. Phys.* **45**, 3972 (1974).
(125) B. Lax, R. L. Aggarwal and G. Favrot, *Appl. Phys. Lett.* **23**, 679 (1973).
(126) T. J. Bridges and V. T. Nguyen, *Appl. Phys. Lett.* **23**, 107 (1973).
(127) G. D. Boyd, T. J. Bridges, C. K. N. Patel and E. Buehler, *Appl. Phys. Lett.* **21**, 553 (1972).
(128) D. H. Auston, A. M. Glass and P. LeFur, *Appl. Phys. Lett.* **23**, 47 (1973).
(129) D. W. Faries, K. A. Gehring, P. L. Richards and Y. R. Shen, *Phys. Rev.* **180**, 363 (1969).
(130) P. K. Cheo and M. Gilden, *Opt. Lett.* **1**, 38 (1977).
(131) P. K. Cheo, in *Laser Spectroscopy III* (J. L. Hall and J. L. Carlsten, eds.), Springer-Verlag, Berlin, 1977, p. 394.
(132) V. J. Corcoran, R. E. Cupp, J. J. Gallagher and W. T. Smith, *Appl. Phys. Lett.* **16**, 316 (1970).
(133) V. J. Corcoran and W. T. Smith, *Appl. Opt.* **11**, 269 (1972).
(134) V. J. Corcoran, J. M. Martin and W. T. Smith, *Appl. Phys. Lett.* **22**, 517 (1973).
(135) E. Bonek and H. Korecky, *Appl. Phys. Lett.* **25**, 740 (1974).
(136) S. N. Bagayev, L. S. Vasilenko, V. G. Goldort, A. K. Dmitriyev, A. S. Dychkov and V. P. Chebotayev, *Appl. Phys.* **13**, 291 (1977).
(137) P. P. Sorokin, J. J. Wynne and J. R. Lankard, *Appl. Phys. Lett.* **22**, 342 (1973).
(138) J. J. Wynne, P. P. Sorokin and J. R. Lankard, in *Laser Spectroscopy* (R. G. Brewer and A. Mooradian, eds.), Plenum Press, New York, 1974, p. 103.
(139) P. A. Kärkkäinen, *Appl. Phys.* **13**, 159 (1977).
(140) J. Ducuing, R. Frey and F. Pradère, in *Tunable Lasers and Applications* (A. Mooradian, T. Jaeger and P. Stokseth, eds.), Springer-Verlag, Berlin, 1976, p. 81.
(141) R. L. Byer, *ibid.*, p. 70.
(142) S. J. Brosnan, R. N. Fleming, R. L. Herbst and R. L. Byer, *Appl. Phys. Lett.* **30**, 330 (1977).
(143) J. Cahen, M. Clerc and P. Rigny, *Opt. Commun.* **21**, 387 (1977).
(144) R. S. McDowell, L. B. Asprey and R. T. Paine, *J. Chem. Phys.* **61**, 3571 (1974).
(145) N. Lee, R. L. Aggarwal and B. Lax, *J. Appl. Phys.* **48**, 2470 (1977).
(146) L. F. Mollenauer and D. H. Olson, *Appl. Phys. Lett.* **24**, 386 (1974).
(147) L. F. Mollenauer and D. H. Olson, *J. Appl. Phys.* **46**, 3109 (1975).

(148) Yu. L. Gusev, S. I. Marennikov and V. P. Chebotayev, *Appl. Phys.* **14**, 121 (1977).
(149) L. F. Mollenauer, *Opt. Lett.* **1**, 164 (1977).
(150) H. Welling, G. Litfin and R. Beigang, in *Laser Spectroscopy III* (J. L. Hall and J. L. Carlsten, eds.), Springer-Verlag, Berlin, 1977, p. 370.
(151) D. A. G. Deacon, L. R. Elias, J. M. J. Madey, G. J. Ramian, H. A. Schwettman, and T. I. Smith, *Phys. Rev. Lett.* **38**, 892 (1977).
(152) D. A. G. Deacon, L. R. Elias, J. M. J. Madey, H. A. Schwettman and T. I. Smith. in *Laser Spectroscopy III* (J. L. Hall and J. L. Carlsten, eds.), Springer-Verlag, Berlin, 1977, p. 402.
(153) A. R. H. Cole, compiler, *Tables of Wavenumbers for the Calibration of Infrared Spectrometers*, 2nd ed., Pergamon, Oxford, 1977.
(154) K. N. Rao (Ohio State Univ.), unpublished grating spectra of NH_3.
(155) J. S. Knoll, G. L. Tettemer, W. G. Planet, K. N. Rao, D.-W. Chen and L. A. Pugh, *Appl. Opt.* **15**, 2973 (1976).
(156) R. A. McClatchey, W. S. Benedict, S. A. Clough, D. E. Burch, R. F. Calfee, K. Fox, L. S. Rothman and J. S. Garing, Air Force Cambridge Research Labs. Report No. AFCRL-TR-73-0096 (1973).
(157) S. R. Drayson, Univ. of Michigan High Altitude Engineering Lab. Technical Report 036350-4-T (1973).
(158) G. P. Montgomery and J. C. Hill, *J. Opt. Soc. Am.* **65**, 579 (1975).
(159) A. Fayt, D. VanLerberghe, J. P. Kupfer, H. P. Pascher and H. G. Häfele, *Mol. Phys.* **33**, 603 (1977).
(160) F. R. Petersen, D. G. McDonald, J. D. Cupp and B. L. Danielson, in *Laser Spectroscopy* (R. G. Brewer and A. Mooradian, eds.), Plenum Press, New York, 1974, p. 555.
(161) K. M. Evenson, J. S. Wells, F. R. Petersen, B. L. Danielson and G. W. Day, *Appl. Phys. Lett.* **22**, 192 (1973).
(162) C. Freed, A. H. M. Ross and R. G. O'Donnell, *J. Mol. Spectrosc.* **49**, 439 (1974).
(163) R. T. Menzies and M. S. Shumate, *IEEE J. Quantum Electron.* **QE-9**, 862 (1973).
(164) C. Freed, R. G. O'Donnell and A. H. M. Ross, *IEEE Trans. Instrum. Meas.* **IM-25**, 431 (1976).
(165) J. Reid and K. Siemsen, *Appl. Phys. Lett.* **29**, 250 (1976).
(166) J. Reid and K. Siemsen, *J. Appl. Phys.* **48**, 2712 (1977).
(167) K. J. Siemsen and B. G. Whitford, *Opt. Commun.* **22**, 11 (1977).
(168) W. Berger, K. Siemsen and J. Reid, *Rev. Sci. Instrum.* **48**, 1031 (1977).
(169) J.-P. Monchalin, M. J. Kelly, J. E. Thomas, N. A. Kurnit, and A. Javan, *J. Mol. Spectrosc.* **64**, 491 (1977).
(170) N. G. Nereson and H. Flicker, *Opt. Commun.* **23**, 171 (1977).
(171) R. S. Eng, H. Kildal, J. C. Mikkelsen and D. L. Spears, *Appl. Phys. Lett.* **24**, 231 (1974).
(172) H. Kildal, R. S. Eng and A. H. M. Ross, *J. Mol. Spectrosc.* **53**, 479 (1974).
(173) T. R. Todd, C. M. Clayton, W. B. Telfair, T. K. McCubbin and J. Plíva, *J. Mol. Spectrosc.* **62**, 201 (1976).
(174) C. Amiot, *J. Phys. B* **10**, L317 (1977).
(175) J. J. Hillman, T. Kostiuk, D. Buhl, J. L. Faris, J. C. Novaco and M. J. Mumma, *Opt. Lett.* **1**, 81 (1977).
(176) R. L. Barger and J. L. Hall, *Appl. Phys. Lett.* **22**, 196 (1973).
(177) T. G. Blaney, G. J. Edwards, B. W. Jolliffe, D. J. E. Knight and P. T. Woods, *J. Phys. D* **9**, 1323 (1976).
(178) K. M. Evenson, J. S. Wells, L. M. Matarrese and L. B. Elwell, *Appl. Phys. Lett.* **16**, 159 (1970).

(179) H. E. Radford, F. R. Peterson, D. A. Jennings and J. A. Mucha, *IEEE J. Quantum Electron.* **QE-13**, 92 (1977).

(180) L. O. Hocker, A. Javan, D. R. Rao, L. Frenkel and T. Sullivan, *Appl. Phys. Lett.* **10**, 147 (1967).

(181) C. H. Townes and A. L. Schawlow, *Microwave Spectroscopy*, McGraw-Hill, New York, 1955, Ch. 13.

(182) F. A. Blum, K. W. Nill, A. R. Calawa and T. C. Harman, *Chem. Phys. Lett.* **15**, 144 (1972).

(183) R. S. Eng, A. R. Calawa, T. C. Harman, P. L. Kelley and A. Javan, *Appl. Phys. Lett.* **21**, 303 (1972).

(184) M. Herzberger and C. D. Salzberg, *J. Opt. Soc. Am.* **52**, 420 (1962).

(185) C. D. Salzberg and J. J. Villa, *J. Opt. Soc. Am.* **48**, 579 (1958).

(186) C. D. Salzberg and J. J. Villa, *J. Opt. Soc. Am.* **47**, 244 (1957).

(187) H. Flicker, J. P. Aldridge, H. Filip, N. G. Nereson, M. J. Reisfeld and W. H. Weber, *Appl. Opt.* **17**, 851 (1978).

(188) C. Freed, D. L. Spears, R. G. O'Donnell and A. H. M. Ross, in *Laser Spectroscopy* (R. G. Brewer and A. Mooradian, eds.), Plenum Press, New York, 1974, p. 171.

(189) D. L. Spears and C. Freed, *Appl. Phys. Lett* **23**, 445 (1973).

(190) L. W. Aukerman and J. W. Erler, *Opt. Lett.* **1**, 178 (1977).

(191) E. D. Hinkley, *Appl. Phys. Lett.* **16**, 351 (1970).

(192) R. K. Hanson, *Appl. Opt.* **16**, 1479 (1977).

(193) E. D. Hinkley, *Opto-electronics* **4**, 69 (1972).

(194) G. A. Antcliffe and J. S. Wrobel, *Appl. Opt.* **11**, 1548 (1972).

(195) R. K. Hanson, P. A. Kuntz and C. H. Kruger, *Appl. Opt.* **16**, 2045 (1977).

(196) M. E. Delany, *Sci. Prog.* (*Oxford*) **47**, 459 (1959).

(197) L. B. Kreuzer, *J. Appl. Phys.* **42**, 2934 (1971).

(198) C. F. Dewey, R. D. Kamm and C. E. Hackett, *Appl. Phys. Lett.* **23**, 633 (1973).

(199) C. F. Dewey, *Proc. Soc. Photo-Opt. Instrum. Eng.* **49**, 13 (1975).

(200) E. L. Kerr and J. G. Atwood, *Appl. Opt.* **7**, 915 (1968).

(201) L. B. Kreuzer, N. D. Kenyon and C. K. N. Patel, *Science* **177**, 347 (1972).

(202) L. B. Kreuzer, *Anal. Chem.* **46**, 235A (1974).

(203) M. C. Teich, *Proc. IEEE* **56**, 37 (1968).

(204) T. G. Blaney, *Space Sci. Rev.* **17**, 691 (1975).

(205) M. M. Abbas, M. J. Mumma, T. Kostiuk and D. Buhl, *Appl. Opt.* **15**, 427 (1976); **16**, 2793 (1977).

(206) T. Kostiuk, M. J. Mumma, M. M. Abbas and D. Buhl, *Infrared Phys.* **16**, 61 (1976).

(207) R. T. Ku and D. L. Spears, *Opt. Lett.* **1**, 84 (1977).

(208) E. Wiesendanger, *Space Sci. Rev.* **17**, 721 (1975).

(209) R. T. Menzies and M. S. Shumate, *Science* **184**, 570 (1974).

(210) B. J. Peyton, A. J. DiNardo, S. C. Cohen, J. H. McElroy and R. J. Coates, *IEEE J. Quantum Electron.* **QE-11**, 569 (1975).

(211) R. T. Menzies and R. K. Seals, *Science* **197**, 1275 (1977).

(212) D. W. Peterson, M. A. Johnson and A. L. Betz, *Nature* (*London*) **250**, 128 (1974).

(213) M. A. Johnson, A. L. Betz, R. A. McLaren, E. C. Sutton and C. H. Townes, *Astrophys. J.* **208**, L145 (1976).

(214) A. L. Betz, M. A. Johnson, R. A. McLaren and E. C. Sutton, *Astrophys. J.* **208**, L141 (1976).

(215) A. L. Betz, R. A. McLaren, E. C. Sutton and M. A. Johnson, *Icarus* **30**, 650 (1977).

(216) A. L. Betz, E. C. Sutton and R. A. McLaren, in *Laser Spectroscopy III* (J. L. Hall and J. L. Carlsten, eds.), Springer-Verlag, Berlin, 1977, p. 31.

(217) R. T. Menzies, *Appl. Opt.* **10**, 1532 (1971).
(218) R. T. Menzies, *Opto-electronics* **4**, 179 (1972).
(219) E. D. Hinkley and P. L. Kelley, *Science* **171**, 635 (1971).
(220) M. Mumma, T. Kostiuk, S. Cohen, D. Buhl and P. C. von Thuna, *Nature (London)* **253**, 514 (1975).
(221) M. A. Frerking and D. J. Muehlner, *Appl. Opt.* **16**, 526 (1977).
(222) R. T. Menzies, *Appl. Opt.* **15**, 2597 (1976).
(223) H. Walther, in *Laser Spectroscopy of Atoms and Molecules* (H. Walther, ed.) Springer-Verlag, Berlin, 1976, p. 1.
(224) F. Y. Chu and T. Oka, *J. Appl. Phys.* **46**, 1204 (1975).
(225) A. S. Pine and K. W. Nill, *Opt. Commun.* **18**, 57 (1976).
(226) M. P. Sinha, A. Schultz and R. N. Zare, *J. Chem. Phys.* **58**, 549 (1973).
(227) R. E. Smalley, L. Wharton and D. H. Levy, *Acc. Chem. Res.* **10**, 139 (1977).
(228) S. E. Novick, P. Davies, S. J. Harris and W. Klemperer, *J. Chem. Phys.* **59**, 2273 (1973).
(229) T. E. Gough, R. E. Miller and G. Scoles, *Appl. Phys. Lett.* **30**, 338 (1977).
(230) D. N. Travis, J. C. McGurk, D. McKeown and R. G. Denning, *Chem. Phys. Lett.* **45**, 287 (1977).
(231) J. P. Aldridge, H. Filip, K. Fox, H. Galbraith, R. S. McDowell and D. F. Smith, Conference on Lasers for Isotope Separation, Albuquerque, New Mexico, 1976.
(232) W. Brunner and H. Paul, *Opt. Commun.* **19**, 253 (1976).
(233) N. Dutta, R. T. Warner and G. J. Wolga, *Opt. Lett.* **1**, 155 (1977).
(234) E. Arimondo, P. Glorieux and T. Oka, in *Laser Spectroscopy III* (J. L. Hall and J. L. Carlsten, eds.), Springer-Verlag, Berlin, 1977, p. 287.
(235) H. J. Gerritsen and S. A. Ahmed, *Phys. Lett.* **13**, 41 (1964).
(236) K. Sakurai and K. Shimoda, *J. Phys. Soc. Jpn.* **21**, 1842 (1961).
(237) K. Uehara, K. Sakurai and K. Shimoda, *J. Phys. Soc. Jpn.* **26**, 1018 (1969).
(238) A. S. Pine, *J. Mol. Spectrosc.* **54**, 132 (1975).
(239) K. Fox, J. P. Aldridge, H. Flicker, R. F. Holland, R. S. McDowell and N. G. Nereson, to be published.
(240) J. Häger, W. Hinz, H. Walther and G. Strey, *Appl. Phys.* **9**, 35 (1976).
(241) H. Flicker, R. S. McDowell, N. G. Nereson and K. Fox, to be published.
(242) T. Kasuya, *Jpn. J. Appl. Phys.* **11**, 1575 (1972).
(243) J. P. Sattler and G. J. Simonis, *IEEE J. Quantum Electron.* **QE-13**, 461 (1977).
(244) K. W. Nill, A. J. Strauss and F. A. Blum, *Appl. Phys. Lett.* **22**, 677 (1973).
(245) K. Sakurai, K. Uehara, M. Takami and K. Shimoda, *J. Phys. Soc. Jpn.* **23**, 103 (1967).
(246) A. V. Nowak and J. I. Steinfeld, *J. Chem. Phys.* **57**, 5595 (1972).
(247) R. S. McDowell, in *Laser Spectroscopy III* (J. L. Hall and J. L. Carlsten, eds.), Springer-Verlag, Berlin, 1977, p. 102.
(248) R. S. McDowell, H. W. Galbraith, M. J. Reisfeld and J. P. Aldridge, to be published.
(249) K. W. Nill, F. A. Blum, A. R. Calawa and T. C. Harman, *Appl. Phys. Lett.* **19**, 79 (1971).
(250) R. T. Ku, E. D. Hinkley and J. O. Sample, *Appl. Opt.* **14**, 854 (1975).
(251) M. Wahlen, R. S. Eng and K. W. Nill, *Appl. Opt.* **16**, 2350 (1977).
(252) W. G. Planet, J. R. Aronson and J. F. Butler, *J. Mol. Spectrosc.* **54**, 331 (1975).
(253) J. R. Aronson, P. C. von Thüna and J. F. Butler, *Appl. Opt.* **14**, 1120 (1975).
(254) J. P. Aldridge, R. F. Holland, H. Flicker, K. W. Nill and T. C. Harman, *J. Mol. Spectrosc.* **54**, 328 (1975).
(255) F. A. Blum and K. W. Nill, in *Laser Spectroscopy* (R. G. Brewer and A. Mooradian, eds.), Plenum Press, New York, 1974, p. 493.
(256) M. J. Reisfeld and H. Flicker, *J. Mol. Spectrosc.* **69**, 330 (1978).

(257) H. Flicker, N. G. Nereson and J. P. Aldridge, to be published.
(258) B. Lehmann, M. Wahlen, R. Zumbrunn, H. Oeschger and W. Schnell, *Appl. Phys.* **13**, 153 (1977).
(259) W. H. Weber, P. D. Maker and C. W. Peters, *J. Chem. Phys.* **64**, 2149 (1976).
(260) W. H. Weber, J. P. Aldridge, H. Flicker, N. G. Nereson, H. Filip and M. J. Reisfeld, *J. Mol. Spectrosc.* **65**, 474 (1977).
(261) R. T. Menzies, J. S. Margolis, E. D. Hinkley and R. A. Toth, *Appl. Opt.* **16**, 523 (1977).
(262) S. D. Smith, C. R. Pidgeon, R. A. Wood, A. McNeish and N. Brignall, in *Laser Spectroscopy* (R. G. Brewer and A. Mooradian, eds.), Plenum Press, New York, 1974, p. 523.
(263) F. A. Blum, K. W. Nill, P. L. Kelley, A. R. Calawa and T. C. Harman, *Science* **177**, 694 (1972).
(264) R. S. Eng, P. L. Kelley, A. Mooradian, A. R. Calawa and T. C. Harman, *Chem. Phys. Lett.* **19**, 524 (1973).
(265) R. S. Eng, P. L. Kelley, A. R. Calawa, T. C. Harman and K. W. Nill, *Mol. Phys.* **28**, 653 (1974).
(266) P. L. Kelley, R. A. McClatchey, R. K. Long and A. Snelson, *Opt. Quantum Electron.* **8**, 177 (1976).
(267) C. K. N. Patel, E. G. Burkhardt and C. A. Lambert, *Science* **184**, 1173 (1974).
(268) M. A. Guerra, M. Ketabi, A. Sanchez, M. S. Feld and A. Javan, *J. Chem. Phys.* **63**, 1317 (1975).
(269) W. H. Weber, P. D. Maker, K. F. Yeung and C. W. Peters, *Appl. Opt.* **13**, 1431 (1974).
(270) R. A. Wood, R. B. Dennis and J. W. Smith, *Opt. Commun.* **4**, 383 (1972).
(271) G. A. Antcliffe, S. G. Parker and R. T. Bate, *Appl. Phys. Lett.* **21**, 505 (1972).
(272) K. W. Nill, F. A. Blum, A. R. Calawa and T. C. Harman, *Chem. Phys. Lett.* **14**, 234 (1972).
(273) R. S. McDowell, *Proc. Soc. Photo-Opt. Instrum. Eng.* **113**, 160 (1977).
(274) R. S. McDowell, *Proc. Electro-Optics/Laser '77 Conf.*, Anaheim, Cal., Oct. 1977, p. 589.
(275) R. S. McDowell, L. J. Radziemski, H. Flicker, H. W. Galbraith, R. C. Kennedy, B. J. Krohn, N. G. Nereson, J. D. King and K. Fox, *Opt. Lett.* **2**, 97 (1978).
(276) J. P. Aldridge, H. Filip, H. Flicker, R. F. Holland, R. S. McDowell, N. G. Nereson and K. Fox, *J. Mol. Spectrosc.* **58**, 165 (1975).
(277) R. S. McDowell, H. W. Galbraith, B. J. Krohn, C. D. Cantrell and E. D. Hinkley, *Opt. Commun.* **17**, 178 (1976).
(278) R. S. McDowell, H. W. Galbraith, C. D. Cantrell, N. G. Nereson, P. F. Moulton and E. D. Hinkley, to be published.
(279) I. M. Beterov, V. P. Chebotayev and A. S. Provorov, *Opt. Commun.* **7**, 410 (1973).
(280) M. Dubs and Hs. H. Günthard, *Chem. Phys. Lett.* **47**, 421 (1977).
(281) A. S. Pine and P. F. Moulton, *J. Mol. Spectrosc.* **64**, 15 (1977).
(282) J. Moret-Bailly, *Cah. Phys.* **15**, 237 (1961).
(283) J. Moret-Bailly, *J. Mol. Spectrosc.* **15**, 344 (1965).
(284) K. T. Hecht, *J. Mol. Spectrosc.* **5**, 355, 390 (1960).
(285) B. Bobin and K. Fox, *J. Phys. (Paris)* **34**, 571 (1973).
(286) B. J. Krohn, *J. Mol. Spectrosc.* **68**, 497 (1977); Los Alamos Scientific Lab. Report LA-6554-MS (1976).
(287) W. G. Harter and C. W. Patterson, *J. Chem. Phys.* **66**, 4872 (1977).
(288) C. W. Patterson and W. G. Harter, *J. Chem. Phys.* **66**, 4886 (1977).
(289) C. D. Cantrell and H. W. Galbraith, *J. Mol. Spectrosc.* **58**, 158 (1975).
(290) F. A. Blum, K. W. Nill and A. J. Strauss, *J. Chem. Phys.* **58**, 4968 (1973).

(291) D. Papoušek and V. Špirko, *Top. Curr. Chem.* **68**, 59 (1976).
(292) K. Shimoda, in *High-Resolution Laser Spectroscopy* (K. Shimoda, ed.), Springer-Verlag, Berlin, 1976, p. 11.
(293) C. K. N. Patel, *Appl. Phys. Lett.* **25**, 112 (1974).
(294) S. S. Penner, *Quantitative Molecular Spectroscopy and Gas Emissivities*, Addison-Wesley, Reading, Mass., 1959.
(295) R. H. Dicke, *Phys. Rev.* **89**, 472 (1953).
(296) F. A. Blum, K. W. Nill, A. R. Calawa and T. C. Harman, *Appl. Phys. Lett.* **20**, 377 (1972).
(297) I. M. Mills, *Annu. Rep. Prog. Chem.* **55**, 55 (1958).
(298) W. B. Person and D. Steele, in *Molecular Spectroscopy*, Vol. 2, Chem. Soc. Specialist Periodical Reports, London, 1974, p. 357.
(299) K. Fox and W. B. Person, *J. Chem. Phys.* **64**, 5218 (1976).
(300) H. Filip, R. F. Holland, K. C. Kim and N. G. Nereson, unpublished data cited in Ref. (299).
(301) P. N. Schatz and D. F. Hornig, *J. Chem. Phys.* **21**, 1516 (1953).
(302) K. Fox, *Opt. Commun.* **19**, 397 (1976).
(303) E. Weitz and G. Flynn, *Ann. Rev. Phys. Chem.* **25**, 275 (1974).
(304) K. Shimoda, in *Laser Spectroscopy of Atoms and Molecules* (H. Walther, ed.), Springer-Verlag, Berlin, 1976, p. 197.
(305) K. Shimoda, in *Laser Spectroscopy III* (J. L. Hall and J. L. Carlsten, eds.), Springer-Verlag, Berlin, 1977, p. 279.
(306) C. K. Rhodes, M. J. Kelly and A. Javan, *J. Chem. Phys.* **48**, 5730 (1968).
(307) I. Burak, A. V. Nowak, J. I. Steinfeld and D. G. Sutton, *J. Chem. Phys.* **51**, 2275 (1969).
(308) J. I. Steinfeld, I. Burak, D. G. Sutton and A. V. Nowak, *J. Chem. Phys.* **52**, 5421 (1970).
(309) D. S. Frankel and J. I. Steinfeld, *J. Chem. Phys.* **62**, 3358 (1975).
(310) J. I. Steinfeld and C. C. Jensen, in *Tunable Lasers and Applications* (A. Mooradian, T. Jaeger and P. Stokseth, eds.), Springer-Verlag, Berlin, 1976, p. 190.
(311) D. S. Frankel, *J. Chem. Phys.* **65**, 1696 (1976).
(312) D. S. Frankel, *Opt. Commun.* **18**, 31 (1976).
(313) P. L. Houston, A. V. Nowak and J. I. Steinfeld, *J. Chem. Phys.* **58**, 3373 (1973).
(314) P. F. Moulton, D. M. Larsen, J. N. Walpole and A. Mooradian, *Opt. Lett.* **1**, 51 (1977).
(315) R. G. Brewer, *Science* **178**, 247 (1972).
(316) R. L. Shoemaker, in *Laser Applications to Optics and Spectroscopy* (S. Jacobs, M. Sargent, J. F. Scott and M. O. Scully, eds.), Addison-Wesley, Reading, Mass., 1975, p. 453.
(317) V. S. Letokhov, *Science* **190**, 344 (1975).
(318) T. Shimizu, *Appl. Spectrosc. Rev.* **11**, 163 (1976).
(319) V. S. Letokhov, in *High-Resolution Laser Spectroscopy* (K. Shimoda, ed.), Springer-Verlag, Berlin, 1976, p. 95.
(320) V. S. Letokhov and V. P. Chebotayev, *Non-linear Laser Spectroscopy*, Springer-Verlag, Berlin, 1977.
(321) K. Shimoda and T. Shimizu, *Prog. Quantum Electron.* **2**, 45 (1972).
(322) W. E. Lamb, *Phys. Rev.* **134**, A1429 (1964).
(323) R. L. Barger and J. L. Hall, *Phys. Rev. Lett.* **22**, 4 (1969).
(324) E. E. Uzgiris, J. L. Hall and R. L. Barger, *Phys. Rev. Lett.* **26**, 289 (1971).
(325) A. C. Luntz and R. G. Brewer, *J. Chem. Phys.* **54**, 3641 (1971).
(326) J. L. Hall and C. Bordé, *Phys. Rev. Lett.* **30**, 1101 (1973).
(327) J. L. Hall and J. A. Magyar, in *High-Resolution Laser Spectroscopy* (K. Shimoda, ed.), Springer-Verlag, Berlin, 1976, p. 173.

(328) J. L. Hall, C. J. Bordé and K. Uehara, *Phys. Rev. Lett.* **37**, 1339 (1976).
(329) N. G. Basov, I. N. Kompanets, O. N. Kompanets, V. S. Letokhov and V. V. Nikitin, *JETP Lett.* (*Engl. Transl.*) **9**, 345 (1969).
(330) P. Rabinowitz, R. Keller and J. T. LaTourrette, *Appl. Phys. Lett.* **14**, 376 (1969).
(331) M. W. Goldberg and R. Yusek, *Appl. Phys. Lett.* **17**, 349 (1970).
(332) P. Rabinowitz, Thesis, Polytechnic Inst. of Brooklyn (1970); also available as Polytechnic Inst. Brooklyn Dept. Electrophysics Report PIBEP-70-065 (1970).
(333) N. G. Basov, O. N. Kompanets, V. S. Letokhov and V. V. Nikitin, *Sov. Phys. JETP* (*Engl. Transl.*) **32**, 214 (1971).
(334) M. Ouhayoun and C. J. Bordé, *Metrologia* **13**, 149 (1977).
(335) Yu. A. Gorokhov, O. N. Kompanets, V. S. Letokhov, G. A. Gerasimov and Yu. I. Posudin, *Opt. Commun.*, **7**, 320 (1973).
(336) O. N. Kompanets, A. R. Kukudzhanov, V. S. Letokhov, V. G. Minogin and E. L. Mikhailov, *Sov. Phys. JETP* (*Engl. Transl.*) **42**, 15 (1976).
(337) E. N. Bazarov, G. A. Gerasimov and Yu. I. Posudin, *Opt. Spectrosc.* (*U.S.S.R.*) **38**, 354 (1975).
(338) E. D. Hinkley, ed., *Laser Monitoring of the Atmosphere*, Springer-Verlag, Berlin, 1976.
(339) E. D. Hinkley, *Opt. Quantum Electron.* **8**, 155 (1976).
(340) I. Melngailis, *IEEE Trans. Geosci. Electron.* **GE-10**, 7 (1972).
(341) R. A. Toth, R. L. Abrams, G. Birnbaum, S. T. Eng, R. A. McClatchey, P. E. Nordal and S. O. Olsen, *Opt. Quantum Electron.* **8**, 191 (1976).
(342) R. T. Menzies, F. Allario, D. Duewer, D. T. Gjessing, K. Gürs, C. G. Little, T. Lund, J. Nordø, B. Ottar, G. E. Peckham and K. W. Rothe, *Opt. Quantum Electron.* **8**, 185 (1976).
(343) P. L. Hanst, J. A. Cooney, E. Hesstvedt, P. L. Kelley, J. J. Kennedy, J. E. Lovelock, C. K. N. Patel and G. Wang, *Opt. Quantum Electron.* **8**, 187 (1976).
(344) N. Laulainen, *Minor Gases in the Earth's Atmosphere: A Review and Bibliography of Their Spectra*, Project Astra Publ. 18, Univ. of Washington, Seattle (1972).
(345) E. G. Burkhardt, C. A. Lambert and C. K. N. Patel, *Science* **188**, 1111 (1975).
(346) C. K. N. Patel, *Opt. Quantum Electron.* **8**, 145 (1976).
(347) T. Henningsen, M. Garbuny and R. L. Byer, *Appl. Phys. Lett.* **24**, 242 (1974).
(348) J. Reid, J. Shewchun, B. K. Garside and E. A. Ballik, *J. Opt. Soc. Am.* **67**, 1363 (1977).
(349) R. T. Menzies, in *Laser Spectroscopy III* (J. L. Hall and J. L. Carlsten, eds.), Springer-Verlag, Berlin, 1977, p. 325.
(350) E. D. Hinkley, A. R. Calawa, P. L. Kelley and S. A. Clough, *J. Appl. Phys.* **43**, 3222 (1972).
(351) S. T. Eng and E. Max, in *Tunable Lasers and Applications* (A. Mooradian, T. Jaeger and P. Stokseth, eds.), Springer-Verlag, Berlin, 1976, p. 348.

Chapter 2

THE VIBRATIONAL SPECTRA OF CARBON MONOXIDE CHEMISORBED ON THE SURFACES OF METAL CATALYSTS – A SUGGESTED SCHEME OF INTERPRETATION

N. Sheppard and T. T. Nguyen

School of Chemical Sciences, University of East Anglia, Norwich NR4 7TJ, U.K.

1 INTRODUCTION

1.1 Infrared and Raman Spectra of Chemisorbed Molecules

The spectroscopic method that has made the greatest contributions to the study of the structures of molecules adsorbed on surfaces has been infrared spectroscopy. Since the pioneering work of Terenin in the late 1940s (initially concerned mainly with physical adsorption)[1] and of Eischens in the mid-1950s (mainly concerned with chemisorption),[2] there has grown up a large and important literature, summarized to date in three books.[3–5] From the chemical point of view, the most important aim of this work has been to identify the structures of species formed by the chemisorption of molecules on surfaces of catalytic importance. Two main types of such surfaces have received the most attention.

The first of these types constitutes the oxides of the lighter elements silicon and aluminium which, because of their catalytic importance, are readily available in high-area forms. In addition to different forms of pure silica or alumina there are other catalytically important adsorbents derived from them, viz. the silica–alumina cracking catalysts and the zeolites. The latter are crystalline silica–aluminas with replaceable metal cations. Infrared work on such surfaces has recently been reviewed in detail.[5,6]

The second type of catalyst that has been extensively studied by infrared spectroscopy comprises the finely divided metals. These are usually stabilized in high area form by deposition on supports of the finely divided oxide types just mentioned. Little[3,7] and Pritchard[8] have reviewed infrared studies on metal surfaces in general. This present review article is specifically concerned with infrared studies of carbon monoxide adsorption on such metal catalysts.

Another type of catalyst which has been studied to only a limited extent is the family of heavy-metal oxide catalysts. The main difficulties in such work have been (a) the preparation of these oxides in sufficiently high area form to give measurable absorption bands from adsorbed molecules and (b) the overcoming of heavy scattering of infrared radiation by these high refractive index materials. The latter difficulty makes infrared transmission studies particularly difficult but newer spectroscopic techniques of high sensitivity, such as Fourier-transform infrared interferometry, show signs of opening up this important field. A very good start has been made by the late Professor Kokes[9] and his colleagues by their identification of an allylic species from the chemisorption of propylene on zinc oxide. Folman and his colleagues[10] pioneered the infrared study of adsorption on alkali-halide surfaces, where the infrared transmission is particularly favourable.

More recently, laser Raman spectroscopy has begun to make substantial contributions to the study of the structures of species adsorbed on catalyst surfaces and this work has recently been reviewed.[11,12] However, to date most of the experiments have been concerned with adsorption on the silicas and aluminas because of their high areas (to give good sensitivity) and their white or off-white colours. Because finely divided metal catalysts are highly coloured, or more often black, for such adsorbents there are major problems from sample heating and adsorbate decomposition in the laser beams used for excitation of Raman spectra. However, attempts are being made in several laboratories to overcome this difficulty. Also, successful Raman work on heavy-metal oxides has been initiated,[13] and some successful studies have been made of adsorption from aqueous solutions on metal electrodes.[14]

1.2   Infrared Spectra of CO Chemisorbed on Metal Catalysts

The infrared absorption bands resulting from the chemisorption of CO on metals, particularly the bands associated with νCO bond-stretching modes, are very strong and readily measured. Hence, not infrequently, the infrared spectrum from adsorbed CO is measured with a view to characterizing a particular preparation of a metal catalyst. It is found that rarely do two finely divided catalysts derived from the same metal give the same CO spectra. Even when obviously aberrant spectra, such as those from incompletely reduced metals, are excluded there often remain very substantial spectral differences. As a result the literature is confusing and inconsistent, but on the other hand there are many data which are potentially very valuable if they could be interpreted. This review represents a first comprehensive attempt to interpret the already published experimental data in terms of differing surface structures of the metal catalysts. With a few exceptions, the literature coverage is up to mid-1977.

For those samples which are judged to be well reduced, i.e. essentially pure metal, and free of significant surface contamination, our main aim will be to interpret the CO spectra in terms of:

(a) The chemical nature of the adsorbed species;
(b) The type of sites likely to be consistent with the presence of that species; and
(c) The surface crystal planes that are likely to provide the sites so identified.

In relation to individual crystal faces, we shall take into account the fractional surface coverage and the size of faces as significant variables. For small metal particles the nature of the support may also be of relevance.

A reason for attempting such an interpretation at this time is the recent publication of results on the vibrational frequencies of CO chemisorbed on specified individual single-crystal planes of several metals. Work of this type involving CO was pioneered by Pritchard and his colleagues[15] in relation to different crystal planes of copper. They used the reflection-absorption infrared technique (r.a.-i.r.) due to Francis and Ellison[16] and to Greenler.[17] In such work the absorption of radiation from an infrared beam reflected off a metal surface at a high angle of incidence gives information about the frequencies of vibrations of the adsorbate. Those that are active are the vibrations that exhibit dipole changes perpendicular to the metal surface. Bradshaw and Hoffmann[18] have very recently made similar studies for CO on Pd, and Horn and Pritchard[19] for CO on Pt.

Within the past 18 months very valuable additional results have come from the electron energy-loss (EELS) technique as applied to vibrational spectra.[20,21] The selection rules and factors determining the intensities of energy absorption are closely similar in EELS and r.a.-i.r. spectroscopy.[21] The EELS method has an advantage of one to two orders of magnitude greater sensitivity than the infrared method, and a wider accessible range of energies, i.e. effective wavenumbers. The r.a.-i.r. method is at present limited to the wavenumber range in excess of 600 to 800 cm^{-1} by the available window materials. The EELS method has a disadvantage of about an order of magnitude less resolution than the infrared method but, despite this limitation, extremely valuable results have been obtained for CO on Pt and Ni by Ibach and his colleagues[22] and by Andersson[23] respectively. The EELS results give the added bonus of information about frequencies associated with the νM—C bond-stretching modes in addition to those of the νCO type.

Both the r.a.-i.r. and EELS methods require the use of ultra-high vacua in the 10^{-10} Torr (1 Torr = 133.32 N m^{-2}) range in order to effect the cleaning, and retention of cleanliness, of the low-area single-crystal surfaces. Also the measurement of electron energies can only be made in the presence of very low pressures of gas-phase molecules. The latter limitation is not present for reflection studies involving electromagnetic radiation as a probe, but there is a sense in which both the EELS and r.a.-i.r. techniques are applied under idealized conditions compared with those used for the preparation and application of oxide-supported metal catalysts. The latter require normal high vacua techniques (10^{-6} Torr) at best, and even these pressures are idealized in relation to the conditions of use of normal 'working' catalysts in the laboratory or in industry.

Nevertheless the complexities and subtleties of surface structures, as will be discussed below for the metals, are such that simplification is probably essential for progress to be made. And, after all, it is doubtless these subtleties and complexities which enable solid-state heterogeneous catalysts to open up so many very valuable reaction pathways that would otherwise be blocked by the slowness of thermodynamically feasible chemical reactions. It should be borne in mind that, by selectively opening up particular reaction steps amongst consecutive or parallel reaction possibilities, catalysts also enable the selective isolation of a wide variety of very valuable products by the methods of kinetic control.

2 ADSORPTION SITES ON METAL SURFACES

As a preliminary to attempting to obtain an understanding of the complex features of the infrared spectra of CO chemisorbed on metal surfaces, it is necessary to consider certain features of the surfaces themselves.[24] For the transition metals of Periods III, IV, and V, Table 1 lists (i) the outer electronic structures of isolated atoms in terms of the occupancy of the outer d and s orbitals, (ii) the atomic radii in Å within the bulk metals and (iii) the type of crystal structure exhibited by each metal.[25] The majority of metals that we shall be interested in have the close-packed face-centred cubic structure (f.c.c.), and hence our discussion of different available sites for adsorption on metals will be given particularly in terms of this structure.

We shall first give attention to the idealized crystal planes of types (111), (100) and (110) and proceed from there to discuss imperfections in these (often termed steps and kinks) and the so-called high-index planes. Finally we shall discuss possible additional features of the surfaces of small metal particles such as are present in supported-metal catalysts.

2.1 The Topography of Metal Surface Planes

The pattern of surface atoms on the (111), (100) and (110) planes of a f.c.c. metal lattice are illustrated in Fig. 1. The symmetries of these surface meshes reflect the 3-fold, 4-fold and 2-fold symmetry axes, respectively, which emerge perpendicular to these surfaces.

For the close-packed f.c.c. (111) plane, and very probably also for the (100) plane, the second layer of atoms is likely to be quite inaccessible, in the sense of the possibility of forming a valence bond, to a molecule of the size of CO. Typical surface internuclear distances between metal atoms are 2.5 to 2.9 Å

TABLE 1
Basic data on the transition metals

Metal	Lattice[b] type	Radius[c] /Å	Electronic structure[a]	Metal	Lattice[b] type	Radius[c] /Å	Electronic structure[a]	Metal	Lattice[b] type	Radius[c] /Å	Electronic structure[a]
Sc	c.p.h.	1.66	$3d^1 4s^2$	Y	c.p.h.	1.80	$4d^1 5s^2$	La[a]	c.p.h.	1.86	$5d^1 6s^2$
Ti[a]	c.p.h.	1.46	$3d^2 4s^2$	Zr[a]	c.p.h.	1.58	$4d^2 5s^2$	Hf	c.p.h.	1.57	$5d^2 6s^2$
V	b.c.c.	1.31	$3d^3 4s^2$	Nb	b.c.c.	1.43	$4d^4 5s^1$	Ta	b.c.c.	1.43	$5d^3 6s^2$
Cr[a]	b.c.c.	1.25	$3d^5 4s^1$	Mo	b.c.c.	1.36	$4d^5 5s^1$	W[a]	b.c.c.	1.37	$5d^4 6s^2$
Mn[a]	A6	1.29	$3d^5 4s^2$	Tc	c.p.h.	1.36	$4d^6 5s^1$	Re	c.p.h.	1.37	$5d^5 6s^2$
Fe[a]	b.c.c.	1.24	$3d^6 4s^2$	Ru	c.p.h.	1.32	$4d^7 5s^1$	Os	c.p.h.	1.33	$5d^6 6s^2$
Co[a]	f.c.c.	1.25	$3d^7 4s^2$	Rh	f.c.c.	1.34	$4d^8 5s^1$	Ir	f.c.c.	1.35	$5d^7 6s^2$
Ni[a]	f.c.c.	1.24	$3d^8 4s^2$	Pd	f.c.c.	1.37	$4d^{10} 5s^0$	Pt	f.c.c.	1.38	$5d^9 6s^1$
Cu	f.c.c.	1.27	$3d^{10} 4s^1$	Ag	f.c.c.	1.44	$4d^{10} 5s^1$	Au	f.c.c.	1.44	$5d^{10} 6s^1$
Zn	c.p.h.	1.33	$3d^{10} 4s^2$	Cd	c.p.h.	1.48	$4d^{10} 5s^2$	Hg	A10	1.50	$5d^{10} 6s^2$

[a] Other allotropic modifications are known.

[b] c.p.h. = close-packed hexagonal (A3); b.c.c. = body-centred cubic (A2); f.c.c. = face-centred cubic (A1); other crystal structures are denoted by the Strukturbericht symbols.

[c] The metallic interatomic distance is twice this value.

[d] The outer electronic structures of the isolated atoms, from F. A. Cotton and G. Wilkinson, *Advanced Inorganic Chemistry*, Interscience, New York, 1972.

(Table 1), and the van der Waals diameter of a CO molecule is about 3.5 Å.[†] However, on the (110) plane it is possible that a CO molecule adsorbed at the centre of the rectangular surface mesh might interact also with the atom in the next layer at that location.

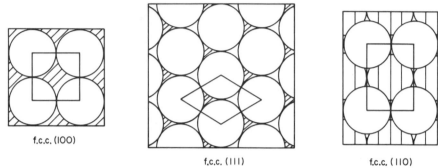

f.c.c. (100)   f.c.c. (111)   f.c.c. (110)

Fig. 1. Patterns of surface atoms on the (100), (111) and (110) faces of a f.c.c. metal lattice.

On each of the above crystal planes, CO adsorption could involve the interaction of the adsorbed species with a single metal atom, or with pairs of equivalent metal atoms. Interactions with 3 (for the (111) plane) or 4 (for the (100) and (110) planes) equivalent metal atoms are also possible. Van Hardeveld and Hartog[26] and Nicholas[27] have considered these various sites in a systematic manner. We shall adopt a notation given by Nicholas; this is the same as van Hardeveld and Hartog's notation except that, for simplicity, their second suffix denoting the number of next-nearest neighbours is not used.

2.2   Adsorption on Single-atom Sites

A metal atom within a f.c.c. crystal is coordinated by 12 nearest neighbours. The single-atom sites on different surface planes themselves differ in terms of the residual coordination by nearest-neighbour metal atoms. On the (111), (100) and (110) planes these coordination numbers are 9, 8 and 7 respectively. These are denoted as C_9, C_8 and C_7 sites, with the implication that the lower the value of the coordination number the greater is the number of unsaturated valencies at the site. This implies a qualitatively greater availability of electrons for bond-formation to adsorbed species.

In coordination chemistry, ligands such as CO normally exhibit a maximum coordination number of 6, with octahedral symmetry around the metal atom. Counting 2 of the 12 metal coordinations in the bulk metal as the equivalent of

[†] There would, of course, be less restriction of access to second-layer metal atoms for a uniquely small atom such as that of hydrogen; this is worth bearing in mind in view of the dependence of the infrared spectra of some adsorbed CO species on the presence or absence of hydrogen co-adsorption.

1 CO coordination, the maximum unsatisfied CO coordinations on (111), (100) and (110) of f.c.c. metals would formally correspond to $1\frac{1}{2}$, 2 and $2\frac{1}{2}$ respectively. In practice, on steric grounds, the number of additional bonds formed seems likely to be 1 each on (111) and (100) planes because other metal atoms surround the adsorbing atom in the same plane. The ridges of metal atoms on (110) faces might in principle accommodate two CO molecules; but as the maximum fractional coverage, θ, on any of these planes is $\theta = 1$, we shall assume that even on (110) planes there is no more than a single adsorbed CO molecule per surface metal atom (see also Sections 5.2 and 10).

2.3 Adsorption on Multiple Atom Sites

In principle, sites for equivalent adsorption to 2 metal atoms (B_2 sites)[†] are available on all three types of surface planes. On (111) and (100) the appropriate spacing available is the close-packed spacing, which we shall label a. However, as mentioned above, the individual atoms on these two planes differ in their detailed bonding capacities. On the (110) plane some pairs of atoms are separated by a and others by the longer spacing of $a\sqrt{2}$. On (111) planes there is a 3-fold triangular adsorption site designated B_3; on (100) a 4-fold square adsorption site denoted B_4; and on (110) a 4-fold rectangular site, denoted B_5. The latter site is designated B_5 because it is the one, mentioned earlier, that may involve some interaction of the adsorbed species with a 5th, non-equivalent, metal atom in the second layer. For completeness it should be noted that the 3-fold adsorption sites on the (111) surface can be sub-divided into two equal sets. In one of these there is a metal atom to be found directly below in the second layer and in the other there are no such second-layer atoms. In the literature on transition-metal cluster compounds it is customary to describe CO molecules bonded to single metal atoms as *terminal*.[28] In the adsorption literature the analogous term is *linear*, and we shall use the latter description in this review. CO molecules bonded to more than one metal atom are denoted '*edge-bridged*' (2 atoms) or '*face-bridged*' (3 or 4 atoms) in the cluster-compound literature: we shall use the descriptions '*2-fold bridged*' or '*3-fold bridged*' etc. as the description 'edge' has a different connotation in the adsorption literature.

Recent theoretical studies by Doyen and Ertl,[29] by Blyholder[30] and by Politzer and Kasten[31] suggest that, when both linear and bridged sites are available, the latter (and particularly the 4-fold bridged sites) are likely to be more stable for the bonding of CO to a nickel surface. Less energy difference between linear or bridged sites is found on the (111) face of Ni according to calculations.[29] We shall take these theoretical conclusions to be indicative rather than definitive, bearing in mind (see later) that experimental evidence strongly favours the predominance of linear sites on Pt.

[†] We shall once again omit the upper suffices used in van Hardeveld and Hartog's more complete notation.[26]

2.4   Out-of-register Adsorption Sites

In the above discussion we have assumed that molecules are likely to be adsorbed on one or another of the more symmetrical sites on a metal surface. Low energy electron diffraction (LEED) provides an experimental means of exploring the surface crystallography associated with metal surfaces and adsorbed overlayers. Typically the early stage of adsorption of molecules is accompanied only by a general increase of background scattering of electrons, presumably reflecting chemisorption on different sites at random distances with respect to each other. However, usually at certain well-defined fractional coverages, e.g. $\theta = \frac{1}{4}, \frac{1}{3}, \frac{1}{2}$ etc. sharp diffraction patterns are obtained which give information about the pattern and spacings of atoms in symmetrical and regular adsorbed overlayers. Frequently these patterns are what would be expected through regular adsorption on the types of sites discussed above, although it is important to realize that the LEED measurements do not normally provide direct information about the *locations* of the 2-dimensional lattices formed by adsorbed molecules with respect to the underlying lattice of surface metal atoms. Thus, for example, a centred (2×2) structure, as has been observed for CO adsorbed in Ni(100),[32] could denote CO molecules adsorbed on 4-fold bridged sites on every other square mesh *or*, equally well, adsorption of CO over every other metal atom on linear sites.

More recently, increasing numbers of LEED measurements, usually at high surface coverages, have shown the presence of adsorbed overlayers which are not simply related to the unit mesh of the metal surface.[32] These are often described as being *compressed* (because of the high coverage) or *out-of-register* structures. They can frequently be understood in terms of *close-packing of the adsorbed molecules* in one or two dimensions, without regard to the underlying patterns of metal atoms. Such observations clearly have implications for the nature of the valence forces holding molecules to metal surfaces, and equally for the interpretation of infrared spectra from adsorbed molecules. These phenomena are at least explicable in terms of the oversimplified model of a plane metal surface with valence electrons uniformly available at all locations.

It has, however, been suggested recently that in some cases it may not be possible to distinguish, in the LEED pattern, between a truly close-packed overlayer and one in which individual adsorbed molecules still occupy well-defined sites (linear, 2 fold-bridged, etc.) at positions *near* ideal close-packed positions.[33] These could occur in a random manner in different parts of the adsorbed layer. The LEED pattern in such cases would represent an average from a disordered structure, and might only reflect the mean spacing between adsorbed molecules.

2.5   Metal Surface Reconstructions

In the above discussion we have implicitly assumed that the metal surface formed is of the type expected as a planar termination of the underlying 3-dimensional metal lattice. However, LEED experiments have shown that this is not always the case. The evidence is in the form of diffraction patterns of unexpected symmetry and/or complexity, obtained either from the clean metal surface itself or after adsorption of molecules. Such unexpected metal surfaces are described as *reconstructed*. Examples of reconstructed metal surfaces are provided by LEED studies of clean-metal (100) faces on Pt, Ir, and Au.[32] In each case a complex pattern is observed which can be reasonably interpreted in terms of a close-packed (111)-type top layer of metal atoms. In these cases it is the top layer of metal atoms that is out of register with the underlying lattice.

2.6   Terraces, Edges and Kinks: High-index Planes

Even a well-cut and well-annealed single crystal face of the type that we have been considering will, in fact, have a considerable number of faults on the atomic scale. These may consist of the ends of the screw dislocations which often provide the growing points for the next layer of atoms on top of a crystal. There will also be projections or islands of atoms, and similarly holes representing incomplete sections of surfaces. Such faults are represented schematically in Fig. 2.

In most cases these faults have the effect of producing one-atom or two-atom deep steps which provide different types of adsorption sites from those available on the perfect crystal planes. Such sites can be produced systematically if a crystal plane is deliberately cut at a small angle to a plane such as either (111) or (100). The sites themselves are termed '*step sites*' and '*kink sites*', the more abundant sites of the dominant crystal plane being then referred to as '*terrace sites*'. Such phenomena are visually in evidence from field-ion microscopic studies of metal tips.[34] The small-angle planes themselves are termed high-index planes and it is becoming rather widely found and assumed that adsorption on such planes (presumably at these additional types of sites) leads to particularly strong bonding of adsorbed molecules to the surface.[35] For example, it has been

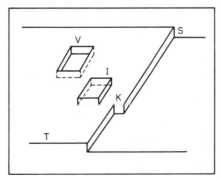

Fig. 2. Schematic representation of faults on surfaces showing a step, S; a terrace, T; a kink, K; a vacancy on surface, V; and an island, I.

claimed that CO is adsorbed without dissociation on (111) and (100) planes of Pt but with dissociation on the 'high-index' planes.[35]

The cutting of high-index planes provides a systematic way of producing a given proportion of step and kink sites with respect to a majority of planar or terrace sites. However it is somewhat misleading to use the term 'high-index' to denote the presumably more active step sites themselves. Thus, for example, the (110) surface described earlier can be considered as a regular array of 1-step sites relative to 'terraces' of (100) planes of unit depth, i.e. the surface consists entirely of 'step' sites!

'Outside' atoms at step sites consist of surface atoms of particularly low metal coordination number. For steps which are several atoms in depth these are the same type of sites that constitute the edges of individual 3-dimensional crystals. In addition the atoms at the 'inside' of the steps provide bridged sites involving 4 or 5 atoms such as the B_5 sites exhibited by the (110) surface. It does not yet seem to have been firmly established whether it is the 'outside' or 'inside' sites that are most active in chemisorption. Which is the case may well differ from one adsorbate to another.

2.7 Additional Features in the Surfaces of Metal Particles

A typical supported metal catalyst has metal particles ranging from a few tens to a few hundred Ångstroms in diameter. The larger particles are often polygonal in outline in electron micrographs with triangular, square, pentagonal or hexagonal cross-sections.[24] These outlines probably denote particles of tetra-hedral or cubic or hexagonal shapes or others formed by twinning processes based on tetrahedral sub-crystals. It is considered most likely that in thermo-dynamic equilibrium the surfaces of such f.c.c. metallic crystals would be composed of facets of (111) or (100) types, e.g. in cubo-octahedra. Often in reality the corners and edges of such images are rounded and many small particles are near circular in cross-section.

If the crystallites were perfectly formed then, for a given total mass of metal, as the crystal diameter became smaller an increasing proportion of atoms would be located at corners (with typical metal coordination numbers of 3 or 4) or along edges (with typical coordination numbers of 5, 6 or 7). Van Hardeveld and Hartog[26] have looked into the statistics of occurrence of atoms with different metal coordination numbers as a function of mean metal particle size. It is shown that there are relatively few corner sites for crystallites of mean diameter greater than 5 atomic diameters (e.g. greater than about 10–20 Å for typical metals such as Ni, Pd or Pt). However, edge atoms provide a meaningful proportion of sites (10% or more) even for crystallites of dimensions of 25 atomic diameters or 50–100 Å. The latter is a typical range of metal particle sizes for oxide-supported metal catalysts.

Metal crystallites with rounded corners or edges will have more sites of the edge and corner type at the atomic level. Here one is considering the same types of sites denoted earlier as 'step' or 'kink' sites on imperfect or terraced crystal planes. Hence the calculations of the proportions of such sites based on perfectly shaped crystallites gives a minimum evaluation of their numerical importance. Clearly, 'step-sites' in particular (of either the 'outside' or 'inside' varieties) must be taken into account in interpreting the spectra from normal supported metal catalysts.

Finally with supported metal catalysts there will exist metal atoms which may have different adsorption properties because they are adjacent to the surface of the support material.[36]

3 SPECTROSCOPIC PHENOMENA ASSOCIATED WITH THE INTERACTION OF ADSORBED MOLECULES ON THE SAME CRYSTAL FACES

The discussion so far has been concerned with the different types of sites likely to be presented by metal surfaces. However if, for example, there are considerably more stable sites for chemisorption on one particular type of crystal face than on another, there will be a tendency (assuming either surface mobility, or mobility via a dynamic equilibrium of adsorbed species with the gas phase) for certain crystal planes to achieve high coverage first. This may occur even after only a relatively small proportion of the total surface sites has been covered.

Additional phenomena arising from interactions of adjacent adsorbed molecules are likely to come into play when the coverage becomes more than a small fraction of the total. These phenomena are likely to have at least two origins, although the overall effect may well reflect a combination of both. On the one hand, the adsorption of a molecule on one site may affect the electron density and hence the strength of the chemisorption bond at an adjacent site. In principle, the electron densities of all metal atoms in the particle would be affected in different degrees, but it seems reasonable to assume that it is the immediately adjacent surface atoms that will be most affected.[18] Secondly, there may be lateral 'across-space' electrical or steric interactions between nearby adsorbed molecules.[18]

We shall first consider the latter type of interaction, bearing in mind that we are interested in the manner in which the interaction affects vibrational frequencies. Hammaker et al.[37] and van Hardeveld and Hartog[38] have considered such effects explicitly for the adsorption of CO and N_2 on metal surfaces. From studies of the spectra obtained by mixtures of isotopically substituted adsorbates (^{12}CO and ^{13}CO, $^{14}N^{14}N$, $^{14}N^{15}N$, and $^{15}N^{15}N$) they have reached the conclusions that the effects are considerable. The spectroscopic manifestations of such interactions can be appreciated in qualitative terms for the simplified model of a linear array of adjacent parallel oscillating molecules.

Let $\tilde{\nu}_0$ be the wavenumber of an isolated oscillator corresponding to a basic force constant k, and k' the interaction constant between adjacent molecules.

Let the reduced mass for a single oscillator be μ. For a single CO oscillator, $\tilde{v}_0 = (k/\mu)^{\frac{1}{2}}/2\pi c$ where c is the velocity of light. For a pair of adjacent oscillators there will be two normal modes, one in which the two molecules vibrate in-phase and the other in which they vibrate out-of-phase. There will be a resulting pair of fundamental frequencies split by a wavenumber difference, $\Delta\tilde{v}$, dependent on the magnitude of k'. If k' has one sign the in-phase vibration will be higher in wavenumber and the out-of-phase one lower; for k' of the opposite sign the reverse will be true. If we add a third vibrating molecule to the sequence an additional interaction constant k'' for the interaction between next-to-nearest neighbours will, in principle, have to be taken into account. For an infinite linear array of adsorbed molecules there will be an analogous number of normal modes of vibration leading to a continuum of vibrational frequencies. The precise frequency of a particular normal mode will depend on the form of the vibration as determined by the phase difference between adjacent oscillators. However the infrared intensity depends on the square of the dipole change between the two extremes of the vibration, and clearly this will be greatest for that normal mode in which all the parallel oscillators are in phase, so that the individual vibrational dipole changes reinforce each other. For an infinite one-dimensional situation all other modes will have zero intensity as they will arise from sets of oscillators vibrating to give rise to dipole changes in the opposite sense. For a finite series of oscillators, the in-phase mode will remain much the strongest in the infrared spectrum. An observed wavenumber of $\tilde{v}_0$ for a single isolated oscillator will gradually move out from $\tilde{v}_0$ to a new limiting value, depending on the magnitudes of the interaction constants, k', k'' etc. as the number of oscillators increases.

The infrared absorption bands attributed to CO stretching modes of metal carbonyls are very intense, corresponding to large vibrational dipole changes. In such cases the interaction constant k' is likely to reflect primarily dipolar interactions, leading to the intense in-phase mode occurring at a higher frequency than $\tilde{v}_0$. The argument can be generalized to two dimensions.

In agreement with the predictions of this model it is normal for the vCO frequencies of adsorbed molecules to increase with increasing surface coverage so that even adsorption on a single crystal plane does not lead to a fixed infrared frequency. However, this observed effect could alternatively in part also arise from a change in the basic force constant (k) with coverage, resulting from electronic effects of neighbouring adsorbed molecules as discussed earlier and as envisaged by Blyholder.[39]

Qualitative arguments similar to the above could apply to the coupled vibrations of other parallel adjacent oscillators, such as bridged CO groups.

4 DO BRIDGED SPECIES EXIST ON METAL SURFACES?

In their pioneering studies of the spectra of CO adsorbed on silica-supported metals, Eischens and his colleagues[2,40] drew on the then small literature on the infrared spectra of metal carbonyls in order to make their well known distinction between 'linear' and 'bridged' ('2-fold bridged' in the notation used in this article) adsorbed species. At that time the ranges 2100 to 1950 cm^{-1} seemed applicable to linear (terminal) CO bonding, and 1900 to 1800 cm^{-1} for bridged bonding in metal carbonyls. Eischens et al.[41] pointed to the fact that many of the absorptions that they observed from adsorbed CO fell in the intermediate wavenumber range of 2000 to 1900 cm^{-1}, but preferred the assignment of these bands to bridged species because of the strong overlapping of these absorptions with others in the 1900 to 1800 cm^{-1} region. They were, however, uncertain how to assign a single Fe/CO absorption band near 1960 cm^{-1}.[41] Subsequently Blyholder[39] pointed to later infrared evidence from the metal-carbonyl literature, that certain undoubtedly linearly bonded CO groups could give absorption bands well below 2000 cm^{-1}. While not denying the existence of bridged groups, he did raise the question whether this was a necessary hypothesis. He envisaged, on sound *qualitative* theoretical grounds, which are generally accepted in the literature on metal carbonyls, that a range of linear CO frequencies could be accounted for in terms of different degrees of back-bonding by d-electrons from the metal into anti-bonding orbitals of the CO molecule so as to give a structure resembling $M\!=\!C\!=\!O$ rather than the conventional $\overset{-}{M}\!-\!\overset{+}{C}\!\equiv\!O$ formulation based on the electronic structure of CO itself. Different compounds would have structures, and frequencies, between these extremes, and Blyholder envisaged that the range of wavenumbers could be wide enough (≈ 2100 to 1800 cm^{-1}) to encompass the whole range of absorption bands observed by Eischens et al. for CO on metals. He supported these ideas with molecular orbital calculations[42] and pointed to many phenomena in the infrared literature that could be interpreted on this hypothesis. The idea was that exposed metal atoms on edges and corners of metal crystallites (those with particularly low values of n based on the C_n notation used in Sections 2.1 and 2.2) would have the highest electron density for back-bonding from the metal d orbital into the π^* anti-bonding orbital of CO, and hence lowest νCO frequencies. By comparison, metal atoms in the main faces, with high n, would give little back-bonding and high νCO frequencies. The former were considered to be responsible for the low frequency bands which Eischens et al. had assigned to bridged species, and the latter for the higher frequency bands already assigned to linear species. Blyholder's interpretations of the infrared spectra were attractive and obtained substantial support, e.g. from van Hardeveld and Hartog.[43]

However, during the last 5 years a variety of lines of experimental evidence have pointed to the correctness of Eischen's original explanation in terms of linear and bridged sites, with a generalization of the latter category to include B_3 and B_4 sites as well as B_2 ones.[36] Also, as a result of further theoretical calculations, Blyholder[30] himself has concluded that the strongest CO adsorption and the weakest CO bond-order (and hence the lowest νCO frequencies) may be associated with multi-bridged species. However, this has been a long-standing controversy, and it is important to understand the main lines of evidence on both sides. These are as follows:

(a) *Model coordination compounds.* In retrospect it is seen that the abnormally low νCO frequencies found from linear CO species in transition-metal coordination compounds,[39] were always associated with the presence of negative charges on the metal atoms or of other metal ligands attached to the same metal atom, such as amines and phosphines, which are particularly good electron donors to the metal but poor d-electron acceptors. These ligands promote d-electron donation to the CO groups and lower their frequencies. However, in metal catalysts or in metal carbonyls, the only other ligands are other metal atoms or the less strongly electron-donating CO groups.

(b) *Metal alloys.* Recent infrared studies by Soma-Noto and Sachtler[44] of CO adsorbed on Pd/Ag alloys have shown that dilution of Pd (on which most CO bonding gives low frequency bands) by Ag (on which only very weak infrared bands are observed—see Section 6.5) leads to a rapid growth of the higher frequency bands on Pd at the expense of low frequency bands. This is readily accounted for if the low frequency bands are from bridged species which require adjacent pairs of Pd atoms. The latter become less frequent in occurrence as the proportion of Ag atoms increases, although the total effect observed seems larger than expected on that factor alone.[45] On Blyholder's model[39] the complete d-shell of the Ag should donate to vacant d orbitals in Pd to give higher electron densities and hence lower CO frequencies. This implies that both high and low frequency bands, postulated to correspond to different C_n sites on Pd, should move to lower frequencies. The frequency shift predicted on Blyholder's model is observed on a limited scale with the Pd/Ag system[45] and, as Blyholder noted,[39] had also been observed in some earlier measurements on Ni/Cu alloys by Eischens.[46] However Blyholder's hypothesis seems to have nothing predictive to say about the more spectacular intensity increase and decrease of the high and low frequency bands respectively with increasing Ag content within the alloys.

Similar work has been carried out by Soma-Noto and Sachtler[47] and by Dalmon et al.[48] on the Ni/Cu alloy system and interpreted in the same way. Hobert[49] had previously studied the Ni/Cu system with particular emphasis on the frequencies of the bands and, as already mentioned, Eischens[46] had obtained infrared spectra on Pt/Pd and Ni/Cu alloy systems. Eischens, of course, had no difficulty in understanding the band intensities on his 'linear' and 'bridged' CO model but did not at that time (prior to Blyholder's hypothesis) find a satisfactory explanation of the CO-band frequency shifts on the Ni/Cu systems.

(c) *Matrix-isolated MCO species.* Inert-gas, matrix-isolation work on metals and CO allow the measurement of the infrared frequencies of the 3-atom species MCO (M = metal). Moskovits and Ozin[50] have made such measurements and pointed out that, on Blyholder's hypothesis, this species should be the most favourable one for d → π^* back donation to CO and should therefore set a lower limit for vCO frequencies in linear species. Because many of the low frequency bands from CO on metal catalysts occur at even lower frequencies than those of the MCO species, they too prefer Eischen's assignment in terms of bridged species.

(d) *Combined infrared and magnetic measurements.* Dalmon, Primet, Martin and Imelik[36,48] have used magnetic criteria to measure the average number of bonds, n, formed to metal atoms per adsorbed CO molecule for oxide-supported Ni/Cu alloys[48] and for a variety of preparations of Ni.[36] They have made infrared spectroscopic studies on the same preparations and show that for the Ni/Cu alloys, the magnetically determined values of n, and the varying integrated intensity ratios of the low frequency and high frequency bands, are in good agreement if the low frequency bands are assigned to the 2-bridged species, $Ni_2(CO)$. There were indications of smaller contributions from 3- and/or 4-bridged species. Results from a range of Ni preparations are similarly best interpreted in terms of predominantly $Ni_2(CO)$ species for assignment of the low frequency bands. $Ni_3(CO)$ and $Ni_4(CO)$ species are presumed to absorb in the lower wavenumber tail to the 'bridged' absorption band in the region of 1800 to 1850 cm^{-1}.[36]

(e) *Internal evidence from the infrared spectra.* In virtually all cases the infrared spectra themselves show a substantial gap between the narrow absorption region assigned to 'linear' species and the much broader absorption region assigned to 'bridged' species. This suggests a qualitative rather than a quantitative distinction between the species giving rise to the two sets of absorption bands.

(f) *Spectral variability between different metals.* The Blyholder hypothesis can, as he pointed out,[39] account for different intensities observed in the high and low frequency regions for different catalyst preparations of the same metal. When the high frequency bands are stronger than the low frequency ones the conclusion would be that the particular sample had more well-defined crystal faces. However, major differences between different metals, where the high frequency bands are very dominant on Pt and the low frequency bands are dominant on Pd, seem to be more difficult to account for.[2] It seems most unlikely that all Pt preparations are well crystalline and all Pd ones are poorly crystalline as far as their outer faces are concerned. For Ni, bands in the two regions are more comparable in intensity but the low frequency absorption remains somewhat stronger, even when the sample has been reduced at 900 °C, when crystalline faces would have been expected.[36]

The six lines of evidence cited above all point to the correctness of Eischens' original interpretation of the low frequency bands in terms of bridged species, together with smaller contributions from $Ni_3(CO)$ and $Ni_4(CO)$ than from $Ni_2(CO)$.

However, the frequency shifts cited in connection with the work on Pd/Ag and Ni/Cu alloys point to the Blyholder d → π^* hypothesis being correct *as* *applied separately to linear and bridged species*, but in each case over a much smaller range of wavenumbers (*ca.* 50 cm^{-1}) than originally envisaged. Within this narrower range, the hypothesis may also help to account for multiple infrared absorption components found within the 'linear' region as cited below in the discussions of results with individual metals. This more limited application of the Blyholder hypothesis is also confirmed by the effects of electron-donating adsorbates in lowering infrared frequencies of co-adsorbed CO.[51,52]

In relation to his 'linear' and 'bridged' model, Eischens pointed out at an early stage[40] that bridged COs in metal carbonyls had a rather lower wavenumber range (*ca.* 1900 to 1800 cm^{-1}) than the postulated bridged species on metals (*ca.* 2000 to 1750 cm^{-1}). Two things can be said about the differences between these systems. In the metal carbonyls the bridged COs are attached to metals which invariably have several (usually three or more) other CO ligands attached to them. These metal atoms may therefore be in a different electronic state from metal atoms which, in metal surfaces, have no (or, at the maximum, one) other CO molecules attached to each metal atom. Related to the different electronic structures, the metal–metal distances in metal carbonyls are also usually 0.1 to 0.3 Å greater than in bulk metals.[53] This difference will lead to a somewhat greater magnitude of the M—C—M angle in the bridged complexes, to a hybridization at the carbon atom closer to that required by a double-bonded C=O group, and hence to lower CO frequencies. Confirmation that COs bridged between metal atoms without additional CO molecules bonded to them do absorb at wavenumbers greater than 1900 cm^{-1} comes from some recent CO/Ni and CO/Cu matrix-isolation studies by Moskovits and Hulse[54,55] designed to obtain infrared bands from CO/metal complexes of formula M_nCO (M = metal, $n = 2, 3 \ldots$). They assign bands in the region of 1960 cm^{-1} to 2-fold bridged CO molecules and in the 1930 cm^{-1} region to 3-fold bridged COs. It would be interesting to extend these studies to encompass larger metal clusters prepared under matrix-isolated conditions.

In the literature on metal carbonyls, relatively few infrared measurements have been made on 3-metal bridged CO in metal clusters of authenticated structure[28,56] and none, to our knowledge, on 4-metal bridged CO. However, excluding the matrix isolation work of Moskovits *et al.* mentioned above, the 3-fold bridged species so far studied by infrared spectroscopy absorb between 1800 and 1650 cm^{-1}, i.e. consistently below 2-fold bridged species in the metal carbonyls. On the metal surfaces it therefore seems reasonable to assume that the 3-fold bridged COs absorb at lower wavenumber than the 2-fold bridged ones, and possibly (but not certainly) that 4-fold bridged ones absorb at lower wavenumbers still. Such assignments have already been made by Dalmon, Primet, Martin and Imelik[36,48] and by Bradshaw and Hoffmann.[18]

In the remainder of this review we shall assume that Eischens' interpretation of the lower frequency bands in terms of bridged species is correct except for the possibility of its extension to multiple metal–atom bridges. It would be too consuming of space to present always the two points of view.

5   A GENERAL STRATEGY FOR THE INTERPRETATION OF ABSORPTION BANDS FROM CO ON METALS

5.1   The Assignment of Absorption Bands to Vibrational Modes of Different Adsorbed Species

For simplicity we have adopted a particular, and relatively straightforward, strategy for interpreting the many infrared spectra from CO adsorbed on metals, based on our discussions in Section 4. We list the assumptions implied in the strategy below; should any of them prove to be invalid, our interpretations will require systematic modification.

We assume that particular types of adsorbed CO species are associated with absorption bands in reasonably well defined spectral regions. These wavenumber regions are only approximate because within them there are variations of wavenumbers of analogous species from metal to metal, e.g. in the range 2130 to 2000 cm^{-1}, attributed below to linearly adsorbed CO species, the group IB metals Cu, Ag and Au give bands at considerably higher mean values than do the group VIII metals. The wavenumber of 1880 cm^{-1}, chosen to separate 2-fold bridged species from 3- or 4-fold bridged ones, is somewhat arbitrary, and may be exceeded for high coverage from the latter types of species on (111) or (100) planes—see later discussion.

It should be carefully noted that there is considerable evidence, considered later, that a given type of crystal plane can accommodate more than one type of adsorbed species of the linear, 2-fold and multi-fold bridged types.

The wavenumber regions chosen follow below.

5.1.1   2200 to ca. 2130 cm^{-1}

Bands in this region are interpreted as arising from CO adsorbed on incompletely reduced salts, or metals that have become oxidized, e.g. from Fe(II) or Cu(II) species as in Fe^{2+} or Cu^{2+}. All other absorption bands in the lower frequency ranges discussed below are assumed to arise from CO adsorbed on metal in the zero oxidation state, e.g. (CuO).

5.1.2   ca. 2130 to ca. 2000 cm^{-1}

(i) Absorption bands in this region are interpreted as arising from linearly bonded CO molecules. However, the number of possible one-atom sites is great and so this is perhaps the region for which it is most difficult to make definitive assignments.

(ii) Separate absorption bands in this region (that often individually rise in frequency with increasing coverage—Section 6) may be identified with CO adsorption on metal atoms in different environments, e.g. on different crystal planes, edges, etc. The expected sequence of frequencies for a pure metal would be (111) plane, C$_9$ sites > (100) plane, C$_8$ sites etc. i.e. in descending order of residual coordination of the metal atoms concerned. The expectation is (Section 4) that the strength of adsorption will be greater the lower is n in C_n and, in agreement with that idea, the almost invariable experimental finding is that on increasing coverage the lowest frequency bands appear first, followed successively by those at higher frequencies.

(iii) Alternative possibilities for assignment of absorptions in the linear-CO region are sites where uncharged metal atoms are adjacent to charged metal atoms, as with incompletely reduced metals, or when metal atoms are in contact with the oxide support.[36]

(iv) It is also possible that higher frequency bands in this region may be associated with multiple adsorption of CO on the same metal atoms, M,[57] although this is considered to be unlikely on well-formed crystal planes (Section 2.2). $M(CO)_2$ and $M(CO)_3$ groups in coordination compounds usually give two very strong infrared bands separated by 50 to 100 cm^{-1}. Such phenomena are rarely observed for CO adsorbed on metals, but it must be noted that if the two-fold or three-fold axes of these groups are perpendicular to the surface, the operation of the metal-surface selection rule for metal particles[58] would only allow the in-phase and higher frequency vibration of higher symmetry to be infrared active.

(v) It should be noted that there is usually a clear-cut intensity minimum, separating bands in this range from those in range in Section 5.1.3.

5.1.3   ca. 2000 cm^{-1} to ca. 1880 cm^{-1}

(i) Absorption bands in this region are interpreted as arising from CO species bridging two metal atoms, i.e. on B_2 sites (Section 2.3).

(ii) The separate absorption bands observed (each of which may increase in frequency with increasing coverage) are interpreted as arising from B_2 sites on different crystal planes, etc. Frequencies are expected to decrease in the order $(111) > (100) > (110)$. Once again the lower frequency bands are normally the first to appear and we assume that these are associated with adsorption on pairs of metal atoms with the lowest numbers of coordinating metal-atom neighbours.

5.1.4   The region 1880 to 1650 cm^{-1}

When the spectra from adsorbed CO are dominated by bands from bridged species, it is the low-frequency bands in this final region that appear first, and hence correspond to the most strongly held CO species. We shall initially assume that they are associated with multi-centre adsorption sites with decreasing frequencies as follows: $B_3(111)$ plane $> B_4(100)$ plane $> B_5(110)$ plane. This sequence is in agreement with theoretical predictions, by Doyen and Ertl[29] and by Blyholder,[30] of the strength of binding at different types of metal sites but it is not necessarily definitive. In principle, the strength of binding to the B_5 site will depend on the strength of bonding to the 5th atom in the second layer (see Sections 6.4 and 10.1.2).

5.2   The Dependence of Spectra on Surface Coverage

In the ensuing discussion of the results obtained with different metals we shall start off by considering results obtained on single-crystal plane surfaces where such data are available. As discussed earlier in Section 3, we may normally expect that when molecules are adsorbed on adjacent sites their frequencies will change, either due to a change in strength of bonding to such adjacent sites, or through vibrational coupling. In either case a different type of dependence of observed frequency versus fractional surface coverage, θ, may be expected, depending on whether adjacent adsorbed molecules repel each other, have no effect on each other so that adsorption is random, or attract each other. Given mobility on the surface, the two extreme cases lead respectively to a maximization of the distances between adsorbed molecules, or the minimization of distances leading to island formation.

For a model of an infinitely extensive single-crystal plane the 'repulsive' model will lead to a rather narrow absorption band (corresponding in position to the frequency of the coupled in-plane vibrations of all the adsorbed molecules—see Section 3) which will change gradually in position with increasing coverage. The 'attraction' extreme will lead to a very rapid change of frequency with coverage from the value for an 'isolated' molecule towards the extreme value corresponding to full coverage with nearest neighbour adsorbed molecules. In this latter case, given limited spectral sensitivity, it will be difficult experimentally to locate the absorption for an isolated molecule; under such conditions it may appear simply that the observed frequency of absorption hardly changes at all with coverage. In the intermediate case of random adsorption, different 'clusters' of adjacent adsorbed molecules will occur, each with its own separate contribution at a different frequency, i.e. for intermediate coverages a broad absorption region will be observed overall, possibly with sub-structure. However, of course, as θ tends to its maximum value, the spectrum in each case approaches the same limiting extreme of a sharp absorption at the highest (or lowest) frequency.

With finely divided metals the same types of spectral behaviour might be observed. However, several limiting absorption bands may occur at high coverage, corresponding to different types of crystal faces. Also, for each type of face, there may be somewhat different extreme frequencies depending on the sizes of the crystal faces. In chemical terms the most meaningful spectra will be obtained at low coverage (molecules adsorbed on isolated sites) or at high coverage (molecules adsorbed on sites with all neighbouring allowed sites occupied).

The superposition of species effects and coverage effects as detailed in Sections 5.1 and 5.2 goes some way towards explaining why the interpretation of vibrational spectra from CO adsorbed on metals, for which literature extends back over more than 20 years, remains controversial and difficult.

6 CO SPECTRA FROM ADSORPTION ON INDIVIDUAL METALS

The metals whose adsorbed-CO vibrational spectra have been most studied are the catalytically important ones, Ni, Pd and Pt, and also Cu. As described earlier in this review, in recent years single-crystal studies involving specified surface planes have also been made for each of these metals, either by reflection-absorption infrared spectroscopy (r.a.-i.r.) or, very recently, by the alternative very sensitive technique of electron energy-loss spectroscopy (EELS).

For finely divided metal catalysts the infrared sensitivity is more than adequate but there is then the disadvantage that it is not clear what surface planes are exposed by the metal particles. It has recently been suggested by Pearce and Sheppard[58] that the 'metal-surface selection rule' remains of importance for normal finely divided metal adsorbents, although it must be relaxed for exceptionally small metal particles—perhaps those of less than 20 Å.

6.1   Nickel

6.1.1   Single-crystal surfaces

EELS spectra have been obtained for CO on Ni(100),[23] and on the crystal plane with specified pre-adsorption of oxygen,[59] by Andersson. Bertolini *et al.*[60] have reported similar experiments with CO adsorbed on Ni(111). Typical spectra in the vCO region are shown in Fig. 3.

On Ni(100) at 173 K with a coverage, θ, of 0.3 the dominant vCO absorption is near 1932 cm^{-1} ($\pm 10 \text{ cm}^{-1}$) and lower wavenumber absorptions occur at 656 cm^{-1} (weak) and 350 cm^{-1} (strong). These bands have been assigned by Andersson respectively to vCO and antisymmetrical and symmetrical vC—M vibrations of a 2-centre bridged-CO species.[23] At the same coverage but the higher temperature of 293 K a new band of considerable intensity appears at 2065 cm^{-1} together with a companion band at 480 cm^{-1}. These are convincingly attributed to vCO and vCM vibrations of a linear MCO species.[23] When the coverage has increased to 0.5 at 293 K the latter two are much the strongest bands and at that coverage the low energy electron diffraction (LEED) pattern shows a $c(2 \times 2)$ surface mesh. At $\theta = 0.61$ at 173 K broader absorptions centred near 2009 cm^{-1} (half-width *ca.* 250 cm^{-1}) and 436 cm^{-1} are interpreted as reflecting an out-of-register adsorbed layer with a variety of sites giving rise to bands with different wavenumbers.[23]

From Ni(100) on which a quarter of a monolayer of oxygen has been pre-adsorbed to give a $p(2 \times 2)$, $\theta = \frac{1}{4}$, surface overlayer, Andersson[59] obtained two vCO bands at 1751 and 1932 cm^{-1} at 175 K which moved to 1778 and 1972 cm^{-1} at higher coverage ($\frac{1}{4}$ coverage giving a $p(2 \times 2)$ mesh from CO). Whereas initially the two bands were of comparable intensity, at $\theta = \frac{1}{4}$ the higher wavenumber band was much the stronger and there occurred a companion low wavenumber band at 370 cm^{-1}. The 1972 cm^{-1} band is assigned to a 2-metal-atom bridged site, the 370 cm^{-1} band to the symmetrical νM—C stretching mode (*cf.* the similar assignments at somewhat lower wavenumbers on the clean Ni surface) and the 1795 cm^{-1} band to adsorption in the 'hollow' between four nickel atoms, i.e. B$_4$ sites.[59]

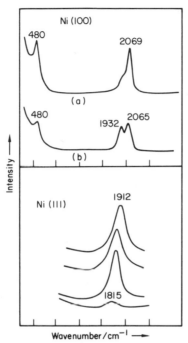

Fig. 3. Electron energy-loss spectra from (a) the Ni(100) c (2×2) CO structure at 293 K, (b) 0.3 L exposure of CO on Ni(100) at 293 K. (After Andersson, Ref. 23.) 1 L (Langmuir) = 10^{-6} Torr s.

Electron energy-loss spectra from CO on Ni(111) with increasing CO exposures from less than 0.05 L to *ca.* 10 L. (After Bertolini, Dalmai-Imelik and Rousseau, Ref. 60). [1 meV $\equiv$ 8.0656 cm^{-1}]

For Ni(100) with a $\frac{1}{2}$ coverage by $c(2 \times 2)$ mesh of oxygen, the CO adsorption is very much weaker but it is otherwise similar to that discussed above except that, at high CO pressures, a νCO band occurs at 2138 cm^{-1}; this band disappears when the CO is removed at low pressures. It seems sensible to assign this band to adsorption on partly oxidized sites, as suggested under the general strategy (Section 5.1).

Finally, Bertolini *et al.*[60] found a single νCO absorption band from CO on Ni(111) at room temperature which varies in wavenumber from 1815 to 1912 cm^{-1} with increasing coverage. Although they do not make a definite assignment to this band, it is most probably associated with CO adsorption onto B$_3$ sites on the (111) surface.

Similar studies on other well-defined surfaces of Ni would doubtless show some different and some similar results. However, the results obtained so far on Ni(100) and Ni(111) provide a range of bands which can be classified very satisfactorily in terms of the general strategy specified earlier. In summary these are: *ca.* 2138 cm^{-1}, linear CO on oxidized sites; *ca.* 2065 cm^{-1} linear CO; *ca.* 1930 cm^{-1}, CO at B$_2$ sites (*ca.* 1970 cm^{-1} on slightly oxidized Ni); 1815 cm^{-1}, CO at B$_3$ sites on (111) planes; and 1750 cm^{-1}, CO at B$_4$ sites on (100) planes. The wavenumbers quoted above are those at which the bands appear at low coverage. In the case of the B$_3$ sites on Ni(111) planes there is a particularly large wavenumber shift on increased coverage from 1815 to 1912 cm^{-1} which causes the band to cross into the general region assigned in Section 5.1 to B$_2$ sites. This large shift implies repulsive interactions between the adsorbed molecules (Section 5.2). For comparison with experimental data from other more finely divided Ni samples, the frequencies discussed above are listed in Table 2 (a).

6.1.2   Evaporated metal films

A number of studies have been made of CO adsorption on evaporated films, usually by infrared transmission methods, as summarized in Part (b) of Table 2. These include several attempts to carry out adsorption in very high vacua[64,68] but not infrequently acceptable transmission or sufficiently strong absorption bands are obtained only when the Ni is evaporated in the presence of gaseous CO[63,65,66,68] or an inert gas.[68]

There are possible complications caused by epitaxial phenomena depending on the infrared-transmitting substrate used. If this leads to preferred surface planes then atypical spectra may be obtained. In the case of a study by Eckstrom and Smith[67] the evaporation procedure in the presence of a gas was carried out deliberately in order to develop what were believed to be (110) faces. Another way in which evaporated films may differ from the oxide-supported metals to be discussed below is that they may give rise to larger crystallites.[63]

In two studies, by Bradshaw and Pritchard[65,66] and Garland et al.,[63] unusually low-wavenumber absorptions have been observed between 1620 and 1590 cm^{-1}. In each case these arise from experiments where the metal is evaporated in the presence of CO gas. A suggested assignment of these to M$_2$C=O . . . M species[63] would be consistent with a certain degree of occlusion of CO within the surfaces of the particles. Alternatively the high temperature of the evaporation filament might lead to such unusual surface species.

To judge by the high frequencies of the bands observed in the reflection study of Ni films by Gardner and Petrucci,[62] their films were somewhat oxidized.

6.1.3   Supported metal particles

The substantial amount of experimental data relating to these types of Ni samples is summarized in Table 2 (c), with some sub-classification according to the support material used.[2,36,41,43,48,49,52,70–81] In this table the wavenumbers of the most prominent bands are underlined.

TABLE 2
Vibrational wavenumbers/cm⁻¹ for carbon monoxide chemisorbed on nickel surfaces

1st author and year	Ref. no.	Substrate or support	νCO (linear)	νCO (bridged)	νCM	Comments
(a) Single crystals						
Andersson, 1977	23	(100) face	≈2010 2065 2069	1932[a] 1932 (1930) 1932	658 359 $\theta = 0.3$ 173 K 480 (360)[b] $\theta = 0.3$ 293 K 480 $\theta = 0.5$ 293 K	
Andersson, 1977	59	(100) face	<i>c</i> 1972	1751 → 1775	low	low $\bigg\}$ $\theta = \frac{1}{4}$ of oxygen preadsorption high low θ
Bertolini *et al.*, 1977	60	(111) face		1912 → 1815		high θ
(b) Evaporated films						
Pickering, 1959	61	glass	2055			
Gardner, 1960	62	glass	2174, 2115 2060			
Garland, 1965	63	CsI or CaF₂	2085 ≈2050 2025	1925 1880 → 1830	1620 1620	60 Å particles low θ $\Big\}$ 200 Å particles high θ
Baker, 1968	64	CaF₂	2058 2050	1920 1890 1880	1620	low θ
Bradley, 1969	87	KBr				
Bradshaw, 1969	65	NaCl	2085 2020 2020	1860 1850	1570	high θ
Eckstrom, 1970	67	(110) on Al	2056	1920	1570	easily pumped off

TABLE 2—*continued*

1st author and year	Ref. no.	Substrate or support	νCO (linear)	νCO (bridged)	νCM	Comments
Hayward, 1971	68	—	2075	1950		
			2060	1915		evap. in Ar
			2058 2034	1915		evap. in CO
Queau, 1972	51a	NaCl		1890		
McCoy, 1973	69	glass	2010	1975		
			2060	1900		

(c) Supported metal particles

1st author and year	Ref. no.	Substrate or support	νCO (linear)	νCO (bridged)	νCM	Comments
Eischens, 1954	2	SiO₂	(2192) 2033	1908		
Eischens, 1956	41	SiO₂	2040 2020	1912 1850		low θ
			2079 2058	1870		high θ
Eischens, 1956	46	SiO₂	2030	1920 ≈ 1870		low θ
O'Neill, 1961	71	SiO₂	2020	1912 1880		high θ
Cho, 1964	72	SiO₂	2075 (2050)	1920 1960		
Hobert, 1966	49	SiO₂	2075 2050	1930 1950	1830	
Hobert, 1968	73	SiO₂	2045	1950	1820	
Ferreira, 1970	75	SiO₂ 2180 2115	2075 2058	1950	1830	
van Hardeveld, 1972	43	SiO₂	2075 2050	1950	1820	214 Å particles
			2080 2057 (2030)	1940		70 Å
			2080 2057 (2030)	1930 1860	1830	70 Å
			2080 2057 (2030)	1950		21 Å
			2082 2055 2035	1917	1810	20 Å
Marx, 1972	77	SiO₂	2080 2040	1930 1880	1820	500 K reduction
			2040	1960 1880		900 K reduction
Dalmon, 1975	48	SiO₂	2090 2065	1990	1840	
			2058	1945		

1st author and year	Ref. no.	Substrate or support	νCO (linear)	νCO (bridged)	νCM	Comments
Soma-Noto, 1974	47	SiO_2	(2060) 2035	1960		H_2 free
Primet, 1976	79	SiO_2	2040 → 2070 2080	1940		H_2 covered surface / room temperature / after heating to 533 K
Heal, 1977	80	SiO_2	2055 2030	1930 1930	1800 1800	surface deposited with 'C'
Van Dijk, 1976	73b	SiO_2	2055 2195	1930		unreduced,
Primet, 1977	36	SiO_2	2195 2077 2045	1925		5% reduced; 30 Å particle
			2077 2045	≈1830 1940		100% reduced; 25 Å
			2075 2040	1820 1935		100% reduced; 63 Å
			2075 2045	1820 1940		100% reduced; 95 Å
Martin, 1977	81	SiO_2	(2060) 2035	1940 1820 1915		room temperature
			2025	1935 1820		after heating to 380 K
			2005	1920 1820		after heating to 480 K
O'Neill, 1961	7_	Al_2O_3	2040 → 2070	1945 (1900)		low θ
				←1958		high θ
Garland, 1959	70a	Al_2O_3	(2045) 2075	≈1910 1960		1.5% Ni
Yates, 1961	70b	Al_2O_3	2080 2045	≈1910 1970		10% Ni
			2080 2045	≈1910 1960		25% Ni
O'Neill, 1961	71	TiO_2	2090 ≈2030	≈ 1940		low θ
			2080	1925		high θ
Blyholder, 1969	74	paraffin	2080 2075	≈1925 1935	≈1810	
1971	76	argon matrix	2080 2075	1925	≈1810	
1972	52	paraffin	2060	1920		

[a] Underlining denotes relatively strong absorptions.

[b] Figures in brackets are for ill-defined peaks.

[c] Arrows show band positions changing with surface coverages θ.

A particularly detailed study of CO adsorbed on Ni/SiO_2 preparations has recently been made by Primet et al.[36] They explored spectra as a function of metal-particle size, the degree of reduction, and the fractional surface coverage. They showed that the complete reduction of the hexamminenickel(II) nitrate to metallic nickel requires a temperature of reduction in hydrogen of about 600 °C. When reduction was complete they showed that the peak intensities of the linear-CO bands in the 2080 to 2040 cm^{-1} region were about equal to, or slightly less than, those of the strongest bridge-CO band between 1940 and 1930 cm^{-1}. However, in terms of integrated intensities, the overall absorption in the bridge-CO region was markedly greater. These results were for 'irreversibly adsorbed' CO, i.e. when the gas-phase CO had been evacuated after the initial adsorption.

The relative intensities of the two high-wavenumber sub-bands in the ranges 2080 to 2070 and 2050 to 2040 cm^{-1} varied from preparation to preparation, the former band being somewhat more intense at low reduction temperatures, or with higher CO pressures. Typical spectra obtained by these authors are illustrated in Fig. 4. In all the spectra there is additional absorption, as a tail to the main ca. 1940 cm^{-1} band, near 1800 cm^{-1} and, in some cases, a distinct shoulder is observed near 1810 cm^{-1}. The authors suggest that the latter band may represent multi-centre adsorption of CO, e.g. in the centre of triangles of 3 metal atoms on (111) planes. This suggestion fits in well with the bands observed on (111) crystal planes of Ni as discussed above. In the spectrum of a sample that had been reduced at 900 °C, and had the largest metal particles, a second band in the 2000 to 1850 cm^{-1} region occurred at 1920 cm^{-1} and probably corresponds to the 'high-coverage' situation found for Ni(111). The large change in wavenumber of the Ni(111) CO-absorption with coverage may also be dependent on the size of the crystal faces and these are likely to be larger for the metal particles reduced at high temperature.

Primet et al.[36] have discussed at some length the origins of the bands in the 2080 to 2070 and 2050 to 2040 cm^{-1} ranges. Their assignment of the lower wavenumber bands to CO adsorbed on 'unperturbed' Ni atoms is very probably correct, although linear-CO bands in precisely this range have not yet been observed in studies of single crystal planes. The bands near 2065 cm^{-1} observed from CO on (100) planes probably contributes to the strong region of overlap of the two bands mentioned, and some other authors do find maxima in the region 2055 to 2060 cm^{-1} (see Table 2 (c)).

The band at ca. 2080 cm^{-1} is particularly prominent in spectra from incompletely reduced metal samples and from those with small metal particles. Yates and Garland[70] have previously assigned bands in that region to 'dispersed', i.e. non-crystalline, Ni. This would be consistent with the views of Primet et al., although whether the dispersal is in the form of isolation of Ni sites in unreduced metal, or at the metal/oxide interface,[36] or whether the high frequency is caused by $M(CO)_2$ groups which form at isolated sites at high coverage, remains uncertain.[36,43,46,71] We favour the former type of assignment rather than the latter and note that deliberate contamination of Ni surfaces by H_2S[77] leads to dominant bands in the 2090 cm^{-1} region. Van Hardeveld and Hartog[43] also studied CO spectra on nickel samples with different particle sizes, although with a less consistent pattern of results than those obtained by Primet et al. They interpreted their results on the 'all-linear' Blyholder model. They, as have others,[65,80] noted spectral complications near 2065 cm^{-1} due to Ni(CO)$_4$ formation and this led them to assign the highest wavenumber band to Ni(CO)$_n$ species.

Primet et al.[36] identified, convincingly, weak but sharp bands at 2195 cm^{-1} from poorly reduced samples as resulting from adsorption of CO on Ni^{2+} ions. Many other workers, starting with Eischens et al.,[2] have studied the infrared

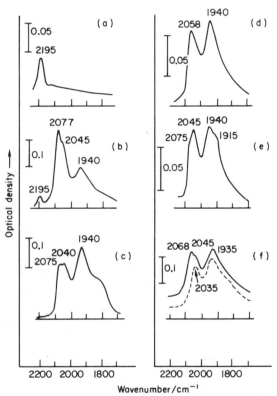

Fig. 4. Infrared spectra from CO irreversibly adsorbed at 25 °C on various Ni/SiO$_2$ samples that were prepared from hexammine nickel(II) nitrate on SiO$_2$ by heating in a stream of H$_2$ (2 dm³ h^{-1}) for 15 h at specified temperatures. (a) Heated at 200 °C, metal particle size 30 Å, zero effective reduction; (b) heated at 350 °C, particle size 35 Å, 0.05 degree of reduction; (c) and (d) heated in H$_2$ at 650 °C, particle size 63 Å, fully reduced; (e) heated in H$_2$ at 900 °C, particle size 90 Å, fully reduced. In spectrum (f) the same sample is used as in (c) and (d) but the adsorption temperature was −196 °C, with the spectrum recorded between −100 and −50 °C (full line) and at room temperature (broken line). (After Primet, Dalmon and Martin, Ref. 36.)

spectra from CO chemisorbed on Ni. Some other spectra are also illustrated in Fig. 4. The various bands observed have been sub-classified into characteristic wavenumber regions in Table 2. Although these regions are somewhat arbitrary, the number of regions chosen is usually determined by the fact that individual samples have shown bands simultaneously in two or more of these in each of the 'linear' and 'bridged' regions. The main uncertainty in this respect relates to the region 1900 to 1800 cm^{-1} where often, but not always, the bands observed are shoulders on a sloping background decreasing from a maximum above 1900 cm^{-1}. The bands observed seem often to cluster around 1880 or 1820 cm^{-1} and these might represent different sites. On the other hand Table 2 (c) shows little evidence of such absorption maxima being observed simultaneously on the same sample, and this is the very region where studies of CO on Ni(111) show a single band shifting between 1810 and 1910 cm^{-1} with increasing coverage.[60] Similar shifts to high wavenumbers might occur with increasing sizes of crystallite faces. We are therefore uncertain whether absorption in the 1900 to 1800 cm^{-1} range represents CO at a single site or two different sites.

We suggest assignments for the various bands in Table 3. In many respects our classification is a development of that proposed much earlier by Yates and Garland,[70] except that we tend to designate their 'semicrystalline' sites as sites on crystal planes where adsorption would be expected to be weaker. The wavenumber ranges in Table 3 are typical for silica-supported Ni; somewhat higher values in the 1950 to 2000 cm^{-1} region seem to be observed consistently for CO on Ni supported on alumina[70,71] or titania.[71] The assignments of sites in terms of particular crystal planes are made by analogy with the results so far obtained on metal single crystals but, because the latter studies have been entirely confined to Ni(100) and (111) planes at this stage, these assignments may be expected to be made more precise subsequently. We are proposing a tentative pattern against which subsequent experimental work can be evaluated.

An unusual spectrum with an exceptionally strong linear-CO band at 2080 cm^{-1} was observed by Marx et al.[77] from an Ni/SiO$_2$ sample that had been reduced from Ni(NO$_3$)$_2$ at the exceptionally high temperature of 900 °C; on the other hand, a similar high-temperature reduction of the nickel ammine did not give an abnormal spectrum.[36] It is possible that the abnormal spectrum from Marx et al. results from a reaction of Ni with the oxide support at that highest temperature. We also note that Primet and Sheppard[79] found that the stronger linear-CO band moved from 2040 to 2070 cm^{-1} in the presence of co-adsorbed hydrogen. However, this probably represents an H$_2$-induced change in wavenumber on a particular type of site rather than a change of site.

Raising the temperature of an Ni/CO sample in the presence of gaseous CO[80,81] leads to higher frequency bands being replaced by lower frequency ones but, because of surface-contamination effects resulting from disproportionation of CO into CO$_2$ and C,[81] we shall not discuss these results in detail. However, in one case Garland et al.[63] observed a similar result in the bridging-CO region for an evaporated Ni film on continued pumping at ambient tempera-

TABLE 3
A suggested interpretation of absorption bands from CO chemisorbed on Ni

Wavenumber range	Comments	Possible sites
Linear species		
$2090-2070$ cm^{-1}	Weakly held; sometimes associated with small particles or partially reduced Ni	Isolated Ni atoms or non-crystalline Ni, e.g. next to oxygen atoms or oxide support
$2065-2050$ cm^{-1}	Moderately strongly held[a]	Ni(100)[23]
$2045-2025$ cm^{-1}	Strongly held; occurs at lowest coverage	Lower coordination sites, (110), etc.
Bridged species		
$1975-1950$ cm^{-1} ⎫		B$_2$ on slightly oxidized Ni(100)[59]
$1950-1930$ cm^{-1} ⎪	Often blend together; all are strongly held and give strong absorptions	B$_2$ on Ni(100)[23] at lower coverage; uncertain for high coverage
$1925-1910$ cm^{-1} ⎭		B$_2$ on lower coordination sites or B$_3$ on Ni(111) for large crystals[b]
$1890-1860$ cm^{-1} ⎫	Strongly held; sometimes interconvert; lowest wavenumbers at lowest coverages	B$_3$ on Ni(111) as a function of coverage and crystallite size[60]
$1840-1810$ cm^{-1} ⎭		
$1775-1750$ cm^{-1}		B$_4$ as observed on oxidized Ni(100)[59]
Other bands		
$\approx 1620-1590$ cm^{-1}	Rarely observed[63,65,73]	Possibly Ni$_2$CO . . . Ni, i.e. 'horizontal species'[63]

[a] In the presence of substantial CO, gaseous Ni(CO)$_4$ may absorb here.

[b] On large crystal planes at high coverage the B$_3$, Ni(111), site can give an absorption maximum as high as 1915 cm^{-1}.[60]

ture. The effect was more marked with increasing particle size and can probably be related to the shift of the B$_3$ frequency with coverage on the Ni(111) plane.[60]

6.2 Palladium

6.2.1 Single-crystal surfaces

A very significant piece of work has recently been carried out by reflection-absorption infrared spectroscopy on CO adsorbed on Pd(100), (111) and (210) planes, by Bradshaw and Hoffmann.[18] This follows earlier work by the same authors on polycrystalline films to be discussed below.[87,93]

On Ni(100), discussed in Section 6.1, CO absorption bands appeared near 1932 and 2065 cm^{-1}; they shifted little with coverage but the latter became dominant at the expense of the former at higher coverages. CO on Pd(100) at 300 K exhibits a very different behaviour in that a band at 1895 cm^{-1} at low coverages shifts gradually to 1930 cm^{-1} at a coverage of about 0.4 and then more rapidly (in coverage terms) to an upper limit of 1983 cm^{-1} at $\theta = 0.61$.

The wavenumber changes with coverage denote intermolecular interactions which increase with coverage, and the higher rate of change of wavenumber coincides with the 'compressed-CO' region where the adsorbed CO molecules are being forced together.[18] In the region below compression, $\theta \approx 0.5$, the LEED data also provide a very strong indication that the species concerned is the 2-fold bridged one, B_2. This, therefore, gives rise to a band at 1893 cm^{-1} for isolated bridge-CO species which shifts to 1930 cm^{-1} for a complete layer. A weak band at 2096 cm^{-1} occurred for rapid high-coverage adsorption at 300 K, but annealing of the sample led to its disappearance.

For CO on Pd(111) a similar behaviour was observed, with an absorption starting at 1820 cm^{-1} at low coverage, increasing smoothly to 1840 cm^{-1} at $\theta \approx 0.3$ and then more rapidly through a region of broad, ill-defined absorption, to a well-defined band at 1936 cm^{-1} for $\theta = 0.5$. Higher coverages led to a final shift to 1946 cm^{-1} and the appearance of an additional linear-CO band (under equilibrium conditions) at 2092 cm^{-1}. This sequence of spectra was convincingly interpreted in terms of adsorption on B_3 sites (1820 to 1840 cm^{-1}); a transition then occurs to bridge B_2 species (1890 to 1946 cm^{-1}) through a transition region where both B_2 and B_3 sites are present. The linear-CO species absorbing at 2092 cm^{-1} is presumed to be from CO adsorbed on isolated metal-atom sites left over from the other 2-dimensional meshes. The general results on Ni(111) mentioned earlier are similar to the first phase of CO on Pd(111), i.e. starting near 1812 cm^{-1} and moving up towards 1920 cm^{-1}, at least before the transition to a B_2 species occurs. As remarked by Bradshaw and Hoffmann,[18] on Pd one has the case where the spectrum observed depends very much, *both* on the type of the adsorbed species, *and* on the coverage. The spectral data are summarized in Table 4(a).

Pd(210) has an open structure in the top layer with interatomic metal distances of 3.88 Å, compared with 2.73 Å for interatomic metal contact. The observed infrared spectra bear a surprisingly close relation to those observed on Pd(100), with wavenumbers increasing from 1878 to 1996 cm^{-1} and a greater rate of change with coverage above 1945 cm^{-1}. This seems best reconciled with B_2 *bridge-bonding between atoms in the first and second layers* of the open surface structure.

In summary, Bradshaw and Hoffmann[18] give the following assignments for Pd

B_3 sites 1820 to 1840+ cm^{-1} on (111) planes

B_2 sites $\begin{cases} 1890 \text{ to } 1930 \text{ cm}^{-1} \text{ on (100) planes} \\ 1890 \text{ to } 1946 \text{ cm}^{-1} \text{ on (111) planes} \\ 1898 \text{ to } 1945 \text{ cm}^{-1} \text{ on (210) planes} \end{cases}$

Compressed sites $\begin{cases} 1950 \text{ to } 1983 \text{ cm}^{-1} \text{ on (100) planes} \\ 1950 \text{ to } 1995 \text{ cm}^{-1} \text{ on (210) planes} \end{cases}$

Whereas it seems reasonable to suppose that, as for the case of CO on

Pt,[37,84] dipolar coupling plays a substantial role in causing the coverage-dependent frequency shifts for a given type of adsorbed species, other interactions of the through-metal type or in the form of direct repulsive forces may play a role (see Section 3). Bradshaw and Hoffmann are probably correct to assume that direct repulsion, leading indirectly to weakened chemisorption, plays an important role in the large wavenumber shifts with coverage in the 'compressed' layers.

Some of Bradshaw and Hoffmann's spectra are illustrated in Fig. 5.

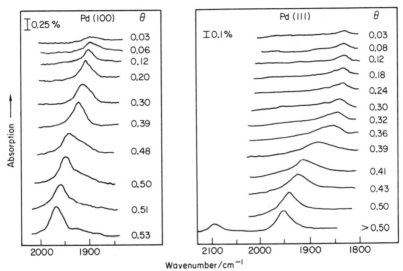

Fig. 5. Infrared reflection-absorption spectra from CO on Pd(100) and on Pd(111) planes at 300 K as a function of coverages, θ. (After Hoffmann and Bradshaw, Ref. 18.)

6.2.2 Evaporated metal films

Spectra from the literature[51a,57,68,82,83,85–88] are summarized in Table 4(b). It is seen that the strongest feature is normally a broad band centred between 1890 and 1920 cm^{-1} due to bridged CO, with much weaker bands between 2100 and 2000 cm^{-1} due to linear CO. Exceptions to the above generalizations are the spectrum obtained by Rice and Haller,[88] which has its bridge-CO band-maximum at 1940 cm^{-1}, and the spectra by Hayward and McManus[68] which give maxima (of unspecified intensity) at 1980 cm^{-1}. The latter relates to Bradshaw and Hoffmann's[82,83] reflection/absorption studies on polycrystalline Pd deposited on a glass substrate. These show a single absorption band which moves from 1925 to 1985 cm^{-1} with increasing coverage. The latter behaviour is somewhat similar to that observed by the same authors for adsorption on Pd(100) or (210) planes,[18] and discussed in Section 6.2.1.

Rice and Haller's work, using polarized infrared radiation with attenuated

TABLE 4
Vibrational wavenumbers/cm^{-1} for CO chemisorbed on Pd

1st author and year	Ref. no.	Substrate or support	νCO (linear)	νCO (bridged)	Comments
(a) Single crystals					
Bradshaw, 1977	18	(100) face		1885[a]	θ low
				→b 1930	$\theta = 0.4$
				1983	$\theta = 0.61$
	18	(111) face	2092	1820	θ low
				1865[c]	$\theta = 0.3$
				1946	$\theta \approx 0.6$
	18	(210) face		1878	θ low
				1940	$\theta \approx 0.35$
				1985	$\theta \approx 0.45$
(b) Evaporated metal films					
Garland, 1965	57	CaF$_2$	2085	1910 1910 / 1840 1840	
Nash, 1965	85	NaCl		1970	
Harrod, 1967	86	NaCl	<1980	1890 ——	exploding wire in CO
Bradley, 1969	87	KBr		1900 ——	exploding wire in CO
Hayward, 1971	68		1980	1920	*in vacuo*
			1980	1902 ——	evaporated in CO
Queau, 1972	51a	NaCl	2090 2010		

1st author and year	Ref. no.	Substrate or support	νCO (linear)	νCO (bridged)	Comments
Rice, 1974	88	KBr	2050	1930 1890 1830	a.t.r.—polarization measurements
Bradshaw, 1975	82	glass		1920	low θ at 420 K (Somewhat different results at 230 K) ; high θ
Hoffmann, 1976	83	glass		1987	
(c) Particularly finely-divided metal particles					
Clarke, 1967	89	SiO₂	2080	1980	
van Hardeveld, 1972	43	SiO₂	2088		
Naccache, 1973	90	zeolites	2100	1940 1920 1920	<15 Å diameter particles
Figueras, 1973	91	Al₂O₃	2075	1970 1935 1895	
(d) Supported metal particles					
Eischens, 1954	2	SiO₂	2053	1916 1825 1786	
Eischens, 1956	41	SiO₂		1876 1843	
Eischens, 1956	46	SiO₂		1930 1912 1885 1835	
Kavtaradze, 1961	92	SiO₂	2085	1990	
Kavtaradze, 1965	94	SiO₂ ?	2050	1910	
Clarke, 1967	89	SiO₂	2080	1985 1940 1920 1885 1865	larger particles, low θ
Baddour, 1970	96	SiO₂	2060 2035	1985 1970 1920	high θ } before 'break-in'
			2085	1985 1965 1920 1885	low θ
	96	SiO₂	(2065)	1965 1890	low θ } after 'break-in'
			2090	1985 1920 1890	high θ
van Hardeveld, 1972	43	SiO₂	2086 2060	1982 1950 1920 1830	medium particles (≈105 Å), low θ
Soma-Noto, 1974	44	SiO₂	2090	1990 1930 1875 1815	high θ

TABLE 4—continued

1st author and year	Ref. no.	Substrate or support	νCO (linear)	νCO (bridged)	Comments
Palazov, 1975	97	SiO$_2$	2070	1970 — 1900 — 1830	low θ
			2095	1980 — 1900	high θ oxidized
			2135 2103		
Kember, 1975	98	SiO$_2$	2065 2085	1930 1890	low θ
				1980 — 1930 — 1840	high θ
Sokolova, 1974	101	Al$_2$O$_3$	2050	1880	
van Hardeveld, 1972	43	Al$_2$O$_3$	2094	1982 1942	45 Å particles

[a] Underlining denotes relatively strong absorptions.
[b] Arrows show absorptions changing with coverages.
[c] Figures between horizontal lines are maxima of very broad absorptions.

total reflection techniques,[88] suggests that the lower-frequency bridged-CO absorptions, in particular, may arise from CO groups which are not completely perpendicular to the metal surface.

6.2.3 Particularly finely divided metal particles

The spectra of samples that are measured to be, or are inferred from their method of preparation to be, very finely divided are summarized in Table 4(c).[43,89-91] The evidence for the degree of subdivision is sometimes direct, as in the spectrum obtained by van Hardeveld and Hartog[43] where the metal particles were measured to be less than 15 Å in diameter on average, or sometimes indirect, as in the spectrum obtained by Clarke et al.,[89] where the metal coverage was obtained by multiple impregnations with small amounts of metal. In the studies by Naccache et al.[90] and Figueras et al.[91] on zeolites, the metal is thought to be 'atomically dispersed' on zeolite surfaces. All these spectra have one feature in common, namely abnormally strong linear-CO bands in the highest wavenumber range between 2070 and 2110 cm^{-1} relative to the bridged-CO bands between 2000 and 1800 cm^{-1}. Small metal particles, down to individual atoms, should have the common property that they exhibit fewer pairs of surface atoms for bridged-CO-bonding. This seems to be the probable cause of the relative abundance of linearly-adsorbed CO on these samples, and is analogous to the case of Pd/Ag alloys that are dilute in Pd.[44] For very small metal particles the underlying support can have a substantial electronic influence.[91] These high frequency linear-CO bands seem to be analogous to those observed with Ni and attributed by Primet et al.[36] to isolated metal atoms on incompletely reduced metal, or to metal atoms in contact with the oxide support as discussed in Section 6.1.3.

6.2.4 Supported metal particles

Data from the literature[2,40,41,43,44,46,89,92-99] are summarized in Table 4(d) and typical spectra are illustrated in Fig. 6.

Eischens and his colleagues[2,41] were the first to show that CO on palladium has an infrared spectrum which implies a dominance of bridge-bonded CO molecules on polycrystalline metal surfaces. In a detailed discussion of the CO/Pd system, Eischens, Francis and Pliskin[41] pointed out that the broad region of absorption (between about 1950 and 1700 cm^{-1} in their spectra) associated with bridged species seem to be subdivided into a series of components which exhibited sub-maxima. They observed that a low wavenumber component with a maximum near 1835 cm^{-1} appeared first (it also had a low wavenumber tail extending down towards 1700 cm^{-1}), followed in sequence by others with, at high coverage, maxima near 1895, 1910, and 1930 cm^{-1}, and with a substantial shoulder (illustrated but not mentioned by them) near 1950 cm^{-1}. There was also a tendency for each sub-maximum to move to higher wavenumber as it grew in intensity with increasing surface coverage. In fact these frequency shifts make it difficult to identify unambiguously the corresponding features in con-

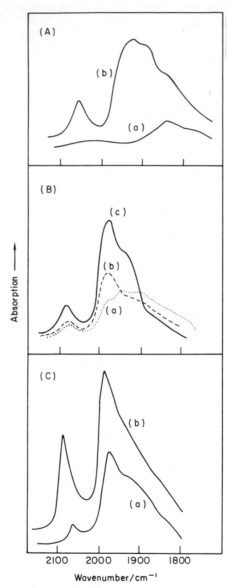

Fig. 6. Infrared spectra from CO chemisorbed on silica-supported Pd. (A) At (a) low and (b) high coverages. (After Eischens, Francis and Pliskin, Ref. 41.) (B) At a high coverage (a) prior to break-in, (b) partial break-in, (c) complete break-in. (After Baddour, Modell and Goldsmith, Ref. 96.) (C) At (a) low and (b) high coverages. (After Palazov, Chang and Kokes, Ref. 97.)

secutive spectra so that there is some doubt about the number of separate sub-maxima. But to judge from the spectrum at high coverage there must be at least four sub-bands, by then located near $1950 \, cm^{-1}$ (shoulder), 1930, 1895, and $1840 \, cm^{-1}$. Furthermore, with the exception of the final shoulder near $1950 \, cm^{-1}$, each successive sub-band finally exceeded the previous one in peak intensity. Eischens and his colleagues reported,[41] but did not illustrate, spectra in which the removal of sub-bands by evacuation occurred in the reverse sequence to their appearance. They interpreted the largely independent sub-bands as arising from different areas of the surface, each one essentially homogeneous, and each exhibiting a different strength of bridge-bonding of CO. Because the sub-bands appeared successively from low frequencies to high, it is clear that those of lowest frequencies represent the most strongly adsorbed molecules. They expressed the view that: 'it is possible to identify them [the homogeneous areas of surface] with the major crystal planes'. They also pointed out that the successive coverage of sections of the metal surface with molecules with increasing strengths of adsorption, could be one cause of the commonly found decreasing heat of adsorption with increasing coverage.

More recently Palazov et al.[97] obtained a set of spectra whose behaviour with increasing coverage differed very markedly from that observed by Eischens et al.[41] In the latter case each additional adsorption led to increased spectral absorption that overlay bands already present. But Palazov and his colleagues[97] found that, for the bridge-CO region, as the high frequency bands increased, their lower frequency bands *decreased* in intensity leading to the suggestion that low frequency species were perhaps being converted to high frequency ones with increasing adsorption. Furthermore, the extreme bridge-CO band at $1980 \, cm^{-1}$[97] was considerably higher in wavenumber than the $1950 \, cm^{-1}$ absorption observed by Eischens et al.[41]

A connection between the two sets of results discussed above is provided by the work of Baddour et al.[96] They described how the profile of the absorption bands from CO on Pd varied with pretreatment of the metal sample with mixtures of CO and O_2 at different temperatures, followed by re-reduction with hydrogen. They found systematic changes of infrared spectra from CO with the above treatment. Before the CO/O_2 treatment the spectra had similar profiles and behaved very much like those reported by Eischens[41] with respect to increasing coverage of CO. After the treatment the overall profile (including the frequency of the strongest bridge-CO absorption band) and the behaviour with coverage showed most of the characteristics which were later reported by Palazov et al.[97] They attributed the changes to catalyst 'break-in' with the CO/O_2 reaction which they suggested consisted of 'a redistribution of exposed crystallographic planes resulting from the surface diffusion of palladium atoms or palladium-oxygen complexes'. They considered that little change in total metal area accompanied 'break-in' and postulated that similar phenomena might be initiated by controlled heating of such catalysts in the absence of oxygen. In fact Palazov et al.[97] obtained their catalyst without any oxygen treatment and similar CO spectra after hydrogen reduction alone have also been obtained in this laboratory by Kember.[98]

The Palazov-type results can be understood without difficulty by comparison with Bradshaw and Hoffmann's results[18] on Pd(100) and (111) planes discussed in Section 6.2.1. These provide for bands associated with the same crystal plane moving with increasing coverage from 1890 to 1983 cm^{-1} on (100) planes and from 1820 to 1946 cm^{-1} on (111) planes. Thus both the upper limiting bridged-CO band and the removal of low wavenumber bands to make way for higher wavenumber ones in the Palazov spectra are readily accounted for. It is more difficult to account for the earlier Eischens results,[41] corresponding to a catalyst that has not been broken in, on the basis of the single crystal results.

Baddour et al.[96] compared spectra as a function of degree of break-in with the same pressure of gaseous CO. They showed that, prior to 'break-in', the CO spectra showed much more absorption at low wavenumbers, between 1940 and 1800 cm^{-1}, and much less absorption between 1950 and 1990 cm^{-1} as shown in Fig. 7. This was true even for samples which at a relatively high CO pressure, and hence high coverage, gave 'broken-in' spectra as expected for high coverage results on a mixture of (100) and (111) planes. As a given crystal plane of appreciable size must reach saturation under these conditions, one possible explanation of the results is that there is a much smaller proportion of the low-index planes prior to break-in, and a much higher proportion of adsorption on other sites of high adsorption strength, e.g. on (110) planes or similar sites on defect-rich poorly crystalline regions of the surfaces.

On the basis of this picture, 'break-in' consists of the formation of crystallites with well-defined faces from more amorphous metal conglomerates of similar overall size. This picture probably contains a great deal of truth. However, as there are very large frequency shifts with coverage on the large single-crystal faces, and as the interactions between adsorbed molecules probably involves appreciable interaction with other adsorbed molecules 2 or 3 sites removed, then it is probably also true that the saturation frequencies of individual types of crystal planes also varies with, and increases with, the mean face diameter.

Based on the single crystal results, we feel confident in assigning the two strongest bridge-CO bands near 1985 and 1955 cm^{-1} to (100) and (111) planes, respectively; the residual 'tail' to lower wavenumbers between, say, 1930 and 1850 cm^{-1}, then represents either a proportion of (110) or similar planes and/or a proportion of (100) or (111) planes of small diameter. In our view this is the best example so far where the infrared spectrum from adsorbed CO can be convincingly interpreted in terms of the nature of the surfaces of the metal crystallites.

The spectrum itself gives the impression that (100) planes are most numerous even although the intensities of the two main bands are badly overlapped. There is, of course, no guarantee that the intensity per adsorbed CO molecule is identical on the (100) and (111) faces. However the retention of similar overall spectral areas in the 'broken-in' and non-'broken-in' samples does suggest qualitatively that the intensities associated with bridge-CO sites do not vary greatly with the frequencies of the associated absorption bands.

The linear absorption bands are much weaker on Pd compared with Ni. For high coverage on the 'broken-in' samples we interpret the high wavenumber absorptions near 2090 cm^{-1}, which are readily removed by evacuation, as linear

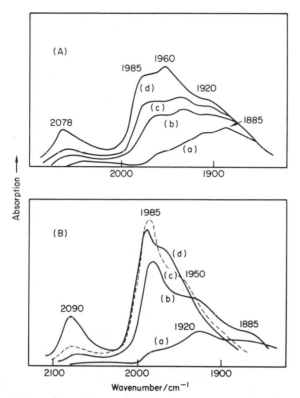

Fig. 7. Infrared spectra from CO chemisorbed on Pd/SiO$_2$ samples. (A) Before break-in. CO partial pressure/Torr (a) 0.005; (b) 0.146; (c) 0.67; (d) 30. (B) After break-in. CO partial pressure/Torr: (a) 0.008; (b) 0.109; (c) 0.30; (d) 110. (After Baddour, Modell and Goldsmith, Ref. 96.)

'fill-in' sites on (111) planes. The other, more strongly retained absorptions in the 2060 cm^{-1} region we tentatively assign to linear-CO adsorption on other sites, (110) planes, etc. Because of the great shifts of band frequencies with coverage, and probably with size of faces, the detailed interpretation of the spectra from unbroken-in samples is more hazardous than in the case of Ni. However, we consider that on these samples individual absorption frequencies can be interpreted on the same lines as indicated in Section 5 under 'general strategy' *at coverages when individual absorptions appear for the first time.* With this reservation we find that we can qualitatively support Eischens'[41] original views.

Palazov et al.[97] also made some interesting observations on how the spectra from CO on Pd vary with heating the catalyst in the presence of gaseous CO. These results are very similar to temperature-dependent results on Ni[81] and, because they are subject to the same potential hazard of associated surface contamination from C, we shall not discuss them further here. They do, however, merit further investigation. The temperature-dependent measurements did appear to reveal a correlation between the ca. 2060 cm^{-1} linear-CO and the 1990 cm^{-1} bridge-CO absorption bands in the sense that both decreased together with increasing temperature.[97] However measurements by Kember[98] indicate that this, while sometimes true, is not always the case. It seems more likely that these simply represent two species of similar temperature sensitivity. Other temperature- and coverage-dependent spectra on Pd have been measured by Kavtaradze and Sokolova,[94] and Sokolova[100,101] has made temperature-dependent measurements relating to CO on Ir/Pd and Pd/Ag alloys.

6.3 Platinum

6.3.1 Single-crystal surfaces etc.

Our starting point here is two recent papers concerned with CO adsorption on Pt(111), one by Ibach and his colleagues using EELS,[22] and one by Horn and Pritchard using r.a.-i.r.[19] They are supported by two papers by King and his colleagues in which the r.a.-i.r. method was applied to CO adsorbed on a polycrystalline Pt ribbon with predominantly (111) facets,[84,102] and one by Hoffmann and Bradshaw[83] on a thick, evaporated film of Pt. Typical spectra are shown in Fig. 8.

The r.a.-i.r. results are all rather similar, but the greatest details are given by Horn and Pritchard.[19] At 295 K and low coverages absorption is first observed as a band at 2065 cm^{-1} with a half-width of ca. 20 cm^{-1}. This band is attributable to isolated, adsorbed CO molecules. As the coverage increases, the absorption peak moves, with a new band emerging at 2082 cm^{-1} and then shifting to 2089 cm^{-1} with a final half-width of ca. 15 cm^{-1}. The results at 80 K are similar, except that less of the low wavenumber band is seen and the 2082 cm^{-1} band initially grows with very little change of wavenumber, suggesting 'island' or domain formation. It is probable that the attractive forces are sufficiently weak that there is appreciable domain disorder and more isolated molecules at 295 K. The results on the (111) ribbon[84,102] differ mainly in that the final high absorption band occurs at 2101 cm^{-1}. In all cases the last increases in surface coverage led to a shift of this band to higher wavenumber with little enhancement of intensity.

The EELS results[22] obtained at 320 K were very similar in the 2050 to 2100 cm^{-1} region and gave a band shifting from 2075 cm^{-1} to about 2100 cm^{-1} at saturation (surface coverage of 0.25), together with a companion vM—C bond-stretching band at 468 cm^{-1}. However, starting at a surface coverage of about 0.13, a second vCO band was observed at 1870 cm^{-1} with a half-width of

ca. 65 cm^{-1}. This grew to an intensity of about half that at 2100 cm^{-1} and had
a companion νM—C band at about 363 cm^{-1}. The low frequency νCO band was
not observed in any of the r.a.-i.r. studies, although Shigeishi and King[102]
searched the appropriate region; however, its lower intensity and greater width
militates against its successful observation in a region of strong water-vapour
absorption in the infrared spectra. The poorer resolution of the EELS experiments makes the two bands of *apparently* similar width.

Ibach *et al.*[22] relate the *ca.* 2090 cm^{-1} band to a linear MCO species corresponding to a ($\sqrt{3} \times \sqrt{3}$) 30° surface mesh and the final spectrum to a $c(4 \times 2)$
mesh (coverage $= \frac{1}{4}$) with equal numbers of linear and 2-fold B$_2$ bridged species.
Horn and Pritchard consider this model, and an alternative one where the *ca.*
2090 cm^{-1} band corresponds to B$_3$ species and the 1870 cm^{-1} band to unsym-
metrical B$_2$ species. They point out that the latter model more readily accounts
for the breadth of the 1870 cm^{-1} band and, as has previously been noted, there
is some theoretical support for multi-centre bonding sites.[29,30] However, we
prefer Ibach's assignment to linear and bridged B$_2$ species. We note that the

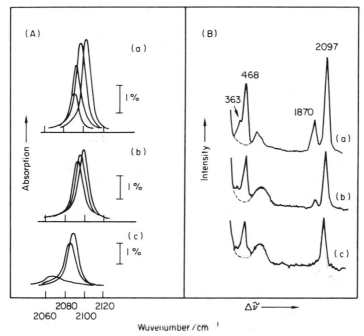

Fig. 8. (A) Infrared reflection–absorption spectra from CO on Pt(111) with increasing
surface potentials (from left to right). (a) At 80 K; (b) additional adsorption at 80 K
after adsorption at 295 K; (c) at 295 K. (After Horn and Pritchard, Ref. 19.) (B)
Electron energy-loss spectra from CO on Pt(111); (a) at 350 K, at ambient CO
pressure of 6.5×10^{-7} Pa; (b) at 320 K, high coverage 0.25 L exposure; (c) at 320 K,
low coverage 0.12 L exposure. (After Froitzheim, Hopster, Ibach and Lehwald,
Ref. 22.)

bridge-CO wavenumber is marginally lower than the range we have assigned to B_2 species in Section 5, i.e. it would be not inconsistent to assign it to a B_3 site. However, the LEED results militate against this. Further studies on (100) and (110) single crystal planes of Pt would be very valuable.

6.3.2 Evaporated metal films

Spectra from CO adsorbed on evaporated metal films have been reported in a number of papers.[40,51a,57,68,83,86,87] The spectra observed have a strong general similarity to those obtained on supported metal particles (Section 6.3.3 below). This is in the sense that the dominant band in both peak intensity and in area is almost invariably the one in the linear-CO region between 2030 and 2070 cm^{-1}. However, more often than not, there is a weaker and broader bridge-CO band in the region 1800 to 1875 cm^{-1}, and, in one case for an evaporated film,[86] the integrated intensity of the absorption is comparable with that of the linear-CO species. The latter is interesting in implying that it is possible, but not usual, to prepare the Pt samples which are strong bridge-CO adsorbers. The results are summarized in Table 5(b).

There is a tendency for the linear-CO groups on evaporated metal films to have lower stretching frequencies than those observed for supported metal samples or for CO on Pt(111) planes. This may be a reflection of epitaxial effects from the substrate on which the film is evaporated, implying that (111) planes may not be the dominant ones. However, in a number of cases, films were evaporated in the presence of gaseous CO and this could have led to contamination from dissociated CO.

6.3.3 Supported metal particles

Many studies have been made of the infrared spectrum of CO on supported Pt.[2,37,40,41,46,103–119] These are summarized in Table 5(c) and are subdivided according to the support used. At high coverage the linear-CO band almost invariably falls in the wavenumber range 2070 to 2095 cm^{-1} and this is in good agreement with the results for Pt(111)[19,22] planes. However, of course, it remains to be seen what linear-CO band wavenumbers result from adsorption on other single crystal planes of Pt.

A study of the linear-CO-group frequency with particle size has been made by Dalla Betta[115] who claims that smaller metal particles give somewhat lower νCO wavenumbers (2093 cm^{-1} for 100 Å particles; 2077 cm^{-1} for 10 Å particles). As with the work on Pt ribbon, the linear-CO band wavenumber increases with increasing coverage on oxide-supported samples[51b,105] and this has been discussed in terms of through-metal interactions[51b] or dipolar coupling.[37]

Oxidation causes the linear-CO-group band to shift upwards to 2120 cm^{-1}[51b,105,118] and in one case an additional weak band has also been observed at 2170 cm^{-1}.[105]

Weaker and broader absorption bands attributable to bridged CO groups have frequently been observed on oxide-supported metal samples. Their wavenumbers

TABLE 5
Vibrational wavenumbers/cm^{-1} for CO chemisorbed on Pt

1st author and year	Ref. no.	Substrate or support	νCO (linear)	νCO (bridged)	νCM	Comments
(a) Single crystals etc.						
Horn, 1977	19	(111) face	2065^a $\;$ 2089 $\;\;^b$			low θ
Froitzheim, 1977	22	(111) face	2075			high θ / low θ
Shigeishi, 1976	102	(111) face	2100 → 2065	1870		high θ / low θ
Low, 1970	109	Pt foil	2100 → 2090			high θ
						} polycrystalline ribbon
(b) Evaporated metal films						
Eischens, 1958	40	CaF$_2$	2040			
Queau, 1972	51a	NaCl	2040	≈ 1800		
Garland, 1965	57	CaF$_2$ or CsI	2053 $\;$ 2030	1850 $\;$ 1840	570 $\;$ 477	evaporated in CO / evaporated *in vacuo*
Harrod, 1967	86	NaCl	2070	1800^c ———		
Bradley, 1969	87	KBr	2075 $\;$ 2063 $\;$ 2050	1850		evaporated *in vacuo* / evaporated in argon
Hayward, 1971	68		2180 $\;$ 2040	1874		evaporated in CO

TABLE 5—*continued*

1st author and year	Ref. no.	Substrate or support	νCO (linear)	νCO (bridged)	νCM	Comments
(c) *Supported metal particles*						
Eischens, 1954	2	SiO₂	2070	1828		
1956	41, 46	SiO₂	2070	1818		
1958	40	SiO₂	2050	1845		after treatment with H₂
Heyne, 1966	105	SiO₂	2038			low θ
1967	105	SiO₂	2070			high θ
Brown, 1976	117	SiO₂	2070	≈1800		
Eischens, 1958	40	Al₂O₃	2050	1818		
Kavtaradze, 1966	104	Al₂O₃	2070	1800		
Aragano, 1969	107	Al₂O₃	2170 & 2080 / 2120			oxidized
Kavtaradze, 1970	108	Al₂O₃	2080 → 2050 → 2010	1820		room temperature
				—		heat in H₂ at 100 °C
				1780		heat in H₂ at 300 °C
Sokolova, 1972	111	Al₂O₃	2060			

1st author and year	Ref. no.	Substrate or support	νCO (linear)	νCO (bridged)	νCM	Comments
Primet, 1973	51b	Al₂O₃	2050	1870 →		low θ
	112	Al₂O₃	→ 2080	1845		high θ
			→ 2120			oxidation
Palazov, 1973	113	Al₂O₃	2075			
Unland, 1973	114	Al₂O₃	2090			
Kikuchi, 1974	119	Al₂O₃	2080 → 2120			
Dalla Betta, 1975	115	Al₂O₃	2093 / 2077	1853 (1605)[d]		oxidized; 120 Å particles; 10 Å particles; no νCO shift with H₂
Basset, 1975	116	Al₂O₃	2065			
Bolivar, 1976	118	Al₂O₃	2074 → 2117	1860		
Eischens, 1958	40	KBr	2000	— 1850		
Blyholder, 1970	106	oil	2045	1815	476	heat in oxygen
Cooney, 1977	14	Pt electrode	2096 2081		480	480 → 560 on oxidation

[a] Underlining denotes relatively strong absorptions.
[b] Arrows show absorptions changing with increasing coverages or oxidation.
[c] Figures between horizontal lines are maxima of very broad absorptions.
[d] Wavenumbers in brackets denote ill-defined peaks.

are variable (1875 to 1780 cm^{-1}). In a few cases they are reasonably intense[40,106,111] and they seem to be more pronounced with Pt/Al$_2$O$_3$[40,111] than with Pt/SiO$_2$[40] samples.

Work has been carried out on Pt/Pd alloys[46] and on Pt/Ir alloys.[111]

Bands attributable to linear CO groups have been observed on a Pt electrode in aqueous solution.[14]

6.4   Copper

6.4.1   Single crystal surfaces

The most detailed study of the vibrational spectra of molecules adsorbed on single crystal surfaces has been made by Pritchard and his colleagues using reflection-absorption infrared techniques on the Cu/CO system.[15,120–124] They have studied the r.a.-i.r. spectra from CO on the (100), (111), (110), (211), (311), and (755) crystal planes of copper. They correlated the infrared absorptions with surface potential changes which invariably increased to a maximum with increasing coverage and then decreased again. These surface potentials were always positive, in contrast to results with Fe, Co and Ni where they are negative.

It is valuable to compare the infrared spectra at low coverage, when the νCO frequencies are most likely to be characteristic of individual adsorption sites, at the maximum surface potential, when an ordered adsorbed layer is most likely to be present, and at the saturation coverage, where 'compressed' or 'out-of-register' structures tend to be in evidence as shown by LEED measurements.

In Table 6 Pritchard's experimental results are collected together and typical spectra are illustrated in Fig. 9. The planes (100) and (111) give single bands near 2080 cm^{-1} at low coverages. These shift somewhat to higher wavenumbers for (100) and to lower ones for (111) planes[122] with increase of coverage.

The latter behaviour is unusual in that it is in the opposite direction to the effects described above with increasing CO coverage on Pd and Pt. However with Cu it also occurs for the higher wavenumber bands on the (211), (311), and (755) planes up to the coverage giving a maximum surface potential. It also occurs (Section 6.5) for CO adsorption on Ag and Au. The lowering of wavenumber of νCO with increasing coverage relative to the gas-phase value at 2143 cm^{-1} could imply a strengthening of adsorption with increasing coverage. Grimley[125] has suggested, on theoretical grounds, that electronic interactions of adsorbed molecules through the metal substrate can lead to strengthened or weakened adsorption depending on the distance of separation. Chesters *et al.*[121] have suggested that an excess of charge accumulation on the Group IB metal surfaces resulting from predominantly σ-bonding from CO could nevertheless lead to some back donation.

The (110) plane[124] gives rise to two absorption bands at low CO coverage; these blend together at higher coverage. One of these bands (at 2088 cm^{-1}) is not very different in wavenumber from that given by CO on the (100) plane but

TABLE 6
Wavenumbers/cm^{-1} and intensities of infrared absorption bands from CO chemisorbed on single-crystal surfaces of copper at 77 K as studied by Pritchard et al.[15, 120-124]

Crystal face	Ref.	Low coverage	Surface potential maximum	Saturation coverage
(111)	120, 122	2080	2076^a	2070
(100)	15, 121, 122, 123	2079	2086^b	2088
(110)	120, 122, 124	2088	2093	2094
(755)	122	2093(w, bd) 2112(m, sh)	2066(w) 2098(s)	2073(vw) 2106(s)
(211)	122	2095(w) 2110(mw)	2100(s, v.bd)	2110(s, sh)
(311)	122	2093(m) 2110(m)	2096(ms) 2102(s)	2093(ms) 2103(s)

(s) = strong; (m) = medium; (mw) = medium weak; (w) = weak; (sh) = sharp; (v.bd) = very broad.
Underlining denotes relatively strong absorptions.
^{a} ($\sqrt{3} \times \sqrt{3}$) 30° mesh.
^{b} c (2×2) mesh.

the other (at 2104 cm^{-1}) is notably higher. Similar pairs of absorption bands are found at low coverage for the (755), (211) and (311) planes. In the simplest and most regular form these planes can be expected to consist of 6-, 3-[122] and 1-atom rows,[175] respectively, of the (111) type, forming terraces separated by 1-atom steps of the (100) type. We note that in the first two cases there are, in principle, three types of single-atom sites available, i.e. C_9 sites on the (111) terraces, C_7 sites on the outer edges of the steps, and C_{10} sites on the inner part of the steps.

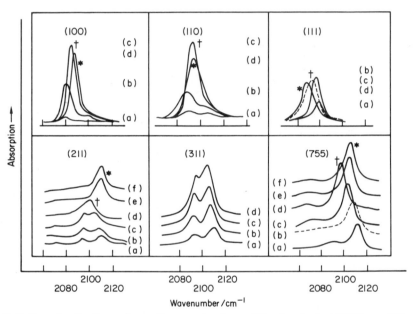

Fig. 9. Infrared reflection–absorption spectra from CO adsorbed at 77 K on different single-crystal planes of Cu. Spectra were recorded with increasing coverages in the sequences (a), (b) etc. Spectra corresponding to, or near, maximum surface potentials are indicated by †. Those corresponding to saturation coverages are indicated with *.
(After Pritchard *et al.*, Refs 122–124.)

For the (311) planes there are only C_7 and C_{10} sites in equal numbers. For the (211) and (311) planes it is clearly tempting to associate the new high wavenumber bands with the step sites. The relative intensities and wavenumbers of the bands at low CO coverage (Fig. 9) on these two planes are best accommodated by assuming that the high wavenumber band near 2110 cm^{-1} is associated with the C_{10} sites, and the lower wavenumber bands near 2093 cm^{-1} with the C_7 and C_9 sites together.

At low CO coverage on (110) planes the two absorptions have been attributed by Pritchard *et al.*[124] to two domains of identical linear-CO species on C_6 sites which differ in the way in which adjacent rows of adsorbed molecules are related to each other. However, an alternative possible explanation is in terms of adsorption on two different sites once again, viz. on C_6 sites (2080 cm^{-1}) and C_{10} sites (2110 cm^{-1}). This is an interesting point because the same locations on (110) planes have been designated above as B_5 sites (on the assumption that they will involve appreciable bonding to all 5 rather than to the one central atom) with tentatively postulated frequencies at the opposite extreme of the νCO range! It is, of course, possible that different metals provide different bonding patterns at the same location and, in contrast to the other metals so far considered, copper has a complete d shell. It should be emphasized that the above interpretations are necessarily speculative and that the frequencies do not correlate in detail with the value of n in C_n such as was predicted earlier. Also, on any interpretation, it seems difficult to reconcile the very different low coverage spectra on (111) and (755) planes where C_9 sites of the (111) type are expected to be dominant in each case. Perhaps the (755) plane has a different arrangement of surface atoms.[122]

For comparison with infrared spectra from CO on evaporated metal films or supported metal particles, it is probable that the high CO-coverage results from the single crystals are of relevance. At saturation, the single dominant bands fall in the wavenumber sequence (111), 2070 < (100), 2088 < (110), 2094 < (755), (311), (211), *ca.* 2110 to 2105 cm^{-1}. The low-index planes give CO bands with significantly lower wavenumbers than do the high-index planes.[122]

6.4.2 Evaporated metal films

The results[66,121,122,126–130] are collected together in Table 7. For the most part they are extremely uniform, with absorption bands at 2104 ± 2 cm^{-1}. An exceptional result is for copper evaporated onto an MgO substrate[122] (see further discussion in Section 6.4.3). In two cases there are signs of additional absorption near 2090 cm^{-1}. It is clear that the infrared band wavenumbers are much closer to expectation for higher-index faces and this correlation is supported by surface potential measurements.[122] A slightly higher wavenumber was observed for a massive copper sample prepared under less satisfactory vacuum conditions by electropolishing.[126]

6.4.3 Supported metal particles

Here the results are more numerous[2,40,72,74,122,131–139] and the CO bands observed are more variable in wavenumber. However, there is clear-cut evidence[122,138] that the bands at higher wavenumbers (*ca.* 2120 cm^{-1}) are associated with less well-reduced samples. Further reduction leads to an absorption between 2110 and 2100 cm^{-1} with a mean value, 2105 cm^{-1}, very close to that obtained with evaporated Cu films. Deliberate oxidation causes the wavenumber to rise again.[40,122] The only strong bands with wavenumbers below 2100 cm^{-1} were near 2095 cm^{-1} as observed by Gardner and Petrucci[132] and Pearce,[138] each of whom used very high reduction temperatures, and at the exceptionally low value of 2081 cm^{-1} obtained by Pritchard[122] for copper

TABLE 7
Vibrational wavenumbers/cm^{-1} for CO chemisorbed on Cu[e]

1st author and year	Ref. no.	Substrate or support	νCO >2120	2100	2080	<2080	Comments[d]
(a) Single crystals							
Chesters, 1970	15	(100) face			2094[a]		
Pritchard, 1975	122	(100) face			2088[a]		
Horn, 1976	123						
Pritchard, 1975	122	(111) face				2070[a]	
Horn, 1977	124	(110) face			2094[a]		
Pritchard, 1975	122	(211) face		2110[a]			
Pritchard, 1975	122	(311) face		2103[a]	2093[a]		
Pritchard, 1975	122	(755) face		2106[a]		(2073)[a]	
(b) Evaporated films etc.							
Drmaj, 1970	126	Solid Cu		2110			electropolished, also higher wavenumber bands
Bradshaw, 1968	127	glass		2105			
Pritchard, 1970	128	glass		2105	(2092)		
Chesters, 1972	121	glass		2105	(2090)		
Pritchard, 1975	122	glass		2102			
Pritchard, 1975	122	Al$_2$O$_3$		2106			
Pritchard, 1975	122	MgO			2082		
Tompkins, 1971	129	Ta		2105[b]			
Bradshaw, 1970	66	NaCl		2103			
Stobie, 1976	130	CaF$_2$		2102			

supported on MgO. In some cases a low wavenumber shoulder was observed near 2060 cm^{-1}.[40,134,138]

Only the MgO result corresponds to expectation for low index faces of the (100) or (111) types, and it was mentioned earlier that a similar result was obtained for Cu evaporated onto MgO. This latter result at first sight seemed surprising in view of the substantial thickness of *ca.* 4000 Å for the evaporated film. However the strong correlation between the results for films and particles on MgO has led Pritchard[122] to argue that this ionic and crystalline support is capable of promoting long-range epitaxial effects. It seems probable that MgO gives mainly (100) faces to the Cu crystallites. Other than with MgO, the nature of the support seems to have relatively minor effects on the wavenumbers of the infrared bands of CO on Cu.

The main conclusion drawn by Pritchard[122] is that low-index (111) or (100) faces are rarely found with evaporated films or with supported copper catalysts. There is evidence that, in thermodynamic terms, there is little energy difference between different faces[140] and it may be that copper has a greater tendency to form smooth poorly-crystalline surfaces than do other metals.

Bands between 2140 and 2110 cm^{-1} seem to be reliably assigned to partially oxidized copper. For adsorption on CuO, Gardner[132] has assigned bands at

TABLE 7—*continued*

1st author and year	Ref. no.	Substrate or support	vCO >2120	2100	2080	<2080	Comments[a]
(c) Supported metal particles							
Eischens, 1954	2	SiO₂	2128[e]				r.t. 200–350 °C
Eischens, 1958	40	SiO₂		<u>2100</u>			
Eischens, 1958	40	SiO₂	2120				O₂ added
Kavtaradze, 1962	131	SiO₂	2120				r.t. 300–380 °C
Gardner, 1963	132	SiO₂	2136		2095		r.t. 450 °C oxidized
Cho, 1964	72	SiO₂		2100[e]			r.t. 350 °C
Seanor, 1965	133	SiO₂	2132				oxidized
Smith, 1965	134	SiO₂	2125 –	2100		(2070)	r.t. 140 °C
Cukr, 1970	135			2100			
Kavtaradze, 1970	136	SiO₂		2110			
London, 1973	137	SiO₂	2140				on CuO
Pearce, 1974	138	SiO₂	(2120)	<u>2108</u>			r.t. 300 °C
				<u>2105</u>			r.t. 400–500 °C
					<u>2093</u>	2060	r.t. 700 °C
Pritchard, 1975	122	SiO₂		2104			r.t. 140 °C
				2100			r.t. 350 °C
Kavtaradze, 1962	131	Al₂O₃	2120				r.t. 300–350 °C
Smith, 1965	134	Al₂O₃		2110			r.t. 140 °C
Kavtaradze, 1967	139	Al₂O₃	2120				r.t. 300 °C
Kavtaradze, 1970	136	Al₂O₃		2110			
Pritchard, 1975	122	Al₂O₃	2124				r.t. 140 °C
				2108			r.t. 350 °C
Pritchard, 1975	122	MgO			2081		r.t. 140 °C
Blyholder, 1969	74	paraffin	2120				

[a] Value observed at saturation coverage.
[b] Also absorption at 2140 with 2105 increasing to 2120 cm⁻¹ on oxidation.
[c] Also an additional weak and broad absorption near 1850 cm⁻¹.
[d] r.t. – reduction temperature.
[e] More intense bands are underlined.

2177 and 2127 cm⁻¹, and Pearce[138] one at 2215 cm⁻¹. Also London[137] assigned the band at 2140 cm⁻¹ to CO on CuO. Pearce argued that bands near 2130 cm⁻¹ are from CO on Cu₂O, and this is probably correct.

In a few cases weak and broad absorption bands have been positively identified near 1850 cm⁻¹.[2,72] These have been assigned by Eischens[2] to bridged-CO species. With silica, in particular, this is a difficult region to investigate because of background absorption. Accordingly these bands may be more prevalent than has been reported. As with the similarly weak bands from CO on Pt, they merit further investigation, e.g. by the application of EELS techniques.

Moskovits and Hulse[54] have studied the adsorption of CO on multiple metal-atom clusters in inert gas matrices. As n increases from 2 to >4 in Cu$_n$CO the band shifts from 2128 to 2090 cm⁻¹, in good agreement with the results on metal particles.

6.5   Silver and Gold

We now pass to metals for which no single crystal work has been carried out, with the exception of tungsten (Section 6.8.3). Our discussions of the spectra hence will be less detailed, and we shall consider groups of related metals together. We commence with silver and gold which, with copper, are Group IB metals with completed d-electron shells. In Table 8 we collect together the published results for Ag[66,121,132,138,141,142] and Au[66,121,142-146].

The results on evaporated metal films are very consistent and comprise absorptions at *ca.* 2160 cm^{-1} for Ag, and *ca.* 2120 cm^{-1} for Au. Well-reduced supported samples[147] give bands at similar wavenumbers for CO adsorption

TABLE 8
Vibrational wavenumbers/cm^{-1} for CO chemisorbed on silver and gold[b]

1st author and year	Ref. no.	Substrate or support	νCO						Comments
(a) Silver									
(i) Evaporated films									
Bradshaw, 1970	66	glass	2160						ads. at −160 °C
Chesters, 1972	121	glass	2155						ads. at −196 °C
(ii) Supported metal particles									
Gardner, 1963	132	SiO₂	2165						AgNO₃ heated to 250 °C
Keulks, 1970	141	SiO₂	2180						pretreated with O₂
Pearce, 1974	138	SiO₂	2179						oxidized Ag
					2085	**2058**	2015		high coverage[a]
						2064	**2015** &	1884	low coverage[a]
				2166	2140	2095		2055	ads. at −110 °C
Kavtaradze, 1962	142	Al₂O₃	2182						ads. at −150 °C
Keulks, 1970	141	Al₂O₃	2180						O₂ pretreatment
(b) Gold									
(i) Evaporated films									
Bradshaw, 1970	66	NaCl	2120						ads. at −160 °C
Kottke, 1972	143	Ta foil	2115						ads. at 25 °C
Chesters, 1972	121	glass	2120						ads. at −196 °C
(ii) Supported metal particles									
Yates, 1969	144	SiO₂	2175						partially reduced
				2110					r.t. 250 °C
				≈2135					CO/O₂
Kavtaradze, 1962	142	Al₂O₃	2174						
Guerra, 1967	145	SiO₂			2075				
Guerra, 1969	146	SiO₂			2100				heating to 375 °C

[a] Pretreatment with hydrogen.
[b] More intense bands are underlined.

on Ag at low temperature[138] and for adsorption on Au at room temperature,[144–146] although it should be noted that pre-treatment with H_2 is needed
to obtain CO adsorption on supported Ag.[138] However, at room temperature,
CO adsorbed on reduced Ag gives a dominant infrared absorption at *ca.*
2060 cm^{-1} at high coverages, and the band at 2166 cm^{-1} obtained from samples
at low temperatures changes to 2060 cm^{-1} on allowing the sample to warm;[138]
this process is only partially reversible. The low temperature species is regarded
as a precursor to the room temperature one. The spectrum from CO on Ag at
room temperature further changes reversibly to a pair of bands at 2015 cm^{-1}
and 1884 cm^{-1} on reducing the surface coverage by evacuation. Pearce[138]
assigned these bands to linear- and a bridge-CO species, respectively. Oxidized
samples give somewhat higher CO band wavenumbers for both silver and gold.

The three Group IB metals have several spectroscopic features in common,
i.e. (i) a great preponderance of linearly adsorbed species, (ii) a tendency for
band wavenumbers to shift to *lower values* with increasing coverage and (iii) a
tendency for enhanced adsorption at low temperatures. However, the wavenumbers themselves do not fall into regular sequences, as shown below:

Reduced metal: Cu, *ca.* 2105 cm^{-1}; Ag, *ca.* 2160 cm^{-1} (low temperature) and
ca. 2060 cm^{-1} (room temperature); Au, *ca.* 2110 cm^{-1}.
Oxidized metal: Cu, 2130 cm^{-1}, Ag, 2180 cm^{-1}, Au, 2175 cm^{-1}.

These are discussed further in Section 10.1.2.

6.6   Iron, Cobalt and Other Metals of the First Transition Series

6.6.1   Iron

The chemisorption of CO on iron surfaces has been studied by infrared
spectroscopy by a considerable number of workers because of the importance of
this catalyst in the Fischer-Tropsch process and in ammonia synthesis. However,
there are particular problems associated with the interpretation of these spectra
in that the bands at highest frequencies observed on well-reduced catalysts are
in the low frequency end of the range that we have associated with the linear
species, and other bands occur in the high-frequency end of the range which we
have taken to be associated with bridged species. The question is whether these
latter bands are to be assigned to linear or to bridged species. The situation is
complicated by the fact that iron has a body-centred cubic structure in contrast
to the face-centred cubic structures of the metals whose spectra we have so far
discussed. Non-f.c.c. structures become increasingly common as one moves from
the right to the left of the transition metals in the Periodic Table. Finally, for
iron[148] and for certain other transition elements, there is evidence for dissociative adsorption near room temperature. This can complicate matters by leading
to surfaces contaminated with carbon and/or oxygen.

The results for evaporated iron films[51a,64,65,68] and for supported metal
particles[40,72,74,132,149–153] are collected in Table 9. Usually there are not

TABLE 9
Vibrational wavenumbers/cm^{-1} for CO adsorbed on cobalt to titanium in the first transition metal series[a]

1st author and year	Ref. no.	Substrate or support	νCO					Comments
Iron								
(a) Evaporated films								
Baker, 1968	64	CaF$_2$			1950			at −103 °C
					1900			at 25 °C
Bradshaw, 1969	65	NaCl		2040	1960			at −160 °C
					1930			at 25 °C
Hayward, 1971	68	CaF$_2$	2015		1915			
					1980			
Queau, 1972	51a	NaCl			1915			evaporated in CO
(b) Supported metal particles								
Eischens, 1958	40	SiO$_2$		2020	1960			
Blyholder, 1962	149	SiO$_2$		2020	1980	(1887)		
Cho, 1964	72	SiO$_2$		2005		(1870)		
Heal, 1976	150	SiO$_2$	2169	2035	1980			1980 remains on evac.
Tanaka, 1972	151	Argon		2030	1980		580	at −230 °C
Blyholder, 1962	149	Oil		2015	1950		580	
					1925			
Blyholder, 1966	152	Oil			1970		580	isotopic studies
Blyholder, 1969	74	Oil			1980			
Neff, 1976	153	Oil			1940			
Cobalt								
(a) Evaporated films								
Baker, 1968	64	CaF$_2$			1970			1990 at −103 °C
Bradshaw, 1970	66	NaCl		2040				−160 °C
					1975			25 °C
Hayward, 1971	68	—		2032,		1856		evaporated in CO
				2016				
Queau, 1972	51a	NaCl			1980	1880		
Wojtczak, 1975	156	NaCl			1960	1815		evaporated in CO

more than two absorption bands near 2020 and 1950 cm^{-1}. The latter is very frequently, but not invariably, the dominant one; sometimes it is the only one. The lower wavenumber band has a mean value of about 1935 cm^{-1} for the evaporated films but a somewhat higher mean of about 1970 cm^{-1} for the supported metal particles. This absorption clearly arises from the principal associatively adsorbed CO species. Bradshaw and Pritchard[66] mentioned that initial adsorption of CO on iron did not appear to give rise to CO absorption bands and speculated whether a CO species with its bond parallel to the metal surface was first adsorbed. Another possibility is that at low coverage dissocia-

TABLE 9—*continued*

1st author and year	Ref. no.	Substrate or support	νCO			Comments
(b) Supported metal particles						
Gardner, 1960	62	SiO$_2$	2179, 2160	2091		
Cho, 1964	72	SiO$_2$		<u>2070</u>, 2025	1930	
Ferreira, 1970	75	SiO$_2$	2180, 2130	2095, 2065, 2040		
Heal, 1976	150	SiO$_2$	2181	2060, 2034 2020		with gaseous CO retained on evac.
Kavtaradze, 1964	157	Al$_2$O$_3$		2070	<u>1950</u> 1820	2140 cm^{-1} band removed on pumping
Blyholder, 1969	74	Oil		<u>2000</u>	1880	
Manganese						
Baker, 1968	64	CaF$_2$		2080, 2000		evaporated in CO
Hayward, 1971	68	—		2080, 2000	1770	evaporated in CO
Blyholder, 1969	74	Oil		1950	1890	
Chromium						
Baker, 1968	64	CaF$_2$		1930		evaporated in CO
Hayward, 1971	68	—		1970		evaporated in CO
Blyholder, 1969	74	Oil		1940		
Vanadium						
Blyholder, 1969	74	Oil		≈ 1920		
Titanium						
Hayward, 1971	68	—	2165	2060		

[a] More intense bands are underlined.

tive adsorption occurs,[148] but Bradshaw and Vierle[154] later suggested an alternative explanation for this delayed appearance of νCO absorptions.

Eischens[40] originally assigned the *ca.* 1960 cm^{-1} absorption band to a linear rather than a bridged species. Blyholder[149] naturally preferred that type of interpretation, and it has been shown[50,54] that the species FeCO absorb at 1898 cm^{-1}, so that such a wavenumber is not impossible for a linear species. However, Eischens' original assignment[40] was based on the consideration that bridged species in metal carbonyls normally absorb below 1900 cm^{-1}. More recently (Section 4) it has become apparent that there is a systematic difference between the wavenumbers of bands due to bridged species adsorbed on surfaces and in metal carbonyl compounds. Hence it would now be more reasonable to consider the *ca.* 1970 cm^{-1} absorption bands as assignable to bridged species (see further discussion in Section 10.1.2). Because the spectrum of CO on Fe rarely shows more than two νCO absorption bands, a single-crystal EELS study combined with electron diffraction data would seem to be particularly worthwhile.

The *ca.* 2025 cm^{-1} absorption seems assignable without difficulty to a linear species, and the absorption near 580 cm^{-1} observed by Blyholder[149,151,152] for CO on Fe in oil or argon matrices have been assigned to an MCO angle bending mode on the basis of isotopic studies.[152] An alternative possibility is that this band might be assignable to a νM—C vibration of the associatively adsorbed species.[58]

Eischens and Pliskin[40] found difficulty in completely reducing iron samples, and Heal[150] showed that a trace of Cu facilitated the reduction of the nitrates. A band observed by Heal[150] at 2169 cm^{-1} is presumably to be assigned to CO adsorbed on an oxidized Fe surface. Voroshilov *et al.*[155] have assigned bands at 2180 cm^{-1} to adsorption on Fe_2O_3, 2070 cm^{-1} to adsorption on FeO, and 2020 cm^{-1} to adsorption on Fe.

Cho and Schulman[72] studied CO adsorption on Fe/Ni alloys.

6.6.2 Cobalt

Spectra of CO adsorbed on evaporated films of cobalt are not dissimilar to those of CO on iron, with weaker bands at *ca.* 2030 cm^{-1} and stronger ones near 1970 cm^{-1}.[51a,64,66,68,156] However, the supported metal samples,[62,72,74,75,150,157] unlike those of Fe, show a number of additional linear-CO bands between 2050 and 2100 cm^{-1}, and are in general dominated by absorptions in the linear-CO region. Heal[150] assigns the two or three bands in the 2100 to 2000 cm^{-1} region to multi-linear species of the M(CO)$_n$ type.

Bands near 2180 cm^{-1} are attributable to CO adsorbed on incompletely reduced Co.[62,75,150] It seems that it is difficult to reduce Co, or alternatively that adsorbed carbon monoxide is partly dissociated at room temperature leading to re-oxidation of the surface.

Cho and Schulman[72] studied CO adsorption on Co/Ni alloys.

6.6.3 Manganese, chromium, vanadium and titanium

The infrared spectra from CO adsorbed onto the above metals have been relatively little studied. However, Blyholder and Allen[74] obtained spectra from CO on Mn, Cr and V in the form of small metal particles in oil. They interpreted the trends in the wavenumbers of the stronger bands with the help of molecular orbital theory, using Blyholder's assumption that the bands in question arise from linear-CO species.

For chromium in oil the results[74] agree with those obtained from evaporated films,[64,68] but for manganese there are substantial differences,[64,68] with much stronger linear-CO absorptions from the evaporated films.

6.7 Rhodium, Ruthenium and Molybdenum: The Second Series of Transition Metals

6.7.1 Rhodium

The results for CO adsorbed on rhodium are collected in Table 10. With evaporated films[51a,57,67,68,86,156,158] the results are somewhat variable. Linear-CO bands are normally dominant. However, there is rather consistently a bridge-CO absorption in the region 1885 to 1820 cm^{-1} and this is sometimes rather strong.[86] Its low wavenumber suggests 3-fold or 4-fold bridged species on (111) or (100) planes. On NaCl[51a,86,156] the linear-CO bands fall close to 2010 cm^{-1}, suggesting an epitaxial effect; otherwise they fall between 2055 and 2080 cm^{-1} (Table 10).

The spectra from CO on supported metal particles include the results of detailed studies by Yang and Garland,[159] who made the first studies on rhodium, and by Pearce.[138] These authors are in good agreement in assigning a pair of bands near 2100 and 2030 cm^{-1} to sites on unsintered samples, a normally dominant band at 2060 cm^{-1} which grows relative to the other on sintering, to a linear species, and a band of variable wavenumber and intensity between 1925 and 1780 cm^{-1} to bridged species. In Pearce's study[138] of Rh/SiO$_2$ it is shown that the latter band becomes weaker and moves to low frequency as the temperature of reduction increases to 700 °C and the particle sizes become larger. Pearce has suggested that sintering removes high-index planes on which the bridged species adsorb. The bridge-CO band can also be strong on Rh/Al$_2$O$_3$.[136]

The main linear-CO band between 2050 and 2065 cm^{-1} on supported metal samples correlates reasonably with analogous bands obtained with evaporated metal films except when NaCl is the substrate for the latter. The additional pair of bands found near 2095 and 2030 cm^{-1} on unsintered[159] or lightly sintered[138] samples do not seem to appear with evaporated films. They presumably arise from irregular non-crystalline surfaces of the particles. The presence of two such bands of similar intensity led Yang and Garland[159] to assign them to a Rh(CO)$_2$ surface species, which can give two bands by coupling of the vibrations of the two equivalent CO groups. The two bands in question were dominant at 2095 and 2027 cm^{-1} with a 2% unsintered metal sample.[57] Guerra et al.[145] has questioned the Rh(CO)$_2$ assignment on the grounds that the ratio of adsorbed CO molecules to metal atoms on their samples would suggest that such CO-rich species cannot be present at high concentration; they also consider that the intensities of the two bands do not always vary together. They propose some alternative assignments, e.g. to Rh(CO)(CO) species with a second non-equivalent linear CO group. However their spectra differ somewhat from those of Yang and Garland[159] and Pearce.[138]

We note that, if the metal particles are large enough, the 'metal-surface selection rule'[58] would cause the out-of-phase vCO vibration of an Rh(CO)$_2$ group to be forbidden in infrared absorption as its dipole change is expected to be parallel to the surface. On the other hand, the pair of bands under discussion

TABLE 10
Vibrational wavenumbers/cm^{-1} for CO chemisorbed on rhodium, ruthenium and molybdenum

1st author and year	Ref. no.	Substrate or support	νCO					Comments
Rhodium								
(a) Evaporated films								
Garland, 1965	57	CaF$_2$ (2111) or CsI		2055[a]		1905	1852	evaporated in CO
Harrod, 1967	86	NaCl			2000		1820	
Eckstrom, 1970	67	metal	2078	2060				(110) crystallites?
Hayward, 1971	68	—		2055			1820	evaporation in CO
Queau, 1972	51a	NaCl		2020		1885		evaporation in CO
Wojtczak, 1975	156	NaCl		2015		1860		evaporation in CO
Wells, 1977	158	Ta		2060				— low coverage
				2080 [b]				— high coverage
(b) Supported metal particles								
Guerra, 1967	145	SiO$_2$		2065	2005	1895		
Kavtaradze, 1970	136	SiO$_2$		2050		1860		
Pearce, 1974	138	SiO$_2$	2105[c]	2065	(2040)[d]	1920		unsintered
			2095[c]	2060	2030	1920		sintered, r.t. 250 °C
				2060			1885	sintered, r.t. 350 °C
				2060			1780	sintered, r.t. 700 °C
Yang, 1957	159	Al$_2$O$_3$	2095		2027			2% Rh, unsintered
		Al$_2$O$_3$	2095	2055	2027	1905		8–16% Rh, unsintered
		Al$_2$O$_3$	2108	2062	2040	1925		8–16% Rh, sintered
Kavtaradze, 1970	136	Al$_2$O$_3$		2060			1870	
Sokolova, 1972	160	Al$_2$O$_3$		2030			1860	

may well occur in spectra from CO on small metal particles. If $M(CO)_2$ groups do occur on metal surfaces this spectrum from CO on rhodium is the one most likely to signify their existence. But more work is needed before this can be accepted. Alternatively it is possible that the 2095 cm^{-1} band is associated with incompletely reduced metal, or with metal atoms adjacent to the surface of the oxide support, as has been suggested for high frequency linear-CO bands from CO on Ni (Section 6.1).

Sokolova[160] has studied CO adsorption on Rh/Ir alloys.

6.7.2 Ruthenium

An appreciable number of infrared studies have been made for CO on ruthenium.[94,103,114,115,145,161–163] There is a consistency in the wavenumbers of bands observed above 2000 cm^{-1}, viz. *ca.* 2140 cm^{-1}, *ca.* 2070 cm^{-1}, and *ca.* 2030 cm^{-1}. In Lynds' original investigation[103] only the two higher wave-

TABLE 10—*continued*

1st author and year	Ref. no.	Substrate or support	νCO						Comments
Ruthenium									
Supported metal particles									
Lynds, 1964	103	SiO$_2$	2143	2083					1.5% Ru
Guerra, 1967	145	SiO$_2$			$\approx$2000		1910		overlapping bands
Abhivant, 1972	161	SiO$_2$	(2146)			2040			
Kobayashi, 1973	162	SiO$_2$				2040	1980		not run *in situ*
Brown, 1976	163	SiO$_2$	2150	2080		2030			reduced sample
	117	SiO$_2$	2135	2080		2030		(1800)	reoxidized sample
Lynds, 1964	103	Al$_2$O$_3$	2125	2060					
Unland, 1973	114	Al$_2$O$_3$		2060			1970		very weak spectrum
Dalla Betta, 1975	115a	Al$_2$O$_3$				2028			91 Å particles[e]
		Al$_2$O$_3$	2147	2086		2029			45 Å particles[e]
		Al$_2$O$_3$	2137	2073		2050			14 Å particles[e]
Kavtaradze, 1965	94	SiO$_2$ or Al$_2$O$_3$	2160	2080		2020	1780		
Dalla Betta, 1977	115b	Al$_2$O$_3$				2043			
Molybdenum									
Hayward, 1971	68				2056	2032	1985		evaporation in CO
Nash, 1965	85	NaCl			<2070				exploded wire

[a] Underlining denotes relatively strong absorptions.
[b] Arrows show absorptions changing with coverages.
[c] Also weak bands near 2150 and 2180 cm^{-1}.
[d] Wavenumbers in brackets denote ill-defined peaks.
[e] Reduction treatment incompletely specified.

number bands occurred. In several other cases[94,115,163] it is the lowest wavenumber band of the three which has the greatest intensity. Dalla Betta[115] showed that this band was the strongest, or the only band, when large metal particles were present; Brown and Gonzalez,[163] aiming at accounting for differences previously obtained, showed that the 2030 cm^{-1} band was much the strongest for a newly reduced Ru sample, but that the 2080 cm^{-1} absorption became strongest after controlled re-oxidation of metal samples.

The most straightforward interpretation is[163] that the *ca.* 2030 cm^{-1} band is attributable to the linear and dominant species on fully reduced Ru, the *ca.* 2080 cm^{-1} band is from linear CO on partially oxidized Ru, and the *ca.* 2140 cm^{-1} band is from CO on strongly oxidized Ru, e.g. ruthenium oxide. Earlier suggestions that Ru(CO)$_n$ species ($n > 2$) give rise to the higher frequency bands[115,162] seem to be less probable.

Brown and Gonzalez' conclusions[163] are consistent with Dalla Betta's results[115] if it is assumed that the smaller metal particles are less thoroughly

TABLE 11
Vibrational wavenumbers/cm^{-1} for CO chemisorbed on iridium, osmium, rhenium and tungsten

1st author and year	Ref. no.	Substrate or support	νCO			Comments
Iridium						
(a) Evaporated films						
Harrod, 1967	86	NaCl	<u>2050</u>		<u>1900</u>^{a}	
Baker, 1968	64	CaF$_2$	1970			adsorption at −103 °C
(b) Supported metal particles						
Lynds, 1964	103	SiO$_2$	2044			low coverage
			$\overset{g}{\swarrow}$ 2074			high coverage
Guerra, 1967	145	SiO$_2$	2080	<u>2030</u> (1993) (1900)^b		2080 cm^{-1}, goes on pumping
van Hardeveld, 1972	43	SiO$_2$	<u>2078</u> (2054)	<u>2048</u>		100 Å particles 8 Å particles
Ravi, 1968	164	SiO$_2$	2070			
Lynds, 1964	103	Al$_2$O$_3$	2070			also weak band at 2120 cm^{-1}
Kavtaradze, 1966	104	Al$_2$O$_3$	<u>2070</u> 2000		1860, 1720	
Unland, 1973	114	Al$_2$O$_3$	$\approx$ 2050			
Bozon-Verduraz, 1974	165	Al$_2$O$_3$	<u>2065</u>		1850	
Osmium						
Guerra, 1967	145	SiO$_2$	(2080) <u>2010</u>		1860	
Kavtaradze, 1966	104	Al$_2$O$_3$	$\approx$ 2040		$\approx$ 1925 $\approx$ 1745	weak spectra

reduced, or are modified by proximity to the surface of the oxide support. This is reminiscent of the situation with Ni (Section 6.1). Only a few weak bands have been observed for ruthenium in the bridge-CO region, with the exception of results by Kobayashi and Shirasaki[162] wherein a strongish absorption band was reported to occur just below 2000 cm^{-1}; but in this case the experimental procedures did not allow for *in situ* examination of the spectra of the sample in an evacuated infrared cell. Only one infrared study has been made of CO on other transition metals of the second series. Hayward[68] has studied CO on a film of molybdenum evaporated in an atmosphere of CO. Linear species predominated.

6.8 Iridium, Osmium, Rhenium, Tungsten and Tantalum: The Third Series of Transition Metals

For metals of the Third Transition Series, iridium and tungsten have been

TABLE 11—*continued*

1st author and year	Ref. no.	Substrate or support	νCO				Comments
Rhenium							
Guerra, 1967	145	SiO$_2$		<u>2040</u>	<u>2000</u>	(1950) (1890)	
Bolivar, 1976	118	Al$_2$O$_3$	(2105)	<u>2035</u>		1950	
Tungsten							
(a) Single crystals							
Froitzheim, 1977	166	(100) face	$\{$2081^c				363^{c,f} α-Co, high coverage
						629^{c,e} 548^{c,f}	β-CO, low coverage
Backx, 1977	167	(111) face	$\{$	1993^d			α-CO, high coverage
						565^{d,f}	β-CO, low coverage
		(110) face	$\{$	1993^d		403^{d,f}	α-CO, high coverage
						565^{d,f}	β-CO, low coverage
(b) Evaporated films etc.							
Yates, 1972, 1973	168	metal ribbon	$\{$2128				α_1-CO
			2090				α_2-CO
Baker, 1968	64	CaF$_2$		1970			evaporated in CO
Hayward, 1971	68		2085	1975	1915		evaporated in CO
	68	CaF$_2$	2075				evaporated with CaF$_2$
Blyholder, 1973	170a	oil		(1950)	<u>1920</u>		
Tantalum							
Hayward, 1971	68		2096				evaporated in CO

^{a} Underlining denotes relatively strong absorptions.
^{b} Wavenumbers in brackets denote ill-defined peaks.
^{c} Resolution about 55 cm^{-1}.
^{d} Resolution about 160 cm^{-1}.
^{e} Assigned to νMO.
^{f} Assigned to νMC.
^{g} Arrow shows absorption changing with coverage.

studied in some detail (the latter with the help of single crystal studies utilizing EELS) and isolated spectroscopic studies have been made for osmium and rhenium.

6.8.1 Iridium

The published results[43,64,86,103,104,117,145,164,165] are summarized in Table 11. The majority of papers are concerned with silica or alumina-supported iridium, and in nearly all cases the CO spectrum is dominated by a strong band near 2075 cm^{-1} (2045 cm^{-1} at low coverage) from a linear species. A few weak bands from bridged species are observed below 1900 cm^{-1}. The main exception to the above generalization arises from the spectrum reported by Guerra and Schulman,[145] where the strongest band is near 2030 cm^{-1}. The reason for this difference is not apparent. However, the two studies of CO adsorption on evaporated films,[64,86] while differing from each other, do give bands at wavenumbers similar to those observed by Guerra and Schulman.[145] A judgement of which of these represents an authentic spectrum of CO on iridium must await further work.

Alloys of iridium with Pt, Pd, and Rh have been studied by Sokolova.[100,111,160]

6.8.2 Osmium and rhenium

Guerra and Schulman[145] have studied silica-supported osmium and rhenium and find bands in the linear-CO region to be the strongest (Table 11). Kavtaradze and Sokolova[104] obtained very weak spectra from CO on alumina-supported osmium but did not illustrate them. Bolivar et al.[118] have studied Re on alumina as part of a study of Pt/Re alloys.

6.8.3 Tungsten

Some very recent results obtained by EELS for CO chemisorbed on W(100) by Ibach et al.[166] and on W(110) and on W(111) by Backx et al.[167] have added substantially to earlier work on tungsten ribbons by Yates, King and colleagues[168a,b] as shown in Table 11.

The chemisorption of CO on tungsten has been studied by a wide range of physical techniques and the results prior to 1970 have been reviewed by Ford.[169] From the spectroscopic point of view the significant points are that CO adsorbs on W both dissociatively (β-state) and associatively (α-state). The α-state is relatively weakly held and forms mainly after coverage by the β-state has been essentially completed. The α-state can also be subdivided into two sub-states, α_1 and α_2 which desorb by different mechanisms. At low temperature a 'virgin' state is formed which transforms to the β-state on warming; it is regarded as a precursor to β and is thought to be molecularly adsorbed.

The reflection-absorption infrared method is limited in the wavenumber range that is accessible so that it is not possible to observe the bands associated with νMO or νMC vibrations which would occur due to dissociative adsorption in the β-state. However, Yates, King and their colleagues[168a,b] have convincingly assigned overlapping bands from CO on a tungsten ribbon at 2128 cm^{-1} to α_1-CO and at 2090 cm^{-1} to α_2-CO. The bands clearly arise from linearly bonded species.

Although the EELS method has substantially less resolution it has much greater sensitivity and has virtually the whole wavenumber region available to it so that it can be used to study both the α- and the β-states. Froitzheim et al.[166] convincingly identified high-coverage bands at 2081 and 363 cm^{-1} as νCO and νCM for the α-state on (100) planes, and low-coverage bands at 629 and 548 cm^{-1} as νMO and νMC, respectively, from the dissociatively adsorbed β-state. Backx et al.[167] identify bands at 1993 cm^{-1} from CO on (111) and (110) planes as arising from CO in the α-state and a 403 cm^{-1} band on (110) planes as arising from the νCM companion band. The increase in νCM coupled with a decrease in νCO is what is expected for a partial transition from an $\overset{-}{M}$—$C{\equiv}\overset{+}{O}$ bonding pattern towards $M{=}C{=}O$. A band at about 565 cm^{-1} from CO on (111) and (110) planes clearly arises from β-CO; because the band half-widths are substantially greater than for CO on (100) planes, 160 cm^{-1} compared with 55 cm^{-1}, this may represent an overlap of two separate bands.

Backx et al.[167] assigned the 1993 and 403 cm^{-1} bands to 'disordered' structures. The former has a half-width of about 250 cm^{-1} and higher resolution might show that there are adjacent, at present unresolved, bands. There is reasonable agreement between the wavenumber of νCO for the α-state on (100) planes[166] and those measured by Yates and King[168a,b] for CO on a tungsten filament.

Turning next to the infrared results obtained from CO on evaporated films, as reported by Hayward[68] and Baker,[64] the principal bands at ca. 2080 and ca. 1975 cm^{-1} agree well with those obtained for the α-state on (100) and (111) or (110) planes, respectively. No studies have been made with oxide-supported W, but Blyholder and Tanaka[170a] have published a single spectrum of CO on W in oil with a rather lower wavenumber band at 1920 cm^{-1} with a substantial shoulder at 1950 cm^{-1}.

6.8.4 Tantalum

A single measurement on an evaporated film of tantalum[68] revealed a linear-CO band at 2096 cm^{-1}.

7   THE ADSORPTION OF CO ON METAL ALLOYS

Certain metal alloys are well known catalysts and hence it is not surprising that a number of binary alloy systems have been studied by CO adsorption and infrared spectroscopy. Alloy systems are obviously more complex than single metals, e.g. in terms of whether the metals remain mixed on the surfaces of the oxide-supporting materials or crystallize separately, and in terms of the extent to which the surfaces of alloy particles have a metallic composition close to that of the bulk.

We do not have space here to discuss the results on alloys in detail, although some of these studies have already been mentioned in Section 4 because of their bearing on the discussion as to whether or not bridged-CO species exist. For convenience we list here the binary alloy systems that have been studied, the two metals concerned being listed in order of their atomic numbers: Fe/Ni;[72] Co/Ni;[72] Ni/Cu;[46–49] Rh/Ir;[160] Pd/Ag;[101] Pd/Ir;[100] Pd/Pt;[46] Ir/Pt.[111]

The effect of Hg on the νCO bands on Ni has been investigated.[73]

8   THE EFFECTS ON νCO ABSORPTIONS OF OTHER CO-ADSORBED GASES

Pre- or post-adsorption of other gases with CO can lead to changes in the frequencies of the νCO bands or alternatively to the disappearance of these bands due to chemical reaction.

The effects of oxygen, in so far as they cause changes in CO band wavenumbers, are recorded in the Tables and discussed below in Section 10. The reaction of CO with O_2 over Pd has led to the 'break-in' phenomenon, discussed earlier[96] (Section 6.2.4), probably caused by reactive heating of the metal particles. The addition of oxygen to CO adsorbed on Fe led to the disappearance of the CO absorption.[149b] Additional bands have been observed, probably caused by oxidation of CO to CO_2 followed by interaction of the latter with the metal surface of Ni[40] and Fe.[149b]

Primet and Sheppard[79] and Martin et al.[81] have shown that co-adsorption of H_2 with CO leads to an upward shift of the linear-CO band from 2040 to 2070 cm^{-1}. Eischens and Pliskin[40] and Heyne and Tompkins[105] showed that addition of H_2 to CO adsorbed on silica-supported Pt leads to a lowering of the CO wavenumber by 20 cm^{-1}. Others have not observed this effect with Pt/Al$_2$O$_3$.[116] However prolonged treatment of Pt/Al$_2$O$_3$ with H_2 at elevated temperatures does lead to substantial shifts to low wavenumber.[108,111] The possibilities of a chemical reaction between CO and H_2 over metals is of interest from the point of view of the Fischer-Tropsch synthesis. Blyholder and Neff[149c] showed that an H_2/CO interaction over Fe at 180 °C led to the production of CH$_4$. Leisegang and colleagues have found[75,80,150] that with Fe, CO and Ni the linear-CO species from chemisorbed CO, not the bridged ones, are involved in the methanation reaction. Dalla Betta and Shelef[115b] showed that the CO/H$_2$ interaction over Ru/Al$_2$O$_3$ at elevated temperatures (>250 °C) led to a lowering of νCO from 2043 to 1998 cm^{-1}. Other products that were formed (formate species, hydrocarbons and water) were shown to be adsorbed on the alumina, but the presence of the metal was not necessary for their formation.

Several systematic studies have been made of the effect of electron-donating and electron-withdrawing co-adsorbates on the νCO frequencies.[51a,51b,52,77,107,113,116,145,146,153,170b,171] The co-adsorbates so far studied include NH$_3$,[51b,171] amines,[51,171] hydrazine,[171] pyridine,[51b] ethyl isocyanide,[51a] sulphur-containing compounds[70a] and H$_2$S,[77] trimethyl phosphite,[171] BF$_3$,[173] and benzene.[51b,113,116] In general the electron-donating molecules (Lewis bases) cause the νCO band frequency to drop and the electron-withdrawing molecules (Lewis acids) cause the νCO frequency to rise. In other words, by donating (or withdrawing) electrons from the metal the $d \rightarrow \pi$ back-donation into the π^*-antibonding orbital of the CO is enhanced (or reduced).[39,51a,51b,52] Thus, for example, for CO adsorbed on Fe, co-adsorption of BF$_3$ leads to a rise in the wavenumber of νCO from 1950 to 1980 cm^{-1},[170b] but co-absorption of trimethylamine causes a drop to 1920 cm^{-1}.[171]

For a series of Lewis bases, the shifts to lower frequencies have been shown to increase with lowered first ionization potential of the base.[51b]

The co-adsorption of benzene leads to a lowering of the linear-CO band on Pt by 40 to 55 cm^{-1}; this has been proposed as evidence for π-donation (and hence π-bonding) of the benzene molecules to the Pt surface.[51b,113,116] Subsequent addition of hydrogen caused the restoration of the CO band wavenumber almost back to its original value when the adsorbed benzene was replaced by σ-bonded cyclohexyl groups.[113,116] Adsorption of CO after olefinic hydrocarbons have been pre-adsorbed has been shown by Pearce and Sheppard[58] and Pearce[138] to remove the more labile chemisorbed hydrocarbon species but to retain others. This has helped substantially in the analysis of the complex spectra from chemisorbed hydrocarbons.[58] An interaction of CO with ethylene pre-adsorbed on an evaporated-iron film was interpreted by Blyholder and Goodsel[172] as leading to the formation of a surface isopropoxide by an insertion mechanism. Competitive chemisorption of CO and ethylene on Ni, Co, Rh and Pt films has also been studied.[156]

The reaction of CO and NO over a series of metals has been shown to give rise to chemisorbed isocyanate species.[114,117,173]

9　TYPES AND METHODS OF PREPARATION OF METAL SAMPLES FOR VIBRATIONAL SPECTROSCOPY

We have seen that different methods of preparation of samples of the same metal can lead to very different spectra. These differences are real, i.e. for the most part they fall well outside any experimental errors associated with the spectroscopic measurements. It is therefore appropriate to consider briefly the different methods of preparation of the metal sample in relation to the different structures of the surfaces produced.

In principle, the simplest situation seems to pertain to the single-crystal or similar studies of polycrystalline bulk metal samples. An essential requirement is the use of ultra-high vacuum (UHV) techniques so that the small surface of metal available can be kept clean once it has been prepared. However, before that, it is necessary to prepare a clean surface, and this may be difficult. A normal way of cleaning a metal surface is to heat the metal to a high temperature so as, for example, to vaporize oxides, etc. from the surface.[168a,b] However, in the process other impurities, such as carbon, in the bulk of the metal can diffuse to the surface. Sometimes repeated treatments are necessary until all the bulk impurities have been removed. Alternatively a new surface may be generated by bombardment with inert gas ions.[120-122] This will leave an irregular metal surface which then needs to be annealed at a high enough temperature to enable the metal atoms to relax to a predominantly single (or multiple) crystal surface. Other UHV techniques such as Auger spectroscopy and LEED can be used to monitor the surface once prepared. The adsorption of gases on these surfaces are studied by EELS or r.a.-i.r. methods, the main problems being the limited sensitivity of the infrared method and the limited resolution of the EELS method.

The next alternative is to use metal films prepared by evaporation onto a substrate surface from a heated filament. The main variables in these experiments are the temperature and nature of the substrate surface, e.g. amorphous, as with glass[61,62,69] or polycrystalline as with alkali halide[51a,64–66,86] or MgO surfaces,[122] and the presence and composition of a gas phase. The infrared transmission of films prepared in this manner is a very sensitive function of the conditions of preparation.[63–66,68] For transmission to be appreciable the thin film must normally consist of 'islands' of metal particles which are not too large in diameter and are separated by 'holes' through which the radiation can pass. If the metal particles are too large, then distortions of the absorption spectra occur in the form of abnormal transmission regions close to the frequencies of the absorption bands.[64,65,138] They are caused by rapid refractive-index changes across the absorption region. Ideally the evaporated films should be prepared in an ultra-high vacuum,[68,86] but sometimes it is not possible by this means to prepare films with adequate transmission properties. Evaporation in an inert gas[67,68,85] sometimes helps to produce deposited films with the right particle sizes, but often measurable spectra can only be obtained by evaporation in the presence of a small pressure of CO itself.[57,68,85,87] Although these spectra are of interest, it is probable in many cases that contact of CO with hot metal particles may have led to decomposition of the gas to give carbon or oxygen impurities on the surface. The results of such experiments must be treated with caution.

The alternative method with evaporated films is to form thick coherent films in ultra-high vacuum[122,128,129] and then to obtain spectra by the methods used for single crystalline or polycrystalline bulk metal samples.

The great majority of published infrared results for CO on metals have been obtained with oxide-supported samples of the general type used in the laboratory and industry, although usually prepared under higher standards of vacuum and chemical purity than are used for working catalysts. However, their relation to the latter make them of particular interest. The fact that infrared spectra can be obtained in the presence of gases, and even from working reaction systems,[9,174] heightens the interest in such work. Usually a metal salt, e.g. nickel nitrate or palladium chloride, is deposited from solution onto the surface of a finely powdered oxide such as silica or alumina. A coherent disc is pressed from the mixture and then the salt is reduced to the metal by hydrogen at an appropriate temperature in situ in a cell with infrared-transparent windows. The disc usually retains a substantial porosity so that the metal of a reduced catalyst can be in ready equilibrium with species in the gas phase. The disc may be held in place in the infrared beam in a metal or glass holder that can be heated to 400 or 500 °C.[3] Alternatively, particularly if higher reduction temperatures are necessary, the disc may be transported to a separate furnace part of the cell for carrying out the reduction process. For this purpose it is usually attached to a glass or silica framework that can be lifted from the outside with the help of an incorporated magnet.[3,7] The latter type of cell is more flexible as far as temperature treatment of the sample is concerned, but the former type usually enables spectroscopic work to be carried out more readily with the catalyst sample at an elevated temperature, or cooled down to liquid N_2 temperature.

The principal advantage of oxide-supported catalysts is that, up to a substantial temperature, the metal particles formed by reduction of the metal salt are not mobile over the oxide surface so that small particles are retained which give a high total area for the metal sample. Eischens and his colleagues[2,40] did the pioneering work on preparing such infrared transmitting metal samples. The infrared beam, in effect, interacts with many monolayer equivalents of adsorbed molecules on passing through the sample with its opaque metal particles separated by transparent oxide particles.

The obvious experimental variables are the time and temperature associated with the reduction by H_2, and the loading of the oxide with the metal salt. High loadings of salt, and hence of metal after reduction, seem usually to be associated with the production of larger metal particles, although obviously the initial degree of dispersion of the metal salt makes a difference. Eischens[40,41] has suggested that metal particles of diameter greater than about 300 Å, the electron mean free path, lead to excessive light absorption by the metal.

Many catalysts prepared by the method described above, the so-called impregnated catalysts, have ranges of particle sizes from 30 to 150 Å, with mean values of 75 to 100 Å. Other special methods can be used to prepare samples with smaller mean particle sizes.[36,43,175]

In some cases the attachment of individual metal ions to particular sites on the internal porous framework of crystalline zeolites can lead, it is believed, to single atoms of neutral metal after reduction.[90,91] An increase of temperature of reduction will normally lead to more completely reduced metal particles[36,122,138] and, at sufficiently high temperature, to crystallization and the development of well-defined faces. There is increasing evidence that a higher temperature reduction leads to improved uniformity in both these respects. The degree of crystallinity of the metal particles is probably the significant difference between metal catalysts that are, or are not, 'broken-in'.[96] However, at too high a temperature, mobility of metal atoms across the oxide support becomes possible, leading to lowered surface areas through sintering, and also chemical reaction between the metal and the support may occur.[40]

In some cases an apparently identical reduction procedure can lead to rather different infrared spectra from adsorbed CO, depending on the nature of the oxide support.[40,71,122] Sometimes less obvious effects, such as different degrees of porosity of different discs or the different retention of reduction products by the surface of the support, may play a role in the efficiency of the reduction process. Assuming that reduction to the metal is fully achieved, other effects may result from different degrees of electron transfer across the metal/

support interface (an effect which is most likely to be significant for small metal particles;[91] a net negative charge on a metal particle is expected to lower the frequency of a CO species)[176] or epitaxial effects whereby the oxide support promotes the formations of crystallites or particular planes on crystallite surfaces, as deduced by Pritchard et al. for Cu particles grown on magnesia surfaces.[122]

One of the disadvantages of oxides as metal supports is that these are to a considerable extent ionic in character and hence have very strong infrared absorptions of their own. Thus in the mid-infrared range (4000 to 400 cm^{-1}) silica has little transparency below 1300 cm^{-1}, alumina below 1150 cm^{-1}, and magnesia below 800 cm^{-1}. For work with CO this means that the MCO angle-bending frequencies (≈ 600 cm^{-1}) and the νMC bond-stretching frequencies (≈ 500 cm^{-1}) are not accessible.

Blyholder[149] developed an alternative method whereby the metal is evaporated to give small particles into a thin film of paraffin oil. There can be no doubt that in principle this method does lead to some contamination of the metal surface with carbon or hydrocarbon residues. However, very similar spectra are usually obtained from CO adsorbed on these metal particles as on oxide-supported ones. Probably CO is sufficiently strongly adsorbed to displace the hydrocarbon residues. The advantage of Blyholder's procedure is that the lower frequency region is now readily available and he has convincingly identified a number of νMC frequencies by this means.[106,149,151]

Blyholder has developed an improvement on his oil technique by isolating metal particles in inert gas matrices at very low temperatures.[76,177] This work overlaps with more traditional matrix-isolation techniques whereby CO is made to react with single metal atoms or clusters of a few such atoms.[50,54,55] These techniques, as we have seen in Section 4, have also given very valuable results.

For most work on CO with supported metal samples, standard infrared techniques are suitable. This is because the CO bands are relatively intense. However in cases where the pressed discs scatter or absorb too much radiation, the increased sensitivity of Fourier-transform interferometric infrared techniques can be of great assistance.[178] The use of a computer coupled to the spectrometer also can be of great value in ratioing out complex backgrounds, as from the oxide support, and improving signal/noise ratios by spectrum accumulation.[58,138] For reflection-absorption studies, when the CO absorption bands are typically about 1 % or less in absorption strength, the use of low-temperature photoconductive detectors of high sensitivity—possibly coupled with wavelength modulation—can lead to much improved spectra.[122]

10   CONCLUSIONS

The writing of this review article has had three aims. The first was archival in nature in that we have attempted to collect together references and data from all known papers involving the vibrational bands of CO on metal surfaces. The literature is already very large, reflecting the great practical importance of knowledge about metal catalysts. It is hence important that newcomers to the field are enabled to compare their results with those of earlier workers. The major tables and the lists of references embody this aim.

The second aim was to look across the field in a panoramic manner to discern regularities and trends in hopes of working out a consistent scheme of spectral interpretation. When one collects the data from the literature, this task alone seems to be a very daunting one. This is because only a few transition metals have been studied in great detail (copper, nickel, palladium and platinum), a few have been studied in moderate detail (rhodium, iron and tungsten), and many others have been studied by only a few laboratories or not at all. If most laboratories obtained the same results with the same metal the present literature might have proved to be adequate. However, in fact spectra obtained in different laboratories for CO adsorbed on the same metal can show bewildering differences. These spectral differences are real and reflect the different detailed topographical forms and degrees of cleanliness presented by the metal surfaces to gaseous CO.

Relevant experimental differences are whether the sample investigated is in the form of a single metal crystal, of an evaporated metal film, or of supported-metal particles (Section 9). In the latter two cases differing degrees of crystallinity and sizes of the metal particles can clearly affect the observed spectra; in addition, epitaxial or electronic effects of the supporting substrate can be of importance; and finally the degree of reduction (or of re-oxidation) of metal particles can also have major influences on the spectra observed. The interplay of all these effects can be seen in particular examples. Hence even a panoramic view can only be achieved by the exercise of judgement by the reviewers in paying more attention to one set of spectra than to another. This must be borne in mind in reading this conclusion section.

We have earlier given reasons for preferring the linear/bridged interpretation scheme of Eischens over the all-linear scheme of Blyholder (Section 4), although we have retained features of the latter scheme in adopting the former. This choice, too, is a matter of judgement; we believe that it is a sound one.

The third and final aim was to see to what extent the recently achieved results on particular crystallographic faces of metal single crystals can be used to interpret the spectra from supported metal particles, i.e. to see to what extent the CO spectra can provide reliable information about the surface structures of working catalysts. This aim will certainly be more readily achievable later, when more single crystal results have been published, but an interim aim is to point to the future importance of such work.

10.1　A Panoramic View

10.1.1　Oxidation or incomplete reduction of supported metal particles

In our scheme of interpretation proposed in Section 5 we suggested that the region 2200 to 2130 cm^{-1} might be characteristic of CO adsorbed on positively charged metal sites in salts or oxides. The lower limit of this range coincides closely with the wavenumber of gaseous CO (2143 cm^{-1}). Electron withdrawal by the M^{n+} species can be expected to contribute to a CO bonding pattern that is closer to that of a pure triple bond, $\overset{-}{C}\equiv\overset{+}{O}$, with a positively charged oxygen atom. Smaller high frequency shifts also result from coupling of the CO bond-stretching vibration to the much lower frequency νM—C vibration.

The collected results taken from the tables confirm our suggested range, the wavenumbers/cm^{-1} in question being as follows:

Cu, 2215;	Ni, 2195;	Co, 2180;	Fe, 2169;	Ti, 2165
Ag, 2180;	Pd, (2135);	Rh, (2150, 2180);	Ru, 2140	
Au, 2175;	Pt, 2180			

Although clear-cut patterns of wavenumber are not discernible, it has to be remembered that the metals can have different oxidation states. Pearce[138] has attributed the 2215 cm^{-1} absorption to CO adsorption on CuO; Voroshilov et al.[155] have observed a band at 2180 cm^{-1} for adsorption of CO on Fe_2O_3; and Eischens[40] has observed a band at 2195 cm^{-1} from CO on NiO.

Based on the appearance or otherwise of these absorption bands, the spectroscopic studies show that Co, Fe and Ru are metals that are particularly difficult to reduce, and that Cu, Ag, and Au require particular care to achieve full reduction of supported samples. The appearance of any of the above absorption bands in a spectrum implies that the sample is very poorly reduced. Although the bands are rarely strong they tend to be sharp and readily discernible.

In a number of cases other abnormally high frequency linear-CO bands have been observed when reduction has been substantial but incomplete, or limited re-oxidation has been deliberately brought about or, sometimes, as in the case of Pd, the metal particles simply are thought to be very small. Absorptions which seem to fit this pattern have been observed at the following wavenumbers/cm^{-1}:

Cu, 2130;	Ni, 2080;	Co, 2090	
Ag, —;	Pd, (2090);	Rh, 2095;	Ru, 2080
Au, 2135;	Pt, 2120;	Ir, 2070;	Os, 2080

A characteristic of these absorptions is that they are normally 20 to 50 cm^{-1} higher than the principal linear-CO absorption band observed for highly reduced metal samples. They have been variously explained as possibly indicating (i) non-crystalline regions of surface,[70b,89-91] (ii) sites of multiple-CO adsorption[36,43,46,57,71,145] or (iii) sites adjacent to oxygen atoms either on the metal surface itself or on the adjacent surfaces of the oxide support.[36,91,122,138] Blyholder's model predicts that isolated metal atoms, such as those on corners or edges of crystallites, should give the *lowest* and not the highest wavenumbers for single CO adsorption, and it is probably this consideration that has led others to prefer the assignment of these bands to $M(CO)_2$ species, etc.[43] Our preference is for explanation (iii).[36] If $M(CO)_2$ species occur, the most likely metal is rhodium[159] because a high *and* low wavenumber linear-CO band is given by CO on small metal particles. The absorption at 2090 cm^{-1} from CO on Pd appears to occur both for small Pd particles and also (weakly) for large crystallites (Table 4). It would be particularly interesting to see whether such absorptions consistently dominate spectra from 'atomically dispersed' metals on zeolites such as those already studied for Pd.[91]

It is, of course, possible that abnormally high-wavenumber bridge-CO bands will occur from the same cause. However, the highest contender is the bridge-CO band of CO on Pd near 1985 cm^{-1}, but this has been obtained on catalyst samples which appear to have been well reduced.[97,98]

10.1.2 Well-reduced samples of oxide-supported metals

Having conceptually separated off the above absorptions from the remainder, we now wish to see to what extent the latter can be interpreted in terms of linear and bridged species. We note that, on the whole, spectra obtained by transmission or reflection from evaporated metal films are more variable than those from supported metal particles (although for a given metal there is usually a statistical 'family resemblance' between the two types of spectra). Hence, in attempting a panoramic view we shall concentrate on results obtained with supported metal particles. Perhaps the temperature of condensation and subsequent sintering processes play important parts in determining the nature of the surfaces of evaporated metal films. It is also not improbable that, when recourse has to be made to evaporating from a very hot metal filament in the presence of CO in order to obtain acceptable spectra, dissociative adsorption—leading to contamination of the metal surface with C or O—occurs for metals which at room temperature would only be expected to give associative adsorption. Such 'contamination' effects can also occur at ambient temperatures, and so affect the CO spectra, for metals such as Fe,[148] Mo and W.[169]

In Fig. 10 we attempt a panoramic overview of results on oxide-supported metals. In order to reduce the variables that affect the spectral comparison, the spectra chosen have been selected as representing (i) well-reduced metals, (ii) where choice is possible, larger particle sizes, and (iii) conditions of high-CO coverage. Spectra from Ni, Pd, Pt and the higher-frequency band of CO on Cu can reasonably be regarded as 'typical' in relation to a large number of published results. For Ag, Au, Fe, Rh and Ir the spectra shown have been selected by us as the 'best' available, usually by the criterion that they are free of the 'oxidation' bands discussed above. The situation is much less certain for other metals as both few and also variable spectral results have been reported for them.

In several cases, e.g. Rh, Ru and Re, the proportion of linear-CO to bridge-CO absorptions vary widely between different investigations (Tables 10 and 11). Even platinum and iridium, which normally show only very weak bridge-CO

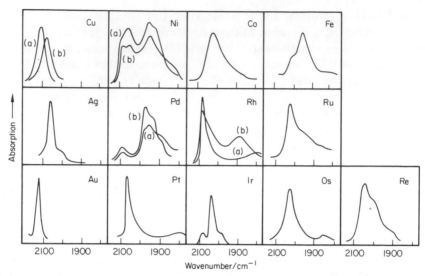

Fig. 10. Some typical infrared spectra from CO chemisorbed *at high coverage* on metals supported on silica unless otherwise stated. Cu, (a) silica support; (b) magnesia support (after Pritchard, Catterick and Gupta, Ref. 122); Ag (after Pearce, Ref. 138); Au (after Yates, Ref. 144); Ni, (a) metal particle size 95 Å, reduced at 900 °C, (b) metal particle size 63 Å, reduced at 650 °C (after Primet, Dalmon and Martin, Ref. 36); Pd, (a) prior to break-in; (b) after break-in (after Baddour, Modell and Goldsmith, Ref. 96); Pt, (after Eischens, Pliskin and Francis, Ref. 2); Co, *low coverage spectrum* (after Heal, Ref. 150); Rh, (a) sample reduced at 700 °C; (b) sample reduced at 350 °C (after Pearce, Ref. 138); Ir (after Guerra and Schulman, Ref. 145); Fe (after Eischens and Pliskin, Ref. 40); Ru (after Brown and Gonzalez, Ref. 163); Os (after Guerra and Schulman, Ref. 145); Re (after Guerra and Schulman, Ref. 145).

absorptions, have given a few spectra with strong bridge-CO bands observed from samples of evaporated metal films.[86]

Let us next reconsider the question of whether the absorption bands from CO on Fe near 1970 cm^{-1} ought to be assigned to linear or bridged species. We take what is probably the minority view—that these bands arise from bridged species—on the following grounds:

(a) The mean values for νCO band wavenumbers for the all-linear (in the CO sense) metal carbonyls are as follows:[176] $Ni(CO)_4$, 2066; $CoH(CO)_4$, 2067; $Fe(CO)_5$, 2045 (1993); $Mn_2(CO)_{10}$, 2013 (infrared data); $Cr(CO)_6$, 2013 cm^{-1}. There is, to be sure, again the ambiguity for $Fe(CO)_5$ in that one band has been postulated to change substantially in wavenumber from the gas to the liquid state. This is the reason for the alternative value of 1993 cm^{-1}. With $Fe_3(CO)_{12}$ the infrared bands from linear-CO groups are at 2043, 2020, 1997 cm^{-1}; again suggesting that just less than 2000 cm^{-1} is the lowest wavenumber for a linear-CO group, even with inter-CO coupling.

(b) That in addition to the strongest absorption near 1970 cm^{-1}, weaker bands are found in the region above 2000 cm^{-1} for assignment to linear species.

(c) The *ca.* 1970 cm^{-1} bands are very broad ($\Delta \tilde{v}_{\frac{1}{2}}$; $60\text{–}70 \text{ cm}^{-1}$) and this contrasts with the general sharpness of bands in the linear-CO region, even for Fe itself.[80,150] Except when they split into clear-cut sub-bands, as with Pd, the bridge-CO absorption bands are usually broad.

We, therefore, retain our interpretation scheme which says that bands between 2130 and 2000 cm^{-1} are to be assigned to linear species. Within that scheme the wavenumbers of the strongest absorption bands in the linear-CO region observed on the different metals at high coverage may be summarized as follows ($\tilde{v}/\text{cm}^{-1}$):

Cu, 2105 (0);	Ag, 2060 (0);	Au, 2110 (0)
Ni, 2055 (2);	Pd, 2085 (0);	Pt, 2080 (1)
Co, 2030 (3);	Rh, 2060 (2);	Ir, 2030 (3)
Fe, 2030 (4);	Ru, 2030 (3);	Os, (2025) (4)
Mn, (2000) (5);		Re, (2035) (5)
Cr, — (5);	Mo, — (5);	W, 2100 (6)
V,		Ta, (2096) (7)
Ti, (2060) (8);		

Uncertain or poorly characterized values are given in brackets. Our wavenumbers differ in detail from those collected together by Guerra[146] in that we have not always used the values reported by Guerra and Schulman,[145] and we have added data for W, Ti and Ta.

Guerra[145,146] has suggested that there is a correlation between the CO force constants (derived from the frequencies) and the number of d-band holes in the electronic structure of the metal atoms. The latter are listed in brackets behind the wavenumbers. It is seen that for the first 4 elements in each period the correlation is rather successful, particularly in accounting for the variations in wavenumbers in the Ni, Pd, Pt and Co, Rh, Ir sequence. Although the correlation fails for Ti, W and Ta, it is at the left-hand end of the periods that dissociative (β) adsorption of CO occurs, so that the electronic structures of the metal atoms may be different for the associative (α) adsorption of linear species.

Blyholder and Allen[74] gave qualitative arguments, backed up by molecular orbital calculations, for linear M·CO wavenumbers decreasing on going from Cu to V in the first transition series. A factor of relevance was that the d-orbitals are more strongly contracted for elements of higher atomic number in the same period; considerations of just the *number* of d-electrons available for back-bonding might have led to a predicted decrease of vCO with increasing atomic number of the metal.[146] Although we do not accept Blyholder's series of frequencies[74] as all belonging to linear species, the trend observed above for the linear species within each period for Cu to Fe, Ag to Ru and Au to Os are in agreement with Blyholder's qualitative predictions.

Kavtaradze and Sokolova[110] have also surveyed the infrared spectra from CO on metals. They have concluded that $M(CO)_2$ surface species are unlikely, and that 2.85 Å may be the upper-limit of the metal–metal internuclear distance for the formation of bridged COs. Although this does not contradict their assertion, the fact that Pt gives nearly all linear species and Pd nearly all bridged ones, although the two metals have virtually identical internuclear distances (Table 1), shows that the latter parameter is not the only significant one in determining the *degree* to which bridged species are predominant.

In the above classification of the linear-CO band wavenumbers we have over-simplified matters by choosing only the strongest absorptions and ignoring the effect of different crystal planes on the linear-CO values. We have made no attempt to make a similarly straightforward list of typical bridge-CO band wavenumbers because, as has been seen earlier, e.g. for Ni and Pd, the positions of the absorption bands are very sensitive functions of the type of crystal plane and of the coverage.

As indicated earlier, we still regard the frequency boundary between 2-fold bridged and 3- or 4-fold bridged species to be rather ill-defined, partly because of coverage-dependent frequencies. However, the single crystal work on Ni and Pd does support the suggestion that B_3 and B_4 sites are expected to give lower vCO frequencies than B_2 sites *at the same degree of coverage*. The work on Cu(110) (Section 6.4) does, however, raise the *possibility* that B_5 sites on such planes give absorption bands at much higher frequencies, in the linear-CO region. Further investigation would be very valuable for CO on (110) planes of other metals. B_5 sites were originally suggested by van Hardeveld and van Montfoort[175] as the sites for adsorption of adsorbed N_2 molecules that give infrared absorption bands. There are many analogies between linear-CO and -N_2 interactions with transition metals,[50] and the N_2 band wavenumbers are sufficiently close to those of the gas-phase molecule to warrant a description of the adsorbed species as 'linearly' adsorbed to one metal atom. CO and N_2 are, of course, isoelectronic.

10.2 Comparisons between vCO Absorption Bands on Single Crystal Surfaces and on Oxide Supported Metal Particles

Finally we turn to survey the extent to which we have been able to apply the results recently obtained for CO on single crystal surfaces to interpret the infrared spectra from supported metal particles. This experimental enterprise was pioneered by Pritchard et al. for Cu.[122] Comparisons are most likely to be successful when the supported metal particles are large and have been reduced or prepared at relatively high temperatures so as to give well defined crystal faces.

In Fig. 11 we have collected together results from typical supported metal samples, sometimes for both high- and low-surface coverages with CO, for Ni, Pd, Pt and Cu. Over each spectrum there is a schematic representation of the single crystal results. There is a good general resemblance between the frequencies and band intensities obtained on single crystals and on particles of the same metal, even although at this stage the numbers of single-crystal planes that have been explored is rather limited. Thus the single crystal work on Ni has sometimes given intense linear-CO and sometimes intense bridge-CO bands;[23,60] on single crystals of Pd the bridge-CO bands have so far been dominant;[18] with Pt the linear-CO bands are dominant except at the highest coverages;[19,22] and for Cu the bands are predominantly of the linear-CO type.[122] These patterns follow closely those of spectra observed with the same metals in supported form, even although they change very substantially from one metal to the next. This finding is encouraging.

For Cu we accept Pritchard's conclusions,[122] namely that it is only on MgO as the support that the metal particles have predominantly low-index planes, probably (100) for reasons of epitaxy. The next most interesting example is Pd because of the substantial variation in spectra from the supported catalysts before and after 'break-in'.[96] The changes in spectra with coverage for the 'broken-in' samples are as expected from Bradshaw and Hoffmann's single-crystal results[18] which show that on (100), (111) and (210) planes bridge-CO bands occur which shift markedly to high wavenumber with increasing coverage. As concluded in Section 6.2, high coverage spectra strongly suggest that for the supported metals the *ca.* 1985 cm^{-1} and *ca.* 1960 cm^{-1} absorption bands are to be assigned to CO at (100) and (111) planes, probably with adsorption on B$_2$ sites. The (210) plane is an alternative, but intrinsically less probable, assignment for the 1985 cm^{-1} band. At high coverage the (111) plane also contributes to the weak linear-CO absorption near 2085 cm^{-1}. If these interpretations are correct we see that 'break-in' consists of a relative growth of both (100) and (111) planes, with the former increasing with respect to the latter. The extra absorption bands in the lower wavenumber range (1900 to 1800 cm^{-1}), which occur even for high coverage for the samples that have not been 'broken-in', suggests that these catalysts may also contain (100) and (111) crystal faces of rather low total diameter (Section 6.2). In such cases the maximum shift to high wavenumber with increasing coverage is limited in extent. Our assignments are indicated in Fig. 11.

For Ni the interpretation of the spectra is more difficult. The absorption band in the 1900 to 1800 cm^{-1} region can again reasonably be accounted for in terms of (111) planes of different sizes. In the spectrum obtained by high-temperature reduction, where the crystallite faces are likely to be large and well formed, the tail below 1900 cm^{-1} is substantially reduced in area and a maximum at *ca.* 1910 cm^{-1} corresponds closely to the upper limit of the bands on the (111) plane at full coverage.[60] The (100) plane seems likely to contribute to the *ca.* 2070 cm^{-1} absorption in the linear-CO region at high coverage and possibly to the 1935 cm^{-1} absorption at low coverage.[23] On the (100) single crystal plane the former band grows at the expense of the latter with increasing coverage. It remains to be seen whether (110) faces of Ni account for the lower-wavenumber

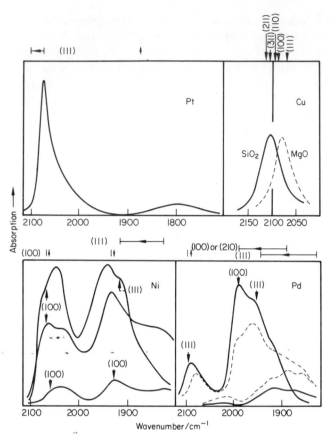

Fig. 11. Infrared spectra from oxide-supported metal particles (Pt,[2] Cu,[122] Ni,[36] Pd[96] compared with literature data from single crystal studies (Pt,[19,22] Cu,[122] Ni,[23,60] Pd[18]). The single-crystal results are summarized schematically at the top of each spectrum. For these, a horizontal arrow denotes a band which shifts and increases in intensity with increasing coverage; a vertical arrow next to a vertical line denotes an essentially stationary band which increases (↑) or decreases (↓) in relative intensity with increasing coverage; a vertical broken line denotes a relatively weak band.

For Pt: there is uncertainty whether the metal particles exhibit (111) faces because, at high coverage, under which conditions the spectrum on the supported Pt sample has been obtained,[2] both the linear-CO[19,22] and bridge-CO bands[22] on (111) faces fall at somewhat higher wavenumbers.

For Cu: (Pritchard et al., Refs. 122–124). The spectra of CO on Cu/SiO$_2$ indicate absorption on high-index planes, but those from CO on Cu/MgO indicate absorption on low-index planes, probably (100) through epitaxy.

For Ni: the upper spectrum denotes high-coverage adsorption on crystals of 90 Å diameter. These had been reduced at 900 °C. The lower spectra are from high- and low-coverage adsorption on 63 Å particles reduced at 650 °C (Primet, Dalmon and Martin, Ref. 36). Only partial assignments, as indicated, are possible by comparison with the single-crystal results (see the discussion in the text).

For Pd: spectra from high and low coverage on 'broken-in' (solid lines) and non-linear-CO absorption and whether these faces contribute also to absorption in the bridge-CO region, perhaps in the 1930 to 1940 cm^{-1} region.

Finally, for Pt the *low coverage* results on (111) planes[19,22] agree well with the observation of an intense linear-CO band near 2070 cm^{-1} but the high coverage shift to *ca.* 2100 cm^{-1}[22,102] does not seem to occur with fully reduced supported-Pt catalysts. Also the high coverage (111) EELS results[22] show a bridge-CO band at *ca.* 1870 cm^{-1} whereas the bridge-CO band normally observed from the supported catalysts is weaker and is centred between 1800 and 1820 cm^{-1}. It is possible that the supported Pt catalysts exhibit mainly (100) rather than (111) faces or, alternatively, as with Cu, that higher-index planes are involved. In comparing the EELS and infrared results it must be remembered that there is substantially lower resolution available with EELS. This means that the peak height of the linear-CO band, which is very sharp in the infrared spectra, is much reduced in the EELS spectrum relative to that of the naturally broad bridge-CO band. However, the relative areas should remain comparable in the two spectra. More single-crystal faces need to be explored if we are to be able to answer these questions. Single-crystal work on (110) planes would be particularly valuable for Ni, Pd and Pt. However, the prospects for the future are very promising.

One of the outstanding problems for the bonding of CO on metals is why, for example, from the infrared evidence, CO adsorbed on Pt mostly occurs in the linear form, CO on Pd mostly occurs in the bridge form, and CO on Ni occurs strongly in both forms. These were the conclusions of the earliest study by Eischens *et al.*[2] of CO adsorbed on finely divided metal catalysts. As we have seen, the more recent single-crystal results indicate a similar pattern of results on the low-index planes of these metals. This implies that an explanation for these differences is not to be found in terms of similar species on different metals being present on the same type of crystal plane from but with the different metals adopting different predominant planes on the particles. For example, whereas on the Ni (111)[60] and Pd (111)[18] planes bridge sites, probably of the B$_3$ type, predominate for CO adsorption, on the Pt (111) planes linear sites predominate with bridged species only occurring in less abundance at high coverage.

Equally it is not necessarily true, as might have been envisaged, that one crystal plane gives one type of adsorbed species, and another gives a different one. Often linear and bridged species occur on the same crystal plane but in proportions that vary with coverage. The phenomena are complex and explanations for these differences must be sought in terms of differences in chemical bonding, allied to topology, between individual metals and CO.

'broken-in' (dashed lines) silica-supported samples are illustrated (Baddour, Modell and Goldsmith, Ref. 96); a very satisfactory assignment is proposed on the basis of the single-crystal results (Bradshaw and Hoffmann, Ref. 18). As with Ni, a reduction of a low-wavenumber 'tail' of absorption, below 1900 cm^{-1}, seems to be associated with a growth of size of (111) faces on the metal particles of the 'broken-in' sample.

We finish by pointing out that the many possibilities of different metal sites and different species resulting from CO adsorption means that vibrational spectroscopy by itself cannot hope to give complete information about any system. Other techniques such as surface potential measurements, other electron spectroscopies, low-energy electron diffraction (LEED), etc. provide important information, particularly for adsorption on single crystal planes of metals. It is inappropriate to review the results from these other techniques here. However, we may note that the assignments we have made of structures to surface species based on the single crystal studies either follow those of the original authors, who have taken the above types of information into account, or choose amongst the alternatives offered against the background of such evidence.[60] Sometimes the LEED evidence, in particular, provides reliable information about the pattern and spacing of adsorbed molecules on the surface but still leaves open the precise site to be chosen. In some ways LEED amongst the diffraction methods, and vibrational spectroscopy amongst the spectroscopic methods, are particularly complementary.

Finally, the infrared method in particular seems best suited to connect single crystal and small particle studies so that the former rather 'academic' studies can begin to throw light on the structures and behaviours of working metal catalysts.

REFERENCES

(1) A. N. Terenin, *Zh. Fiz. Khim.* **14**, 1362 (1940).
(2) R. P. Eischens, W. A. Pliskin and S. A. Francis, *J. Chem. Phys.* **22**, 1786 (1954).
(3) L. H. Little, *Infrared Spectra of Adsorbed Species*, Academic Press, London, 1966.
(4) M. L. Hair, *Infrared Spectroscopy in Surface Chemistry*, Dekker, New York, 1967.
(5) A. V. Kiselev and V. I. Lygin, *Infrared Spectra of Surface Compounds*, John Wiley, New York, 1975 (Russian Edition, 1972).
(6) C. H. Rochester and M. S. Scurrell, in *Surface and Defect Properties of Solids*, Vol. 2 (M. W. Roberts and J. M. Thomas, eds.), Specialist Periodical Reports, Chemical Society, London, 1973, p. 114.
(7) L. H. Little, in *'Chemisorption and Reactions on Metallic Films'*, Vol. I (J. R. Anderson, ed.), Academic Press, London, 1971, p. 489.
(8) J. Pritchard, in *Surface and Defect Properties of Solids*, Vol. 1 (M. W. Roberts and J. M. Thomas, eds.), Specialist Periodical Reports, Chemical Society, London, 1972, p. 222.
(9) A. L. Dent and R. J. Kokes, *J. Am. Chem. Soc.* **92**, 6709 (1970).
(10) Y. A. Kozirovski and M. Folman, *J. Chem. Phys.* **41**, 1509 (1964).
(11) T. A. Egerton and A. H. Hardin, *Catal. Rev.* **11**, 71 (1975).
(12) R. P. Cooney, G. Curthoys and T. T. Nguyen, *Adv. Catal.* **24**, 293 (1975).
(13) T. T. Nguyen and N. Sheppard, unpublished work.
(14) R. P. Cooney, M. Fleischmann, and P. J. Hendra, *Chem. Commun.* 235 (1977).
(15) M. A. Chesters, J. Pritchard and M. L. Sims, *Chem. Commun.* 1454 (1970).
(16) S. A. Francis and A. H. Ellison, *J. Opt. Soc. Am.* **49**, 131 (1959).
(17) R. G. Greenler, *J. Chem. Phys.* **44**, 310 (1966); **50**, 1963 (1969).

(18) (a) A. M. Bradshaw and F. Hoffmann, *Surface Science* **72**, 513 (1978);
(b) F. M. Hoffmann and A. M. Bradshaw, Proc. 7th Int. Vac. Congress and 3rd Int. Conf. Solid Surfaces, Vienna, 1977.

(19) K. Horn and J. Pritchard, *J. Phys. (Paris)* **38**, C4-1 (1977).

(20) F. M. Propst and T. C. Piper, *J. Vac. Sci. Technol.* **4**, 53 (1967).

(21) H. Froitzheim, H. Ibach and S. Lehwald, *Phys. Rev.* **B14**, 1362 (1976).

(22) H. Froitzheim, H. Hopster, H. Ibach and S. Lehwald, *Appl. Phys.* **13**, 47 (1977).

(23) S. Andersson, *Solid State Commun.* **21**, 75 (1977).

(24) J. R. Anderson, *Structure of Metallic Catalysts*, Academic Press, London, 1975.

(25) G. C. Bond, *Catalysis by Metals*, Academic Press, London, 1962; Appendix I.

(26) R. van Hardeveld and F. Hartog, *Surface Science* **15**, 189 (1969).

(27) J. T. Nicholas, *An Atlas of Models of Crystal Surfaces*, Gordon and Breach, New York, 1965.

(28) P. Chini, G. Longoni and V. G. Albano, *Adv. Organomet. Chem.* **14**, 285 (1976).

(29) G. Doyen and G. Ertl, *Surf. Sci.* **43**, 197 (1974).

(30) G. Blyholder, *J. Phys. Chem.* **79**, 756 (1975).

(31) P. Politzer and S. D. Kasten, *J. Phys. Chem.* **80**, 385 (1976).

(32) R. Mason and M. Textor, in *Surface and Defect Properties of Solids*, Vol. 5 (M. W. Roberts and J. M. Thomas, eds.), Specialist Periodical Reports, Chemical Society, London, 1976, p. 189.

(33) J. Pritchard, personal communication.

(34) E. W. Müller and T. T. Tsong, *Prog. Surf. Sci.* **4**, 1 (1974).

(35) B. Lang, R. W. Joyner and G. A. Somorjai, *Surf. Sci.* **30**, 454 (1972).

(36) M. Primet, J. A. Dalmon and G. A. Martin, *J. Catal.* **46**, 25 (1977).

(37) R. M. Hammaker, S. A. Francis and R. P. Eischens, *Spectrochim. Acta* **21**, 1295 (1965).

(38) R. van Hardeveld and A. van Montfoort, *Surf. Sci.* **17**, 90 (1969).

(39) G. Blyholder, *J. Phys. Chem.* **68**, 2772 (1964).

(40) R. P. Eischens and W. A. Pliskin, *Adv. Catal.* **10**, 1 (1958).

(41) R. P. Eischens, S. A. Francis and W. A. Pliskin, *J. Phys. Chem.* **60**, 194 (1956).

(42) G. Blyholder, in *Proc. 3rd Int. Congress Catalysis, Amsterdam, 1964* (W. M. H. Sachtler, G. C. A. Schuit and P. Z. Zwietering, eds.), North-Holland, Amsterdam, 1965, p. 64.

(43) R. van Hardeveld and F. Hartog, *Adv. Catal.* **22**, 75 (1972); Proc. 4th Inter. Congress of Catalysis (Moscow).

(44) Y. Soma-Noto and W. M. H. Sachtler, *J. Catal.* **32**, 315 (1974).

(45) M. Primet, M. V. Mathieu and W. M. H. Sachtler, *J. Catal.* **44**, 324 (1976).

(46) R. P. Eischens, *Z. Elektrochem.* **60**, 782 (1956).

(47) Y. Soma-Noto and W. M. H. Sachtler, *J. Catal.* **34**, 162 (1974).

(48) J. A. Dalmon, M. Primet, G. A. Martin and B. Imelik, *Surf. Sci.* **50**, 95 (1975).

(49) H. Hobert, *Z. Chem.* **6**, 73 (1966).

(50) M. Moskovits and G. A. Ozin, in *Vibrational Spectra and Structure* (J. R. Durig, ed.), Vol. 4, Elsevier, Amsterdam, 1975, p. 187.

(51) (a) R. Queau and R. Poilblanc, *J. Catal.* **27**, 200 (1972); (b) M. Primet, J. M. Bassett, M. V. Mathieu and M. Prettre, *J. Catal.* **29**, 213 (1973).

(52) G. Blyholder and R. W. Sheets, *J. Catal.* **27**, 301 (1972).

(53) L. E. Sutton, ed., Chemical Society, London, 1958 and 1965. *Tables of Interatomic Distances and Configurations in Molecules and Ions*.

(54) M. Moskovits and J. E. Hulse, *Surf. Sci.* **61**, 302 (1976); *J. Phys. Chem.* **81**, 2004 (1977).

(55) J. E. Hulse and M. Moskovits, *Surf. Sci.* **57**, 125 (1976).

(56) E. R. Corey, L. F. Dahl and W. Beck, *J. Am. Chem. Soc.* **85**, 1202 (1963).

(57) C. W. Garland, R. C. Lord and P. F. Triano, *J. Phys. Chem.* **69**, 1188 (1965).

(58) H. A. Pearce and N. Sheppard, *Surf. Sci.* **59**, 205 (1976).
(59) S. Andersson, *Solid State Commun.* **24**, 183 (1977).
(60) J. C. Bertolini, G. Dalmai-Imelik and J. Rousseau, *Surf. Sci.* **68**, 539 (1977).
(61) H. L. Pickering and H. C. Eckstrom, *J. Phys. Chem.* **63**, 512 (1959).
(62) R. A. Gardner and R. H. Petrucci, *J. Am. Chem. Soc.* **82**, 5051 (1960).
(63) C. W. Garland, R. C. Lord and P. F. Triano, *J. Phys. Chem.* **69**, 1195 (1965).
(64) F. S. Baker, A. M. Bradshaw, J. Pritchard and K. W. Sykes, *Surf. Sci.* **12**, 426 (1968).
(65) A. M. Bradshaw and J. Pritchard, *Surf. Sci.* **17**, 372 (1969).
(66) A. M. Bradshaw and J. Pritchard, *Proc. R. Soc.* **A316**, 169 (1970).
(67) H. C. Eckstrom, G. G. Possley, S. E. Hannum and W. H. Smith, *J. Chem. Phys.* **52**, 5435 (1970).
(68) D. O. Hayward (1963) and J. C. McManus (1966), cited by D. O. Hayward, in *Chemisorption and Reactions on Metallic Films*, Vol. I (J. R. Anderson, ed.), Academic Press, London, 1971, p. 225.
(69) E. F. McCoy and R. St. C. Smart, *Surf. Sci.* **39**, 109 (1973).
(70) (a) C. W. Garland, *J. Phys. Chem.* **63**, 1423 (1959); (b) J. T. Yates and C. W. Garland, *J. Phys. Chem.* **65**, 617 (1961).
(71) E. C. O'Neill and D. J. C. Yates, *J. Phys. Chem.* **65**, 901 (1961).
(72) J. S. Cho and J. H. Schulman, *Surf. Sci.* **2**, 245 (1964).
(73) H. Hobert and J. Thieme, *Z. Chem.* **10**, 346 (1968).
(74) G. Blyholder and M. C. Allen, *J. Am. Chem. Soc.* **91**, 3158 (1969).
(75) L. G. Ferreira and E. C. Leisegang, *J. S. Afr. Chem. Inst.* **23**, 136 (1970).
(76) G. Blyholder and M. Tanaka, *J. Colloid Interface Sci.* **37**, 753 (1971).
(77) G. Marx, H. Hobert, V. Hopfe, B. Knappe, W. Vogelsberger, P. Mackrodt and K. Meyer, *Z. Chem.* **12**, 444 (1972).
(78) (a) J. Ansorge, M. Primet, J. A. Dalmon and G. A. Martin, *C.R. Acad. Sci. Ser. C* **281**, 607 (1975); (b) W. L. van Dijk, J. A. Groenewegen and V. Ponec, *J. Catal.* **45**, 277 (1976).
(79) M. Primet and N. Sheppard, *J. Catal.* **41**, 258 (1976).
(80) M. J. Heal, E. C. Leisegang and R. G. Torrington, *J. Catal.* **42**, 10 (1976).
(81) G. A. Martin, M. Primet and J. A. Dalmon, *J. Catal.*, in press.
(82) A. M. Bradshaw and F. Hoffmann, *Surf. Sci.* **52**, 449 (1975).
(83) F. Hoffmann and A. M. Bradshaw, *J. Catal.* **44**, 328 (1976).
(84) A. Crossley and D. A. King, *Surf. Sci.* **68**, 528 (1977).
(85) C. P. Nash and R. P. de Sieno, *J. Phys. Chem.* **69**, 2139 (1965).
(86) J. F. Harrod, R. W. Roberts and E. F. Rissman, *J. Phys. Chem.* **71**, 343 (1967).
(87) J. N. Bradley and A. S. French, *Proc. R. Soc.* **A313**, 169 (1969).
(88) R. W. Rice and G. L. Haller, *J. Catal.* **40**, 249 (1974).
(89) J. K. A. Clarke, G. Farren and H. E. Rubalcava, *J. Phys. Chem.* **71**, 2376 (1967).
(90) C. Naccache, M. Primet and J. P. Mathieu, *Adv. Chem. Ser.* **121**, 266 (1973).
(91) F. Figueras, R. Gomez and M. Primet, *Adv. Chem. Ser.* **121**, 480 (1973).
(92) N. N. Kavtaradze, E. G. Boreskova and V. J. Lygin, *Kinet. Katal.* **2**, 349 (1961). [Russian, p. 378.]
(93) N. N. Kavtaradze, N. P. Sokolova, V. M. Lukyanovich and E. I. Erko, *Kinet. Katal.* **5**, 968 (1964). [Russian, p. 1095.]
(94) N. N. Kavtaradze and N. P. Sokolova, *Dokl. Phys. Chem.* **162**, 420 (1965). [Russian, p. 847.]
(95) R. F. Baddour, M. Modell and U. K. Heusser, *J. Phys. Chem.* **72**, 3621 (1968).
(96) R. F. Baddour, M. Modell and R. L. Goldsmith, *J. Phys. Chem.* **74**, 1787 (1970).
(97) A. Palazov, C. C. Chang and R. J. Kokes, *J. Catal.* **36**, 338 (1975).
(98) D. R. Kember, Ph.D. Thesis, University of East Anglia, Norwich, England (1976).

(99) N. N. Kavtaradze and N. P. Sokolova, *Dokl. Acad. Sci.* **138**, 616 (1961).
(100) N. P. Sokolova, *Russ. J. Phys. Chem.* **46**, 95 (1972). [Russian p. 170.]
(101) N. P. Sokolova, *Russ. J. Phys. Chem.* **48**, 744 (1974). [Russian p. 1274].
(102) R. A. Shigeishi and D. A. King, *Surf. Sci.* **58**, 379 (1976).
(103) L. Lynds, *Spectrochim. Acta.* **20**, 1369 (1964).
(104) N. N. Kavtaradze and N. P. Sokolova, *Dokl. Phys. Chem.* **168**, 295 (1966). [Russian, p. 140.]
(105) H. Heyne and F. C. Tompkins, *Proc. R. Soc.* **A292**, 460 (1966); *Trans. Faraday Soc.* **63**, 1274 (1967).
(106) G. Blyholder and R. Sheets, *J. Phys. Chem.* **74**, 4335 (1970).
(107) E. S. Argano, S. S. Randhava and A. Rehmat, *Trans. Faraday Soc.* **65**, 552 (1969).
(108) N. N. Kavtaradze and N. P. Sokolova, *Russ. J. Phys. Chem.* **44**, 93 (1970). [Russian, p. 171].
(109) M. J. D. Low and J. C. McManus, *Chem. Commun.* 1454 (1970).
(110) N. N. Kavtaradze and N. P. Sokolova, *Russ. J. Phys. Chem.* **41**, 225 (1972).
(111) N. P. Sokolova, *Russ. J. Phys. Chem.* **46**, 55 (1972). [Russian, p. 967.]
(112) M. Primet, J. M. Basset, M. V. Mathieu and M. Prettre, *J. Catal.* **28**, 368 (1973).
(113) A. Palazov, *J. Catal.* **30**, 13 (1973).
(114) M. L. Unland, *J. Catal.* **31**, 459 (1973).
(115) (a) R. A. Dalla Betta, *J. Phys. Chem.* **79**, 2519 (1975); (b) R. A. Dalla Betta and M. Shelef, *J. Catal.* **48**, 111 (1977).
(116) J. M. Basset, G. Dalmai-Imelik, M. Primet and R. Martin, *J. Catal.* **37**, 22 (1975); M. Primet and M. V. Mathieu, *J. Chim. Phys.* **72**, 659 (1975).
(117) M. F. Brown and R. D. Gonzalez, *J. Catal.* **44**, 477 (1976).
(118) C. Bolivar, H. Charcosset, R. Frety, M. Primet, L. Tournayan, C. Betizeau, G. Leclercq and R. Maurel, *J. Catal.* **45**, 163 (1976).
(119) E. Kikuchi, P. C. Flynn and S. E. Wanke, *J. Catal.* **34**, 132 (1974).
(120) J. Pritchard, *J. Vac. Sci. Technol.* **9**, 895 (1972).
(121) M. A. Chesters, J. Pritchard and M. L. Sims, in *Adsorption Desorption Phenomena* (F. Ricca, ed.), Academic Press, London, 1972, p. 277.
(122) J. Pritchard, T. Catterick and R. K. Gupta, *Surf. Sci.* **53**, 1 (1975).
(123) K. Horn and J. Pritchard, *Surf. Sci.* **55**, 701 (1976).
(124) K. Horn, M. Hussain and J. Pritchard, *Surf. Sci.* **63**, 244 (1977).
(125) T. B. Grimley, *Proc. Phys. Soc. London* **90**, 751 (1967).
(126) D. T. Drmaj and K. E. Hayes, *J. Catal.* **19**, 154 (1970).
(127) A. M. Bradshaw, J. Pritchard and M. L. Sims, *Chem. Commun.* 1519 (1968).
(128) J. Pritchard and M. L. Sims, *Trans. Faraday Soc.* **66**, 427 (1970).
(129) H. G. Tompkins and R. G. Greenler, *Surf. Sci.* **28**, 194 (1971).
(130) R. W. Stobie, B. Rao and M. J. Dignam, *Surf. Sci.* **56**, 334 (1976).
(131) N. N. Kavtaradze and N. P. Sokolova, *Dokl. Phys. Chem.* **146**, 747 (1962). [Russian, p. 1367.]
(132) R. A. Gardner and R. H. Petrucci, *J. Phys. Chem.* **67**, 1376 (1963).
(133) D. A. Seanor and C. H. Amberg, *J. Chem. Phys.* **42**, 2967 (1965).
(134) A. W. Smith and J. M. Quets, *J. Catal.* **4**, 163 (1965).
(135) N. Cukr, *Chem. Listy* **64**, 785 (1970).
(136) N. N. Kavtaradze and N. P. Sokolova, *Russ. J. Phys. Chem.* **44**, 603 (1970). [Russian, p. 1088.]
(137) J. W. London and A. T. Bell, *J. Catal.* **31**, 32 (1973).
(138) H. A. Pearce, Ph.D. Thesis, University of East Anglia, Norwich, England (1974).
(139) N. N. Kavtaradze and N. P. Sokolova, *Dokl. Phys. Chem.* **172**, 39 (1967). [Russian, p. 386.]
(140) M. McLean and B. Gale, *Philos. Mag.* **20**, 1033 (1969).

(141) G. W. Keulks and A. Ravi, *J. Phys. Chem.* **74**, 783 (1970).
(142) N. N. Kavtaradze and N. P. Sokolova, *Russ. J. Phys. Chem.* **36**, 1529 (1962). [Russian, p. 2804.]
(143) R. A. Kottke, R. G. Greenler and H. G. Tompkins, *Surf. Sci.* **32**, 231 (1972).
(144) D. J. C. Yates, *J. Colloid Interface Sci.* **29**, 194 (1969).
(145) C. R. Guerra and J. H. Schulman, *Surf. Sci.* **7**, 229 (1967).
(146) C. R. Guerra, *J. Colloid Interface Sci.* **29**, 229 (1969).
(147) P. Harriott, *J. Catal.* **21**, 56 (1971).
(148) K. Kishi and M. W. Roberts, *J. Chem. Soc., Faraday Trans. 1* **71**, 1715 (1975).
(149) (a) G. Blyholder, *J. Chem. Phys.* **36**, 2036 (1962); (b) G. Blyholder and L. D. Neff, *J. Phys. Chem.* **66**, 1464 (1962); (c) *idem* **66**, 1664 (1962).
(150) (a) M. J. Heal, Ph.D. Thesis, University of Capetown, South Africa (1976); (b) M. J. Heal, E. C. Leisegang and R. G. Torrington, *J. Catal.* **51**, 314 (1978).
(151) M. Tanaka and G. Blyholder, *J. Phys. Chem.* **76**, 3180 (1972).
(152) G. Blyholder, *J. Chem. Phys.* **44**, 3134 (1966).
(153) L. D. Neff and J. L. Wallace, *J. Catal.* **44**, 332 (1976).
(154) A. M. Bradshaw and O. Vierle, *Ber. Bunsenges. Phys. Chem.* **74**, 630 (1970).
(155) T. G. Voroshilov, N. K. Lunev, L. M. Roev and M. T. Rusou, *Dopov. Akad. Nauk Ukr. RSR Ser. B* **4**, 319 (1975); *Chem. Abst.* **83**, 103698 b.
(156) J. Wojtczak, R. Queau and R. Poilblanc, *J. Catal.* **37**, 391 (1975).
(157) N. N. Kavtaradze and N. P. Sokolova, *Russ. J. Phys. Chem.* **38**, 548 (1964). [Russian, p. 1004.]
(158) M. G. Wells, N. W. Cant and R. G. Greenler, *Surf. Sci.* **67**, 541 (1977).
(159) A. C. Yang and C. W. Garland, *J. Phys. Chem.* **61**, 1504 (1957).
(160) N. P. Sokolova, *Dokl. Phys. Chem.* **202**, 85 (1972). [Russian, p. 646.]
(161) P. Abhivantanaporn and R. A. Gardner, *J. Catal.* **27**, 56 (1972).
(162) M. Kobayashi and T. Shirasaki, *J. Catal.* **28**, 289 (1973); **32**, 254 (1974).
(163) M. F. Brown and R. D. Gonzalez, *J. Phys. Chem.* **80**, 1731 (1976).
(164) A. Ravi, Ph.D. Thesis, University of East Anglia, Norwich, England (1968).
(165) F. Bozon-Verduraz, *Ann. Chim.* **9**, 77 (1974).
(166) H. Froitzheim, H. Ibach and S. Lehwald, *Surf. Sci.* **63**, 56 (1977).
(167) C. Backx, R. F. Willis, B. Feuerbacher and B. Fitton, *Surf. Sci.* **68**, 516 (1977).
(168) (a) J. T. Yates and D. A. King, *Surf. Sci.* **30**, 601 (1972); (b) J. T. Yates, R. G. Greenler, I. Ratajczykowa and D. A. King, *Surf. Sci.* **36**, 739 (1973).
(169) R. R. Ford, *Adv. Catal.* **21**, 51 (1970).
(170) (a) G. Blyholder and M. Tanaka, *Bull. Chem. Soc. Jpn* **46**, 1876 (1973); (b) R. Sheets and G. Blyholder, *J. Am. Chem. Soc.* **94**, 1434 (1972).
(171) R. Sheets and G. Blyholder, *Appl. Spectrosc.* **30**, 602 (1976).
(172) G. Blyholder and A. J. Goodsel, *J. Catal.* **23**, 374 (1971).
(173) M. L. Unland, *J. Phys. Chem.* **77**, 1952 (1973); *Science* **179**, 567 (1973).
(174) N. Sheppard, N. R. Avery, B. A. Morrow and R. P. Young, in *Chemisorption and Catalysis* (A. R. West, ed.), Inst. Petroleum, London, 1971.
(175) R. van Hardeveld and A. van Montfoort, *Surf. Sci.* **4**, 396 (1966).
(176) D. M. Adams, *Metal-Ligand and Related Vibrations*, Arnold, London, 1967.
(177) G. Blyholder, M. Tanaka and J. D. Richardson, *Chem. Commun.* 499 (1971).
(178) P. R. Griffiths, *Chemical Infrared Fourier Transform Spectroscopy*, Wiley & Sons, New York, 1975.

Chapter 3

THE VIBRATIONAL SPECTROSCOPY OF WATER

James R. Scherer

Western Regional Research Center, Science and Education Administration, U.S. Department of Agriculture, Berkeley, California 94710, U.S.A.

1   INTRODUCTION

1.1   Spectra and Structure

Over the past several years there have been many books and reviews written on the subject of the structure and spectroscopy of water in its various forms.[1–20] It is clear from these sources that there is considerable ambiguity about the correlation of observed vibrational spectra with molecular structure. To some it may come as no surprise that the determination of structure from observed spectra is a more uncertain process than the reverse operation. It is this reviewer's opinion that the controversy regarding the structure of liquid water has reached its present state because of zealous correlation of spectral observation with proposed structure without adequate regard for spectroscopic considerations. For example, infrared and Raman band profiles from an assumed symmetric distribution of oscillators should be inherently asymmetric. Yet it has been common practice to fit the observed data with symmetric band-shape functions.[5] Quantitative estimates of the effect of Fermi resonance, anharmonicity or intermolecular coupling have been attempted in a few cases but, by and large, these problems have been ignored because of the complications that they present.

The scarcity of detail in Raman spectral data for H_2O in the solid, liquid and near-gaseous state is seen in Fig. 1.[21–23] Infrared data of liquid water[24,25] and ice[26–28] have fewer distinct features and are correspondingly difficult to interpret. The OH-stretching bands shift from above 3600 cm^{-1} at high temperature and low density to below 3200 cm^{-1} in the spectra of ice at low temperature. The bandwidths are greatest in the spectra of the liquid near room temperature but the band structure is the most complex for ice at low temperature. Fortunately, important clues for interpreting the liquid state data come from other

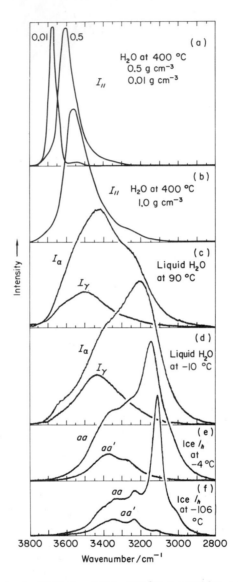

Fig. 1. Raman scattering by H_2O at -106 to $400\ ^\circ C$. (a) $400\ ^\circ C$ at 0.01 and $0.5\ g\ cm^{-3}$ density; (b) $400\ ^\circ C$ at $1.0\ g\ cm^{-3}$ density; (c) $90\ ^\circ C$, isotropic (I_α) and anisotropic (I_γ) scattering; (d) $-10\ ^\circ C$, I_α and I_γ; (e) ice at $-4\ ^\circ C$, aa and aa' scattering; (f) ice at $-106\ ^\circ C$, aa and aa'. ((a), (b): Lindner, Ref. 23; (c), (d): Scherer, Go and Kint, Ref. 22; (e), (f): Scherer and Snyder, Ref. 21).

sources, i.e. studies of water in the gas phase, in dimers, hydrogen-bonding solvents, hydrates and ice.

1.2 Mixture and Continuum Models

Briefly, mixture models of liquid water assume the existence of a small number (nine or less) of species that differ in the number and configuration of hydrogen bonds. The spectra of the liquid are usually separated into components which are said to arise from the different species.

Continuum models assume that all water molecules are four-coordinated as in ice, but that the hydrogen bonds are irregular and distorted, giving rise to a continuous distribution of hydrogen bond strengths and a correspondingly broad OH stretching spectrum. The observation of a weak band near 3650 cm^{-1} in the Raman spectrum of liquid HOD[29] has been interpreted as evidence of broken hydrogen bonds, or at least very weak hydrogen bonds. Consequently continuum approaches that have attempted to account for the observed spectra[30,31] have had to be modified[32] to account for these observations.

It is not this reviewer's intention to consider these two opposing theories in much detail. A lucid account of the problems of both approaches has been given by Eisenberg and Kauzmann.[5] In the following, references to mixture and continuum models will be avoided so as to focus more on the spectroscopic problems that obscure the relation between spectra and structure. In Sections 2 to 3 we shall review the tools of spectral analysis. In Sections 4 to 7 we shall consider water in increasingly complex molecular interactions in order to prepare firm spectroscopic grounds for the interpretation of the spectra of liquid water in Section 8. In Section 9 we shall summarize conclusions about the spectra and structure of liquid water.

In the following sections the vibrational modes of the H_2O (D_2O) molecule will usually be designated as v_1 for a symmetric stretching vibration, v_2 for a H—O—H bending vibration, and v_3 for an antisymmetric stretching vibration. The stretching vibration of a single O—H bond, as in RO—H or DO—H, will be designated v_{OH} with the insertion of a tilde being used to signify the use of wavenumber values for these modes, viz. $\tilde{v}$.

2 INFLUENCE OF PERTURBATIONS ON SPECTRA

2.1 Hydrogen Bonding

2.1.1. Frequencies

Considering the importance of the connection between hydrogen bonding and the properties of liquid water, it might seem too conservative to view hydrogen bonding as a perturbation acting on a free water molecule. Nevertheless, this approach is helpful in relating water spectra to water structure.

Correlations between the frequencies of ν_{OH} or ν_{OD} of the single OH or OD oscillator as a function of the O $\cdots$ O distance are well known.[2,3,8,33,34] The most recent correlation, by Novak,[35] shown in Fig. 2, considers $R_{O\ldots O}$ distances from 2.43 Å to 2.90 Å. Kamb[3] has correlated the ν_{OH} and ν_{OD} frequencies of HOD from various forms of ice where $R_{O\ldots O}$ extends from 2.76 to 2.95 Å ($\tilde{\nu}_{OH}$ = 3277 to 3477 cm^{-1}). Falk[8,36] has determined a similar correlation for ν_{OD} of HOD using data from crystalline hydrates and ices. This correlation has the form

$$\tilde{\nu}_{OD} = 2727 - \exp(20.96 - 5.539\ R_{O\ldots O}) \tag{1}$$

The portions of these curves that pertain to liquid water and ice are above $R_{O\ldots O}$ = 2.76 Å. Their asymptotic limits[37] are the gas-phase wavenumbers for HOD: $\tilde{\nu}_{OH}$ = 3707, $\tilde{\nu}_{OD}$ = 2727 cm^{-1}.

At present there are no useful correlations between $R_{O\ldots O}$ and the force constant for O—H bond stretch. However, it is relatively easy to compute the frequencies for a given set of force constants if we assume no intermolecular

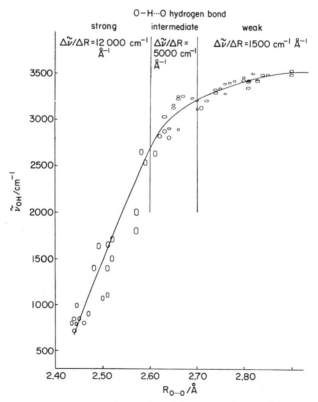

Fig. 2. Correlation of uncoupled ν_{OH} band wavenumbers with O $\cdots$ O distances (Novak, Ref. 35).

coupling. This approach has been used by Burneau and Corset[38] to show how the vibrational frequencies of H_2O, D_2O and HOD depend on the r_{O-H} force constant. The dependence will be discussed more fully in later sections.

The HOH bending mode, ν_2, seems to increase in wavenumber with increased strength of hydrogen bonding.[2,39,40] However, this correlation does not always hold. The bending mode of water complexed with two molecules of dimethyl-sulfoxide (DMSO) is about 23 cm^{-1} higher than the same mode in the complex with hexamethylphosphorotriamide (HMPT) even though ν_1 (and ν_3) has nearly the same wavenumber for the two complexes.[40] The bending modes in

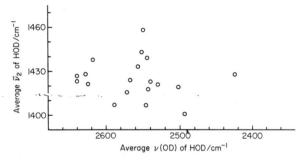

Fig. 3. Bending mode wavenumbers ν_2 vs. ν_{OD} of isotopically dilute HOD for a series of hydrates. (Falk and Knop, Ref. 8.)

hydrates[8] show a general increase in wavenumber with increasing hydrogen-bond strength. However, there are many bending modes with wavenumbers that are *below* the gas-phase values. Wavenumber correlations for ν_2 of HOD with ν_{OD} are shown in Fig. 3. Clearly there does not seem to be any rigorous correlation of the ν_2 wavenumber with hydrogen-bond strength. Therefore, it seems likely that, within the bandwidth of $\tilde{\nu}_2$, there is no direct correlation of band wavenumbers to the low side of $\tilde{\nu}_2$ with stretching mode wavenumbers to the high side of $\tilde{\nu}_{OH}$. Walrafen[41] has measured the Raman band depolarization ratios over the bending region for liquid H_2O and D_2O. He finds that the ν_2 band is more anisotropic above the band maximum, $\tilde{\nu}_{max}$, and more isotropic below $\tilde{\nu}_{max}$. He interprets this as evidence for two different hydrogen-bonded species. An alternative explanation is that the bending modes are strongly intermolecularly coupled, thereby causing a difference in the distribution of anisotropy over the band. The ν_2 Raman band of liquid water narrows with increasing temperature.[22] This may signify less intermolecular coupling at higher temperatures. In the polarized spectrum of single crystal ice, I_h,[21] the anisotropic component of scattering (*ca*) is at a higher frequency than the isotropic (*cc* and *aa*) components of ν_2 for both D_2O and H_2O. There is also evidence from the HOD spectrum of ice that the ν_2 modes must be highly coupled in pure H_2O and D_2O ice. This will be discussed later.

Finally, it will be shown later that Fermi resonance of ν_1 with $2\nu_2$ produces unique features in the spectrum of hydrogen-bonded water. If the frequency of v_2 (and hence $2v_2$) increases as that of v_1 decreases, the resonance perturbation between levels leads to no intensity at the $2v_2$ position, even for small resonance interaction constants. However, interactions between v_1 and an uncorrelated distribution of $2v_2$ levels seems to reproduce the observed spectra.

2.1.2 Intensities

Infrared band intensities depend on the square of the variation of dipole moment with normal coordinate, $(\partial p_j/\partial Q_i)^2$. However, Raman band intensities depend on the variation of polarizability $(\partial \alpha_{jk}/\partial Q_i)^2$ with normal coordinate. Whereas there is an abundance of data that correlates infrared intensities with the strength of hydrogen bonding,[2] there is a complete absence of information regarding the dependence of polarizability derivatives, α'_{jk}, on hydrogen bonding. In the following section it will be shown how Raman depolarization measurements on v_{OH} or v_{OD} of HOD in H_2O or D_2O provide a measure of the ratio of mean bond polarizability to anisotropy derivatives, α'_b/γ'_b, which vary with hydrogen-bond strength. However, there have been no measurements of the absolute variation of α'_b with hydrogen bond strength. Glew and Rath[42] have measured the infrared intensities of v_1 and v_3 of H_2O and v_{OD} of HOD in a variety of hydrogen-bonding solvents. They find a linear correlation between the increase in integrated band areas and the frequencies of v_{OH}, v_1 and v_3. Lindgren and Tegenfeldt[43] have correlated infrared intensity ratios I_B/I_F (B = bonded, F = free) with v_{OH} of HOD for a series of hydrates. They find that $(I_B/I_F)/\Delta\tilde{v}$ is ≈ 0.042 for $\Delta\tilde{v} < 100$ cm^{-1} and ≈ 0.015 for $\Delta\tilde{v} \approx 400$ cm^{-1}. Their correlations are approximately consistent with those of Glew and Rath.

2.2 Anharmonicity

The anharmonic nature of the OH bond potential function significantly affects the vibrational frequencies, band intensities and resonance interactions of water.[14,15,44] The anharmonicity has two sources. Mechanical anharmonicity comes from cubic and quartic terms in the expansion of potential energy in dimensionless normal

$$V/hc = \tfrac{1}{2} \sum_{i=1}^{3} \omega_i q_i^2 + \sum k_{ijl} q_i q_j q_l + \sum k_{ijlm} q_i q_j q_l q_m \tag{2}$$

coordinates[45] where the k_{ijl} and k_{ijlm} terms are the higher-order force constants in dimensionless normal coordinates and ω_i is the harmonic frequency. Electrical anharmonicity depends on quadratic and higher terms in the expansion of the instaneous dipole moment and polarizability in terms of the normal coordinates. Nothing is known about the latter kind of anharmonicity for hydrogen-bonded systems. Mechanical anharmonicity affects the observed vibrational energy as follows.[14,46]

$$G(v_1, v_2, v_3) = \sum_i \omega_i(v_i + \tfrac{1}{2}) + \sum_{i,j} x_{ij}(v_i + \tfrac{1}{2})(v_j + \tfrac{1}{2}) \tag{3}$$

where $G(v_1, v_2, v_3)$ is the vibrational energy for states having quantum numbers v_i. 1, 2, and 3 refer to symmetric stretch, HOH bend, and antisymmetric stretch, respectively, and x_{ij} is the anharmonic contribution to the energy. The six anharmonic constants x_{ij} are evaluated from observed overtone and combination bands. The values of x_{ij} obtained for the free water molecule,[47,48] water in CCl_4, and a CCl_4 solution of a 1:1 complex of hexamethylphosphorotriamide (HMPT) and water[49] are given in Table 1. The anharmonicity (x_{33}) of the 'free' OH stretch in the 1:1 complex of H_2O with HMPT $((H_2O)_{1-1})$ is -83 cm^{-1}, and that for the 'free' OD stretch in $((D_2O)_{1-1})$ is -42 cm^{-1}. These values are nearly the same for x_{33} (OH) and x_{11} (OD) of HOD. Thus, the anharmonicities indicate that asymmetric hydrogen-bonding of the H_2O or D_2O water molecule decouples the OH or OD stretching coordinates. The calculated normal coordinates that are shown in a later section also indicate that decoupling is a function of the strength of hydrogen bonding. The dependence of x_{ij} on the OH force constant for symmetric and asymmetric hydrogen-bonded water is graphically illustrated in Ref. 38.

TABLE 1
Anharmonicity coefficients/cm^{-1} for H_2O, D_2O and HOD in gas phase[47,48] and in hydrogen-bonding and non-hydrogen-bonding solvents[49].^{a}

	(H_2O)			(H_2O)$_{1-1}$
	Vapor		CCl_4	HMPT + CCl_4
x_{11}	-43		-61	$-185?$
x_{12}	-16		-19	-7
x_{13}	-166		-169	0
x_{22}	-17		-16	-22
x_{23}	-20		-25	-17
x_{33}	-48		$-$	-83
	(D_2O)			(D_2O)$_{1-1}$
x_{11}	-23		-25	$-$
x_{12}	-8		-11	$-$
x_{13}	-87		-85	-10
x_{22}	-9		-9	-14
x_{23}	-11		$-$	-11
x_{33}	-26		$-$	-42
	(HOD)		(HOD)$_{1-D-1}$	(HOD)$_{1-H-1}$
x_{11}	-43		$-$	$-$
x_{12}	9	-19	$-$	$-$
x_{13}	-13	-12	$-$	$-$
x_{22}	-12	-14	-12	$-$
x_{23}	-20	-25	-23	$-$
x_{33}	-83	-83	-82	-44

^{a} HMPT is hexamethylphosphorotriamide. (HOD)$_{1-D-1}$ refers to asymmetrically hydrogen-bonded HOD with the stronger hydrogen bond on the D atom.

The observed anharmonic constants and rotational constants for the different vibrational states of gaseous H_2O, D_2O and HOD were used by Smith and Overend[50] to calculate a quartic force field. Corrections for resonance between states giving rise to vibrational frequencies $2\tilde{v}_1$ and $2\tilde{v}_3$[46] and between $2\tilde{v}_2$ and $\tilde{v}_1$ (Fermi resonance) were found to be important. From their treatment, the cubic normal-coordinate force constant, k_{122}, which governs the Fermi resonance between v_1 and $2v_2$ of H_2O, was found to be only 72 cm^{-1} instead of 302 cm^{-1} reported in an earlier paper by Pariseau,[51] 255 cm^{-1} by Kuchitsu and Morino,[45] 167 cm^{-1} by Hoy et al.[52] and 92 cm^{-1} by Speirs and Spirko.[53] The effect of this low value of the resonance constant will be discussed next.

2.3 Fermi Resonance

The observed separation of two transitions of a Fermi diad,[46] X, is given by

$$X = (\Delta^2 + 4W^2)^{\frac{1}{2}} \qquad (4)$$

where Δ is the separation between the unperturbed transitions and W is the Fermi interaction constant. The ratio of intensities of the Raman bands associated with transitions to the upper and lower levels of the diad[54] is

$$\frac{I_u}{I_l} = \left[\frac{(X+\Delta)^{\frac{1}{2}}(\alpha_u/\alpha_l) \mp (X-\Delta)^{\frac{1}{2}}}{\pm(X+\Delta)^{\frac{1}{2}} + (X-\Delta)^{\frac{1}{2}}(\alpha_u/\alpha_l)} \right]^2 \qquad (5)$$

where α_u/α_l is the ratio of matrix elements of the polarizability for the transitions from the ground state to the unperturbed upper and lower levels of the diad. If we assume the matrix element of the overtone to be zero, eqn. (5) reduces to

$$I_u/I_l = (X-\Delta)/(X+\Delta) \qquad (6)$$

The Fermi interaction constant has the form[50]

$$W = \langle v_1, v_2, v_3 | H'/hc | v_1 - 1, v_2 + 2, v_3 \rangle \qquad (7)$$

$$= \frac{k_{122}}{2} \left[\frac{v_1}{2} (v_2 + 1)(v_2 + 2) \right]^{\frac{1}{2}} \qquad (8)$$

where v_1, v_2 and v_3 are the vibrational quantum numbers for the fundamentals, H'/hc is the anharmonic term in the Hamiltonian, and k_{122} is the cubic force constant in dimensionless normal coordinate space. The resonance between v_1 and $2v_2$ requires that $v_1 = 1$, $v_2 = 0$, $v_3 = 0$ and $W = k_{122}/2$.

In their studies of gaseous HOD, Benedict et al.[47] found a case of nearly exact Fermi resonance ($\Delta \approx 0$) between rotational levels in the $v_1 + v_2$ and $3v_2$ infrared bands, which gave rise to a splitting of 45.3 cm^{-1}. For these transitions eqn. (8) reduces to $W = k_{122}\sqrt{3}/2$, which, when combined with eqn. (4), leads to a value of 26 cm^{-1} for k_{122}. The Smith-Overend force field predicts a value of 26 cm^{-1} for k_{122} of HOD and this agreement gives us confidence in their calculated values of 72 cm^{-1} and 50 cm^{-1} for k_{122} of H_2O and D_2O.

There has been a great deal of controversy over whether there is or is not Fermi resonance between v_1 and $2v_2$ in the liquid state. Unfortunately (or fortunately?), recognition of this resonance is not as simple as the two opposing sides have indicated. The magnitude of the resonance constant and the distribution of energy states involved can combine to give unusual band shapes[55–59] that are not simple sums of component bands. In special cases, broad spectral bands appear to have sharp holes[55,56] that appear as transmission spikes in infrared spectra, or intensity spikes in Raman spectra. These features have been termed 'Evans holes'.[58] In Fig. 4 are calculated spectra showing Fermi resonance between (a) a narrow distribution of fundamentals with a narrow distribution of overtones, (b) a broad distribution of fundamentals with a narrow distribution of overtones and (c) a broad distribution of fundamentals with a broad distribution of overtones. On the left of this figure the overtone distribution is located 150 cm^{-1} to the low wavenumber side of the fundamental (3450 cm^{-1}) distribution; on the right the centers of both distributions are coincident. Gaussian band shapes were assumed. The half-widths are 60 and 350 cm^{-1} for the fundamental distributions and 60 and 120 cm^{-1} for the overtone distributions. The magnitude of W is assumed to be 36 cm^{-1}. In

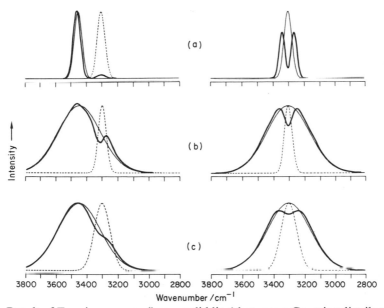

Fig. 4. Result of Fermi resonance (heavy solid line) between a Gaussian distribution of fundamentals (light solid line) and overtones (broken line) separated by 150 cm^{-1} and 0 cm^{-1} (right) with a resonance constant, W, of 36 cm^{-1}. (a) both distributions with half-widths of 60 cm^{-1}; (b) fundamental half-width is 350 cm^{-1}, overtone half-width 60 cm^{-1}; (c) fundamental half-width is 350 cm^{-1}; overtone halfwidth is 120 cm^{-1}.

Fig. 5 are spectra from equivalent calculations with $W = 70$ cm^{-1}. The calculations were made assuming[58] that the overtone frequencies are not correlated with the fundamental frequencies. The shape of the overtone distribution $(I_v^\circ/\sum_{\text{band}} I_v^\circ)$ is assumed to be related to the probability of interaction of overtone I_v° with a given fundamental I_v^f. The resulting intensities for the diad were weighted by this probability and the intensity at a given frequency in the resulting spectrum is generated by summing the intensities from all possible diads. Bratos[59] and others[58] have noted that correlated $2v_2$ and v_1 distributions lead to no intensity at the position of maximum Fermi resonance whereas uncorrelated distributions seem to give results closer to experimental observations. The Evans holes[58] produced in these calculated spectra have characteristics determined by the width of the overtone distribution and the magnitude of the resonance constant. Thus, a small value of W and a narrow overtone distribution gives rise to narrow sharp holes. Increasing the width of the overtone distribution makes the hole more shallow but does not widen the base of the hole. Increasing the magnitude of W widens the base of the hole.

Specific examples of these Fermi resonance interactions will be discussed in later sections. In general, evidence for this perturbation has been found for water in hydrogen-bonding solvents, hydrates, ice and liquid water. Consideration of these cases in detail shows that Fermi resonance must be taken into account in the analysis of water spectra. The perturbation is small, but decidedly not negligible.

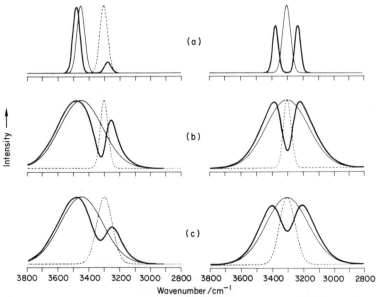

Fig. 5. Result of Fermi resonance (heavy solid line) between a Gaussian distribution of fundamentals (light solid line) and overtones (broken line) separated by 150 cm^{-1} (left) and 0 cm^{-1} (right), with a resonance constant, W, of 70 cm^{-1}. Half-widths as in Fig. 4.

2.4 Intermolecular Coupling of Vibrations

There have been few attempts to address the question of whether or not there is intermolecular coupling in liquid water. Studies of the spectra of ice[21,60–63] indicate that intermolecular coupling of stretching vibrations of water molecules in the ice I_h lattice is strong. From a study of the infrared spectra of dilute HOD in an H_2O matrix, Haas and Hornig[60] were able to observe bands due to in-phase, v^+, and out of phase, v^-, components of the v_{OD} vibrations of
$$\text{HO—D} \cdots \overset{\text{H}}{\text{O}}\text{—D}$$
dimers. From the separation of v^- and v^+ (49 cm^{-1}) and the observed intensities, they determined that (at -195 °C) the band at 2442 cm^{-1} was from the v^- vibrations and the band at 2393 cm^{-1} from v^+ vibrations. The coupling constant between O—D bonds was found to be -0.123 mdyn Å^{-1}, which is of the same order of magnitude as the intramolecular coupling constant between adjacent OD stretching coordinates in D_2O. Given a network of N water molecules separated by single hydrogen bonds (i.e. ice), the spectrum in the OH (and OD) stretching region has been calculated[62] assuming no oxygen motion and no dependence on HOH bending. The potential function that was used had the form

$$2V = \sum_{}^{N} k_1(\Delta r_{ij}^2 + \Delta r_{ik}^2) + 2 \sum_{}^{N} k_2 \, \Delta r_{ij} \, \Delta r_{ik}$$
$$+ 2 \sum k_3 \, \Delta r_{ij} \, \Delta r_{lm} + 2 \sum k_4 \, \Delta r_{ik} \, \Delta r_{lm} \tag{9}$$

where the i, j, k, l and m indices are defined by the geometry H_k—O_i—$H_j \cdots O_l$—H_m and the last two sums are taken over all sets of near neighbor oscillators. The constants k_3 and k_4 arise from transition dipole coupling.[13,60,61,64,65] Whereas k_3 has only one value for its orientation of coordinates, k_4 can have four possible values. The calculated spectra[62] have a general resemblance to the observed spectra. More recent calculations that allow for oxygen motion give a better account of the spectrum.[66]

Recently, Ritzhaupt and Devlin[67] have obtained the infrared spectrum of vibrationally decoupled D_2O in a glassy H_2O matrix by simultaneous deposition of H_2O and D_2O molecular beams on a CsBr substrate held at 90 K. These spectra show two peaks at 2473 and 2378 cm^{-1} which they assign to v_3 and v_1, respectively. According to Burneau and Corset,[38] a hydrogen-bonded water molecule having v_3 at *ca.* 2473 cm^{-1} should have a separation between v_3 and v_1 of *ca.* 85 cm^{-1} which would place v_1 near 2388 cm^{-1}. The expected Fermi resonance with $2v_2$ at 2400 cm^{-1} would have a tendency to push v_1 to lower wavenumbers. The OD stretch for DOH in glassy H_2O is at 2437 cm^{-1}[68] which is *ca.* 36 cm^{-1} lower than the observed value for v_3 for isolated D_2O but 59 cm^{-1} higher than the observed value for v_1. This also suggests that Fermi resonance with $2v_2$ may be pushing the observed maximum of v_1 to lower wavenumbers.

It is worth mentioning at this point that, even though the D_2O vibrations in glassy H_2O are decoupled, the observed v_1 and v_3 infrared bands have half-widths of the order of 100–150 cm^{-1}. The width of these bands is about the same as those for the uncoupled OD stretches of HOD in liquid water. It seems likely that the band width in these two cases is the result of distortion of the O—D $\cdots$ O configurations. Intermolecularly decoupled H_2O in a D_2O matrix has not yet been observed. Whether intermolecular coupling is a factor that must be considered in the dynamics of liquid water will be considered in Section 8.

3 ANALYTICAL TOOLS

3.1 Normal Coordinates of Water

A rigorous calculation of the normal coordinates of liquid water would require a detailed knowledge of structure and the intra- and intermolecular force constants for numerous hydrogen-bonding states. Unfortunately, not enough is known about the molecular constants of water in the liquid state to undertake this approach. A simpler task is to consider hydrogen bonding as a perturbation acting on the force constants of the isolated water molecule. This approach neglects anharmonicity differences between hydrogen-bonded states, and inter-molecular coupling. Nevertheless, some appreciation may be obtained of the degree of internal-coordinate decoupling caused by hydrogen bonding and isotopic substitution.

The internal coordinates, R_i, of the water molecule may be defined as the two OH stretching coordinates, Δr_1 and Δr_2, and the valence angle bending coordinate, $\Delta \alpha$. The potential energy is defined by $2V = \tilde{R}FR$ where F is the force constant matrix and $\tilde{R}$ is the transpose of R. Force constants have been determined by Nibler and Pimentel[69] from harmonic[47,48] and observed frequencies. The observed and harmonic wavenumbers are listed in Table 2 and the force constants in Table 3. The totally symmetric OH stretch, v_1, of H_2O (and D_2O) has very little contribution from the bending coordinate. Similarly, the bending vibration, v_2, has little contribution from the OH stretching coordinate. By symmetry, v_3 cannot interact with either v_1 or v_2. However, in HOD, the intramolecular coupling between the OH and OD bond stretches is almost

TABLE 2
Harmonic ($\tilde{\omega}$) and observed ($\tilde{v}$) wavenumbers/cm^{-1} for water in the gas phase[47,48]

	H_2O		D_2O		HOD	
i	$\tilde{v}_i$	$\tilde{\omega}_i$	$\tilde{v}_i$	$\tilde{\omega}_i$	$\tilde{v}_i$	$\tilde{\omega}_i$
1	3656.7	3832.2	2671.5	2763.8	3707.5	3889.8
2	1594.6	1648.5	1178.3	1206.4	1403.4	1441.4
3	3755.8	3942.5	2788.1	2888.8	2726.7	2824.3

eliminated because of the large separation between the energy levels of the OH and OD oscillators. As a result, the $\tilde{\nu}_{OH}$ and $\tilde{\nu}_{OD}$ wavenumbers of HOD are approximately halfway between $\tilde{\nu}_1$ and $\tilde{\nu}_3$ for H_2O and D_2O, respectively.

Since stretching frequencies depend on the force constant of the bond being stretched[70] and since the changes in the frequencies of ν_{OH} and ν_{OD} depend on the strength of hydrogen bonding,[33,34] we may, to a first approximation, calculate the decrease in the frequencies of ν_{OH} and ν_{OD} by lowering the r_{OH} and r_{OD} stretching force constants and ignore the terms coupling Δr_{OH} and Δr_{OD} to the adjacent molecules. Burneau and Corsett[38] have calculated the effect that hydrogen bonding of a single OH or both OH bonds of an H_2O molecule has on the vibrational frequencies and normal coordinates. Two basic types of hydrogen-bonded water molecules were considered: one having only one hydrogen bond (1:1 complex) and the other having two hydrogen bonds (1:2 complex). Starting with the harmonic force constants of Nibler and Pimentel, they lowered the force constant of the hydrogen bonded OH or OD by as much as 22%. Figure 6 shows the variation of calculated $\tilde{\omega}_i$ and observed $\tilde{\nu}_i$ as a function of the percentage change in f_r. The f_r force constants for the 1:2 complex are assumed to be equal. The transformation, L, between internal coordinates, R_i, and normal coordinates, Q_i, is defined as

$$\begin{bmatrix} \Delta r_1 \\ \Delta \alpha \\ \Delta r_2 \end{bmatrix} = \begin{bmatrix} l_{11} & l_{12} & l_{13} \\ l_{21} & l_{22} & l_{23} \\ l_{31} & l_{32} & l_{33} \end{bmatrix} \begin{bmatrix} Q_1 \\ Q_2 \\ Q_3 \end{bmatrix} \tag{10}$$

The jth column in the matrix $[l_{ij}]$ gives the variation in the ith internal coordinate per unit change in the jth normal coordinate. The ratio l_{31}/l_{11} gives the proportion of Δr_2 to Δr_1 in the Q_1 (ω_1) normal coordinate. For the symmetric 1:2 complex the ratio $l_{31}/l_{11} = +1$ (ω_1 = symmetric stretch) and $l_{13}/l_{33} = -1$ (ω_3 = antisymmetric stretch). However, for the asymmetric complexes, the decoupling of symmetric and antisymmetric stretching coordinates depends on the strength of the hydrogen bond. In Fig. 7 are the l_{ms}/l_{ss} ratios calculated by Burneau and Corset for $(H_2O)_{1-1}$, $(D_2O)_{1-1}$, $(HOD)_{1-H-1}$ and $(HOD)_{1-D-1}$; m and s are indices that identify the L-matrix elements. The notation $(HOD)_{1-H-1}$ signifies a 1:1 complex with the hydrogen atom bonded. Two

TABLE 3
Quadratic force constants for an isolated water molecule[69]

Coordinate force constant	Δr f_r/mdyn Å^{-1}	$\Delta \alpha$ f_α/mdyn Å rad^{-2}	$\Delta r_1 \Delta r_2$ f_{rr}/mdyn Å^{-1}	$\Delta r \Delta \alpha$ $f_{r\alpha}$/mdyn rad^{-1}
From ω_i	8.453 ± 0.005	0.696 ± 0.004	-0.100 ± 0.005	0.231 ± 0.065
From ν_i	7.567 ± 0.111	0.730 ± 0.067	-0.263 ± 0.133	-0.429 ± 0.189

points are immediately apparent from these figures. The first is that asymmetric hydrogen bonding partially decouples v_1 and v_3 vibrations of $(H_2O)_{1-2}$ (or $(D_2O)_{1-2}$) but not as well as the substitution of a D (or H) atom. The second point is that the decoupling of the OH and OD coordinates of HOD is nearly independent of hydrogen-bond strength. However, the OD stretch tends to have a slight symmetric-stretch character and the OH stretch tends to have an anti-symmetric-stretch character. These diagrams will be discussed more fully in later sections.

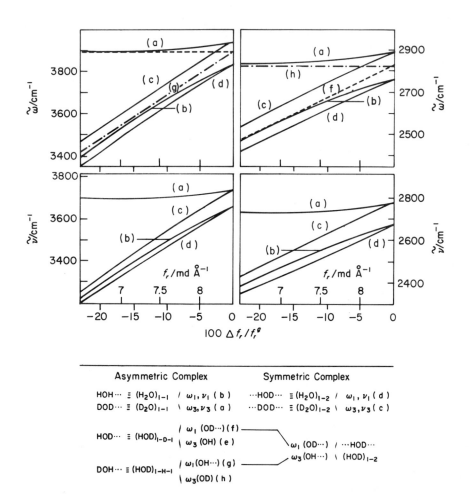

Fig. 6. Dependence of harmonic ($\tilde{\omega}$) and observed ($\tilde{v}$) mode wavenumbers on per-centage change of OH-stretching force constant for the hydrogen-bonded OH bond in symmetrically and asymmetrically hydrogen-bonded H_2O, D_2O and HOD. (Burneau and Corset, Ref. 38.)

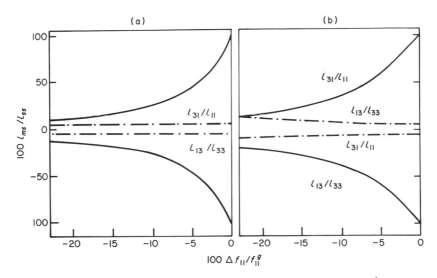

Fig. 7. Relative eigenvectors for asymmetric complex of H_2O, D_2O and HOD as a function of percentage change in OH stretching force constant of hydrogen-bonded OH. (a) — $(H_2O)_{1-1}$, —·— $(HOD)_{1-D-1}$; (b) — $(D_2O)_{1-1}$, —·— $(HOD)_{1-H-1}$ (Burneau and Corset, Ref. 38.)

3.2   Band Fitting

The widths of vibrational bands having a well-defined normal coordinate are, in general, quite small. However, bands in the vibrational spectra of water are extremely broad and this cannot be attributed to the combined natural widths from a small number of molecular species.[5] The widths of the uncoupled OH and OD stretching bands of HOD in liquid H_2O and D_2O indicate a broad distribution of the O—H bond strengths or considerable distortion or disorder in the hydrogen-bonded environment of the uncoupled oscillator.[71–73]

Let us consider the expected shape of the infrared and Raman bands from an assumed symmetric distribution of uncoupled OH oscillator frequencies. The band from an individual oscillator with a specific geometry should be narrow[5] and we expect the infrared intensity at any frequency v_i to be the product of the dipole moment changes $(\partial p/\partial Q_i)^2$ for the oscillator (Q_i) and the number of such oscillators. However, hydrogen bonding is known to increase the intensity of OH and OD stretching bands.[2] The absorptivity varies linearly,[36,42,43] with the shift of the OH (or OD) frequency from its vapor phase wavenumber value of 3707 (or 2727) cm^{-1}. Because of this dependence of $(\partial p/\partial Q_i)$ on hydrogen bonding, we expect the observed infrared band of v_{OH} or v_{OD} to have more intensity below the wavenumber of the band maximum than above it. Before applying band-fitting analysis we should either correct the observed spectrum for this asymmetry or incorporate the asymmetry into the function used to fit the observed data. The former approach has been applied in an analysis of shapes of ν_{OD} and ν_{OH} infrared bands by Falk.[36]

Raman band polarization measurements yield information about the spherical and anisotropic components of the polarizability derivative tensor. We define the laser excitation and scattering geometries by the notation $X_i(X_j X_k) X_l$ where X refers to a Cartesian coordinate direction:[74] X_i is the direction of propagation of the laser beam, X_j is its direction of polarization, X_l refers to the direction in which the scattered light is observed and X_k indentifies the component of polarization that is being measured. The Raman intensity expected from a single oscillator is

$$Z(XX)Y : I_{\parallel} \propto K_{v,T}(45\bar{\alpha}'^2 + 4\bar{\gamma}'^2) \qquad (11)$$

and

$$Z(XZ)Y : I_{\perp} \propto K_{v,T}(3\bar{\gamma}'^2) \qquad (12)$$

where $\bar{\alpha}'$ is the mean value of the derived polarizability tensor, $(\partial\bar{\alpha}/\partial Q_i)$, and $\bar{\gamma}'$ is its anisotropy, $(\partial\bar{\gamma}/\partial Q_i)$.

$$K_{v,T} = \frac{(\nu_L - \nu_i)^4}{\nu_i(1 - e^{-h\nu_i/kT})} \qquad (13)$$

where ν_L is the excitation frequency, and ν_i is the vibrational frequency of the oscillator. We assume that the $I_{\parallel}$ and the $I_{\perp}$ data have already been corrected for non-uniform intensity response of the instrument as a function of frequency.[75] These data are easily transformed to isotropic, I_{α}, and anisotropic, I_{γ}, spectra[76] with the advantage that strictly antisymmetric vibrations cannot appear in the I_{α} spectrum.

$$I_{\alpha} = K_{v,T}(45\bar{\alpha}'^2) \qquad (14)$$

$$I_{\gamma} = K_{v,T}(4\bar{\gamma}'^2) \qquad (15)$$

The Boltzmann factor in $K_{v,T}$ may be ignored for OH and OD stretching vibrations even at high temperatures. However, the $(\nu_L - \nu_i)^4/\nu_i$ term makes the observed intensity in the 3600 cm^{-1} region about 24% less than it would be (relative to the same intensity at 3200 cm^{-1}) had the factor not been present.[58] If we assume that $\bar{\alpha}'$ and $\bar{\gamma}'$ are independent of hydrogen-bond strength, the concentrations of species are proportional to $(45\bar{\alpha}'^2)$ and $(4\bar{\gamma}'^2)$ spectra and not I_{α} or I_{γ}. Similarly, resonance perturbations involving intensity transfer between vibrational levels must be made on the $(45\bar{\alpha}'^2)$ and $(4\bar{\gamma}'^2)$ spectra. As a result of these factors, Raman band shapes have terms which make them inherently asymmetric and this asymmetry cannot be neglected.

Unlike the case with infrared band intensities, there have been no studies of the dependence of $\bar{\alpha}'$ and $\bar{\gamma}'$ on hydrogen bonding. Some dependence may be inferred from the behavior of the uncoupled OH and OD bands of HOD with temperature. Walrafen[77] reports a 25% decrease in the observed intensity of the OD stretch over the range of 0 to 100 °C. Using more accurate techniques and intensity corrections, Scherer et al.[22] find that the integrated intensity of the $(45\bar{\alpha}'^2 + 4\bar{\gamma}'^2)$ spectrum of ν_{OH} decreases by 15% when the temperature changes from 10 to 90 °C. The corresponding decrease for ν_{OD} is 17%. The wavenumber of the band maximum shifts upward by *ca.* 50 cm^{-1} in both cases. This indicates that the polarizability derivatives decrease as the hydrogen-bond strength decreases; Lindner's[23] measurements of the ν_{OD} band at temperatures up to 400 °C at constant density show that the intensity decrease is greater at higher temperatures than at lower temperatures, even though the shift in the position of the band maximum is much smaller at higher temperatures. However, most of this intensity decrease occurs in the region between the low and high temperature band maxima. These observations seem to indicate that $\partial\alpha/\partial Q$ decreases with decreased hydrogen-bond strength. Falk[36] found that when the infrared OH and OD bands are corrected for the increase in intensity with hydrogen bonding,[43] the resulting curve compares favorably with the $(45\bar{\alpha}'^2 + 4\bar{\gamma}'^2)$ spectra[22] in the region of the band maximum and at lower frequencies. This is to be expected if there is little or no dependence of $\partial\alpha/\partial Q$ on hydrogen bonding in this region. At higher frequencies, however, the corrected infrared data do not agree with the Raman data. The discrepancy probably is a result of dependence of the polarizability derivative on strength of hydrogen bonding. Clearly, a careful study of the effect of hydrogen bonding on Raman intensities would provide an important missing link in our understanding of the Raman spectra of water. In the absence of such work, intensity interpretations should be based on $45\bar{\alpha}'^2$ and $4\bar{\gamma}'^2$ data rather than observed Raman data.

Observed infrared and Raman data have been fitted with band-shape functions that are Gaussian (3 parameter), Lorentzian (3 parameter), product function of Gaussian and Lorentzian (4 parameter), and skew product (5 parameter). These have the following forms:[78,79]

$$\text{Gaussian } I_\nu = I_0 \exp\left[-(4\ln 2)\left(\frac{\nu-\nu_0}{G}\right)^2\right] \tag{16}$$

$$\text{Lorentzian } I_\nu = \frac{I_0}{1+4\left(\dfrac{\nu-\nu_0}{L}\right)^2} \tag{17}$$

$$\text{Product } I_\nu = \frac{I_0 \exp\left[-(4\ln 2)\left(\dfrac{\nu-\nu_0}{G}\right)^2\right]}{1+4\left(\dfrac{\nu-\nu_0}{L}\right)^2} \tag{18}$$

$$\text{Skewed Product } I_\nu = \frac{I_0 \exp\left[-f^2\left(\dfrac{\nu-\nu_0}{Y}\right)^2 A\right]}{1+(1-f)^2\left(\dfrac{\nu-\nu_0}{Y}\right)^2 A}$$

$$A = 1 + a(\nu-\nu_0) + a^2(\nu-\nu_0)^2/2 \tag{19}$$

where v_0 is the band center, I_0 is the peak height at v_0, G is the half-width (width at half-height) for the Gaussian function, L is the half-width for the Lorentzian function, f is the fraction Gaussian, Y a parameter related to band half-width and a is an asymmetry parameter.

Walrafen has claimed that the v_{OD} Raman bands of HOD may be fitted well with two,[29,77] three[77] and four[80,81] Gaussian bands. A three band Gaussian fit was also claimed to match the v_{OD} infrared band contour.[77] However, Clarke and Glew were able to fit the infrared data with one, two or four bands (using progressively bolder assumptions) having the skewed product form.[79] They find that the component infrared bands are only about 47% Gaussian. It is difficult to evaluate Walrafen's Gaussian band decompositions for his Raman data because neither residuals nor sums of component bands are shown with the observed data. An additional problem with these Raman data is that the backgrounds are not well defined and in all cases they were established with straight lines drawn between arbitrary points on the band wings.[6,77] In more recent work,[22] using digital subtraction of H_2O and D_2O from the HOD spectra, the wings of the OD stretch are seen to extend down to 2100 cm^{-1} whereas Walrafen's data show wings only down to 2250 cm^{-1}. The Lorentzian components of these bands are determined to a great extent by these extended wings. The two-band decompositions in Ref. 22 are not comparable with Walrafen's work because they are applied to the $45\bar{\alpha}'^2$ and $4\bar{\gamma}'^2$ spectra and not to the observed spectral data. These decompositions indicate that the major v_{OD} band at 2520 cm^{-1} (at 10 °C) has wavenumber values of G and L of 220 and 260 cm^{-1}, respectively. In the fractional Gaussian formalism of eqn. (19), this band is only 50% Gaussian. A major point for making these comparisons is to emphasize that very little is known about the band shape expected from a hydrogen-bonded species. Why then should an observed band that has only *two* broad bumps be fitted with any more than *two* bands? If the band shape for a species is unknown (as is the position and intensity) is there any sense in fitting the HOD band, which only has *two* convincing features, with *four* bands?

3.3   Bond Polarizabilities

Unlike infrared measurements, where the intensity of the OH stretching bands are related to only one quantity, $\partial p/\partial r_{O-H}$, Raman data yield two separately measurable quantities, $\bar{\alpha}'$ and $\bar{\gamma}'$, which may be related to the parallel and transverse bond polarizability change with OH bond stretch, $(\partial \alpha_\parallel/\partial r_{OH}, \partial \alpha_\perp/r_{OH})$. Bond polarizabilities have been determined for liquid water[22] and single crystal ice.[21] Following a procedure developed by Long[82,83] we define molecule-fixed axes in Fig. 8. The polarizability change with bond stretch is $\partial \alpha_{ij}/\partial r_{OH_1} \equiv \alpha'_{ij}$

$$\alpha'_1 = \begin{bmatrix} \alpha'_{xx} & \alpha'_{xy} & \alpha'_{xz} \\ \alpha'_{xy} & \alpha'_{yy} & \alpha'_{yz} \\ \alpha'_{xz} & \alpha'_{yz} & \alpha'_{zz} \end{bmatrix} \tag{20}$$

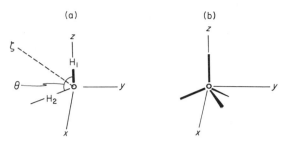

Fig. 8. Molecular axes for bond polarizability calculations. (a) Bond orientation for polarizability-derivative tensor in eqn. (21); (b) orientation of bonds in tetrahedral ice lattice. ζ is the axis bisecting the angle θ.

Since the OH_1 bond has a connecting hydrogen atom, H_2, that we define to be in the yz plane, α'_{xy} and $\alpha'_{xz} = 0$. If we further assume that the OH_1 bond has cylindrical symmetry, then $\alpha'_{yz} = 0$ and $\alpha'_{xx} = \alpha'_{yy}$. Since we will be considering only intensity ratios, we may use ratios of polarizability changes.

$$\boldsymbol{\alpha}'_1 = \alpha'_\perp \begin{bmatrix} 1 & 0 & 0 \\ 0 & 1 & 0 \\ 0 & 0 & \alpha'_\| / \alpha'_\perp \end{bmatrix} \tag{21}$$

The simplest bond-polarizability model has only one parameter, $\alpha'_\| / \alpha'_\perp$. The mean bond-polarizability and anisotropy derivatives[84] are

$$\alpha'_b = \tfrac{1}{3}(2 + \alpha'_\| / \alpha'_\perp)\alpha'_\perp$$

and

$$\gamma'^2_b = (1 - \alpha'_\| / \alpha'_\perp)^2 \alpha'^2_\perp \tag{22}$$

The polarizability change for bond $O—H_2$ may be obtained by a similarity transform of $\boldsymbol{\alpha}'_1$

$$\boldsymbol{\alpha}'_2 = \mathbf{R}^{-1} \boldsymbol{\alpha}'_1 \mathbf{R} \tag{23}$$

where $\mathbf{R}$ is the rotation transformation about axis ζ (see Fig. 8) that carries H_1 into H_2 (angle of rotation $= 180°$). The ζ axis lies in the yz plane and bisects the $H_2—O—H_1$ angle, θ.

The total polarizability change for a normal coordinate Q_k is

$$\boldsymbol{\alpha}'_T = \boldsymbol{\alpha}'_1 l_{1k} + \mathbf{R}^{-1} \boldsymbol{\alpha}'_1 \mathbf{R} l_{3k} \tag{24}$$

where $l_{1k} = (\partial r_1 / \partial Q_k)$ and $l_{3k} = (\partial r_2 / \partial Q_k)$ and the mean polarizability and anisotropy invariants of $\boldsymbol{\alpha}'_T$ are

$$\bar{\alpha}'_T = \alpha'_b l_{+k} \alpha'_\perp$$

and

$$\bar{\gamma}'^2_T = \gamma'^2_b [l^2_{+k}(1 + 3\cos^2\theta) + 3l^2_{-k}\sin^2\theta]\alpha'^2_\perp \tag{25}$$

where

$$l_{+k} = l_{1k} + l_{3k} \quad \text{and} \quad l_{-k} = l_{1k} - l_{3k}$$

The instanteous moment induced by light polarized in the X direction is $\alpha'_T E_x$, and the intensity observed in the Y direction is proportional to $(\alpha'_T)^2_{xx} + (\alpha'_T)^2_{xz}$ where the 1st and 2nd terms are the $\parallel$ and $\perp$ polarized components of scattered light.

The $Z(XX)Y$ Raman intensity in the liquid state is obtained by averaging $(\alpha'_T)^2_{xx}$ over all orientations of the water molecule. The result of this averaging[84] has been given in eqn. (11). The intensities, $I_{\parallel}$ and $I_{\perp}$, are obtained by substituting eqn. (25) into eqns. (11) and (12). The depolarization ratio, ρ_k, is therefore

$$\rho_k = \frac{I_{\perp}}{I_{\parallel}} = \frac{\frac{3}{4}[l^2_{+k}(1 + 3\cos^2\theta) + 3l^2_{-k}\sin^2\theta](\gamma'_b/\alpha'_b)^2}{45l^2_{+k} + [l^2_{+k}(1 + 3\cos^2\theta) + 3l^2_{-k}\sin^2\theta](\gamma'_b/\alpha'_b)^2} \tag{26}$$

From a knowledge of the normal coordinates of the uncoupled HOD oscillator and the observed depolarization ratios for ν_{OH} and ν_{OD}, we can determine the ratio γ'_b/α'_b for the OH bond. These measurements will be discussed in Section 8.

Similar information has been obtained from the uncoupled oscillator bands of single crystal ice I_h.[21] The calculated intensities in this case are obtained by averaging the $(\alpha'_T)^2_{xy}$ terms over the 12 different orientations of the HOD molecule in a tetrahedral lattice site (Fig. 8). Assuming the unique axis (c) of the crystal is along the Z direction (a and a' are orthogonal to each other as well as to c) from eqn. (24) we obtain

$$\begin{aligned}
I_k(cc) &= K_{v,T}(81l^2_{+k} + 4(1 + 2l^2_{-k})S^2) \\
I_k(ca) &= K_{v,T}(1 + 2l^2_{-k})S^2 \\
I_k(aa) &= K_{v,T}(81l^2_{+k} + 3(1 + 2l^2_{-k})S^2) \\
I_k(aa') &= K_{v,T}(2(1 + 2l^2_{-k})S^2)
\end{aligned} \tag{27}$$

where $S = \gamma'_b/\alpha'_b$. The intensity data will be discussed in Section 7.

The weak band in the high frequency region of the spectrum of the uncoupled OH and OD oscillator of HOD liquid has been attributed to broken hydrogen bonds,[29,77] very weak hydrogen bonds[12,22] and a band edge formed by 'asymptotic behavior of the OH stretching frequency with hydrogen-bond distance'.[35] If these OH bonds (weakly H-bonded or not) had the same γ'_b/α'_b ratio as strong hydrogen bonds, the depolarization ratio would be constant across the spectrum. However, the observed depolarization ratio is lower[85] in the high region of the spectrum. Figure 9 shows that at 90 °C $\rho_{OH}(3640\ \text{cm}^{-1}) = 0.115$ and $\rho_{OD}(2670\ \text{cm}^{-1}) = 0.078$. The normal coordinates for free OH bonds[38] and slightly hydrogen-bonded OH bonds[22] are nearly the same. Using the latter to evaluate γ'_b/α'_b from eqn. (7), we find this ratio to be 1.30 for weak hydrogen bonds instead of 1.81 for stronger H bonds. In terms of bond polarizabilities, we find that $\alpha'_{\parallel}/\alpha'_{\perp}$ for these weak hydrogen bonds is 3.31 instead

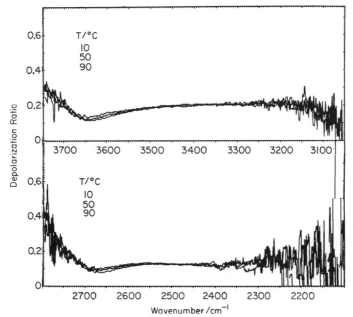

Fig. 9. Depolarization ratio of uncoupled ν_{OH} (top) and ν_{OD} (bottom) of HOD as a function of wavenumber. (Scherer, Go and Kint, Ref. 22.)

of 5.59 for the more strongly hydrogen-bonded OH groups of ice and liquid water. Because of the low dependence of the HOD normal coordinates on the strength of hydrogen bonding, the depolarization ratio of this band measures the dependence of γ_b'/α_b' on hydrogen-bond strength.

4   SPECTRA OF WATER MONOMERS AND DIMERS

The first study of water in a N_2 matrix[86] at 20 K revealed only three bands that could be attributed to a dimeric species, viz. two due to OH stretching (3691 and 3546 cm^{-1}) and one due to HOH bending (1620 cm^{-1}). These observations supported a cyclic structure

$$\begin{array}{c} H-O\cdots H \\ \diagdown\quad\diagdown \\ H\cdots O-H \end{array}$$

for the dimer. In subsequent studies with the same matrix[87] but with higher instrumental resolution, six bands were found that could be associated with a dimer species, viz. four due to O—H stretching (3714, 3698, 3625 and 3547 cm^{-1}) and two due to HOH bending (1600, 1618 cm^{-1}). These assignments favored the open dimer structure

$$\begin{array}{c} H\qquad\quad H \\ \diagdown\qquad\diagup \\ O\cdots H-O \\ \diagup \\ H \end{array}$$

rather than the cyclic structure. Infrared spectra of the mixed water dimer, $H_2O \cdot D_2O$ in an N_2 matrix at 20 K also support the open dimer structure.[88] More recently, two groups, one studying water in D_2 matrices[89] and the other, water in Ar matrices,[90] have concluded that their data support the existence of the cyclic structures in these matrices. Most recently Ayers and Pullin have reinvestigated the infrared spectra of H_2O, D_2O and HOD in Ar matrices[91–94] as well as ^{18}O-enriched samples and Xe-doped Ar matrices of water complexed with HCl and $(CH_3)_2O$. They make distinctions between bands from rotating[95] and non-rotating monomers and point out that bands of non-rotating monomers show a concentration dependence that can lead to confusion between them and dimer bands. Their detailed analysis supports the open-dimer structure. The assignments for the donor and acceptor parts of these structures are listed in Table 4 along with the assignments of Nixon and Tursi[87] for water in the N_2 matrix.

The confusion over the assignments for the two most probable structures can be easily understood in terms of the model normal-coordinate calculations of Burneau and Corset.[38] The cyclic structure may be visualized as two asymmetrically hydrogen-bonded water molecules. We ignore for the moment the effect of the hydrogen-bonded lone-pair electrons on the strength of the OH bond, i.e.

$$\overset{\displaystyle ...\,O-H}{\underset{\displaystyle H}{\diagup}}$$

The principal perturbation of the O—H bond will be through the hydrogen bond directly connected to the hydrogen atom, i.e.

$$\overset{\displaystyle O-H....}{\underset{\displaystyle H}{\diagup}}$$

TABLE 4
Monomer and dimer band wavenumbers/cm^{-1} from H_2O, D_2O and HOD in argon matrices at 7 K[92] and N_2 matrices at 20 K[87]^a

		H_2O	D_2O	HDO
Monomers				
	$\tilde{\nu}_1$	3638 (3632)	2658 (2655)	2710 (2705)
	$\tilde{\nu}_2$	1589 (1597)	1175 (1179)	1399 (1405)
	$\tilde{\nu}_3$	3734 (3725)	2771 (2765)	3687 (3680)
Dimers		$H_2O\cdots$	$D_2O\cdots$	HDO$\cdots$
	$\tilde{\nu}_1$	3634 (3626)	2655 (2650)	2706 (2700)
	$\tilde{\nu}_2$	1594 (1600)	1178 (1181)	1403
	$\tilde{\nu}_3$	3724 (3714)	2766 (2757)	3681 (3668)
		HOH$\cdots$	DOD$\cdots$	HOD$\cdots$
	$\tilde{\nu}_1$	3574 (3547)	2615 (2599)	2639 (2616)
	$\tilde{\nu}_2$	1611 (1618)	1189 (1193)	1398
	$\tilde{\nu}_3$	3710 (3698)	2746 (2738)	3694 (3687)

^{a} N_2 matrix data are given in parentheses.

Referring to Fig. 6, we see that an asymmetric HOH . . . complex involving a weak hydrogen bond (i.e. 6% reduction in O—H force constant) would have one 'free OH' stretching mode with a wavenumber near 3715 cm^{-1} (curve a). The 'bonded' OH stretch (curve b) would be expected to have a wavenumber near 3570 cm^{-1}. We note that no modes are expected with wavenumbers near those of the monomer modes, particularly ν_1.

The open structure has an almost unperturbed water molecule connected (through its lone-pair electrons) to an asymmetrically complexed water molecule. From Fig. 6 we see that the two modes of the acceptor molecule should have wavenumbers close to $\tilde{\nu}_3$ and $\tilde{\nu}_1$ (curves c and d) of a free water molecule (3734 and 3638 cm^{-1}). Whereas the two modes of the asymmetric complex should have wavenumbers, as before, near 3570 cm^{-1} and 3715 cm^{-1}. The observed dimer bands, at 3724, 3624, 3574 and 3710 cm^{-1}, agree almost perfectly with expectations for the open structure. We should note that this structure allows the possibility of a band near $\tilde{\nu}_1$ of the monomer whereas the cyclic dimer does not.

Luck[96] has suggested that coupling between the 'free' OH bonds could give rise to different frequencies for *trans* and *gauche* configurations. Similar coupling of the bonded OH groups would also produce splittings of their OH stretching bands. However, it seems plausible that these splittings would be small and result in two additional bands that should have wavenumbers close to 3715 and 3570 cm^{-1}. This was not observed and, furthermore, the HOD studies involving ^{18}O isotopes[94] gave no indication of such coupling. Finally, the cyclic dimer is expected to have only one infrared active HOH bending mode whereas the open structure has two bending modes. Ayers and Pullin observed two bands attributable to bending modes of the dimers of H_2O, D_2O and HOD. The dimer of HOD involving a hydrogen-bonded OH was not observed, indicating that the OD hydrogen bond is stronger than the OH hydrogen bond.

These studies indicate that water is not a particularly strongly hydrogen-bonding base. In fact, $(CH_3)_2O$[92] lowers the bonded-OH stretch of the 1:1 complex (with water) by 68 cm^{-1} ($\tilde{\nu}_{OH}$ . . . = 3506 cm^{-1}) more than does water (water dimer $\tilde{\nu}_{OH}$ . . . = 3574 cm^{-1}). Yet, hydrogen bonding in ice and liquid water shifts the OH stretching frequency to much lower values. These authors[94] point out that these observations argue strongly for cooperative 3-, 4- and higher-body interactions in larger aggregates.

Magnusson[97,98] has observed two infrared bands from a solution of water in CCl_4 at 3692 cm^{-1} and 3552 cm^{-1} which he attributes to a cyclic dimer. These features were observed by double-beam difference spectra of solutions containing less than 0.008 M water. The magnitude of the difference peaks was about 0.04 of the absorbance of the monomer bands at 3709 and 3618 cm^{-1}. Kollman and Buckingham[99] have pointed out that the additional two bands of the open structure should be very close to ν_1 and ν_3 of the monomer and that it may not be possible to detect dimer bands within 0 to 10 cm^{-1} of ν_1 and ν_3 of the monomer in difference spectra involving such broad bands (half-width 20–30 cm^{-1}). The suggestion has also been made[100] that the cyclic structure may be an intermediate in the interconversion between equivalent linear structures by counter rotation of the two H_2O sub-units. This process may obscure the observation of bands close to those of the monomer.

5   WATER IN HYDROGEN-BONDING BASES

There has been an enormous amount of work concerning the vibrational spectra of water in solvents that are either proton acceptors or have weak interaction with water. In these cases, the OH stretching frequency is lowered by a decrease in the O—H bond-stretching constant because of the interaction with the solvent. Either one or both hydrogen atoms of the H_2O molecule may be involved in this interaction. The complexes formed by this interaction may be labelled symmetric or asymmetric depending on the symmetry of the interaction. Referring to Fig. 6 we see that it would be difficult to distinguish between a symmetric and asymmetric complex if f_r changed by 3%, because the $\tilde{v}_3 - \tilde{v}_1$ separation is nearly the same in both cases. Larger reductions in f_r give rise to much larger $\tilde{v}_3 - \tilde{v}_1$ separations for the asymmetric complexes where one O—H bond remains unperturbed. $\tilde{v}_3$ and $\tilde{v}_1$ of the corresponding symmetric complexes fall at much lower frequencies and are easier to identify. We divide the following discussion into two parts: in the first part we consider weak interactions and, in the second part, stronger interactions involving asymmetric and symmetric complexes.

5.1   Weak Interactions

The effect of the polarizability of a solvent on the fractional frequency shift from gas-phase vibrational frequencies has been studied for a number of oscillators[101–103] by means of 'Kirkwood-Bauer-Magat' diagrams. The KBM relation is

$$\frac{\tilde{v}_{gas} - \tilde{v}_{soln}}{\tilde{v}_{gas}} = f\left(\frac{\epsilon - 1}{2\epsilon + 1}\right) = f\left(\frac{n^2 - 1}{2n^2 + 1}\right)$$

where ϵ is the dielectric constant of the solvent and n is the refractive index. Departures from linearity in plots of $\Delta\tilde{v}/\tilde{v}$ versus $(n^2 - 1)/(2n^2 + 1)$ indicate complex formation between solvent and solute. KBM studies have shown that CCl_4, CS_2, nitromethane, benzene and acetonitrile are relatively inert solvents. The maximum value expected for $\Delta\tilde{v}/\tilde{v}$ of a highly polar solvent (such as water) should be less than 0.02. $\Delta\tilde{v}/\tilde{v}$ has a value of 0.01 for CCl_4. Saumagne and Josien[39,104] have found many halogenated aliphatic and aromatic hydrocarbons that depart from the linear KBM line intersecting the point for CCl_4. However, their values of $\Delta\tilde{v}/\tilde{v}$ are still less than 0.025. The observed infrared spectra of water in these solvents show two well defined peaks that have been assigned to symmetric (lower) and antisymmetric (upper frequency) stretching vibrations of H_2O. The low solubility of water in these solvents makes Raman measurements impracticable. The perturbation of the water molecule by the solvent seems not to destroy the C_{2v} symmetry of the water molecule. Consequently, we have listed the observed wavenumbers of the fundamentals for water in these solvents in the first part of Table 5. The wavenumbers for water in Ar and N_2 matrices are included for comparison.

5.2 The Asymmetric Complex

Asymmetric complexes of water are prepared by dissolving a small amount of water (*ca.* 0.01 to 0.1 M) in a mixture of base and solvent (i.e. 1:4 mole ratio).[39] The dilution of the base with solvent attenuates the formation of symmetric base-water complexes. By varying the ratio of base:solvent, the relative formation of 1:2 and 1:1 complexes with water[39,40,105] can be studied.

The effect of lowering the diagonal stretching force constant of only one OH bond in the water molecule is shown in Fig. 6. The wavenumber of the free oscillator $\tilde{\omega}_3$ (curve a) gradually decreases to a limiting value (curve e) given by the largely uncoupled (by mass difference) OH oscillator of HOD $\cdots$, $\tilde{\omega}_3$ (OH), or completely unbonded HOD. From the normal coordinates in Fig. 7a we see that the l_{13}/l_{33} ratio (l_{33} dominant) is negative, indicating the antisymmetric stretching character of this vibration. From Fig. 6 we immediately recognize that the frequency of a free OH group must lie between the limits of frequency for the free antisymmetric stretch and the free uncoupled oscillator. Gorbunov and Naberukhin[12] have argued that the free OH stretching frequency of water in a highly polar medium should not be very different from a free OH stretching frequency in CCl_4.[106] They point out that the wavenumber of the free OH stretch of water in a 1:1 complex with highly polar solvents such as DMSO and HMPT is very close or above that of the uncoupled HOD oscillator in CCl_4 at 3662 cm^{-1}. Thus it seems reasonable that the wavenumber of the free OH stretch be higher than 3660 cm^{-1} and that of the free OD stretch higher than 2690 cm^{-1}. Support for this lack of dependence on the dielectric constant comes from measurements by Gorbunov and Naberukhin[107] of differences between the wavenumber of the OH stretch of *t*-butyl alcohol (TBA) in CCl_4 and in a hexakaidecahedral[108] cavity of water molecules in a double clathrate of TBA and H_2S. They find that the band due to OH stretching is sharp and is within 5 cm^{-1} of its wavenumber in CCl_4.

A final point to be noted is that the v_1 band of a free H_2O molecule would be observed strongly in the Raman spectrum at a wavenumber ≈ 50 cm^{-1} *lower* than the free v_{OH} of HOD $\cdots$ i.e. ≈ 3660 cm^{-1}.

There have been several measurements[40,42,105] of the infrared spectra of the 1:1 complexes of water in organic solvents. A tabulation of these measurements is presented in Table 6. The high wavenumber bands are sharp, with half-widths from 20 to 50 cm^{-1}. The low wavenumber bands are broad and in some cases have wavenumbers *below* that of v_1 of the 1:2 complex. This probably is due to stronger hydrogen bonding and possibly a larger anharmonicity of the O—H $\cdots$

TABLE 5
Observed wavenumbers/cm^{-1} for symmetrically perturbed H$_2$O (D$_2$O) and H—OD (D—OH)

Solvent	Ref.	H$_2$O (D$_2$O)				H—OD (D—OH)		
		$\tilde{\nu}_3$	$\tilde{\nu}_1$	$\tilde{\nu}_2$	$\tilde{\nu}_3 - \tilde{\nu}_1$	$\tilde{\nu}_{OH}$	$\tilde{\nu}_2$	$\tilde{\nu}_3 - \tilde{\nu}_{OH}$
Gas phase	a	3756 (2788)	3657 (2671)	1595 (1178)	99 (117)	3707 (2727)	1403	49 (61)
Argon	b	3734 (2771)	3638 (2658)	1589 (1175)	96 (113)	3687 (2710)	1399	47 (61)
Nitrogen	c	3725 (2765)	3632 (2655)	1597 (1179)	93 (110)	3680 (2706)	1405	45 (58)
Trichlorotrifluoroethane	e	3721	3628		93			
Hexafluorobenzene	d	3720	3630	1595	90	3676		54
Perfluoro-n-heptyl iodide	d	3716	3622		94			
1,2-Dibromotetrafluoroethane	d	3715	3621		94			
Perfluoro-n-propyl iodide	d	3712	3622		90			
Carbon tetrachloride	d, e, f, g, h, j	3705 (2753)	3613 (2644)	(1178)	92 (109)	3665 (2694)	1405	40 (59)
Tetrachloroethylene	d	3705	3613		92	3662		
Hexachloro-1,3-butadiene	d	3703	3613		90			
Carbon disulfide	f, g	3701	3610		91			
1,1,1-Trichloroethane	d	3698	3609		89	3657		41
Pentachloroethane	d	3691	3608		83	3652		39
Chloroform	d, e, i	3690	3607		83			
Chloropropane	e	3685	3597	1603	88			
Bromobutane	e	3682	3589		93			
Benzene	k, f	3682 (2733)	3596 (2629)		86 (104)	3639 (2670)		43 (63)
Toluene	k, d, j	3681 (2732)	3595 (2628)		86 (104)	3633 (2667)		48 (65)
p-Xylene	k	3680	3592		88	3634		46
Chlorocyclohexane	e	3678	3586	1607	92			
Mesitylene	k	3677	3590 (2625)		87	3630		47
Bromopropane	e	3677	3589		88			
Methylene chloride	d, e, i	3676	3601		75			
α-Methyl-naphthalene	k	3675	3589		86	3633		42
Ethynyl benzene	e	3675	3586		89			
Iodobutane	e	3675	3585		90			

Solvent	Ref.	H$_2$O (D$_2$O)				H—OD (D—OH)		
		$\tilde{\nu}_3$	$\tilde{\nu}_1$	$\tilde{\nu}_2$	$\tilde{\nu}_3 - \tilde{\nu}_1$	$\tilde{\nu}_{OH}$	$\tilde{\nu}_2$	$\tilde{\nu}_3 - \tilde{\nu}_{OH}$
Iodopropane	e	3675	3584		91			
Iodobenzene	e	3673	3583		90			
Bromocyclohexane	e	3673	3588		85			
1,2-Dichloroethane	d	3671	3592	1605	79	3635		36
Nitrobenzene	e	3671	3580	1603	91			
Thiophene	k	3670 (2726)	3586 (2622)		84 (104)	3628 (2657)		42 (59)
Iodocyclohexane	e	3568	3576	1602	92			
Methyl iodide	e	3564	3579		85			
Nitromethane	d,f,e,j	3663	3579	1623	84	3622		41
Anisole	e	3662	3548		114			
Chloroacetonitrile	e	3659	3557	1619	102			
m-Tolunitrile	e	3659	3548		111			
Nitromethane (0 °C)	d	3658	3576		82			
Epichlorohydrin	e	3653	3542	1621	111			
Benzonitrile	e	3650	3545		105			
Benzaldehyde	e	3639	3544		95			
Butyronitrile	e	3638	3543		95			
Acetonitrile	f,e,j,k	3636	3543	1629	93	3585		51
Furfural	e	3621	3538	1632	83			
Butanone	e	3620	3543		77			
Acetone	e,f,j	3615	3535		80			
Acetophenone	c	3612	3535		77			
Cyclohexanone	c	3610	3530		80			
Ethylene oxide (0 °C)	d	3606	3526	1640	80	3542		64
Diethyl ether	e	3590	3518	1628	72			
Dipropyl ether	e	3590	3516		74			
Dibutyl ether	e	3586	3508	1624	78			
Ethylene oxide (−40 °C)	d	3584	3519		65			
1,4-Dioxan	d,e,f,j,k	3584	3517	1639	67			
Tetrahydropyran	e	3580	3512		68			

TABLE 5—*continued*

Solvent	Ref.	H₂O (D₂O)					H—OD (D—OH)	
		$\tilde{\nu}_3$	$\tilde{\nu}_1$	$\tilde{\nu}_2$	$\tilde{\nu}_3-\tilde{\nu}_1$	$\tilde{\nu}_{OH}$	$\tilde{\nu}_2$	$\tilde{\nu}_3-\tilde{\nu}_{OH}$
Tetrahydrofuran	e, d	3572	3499		73	3524		48
Eucalyptol	e	3565	3495	1626	70	3514		48
Tetrahydrofuran (0 °C)	d	3562	3496		66			
Tetrahydrofuran (−40 °C)	d	3552	3489		63			
Hexamethylphosphorotriamide (HMPT)	i, k	3505	3454	1650	51	3470		35
Dimethylsulfoxide (DMSO)	d, e, k, l, o	3494	3444 (2520)	1663 (1217)	50	3465	1463	29
Pyridine	d	3450	3405		55	3405		45
2,6-Lutidine	d	3446	3405		41	3413		33
2-Picoline	d	3446	3405		41	3402		44
2,6-Lutidine (10 °C)	d	3445	3396		49			
4-Picoline (0 °C)	d	3445	3395		50			
2,4,6-Collidine	d	3444	3400		44	3393		51
2-Picoline (0 °C)	d	3442	3395		47			
2,4,6-Collidine (0 °C)	d	3442	3392		50			
4-Picoline	d	3440	3409		31	3413		27
Pyridine (−20 °C)	d	3440	3395		45	3380		60
2,4,6-Collidine (−20 °C)	d	3440	3387		53	3380		60
2-Picoline (−40 °C)	d	3440	3380		60	3375		65
Triethylamine (−20 °C)	d	3422	3365		57			
Triethylamine (30 °C)	d	3410	3368		42	3374		36
Triethylamine (−40 °C)	d	3408	3356	1663	42	3358		50
Ice I_h (−4 °C)	m, n	3270 (2453)	3150 (2330)	1640 (1225)	120 (123)	3314 (2448)	1495	−64 (5)
Ice I_h (−150 °C)	m, n	3221 (2427)	3099 (2294)			3279 (2423)		−58 (4)

^{a} (47, 48).	^{k} (40).
^{b} (91–94).	^{l} (58).
^{c} (87).	^{m} (21).
^{d} (42).	^{n} (61).
^{e} (39).	
^{f} (103).	
^{g} (97, 98).	
^{h} (113).	
^{i} (105).	
^{j} (104).	

TABLE 6
Observed band wavenumbers/cm^{-1} for asymmetrically complexed H$_2$O (and D$_2$O)

Base	Ref.	$\tilde{\nu}_3$	$\tilde{\nu}_1$	$\tilde{\nu}_2$
H$_2$O (dimer in N$_2$)	a	3698 (2738)	3547 (2599)	1618 (1193)
Acetonitrile (CCl$_4$)	b	3684	3546	1621
1,4-Dioxan (CCl$_4$)	b	3688	3516	1618
Tetrahydrofuran (CCl$_4$)	c	3683	3500	—
Eucalyptol (CCl$_4$)	b	3687	3480	1621
Dimethylsulfoxide (CCl$_4$)	b, c	3682	3450	1627
Pyridine (CCl$_4$)	c	3674	3400	
Pyridine (1,2-Dichloroethane)	c	3657	3400	
Pyridine	c	3657	—	
Pyridine (0 °C)	c	3660	—	
HMPT (CCl$_4$)	b, d	3684 (2722)	3385 (2496)	1630
HMPT (CS$_2$)	d	3676 (2716)	3373 (2490)	—
t-Butylammonium bromide (CCl$_4$)	d	3672 (2713)	3366 (2485)	1620
t-Ethylammonium chloride (CHCl$_3$)	d	3662 (2705)	3345 (2490)	1626
Methyl alcohol	c	3679	—	—
Ethyl alcohol	c	3681	—	—
Isopropyl alcohol	c	3678	—	—
t-Butyl alcohol	c	3683	—	—
t-Amyl alcohol	c	3678	—	—
3-Ethyl-3-pentanol	c	3678	—	—
4-Picoline	c	3660	—	—
2,6-Lutidine	c	3660	—	—
2-Picoline	c	3660	—	—
2,4,6-Collidine	c	3657	—	—
2,6-Lutidine (10 °C)	c	3658	—	—
4-Picoline (0 °C)	c	3655	—	—
2-Picoline (0 °C)	c	3660	—	—
2,4,6-Collidine (0 °C)	c	3657	—	—
Triethylamine	c	3680	—	—

^{a} (87). ^{b} (40). ^{c} (42). ^{d} (105).

bond.[105] Burneau and Corset[38] found that the anharmonic constants of water are greatly affected by changes in the normal coordinates (see Section 2.2). Specifically, the anharmonic constant x_{ii} for the free OH or OD stretch in the asymmetric complex equals that for the OH or OD stretch of gaseous HOD. However, $|x_{13}|$ is reduced from the gas-phase values of 166 cm^{-1} (H$_2$O) and 87 cm^{-1} (D$_2$O) to *ca.* 0 cm^{-1} and *ca.* 10 cm^{-1}, respectively. Dependence of anharmonicities on hydrogen bonding has been linked with the width of bands in many hydrogen-bonding systems.[15,44]

5.3   The Symmetric Complex

Infrared spectra of dilute solutions of water in strongly hydrogen-bonding bases tend to exhibit two prominent bands that have been attributed to the anti-symmetric and symmetric stretching vibrations, respectively, of a symmetrically hydrogen-bonded water molecule.[39,40,42,58,103–105,109] Again referring to Fig. 6 we see that the observed band wavenumbers produce a gradual decrease in $\tilde{\nu}_3 - \tilde{\nu}_1$ while the harmonic wavenumber values give almost a constant $\tilde{\omega}_3 - \tilde{\omega}_1$ difference when f_{11} and f_{33} are lowered symmetrically. This observed decrease has been correlated with the strength of hydrogen bonding[42] and changes in the quadratic force field evaluated from observed bands.[110] However, another mechanism is probably responsible for the observed decrease in $\tilde{\nu}_3 - \tilde{\nu}_1$ with increasing hydrogen-bond strength. As the strength of hydrogen bonding increases, the wavenumber of ν_1 moves down into the region of interaction with the first overtone of the HOH bending vibration, $2\nu_2$. The dependence of ν_1, ν_2, ν_3 and $2\nu_2$ of asymmetric and symmetric complexes of water on the diagonal quadratic force constants f_r and f_α has been calculated by Burneau and Corset[38] using Pliva's semi-empirical potential function.[111] Their results are summarized

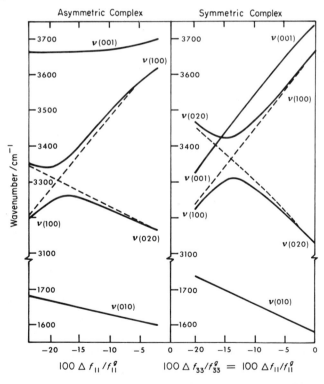

Fig. 10. Calculated wavenumbers for $\nu(100)$, $\nu(001)$, $\nu(010)$ and $\nu(020)$ transitions for asymmetric and symmetric complexes of H_2O as a function of percentage change in OH force constant for the hydrogen-bonded OH. — expected transitions, – – – – transitions corrected for resonance. (Burneau and Corset, Ref. 38.)

graphically in Fig. 10. The change in f_α was assumed to be related to the average percentage change in f_{11} and f_{33}, i.e.

$$\Delta f_\alpha = -\tfrac{1}{2} \left(\frac{\Delta f_{11} + \Delta f_{33}}{f_{11}^g} \right) f_{22}^g$$

f_{33} for the asymmetric complex was taken to be 8.284 mdyn Å^{-1}. The value of k_{122} for a 20% reduction in f_{11} was found to be 121 cm^{-1} for the symmetric complex and 94 cm^{-1} for the asymmetric complex. The difference between $\tilde{v}(100)$ and $\tilde{v}(020)$ equals k_{122} at the point of maximum resonance (point of intersection of the unperturbed transitions). There is reason to believe that these values of k_{122} are still too large (see Section 2.3). However, their calculation demonstrates that this resonance is perhaps the largest factor in accounting for the observed decrease in $\tilde{v}_3 - \tilde{v}_1$. In Fig. 11 are shown the infrared spectra of H_2O and HOD in DMSO[42] and also the isotropic Raman spectrum of H_2O in DMSO.[58] The effect of resonance of v_1 with $2v_2$ is clearly evident at 3300 cm^{-1} in the infrared and Raman spectra of H_2O but absent, as expected, in the HOD spectra. The absence of a v_3 band in the isotropic Raman spectrum makes it convenient to study the resonance-enhanced intensity of the band due to $2v_2$. Using the methods of Section 2.3, the band intensity resulting from a symmetric distribution of fundamental states (mostly Lorentzian, $L = 64$, $G = 170 \text{ cm}^{-1}$) interacting with a Gaussian distribution ($L = 200, G = 79 \text{ cm}^{-1}$) of overtone states in the D_2O-DMSO complex, is shown in Fig. 12. The calcula-

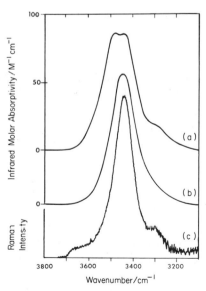

Fig. 11. Infrared spectra of (a) 2 mole% H_2O in DMSO; (b) HOD (5 D_2O/H_2O) in DMSO; (c) Isotropic Raman scattering from 5 mole% H_2O in DMSO. ((a), (b) Glew and Rath, Ref. 42; (c) Scherer, Go and Kint, Ref. 58.)

tion was performed for values of the resonance constant, W, of 20, 25 (the gas phase value for $D_2O^{(50)}$) and 30 cm^{-1}. The curvature in the region of 2450 cm^{-1} is quite sensitive to the magnitude of W and demonstrates the appropriateness of the gas-phase value of 25 cm^{-1} for W. Similar calculations for the H_2O-DMSO complex demonstrated that the value of W for H_2O is not significantly

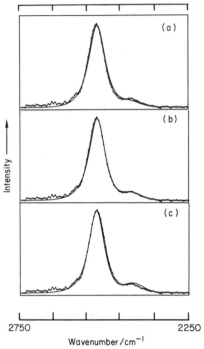

Fig. 12. Calculated and observed $\bar{\alpha}$ spectra for a 5 mole % solution of D_2O in DMSO with $\tilde{W}$ = 20 (a), 25 (b) and 30 cm^{-1} (c).

different from its gas phase value of 36 cm^{-1}. From Section 2.3 we have seen that the result of weak Fermi resonance with a distribution of overtone states on the side of a fundamental band is a shoulder at the overtone position. However, as the frequency of the overtone approaches that of the center of the fundamental band it produces an 'Evans hole' at the position of the overtone. It is interesting to look at a series of different bases from this viewpoint. In Fig. 13 are infrared spectra obtained by Glew and Rath[42] of the symmetric complex of water in ethylene oxide, DMSO, pyridine, 2,4,6-collidine, triethylamine and ice. Leaving aside the problem of ice, we note that the spectra can be qualitatively explained as the gradual shift of low intensity at *ca.* 3280 cm^{-1} in ethylene oxide to a small hole at *ca.* 3300 cm^{-1} for triethylamine. It is not necessary to invoke strong resonance[112] to account for the 'intense shoulder' in *c*, *d* and *e* at 3280 cm^{-1}. Strong resonance would produce spectra similar to those shown in Fig. 5. It is also clear why no absorption maxima have been observed in the region of 3320 cm^{-1} for strong hydrogen-bonding bases such as pyridine and triethyl-amine. The observed band maxima of the modes v_1, v_2, v_3 of H_2O (D_2O) and $v_{OH(OD)}$ and v_2 of HOD in the spectra of symmetric complexes of water with a number of basic solvents are listed in Table 5. From these data we may construct an experimental diagram (Fig. 14) similar to Fig. 10. Since we do not have values of f_{11} for these data we use v_{OH} as the abscissa since, for small Δf_{11}, it is approxi-mately linearly related to f_{11} (see Fig. 6). Figure 14 was constructed as follows.

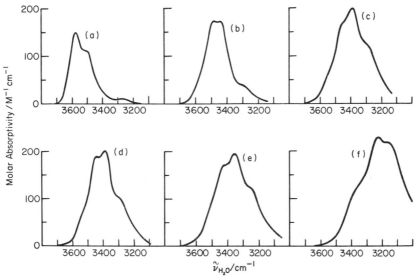

Fig. 13. Infrared spectra of H_2O in (a) ethylene oxide at 0 °C, (b) DMSO at 30 °C, (c) pyridine at − 20 °C, (d) 2,4,6-collidine at − 20 °C. (e) triethylamine at − 44 °C, and (f) of ice at − 40 °C. (Glew and Rath, Ref. 42.)

For those data including HOD measurements we locate the position of $\tilde{v}_{OH}$ on the abscissa and plot values of $\tilde{v}_1$ (○) and $\tilde{v}_3$ (△) on the ordinate. A line is drawn through all $\tilde{v}_3$ points. The $\tilde{v}_{OH}$ values for gaseous HOD, liquid water at − 10 °C and ice are placed on the figure (●). For those measurements lacking $\tilde{v}_{OH}$ data, we locate the observed wavenumber of v_3 on the established linear correlation for $\tilde{v}_3$ and plot the location of $\tilde{v}_1$ at the same abscissa location (□). The locations for observed $2v_2$ bands are denoted by ×. Solid lines are drawn through the v_1 and $2v_2$ data. The dotted line representing unperturbed states was obtained by reflection of the $\tilde{v}_3$ correlation about the line through the HOD data. The dotted line representing unperturbed $2v_2$ states was obtained from the symmetry of the perturbation on the v_1 states. The resulting intersection of the unperturbed v_1 and $2v_2$ states occurs near 3320 cm^{-1}. The dashed continuations of the observed correlations reflect the expectations of the writer, the abilities of

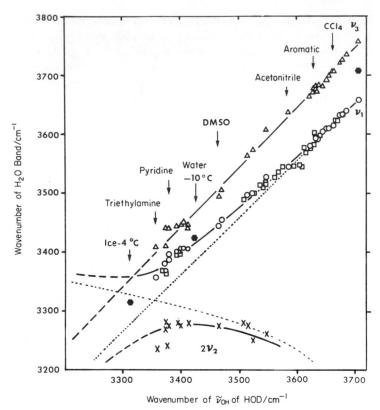

Fig. 14. Correlation of observed $\nu_3(\triangle)$, $\nu_1(\bigcirc, \square)$ and $2\nu_2(X)$ bands of H_2O with ν_{OH} bands of HOD. HOD points for gas, liquid ($-10\,°C$) and solid ($-4\,°C$) are indicated by $\bullet$. (From data in Table 6.)

the illustrator, and the guidance of the data from Fig. 10. We note that the closest approach of observed ν_1 and $2\nu_2$ states is about $100\ \text{cm}^{-1}$ and that this is reasonable for a $\tilde{k}_{122}$ of $70\ \text{cm}^{-1}$ and moderate breadth in the $2\nu_2$ distribution. The parallel nature of the $\tilde{\nu}_3 - \tilde{\nu}_{OH}$ difference has been noted by Glew and Rath.[42] They have determined that

$$(\tilde{\nu}_3 - 3756) = 1.0073(\tilde{\nu}_{OH} - 3707) \tag{28}$$

Shiffer et al.[110] have also correlated $\tilde{\nu}_3 - \tilde{\nu}_1$ and $\tilde{\nu}_3 - \tilde{\nu}_{OH}$ with $\tilde{\nu}_{OH}$. However, their correlation in the region below $3550\ \text{cm}^{-1}$ was based on only four points determined from hydrate data. Their correlation suggests that ν_3 and ν_{OH} approach within $16\ \text{cm}^{-1}$ of each other at $3377\ \text{cm}^{-1}$. Schiffer and Hornig[112] found that the observed $\tilde{\nu}_3 - \tilde{\nu}_1$ difference may be represented by the expression ($\tilde{\nu}$ in cm^{-1})

$$\tilde{\nu}_3 - \tilde{\nu}_1 = 0.1724\,\tilde{\nu}_{OH} - 539.7 \tag{29}$$

Using a larger number of data, Glew and Rath found that

$$\tilde{v}_3 - \tilde{v}_1 = 0.1701\ \tilde{v}_{OH} - 541.5 \tag{30}$$

5.4 Nearly Symmetric Complexes

In the previous two sections we considered the cases of strong symmetric hydrogen bonding and asymmetric hydrogen bonding where one hydrogen atom is nearly free. In dilute solutions of water in HMPT,[105] a sharp weak band at 3686 cm^{-1} is observed which coincides with the free OH stretch in the 1:1 complex observed in H$_2$O/HMPT/CCl$_4$ solutions. This indicates the presence of an asymmetric complex in these solutions. Similarly, solutions of water in DMSO[58] exhibit a weak broad band ($\Delta\tilde{v}_{\frac{1}{2}} \approx 87$ cm^{-1}) at 3640 cm^{-1}. But in spectra of the 1:1 complex of H$_2$O/DMSO/CCl$_4$, a sharp band is found at 3682 cm^{-1}[40] ($\Delta\tilde{v}_{\frac{1}{2}} \approx 13$ cm^{-1}). It seems clear that the 3640 cm^{-1} band must be associated with the stretching vibration of a weakly bonded hydrogen atom in an asymmetric complex i.e. $\cdots$ HOH $\cdots$. On heating to 80 °C this band shifts to 3665 cm^{-1} and becomes sharper ($\Delta\tilde{v}_{\frac{1}{2}} \approx 54$ cm^{-1}).[58] Increased Raman intensity in the region of 3590 cm^{-1} at high temperatures was attributed to a band arising from v_1 vibrations of molecules having two weak hydrogen bonds. In view of the previous discussion and the comments regarding the fitting of non-existent bands (Section 3.2), it seems more appropriate to assign the intensity increase in this region to additional formation of moderately asymmetric complexes from distortion of 1:2 complexes. The sharpness of the high wavenumber edge of the 3665 cm^{-1} band at high temperatures may represent the asymptotic behavior of the v_{OH} band wavenumber in the conversion to nearly free OH bonds. The presence of bands due to free or weakly hydrogen-bonded v_{OH} modes in these spectra indicates that some of the intensity under the v_1 band must be associated with the strongly bonded OH of the asymmetric complex. The band deconvolutions that were made by Scherer et al.,[58] assuming the presence of an asymmetric complex, are not unique but serve to show how increasing temperature or increasing water concentration might affect the proportions of symmetric and asymmetric complex. Efimov and Naberukhin[114-118] have improved a formalism originally proposed by Schiffer and Hornig[112] that uses the width of the HOD uncoupled-oscillator band as a measure of the asymmetry of the 1:1 and 1:2 complexes of H$_2$O with dioxan and DMSO. Their approach avoids the problem of distinguishing between distributions of asymmetric and symmetric H$_2$O molecules and leads to the conclusion that the OH oscillators of an H$_2$O molecule are significantly coupled in spite of the asymmetry of hydrogen bonding.[115] Inclusion of a Fermi-resonance perturbation gives good agreement between their calculated band contours for both infrared and Raman data.[118]

Burneau and Corset's calculations[38,49] show that the decoupling of oscillators produced by asymmetric hydrogen bonding causes a large reduction in

$|x_{13}|$ and a corresponding increase in $|x_{33}|$. These changes are the result of large variations in the cubic and quartic force constants. Whereas k_{113} and k_{333} are zero by symmetry in the symmetric complex, they have values of -100 and -420 cm^{-1}, respectively, for the asymmetric complex with $\Delta f_{11}/f_{11}^q = -0.20$. Decoupling of the oscillators decreases the values of k_{1133} from 200 to -20 cm^{-1} and increases the values of k_{1111} and k_{3333} from 40 and 33 cm^{-1} to 67 and 66 cm^{-1}, respectively. These changes are responsible for the increase in $|x_{11}|$ and $|x_{33}|$ and the large decrease in $|x_{13}|$. If, then, the $1:2$ complex in strongly hydrogen-bonding bases has at a given instant some fraction of its molecules in a perturbed asymmetric state, we would expect[49] that the apparent value of x_{13} as measured by band maxima of the transitions $v(100)$, $v(001)$, $v(101)$, would have a smaller magnitude than the gas-phase values because of the large change in x_{13} from these asymmetric molecules.

6 WATER IN HYDRATES

As we have seen in the last section, water complexed to liquid proton acceptors can form symmetric and asymmetric complexes. If the asymmetry is strong, with one OH weakly hydrogen bonded, we have a $1:1$ complex. If the asymmetry is only slight, we have primarily a $1:2$ complex. The dynamic nature of this system is frozen into a minimum-energy configuration in hydrates, and measurements may be made on water in various specific states of hydrogen bonding with a wide variety of proton acceptors. Nearly all water hydrogens in hydrates appear to be hydrogen bonded to some degree.[8] In this section, we will only consider aspects of hydrate spectroscopy that seem relevant to understanding the spectroscopy of liquid water. A more thorough analysis of hydrate spectroscopy has been given by Hamilton and Ibers[4] and Falk and Knop.[8]

6.1 Symmetry of Hydrogen Bonding

The site symmetry of a water molecule in a hydrate can be C_{2v} or a subset of C_{2v}. The symmetric or asymmetric character of the molecule is determined by the relative strengths of the two O—H bonds. Consequently, if the site symmetry is C_{2v} or C_2, the O—H bonds must have equal strengths. If the two O—H bond strengths are unequal, the site symmetry must be C_s or C_1. The best measure of the O—H or O—D bond strength is the vibrational frequency of the uncoupled oscillator at low HOD concentrations. If hydrogen bonding to a single water molecule is asymmetric, all HOD fundamentals will be doubled (corresponding to the vibrations of $X \cdots HOD \cdots Y$ and $X \cdots DOH \cdots Y$) but the number of H_2O or D_2O fundamentals is not increased by the asymmetry. Limits may be placed on the v_1 and v_3 mode wavenumbers of asymmetric H_2O or D_2O with the aid of Fig. 6. Let $\tilde{v}_3^+$ and $\tilde{v}_1^+$ be the wavenumbers of the modes of a symmetric water molecule where both O—H force constants have the same value as the stronger O—H bond in the asymmetric complex (intersection of a vertical line through curves c and d). Let $\tilde{v}_{OH}^+$ be the wavenumber of the uncoupled oscillator for this molecule. Because of decoupling, $\tilde{v}_{OH}^+$ will also correspond to the highest wavenumber mode of the decoupled HOD oscillator in the asymmetric water molecule. We now lower the force constants of one of the O—H bonds of the symmetric water molecule to the point where the wavenumber of its uncoupled oscillator, $\tilde{v}_{OH}^-$, corresponds to the lower wavenumber uncoupled HOD oscillator of the asymmetric water molecule. This defines the values of $\tilde{v}_1^-$ and $\tilde{v}_3^-$ of a symmetric water molecule having both bonds as weak as the weaker bond in the asymmetric water. It follows that $\tilde{v}_{OH}^+ < \tilde{v}_3(\text{asym}) < \tilde{v}_3^+$, and $\tilde{v}_1^- < \tilde{v}_1(\text{asym}) < \tilde{v}_{OH}^-$.

Band splittings in the spectra of H_2O and D_2O hydrates indicate the presence of molecules with distinctly different environments or multiple equivalent water molecules in the unit cell. The latter effect is called correlation, or factor-group splitting and the magnitude of splitting is a measure of the strength of inter-molecular coupling in the unit cell. The infrared or Raman activity of the fundamentals depends on the symmetry of the vibrations under the factor group. The number of crystallographically distinct water molecules may be determined by observing the number of bands arising from uncoupled H_2O or D_2O v_2 bending modes in a mixture having maximum HOD concentration.[119]

The magnitude and sign of intermolecular force constants between O—H oscillators separated by a hydrogen bond has been explained in terms of coupling of the transition dipoles on the two oscillators.[60] Hydrates that have dimers, chains, or networks of OH oscillators bridged by hydrogen bonds, have spectra that are stongly complicated by intermolecular coupling. The magnitude and sign of the coupling constants between adjacent oscillators in $Li_2SO_4 \cdot H_2O$[65] are in agreement with those determined for ice.[60]

6.2 Bandwidth

Many hydrates have broad OH-stretching bands. Falk and Knop[8] have called attention to differences in the bandwidth of OH-stretching vibrations in the infrared spectra of $LiClO_4 \cdot 3H_2O$[120] and $LiI \cdot 3H_2O$.[121] In the perchlorate, the uncoupled OD oscillator has only a single sharp band at 2618 cm^{-1}, which indicates that the water molecule is symmetric. This band is a singlet at temperatures of -165 to 28 °C. On the other hand, the iodide has two uncoupled-oscillator bands at 2529 and 2642 cm^{-1}, which indicates a pronounced asymmetry in hydrogen bonding. These bands are narrow ($\Delta \tilde{v}_{\frac{1}{2}} \approx 15$ cm^{-1}) at 175 °C, but move closer together and broaden drastically ($\Delta v_{\frac{1}{2}} \approx 100$ cm^{-1}) at higher temperatures. The orientation of the H_2O molecule in the perchlorate and iodide crystal structures is illustrated in Fig. 15 and the temperature-dependence of the infrared spectra is shown in Fig. 16. The two orientations of the asymmetric water molecule in the iodide are of equal energy but are separated by a small potential barrier. Librational motion will tend to decrease the probability of

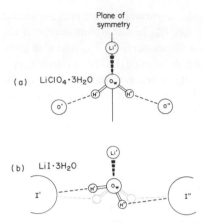

Fig. 15. The environment of the water molecule in LiClO$_4$·3H$_2$O and LiI·3H$_2$O, viewed down the six-fold axis which passes through Li′ and Li″ (eclipsed). (Brink and Falk, Ref. 120.)

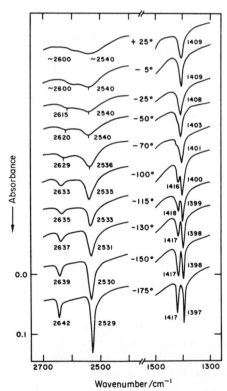

Fig. 16. Infrared spectra of partially deuterated LiI·3H$_2$O (H:D = 97:3) in the OD stretching and HOD bending regions at various temperatures. (Brink and Falk, Ref. 121.)

finding the molecule in one extreme position or the other and also cause the two v_{OD} bands to coalesce at high temperatures. Complete coalescence is not observed for the iodide but is observed in $BaClO_4 \cdot 3H_2O$ and $NaClO_4 \cdot 3H_2O$,[120] where the splitting of v_{OD} from asymmetry is smaller. As we shall see, it seems likely that this type of orientational disorder may be partially responsible for the width of the observed bands of ice and liquid water.

6.3 Fermi Resonance

A great many hydrates exhibit bands in the 3200 to 3300 cm^{-1} region which have been assigned to overtones of v_2 of H_2O and D_2O. When these bands are a hundred or more wavenumbers removed from the stretching vibrations, they seem to be relatively weak. Usually they are sharp because the bands due to the v_2 fundamentals are sharp. It has also been noted that the uncoupled-oscillator wavenumbers of HOD do not fall midway between those of v_3 and v_1 of H_2O and D_2O.[110,122–124] In the case of $CuCl_2 \cdot 2D_2O$, the v_1 band is $ca.$ 9 cm^{-1} closer to v_{OD} than to the v_3 band.[122] The observed position of $2\tilde{v}_2$ is $ca.$ 120 cm^{-1} below that of $\tilde{v}_1$. If $W \approx 25$ cm^{-1} (see Section 2.3) and the separation between unperturbed v_1 and $2v_2$ states is 120 cm^{-1}, the final separation should be 130 cm^{-1} or there would be a shift of $\tilde{v}_1$ toward $\tilde{v}_{OD}$ of 5 cm^{-1}. This magnitude of shift is consistent with the observed data. However, in $Li_2SO_4 \cdot H_2O$ the $\tilde{v}_1$, $\tilde{v}_3$ splitting is such that $\tilde{v}_1$ is further from v_{OD} than $\tilde{v}_3$[124] and, consequently, Fermi resonance cannot be responsible for this behavior.

As the OH-stretching frequency moves into the region of $2v_2$, more dramatic changes take place. The interaction between a broad distribution of fundamental transitions and a sharp distribution of overtones gives rise to an Evans hole (Section 2.3). The calculated spectra in Figs 4 and 5 show that when the center of the v_1 distribution coincides with the center of $2v_2$, weak resonance with a narrow distribution of overtones can produce narrow holes in the observed spectrum. Othen et al.[125] have observed striking examples of this effect in the infrared spectra of $K_2CuCl_4 \cdot 2H_2O$ and $Rb_2CuCl_4 \cdot 2H_2O$. Their spectra are shown in Fig. 17. From Figs 4 and 5 we note that the width of the hole at its base (the separation of the resulting intensity maxima) is sensitive to the magnitude of the resonance constant W and that the depth of the hole is sensitive to the width of the distribution of overtones. In Fig. 16 the width of the hole at its base is 80 cm^{-1} which is consistent with a value of W of 30–40 cm^{-1} or a *weak* Fermi-resonance interaction. These observations show conclusively that even weak Fermi-resonance interactions must be considered in the vibrational assignments of hydrate spectra.

7 SPECTRA AND STRUCTURE OF ICE

There have been several reviews concerning the spectroscopy of the various

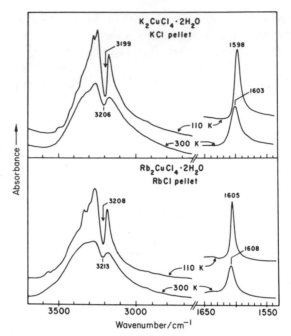

Fig. 17. Infrared spectra of $K_2CuCl_4 \cdot 2H_2O$ and $Rb_2CuCl_4 \cdot 2H_2O$, showing the presence of Evans holes. (Othen, Knop and Falk, Ref. 125).

forms of ice.[1,4,5,7,11,13,126] Because of the similarities of ice I to liquid water, we shall restrict the following discussion to ice I. Ice I exists in two forms. The unfamilar form I_c (cubic ice) is stable below -120 °C. It is formed by warming any of the high pressure phases of ice that have been quenched at liquid-nitrogen temperature and atmospheric pressure to temperatures above -130 °C,[127] or by warming vitreous or glassy ice to temperatures above -130 °C. Vitreous ice is formed by slow deposition from the vapor phase on a substrate held below -196 °C.[11] Besides the familar methods of preparation, ice I_h (hexagonal ice) may be formed by warming ice I_c to temperatures in the range -120 °C[127] to -63 °C.[68] The $I_c \rightarrow I_h$ transition temperature seems to be dependent on the thermal history of the particular sample.

7.1   Structure of Ice

Ice I_h is a uniaxial crystal consisting of puckered sheets of interconnected hexagonal rings of oxygen atoms in chair configurations that are stacked such that the holes of adjacent sheets are directly above one another (the c axis). The 1,3,5-positions of a hexagon on the middle sheet are connected by hydrogen bonds to the hexagon above this plane, and the 2,4,6-positions to the hexagon below the sheet. The structure may be generated by translation of one sheet along c by $r_{O \ldots O}$ and rotation about c by 60°. The hydrogen positions are disordered, with any given H_2O molecule being able to assume any one of the six possible positions around the tetrahedral oxygen lattice site, subject to the restraint that only one hydrogen atom be placed between any two bonded oxygen atoms. In this structure the oxygen atoms connected to a pair of oxygen

atoms along the c axis are in an eclipsed configuration $\rangle\!\!-\!\!\langle$ whereas the con-

figuration about $O \cdots O$ bonds equatorial to the c axis is staggered $\rangle\!\!-\!\!\langle$

This geometrical arrangement is different from that found in cubic ice.

The cubic ice structure may be generated by translating the hexagonal rings of a plane vertically by $r_{O \ldots O}$ and subsequent horizontal translation by $r_{O \ldots O}$ along a path parallel to a line through opposite corners of the hexagon. In this

structure *all* $O \cdots O$ configurations are staggered $\rangle\!\!-\!\!\langle$

The disorder in location of the hydrogen atoms in ice I_c and I_h tends to shift the oxygen atoms from their ideal tetrahedral positions. This disorder contributes to some of the width of the ν_{OH} bands of these forms of ice. Bent hydrogen bonds may contribute to this disorder. The valence angle of water in the gas phase is 104.5° but the O—O—O angles in the ice structure are tetrahedral, 109.47°. Neutron diffraction studies of ice I_h have been interpreted in terms of linear hydrogen bonds[128] but it has been shown that bent hydrogen bonds that preserve the gas-phase valence angle are also consistent with these data.[129,130]

7.2 The Uncoupled Oscillator

The infrared ν_{OH} and ν_{OD} bands of HOD ice shift to lower wavenumbers by 0.20 and 0.15 $cm^{-1} K^{-1}$, respectively,[131] with decreasing temperature. The shift of the corresponding Raman bands is 0.24 and 0.18 $cm^{-1} K^{-1}$.[21] The shift in frequency with decreasing temperature is consistent with a reduction in the linear thermal expansivity.[13] The ν_{OH} and ν_{OD} infrared bands of HOD ice have half-widths of *ca.* 37 cm^{-1} and *ca.* 22 cm^{-1} at -150 °C. The corresponding Raman bands have half-widths of 30 and 20 cm^{-1} at -150 °C. In contrast, ice II, which has an ordered proton structure, has four sharp (half-width $\approx 5 \, cm^{-1}$) ν_{OD} bands that are characteristic of the four crystallographically distinct O—D bonds.[132] These observations suggest that the half-widths in ice I_h must be due in part to the disordered structure.[26] The possibility of non-tetrahedral valence angles also raises the possibility of molecules existing in asymmetric states where one hydrogen atom is more strongly bonded than the other. For reasons similar to those found for the hydrates, it may not be possible to distinguish between the oscillators if the asymmetry is slight and the librational amplitudes are large.

Observations of the Raman spectra of single-crystal ice[21] have revealed the presence of weak bands on the high frequency side of v_{OH} and v_{OD}. Spectra of 3 mol % HOD in H_2O and D_2O ice are shown in Fig. 18. Raman scattering of single-crystal ice involves four independent polarizability-derivative elements: (cc), (ca), (aa) and (aa'). c refers to the c axis and a and a' are mutually perpendicular axes that are perpendicular to the c axis. The baselines in these spectra were obtained by subtraction of stoichiometric amounts of pure H_2O and D_2O spectra. The high-wavenumber shoulders were assigned to binary combinations of v_{OH} and v_{OD} with lattice modes. These observations suggest that part of the complexity of the H_2O and D_2O spectra of ice may be due to similar binary combinations.

Bond polarizability parameters have been determined from measurements of polarized Raman spectra of oriented single crystals of HOD ice.[21] The equations relating to Raman intensities of single-crystal ice to bond polarizability parameters are given in Section 3.3. From an extrapolation of integrated intensity ratios $I(ca)/I(cc)$, $I(ca)/I(aa')$ and $I(aa')/I(aa)$ to infinite dilution, the value of $\gamma_b'/\bar{\alpha}_b'$ for the OH bond of ice at $-4\ °C$ was found to be 1.81. This implies a ratio

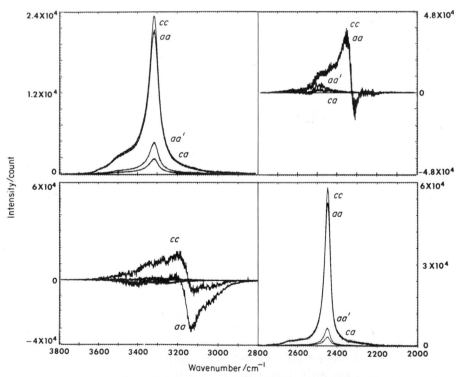

Fig. 18. Raman scattering of single-crystal HOD ice at $-4\ °C$. Top, v_{OH} and residual D_2O scattering. Bottom, v_{OD} and residual H_2O scattering. c refers to the unique crystal axis and a and a' are orthogonal axes perpendicular to c. (Scherer and Snyder, Ref. 21.)

of axial to transverse bond polarizability derivatives $\alpha'_\parallel / \alpha'_\perp$ of 5.59. Using the parameters obtained from HOD ice, the intensities of H_2O and D_2O ice may be calculated. Comparison of these calculations with the observed measurements will be made in a later section.

From infrared intensity measurements, the magnitude of $\partial p / \partial r$ was found to be 4.09 D Å^{-1}.[28] The combined intensities of bands due to ν_1 and ν_3 of H_2O and D_2O ice are also consistent with this value of $\partial p / \partial r$. The magnitude of $\partial p / \partial r$ is also consistent with values obtained from measurements of water in hydrogen-bonding solvents.[42]

7.3   The Coupled Oscillator

7.3.1.   Intermolecular Coupling

It is impossible to discuss the spectra of H_2O and D_2O ice without considering the effect of intermolecular coupling. The coupling of adjacent O—D oscillators in 18 % HOD/H_2O ice gives rise to sub-bands appearing in the infrared spectrum ± 24 cm^{-1} on either side of the uncoupled oscillator band.[60] Similar observations have been made in the Raman spectra of isotopically doped single-crystal ice.[21] The sign of the coupling constant is negative, indicating that the low-

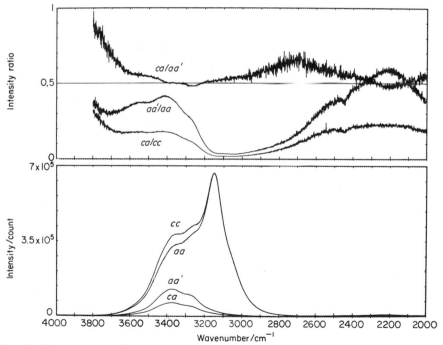

Fig. 19. Raman scattering and intensity ratios of single-crystal H_2O ice at $-4\,°C$. (Scherer and Snyder, Ref. 21.)

wavenumber band is from in-phase coupled OD oscillators and the high-wave-number band is from out-of-phase coupled oscillators. In H_2O ice, the strong, low-wavenumber Raman band has been assigned to the in-phase stretching motion of coupled H_2O oscillators.[61] The strong infrared band at 3220 cm^{-1} must also involve strong intermolecular coupling.[26] In Figs 19 and 20 we show single crystal Raman spectra of H_2O and D_2O ice at $-4\,°C$ in the OH and OD region. The strong infrared bands coincide with the weak Raman bands at 3270 cm^{-1} (H_2O) and 2453 cm^{-1} (D_2O). The uncoupled ν_{OH} and ν_{OD} bands occur at 3314 cm^{-1} and 2448 cm^{-1}. The high wavenumbers of ν_{OH} and ν_{OD} relative to the observed bands in the infrared and Raman spectra are indicative of strong intermolecular coupling.[26] In Fig. 21 we show a diagram, modified from one proposed by Whalley,[126] that illustrates intra- and intermolecular coupling in ice at $-4\,°C$. The observed uncoupled-oscillator transitions (solid vertical lines) are presumed to split under intramolecular coupling by an amount comparable to the gas phase ν_1, ν_3 splitting (i.e. 99 and 117 cm^{-1}). The value of 122 cm^{-1} is an estimate adjusted to fit the assumption that the further splitting due to intermolecular coupling is the same for ν_3 (the higher branch) as for ν_1 (the lower branch). The diagrams account for the near coincidence of

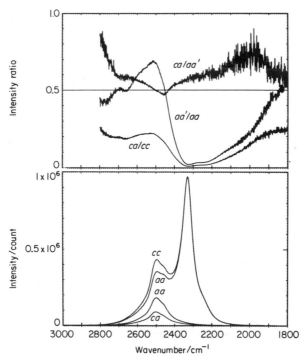

Fig. 20. Raman scattering and intensity ratios of single-crystal D_2O ice at $-4\,°C$. (Scherer and Snyder, Ref. 21.)

v_{OD} with the lowest branch of v_3 (D_2O) corresponding to the observed infrared maximum, and also the 47 cm^{-1} separation of v_{OH} and v_3 (H_2O). The lowest frequency bands of the v_1 and v_3 branches are expected to have a high proportion of in-phase character, and the highest-frequency components of these branches more out-of-phase character. The intermediate region undoubtedly contains bands due to mixtures of v_3 and v_1 vibrations. The intramolecular splitting might be smaller than indicated in Fig. 21 and the intermolecular shifts for v_3 and v_1 probably are not equal[63] (see Section 7.4).

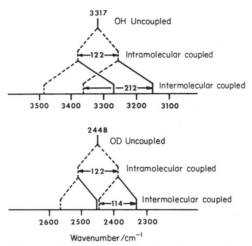

Fig. 21. Schematic diagram showing the relation between the uncoupled-oscillator wavenumbers of HOD ice to intra- and intermolecularly coupled H_2O and D_2O ice at $-4\,^\circ C$.

In Figs 18 and 19 we see that the intensity of (cc) and (aa) scattering in the vicinity of v_1 are equal, but (ca) and (aa') are less than 1% of (cc). The strongly polarized nature of this band is a result of strong intermolecular coupling that puts most of the anisotropy (ca or aa') into the high frequency region. In fact, $\frac{1}{3}$ of the intensity of the (ca) and (aa') spectra must come from v_1 vibrations.

Strong intermolecular coupling is also evident in the residual solvent spectra of Fig. 18. The HOD concentration in these particular samples was 3 mol %. The spectra in the upper half of this figure were obtained by subtracting 97% of a spectrum of pure D_2O ice. The residual spectrum in the OD region should be that of the coupled OD oscillator in the HOD molecule. However, we see that the difference spectrum is negative at ca. 2300 cm^{-1}. Clearly, subtraction of a full 97% of the completely coupled D_2O spectrum removes too much intensity in this region. To a first approximation, since three of the four D_2O molecules surrounding an HOD molecule must have a reduced coupling compared to the situation had they surrounded a D_2O molecule, only 88% (97%–9%) of the D_2O would have spectra like fully coupled D_2O. The remaining OD oscillators,

3% from HOD and 9% from D_2O, would have a spectrum intermediate between that of uncoupled OD and fully coupled D_2O. Consequently, subtraction of 97% fully coupled D_2O produces a difference spectrum with negative intensity in the region of 2300 cm^{-1} and diminished intensity around 2500 cm^{-1}.

7.3.2 Raman Band Intensities

The relations given in eqn. (18) of Section 3.3 for the simple bond-polarizability model reduce to the following ones for v_1 and v_3 of uncoupled H_2O and D_2O oscillators.

$$
\begin{array}{ll}
\qquad v_1 & \qquad v_3 \\
I_1(cc)A/K_{v,T} = 81+4S^2 & I_3(cc)B/K_{v,T} = 8S^2 \\
I_1(ca)A/K_{v,T} = \qquad S^2 & I_3(ca)B/K_{v,T} = 2S^2 \\
I_1(aa)A/K_{v,T} = 81+3S^2 & I_3(aa)B/K_{v,T} = 6S^2 \\
I_1(aa')A/K_{v,T} = \qquad 2S^2 & I_3(aa')B/K_{v,T} = 4S^2 \qquad (31)
\end{array}
$$

where $A = 1/l_{+1}^2\bar{\alpha}_b'^2$, $B = 1/l_{-3}^2\bar{\alpha}_b'^2$ and $S = \gamma_b'/\bar{\alpha}_b'$. The integrated intensities $I^*(ij)$, are defined as

$$
I^*(ij) = \sum_{v_k} (I_{v_k}(ij)A/K_{v,T}) \qquad (32)
$$

The $I^*(ca)/I^*(cc)$, $I^*(ca)/I^*(aa')$, and $I^*(aa')/I^*(aa)$ ratios are computed from the value of S obtained from the HOD data. The results are given in Table 7 under Model I. The agreement of integrated intensity ratios $I^*(ca)/I^*(cc)$ and $I^*(aa')/I^*(aa)$ for the combined v_1 and v_3 vibrations is very good. However, the deviation of $I^*(ca')/I^*(aa')$ from the value of $\frac{1}{2}$ is experimentally significant. It was found that models that retained the tetrahedral symmetry about a central oxygen atom, including a bent hydrogen-bond model,[124,125] could not account for this deviation. However, a model (II, Table 7) which assumed 104.5° valence angles and linear hydrogen bonds for those hydrogen atoms lying on the c axis gave close agreement with the observed $I^*(ca)/I^*(aa')$ ratio. Moreover, it was found that the predicted $I^*(ca)/I^*(aa')$ ratio for the v_3 vibration was less than $\frac{1}{2}$. The observed spectra for both H_2O (and D_2O) in the vicinity of the feature assigned to the in-phase v_3 vibration at 3270 cm^{-1} (2453 cm^{-1}) shows an intensity ratio $I_{ca}/I_{aa'}$ that is less than $\frac{1}{2}$. These intensity studies seem to indicate that water molecules having one hydrogen atom on the c axis may prefer more-linear hydrogen bonding along the c axis. This observation is in agreement with the known shortening of the $O \cdots O$ distance along the c axis.[5,13]

7.3.3 Bandwidths

Variable temperature studies in single-crystal ice have shown that, while there is some slight sharpening of features in the ca and aa' spectra with decreasing temperature, the bandwidths do not change appreciably. The completely isotropic part of the scattering may be obtained, using simple bond-polarizability theory (eqn. 31), by spectral subtraction:

$$aa - 3aa'/2 = cc - 4ca \propto 81\bar{\alpha}_b'^2 \qquad (33)$$

These spectral subtractions are shown for H_2O ice at $-4\,^{\circ}C$ in the upper half of Fig. 22. For comparison, the aa' spectrum is also shown. The lower half of this figure contains the same quantities for H_2O at $-106\,^{\circ}C$. These spectra were scaled so that the integrated intensities of the $I(cc)$ spectra for samples at -4 and $-106\,^{\circ}C$ are equal. It is readily apparent that the great change in band width

TABLE 7
Observed and calculated integrated intensity ratios (eqn. 32) of uncoupled HOD and H_2O (D_2O) for two bond-polarizability models[a]

HOD	Model I				Model II	
	ν_{OH}		ν_{OD}		ν_{OH} calc.	ν_{OD} calc.
	calc.	obs.	calc.	obs		
$I^*(ca)/I^*(cc)$	0.090	0.101	0.073	0.068	0.093	0.078
$I^*(ca)/I^*(aa')$	1/2	0.524	1/2	0.523	0.511	0.541
$I^*(aa')/I^*(aa)$	0.197	0.217	0.158	0.132	0.199	0.154

H_2O	Model I			Model II		
	ν_1 calc.	ν_3 calc.	$\nu_1+\nu_3$ calc. (obs.)	ν_1 calc.	ν_3 calc.	$\nu_1+\nu_3$ calc.
$I^*(ca)/I^*(cc)$	0.035	1/4	0.083 (0.094)	0.042	0.211	0.088
$I^*(ca)/I^*(aa')$	1/2	1/2	1/2 (0.522)	0.792	0.440	0.520
$I^*(aa')/I^*(aa)$	0.072	2/3	0.182 (0.194)	0.053	0.657	0.184

[a] Model I: All HOH angles are assumed to be tetrahedral and the bond-polarizability tensor has cylindrical symmetry (tensor oriented along the OH bond). Model II: All HOH angles are assumed to be 105.4°. H_2Os with two equatorial ($\perp$ to the c axis) hydrogen atoms are positioned so that the HOH bisector coincides with the OOO bisector; H_2Os with one c axis hydrogen atom are positioned so that this atom lies on the c axis. The bond-polarizability tensor is tilted from the O—H bond direction by 7°.[21]

with temperature is due to change in the isotropic spectrum. Since intermolecular coupling increases with decreasing temperature, it cannot be directly responsible for the width of the band at high temperatures. On the other hand it can amplify the effect of instantaneous disorder due to large librational and translation motions.[128] The width of the isotropic spectrum of D_2O ice at $-4\,^{\circ}C$ is comparable to that of H_2O ice at $-106\,^{\circ}C$.[21]

A band about $100\ \mathrm{cm}^{-1}$ to the low-wavenumber side of the strong ν_1 band[21,131] has a temperature-dependence that indicates it is a difference band involving a translational mode, i.e. $\nu_1 - \nu_T$. A band in the infrared spectrum about $100\ \mathrm{cm}^{-1}$ to the low-wavenumber side of the strong ν_3 peak has also been observed[26] but it is not clear whether this might also be a difference band.

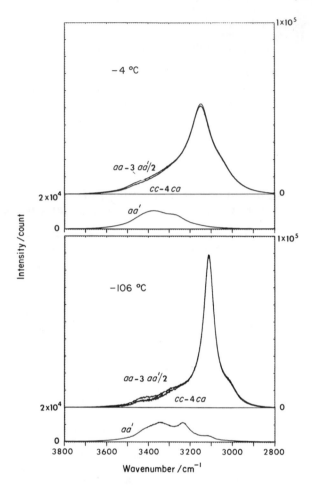

Fig. 22. Isotropic $((aa - 3aa')/2 \approx (cc - 4ca))$ and anisotropic (aa') Raman scattering of single-crystal ice at $-4\,°C$ (top) and $-106\,°C$ (bottom). (Scherer and Snyder, Ref. 21.)

Features in the Raman spectrum of H_2O $(-150\,°C)$ at 3330 and 3415 cm^{-1}, and D_2O at 2488, 2550 and 2640 cm^{-1}, may be associated with combination bands of v_1 and v_3 with lattice modes. These features may be borrowing intensity from underlying intermolecularly coupled OH and OD stretching vibrations. Whalley[64] has assigned the 3420 cm^{-1} and 2550 cm^{-1} bands to anisotropic (out-of-phase) v_1 vibrations. The intensity of these bands seems high for such an assignment. From the splittings suggested in Fig. 21, the anisotropic parts of the v_1 vibrations should be closer to 3370 and 2450 cm^{-1}.

7.4 Amorphous or Vitreous Ice

The infrared spectra of vitreous ice, $H_2O(as)$, tends to be rather featureless with absorption at higher frequencies than either ice I_c or I_h.[68] The Raman spectra show much more detail.[134,135] $H_2O(as)$ at $-183\,°C$ has a strong peak at *ca.* 3120 cm^{-1} with weaker broad bands at *ca.* 3250 cm^{-1} and *ca.* 3350 cm^{-1}.

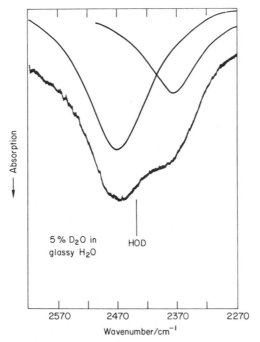

Fig. 23. Infrared spectra of vibrationally decoupled D_2O in vitreous H_2O ice. The position of the ν_{OH} band of vitreous HOD ice is indicated in this figure. (Ritzhaupt and Devlin, Ref. 67).

The similarity of this spectrum to the spectrum of single crystal ice I_h at $-4\,°C$ is remarkable. If one shifts the whole $H_2O(as)$ spectrum (at $-183\,°C$) to higher wavenumbers by only 25 cm^{-1}, there is almost a perfect match in band position and bandwidth with the single crystal spectrum at $-4\,°C$. Similarly, if the spectrum of $D_2O(as)$ at $-173\,°C$ is shifted up by 12 cm^{-1}, it corresponds, feature for feature, with the spectrum of single crystal D_2O ice at $-4\,°C$. We must conclude that the disorder that exists in $H_2O(as)$ at these low temperatures is similar to the disorder that exists in the crystal near the melting point. The bandwidths of the uncoupled-oscillator spectra of $H_2O(as)$ are about twice those of ice I_h at $-4\,°C$ and half those of liquid water at $-10\,°C$. It is puzzling that hexagonal ice at $-4\,^\circ\mathrm{C}$, with its regular oxygen lattice, would have an OH-stretching spectrum so similar to $H_2O(as)$ which is presumed to have no regular crystal structure. One possible explanation is that even though the oxygen lattice is regular in ice I_h at $-4\,^\circ\mathrm{C}$, the bent hydrogen bonds produced by large librational amplitudes give rise to a distribution of hydrogen-bond strengths that is equivalent to that in $H_2O(as)$, i.e. it may no longer be important that the oxygen atoms are in a regular lattice if the hydrogen bonds are severely bent.

The similarity of the spectra of $H_2O(as)$ and ice I_h at $-4\,^\circ\mathrm{C}$ suggests the presence of strong intermolecular coupling in $H_2O(as)$. Vibrationally decoupled D_2O in a $H_2O(as)$ matrix has been prepared by simultaneous deposition of a dilute molecular beam of D_2O and a dense beam of H_2O on a CsBr substrate at $-183\,^\circ\mathrm{C}$.[67] The infrared spectrum is shown in Fig. 23. The component bands have peaks at ca. $2470\ \mathrm{cm}^{-1}$ (v_3) and $2378\ \mathrm{cm}^{-1}$ (v_1). Since the in-phase coupled v_1 band of $D_2O(as)$ is at $2315\ \mathrm{cm}^{-1}$,[134,135] the correlation splitting for v_1 is $63\ \mathrm{cm}^{-1}$. The in-phase coupled v_3 band of $D_2O(as)$ is at $2436\ \mathrm{cm}^{-1}$,[68] which indicates a correlation splitting of only $34\ \mathrm{cm}^{-1}$.[67]

7.5 Fermi Resonance

There has not been much evidence for Fermi resonance in ice I_h or any of the other high-density forms of ice. This seems strange in view of the overwhelming evidence for this perturbation from water in hydrogen-bonding solvents and in hydrates. Weak Fermi resonance may not be obvious in the spectra of ice because of the breadth of the distribution of $2v_2$ states. The Raman spectrum of single-crystal H_2O ice I_h at $-4\,^\circ\mathrm{C}$ in the bending and librational region is shown in Fig. 24. The bending modes at $1650\ \mathrm{cm}^{-1}$ in the spectrum of H_2O and $1225\ \mathrm{cm}^{-1}$ in the D_2O spectrum have small peak heights but have half-widths approaching $200\ \mathrm{cm}^{-1}$. It is conceivable that the overtone distribution might be 300 to $400\ \mathrm{cm}^{-1}$ wide. In the spirit of Section 2.3, Fig. 25 shows the effect of interaction of fundamental distributions, $60\ \mathrm{cm}^{-1}$ (top) and $120\ \mathrm{cm}^{-1}$ (bottom) in half-width, with a broad overtone distribution $350\ \mathrm{cm}^{-1}$ in half-width. The resonance constant, W, was assumed to be $36\ \mathrm{cm}^{-1}$. We see that a weak resonance does not produce any sub-maxima or Evans holes, but does make the observed transitions broader and skewed to the side nearer the center of the overtone distribution. The isotropic spectra of ice in Fig. 22 show an intensity skewing to the region of $2v_2$ which could be indicative of Fermi resonance. Additional evidence may be seen in the observed intensity ratios ca/cc and aa'/aa for H_2O ice and D_2O ice (Figs 19 and 20). Simple bond polarizability theory (Table 7, Model I) predicts that the ratio of ca/cc and aa'/aa for antisymmetric stretches should be $\frac{1}{4}$ and $\frac{2}{3}$, respectively. Fermi resonance would tend to put more intensity into the region of $2v_2$ in the aa and cc spectra with only a small increase in the ca and aa' spectra. As a result the ca/cc and aa'/aa ratios would tend to be depressed in this region. The observed spectra of D_2O ice at $-4\,^\circ\mathrm{C}$ shown in Fig. 20, reveal that the antisymmetric stretching region (2450 to 2550 cm^{-1}) is mostly above the expected $2v_2$ position of 2430 cm^{-1}. Consequently, Fermi resonance does not depress the observed intensity ratios *ca/cc* and *aa'/aa* significantly below the theoretical values of $\frac{1}{4}$ and $\frac{2}{3}$. However, the expected frequency for $2v_2$ of H$_2$O ice is *ca*. 3300 cm^{-1},

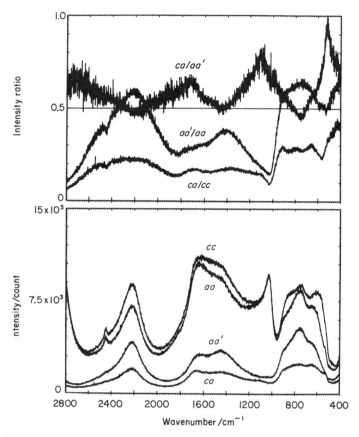

Fig. 24. Raman spectra and intensity ratios of single-crystal H₂O ice in the bending and librational regions. The sharp band at 2450 cm⁻¹ is due to the natural abundance of HOD. (Scherer and Snyder, Ref. 21.)

which is well within the v_3 region (3270–3500 cm^{-1}). Consequently, the observed *ca/cc* and *aa'/aa* ratios are significantly depressed. Furthermore, in the vicinity of 3300 cm^{-1} there is an obvious depression in both these ratios which is even more pronounced at −106 °C. We conclude that the observed intensities in the spectra of ice are consistent with weak Fermi-resonance interaction of the same order of magnitude as occurs in the spectra of hydrates and water bound to organic proton acceptors.

Finally, according to Fig. 14, we see that for ice at $-4\,°C$, the position of v_1 of H_2O, unperturbed by Fermi resonance and intermolecular coupling, should be near $3270\ cm^{-1}$. If intermolecular coupling produces a shift in v_1 of *ca.* $110\ cm^{-1}$ (Fig. 20) then the position of the coupled v_1 band would be $\approx$ $3160\ cm^{-1}$. These transitions are $\approx 140\ cm^{-1}$ from the center of the $2v_2$ distribution, so the shift of v_1 from Fermi resonance should be rather small. These considerations account for the position of v_1 in the spectrum of H_2O ice at $3150\ cm^{-1}$.

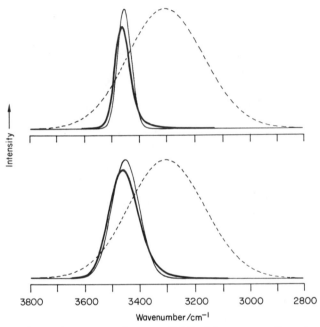

Fig. 25. Result of Fermi resonance (heavy solid line) between a Gaussian distribution of fundamentals (light solid line) and overtones (broken line) separated by $150\ cm^{-1}$, with a resonance constant, $\tilde{W}$, of $36\ cm^{-1}$.

8 LIQUID WATER

Having considered water in increasingly complex interactions, we now consider water in the liquid state. The following discussion will assume that the physics and spectroscopy of this form of water follow the same principles as does water in dimers, hydrogen-bonding bases, hydrates and ice. Specifically, our ideas about liquid water must include the effect of weak Fermi resonance of the OH-stretching band with a distribution of $2v_2$ states, the origins of bandwidths in the simpler systems and particularly ice, and the effects of intermolecular coupling.

8.1   The Uncoupled Oscillator

Infrared bands of the v_{OH} and v_{OD} modes of liquid HOD have been measured over a temperature range of 400 °C.[72,73,112,131,136] Corresponding Raman data[22,23,71,137–139] show band maxima at higher frequencies than the infrared data and this difference has been attributed to the different dependence of the dipole moment and polarizability derivatives on hydrogen-bond strength.[36] Infrared spectra at 10 and 85 °C,[136] and isotropic (and anisotropic) Raman spectra at 10, 50 and 90 °C,[22] are shown in Fig. 26.

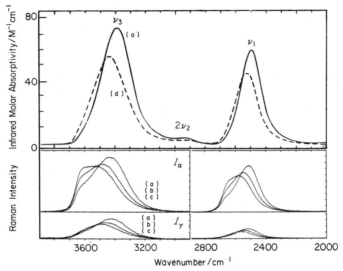

Fig. 26.   Infrared spectra (top) and isotropic (I_α) and anisotropic (I_y) Raman scattering of dilute HOD (liq.) at (a) 10, (b) 50, (d) 85 and (c) 90 °C. (Wyss and Falk, Ref. 136; Scherer, Go and Kint, Ref. 22.)

The widths of these bands are about four times greater than the corresponding bands in ice (Fig. 18) and the band maxima (at 0 °C) are *ca.* 84 (OH) and *ca.* 48 cm^{-1} (OD) above the band maxima of ice at 0 °C.[131] These observations are consistent with more structural disorder[71,131] in the liquid than in ice at 0 °C. It is interesting that the wavenumber of the v_{OH} band in the spectrum of amorphous ice[134] at − 150 °C is only *ca.* 19 cm^{-1} higher than in the spectrum of single-crystal ice at the same temperature but its bandwidth is about four times larger (110 cm^{-1}) than its bandwidth in the spectrum of single crystal ice (30 cm^{-1}).[21] Thus, the disorder introduced by a non-regular array of oxygen atoms seems to increase the bandwidth of the uncoupled oscillator by about a factor of four. The bent hydrogen bonds in such a disordered lattice must also give rise to a broad distribution of hydrogen-bonded states with a variety of asymmetries, having a complex dependence on orientational disorder, as in asymmetric hydrates (Section 6.2). From Section 4 we have seen that breaking a hydrogen bond to an oxygen atom does not appreciably affect the vibrational frequencies of the hydrogens which are valence-bonded to it. From Section 3.1 we have seen that there is little difference between the calculated frequencies of the bonded, uncoupled OH oscillator in DOH $\cdots$ or in $\cdots$ DOH $\cdots$. Without effects due to disorder, the ν_{OH} band should be as narrow in frequency as it is in hydrate spectra or, at worst, appear as a well-resolved doublet. The observed band cannot be the result of a composite of a small number of narrow (or broad) bands with widely separated frequencies.[6,77,79,80] Disorder that gives rise to a broad distribution of hydrogen-bond strengths and perturbations due to hindered translation and rotation[138] must be responsible for the bandwidth of liquid HOD.

8.1.1 Aysmmetric Complexes

The observation of a high-wavenumber shoulder[77] in the region of 3650–3600 cm^{-1} (OH) and 2680–2640 cm^{-1} (OD) in the Raman spectra of liquid HOD (see Fig. 26) has important implications for the structure of liquid water. It is unlikely that these bands are from oscillators that are not hydrogen bonded (see Section 5.2). Both the position ($<$3660 (OH) and $<$2690 cm^{-1} (OD)) and the bandwidth[22] (100–120 cm^{-1} for OH and 70–90 cm^{-1} for OD) indicate that these bands are from weakly hydrogen-bonded OH and OD oscillators of asymmetrically hydrogen-bonded HOD. It seems unlikely that these bands are due to a combination of ν_{OH} and ν_{OD} with the band due to the translational mode at 170 cm^{-1}[140] since they do not shift much with temperature.[6]

8.1.2 Depolarization Ratios

Expressions have been given in Section 3.3 for the depolarization ratio of the uncoupled oscillator (eqn. 26). If the uncoupled oscillator were completely uncoupled, $l_{+OD} = l_{-OD}$ and $l_{+OH} = l_{-OH}$ and the depolarization ratio for ν_{OH} should equal that of ν_{OD}. However, for the major portion of these bands, the measured depolarization ratios are 0.13 for ν_{OD} and 0.20 for ν_{OH}[22,85,139,141] (see Fig. 9). The difference between ρ_{OH} and ρ_{OD} is related to differences between the normal coordinates of the OH and OD stretches. The normal coordinates given in Section 3.1 indicate that ν_{OH} is more antisymmetric and ν_{OD} more symmetric in mixing with the adjacent stretching coordinate. This makes ρ_{OH} higher than ρ_{OD}. From the observed difference between ρ_{OH} and ρ_{OD} and the normal coordinate ratios (Fig. 7), the value of (γ_b'/α_b') was found to be 1.78,[22] with the ratio of longitudinal to transverse bond-polarizability derivatives being 5.38. These bond-polarizability parameters are in excellent agreement with those of ice[21] (see Section 7.2). It has already been pointed out in Section 3.3 that the depolarization ratios of the HOD bands give a measure of the dependence of γ_b'/α_b' on hydrogen bonding.

8.2   The Coupled Oscillator

Is intermolecular coupling in water important? Our first approach in considering this question will be to estimate, on the basis of arguments in previous sections, the position and shape of the expected spectrum if water were not intermolecularly coupled. Following this, we shall consider the effect of intermolecular coupling.

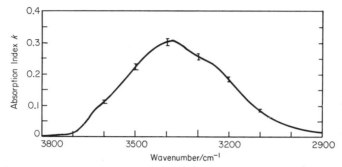

Fig. 27.   Infrared spectrum of liquid H_2O at 26 °C computed from reflectance measurements. (Frech, Ref. 24.)

From Fig. 14 we locate the wavenumber of the uncoupled oscillator v_{OH} for water at -10 °C. The expected positions of v_3 and v_1 of a symmetric complex would be at *ca.* 3460 and *ca.* 3385 cm^{-1}. Since $2v_2$ occurs near 3300 cm^{-1}, we expect Fermi resonance to push v_1 to near coincidence with v_{OH} of the uncoupled oscillator, with a shoulder appearing near 3280 cm^{-1}. The presence of any asymmetric complex would give bands near that of v_{OH} for strongly hydrogen-bonded OHs, and between 3600 and 3700 cm^{-1} for weakly bonded OHs. Thus the infrared spectrum should be intermediate between the DMSO/water spectrum (b) and the 2,4,6-collidine/water spectrum (d) of Fig. 13. The observed infrared spectrum at 26 °C[24] (Fig. 27) shows a maximum near 3400 cm^{-1} but the low-wavenumber shoulder is too intense and falls closer to 3200 cm^{-1} instead of 3300 cm^{-1}. The expected isotropic Raman spectrum should be free of contributions from v_3 and be similar to that of DMSO/water (Fig. 11) with a strong peak at 3435 cm^{-1} and a weaker shoulder at *ca.* 3280 cm^{-1}. The observed isotropic and anisotropic Raman spectra of H_2O are shown in Fig. 28. At 30 °C there are two strong maxima at 3400 cm^{-1} and 3230 cm^{-1} with a shallow dip between them at 3300 cm^{-1}. Broadening of our hypothetical uncoupled spectrum from increased disorder cannot account for the large intensity in the region below 3200 cm^{-1}.

In Section 7.3 we have seen that the correlation splitting of v_1 from intermolecular coupling in ice is of the order of 110 cm^{-1}. If we assume the same order of magnitude coupling in the liquid, the coupled v_1 mode of H_2O at

30 °C would occur at 3300 cm^{-1} and coincide with $2v_2$. Fermi resonance interaction would then produce an Evans hole similar to that shown in the lower-right corner of Fig. 4, with the width of the hole being a function of the $2v_2$ distribution. The isotropic and anistropic Raman spectra of liquid H_2O below 2800 cm^{-1} at 23.8 °C are shown in Fig. 29. The measured half-width of the strongest anisotropic component of v_2 is ≈ 105 cm^{-1}, which is smaller than that for the corresponding band in ice. Therefore we expect to see an Evans hole in the observed spectrum and, in fact, the 30 °C spectrum shown in Fig. 28 does show such a hole.

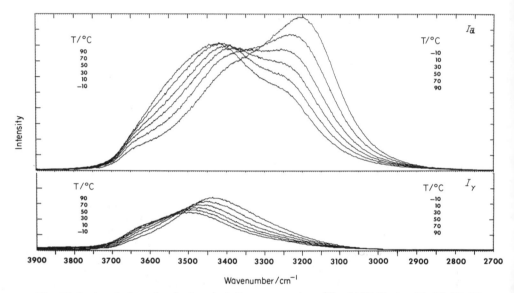

Fig. 28. Isotropic $I_{\bar{z}}$ and anisotropic I_y Raman spectra of liquid H_2O at -10, 10, 30, 50, 70 and 90 °C. (Scherer, Go and Kint, Ref. 22.)

As the temperature is lowered to -10 °C we expect the unperturbed in-phase coupled v_1 oscillator bands to peak at 3275 cm^{-1}. Since the $2v_2$ distribution is above the fundamental distribution by some 30 to 40 cm^{-1}, we expect Fermi resonance to shift the maximum of v_1 down by ca. 30 cm^{-1} to produce a maximum in the range of 3245 cm^{-1}. The effect of Fermi resonance on a single broad band centered at 3277 cm^{-1}, interacting with a Gaussian $2v_2$ distribution at 3340 cm^{-1} (probably 20 cm^{-1} too high), having a half-width of 170 cm^{-1}, is shown in Fig. 30.[22] This figure also shows that a resonance constant in the range of 36 to 46 cm^{-1} gives a close approximation to the observed spectrum from 3100 to 3500 cm^{-1}.

We should also note that at -10 °C, the uncoupled oscillator band from v_{OH} at 3424 cm^{-1} is much closer to the maximum in the anisotropic Raman spectrum

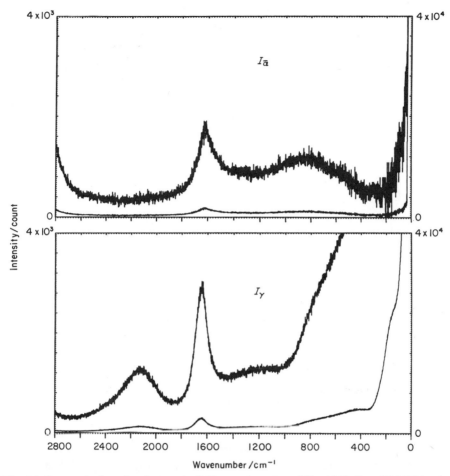

Fig. 29. Isotropic $I_{\bar{z}}$ and anisotropic I_y Raman spectra of liquid H_2O at 23.8 °C in the librational, translational and bending spectral regions. (Scherer, Ref. 145.)

(≈ 3440 cm^1) than to the center of the unperturbed ν_1 distribution (≈ 3275 cm^{-1}). This asymmetric distribution of intensity about the uncoupled oscillator band is similar to that found for ice[21,26] and is indicative of strong inter-molecular coupling.

Kint and Scherer[142] have separated the effects of intermolecular coupling and hydrogen-bond strength in observed Raman spectra by the following experiment. Polarized Raman spectra of pure water were obtained from 2000 to 4000 cm^{-1} at a fixed temperature. Under the same sampling conditions, spectra of a 4 mole% D_2O in H_2O solution were obtained. The stoichiometric equivalent of pure H_2O spectra were subtracted from the HOD solution spectra. The resulting spectra showed the presence of derivative bands in the H_2O solvent region similar to those in Fig. 17. Since there is no change in the strength of hydrogen bonding in the HOD solutions, the resulting difference spectrum must be associated with the difference in intermolecular coupling between the OH oscillators of HOD with its three neighboring H_2O molecules and the H_2O oscillator with its four neighboring H_2O molecules (see Section 7.3). Thus, shifts of bands also indicate changes in intermolecular coupling as well as in hydrogen bonding.

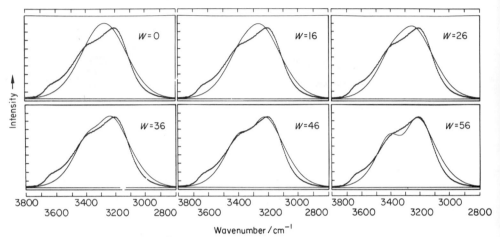

Fig. 30. Fitting the $\bar{\alpha}$ spectra of liquid H_2O at $-10\,°C$ with a single band ($\tilde{v}_0 = 3277$, $L = 800$, $G = 170\ cm^{-1}$) with a $2v_2$ distribution ($\tilde{v}_0 = 3340\ cm^{-1}$, $L = 600$, $G = 170\ cm^{-1}$) and a resonance constant W of 0, 16, 26, 36, 46 and 56 cm^{-1}. (Scherer, Go and Kint, Ref. 22.)

Another consequence of strong intermolecular coupling is that the anisotropic Raman scattering associated with v_1 vibrations will tend to be shifted to higher frequencies. Therefore, band-separation techniques that assume coincidence of bands in the isotropic and anisotropic spectra must be regarded as inaccurate.[22,143]

8.2.1 Asymmetric Complexes

The weak bands at 3650 cm^{-1} and 2700 cm^{-1} in the infrared and Raman spectra of H_2O and D_2O are analogous to the high-wavenumber shoulders in HOD that arise from weakly hydrogen-bonded oscillators. These bands occur at higher wavenumbers than the corresponding bands in HOD, in agreement with arguments that associate them with an asymmetric complex (Section 5.2). The isotropic Raman intensity associated with the stretching of the weakly hydrogen-bonded OH $\cdots\cdots$ (in $\cdots$ HOH $\cdots\cdots$) has $ca.\ \frac{1}{3}$ the intensity associated with the stretch of the adjacent strongly hydrogen-bonded OH $\cdots\cdot$.[22] Therefore, observation of weak isotropic scattering in the high-wavenumber region does not necessarily imply a low concentration of asymmetric complex.

The vibration of the strongly bonded OH $\cdots$ of the asymmetric complex has been assigned to the region of 3545[143] and 3420 cm^{-1}.[22] From consideration of the effects of intermolecular coupling in ice and liquid water, we see that neither of these assignments can be correct. This is because vibrations of the strongly bonded OH $\cdots$ in the asymmetric complex must couple to those of neighboring H_2O molecules which are probably (at low temperatures) more symmetrical. In ice (Section 7.3), the vibrations of the bonded OH of an HOD molecule couple strongly with OH vibrations of the surrounding H_2O lattice. Since intermolecular coupling in water seems to be nearly as strong as in ice, we expect the strongly bonded OH stretch of the asymmetric complex to couple strongly with the v_1 oscillators of symmetric complexes. Consequently, intermolecular coupling seems to destroy any hope of distinguishing the strongly hydrogen-bonded OH of the asymmetric complex from the strongly bonded OHs of the symmetric complexes. Such being the case, there is very little reason for using more than one band (modified by Fermi resonance) to represent bonded oscillators and a second band to represent weakly bonded oscillators to fit the isotropic spectra of liquid H_2O and D_2O.

It has been suggested that most of the water molecules in the liquid state are greatly distorted.[106] This concept of distortion did not take into account either the effect of intermolecular coupling or Fermi resonance on the separation of v_1 and v_3 in the undistorted molecule. Subsequent work has shown that the distortion was over-estimated.[114–118] The isotropic Raman scattering of H_2O and D_2O at low temperatures shows very little intensity in the region of 3650 and 2700 cm^{-1}. Band deconvolutions for water at $-10\ °C$ indicate that the intensity of these features are only 4.5 and 4.7% of the total isotropic scattering for H_2O and D_2O, respectively. Assuming that these bands have $\frac{1}{4}$ the total OH-stretching band intensity from an asymmetric molecule,[22] we find that *ca.* 18% of the total intensity could be due to asymmetric molecules, or the ratio of asymmetric to symmetric molecules is ≈ 0.22. From the isotropic band intensity of HOD at 10 °C we find that the band due to the weakly hydrogen-bonded oscillator has *ca.* $\frac{1}{10}$ of the total band intensity. If the HOD molecules have structures $\cdots HOD \cdots$, $\cdots HOD \cdots\cdots$ and $\cdots\cdots HOD \cdots$ the ratio of asymmetric to symmetric complex, indicated by the above intensity ratio, is 0.25. This is in good agreement with the value deduced from H_2O Raman band-intensity data. This ratio may be higher if the Raman intensity is dependent on hydrogen-bond strength (Section 3.2). In view of the probable continuous nature of H_2O asymmetry,[118] the above intensity argument serves only to show the consistency between the H_2O and HOD data and to give a feeling for the approximate extent of asymmetric bonding.

8.2.2 Isosbestic Points

The attention given to the observation of isosbestic points in Raman data and the contention that these observations support a two-or-more-species model of water[6] deserve some comment. Isosbestic points have been observed in the temperature-dependent infrared spectra of ice, ribose, galactose and penta-erythritol.[144] The author has also observed[145] near-isosbestic points at three frequencies in the OD stretching region of Raman spectra of D_2O ice. Early measurements of the Raman spectra of water,[77,146,147] were not decomposed into the two independent molecular constants, $\bar{\alpha} \equiv 45\bar{\alpha}'^2$ and $\bar{\gamma} \equiv 4\bar{\gamma}'^2$ (see Section 3.2) and the total Raman scattering appeared to have isosbestic points. Recent work[22] has shown that the $\bar{\alpha}$ and $\bar{\gamma}$ spectra of HOD, H_2O and D_2O have no isosbestic points and the occurrence of such regions in the earlier Raman spectra was fortuitous. Raman spectra of HOD at high temperatures and pressures[23,79] show a total absence of isosbestic points. Criticism[6] that these spectra are inaccurate because they do not agree with older Raman data must be discounted because the differences between the relative contributions of $\bar{\alpha}$ and $\bar{\gamma}$ in the recent and older data[22] were not recognized.

What are the probable changes in the structure of liquid water as it is heated? Lindner's high temperature experiments[23] show that the maximum of the ν_{OD} band moves to higher wavenumbers (*ca.* 2637 cm^{-1}) with considerable reduction in the intensity of its low-wavenumber wing as the temperature is increased from 100 to 400 °C at constant (1 g cm^{-3}) density. This is consistent with a continuous weakening of $\cdots$ HOD $\cdots$ bonds to produce structures $\cdots$ HOD $\cdots\cdots$ and $\cdots\cdots$ HOD $\cdots$ and, eventually, structures $\cdots\cdots$ HOD $\cdots\cdots$. Only as the density is dropped from 1 g cm^{-3} at 400 °C to less than 0.5 g cm^{-3} is there an appearance of a band at 2700 cm^{-1} which may be associated with broken hydrogen bonds. These experiments show that at 400 °C and 1 g cm^{-3} density there is still considerable hydrogen bonding of all OH groups.

8.2.3 Stimulated Raman Spectra

Stimulated Raman spectra of liquid H_2O, D_2O and mixtures have been obtained which show bands that are narrower and generally at higher frequencies than those seen in spontaneous Raman spectra.[148–150] The observation of narrow bands was interpreted as unequivocal evidence for the molecular-species model of water structure even though the frequencies of the maxima did not match those from band deconvolutions of the spontaneous Raman spectra. More recent experiments have suggested that the multiple-band structure of the stimulated spectra is due to beating of the laser line with a stimulated line shifted by 60 cm^{-1}, corresponding to a low frequency translational mode.[151,152] The general shift of the stimulated Raman spectrum to higher wavenumbers may also be due to disruption of local water structure by the large electric fields of the laser pulse.[151] The general effect of these large electric fields is to make the band shapes narrower but still maintain the overall spectral contour. The calculated[151] and observed[148] stimulated spectra for H_2O still show a Fermi resonance hole (or shoulder) near 3300 cm^{-1}. Thus it appears that these stimulated Raman spectra cannot be regarded as unequivocal evidence for mixture models.

8.3   Spectra of Salt Solutions

Reviews have been written by Verrall[10] on the infrared spectra and by
Lilley[9] on the Raman spectra of aqueous electrolyte solutions. A recent review
by Irish and Brooker[20] gives an excellent account of the effect of water on
complex inorganic ions. The first two reviews favor the mixture or species
approach to liquid-water structure and both cite the band deconvolutions by
Walrafen[81] as strong evidence for this approach. So far we have seen that
approaches which deconvolute the Raman (or infrared) bands of H_2O into more
than two parts[22,81,151,154] are probably in error. Specifically, the neglect of
weak Fermi resonance between v_1 and $2v_2$ states has led mixture-model advo-
cates to use two bands instead of one to explain the Evans hole near 3300 cm^{-1}.

The uncoupled oscillator spectrum of HOD in salt solutions[81,136,141,155–159]
has two components. The higher-wavenumber v_{OD} component falls in the region
2630 to 2670 cm^{-1} and, from the arguments in Section 5.2, should be assigned
to a very weakly bonded OD stretch.[157] The lower-wavenumber band falls in
the range 2500 to 2520 cm^{-1}, appears to be broader than the higher band, and
diminishes in intensity with increasing salt concentration. Since this component
results from both di-bonded $\cdots$ HOD $\cdots$ and asymmetric $\cdots\cdots$ HOD $\cdots$
molecules, the conversion of di-bonded structures to asymmetric ones would
involve an intensity decrease in the $v_{OD...}$ band because of the equal probability
of forming $\cdots$ HOD $\cdots\cdots$ as well as $\cdots\cdots$ HOD $\cdots$ structures. If the strength
of the OD $\cdots$ bond weakens at high salt concentrations, its position should
merge into the high frequency v_{OD} component and contribute to its intensity.
This seems to be the case for solutions of $Na[ClO_4]$ and $Mg[ClO_4]_2$.[157]

Salts have been classified as 'structure breakers' or 'structure makers' depending on their ability to destroy or promote liquid structure.[10] Unfortunately
the connections between structure and spectra are not strong enough to establish
unequivocally the increase or decrease of 'structure' of salt solutions by measurement of spectral frequency shifts. Consequently, all that can be safely inferred
from shifts of the uncoupled-oscillator spectra is that the O—H bonds are
weaker or stronger than in pure water. The effects that 'structure breaking' and
'structure making' salts have on the Raman spectrum of 10 mole% D_2O and
H_2O[81] is illustrated in Fig. 31. Curve (d) is the spectrum of the H_2O/HOD
solution without any salts. We note that in all cases an Evans hole is seen near
3300 cm^{-1}. The high wavenumber regions show differing degrees of band
structure. 2.6 M $Na[PF_6]$ shows a well-defined v_{OD} peak at 2670 cm^{-1} which
must be from asymmetrically hydrogen-bonded HOD water molecules. From
the observed ratio of v_{OH}/v_{OD} in the spectrum of pure water (1.367) we estimate
that the high-wavenumber v_{OH} band of the uncoupled HOD oscillator or the
asymmetric $\cdots\cdots$ HOH $\cdots$ oscillator should be near 3650 cm^{-1}. A peak is
observed near 3640 cm^{-1} in the spectrum of 2.6 M $Na[PF_6]$ which may confidently
be assigned to the 'nearly free' OH stretch of an asymmetric H_2O molecule.
At higher salt concentrations a second peak appears in the H_2O spectrum at

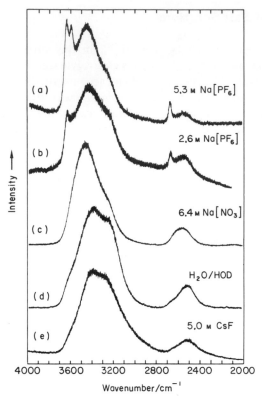

Fig. 31. Raman spectra of salts in solution of 10 mole % D₂O in H₂O. (a) 5.3 M Na[PF₆];
(b) 2.6 M Na[PF₆]; (c) 6.4 M Na[NO₃]; (d) 10 mole % D₂O in H₂O; (e) 5.0 M CsF.
(Walrafen, Ref. 81.)

ca. 3590 cm^{-1}, but no new peaks appear in the ν_{OD} uncoupled oscillator spectrum. Walrafen[81] attributes this peak to 'electrostatic interactions', but a simpler explanation is possible. At these very high salt concentrations we should be forming H_2O molecules that have two weakly hydrogen-bonded OHs. The uncoupled oscillator spectrum would have one peak coincident with the high-wavenumber component of the asymmetric complex at 2670 cm^{-1}. ν_1 should be 50 cm^{-1} lower than the position of the asymmetric or uncoupled oscillator (see Sections 3.1, 5.2 and 6.1) and highly polarized. The observed band meets this requirement and it is also highly polarized.[145] The high frequency ν_{OD} band in the infrared[157,158] and Raman[82,158] spectra of perchlorate solutions also indicates the presence of asymmetric water molecules. The frequency of this band is almost identical to those found in the spectra of perchlorate hydrates.[120] As in hydrate spectra, we expect the width of these bands to be sensitive to the structure of the water/ion complex. Therefore it should not be particularly surprising to find such distinct features absent from some spectra, as in Fig. 31(c). Spectrum (e) of this figure shows the effect of a 'structure making' salt on the water spectrum. Both the uncoupled oscillator band and the H_2O band are more intense in the low frequency region. However, the maxima in the ν_{OD} region and the position of the Evans hole are very similar to the values found in the spectra of pure water. If hydrogen bonding is enhanced in the water structure immediately surrounding the ion by promoting an 'ice-like' lattice around it, we might expect the center of these bands to shift to lower frequencies. However, the lack of four-fold coordination in the water molecules surrounding the ion might also tend to lessen the strength of intermolecular coupling, which would tend to shift these bands back to higher frequencies.[142] These examples demonstrate that it is very risky to deduce structural information from frequency shifts of bands in the spectra of H_2O and D_2O.

9   SUMMARY

A recurring theme in this review is the difficulty of drawing conclusions about the structure of water-complex systems from spectral observations. Indeed, the spectroscopic details have not been well-enough understood to make unambiguous connections between spectra and structure. However, attention to the spectroscopic problems allows us to understand better the limitations of conclusions about the structure of liquid water drawn from observations of spectroscopic data. For this reason the following summary is split into two sections: one, listing conclusions about the spectroscopy of water, and the other (understandably much shorter), about the structure of water.

9.1   Spectroscopic Conclusions

(1) Fermi resonance between OH stretching and $2\nu_2$ states has been observed in the spectra of water in the gas phase, hydrogen-bonding solvents, hydrates, ice and the liquid state. The magnitude of the resonance interaction is small and causes Evans holes or weak shoulders to appear in the observed spectra, depending on the distance between, and widths of, the fundamental and overtone distributions.

(2) Band-fitting procedures that approximate the Evans hole with two bands attributed to molecular species are invalid.

(3) There is very little basis for fitting the uncoupled oscillator spectra of liquid water with any more than two bands. One band is associated with strongly bonded OH $\cdots$ groups and the other from weakly bonded OH $\cdots\cdots$ groups. The assumption of symmetric Gaussian band shapes for infrared or Raman spectra has no theoretical or experimental basis.

(4) Intermolecular coupling between adjacent water molecules is important in ice, amorphous ice and liquid water. It affects the intensity distribution as a function of frequency in polarized Raman spectra and makes the uncoupled oscillator frequencies appear high relative to the observed

infrared and Raman band maxima. Since the strongly bonded OH of an asymmetrically hydrogen-bonded water molecule is strongly coupled to its nearest neighbors, it is impossible to separate its distribution of frequencies from that due to the surrounding di-bonded (tetra-coordinated) molecules. Consequently, it is probably erroneous to fit the H_2O water spectrum with any more than two bands, one with an Evans hole.

(5) Normal-coordinate calculations that distinguish between symmetrically and asymmetrically hydrogen-bonded water are helpful in interpreting the spectra of non-coupled H_2O in hydrogen-bonding solvents, dimers, hydrates, and uncoupled HOD in all hydrogen-bonded systems.

(6) The change in dipole moment with OH bond stretch increases linearly with increasing hydrogen-bond strength (decreasing uncoupled HOD oscillator frequency).

(7) The ratio of longitudinal to transverse polarizability change with OH-bond stretch has a value of *ca.* 5.55 and is the same for liquid water at 0 °C as it is for ice at −4 °C. This ratio is higher for OH bonds that are weakly hydrogen bonded.

(8) There are substantial anharmonicity differences between symmetrically and asymmetrically hydrogen-bonded water molecules which can influence the width of observed OH-stretching bands.

(9) Isosbestic regions in the Raman spectra of water cannot be interpreted as evidence for different molecular species.

(10) Disorder is responsible for the bandwidth in liquid water and amorphous ice. The disorder probably arises from bent bonds, dipole–dipole coupling, and interaction with translational and librational motions.

9.2 Structural Conclusions

(1) Liquid water at low temperatures is similar to ice near the melting point or amorphous ice at −180 °C. It is largely four-coordinated with a small amount of water that has one hydrogen atom that is only weakly hydrogen bonded.

(2) The distortion of hydrogen bonding in the liquid at low temperatures is slightly greater than that in amorphous ice at −180 °C which is, again, slightly greater than in single crystal ice near the melting point. The half-widths of the uncoupled oscillator bands are 250, 120 and 65 cm^{-1} for the OH stretch in these three systems, respectively.

(3) There is evidence for non-tetrahedral HOH valence angles in ice, with some orientational preference for *c* axis hydrogen atoms to form more linear hydrogen bonds.

(4) Heating liquid water involves the formation of larger amounts of asymmetrically hydrogen-bonded water molecules. At 400 °C at a density of 1 g cm^{-3}, most of the water molecules are still weakly hydrogen bonded.

At this point, broken hydrogen bonds are only produced by lowering the density.

(5) The observation of broad bands in the spectra of single crystal ice near the melting point strongly suggests that the width of the corresponding bands in the spectra of liquid water is not due to the presence of a small number of distinctly differently hydrogen-bonded species.

(6) There is little need to invoke a two- (or more) state model to interpret the infrared and Raman spectra of water.

REFERENCES

(1) N. Ockman, *Adv. Phys.* **7**, 199 (1958).
(2) G. C. Pimentel and A. L. McClellan, *The Hydrogen Bond*, Freeman, San Francisco, 1960.
(3) B. Kamb, in *Structural Chemistry and Molecular Biology* (A. Rich and N. Davidson, eds.), Freeman, San Francisco, 1968, p. 507.
(4) W. C. Hamilton and J. A. Ibers, *Hydrogen Bonding in Solids*, W. A. Benjamin, New York, 1968.
(5) D. Eisenberg and W. Kauzmann, *The Structure and Properties of Water*, Oxford University Press, New York, 1969.
(6) G. E. Walrafen, in *Water*, Vol. 1 (F. Franks, ed.), Plenum, New York, 1972, Ch. 5.
(7) F. Franks, in *Water*, Vol. 1 (F. Franks, ed.), Plenum, New York, 1972, Ch. 4.
(8) M. Falk and O. Knop. in *Water*, Vol. 2 (F. Franks, ed.), Plenum, New York, 1973, Ch. 2.
(9) T. H. Lilley, in *Water*, Vol. 3 (F. Franks, ed.), Plenum, New York, 1973, Ch. 6.
(10) R. E. Verrall, in *Water*, Vol. 3 (F. Franks, ed.), Plenum, New York, 1973, Ch. 5.
(11) S. A. Rice, *Top. Curr. Chem.* **60**, 109 (1975).
(12) B. Z. Gorbunov and Yu. I. Naberukhin, *Zh. Struk. Khim.* **16**, 703 (1975).
(13) E. Walley, in *The Hydrogen Bond* (P. Schuster and G. Zundel, eds.), North Holland, Amsterdam, 1976, Ch. 29.
(14) C. Sandorfy, in *The Hydrogen Bond* (P. Schuster and G. Zundel, eds.), North Holland, Amsterdam, 1976, Ch. 13.
(15) D. Hadzi and S. Bratos, in *The Hydrogen Bond* (P. Schuster and G. Zundel, eds.), North Holland, Amsterdam, 1976, Ch. 12.
(16) W. A. P. Luck, in *The Hydrogen Bond* (P. Schuster and G. Zundel, eds.), North Holland, Amsterdam, 1976, Ch. 11.
(17) R. Janaschek, in *The Hydrogen Bond* (P. Schuster and G. Zundel, eds.), North Holland, Amsterdam, 1976, Ch. 3.
(18) J. Brickmann, in *The Hydrogen Bond* (P. Schuster and G. Zundel, eds.), North Holland, Amsterdam, 1976, Ch. 4.
(19) J. W. Perram, in *The Hydrogen Bond* (P. Schuster and G. Zundel, eds.), North Holland, Amsterdam, 1976, Ch. 7.
(20) D. E. Irish and M. H. Brooker, in *Adv. Infrared Raman Spectrosc.*, Vol. 2 (R. J. H. Clark and R. E. Hester, eds.), Heyden, London, 1976, Ch. 6.
(21) J. R. Scherer and R. G. Snyder, *J. Chem. Phys.* **67**, 4802 (1977).
(22) J. R. Scherer, M. K. Go and S. Kint, *J. Phys. Chem.* **78**, 1304 (1974).
(23) H. A. Lindner, Thesis, University of Karlsruhe, Germany, 1970.
(24) R. Frech, Thesis, University of Minnesota, U.S.A., 1968.

(25) L. W. Pinkley, P. P. Sethna and D. Williams, *J. Opt. Soc. Am.* **67**, 494 (1977).
(26) J. E. Bertie and E. Whalley, *J. Chem. Phys.* **40**, 1637 (1964).
(27) J. E. Bertie, H. J. Labbé and E. Whalley, *J. Chem. Phys.* **50**, 4501 (1969).
(28) S. I. Ikawa and S. Maeda, *Spectrochim. Acta, Part A* **24**, 655 (1968).
(29) G. E. Walrafen, *J. Chem. Phys.* **47**, 114 (1967).
(30) B. Curnutte and J. Bandekar, *J. Mol. Spectrosc.* **41**, 500 (1972).
(31) J. B. Bryan and B. Curnutte, *J. Mol. Spectrosc.* **41**, 512 (1972).
(32) B. Curnutte and J. Bandekar, *J. Mol. Spectrosc.* **49**, 314 (1974).
(33) R. C. Lord and R. E. Merrifield, *J. Chem. Phys.* **21**, 166 (1956).
(34) R. E. Rundle and M. Parasol, *J. Chem. Phys.* **20**, 1487 (1952).
(35) A. Novak, *Struct. and Bonding (Berlin)* **18**, 177 (1974).
(36) M. Falk, in *Chemistry and Physics of Aqueous Gas Solutions* (W. A. Adams, ed.), 1975, p. 19.
(37) E. R. Lippincott, J. N. Finch and R. Schroeder, in *Hydrogen Bonding* (D. Hadzi, ed.), Pergamon, New York, 1959.
(38) A. Burneau and J. Corset, *J. Chim. Phys. Phys.-Chim. Biol.* **1**, 142 (1972).
(39) P. Saumagne, Thesis, Université de Bordeaux, France, 1961.
(40) E. Gentric, Thesis, Université de Bretagne Occidentale, France, 1972.
(41) G. E. Walrafen and L. A. Blatz, *J. Chem. Phys.* **59**, 2646 (1973).
(42) D. N. Glew and N. S. Rath, *Can. J. Chem.* **49**, 837 (1971).
(43) J. Lindgren and J. Tegenfeldt, *J. Mol. Struct.* **20**, 335 (1974).
(44) A. Foldes and C. Sandorfy, *J. Mol. Spectrosc.* **20**, 262 (1966).
(45) K. Kuchitsu and Y. Morino, *Bull. Chem. Soc. Jpn* **38**, 814 (1965).
(46) G. Herzberg, *Infrared and Raman Spectra*, Van Nostrand, New York, 1945.
(47) W. S. Benedict, N. Gailar and E. K. Plyler, *J. Chem. Phys.* **24**, 1139 (1956).
(48) N. M. Gailar and F. P. Dickey, *J. Mol. Spectrosc.* **4**, 1 (1960).
(49) A. Burneau and J. Corset, *J. Chim. Phys. Phys.-Chim. Biol.* **1**, 171 (1972).
(50) D. F. Smith and J. Overend, *Spectrochim. Acta, Part A* **28**, 471 (1972).
(51) M. A. Pariseau, Thesis, University of Minnesota, U.S.A., 1963.
(52) A. R. Hoy, I. M. Mills and G. Strey, *Mol. Phys.* **24**, 1265 (1972).
(53) G. K. Spiers and V. Spirko, *J. Mol. Spectrosc.* **56**, 104 (1975).
(54) H. G. Howard-Lock and B. P. Stoicheff, *J. Mol. Spectrosc.* **37**, 321 (1971).
(55) J. C. Evans, *Spectrochim. Acta* **16**, 994 (1960).
(56) J. C. Evans and N. Wright, *Spectrochim. Acta* **16**, 352 (1960).
(57) M. F. Claydon and N. Sheppard, *Chem. Commun.* 1431 (1969).
(58) J. R. Scherer, M. K. Go and S. Kint, *J. Phys. Chem.* **77**, 2108 (1973).
(59) S. Bratos, *J. Chem. Phys.* **63**, 3499 (1975).
(60) C. Haas and D. F. Hornig, *J. Chem. Phys.* **32**, 1763 (1960).
(61) P. T. T. Wong and E. Whalley, *J. Chem. Phys.* **62**, 2418 (1975).
(62) R. McGraw, W. G. Madden, S. A. Rice and M. Sceats, *Chem. Phys. Lett.* **48**, 219 (1977).
(63) E. Whalley, *Can. J. Chem.* **55**, 3429 (1977).
(64) P. T. T. Wong and E. Whalley, *J. Chem. Phys.* **64**, 2359 (1976).
(65) H. P. Hayward and J. Schiffer, *J. Chem. Phys.* **64**, 3961 (1976).
(66) S. Rice, personal communication.
(67) G. Ritzhaupt and J. P. Devlin, *J. Chem. Phys.* **67**, 4779 (1977).
(68) A. H. Hardin and K. B. Harvey, *Spectrochim. Acta, Part A,* **29**, 1139 (1973).
(69) J. W. Nibler and G. C. Pimentel, *J. Mol. Spectrosc.* **26**, 294 (1968).
(70) R. M. Badger, *J. Chem. Phys.* **8**, 288 (1940).
(71) T. T. Wall and D. F. Hornig, *J. Chem. Phys.* **43**, 2079 (1965).
(72) M. Falk and T. A. Ford, *Can. J. Chem.* **44**, 1699 (1966).
(73) E. U. Franck and K. Roth, *Discuss. Faraday Soc.* **43**, 108 (1967).
(74) T. C. Damen, S. P. S. Porto and B. Tell, *Phys. Rev., Ser. 2,* **142**, 570 (1966).

(75) J. R. Scherer and S. Kint, *Appl. Opt.* **9**, 1615 (1970).
(76) J. R. Scherer, S. Kint and G. F. Bailey, *J. Mol. Spectrosc.* **39**, 146 (1971).
(77) G. E. Walrafen, *J. Chem. Phys.* **48**, 244 (1968).
(78) J. Pitha and N. Jones, *NRC Bulletin No. 12*, National Research Council, Ottawa, Canada, 1968.
(79) E. C. W. Clarke and D. N. Glew, *Can. J. Chem.* **50**, 1655 (1972).
(80) G. E. Walrafen, *J. Chem. Phys.* **50**, 567 (1969).
(81) G. E. Walrafen, *J. Chem. Phys.* **55**, 768 (1971).
(82) D. A. Long, *Proc. R. Soc. London, Ser. A* **217**, 203 (1953).
(83) R. E. Hester, in *Raman Spectroscopy* (H. A. Szymanksi, ed.), Plenum, New York, 1967.
(84) E. B. Wilson, J. C. Decius and P. C. Cross, *Molecular Vibrations*, McGraw-Hill, New York, 1955.
(85) M. K. Cunningham, Thesis, Yale University, U.S.A., 1972.
(86) M. Van Tiel, E. D. Becker and G. C. Pimentel, *J. Chem. Phys.* **27**, 486 (1957).
(87) A. J. Tursi and E. R. Nixon, *J. Chem. Phys.* **52**, 1521 (1970).
(88) G. R. Choppin and M. R. Violante, *J. Chem. Phys.* **56**, 5890 (1972).
(89) D. P. Strommen, D. M. Gruen and R. L. McBeth, *J. Chem. Phys.* **58**, 4028 (1973).
(90) B. Mann, T. Neckes, E. Schmidt and W. A. P. Luck, *Ber. Bunsenge. Phys. Chem.* **78**, 1237 (1974).
(91) G. P. Ayers and A. D. E. Pullin, *Spectrochim. Acta, Part A* **23**, 1629 (1976).
(92) G. P. Ayers and A. D. E. Pullin, *Spectrochim. Acta, Part A* **23**, 1641 (1976).
(93) G. P. Ayers and A. D. E. Pullin, *Spectrochim. Acta, Part A* **23**, 1689 (1976).
(94) G. P. Ayers and A. D. E. Pullin, *Spectrochim. Acta, Part A* **23**, 1695 (1976).
(95) R. L. Redington and D. E. Milligan, *J. Chem. Phys.* **37**, 2162 (1962).
(96) W. A. P. Luck, in *Water*, Vol. 2 (F. Franks, ed.), Plenum, New York, 1973, Ch. 4.
(97) L. B. Magnusson, *J. Phys. Chem.* **74**, 4221 (1970).
(98) L. B. Magnusson, *Mol. Phys.* **21**, 571 (1971).
(99) P. A. Kollman and A. D. Buckingham, *Mol. Phys.* **21**, 567 (1971).
(100) P. W. Atkins and M. C. R. Symons, *Mol. Phys.* **23**, 831 (1972).
(101) M. L. Josien, *Pure Appl. Chem.* **4**, 33 (1962).
(102) M. L. Josien, M. P. Leicknam and N. Fuson, *Bull. Soc. Chim. Fr.* 188, **1958**.
(103) E. Greinacher, W. Luttke and R. Mecke, *Z. Elektrochem.* **59**, 23 (1955).
(104) P. Saumage and M. L. Josien, *Bull. Soc. Chim. Fr.* 813, **1958**.
(105) A. Burneau and J. Corset, *J. Chim. Phys. Phys.-Chim. Biol.* **1**, 142 (1972).
(106) D. P. Stevenson, *J. Phys. Chem.* **69**, 2145 (1965).
(107) B. Z. Gorbunov and Yu. I. Naberukhin, *Chem. Phys. Lett.* **19**, 215 (1973).
(108) D. W. Davidson, in *Water*, Vol. 2 (F. Franks, ed.), Plenum, New York, 1973, Ch. 3.
(109) A. L. Narvor, E. Gentric and P. Saumagne, *Can. J. Chem.* **49**, 1933 (1971).
(110) J. Schiffer, M. Intenzo, P. Hayward and C. Calabrese, *J. Chem. Phys.* **64**, 3014 (1976).
(111) D. Papousek and J. Pliva, *Collect. Czech. Chem. Commun.* **29**, 1973 (1964).
(112) J. Schiffer and D. F. Hornig, *J. Chem. Phys.* **49**, 4150 (1968).
(113) D. P. Stevenson, in *Structural Chemistry and Biology* (A. Rich and N. R. Davidson, eds.), Freman, San Francisco, 1968, p. 490.
(114) Yu Ya Efimov and Yu I. Naberukhin, *Mol. Phys.* **30**, 1621 (1975).
(115) Yu Ya Efimov and Yu I. Naberukhin, *Mol. Phys.* **30**, 1627 (1975).
(116) Yu Ya Efimov and Yu I. Naberukhin, *Mol. Phys.* **30**, 1635 (1975).
(117) Yu Ya Efimov and Yu I. Naberukhin, *Mol. Phys.* **33**, 759 (1977).
(118) Yu Ya Efimov and Yu I. Naberukhin, *Mol. Phys.* **33**, 779 (1977).
(119) V. Seidl, O. Knop and M. Falk, *Can. J. Chem.* **47**, 1361 (1969).

(120) G. Brink and M. Falk, *Can. J. Chem.* **48**, 2096 (1970).

(121) G. Brink and M. Falk, *Can. J. Chem.* **49**, 347 (1971).

(122) R. A. Fifer and J. Schiffer, *J. Chem. Phys.* **54**, 5097 (1971).

(123) R. A. Fifer and J. Schiffer, *J. Chem. Phys.* **52**, 2664 (1970).

(124) H. P. Hayward and J. Schiffer, *J. Chem. Phys.* **62**, 1973 (1975).

(125) D. A. Othen, O. Knop and M. Falk, *Can. J. Chem.* **53**, 3837 (1975).

(126) E. Whalley, *Rev. Appl. Spectrosc.* **6**, 277 (1968).

(127) J. E. Bertie, L. D. Calvert and E. Whalley, *J. Chem. Phys.* **38**, 840 (1963).

(128) S. W. Peterson and H. A. Levy, *Acta Crystallogr.* **10**, 70, (1957).

(129) R. Chidambaram, *Acta Crystallogr.* **14**, 467 (1961).

(130) R. Chidambaram and S. K. Sikka, *Chem. Phys. Lett.* **2**, 162 (1968).

(131) T. A. Ford and M. Falk, *Can. J. Chem.* **46**, 3579 (1968).

(132) J. E. Bertie and E. Whalley, *J. Chem. Phys.* **40**, 1646 (1964).

(133) T. C. Sivakumar, D. Schuh, M. G. Sceats and S. A. Rice, *Chem. Phys. Lett.* **48**, 212 (1977).

(134) C. G. Venkatesh, J. B. Bates and S. A. Rice, *J. Chem. Phys.* **63**, 1065 (1975).

(135) P. C. Li and J. P. Devlin, *J. Chem. Phys.* **59**, 547 (1973).

(136) H. R. Wyss and M. Falk, *Can. J. Chem.* **48**, 607 (1790).

(137) G. W. Walrafen, *J. Chem. Phys.* **50**, 560 (1969).

(138) T. T. Wall, *J. Chem. Phys.* **51**, 113 (1969).

(139) W. C. Mundy, L. Gutierrez and F. H. Spedding, *J. Chem. Phys.* **59**, 2173 (1973).

(140) G. E. Walrafen, *J. Chem. Phys.* **44**, 1546 (1966).

(141) R. E. Weston, *Spectrochim. Acta* **18**, 1257 (1962).

(142) S. Kint and J. R. Scherer, *J. Chem. Phys.*, in press.

(143) W. F. Murphy and H. J. Bernstein, *J. Phys. Chem.* **76**, 1147 (1972).

(144) M. Falk and H. R. Wyss, *J. Chem. Phys.* **51**, 5727 (1969).

(145) J. R. Scherer, unpublished work.

(146) G. E. Walrafen and L. A. Blatz, *J. Chem. Phys.* **56**, 4216 (1972).

(147) G. E. Walrafen, *J. Chem. Phys.* **52**, 4176 (1970).

(148) G. E. Walrafen, *Adv. Molec. Relaxation Processes* **3**, 43 (1972).

(149) M. J. Colles, G. E. Walrafen and K. W. Wecht, *Chem. Phys. Lett.* **4**, 621 (1970).

(150) G. E. Walrafen, *J. Chem. Phys.* **64**, 2699 (1976).

(151) M. G. Sceats, S. A. Rice and J. E. Butler, *J. Chem. Phys.* **63**, 5390 (1975).

(152) M. G. Sceats, S. A. Rice and J. E. Butler, *J. Chem. Phys.* **64**, 2700 (1976).

(153) B. G. Oliver and G. J. Janz, *J. Phys. Chem.* **75**, 2948 (1971).

(154) G. E. Rodgers and R. A. Plane, *J. Chem. Phys.* **63**, 818 (1975).

(155) R. D. Waldron, *J. Chem. Phys.* **26**, 809 (1957).

(156) K. A. Hartman, *J. Phys. Chem.* **70**, 270 (1966).

(157) G. Brink and M. Falk, *Can. J. Chem.* **48**, 3019 (1970).

(158) D. M. Adams, M. J. Blandamer, M. C. R. Symons and D. Waddington, *Trans. Faraday Soc.* **67**, 611 (1971).

(159) W. C. Mundy and F. H. Spedding, *J. Chem. Phys.* **59**, 2183 (1973).

Chapter 4

RESONANCE RAMAN SPECTROSCOPY OF NUCLEIC ACIDS

Yoshifumi Nishimura, Akiko Y. Hirakawa, and Masamichi Tsuboi

Faculty of Pharmaceutical Sciences, University of Tokyo, Hongo, Bunkyo-ku, Tokyo, Japan

1 INTRODUCTION

Raman spectroscopy may be regarded as a science having to do with the analysis of a three-dimensional, rather than a two-dimensional, spectrum. We often need to examine the Raman scattered intensity not only as a function of the wavenumber of the scattered beam but also as a function of the exciting light. Such a three-dimensional spectrum is illustrated in Fig. 1. As is seen from this figure, many of the Raman bands of β-uridine-5'-phosphoric acid (UMP) become stronger as the wavelength of the exciting radiation approaches that of an absorption band. This is called a pre-resonance Raman effect. Some of the Raman bands are enhanced to a greater extent than others. The vibrational modes associated with such Raman bands have a close relation with a particular property of the relevant excited electronic state. When the wavelength of the exciting light is brought into coincidence with that of an absorption band of UMP, the so-called rigorous resonance Raman effect is realized. Here, a Raman spectrum can be observed with a UMP solution at a concentration as low as that found suitable for ultraviolet absorbance measurements (*ca.* 10^{-4} M). The characteristics of resonance Raman spectra may be considered to be determined by properties of the excited electronic state concerned as well as of the ground electronic state. How these are determined is the main subject of the present article.

Resonance Raman spectroscopy of nucleic acids does not yet seem to be a very active field in comparison, for example, with resonance Raman spectroscopy of metallo-porphyrins or of rhodopsins.[1] This is partly because the absorption bands of nucleic acids are beyond the wavelength regions of the argon and krypton ion lasers as well as of typical dye lasers, whereas metallo-porphyrins or rhodopsins have their strong absorption bands within these regions. Details of the exictation profiles of most of the Raman bands of nucleic-acid base residues

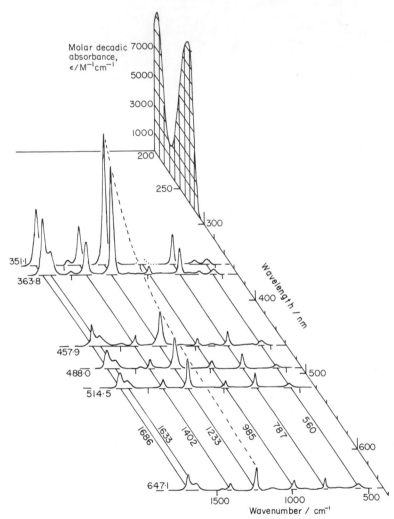

Fig. 1. Raman spectra of β-uridine 5'-phosphoric acid obtained from neutral ^1H_2O solution with exciting lines of various wavelengths.

are yet to be examined. In addition, no detailed assignments of the vibrational spectra of these molecules have yet been possible, because of their high complexities and low symmetries. Normal coordinate treatments[2-5] so far made of the base residues are yet to be refined. Nevertheless, the data we have recently accumulated seem to be sufficient to understand in outline the mechanism of the resonance Raman effects shown by nucleic-acid base residues.

All of the common bases of nucleic acids have strong absorption bands ($\epsilon \approx 10^4$ M^{-1} cm^{-1}) in the 260 nm region (see Fig. 2). Therefore, the most desirable tool for resonance Raman spectroscopy of nucleic acids is a laser tunable in this spectral region. By the use of a frequency doubler in combination with appropriate dyes, an elaborate study of the excitation profiles of the Raman bands of β-adenosine-5'-phosphoric acid has recently been made by Blazej and Peticolas.[6] Similar work on a few other nucleic acids has also been started by Brahms (personal communication). We have been engaged in the use of 257.3 nm c.w. excitation obtained by the use of an argon ion laser (514.5 nm beam) in

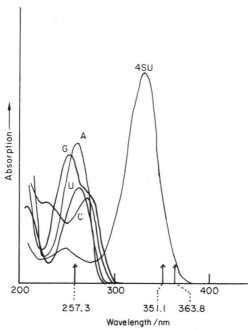

Fig. 2. Absorption spectra of uracil (U), cytosine (C), adenine (A), guanine (G) and 4-thiouracil (4SU) residues, and wavelengths of some lines of the argon and krypton ion lasers and a frequency-doubled argon-ion laser.

combination with a non-linear optical crystal of ammonium dihydrogen phosphate (ADP).[7] The wavelength of this beam is located well within the 260 nm bands of various nucleic acids (Fig. 2), and hence rigorous resonance Raman effects can be observed by its use as the exciting source. The results of such observations form a useful set of data for our discussion below.

The first three sections of this article will be devoted to preparatory descriptions; namely, a brief review of non-resonance or conventional Raman spectroscopy of nucleic acids, a summary of the theory of resonance Raman spectroscopy which is relevant to the later discussion, and a few comments on the nature of the normal vibrations of ring systems. Resonance and pre-resonance Raman effects of regular base residues of nucleic acids will then be discussed. The focus of the discussion will be placed on the correlation between the Raman scattering of each base residue and the nature of its excited electronic states. In the last section, some comments on the possible applications of resonance Raman spectroscopy to the study of nucleic acids in biological systems will be mentioned.

2   A BRIEF REVIEW OF OFF-RESONANCE RAMAN SPECTROSCOPY OF NUCLEIC ACIDS

As an example, a Raman spectrum of purified formylmethionine transfer RNA (tRNA) from *Escherichia coli*, observed by use of 514.5 nm excitation, is shown in Fig. 3. Such a spectrum can be obtained from, for example, 0.2 cm^3 of 5% aqueous solution, and the minimum amount required would be about 0.02 cm^3. This RNA is a single polynucleotide chain with 77 nucleotide residues, of which 8 are those of uridylic acid, 25 cytidylic acid, 15 adenylic acid, and 24 guanylic acid; the remaining 5 are residues of minor nucleotides. It would be helpful to compare such a Raman spectrum with spectra of the homopolymers of the four regular ribonucleotides: polyribouridylic acid (poly(rU)), polyribocytidylic acid (poly(rC)), polyriboadenylic acid (poly(rA)), and polyriboguanylic acid (poly(rG)). The Raman spectra of these four homopolymers in neutral aqueous solutions are given also in Fig. 3. The chemical structure of each nucleotide residue is exactly the same in the homopolymer as in the tRNA. Differences between the Raman spectra of a nucleotide residue in the homopolymer and the tRNA are attributable to differences between their secondary structures. Differences caused by vibrational coupling between the adjacent nucleotide residues would be negligibly small.

In general, every purified nucleic acid gives some thirty to forty Raman bands in the 300–1700 cm^{-1} spectral region. They are mostly caused by vibrations of the base residues, but two strong bands near to 1100 and 810 cm^{-1} are ascribed to the phosphate–ribose main chain. The 1100 cm^{-1} Raman band is assignable to a localized $O\cdots P\cdots O^-$ symmetric stretching vibration.[8–10] Not only its frequency but also its intensity is practically independent of the main-chain conformation.[11] Therefore, this is a useful internal standard for intensity measurements.[12] It is evident, on the other hand, that the Raman band at 810 cm^{-1} is caused by the 'A-type conformation'.[11,13] When the polynucleotide chain takes any other conformation than the A-form, this Raman band shifts out of the 807–814 cm^{-1} region and at the same time becomes weak.[14–20] The RNA double-helix is known to have the A-form main-chain, but the 'A-conformation' does not necessarily occur *only* in the double-helical portion of an RNA structure. The percentage of RNA nucleotides in the 'A-conformation' can be determined by intensity measurements on the 810 cm^{-1} Raman band, with the 1100 cm^{-1} band as the internal standard.[17,21] For each of the completely double-helical polyribonucleotides (poly(rA).poly(rU), poly(rG).poly(rC), etc.), the ratio of the Raman intensities $I(810)/I(1100)$ is 1.64 ± 0.04, while this ratio is 1.53 for *E. coli* 16S ribosomal RNA, 1.38 for *E. coli*

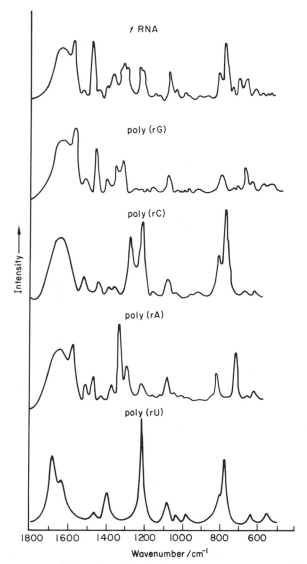

Fig. 3. Raman spectra of formylmethionine transfer RNA of *Escherichia coli*, polyribouridylic acid, polyribocytidylic acid, polyriboadenylic acid, and polyriboguanylic acid in aqueous solutions at neutral pH and room temperature, excited by 514.5 nm radiation.

formylmethionine transfer RNA, and 1.40 for yeast phenylalanine transfer RNA. Therefore, the *A*-form contents of these RNAs are deduced as 93, 84, and 85%, respectively.[21-23]

In the C=O and C=C stretching wavenumber region (1750–1650 cm^{-1}), the uracil residue gives two strong Raman bands. Cytosine and guanine residues, however, give only very weak Raman bands here. On forming the Watson-Crick type adenine–uracil base-pair, a marked change in the Raman spectrum in this region takes place:

	Random coils $\tilde{v}/cm^{-1}$	Double helix $\tilde{v}/cm^{-1}$
Poly(rA–rU).Poly(rA–rU) $\begin{cases} \\ \\ \end{cases}$	1700 (medium) 1662 (strong)	1677 (strong) 1650 (weak)
Poly(rA).Poly(rU) $\begin{cases} \\ \\ \end{cases}$	1698 (medium) 1660 (strong)	1680 (strong) 1631 (weak).

It is interesting that the Raman band wavenumbers in this region depend not only upon whether the molecules are involved in the 'horizontal' hydrogen-bonding but also upon the 'vertical' base sequence.[11,19]

In a double-helical conformation of DNA and RNA, the base residues are arranged with their planes nearly perpendicular to the helical axis and parallel to one another, so that the distance between the adjacent two base-planes is about 3.4 Å. Such a 'stacking' of the base-planes causes a lowering of the ultraviolet absorption intensity at 260 nm (hypochromism). The stacking also causes a decrease in the intensities of some of the Raman bands of the base residues (Raman hypochromism).[11,19,24–27] Some examples of such Raman bands are given below with the percentage hypochromism in each line being given in parentheses:[11,19,26,27]

In Poly(rA).Poly(rU) Uracil: 784 (30), 1231 (52), 1395 (36).
Adenine: 728 (41), 1309 (40), 1339 (10), 1380 (30), 1485 (-25), 1512 (15), 1583 (-18).
In Poly(rA–rU).Poly(rA–rU) Uracil: 783 (35), 1237 (49), 1397 (35).
Adenine: 726 (46), 1302 (28), 1378 (35), 1576 (-14).
In Poly(rA) 725 (35), 1303 (39), 1508 (67).
In Poly (rC) 1296 (20), 1533 (10).

The structure-spectrum correlations so far described are useful for a conformational analysis of various nucleic acids, and especially in interpreting a change in the Raman spectrum of a nucleic acid or a protein/nucleic-acid complex. Some examples of the biological materials subjected to such studies are given below:

Pure nucleic acids: calf-thymus DNA,[18] *Escherichia coli t*RNAs,[16,21,22] yeast *t*RNA,[23] *E. coli* ribosomal RNAs,[21,23] R17 (virus) RNA.[21,28]

Protein nucleic-acid complexes: R17 virus,[28] Pfl and fd viruses,[29] turnip yellow mosaic virus,[30] mouse myeloma chromatin,[31] MS2 phage.[32]

3 THEORY

The underlying principles of the theory of Raman scattering were established long ago,[33] and since then fundamental alterations have not been needed. There are, however, many theories proposed for various practical applications.[34] They are considered to be different from one another only in the approximations adopted to highlight certain special aspects of the Raman effect. Under such approximations some general rules on Raman scattering intensities often emerge. These rules are sometimes useful for constructing a framework for our interpretation of what is observed. In this section, we consider a few of these theories and rules, and make a rapid survey of them to facilitate later discussions.

3.1 A Classical View

In classical theory, Raman scattering is explained by considering that a molecule is polarized by the influence of an electric field, E. Thus, the electric dipole moment, P, induced in the molecule is given by

$$P = \alpha E, \tag{1}$$

where α is the polarizability tensor of the molecule. If E is an alternating field of frequency v_{exc} along a direction σ,

$$E = E_\sigma \cos 2\pi v_{exc} t, \tag{2}$$

where t is the time. In addition, the polarizability $\alpha_{\rho\sigma}$ may also be a periodic function of time t, because the molecule is vibrating along a normal coordinate Q with a frequency v, so that

$$\alpha_{\rho\sigma} = \alpha_{\rho\sigma}^0 + (\partial\alpha_{\rho\sigma}/\partial Q) \cos 2\pi v t. \tag{3}$$

From eqns. (1), (2), and (3),

$$
\begin{aligned}
P_\rho = {}& \alpha_{\rho\sigma}^0 E_\sigma \cos 2\pi v_{exc} t \\
& + \tfrac{1}{2}(\partial\alpha_{\rho\sigma}/\partial Q)E_\sigma \cos 2\pi(v_{exc}+v)t \\
& + \tfrac{1}{2}(\partial\alpha_{\rho\sigma}/\partial Q)E_\sigma \cos 2\pi(v_{exc}-v)t.
\end{aligned}
\tag{4}
$$

This indicates that the molecule should have a dipole oscillation with the frequency

$$v_{sc} = v_{exc} - v \tag{5}$$

(third term), and this is considered to cause Stokes Raman scattering with total intensity over a solid angle 4π:

$$I = \frac{2'\pi^5}{3^2 c^4} v_{sc}^4 I_0 (\partial\alpha_{\rho\sigma}/\partial Q)^2, \tag{6}$$

where c is the light velocity and I_0 is the intensity of the incident laser light. Thus, the Raman scattering intensity should be proportional to $(\partial\alpha_{\rho\sigma}/\partial Q)^2$. In other words, it depends upon how much change is caused in the polarizability of the molecule by a normal vibration along Q. On such a basis, the following general rules are tentatively suggested:

(a) Raman bands are generally more intense for stretching vibrations of covalent bonds than for deformation vibrations.
(b) A Raman band assignable to a C=C stretching vibration is stronger than that assignable to a C—C stretching vibration.
(c) A Raman band becomes stronger with increase in the atomic numbers of the atoms involved in the stretching vibration, all other things being equal.
(d) If two bond-stretching motions are involved in a normal coordinate, the Raman band is more intense when they take place in-phase than when they take place with 180° phase difference. For a cyclic molecule, the Raman band assignable to a vibration in which all of the bonds forming the ring stretch and contract in-phase (ring breathing vibration) is usually the strongest one.

When the frequency v_{exc} of the applied electric field coincides or nearly coincides with a 'natural' frequency v_e of an electronic absorption of the molecule (this is an on-resonance condition), the amplitude of the dipole oscillation of the molecule becomes enormous. It should be inversely proportional to ($v_e^2 - v_{exc}^2 +$ a damping factor). Under such a condition, however, classical theory breaks down.

3.2 Quantum Mechanical View

In quantum mechanical theory, Raman scattered intensity is given by eqn. (6) where $\partial\alpha_{\rho\sigma}/\partial Q$ is replaced by a 'Raman scattering tensor', $(\alpha_{\rho\sigma})_{fi}$, which is represented by the well-known Kramers-Heisenberg expression.[35] Thus,

$$I = \frac{2^7\pi^5}{3^2 c^4} v_{sc}^4 I_0 |(\alpha_{\rho\sigma})_{fi}|^2, \tag{7}$$

and

$$(\alpha_{\rho\sigma})_{fi} = \frac{1}{hc} \sum_{e,k} \left\{ \frac{\langle f|M_\rho|ek\rangle\langle ek|M_\sigma|i\rangle}{v_{ek} - v_i - v_{exc} + i\Gamma_{ek}} + \frac{\langle f|M_\sigma|ek\rangle\langle ek|M_\rho|i\rangle}{v_{ek} - v_f + v_{exc} + i\Gamma_{ek}} \right\}, \tag{8}$$

where M_ρ and M_σ are the dipole moment operators along the ρ and σ directions, respectively. Here, the Raman scattering is considered to be a two-photon process from an initial, $|i\rangle$, to a final state, $|f\rangle$, of the molecule, in which transition moments from the initial to various intermediate states, $|ek\rangle$, and from the intermediate to the final states are involved. None of the transition frequencies ($v_{ek} - v_i$ and $v_{ek} - v_f$) coincides with the exciting laser frequency v_{exc} nor with the frequency v_{sc} of the scattered light (see Fig. 4). Scattering is, however, a process which takes place within a short interval of time Δt, and hence each state of the molecule has an uncertainty ΔE in its energy. The denominator of each term in eqn. (8) takes care of such an uncertainty. Γ_{ek} is the width of the band for the $|ek\rangle$ vibronic state. By the use of eqn. (8), we can understand the rules (a) to (d) to some extent.

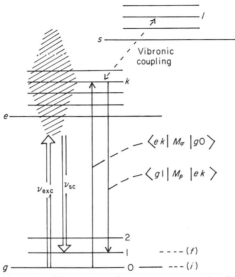

Fig. 4. A schematic drawing illustrating the quantum mechanical theory of Raman scattering.

3.3 Theory of the Resonance Raman Effect

When the exciting frequency v_{exc} becomes close to the transition frequency $v_{ek} - v_i$ for an absorption band of the molecule, a limited number of terms in eqn. (8) become dominant because of their small denominators, so that the relative contributions of the other terms are negligibly small. Equation (8) may now be rewritten as

$$(\alpha_{\rho\sigma})_{g1,g0} = \frac{1}{hc} \sum_k \frac{\langle g1|M_\rho|ek\rangle\langle ek|M_\sigma|g0\rangle}{v_{ek} - v_{g0} - v_{exc} + i\Gamma_{ek}}. \tag{9}$$

Here, initial, $|i\rangle$, and final, $|f\rangle$, states are assumed to be, as usual, the vibrational ground state, $|g0\rangle$, and the first excited vibrational state, $|g1\rangle$, of a particular normal vibration within the electronic ground state.

The vibronic function $|ek\rangle$ is expressed approximately as

$$|ek\rangle = \psi_e(q, Q)\chi_k(Q), \tag{10}$$

where q represents an electronic coordinate, Q a normal coordinate, $\psi_e(q, Q)$ a wave function of the excited electronic state (e) with the nuclear arrangement represented by Q, and $\chi_k(Q)$ a vibrational wave function. This is the Born-Oppenheimer adiabatic approximation.[36] The electronic function is now expanded in a Taylor series of displacements of the nuclear coordinates from the equilibrium arrangement in the electronic ground state, where $Q = 0$.

$$\psi_e(q, Q) = \psi_e(q, Q = 0) + \left(\frac{\partial \psi_e}{\partial Q}\right)_{Q=0} Q + \cdots \tag{11}$$

Then, eqn. (9) becomes

$$
\begin{aligned}
(\alpha_{\rho\sigma})_{10} = \frac{1}{hc} \bigg[&\langle g|M_\rho|e\rangle_0 \langle e|M_\sigma|g\rangle_0 \sum_k \frac{\langle 1|k\rangle\langle k|0\rangle}{v_{ek} - v_{g0} - v_{exc} + i\Gamma_{ek}} \\
&+ \langle g|M_\rho\left(\frac{\partial \psi_e}{\partial Q}\right)_0\rangle \langle e|M_\sigma|g\rangle_0 \sum_k \frac{\langle 1|Q|k\rangle\langle k|0\rangle}{v_{ek} - v_{g0} - v_{exc} + i\Gamma_{ek}} \\
&+ \langle g|M_\rho|e\rangle_0 \langle \left(\frac{\partial \psi_e}{\partial Q}\right)_0|M_\sigma|g\rangle \sum_k \frac{\langle 1|k\rangle\langle k|Q|0\rangle}{v_{ek} - v_{g0} - v_{exc} + i\Gamma_{ek}} \\
&+ \cdots \bigg]
\end{aligned}
\tag{12}
$$

3.3.1. Condon-allowed Raman transitions

For a totally symmetric vibration of a molecule, the first term of the series in eqn. (12) can have a non-zero value, and for such a case this term is considered usually to give the major contribution to $(\alpha_{\rho\sigma})_{10}$. This corresponds to Albrecht's A term,[39] and is written as

$$(\alpha_{\sigma\sigma})_{10} = \frac{1}{hc} \langle e|M_\sigma|g\rangle_0^2 \sum_k \frac{\langle 1|k\rangle\langle k|0\rangle}{v_{ek} - v_{g0} - v_{exc} + i\Gamma_{ek}}. \tag{13}$$

The approximation adopted here is equivalent to assuming that the value of the electronic transition moment remains equal to that at $Q = 0$, and is independent of which vibrational transition is accompanying the electronic transition. This is called the Condon approximation. Thus, in general:

(e) For a totally symmetric vibration of a molecule the resonance Raman scattered intensity is great; (i) when the absorption intensity of the electronic band is large (the Raman scattered intensity is proportional to the square of the absorption intensity); (ii) when some of the products of the Franck-Condon overlap integrals $\langle 1|k\rangle\langle k|0\rangle$ are great; and (iii) when the exciting frequency v_{exc} is close to that of the absorption band under discussion.

3.3.2. Vibronically-allowed Raman transitions

If the vibration along Q is not totally symmetric, but is antisymmetric with respect to a symmetry element, then $\langle 1|k\rangle\langle k|0\rangle$ of the first term of eqn. (12) is always zero, and $\langle g|M_\rho|e\rangle_0\langle e|M_\sigma|g\rangle_0$ is also always zero. If the Raman band attributed to such a vibration is resonance-enhanced, therefore, this should be attributed to the second two terms (or higher terms) but not to the first term in eqn. (12). A variety of theoretical work has recently been published on this subject, and many experimental results have been accumulated and explained by taking these two terms (Albrecht's B term[37-39]) into account. In the resonance Raman spectroscopy of nucleic acids, however, no evidence has so far been obtained indicating that an important contribution comes from these vibronic terms in any of the Raman bands observed.

3.4 Ting's Approximation[40]

We consider here a case where the exciting frequency v_{exc} is fairly close to that of the absorption band $v_{e0} - v_{g0}$, but the frequency difference $v_{e0} - v_{g0} - v_{exc}$ is still much greater than each of the vibrational frequencies v_k in the intermediate (e) state. Thus,

$$v_{e0} - v_{g0} - v_{exc} = v' \gg v_k, \tag{14}$$

where

$$v_k = v_{ek} - v_{e0}. \tag{15}$$

This is regarded as a pre-resonance condition. In such a case, the damping term $i\Gamma_{ek}$ in each denominator in eqn. (13) is neglected, and it becomes $v' + v_k$. Then, by a Taylor expansion,

$$(v' + v_k)^{-1} = v'^{-1} \left(1 + \frac{v_k}{v'}\right)^{-1}$$

$$= v'^{-1} \left(1 - \frac{v_k}{v'} + \ldots\right). \tag{16}$$

In a further approximation, let us assume that the normal vibration under discussion is harmonic in both of the ground (g) and the excited (e) electronic states, that it has an equal vibrational frequency, v'', in both states and that both take place along the same normal coordinate. The potential minimum in the excited state, however, is assumed to be shifted by δ_e from that in the ground state along this normal coordinate (see Fig. 5). On this set of assumptions, it can be shown[40] that

$$\sum_k \langle 1|k\rangle\langle k|0\rangle = 0 \tag{17}$$

and

$$\sum_k k\langle 1|k\rangle\langle k|0\rangle = \delta_e/\sqrt{2}. \tag{18}$$

Therefore, eqn. (13) is now rewritten as

$$(\alpha_{\sigma\sigma})_{10} = \frac{1}{hc} \langle e|M_\sigma|g\rangle_0^2 (\delta_e/\sqrt{2})(v''/v'^2). \tag{19}$$

The rule (e) is now rewritten as:

(e') For a totally symmetric vibration of a molecule, the pre-resonance Raman scattered intensity is great, (i) when $\langle e|M_\sigma|g\rangle_0$ is great, (ii) when the difference, δ_e, between the positions of the potential minima in the electronic ground (g) and excited (e) states along the normal coordinate in question is great (intensity is nearly proportional to δ_e^2), and (iii) v' is small.

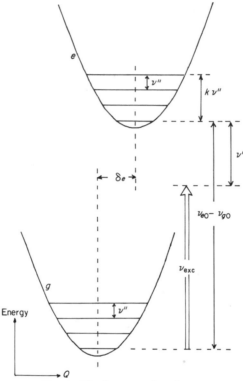

Fig. 5. Ting's approximation.

3.5   Excited State Geometry

Essentially the same rule as (e') may be restated in a slightly different way:

(f) If a Raman band becomes much stronger when the exciting frequency v_{exc} is brought closer to the frequency of an electronic band ($e \leftarrow g$), then the equilibrium conformation of the molecule is distorted along the normal coordinate for the Raman band on going from the ground (g) to the excited (e) electronic states.

As long as this rule is based upon eqn. (19) or upon similar formulae presented by other investigators,[39,41] its validity should be limited to totally symmetric vibrations. Observation of Raman spectra of various molecules at different exciting laser wavelengths, however, suggests that this rule is good not only for

Raman bands corresponding to totally symmetric vibrations but also for those corresponding to non-totally symmetric vibrations.[7,42] A theoretical basis for such a rule for the case of antisymmetric vibrations was discussed by Tsuboi and Hirakawa,[43] and also for the case of degenerate vibrations.[42] It is now understandable that rule (f) is good for any totally symmetric, antisymmetric and degenerate Raman bands, in spite of the difference between the Raman scattering mechanisms for these different types of vibration.

By combining all the data relating to which Raman bands of a molecule are enhanced and which are not when the exciting frequency, ν_{exc}, is brought close to that of the absorption band, we may obtain useful information about the equilibrium geometry of the excited electronic state.

3.6 Conjugated Double-bond Systems

For the resonance Raman effects of conjugated double-bond systems, to which nucleic-acid bases belong, another general trend may be predicted to occur.

Let us take aniline as an example to make the general situation clear. Aniline may be regarded as being intermediate between benzene (a typical conjugated double-bond system) and a nucleic-acid base. It is, however, still a typical conjugated double-bond system. Let us assume that the NH_2 group provides two π-electrons to the conjugated double-bond system of the mono-substituted benzene ring, and regard the problem as that of a 7-orbital, 8-electron system. The 7 molecular orbitals are shown schematically in Fig. 6. Even if the detail

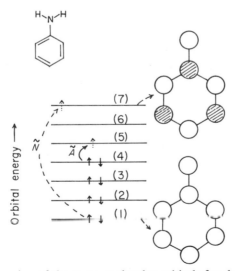

Fig. 6. Schematic drawing of the seven molecular orbitals for the eight π-electrons in aniline. Open and closed circles indicate that the upper branches of the atomic orbitals of the π-electrons are positive and negative, respectively.

of each orbital configuration is not yet fixed, it is known that the lowest-energy orbital should have no node and the highest one should have the highest possible number of nodes (seven) (see Fig. 6). In the highest frequency $\pi^* \leftarrow \pi$ transition ($\tilde{N} \leftarrow \tilde{X}$), therefore, all six C—C bonds and the C—N bond experience a bonding-to-antibonding switch. Hence all seven bonds would become longer on going from the ground ($\tilde{X}$) to this excited ($\tilde{N}$) electronic state. Thus the Raman band for the ring breathing vibration (in which all of the seven bonds stretch and contract in phase) should obtain its intensity from the shortest wavelength $\pi^* \leftarrow \pi$ ($\tilde{N} \leftarrow \tilde{X}$) band. In the longest wavelength $\pi^* \leftarrow \pi$ ($\tilde{A} \leftarrow \tilde{X}$) transition, on the other hand, some bonds would become antibonding, but some others would change from antibonding to bonding. Therefore, a normal mode other than the breathing motion would fit the $\tilde{X}$ to $\tilde{A}$ geometry change. Thus a Raman band, or a few Raman bands for normal vibrations in which some of the C—C and C—N bonds stretch and contract with 180° phase difference with the other bonds, is expected to show a prominent pre-resonance effect when the exciting frequency is brought close to the longest wavelength absorption band.

This is actually found to be the case;[44] in the Raman spectrum of aniline (CH_3OH solution), with 514.5 nm excitation a sharp Raman band at 980 cm^{-1} (assignable to the all-in-phase skeletal stretching vibration) is the strongest one, whereas in the Raman spectrum of the same aniline solution with 363.8 nm excitation another band at 1600 cm^{-1} (which probably corresponds to one of the e_{2g} stretching modes of benzene) is the strongest. The intensity ratio of the 1600 cm^{-1} to 980 cm^{-1} bands is about 1/3 for the 514.5 nm excitation but it is about 3/1 for 363.8 nm excitation.

By generalizing our findings, we obtain:

(g) In a conjugated double-bond system, Raman bands arising from asymmetric skeletal stretching vibrations, rather than those from totally symmetric stretching vibrations, become dominant when the exciting frequency ν_{exc} is brought close to that of the longest wavelength absorption band.

This is in contrast to the general rule (d) described in Section 3.1.

3.7 Duschinsky Effect

The discussion in this section starts from eqn. (13), as did the discussion of Ting's approximation. Ting's approximation was useful for acquiring a general grasp of a particular aspect of the resonance Raman effect, but it involves an oversimplification which makes it unfit for a quantitative explanation of experimental results. This weak point will be covered by some refinements in this section.

Both the equilibrium geometry and the intramolecular force field in the excited (e) electronic state are, in general, appreciably different from those in the ground (g) electronic state. Therefore, the normal modes of vibration are also different in the excited state from those in the ground state. Let us define the normal coordinates in the excited (e) and ground (g) electronic states as

$$\mathbf{Q}^{(e)} = (Q_1^{(e)}, Q_2^{(e)}, \ldots, Q_n^{(e)}) \tag{20}$$

and

$$\mathbf{Q}^{(g)} = (Q_1^{(g)}, Q_2^{(g)}, \ldots, Q_n^{(g)}). \tag{21}$$

The Franck-Condon overlap integrals which appear in eqn. (13) should be considered to be n-fold multiple integrals. To evaluate such integrals we propose to use a set of symmetry coordinates in the ground electronic state,

$$\mathbf{S}^{(g)} = (S_1^{(g)}, S_2^{(g)}, \ldots, S_n^{(g)}). \tag{22}$$

Let us next assume that symmetry coordinates in the excited electronic state are given by the expression

$$\begin{aligned}
\mathbf{S}^{(e)} &= \mathbf{S}^{(g)} + \delta\mathbf{S}^{(e)} \\
&= (S_1^{(g)} + \delta S_1^{(e)}, S_2^{(g)} + \delta S_2^{(e)}, \ldots, S_n^{(g)} + \delta S_n^{(e)}).
\end{aligned} \tag{23}$$

Let us further assume that the normal coordinates in the excited and ground electronic states are related to the symmetry coordinates by the expressions

$$\mathbf{Q}^{(e)} = (\mathbf{L}^{(e)})^{-1}\mathbf{S}^{(e)} \tag{24}$$

and

$$\mathbf{Q}^{(g)} = (\mathbf{L}^{(g)})^{-1}\mathbf{S}^{(g)} \tag{25}$$

respectively. In general, if there is a change in the composition of the normal coordinates in terms of symmetry coordinates on going from the ground to the excited states, the change includes a rotation in coordinate space. Such a rotation is called a Duschinsky effect.[45,46] A Franck-Condon overlap integral $\langle k|0 \rangle = \langle 100 \ldots 0|000 \ldots 0 \rangle$, for example, is now given by

$$\begin{aligned}
\langle k|0 \rangle = \int \ldots \int \chi_{11}^{(e)}(Q_1^{(e)}) \ldots \chi_{n0}^{(e)}(Q_n^{(e)}) \\
\times \chi_{10}^{(g)}(Q_1^{(g)}) \ldots \chi_{n0}^{(g)}(Q_n^{(g)}) J \, \mathrm{d}S_1^{(g)} \, \mathrm{d}S_2^{(g)} \ldots \mathrm{d}S_n^{(g)},
\end{aligned} \tag{26}$$

where $Q_j^{(e)}$ and $Q_j^{(g)}$ are given by eqns. (24) and (25), respectively, and

$$J = \{|(\mathbf{L}^{(e)})^{-1}| \, |(\mathbf{L}^{(g)})^{-1}|\}^{\frac{1}{2}}. \tag{27}$$

Unfortunately, a many-dimensional Franck-Condon overlap integration requires a great amount of computer time.

4   GUIDELINES FOR DETERMINING NORMAL MODES OF VIBRATION FOR A RING SYSTEM

A normal coordinate treatment was carried out for the planar modes of uracil, N,N'-dideutero uracil, C,C'-dideutero uracil, and perdeutero uracil by Susi and Ard;[2] a valence force field was employed. A similar treatment was made by Susi et al.[3] for cytosine and cytosine-d_3. For in-plane vibrations of 1-methyl-uracil, 1-methylcytosine, 9-methyladenine, 9-methylguanine, and their deuterated products, another series of normal coordinate analyses was made by Tsuboi et al.[4,5] Here, the Urey-Bradley-type force field was assumed, and therefore bond-stretch/bond-stretch interaction force constants, which are probably caused by π-orbital rearrangements, must effectively be involved in the non-bonded atom–atom force constants. Each of these calculated frequencies and associated normal modes of vibration can be correlated with an observed Raman and/or infrared band frequency. To fix such a correlation in an unequivocal manner, however, the amount of data we have now is not yet sufficient. We wish to point out here that a powerful set of data will be added by examining the effects of various heavy isotope substitutions ($^{12}C \rightarrow {}^{13}C$, $^{14}N \rightarrow {}^{15}N$, and $^{16}O \rightarrow {}^{18}O$) in nucleic acid bases.

In view of the present status of the regular normal coordinate analysis, we attempt here a slightly different approach to characterizing the molecular vibrations and the Raman bands of the nucleic-acid base residues.

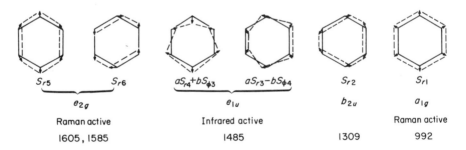

Fig. 7.   Bond-stretching modes of vibration of the benzene ring and their wavenumbers/cm⁻¹.

4.1   Bond-stretching Vibrations in Benzene Ring

For benzene, C_6H_6, there are six normal vibrations in which primarily the C—C bond stretching motions take place. Its twelve internal coordinates, i.e. six C—C stretching (Δr) and six C—C—C deformation ($\Delta \phi$) coordinates (see

Fig. 7), are transformed into the following twelve symmetry coordinates:

$$(a_{1g}) \quad S_{r1} = \frac{1}{\sqrt{6}} (\Delta r_1 + \Delta r_2 + \Delta r_3 + \Delta r_4 + \Delta r_5 + \Delta r_6)$$

$$(b_{2u}) \quad S_{r2} = \frac{1}{\sqrt{6}} (\Delta r_1 - \Delta r_2 + \Delta r_3 - \Delta r_4 + \Delta r_5 - \Delta r_6)$$

$$(e_{1u}) \begin{cases} S_{r3} = \frac{1}{\sqrt{12}} (2\Delta r_1 + \Delta r_2 - \Delta r_3 - 2\Delta r_4 - \Delta r_5 + \Delta r_6) \\ S_{r4} = \frac{1}{2}(\Delta r_2 + \Delta r_3 - \Delta r_5 - \Delta r_6) \end{cases}$$

$$(e_{2g}) \begin{cases} S_{r5} = \frac{1}{\sqrt{12}} (2\Delta r_1 - \Delta r_2 - \Delta r_3 + 2\Delta r_4 - \Delta r_5 - \Delta r_6) \\ S_{r6} = \frac{1}{2}(\Delta r_2 - \Delta r_3 + \Delta r_5 - \Delta r_6) \end{cases} \quad (28)$$

$$(a_{1g}) \quad S_{\phi 1} = \frac{1}{\sqrt{6}} (\Delta\phi_1 + \Delta\phi_2 + \Delta\phi_3 + \Delta\phi_4 + \Delta\phi_5 + \Delta\phi_6)$$

$$(b_{1u}) \quad S_{\phi 2} = \frac{1}{\sqrt{6}} (\Delta\phi_1 - \Delta\phi_2 + \Delta\phi_3 - \Delta\phi_4 + \Delta\phi_5 - \Delta\phi_6)$$

$$(e_{1u}) \begin{cases} S_{\phi 3} = \frac{1}{\sqrt{12}} (2\Delta\phi_1 + \Delta\phi_2 - \Delta\phi_3 - 2\Delta\phi_4 - \Delta\phi_5 + \Delta\phi_6) \\ S_{\phi 4} = \frac{1}{2}(\Delta\phi_2 + \Delta\phi_3 - \Delta\phi_5 - \Delta\phi_6) \end{cases}$$

$$(e_{2g}) \begin{cases} S_{\phi 5} = \frac{1}{\sqrt{12}} (2\Delta\phi_1 - \Delta\phi_2 - \Delta\phi_3 + 2\Delta\phi_4 - \Delta\phi_5 - \Delta\phi_6) \\ S_{\phi 6} = \frac{1}{2}(\Delta\phi_2 - \Delta\phi_3 + \Delta\phi_5 - \Delta\phi_6). \end{cases}$$

Of these twelve, three are redundant. One of the redundant coordinates is $S_{\phi 1}$, and the other two are constructed from S_{r3}, S_{r4}, $S_{\phi 3}$, and $S_{\phi 4}$ by a linear transformation:

$$\begin{aligned} S(\text{redundant})_2 &= aS_{r3} + bS_{\phi 4} \\ S(\text{redundant})_3 &= aS_{r4} - bS_{\phi 3} \\ S(\text{stretch})_3 &= aS_{r4} + bS_{\phi 3} \\ S(\text{stretch})_4 &= aS_{r3} - bS_{\phi 4}, \end{aligned} \quad (29)$$

where

$$\begin{aligned} a &= 2/\sqrt{10} \\ b &= \sqrt{3/5} \end{aligned} \quad (30)$$

The forms of the six skeletal stretching vibrations are shown in Fig. 7 together with the observed vibrational frequencies assignable to these modes.

4.2   Effects of Asymmetrization

Figures 8 and 9 show the results of calculations of normal vibrations of a few hypothetical systems, each of which is constructed from a realistic benzene molecule by a hypothetical modification in force constants or masses of atoms.

A normal coordinate treatment of the 21 in-plane vibrations was made with a valence force field, and the calculated frequencies were brought into agreement with those observed from liquid benzene. It was found that the C—C stretching force constant needed to be fixed at 5.1 mdyn $Å^{-1}$. A trial calculation was then made to determine what happens when one of the six C—C stretching force constants is raised to 6.0 or lowered to 4.0 mdyn $Å^{-1}$, all other parameters being kept unchanged. The result of this trial calculation is shown in Fig. 8. The degenerate vibrations are naturally split into two. For both the e_{2g} and e_{1u} vibrations, the symmetry coordinate of one member of the degenerate pair has no Δr_1 and Δr_4 terms (eqn. (28)). In other words, in such a vibration the bond length of r_1 remains unchanged, and therefore the frequency should be insensitive to the r_1 bond-stretching force constant (Fig. 8). However, the frequency of the other component becomes appreciably higher or lower as the r_1 bond-stretching force constant becomes higher or lower, respectively (Fig. 8).

Another set of calculations was made by increasing the masses of two of the six hydrogen atoms of benzene and by keeping other parameters unchanged; some ideas were obtained as to the correlation between the vibrational spectra of benzene and a *meta*-disubstituted benzene (see upper part of Fig. 9). Next, in such a hypothetical *m*-disubstituted benzene, $C_6H_4X_2$, the C—X bond-stretch-

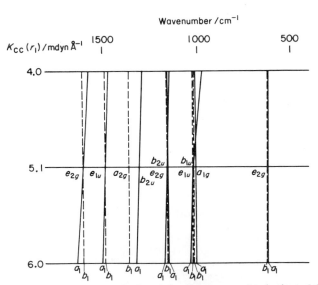

Fig. 8. Vibrational wavenumbers, calculated for benzene and substituted benzenes, in which only one ($K_{CC}(r_1)$) of the six C—C stretching force constants was changed and all other parameters were kept unchanged.

ing force constant (K_{CX}) is increased and other parameters are all kept unchanged. The results of calculations on such systems are shown in the lower part of Fig. 9. It is noticeable that, when the two C—X stretching mode wavenumbers go up from the 1200–1300 cm^{-1} to the 1600–1700 cm^{-1} region, the two ring-breathing modes (whose roots are the e_{2g} vibrations of benzene) go down from 1600 cm^{-1} to the 1300–1500 cm^{-1} region. The vibrational coupling here is found to be greater for the b_1 than for the a_1 vibrations. The ring-breathing (or all-bond in-phase stretching) frequency is sensitive to the mass of the substituent, X, but not to the C—X force constant.

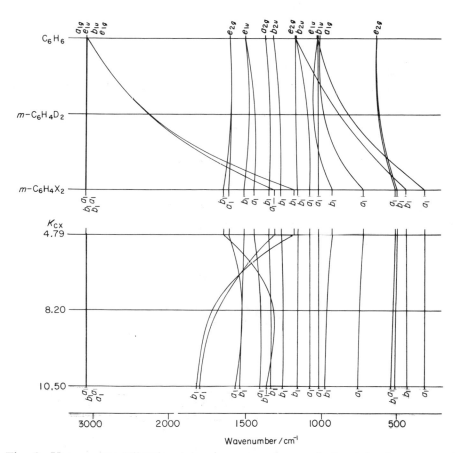

Fig. 9. Upper part: Vibrational band wavenumbers, calculated for benzene and hypothetical benzenes, in which two hydrogen atoms in the *meta* positions change their masses from 1 to 19 a.m.u. and all other parameters are kept unchanged. Lower part: Vibrational band wavenumbers, calculated for the hypothetical *m*-disubstituted benzene $C_6H_4X_2$, in which the mass of X is 19 a.m.u. It is shown how the wavenumbers change when the stretching force constant K_{CX} is changed from 4.79 to 8.20 to 10.5 mdyn Å^{-1}, all other parameters being kept unchanged.

4.3   Heavy Isotope Effects

While deuteration effects upon vibrational frequencies have been widely used for the analysis of Raman spectra, the use of heavy isotope effects (e.g. $^{12}C \rightarrow {}^{13}C$, $^{14}N \rightarrow {}^{15}N$, and $^{16}O \rightarrow {}^{18}O$ effects) has been less extensive. Unlike deuteration, substitution of a heavy isotopic atom is accompanied by a fairly small percentage change in the frequency of the normal mode. In such a case, the isotopic frequency shift, δv_k, is considered to be more significant than the frequency itself as an independent new datum.

An observed value of δv_k is useful first for determining some of the force constant values, k_m, to which δv_k is sensitive. The sensitivity is given[47,48] by

$$\frac{\partial(\delta v_k)}{\partial k_m} = \frac{N v_k}{4\pi^2 c^2} \sum_{j(\neq k)} \frac{(\mathbf{L}^{-1} \widetilde{\delta \mathbf{G} \mathbf{L}^{-1}})_{kj} (\widetilde{\mathbf{L} \mathbf{A}_m \mathbf{L}})_{kj}}{v_k^2 - v_j^2}, \tag{31}$$

where $\delta \mathbf{G}$ is the difference between the inverse kinetic energy matrices of the isotopes and $\mathbf{A}_m$ is a matrix by which the potential energy matrix $\mathbf{F}$ and k_m are related as

$$\mathbf{F} = \sum \mathbf{A}_m k_m. \tag{32}$$

In the approximation used in deriving eqn. (31), it is assumed that the transformation matrix $\mathbf{L}$ between the normal, $\mathbf{Q}$, and symmetry, $\mathbf{S}$, coordinates, $\mathbf{S} = \mathbf{L}\mathbf{Q}$, remains unchanged by isotopic substitution.

Second, from an observed isotope shift we can judge the extent to which the atom in question is involved in the normal vibration of the molecule. It is directly related to the Cartesian displacement,

$$x_a = L_{ak}^x Q_k, \qquad y_a = L_{ak}^y Q_k, \qquad z_a = L_{ak}^z Q_k$$

of the atom a on which the isotopic substitution takes place.[49] Thus,

$$\delta \lambda_k / \lambda_k = [(L_{ak}^x)^2 + (L_{ak}^y)^2 + (L_{ak}^z)^2] \, m_a^2 \delta\left(\frac{1}{m_a}\right), \tag{33}$$

where

$$\lambda_k = 4\pi^2 c^2 v_k^2 \tag{34}$$

and m_a is the mass of the atom a.

Last, a simple formula is given which is useful for estimating an upper limit to the amount of an isotope shift for a given mode of vibration:

$$\delta \lambda_k / \lambda_k = \delta G_{ss} / G_{ss}, \tag{35}$$

where G_{ss} is the diagonal element of the inverse kinetic energy matrix for a symmetry coordinate, S, and δG_{ss} is the difference $(G_{ss}(^{15}N) - G_{ss}(^{14}N)$ or $G_{ss}(^{18}O) - G_{ss}(^{16}O))$ between the G_{ss} values for each molecule. This equation gives an isotopic frequency shift for a hypothetical case where the normal vibration (k) took place entirely along a symmetry coordinate, S.

5   RESONANCE RAMAN EFFECT OF A URACIL RESIDUE

In this section we present a detailed discussion of the resonance and pre-resonance Raman spectra of the uracil residue:

5.1   Pre-resonance Raman Effect

Raman spectra of β-uridine-5'-phosphoric acid (5'-UMP) in neutral aqueous solution, excited at various wavelengths, are reproduced in Fig. 10. In each of such spectra, the intensity ratio I_j/I_s has been determined for each Raman band (j) relative to a chosen standard band (st), i.e. a Raman band at 980 cm^{-1} which is assignable to the symmetric stretching vibration of the $[PO_3]^{2-}$ group.[8,10] The intensity data were derived from area measurements ($\pm 5\%$) and corrected for the spectral sensitivity (illustrated by broken lines in Fig. 10) of the spectrometer and detector system. The scattered beam goes through a polarization scrambler before going into the spectrometer. For most Raman bands, the I_j/I_{st} value was found to become greater on increasing the frequency of the exciting light (v_{exc}). In Fig. 11, observed values of relative intensity $\phi_j(v_{exc})$ are plotted against v_{exc}, where $\phi_j(v_{exc})$ is I_j/I_{st} corrected for the v^4-factor and then normalized relative to the 647.1 nm exciting line, i.e.

$$\phi_j(v_{exc})_{obs} = \frac{(I_j/I_{st})(v_{st}/v_j)^4 \text{ for a given } v_{exc}}{(I_j/I_{st})(v_{st}/v_j)^4 \text{ for } v_{exc} = 15\,454 \text{ cm}^{-1} \text{ (647.1 nm)}}. \tag{36}$$

Here, v_j and v_{st} are the wavenumbers of the scattered radiation corresponding, respectively, to the Raman band (j) under examination and to the Raman band (st) chosen as the intensity standard.

The observed increase of the $\phi_j(v_{exc})$ value with v_{exc} is attributable to a pre-resonance effect. For every observed resonance Raman band, there must be one or more absorption bands responsible for its appearance. If a Raman band (j) is assumed to be caused only by one absorption band ($e \leftarrow g$) and if in addition the pre-resonance condition described in Section 3.4 (given by eqn. (14)) is assumed to be fulfilled, then the Raman scattering tensor is given by eqn. (19). Therefore, its intensity is given by the expression

$$I_j/v_j^4 = C(v_j'')^2 \delta_{ej}^2/(v_{e0} - v_{g0} - v_{exc})^4, \tag{37}$$

where C is a constant independent of j (but dependent on e), $v_{e0} - v_{g0}$ is the frequency of the $0 \leftarrow 0$ transition of the ($e \leftarrow g$) absorption band, v_j'' is the vibra-

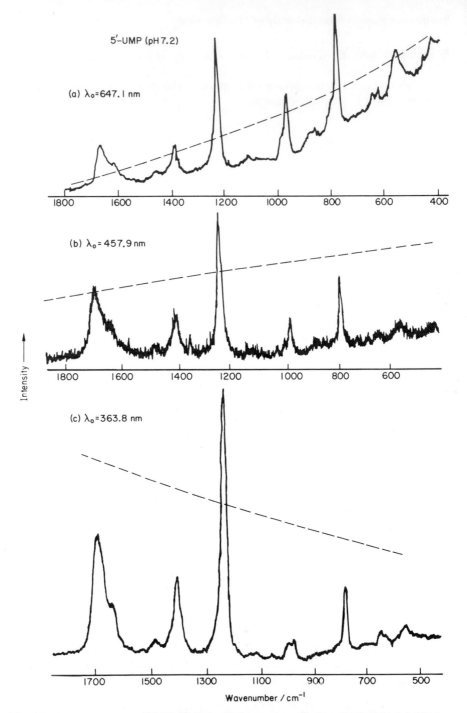

Fig. 10. Raman spectra of 5′-UMP in neutral aqueous solution. Excited by (a) 647.1 nm (Kr), (b) 457.9 nm (Ar), and (c) 363.8 nm (Ar) lines. Broken lines indicate the spectral sensitivity of the monochromator and detector system.

tional frequency of the jth normal vibration (it was assumed to be equal in the e and g states; see Section 3.4), and δ_{ej} is the magnitude of the shift (on going from g to e) of the position of the potential minimum along the normal coordinate j. For the band at 980 cm^{-1}, attributed to symmetric stretching of the $[PO_3]^{2-}$ ion, which is chosen as an internal intensity standard, a similar expression to eqn. (37) can be written. The absorption band associated with the resonance enhancement of this Raman band, however, is known to be located in the shorter wavelength region than 180 nm (5.56×10^4 cm^{-1}), and the change in the frequency denominator caused by a change in ν_{exc} from 647.1 to 351.1 nm is not great. The calculated values $\phi_j(\nu_{exc})$ are found to be practically independent of whether the absorption band of the phosphate group is assumed to be at 180 nm or at 170 nm. Hereafter it is always assumed to be at 180 nm.

Equation (37) is based upon the Ting's approximation (Section 3.4). It is very simple and still fairly good. The numerical differences are very small between those values given by eqn. (37) and those given by the so-called Albrecht's A term[39] (on a higher approximation). Our actual calculations

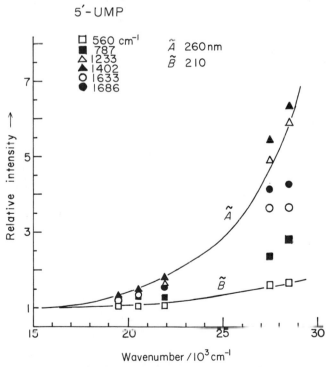

Fig. 11. The Raman intensities of 5'-UMP as a function of the wavenumber, $\tilde{\nu}_{exc}$, of the exciting radiation. Observed values of $\phi_j(\nu_{exc})_{obs}$ (see eqn. (36)) are plotted for the $j = 560, 787, 1233, 1402, 1633,$ and 1686 cm^{-1} Raman bands. Continuous lines indicate $\phi_j(\nu_{exc})_{calc}$ (see eqn. (38)) for the excited electronic state $\tilde{A}$ (260 nm) and $\tilde{B}$ (210 nm).

were, however, made on eqn. (37') instead of eqn. (37).

$$I_j/v_j^4 = C\,\delta_{ej}^2\,\frac{2\{(v_{e0}-v_{g0})^2 + v_{exc}^2\}}{(v_{e0}-v_{g0}-v_{exc})^2(v_{e0}-v_{g0}+v_{exc})^2}. \tag{37'}$$

By substituting eqn. (37') into eqn. (36), the theoretical value of $\phi_j(v_{exc})$ is now given by the expression:

$$\phi_j(v_{exc})_{calc} = \left[\frac{\{(v_{e0}-v_{g0})^2 + v_{exc}^2\}\{5.56\times 10^4 - v_{exc}\}^2\{5.56\times 10^4 + v_{exc}\}^2}{\{v_{e0}-v_{g0}-v_{exc}\}^2\{v_{e0}-v_{g0}+v_{exc}\}^2\{(5.56\times 10^4)^2 + v_{exc}^2\}}\right]^2$$

$$\times \left[\frac{\{(v_{e0}-v_{g0})^2 + (1.54\times 10^4)^2\}\{5.56\times 10^4 - 1.54\times 10^4\}^2 \atop \times \{5.56\times 10^4 + 1.54\times 10^4\}}{\{v_{e0}-v_{g0}-1.54\times 10^4\}^2\{v_{e0}-v_{g0}+1.54\times 10^4\}^2 \atop \times \{(5.56\times 10^4)^2 + (1.54\times 10^4)^2\}}\right]^{-2}. \tag{38}$$

Here, 1.54×10^4 cm^{-1} corresponds to the 647.1 nm laser line and 5.56×10^4 cm^{-1} to the 180 nm absorption band. The uracil residue has absorption bands at 260 $(\tilde{A}\leftarrow\tilde{X})$ and 210 nm $(\tilde{B}\leftarrow\tilde{X})$, leading to $v_{e0}-v_{g0} = 3.85\times 10^4$ and 4.76×10^4 cm^{-1}, respectively. The continuous curves in Fig. 11 represent calculated values of $\phi_j(v_{exc})$ based on these $v_{e0}-v_{g0}$ values and on eqn. (38).

From a comparison of the observed and calculated $\phi_j(v_{exc})$ values (Fig. 11), it is shown to be probable that the Raman bands at 1233 and 1402 cm^{-1} are principally associated with the absorption band at 260 nm. For the Raman bands at 560 and 787 cm^{-1} (ring breathing vibrations), it is apparent that a considerable contribution from the absorption band at 210 nm or other bands of even shorter wavelengths should be taken into account. On the basis of this experimental result and on the basis of eqn. (37'), the δ_{ej} value is considered to be greater for the $v_j'' = 1233$ cm^{-1} or for the $v_j'' = 1402$ cm^{-1} vibration than for other vibrations in the lowest-singlet excited state. On the other hand, the δ_j value for the ring-breathing vibration is rather greater for higher excited states than for that corresponding to the 260 nm band.

5.2   Rigorous Resonance Raman Effect

A rigorous resonance Raman effect of the uracil residue has been examined with 257.3 nm excitation.[50] This laser beam was obtained by the use of an argon ion laser (514.5 nm) in combination with a Coherent Radiation Model 440 UV Generator, which is a continuous-wave frequency doubler utilizing a non-linear optical crystal of ammonium dihydrogen phosphate. The sample of 5'-UMP was dissolved in pure water (no buffer); the concentration was 10^{-4} M and the pH was 6.0 to 6.2. The solution was placed in a silica glass cell, rotating at about 2000 r.p.m. in order to avoid undesirable effects of the laser beam.[51] The result is shown in Fig. 12, along with the results of similar examinations of a few related compounds.

As is seen in Fig. 12(a), six Raman bands at 787, 1233, 1402, 1482, 1636, and 1689 cm^{-1} show a resonance Raman effect associated with the 260 nm band. A comparison of the pre-resonance and resonance Raman spectra of 5′-UMP leads us to the following conclusions:

(i) Resonance effects in the Raman bands of the uracil residue at 1233 and 1402 cm^{-1} (and probably that at 1482 cm^{-1}, also) are associated solely with the 260 nm band.

(ii) The Raman bands at 1633 and 1686 cm^{-1} derive their intensities mainly from the excited electronic state at 260 nm, and partly from higher excited states.

(iii) The ring-breathing vibration at 787 cm^{-1} is only slightly associated

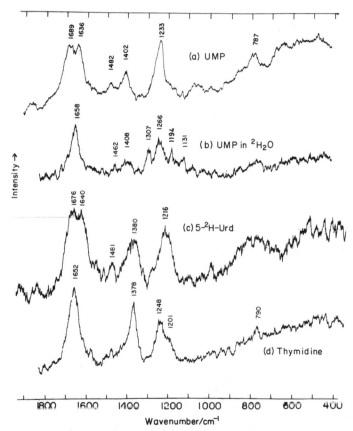

Fig. 12. Resonance Raman spectra of uridine derivatives 10^{-4} molar or 0.004% in neutral aqueous solutions excited by 257.3 nm radiation. (a) β-uridine-5′-phosphoric acid in ^{1}H$_2$O, (b) the same in ^{2}H$_2$O, (c) 5-deuterouridine, (d) thymidine. The spectral response of the monochromator-photomultiplier system used was found to be practically independent of the wavelength in this spectral range.

with the 260 nm band; most of its Raman intensity (with 514.5 nm excitation, for example) comes from higher electronically excited states.

(iv) The relatively weak Raman band at 560 cm^{-1} seems to be associated with some higher frequency absorption bands, but not with the 260 nm band.

5.3   Raman Spectra of Compounds Related to Uracil

In this section, pre-resonance and resonance Raman spectra are shown of various related compounds which are considered to be relevant to the interpretation of the Raman spectrum of the uracil residue. Observed Raman band wavenumbers of uridine and some uridine derivatives are listed in Table 1. Special attention will be paid to the characterization of the six bands at 1689, 1636, 1482, 1402, 1233, and 787 cm^{-1}, which are considered to derive intensity from the 260 nm absorption band (see Fig. 12(a)). Let us call these six vibrations UrI, UrII, UrIII, UrIV, UrV, and UrVI, respectively.

5.3.1.   Deprotonation effect

Figure 13 shows the spectra of 5'-UMP in alkaline aqueous solution, in which the uracil residue has the form

Here, pre-resonance enhancement is found to be prominent for two Raman bands at 1497 and 1290 cm^{-1}. Therefore these two are considered to correspond to the UrIII and UrV vibrations of the neutral uracil residue. This means that the deprotonation at position 3 nitrogen of the uracil residue causes marked shifts of the UrIII and UrV vibrations to higher wavenumbers, i.e. $1482 \rightarrow 1497$ and $1233 \rightarrow 1290$ cm^{-1}, respectively. The Raman band at 1402 cm^{-1} (UrIV) seems to be replaced by two weak Raman bands at 1380 and 1360 cm^{-1}. The deprotonation causes, in addition, shifts of the two Raman bands in the 1600 cm^{-1} region to lower wavenumbers, i.e. $(1638, 1686) \rightarrow (1600, 1629)$ cm^{-1}, and appearance of new stronger Raman bands at 1206 and 1237 cm^{-1}.

The deprotonation should promote delocalization of the π-electrons in the uracil ring, and a lowering of the carbonyl stretching force constants. Hence a general lowering of the wavenumbers of bands in the 1600 to 1700 cm^{-1} region is understandable.

Interpretation of the other spectral changes accompanying the deprotonation is not simple. A possible interpretation is as follows. Let us assume that the intrinsic wavenumbers of the UrIII and UrV vibrations are somewhat higher

TABLE 1
Raman band wavenumbers/cm^{-1} observed for uridine and its derivatives

Compound		UrI	UrII	UrIII	UrIV		UrV				UrVI	
Uridine		1686	1635	1482	1402		1237		1141	873	787	
Uridine-3d[a]	1692	1657	1620	1461	1400	1303	1250	1215	1137	848	782	
Uridine-5d		1676	1623	1469	1372		1214	1170	1123	851	785	
Uridine-3d,5d	1695	1651	1619	1469	1372	1303	1240	1180	1144	827	782	
Uridine-3-deprotonated		1629	1600	1497	1380	1296	1237	1210		875	790	
Thymidine		1667		1420	1378		1244	1190	1144	880	789	749
Thymidine-3d		1664	1632	1482	1381	1311	1247		1160	851	792	740
5-Fluorouridine		1692			1365		1247	1214	1154	872	803	771
5-Bromouridine		1686	1629	1472	1355		1214		1167	868	789	
5-Bromouridine-3d	1698	1657	1629	1456	1355	1303	1243		1144	848	785	
5-Iodouridine		1673	1616	1462	1358		1210		1167	868	785	
5-Iodouridine-3d	1705	1650	1621	1462	1360	1309	1240		1147	855	789	
4-Thiouridine			1619	1482	1372		1243		(1160)[b]		(709)	
4-Thiouridine-3d			1619	1482	1420	1316	1214		(1167)		(709)	
Dihydrouridine	1706			many weak bands					1157	865	811	723
Dihydrouridine-3d	1706			many weak bands					1125	850	798	723

[a] ^{1}H replaced by ^{2}H at the position indicated.
[b] The wavenumbers in parentheses are ascribed to two coupled modes of ring-breathing and $C{=}S$ stretching vibrations.

than those actually observed for the neutral uracil residue. Due to vibrational coupling with the 3-NH in-plane deformation, which would be somewhere in the 1500–1600 cm^{-1} region, both of the UrIII and UrV bands are pushed down (to 1482 and 1233 cm^{-1}, respectively). Therefore, the removal of the position-3 hydrogen causes a shift to higher wavenumbers of each of the UrIII and UrV vibrations. When the UrV vibration is brought up to about 1270 cm^{-1} or so, further vibrational coupling with the 5-CH or 6-CH in-plane deformation may give rise to a complicated feature in this spectral region.

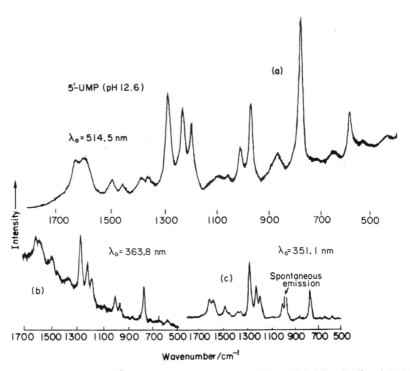

Fig. 13. Raman spectra of β-uridine-5′-phosphoric acid (5′-UMP) in alkaline (pH 12.6) aqueous solution. Excited by (a) 514.5 nm, (b) 363.8 nm, and (c) 351.1 nm lines.

5.3.2. Effect of deuteration at position 3 (see Figs 12(b), 14(b) and 15(b))

The UrV vibration is shifted to a slightly higher wavenumber (1233 → 1249 cm^{-1}), and at the same time a few satellite Raman bands appear both on the high and low wavenumber sides of it. This spectral change on changing 3-NH to ND is somewhat similar to that on changing 3-NH to N$^-$, as mentioned above, and its interpretation may be made in a similar way. The satellite Raman bands, however, may partly be attributed also to vibrational coupling between the 3-ND in-plane deformation and UrV vibrations.

The wavenumber of the UrIV vibration remains almost unchanged, while that of the UrIII vibration is slightly shifted towards lower wavenumbers ($1482 \rightarrow 1461$ cm^{-1}). The spectral change in the 1600 to 1700 cm^{-1} region is complex; instead of the two Raman bands at 1686 cm^{-1} (strong, UrI) and 1633 cm^{-1} (medium, UrII), three new Raman bands are observed for the

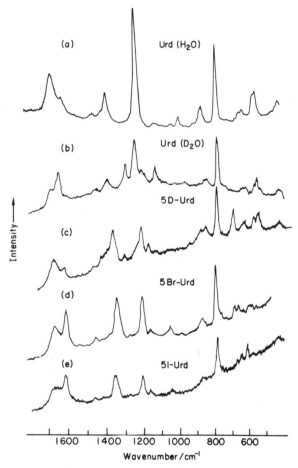

Fig. 14. Raman spectra of uridine and its derivatives in neutral aqueous solutions excited by the 514.5 nm radiation. (a) uridine in ^{1}H$_2$O, (b) uridine in ^{2}H$_2$O, (c) 5-deuterouridine, (d) 5-bromouridine, (e) 5-iodouridine.

3-deuterated-UMP at 1692 (medium), 1657 (strong), and 1620 cm^{-1} (weak). This fact indicates that the 3-NH in-plane bending vibration must occur in the 1600 to 1700 cm^{-1} region. Since 3-ND-uridine has *three* vibrations here, undeuterated uracil residue should have *four* vibrations (three + NH in-plane) in this spectral region; two of these four must give extremely weak Raman bands, so that only two are of appreciable intensity (1686 and 1633 cm^{-1}).

5.3.3. Effect of deuteration at position 5 (see Figs 12(c), 14(c) and 15(c))

The UrIV and UrV vibrations are both shifted slightly towards lower wave-number, i.e. to 1372 and 1214 cm^{-1}, respectively. The fact that the spectral change is not more than this, however, indicates that the 5-CH in-plane deformation does not play a leading part in any of the UrIV and UrV vibrations.

5.3.4. Effect of heavy-atom substitution at position 5 (see Figs 12(d), 14(d, e) and 16)

Raman spectroscopic examinations have been made for substituted uracil residues,

where X$=$CH$_3$, F, Br, or I. Under the pre-resonance condition, five strong Raman bands are found for each of these substituted uracil residues, at about 1680, 1630, 1350, 1210, and 790 cm^{-1}. These are considered to correspond, respectively, to UrI, UrII, UrIV, UrV, and UrVI vibrations of the unsubstituted uracil residues. In addition, a weak Raman band at about 1460 cm^{-1} is always observed, and this is taken as corresponding to the UrIII vibration. The UrIV and UrV frequencies are both somewhat lower in the 5-substituted uracil residue than those for the unsubstituted one. As far as the general features are concerned, however, the resonance Raman spectra of 5-substituted and unsubstituted uracil residues are similar to one another.

5.3.5. Effects of saturation of the C$_6$–C$_5$ bond (see Fig. 17(a))

In the Raman spectrum of dihydrouridine, which contains the residue,

no strong bands are found in the 900 to 1500 cm^{-1} region. It is clear that the C$_5$=C$_6$ double bond, which makes the whole six-membered ring nearly conjugated, is essential for giving rise to the UrIV and UrV vibrations (the C$_5$=C$_6$ double bond is also essential for the 260 nm absorption band). It is noticeable that dihydrouridine gives stronger Raman bands in the 1600–1700 cm^{-1} region, these corresponding to the two C=O groups.

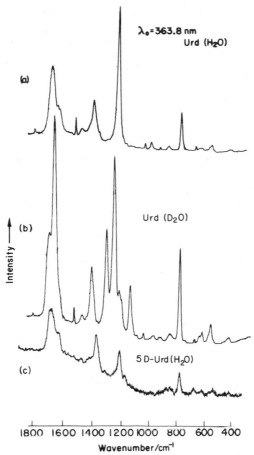

Fig. 15. Raman spectra of uridine and deuterated uridines in neutral aqueous solutions excited by the 363.8 nm radiation. (a) uridine in ^1H_2O, (b) uridine in ^2H_2O (3-deuterouridine), (c) 5-deuterouridine.

5.3.6. Effect of ^{18}O-substitution at position 4

Raman spectroscopic examinations of ^{15}N-substituted uracil residues and ^{18}O-substituted uracil residues have not yet been reported. However, an infrared absorption study was made of uridine-4-^{18}O in a neutral ^2H_2O solution.[52] In the infrared spectrum of 3-ND uracil residue, there appear three absorption bands in the 1600 to 1700 cm^{-1} region. at 1618 (weak), 1657 (strong), and 1691 (medium) cm^{-1}. Position-4 ^{18}O substitution causes a complex isotope effect, with decreases in the wavenumbers of both the 1657 cm^{-1} (-5 cm^{-1}) and the 1618 cm^{-1} bands (-12 cm^{-1}), but no change of the 1691 cm^{-1} band. This observation suggests that the 1691 cm^{-1} band is attributable to the position-2 C=O stretching vibration, in which no position-4 C=O stretching is involved.

Second, it is certain that both the strong 1657 cm^{-1} band (this also is strong in the Raman spectrum) and the weak 1618 cm^{-1} band (this also is very weak in the Raman spectrum) involve the position-4 C═O stretching motion, but neither of these is assignable to the pure 4-C═O stretching vibration. If there were a pure 4-C═O stretching band, it would show an ^{18}O-isotope shift as great as −40 cm^{-1} (eqn. (35)). Because the observed isotope shifts are much smaller, there must be a few complex vibrations in a lower wavenumber region that involve appreciable amount of 4-C═O stretching.

5.4   Assignments of the On-resonance Raman Bands

All of the six Raman bands, UrI to UrVI, are in the skeletal-stretching frequency region. All of these Raman bands, except UrIII, are strong in off-

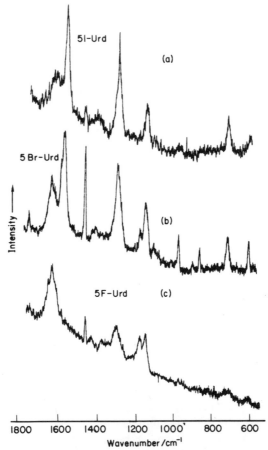

Fig. 16. Raman spectra of uridine derivatives in neutral aqueous solutions excited by 363.8 nm radiation. (a) 5-iodouridine, (b) 5-bromouridine, (c) 5-fluorouridine.

resonance conditions (cf. Section 3.1, rule (a)). In addition, neither position-3 deuteration nor position-5 deuteration causes a wavenumber shift greater than $100\ cm^{-1}$ for any of these Raman bands. Therefore, all of these are assignable primarily to in-plane skeletal bond-stretching vibrations of the neutral uracil residue.

The $787\ cm^{-1}$ band is assignable to a vibration in which all eight skeletal stretching motions take place in-phase.[4,5] On the basis of the general discussion given in Section 3.6, it is understandable that the relative intensity of this band is very strong in an off-resonance Raman spectrum (Fig. 10(a)), while it is very weak in a rigorous resonance Raman spectrum excited within the longest wavelength (260 nm) absorption band (Fig. 12(a)).

In the 1600 to $1700\ cm^{-1}$ region, there are intrinsically four skeletal stretching vibrations expected: $C^2=O$ stretching, $C^4=O$ stretching, and two ring vibrations corresponding to the e_{2g} vibrations of the benzene ring (S_{r5} and S_{r6} in Fig. 7). On the basis of the descriptions given in Section 4.2, however, one of these four is probably pushed down to the 1300 to $1400\ cm^{-1}$ region due to a vibrational coupling. There are thus three bands expected to remain in the 1600 to $1700\ cm^{-1}$ region. The three Raman bands (or three infrared bands) for the position-3 deuterated uracil residue (cf. Sections 5.3.2 and 5.3.3) actually observed in this wavenumber region are considered to be assigned as follows: the $1692\ cm^{-1}$ band to C^2-O stretching, and 1657 and $1620\ cm^{-1}$ bands to a coupled pair of $C^4=O$ and an e_{2g}-type mode. In the undeuterated uracil

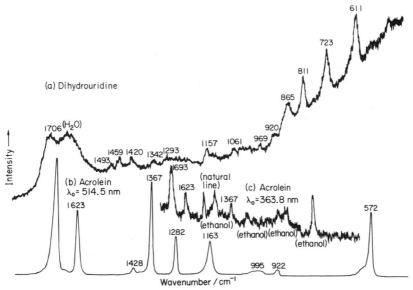

Fig. 17. Raman spectra of (a) dihydrouridine in ^1H_2O excited by 514.5 nm radiation, (b) acrolein (pure liquid) excited by 514.5 nm radiation, and (c) acrolein in ethanol excited by the 363.8 nm radiation.

residue, these three are further disarranged by the N^3—H in-plane bending mode. Of the four vibrations expected in this spectral region, two are missing from the Raman spectrum. One of these must be at 1710 cm^{-1}, because the undeuterated uracil residue gives a strong infrared absorption band at 1710 cm^{-1}.[5] This is assignable to the C^2=O stretching vibration.[53] Thus, the UrI and UrII are probably assignable to a coupled pair of the C^4=O stretching and a ring mode related to an e_{2g} mode of the benzene ring.

The remaining three, i.e. UrIII, UrIV, and UrV Raman bands, are assigned to three of the remaining four ring modes derived from two e_{1u} modes, one b_{2u} mode, and one e_{2g} mode (these being vibrationally coupled to the C^4=O stretching motion).

5.5 Calculation of Normal Vibrations

A normal coordinate treatment has been made of uracil, uracil-3d, uracil-5d, and uracil-3d,5d. The treatment involves a refinement in comparison with what has been done previously;[4,5] the potential function now involves the bond-stretch/bond-stretch interaction terms which take care of the vibrational coupling through rearrangements of the delocalized π-electron orbitals.[54] In our previous article, a discussion was made as to the necessity of introducing a 'Kekulé constant' which once appeared in the potential energy expression of the benzene ring.[55] In other words, it was suggested that even in the uracil ring, a Kekulé form has a special stability. In our present calculation, however, this special stability is effectively introduced (if necessary) by assigning a proper set of values to the bond-stretch/bond-stretch interaction constants, and there is no need to introduce a new potential parameter.

The bond lengths and bond angles in the uracil molecule are assumed to be equal to those given by a crystallographic study of position-5 substituted uracils (T. Katsura et al., personal communication). The calculation was carried out using a HITAC 8800/8700 computer at the University of Tokyo, and the programs, BGLZ, LSMA, and LSMB, written by Shimanouchi and his collaborators.[56]

In Table 2, is shown the set of force constants we finally reached in our present set of trials. The wavenumbers of the in-plane vibrations and the vibrational modes of uracil calculated with this set of force constants are given in Table 3. The nature of each normal mode, k, is well expressed by the 'potential energy distribution'. The internal coordinates, S, are related linearly to the normal coordinates, Q, through the matrix expression

$$S = LQ. \tag{39}$$

The potential energy for a given normal mode of vibration, Q_k, is expressed as $Q_k^2 \sum F_{ij} L_{ik} L_{jk}$. Therefore, the distribution of the potential energy among internal coordinates can approximately be expressed as $F_{ii} L_{ik}^2 (100/\lambda_k)$. This has been calculated as shown in Table 3. The normal modes of vibration are shown in

Fig. 18. We propose to assign these to the UrI to UrVI modes, whose Raman bands are resonance enhanced by interaction with the 260 nm band.

One of the strong points of our present calculation is that the observed deuteration effects are well explained. As may be seen in Fig. 19, the present calculation can reproduce the splitting of the vibration at $1250 \ cm^{-1}$ (UrV) actually observed on introducing deuterium at position 3. It also reproduces the

TABLE 2
The set of force constants for uracil[a]

1	$K(N_1C_2)$	6.380	14	$H(N_1C_2N_3)$	1.619	26	$H(O_2C_2N_1)$	1.034
2	$K(C_2N_3)$	6.380	15	$H(C_2N_3C_4)$	1.166	27	$H(HN_3C_2)$	0.510
3	$K(N_3C_4)$	6.380	16	$H(N_3C_4C_5)$	1.620	28	$H(OC_4N_3)$	1.035
4	$K(C_4C_5)$	6.202	17	$H(C_4C_5C_6)$	0.539	29	$H(HC_5C_4)$	0.304
5	$K(C_5C_6)$	8.700	18	$H(C_5C_6N_1)$	0.539	30	$H(HC_6C_5)$	0.300
6	$K(C_6N_1)$	6.380	19	$H(RN_1C_2)$	0.510	31	$f(\nu_{ring}, \nu_{ring})$	0.896
7	$K(N_1R_7)$	5.397	20	$H(O_2C_2N_3)$	1.034	32	$f(\nu_{C=O}, \nu_{ring})$	1.397
8	$K(C_2O_8)$	11.000	21	$H(HN_3C_4)$	0.510	33	$f(\nu_{C4=O}, \nu_{C=C})$	-0.225
9	$K(N_3H_9)$	5.397	22	$H(O_4C_4C_5)$	1.034	34	$f(\delta_{C=O}, \nu_{ring})$	0.304
10	$K(C_4O_{10})$	10.500	23	$H(HC_5C_6)$	0.302	35	$f(\delta_{NH}, \nu_{ring})$	0.222
11	$K(C_5H_{11})$	5.204	24	$H(HC_6N_1)$	0.302	36	$f(\delta_{CH}, \nu_{ring})$	0.253
12	$K(C_6H_{12})$	5.204	25	$H(RN_1C_6)$	0.508	37	$f(\delta_{C=O}, \nu_{C=O})$	0.857
13	$H(C_6N_1C_2)$	1.166						

[a] K in mdyn $Å^{-1}$, H in mdyn $Å$, f in mdyn.

effects observed on introducing deuterium at position 5, i.e. frequency lowerings of UrII, UrIII, and UrV and no splitting in any of these vibrations.

On the basis of this normal coordinate treatment the following assignments may be made:

UrI at 1686 cm^{-1}. $C^4{=}O$ stretching and a skeletal stretching (similar to that of the $S_{r5}(e_{2g})$ vibration of the benzene ring (see Fig. 7)) take place *in-phase*. This is considered to correspond to the calculated mode at 1648 cm^{-1} (see Fig. 18).

UrII at 1633 cm^{-1}. $C^4{=}O$ stretching and a $S_{r5}(e_{2g})$-like ring motion take place with 180° phase difference. See the calculated mode at 1610 cm^{-1} in Fig. 18.

UrIII at 1482 cm^{-1}. In-phase $C^2{=}O/C^4{=}O$ stretching motion and a vibration that is similar to the $S_{r6}(e_{2g})$ vibration of the benzene ring (see Fig. 7) take place *in-phase*. This probably corresponds to the calculated mode at 1445 cm^{-1} in Fig. 18. As has been suggested in Sections 4.2 and 5.4, the wavenumber of one of the e_{2g}-type bond-stretching modes of the six-membered conjugated double-bond system comes down from the 1600 to the 1400 cm^{-1} region because of the coupling with the stretching motions of the two carbonyl bonds attached at positions 2 and 4.

UrIV at 1402 cm⁻¹. Kekulé-type (b_{2u}) stretching motion (Fig. 7), corresponding to the calculated mode at 1373 cm⁻¹ (Fig. 18).

UrV at 1233 cm⁻¹. An e_{1u}-type motion (Fig. 7), corresponding to the calculated mode at 1284 cm⁻¹ (Fig. 18).

5.6   Correlation with Electronic Structure

Possible structures of the excited electronic states of the uracil residue will now be discussed. It seems to be reasonably certain that the strong absorption

TABLE 3
Calculated wavenumbers/cm⁻¹ and percentage potential energy distribution ($F_{ii}L_{ik}^2\,100/\lambda_k$) among internal coordinates (i). The underline means that the corresponding L-matrix element is negative. In the first column, K means bond-stretching and H means bond-angle bending

Mode	Wavenumber/cm⁻¹								
	1699	1648	1610	1494	1464	1445	1373	1284	793
K (N1C2)	11.3	0.2	1.8	0.7	9.5	<u>8.3</u>	<u>24.8</u>	<u>1.7</u>	<u>6.9</u>
K (C2N3)	9.2	<u>3.2</u>	<u>0.6</u>	4.0	2.9	11.0	29.9	1.7	<u>4.4</u>
K (N3C4)	<u>1.0</u>	6.9	0.0	<u>0.1</u>	16.5	9.4	<u>26.5</u>	9.0	<u>5.3</u>
K (C4C5)	0.1	18.0	0.1	<u>0.0</u>	8.5	<u>7.4</u>	26.5	<u>1.4</u>	6.2
K (C5C6)	0.0	<u>7.5</u>	70.8	<u>0.7</u>	0.2	<u>0.6</u>	<u>9.8</u>	0.8	<u>1.8</u>
K (C6N1)	<u>1.6</u>	0.3	7.4	14.9	<u>3.3</u>	2.1	0.8	37.0	<u>6.7</u>
K (N1R7)	<u>0.0</u>	0.0	0.0	0.0	0.0	<u>0.0</u>	<u>0.0</u>	0.0	0.0
K (C2O8)	75.9	<u>0.0</u>	<u>0.0</u>	6.1	13.2	1.3	0.0	0.0	<u>6.6</u>
K (N3H9)	<u>0.0</u>	<u>0.0</u>	<u>0.0</u>	<u>0.0</u>	<u>0.1</u>	0.1	0.0	<u>0.0</u>	0.0
K (C4O10)	<u>0.7</u>	67.8	9.4	0.0	<u>2.6</u>	15.8	0.0	<u>1.8</u>	4.5
K (C5H11)	0.0	<u>0.0</u>	<u>0.4</u>	<u>0.0</u>	0.0	<u>0.1</u>	0.0	0.0	<u>0.0</u>
K (C6H12)	<u>0.0</u>	<u>0.0</u>	<u>0.4</u>	0.0	<u>0.0</u>	0.0	<u>0.0</u>	0.1	<u>0.1</u>
H (CN1C)	1.6	<u>0.1</u>	<u>2.2</u>	<u>0.3</u>	<u>1.1</u>	0.1	1.2	<u>0.3</u>	<u>7.2</u>
H (NC2N)	<u>10.8</u>	0.0	0.0	0.0	<u>0.0</u>	0.3	<u>0.3</u>	0.2	6.3
H (CN3C)	2.2	2.5	<u>0.0</u>	0.9	1.8	<u>1.7</u>	<u>0.0</u>	0.1	<u>2.6</u>
H (NC4C)	<u>0.0</u>	11.3	<u>0.1</u>	<u>0.0</u>	<u>0.0</u>	<u>0.3</u>	0.0	0.4	4.0
H (CC5C)	<u>0.0</u>	0.5	0.3	0.1	<u>0.4</u>	1.4	<u>0.4</u>	0.2	<u>2.9</u>
H (CC6N)	0.0	0.0	0.4	<u>0.2</u>	0.4	<u>0.3</u>	0.0	<u>1.1</u>	4.1
H (RN1C)	<u>5.1</u>	<u>0.0</u>	<u>1.5</u>	34.9	<u>0.6</u>	0.0	1.9	<u>2.1</u>	0.6
H (OC2N)	1.8	0.0	0.1	2.4	2.5	<u>1.9</u>	<u>2.3</u>	0.0	<u>0.5</u>
H (HN3C)	1.3	<u>8.4</u>	0.4	1.1	14.0	21.4	0.2	<u>0.7</u>	0.4
H (OC4C)	<u>0.0</u>	1.0	0.7	<u>0.0</u>	<u>1.5</u>	5.0	<u>2.0</u>	<u>1.8</u>	2.6
H (HC5C)	0.0	0.3	0.3	<u>0.1</u>	0.0	<u>0.0</u>	0.8	<u>12.9</u>	0.5
H (HC6N)	<u>0.0</u>	<u>0.0</u>	2.5	<u>0.0</u>	<u>0.0</u>	<u>0.0</u>	0.6	<u>4.0</u>	<u>0.6</u>
H (RN1C)	1.9	0.0	5.0	<u>30.2</u>	2.3	<u>0.1</u>	4.6	3.3	0.9
H (OC2N)	1.6	<u>0.0</u>	<u>0.3</u>	2.4	2.3	0.8	3.9	0.2	<u>1.5</u>
H (HN3C)	<u>4.7</u>	3.4	<u>0.2</u>	3.0	21.6	14.0	<u>0.1</u>	0.3	0.1
H (OC4N)	0.0	2.7	<u>0.3</u>	0.0	2.6	<u>3.1</u>	1.4	0.6	0.0
H (HC5C)	<u>0.0</u>	<u>1.2</u>	<u>1.0</u>	0.0	0.0	<u>0.4</u>	<u>0.1</u>	10.2	0.2
H (HC6C)	<u>0.0</u>	0.0	1.1	0.2	<u>0.1</u>	0.3	<u>0.8</u>	7.9	<u>0.5</u>

band at 260 nm is due to its lowest $\pi^* \leftarrow \pi$ transition. For the π-electron system of this base residue, a semiempirical Pariser-Parr-Pople calculation has been made by Nagata *et al.*[57] They assumed that each of the position-1 and position-3 nitrogen atoms provides two π-electrons to the conjugated double-bond system, and regarded the problem as that of an 8-orbital 10-electron system. The eight molecular orbitals are shown schematically in Fig. 20 on the basis of an unpublished part of the results of their calculation (C. Nagata, personal communication). The 260 nm absorption band is assignable to the $(5 \rightarrow 6)$ transition, i.e.

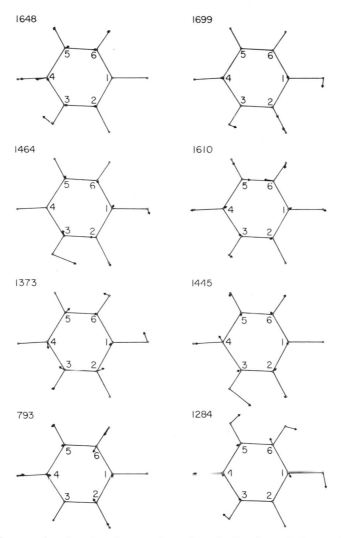

Fig. 18. Wavenumbers/cm^{-1} and normal modes of vibration of the uracil residue, calculated using the set of force constants given in Table 2.

the transition from the 5th molecular orbital to the 6th one, which should have a large oscillator strength according to their calculation.

As may readily be seen in Fig. 20, on going from the 5th to the 6th molecular orbital, the $C^5{=}C^6$ bond should change dramatically from *bonding* to *antibonding*, the $C^4{=}O$ bond should also change from *bonding* to *antibonding*, but the $C^4{-}C^5$ bond should change from *antibonding* to *bonding*. Indeed, as shown in Fig. 21, the calculation of Nagata *et al.*[57] indicates that, on going from the ground $\tilde{X}$ to the excited $\tilde{A}$ $(5 \rightarrow 6)$ electronic state, the greatest bond-order

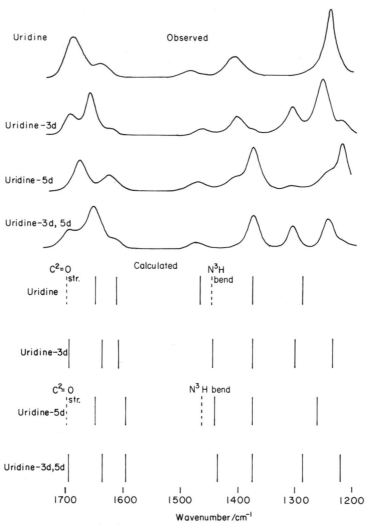

Fig. 19. Some of the observed and calculated Raman band wavenumbers of the uracil residue and its deuterated products.

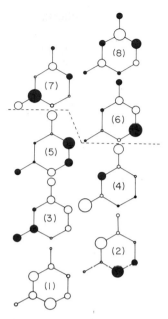

Fig. 20. Schematic drawing of the eight molecular orbitals of the ten π-electrons in the uracil residue (on the basis of an unpublished part of the results of calculation made by Nagata *et al.*[57]). Open and closed circles indicate that the upper branches of the atomic orbitals of the π-electrons are positive and negative, respectively. The size of the circle indicates the approximate value of the coefficient of the particular atomic orbital in the relevant molecular orbital, where (radius)³ = coefficient.

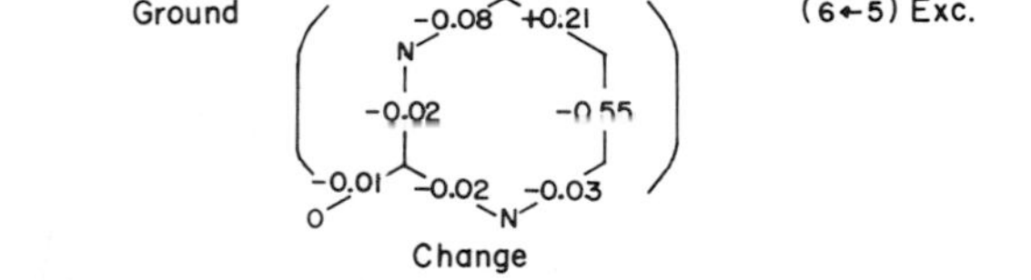

Fig. 21. Bond orders due to the π-electrons in the ground ($\tilde{X}$) and excited ($\tilde{A}$) states of the uracil residue (on the basis of unpublished results of a calculation made by Nagata *et al.*[57]). The changes in the bond orders on going from $\tilde{X}$ to $\tilde{A}$ are also shown.

change takes place at $C^5{=}C^6$; it markedly decreases. The bond-order of the $C^4{=}O$ should also decrease, while that of $C_4{-}C_5$ should increase. It is therefore suggested that, on going from the equilibrium conformation in the $\tilde{X}$ state to that in the $\tilde{A}$ state, an appreciable stretching of the $C^5{=}C^6$ and $C^4{=}O$ bonds and a contraction of the $C^4{-}C^5$ bond may take place. Thus, on the basis of the general rule given in Section 3.5, any vibration in which a large amount of $C^5{=}C^6$ stretching takes place in-phase with the $C^4{=}O$ stretching, but with 180° phase difference with the $C^4{-}C^5$ stretching, is expected to show a resonance effect with the 260 nm band. The actual observations (Sections 5.1 and 5.2) are in agreement with this expectation.

In the higher excited electronic states, most π-electrons are in antibonding orbitals. Therefore, on going from the electronic ground state to such a state most bonds would be elongated. Thus it is understandable that such a higher excited state is primarily responsible for the ring-breathing (UrVI) Raman band in an off-resonance condition. It is not surprising, however, that the ring breathing mode shows a resonance Raman effect in the 260 nm absorption band, because it may involve a small amount of the above mentioned vibrational mode.

For the electronic structure of uracil, an all-valence electron MO—CI calculation has been made by Hug and Tinoco.[58] The above view, based upon the result of the calculation of Nagata et al.,[57] is supported by this more elaborate treatment. Thus, on the basis of Hug and Tinoco's calculation, a marked localization of the monopoles of transitions $\tilde{A} \leftarrow \tilde{X}$ and $\tilde{B} \leftarrow \tilde{X}$ along the acrolein-like fragment $C^6{=}C^5{-}C^4{=}O$ is expected to take place. The deviation from a pyrimidine-like pattern is considered to be so large that it is better to consider $\tilde{A}$ and $\tilde{B}$ as being the two lowest excited states of an α,β-unsaturated ketone, perturbed by those of the urea part of uracil.

5.7   Possibility of a Duschinsky Effect

It is not improbable that the lowering of the bond-orders of the $C^5{=}C^6$ and $C^4{=}O$ bonds just mentioned is so great that their stretching wavenumbers are as low as 1200 to 1300 cm^{-1} in the $\tilde{A}$ state. For acrolein in $\tilde{A}$ state (in which both of the C=C and C=O are longer by 0.1 Å than in $\tilde{X}$, while C—C is shorter by 0.1 Å than in $\tilde{X}$), for example, the C=O and C=C stretching wavenumbers are known to be 1266 and 1410 cm^{-1}, respectively.[59] One should remember that this $\tilde{A}$ state of acrolein is an $(n\pi^*)$ state, whereas the $\tilde{A}$ state of uracil is a $(\pi\pi^*)$ state. Nevertheless, this information may be sufficient to suggest that the lowering of the $C^5{=}C^6$ and $C^4{=}O$ wavenumbers can be from 200 to 400 cm^{-1} on going from $\tilde{X}$ to $\tilde{A}$. If this is so, the vibrational coupling between the $C^5{=}C^6$ stretching, $C^4{=}O$ stretching, and e_{2g}, e_{1u}, and b_{2u}-type ring stretching motions would be greatly different in $\tilde{A}$ from those in $\tilde{X}$. In other words, there must be a Duschinsky effect (see Section 3.7). No significant values of many-dimensional Franck-Condon integrals (eqn. (26)) can be estimated for uracil or for acrolein on the basis of our present knowledge. We can, however, demonstrate how a Raman band in the 1200 to 1300 cm^{-1} region, which is otherwise weak, can become strong by a Duschinsky effect. In showing this we use a very simple model, which does not seem to be realistic, but may be good enough to illustrate the essential features of the situation.

Let us suppose that only two vibrational modes, C=O stretching and 'mode X', whose intrinsic frequencies are 1650 and 1250 cm^{-1}, respectively, need to be taken into account in a given molecule. Let us postulate two cases: case (a), where C=O stretching and X are orthogonal to each other, both in the ground $\tilde{X}$ and an excited electronic state $\tilde{A}$; and case (b), where C=O stretching and X are orthogonal in the $\tilde{X}$ state, but they couple strongly with each other in the upper $\tilde{A}$ state, because in $\tilde{A}$ the C=O stretching wavenumber is lowered to 1250 cm^{-1} and an accidental degeneracy takes place with the X mode. The vibrational wavefunctions for a few lower vibrational states in $\tilde{X}$ and $\tilde{A}$ are shown schematically in Fig. 22. As may be seen in the figure, the Franck-Condon overlap integrals for carbonyl stretching vibrations ($v_1' = 0, 1, \ldots$;

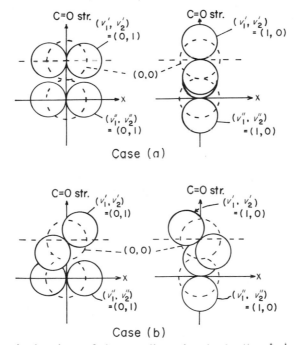

Case (a)

Case (b)

Fig. 22. Schematic drawings of the two-dimensional vibrational eigenfunctions for two hypothetical cases: (a) C=O stretching and X modes are not vibrationally coupled either in the upper ($\tilde{A}$) or ground ($\tilde{X}$) states, and (b) C=O stretching and X mode are strongly coupled in the upper ($\tilde{A}$) state but not in the ground ($\tilde{X}$) state. In both cases the equilibrium bond length of C=O is assumed to be appreciably longer in $\tilde{A}$ than in $\tilde{X}$. v_1' and v_2' are the vibrational quantum numbers for the upper ($\tilde{A}$) state, and v_1'' and v_2'' are those for the ground ($\tilde{X}$) state.

$v_1'' = 0, 1, \ldots$) should have appreciable values, whereas those for X vibrations ($v_2' = 0, 1, \ldots$; $v_2'' = 0, 1, \ldots$) should be very small in case (a). In case (b), on the other hand, the overlap integrals would be great for both of the C=O stretching and X vibrations. Therefore, on the basis of 'rule (e)' described in Section 3.3, an appreciable resonance enhancement of the Raman band assignable to the 'X mode' may take place.

In the Raman spectrum of acrolein, the C^α—H in-plane bending vibration at 1367 cm^{-1} gives a very strong band. Because CH bending vibrations usually give only weak Raman bands, the strong Raman scattering in acrolein may be due to a Duschinsky effect. In our simple model, the C^α—H in-plane bending corresponds to the 'X-mode'. It may further be speculated that the intensity of the 1233 cm^{-1} Raman band of the uracil residue may also be caused by a Duschinsky effect. Here, the UrV mode corresponds to the 'X-mode'.

5.8   Resonance Raman Spectrum of 4-Thiouracil Residue

This is a derivative of the uracil residue in which the position-4 carbonyl is replaced by a thio-carbonyl, viz.

This is a minor base residue which appears occasionally in amino-acid transfer RNAs (tRNAs). Most of the bacterial tRNAs have this residue at position 8. Its Raman spectrum is closely related to that of the uracil residue, and therefore will be discussed here.

4-Thiouridine has its longest wavelength absorption band at 330 nm (see Fig. 2), and a rigorous resonance Raman effect from it is expected to be observed by the use of 363.8 nm excitation. This has been proved to be the case; as is shown in Fig. 23, the Raman spectrum was observed with a solution as dilute as 10^{-4} M. In the resonance condition, six strong Raman bands are observed, at 1619, 1482, 1372, 1243, 1160, and 709 cm^{-1}. The greatest difference from the resonance Raman spectrum of the uracil residue is caused by the C=S stretching vibration. This vibration is considered to be strongly coupled with the ring-breathing vibration and to cause two strong Raman bands at 1160 and 709 cm^{-1}.

The strong Raman band at 1619 cm^{-1} is considered to correspond to the UrII of uracil rather than the C^2=O stretching mode. The latter is observed at 1700 cm^{-1} in the infrared spectrum, but seems to give only a very weak band in the resonance Raman spectrum as it does in the case of the uracil residue. The 1482, 1372, and 1243 cm^{-1} bands are considered to correspond to the 1482 (UrIII), 1404 (UrIV), and 1233 cm^{-1} (UrV) bands of the uracil residue, respectively.

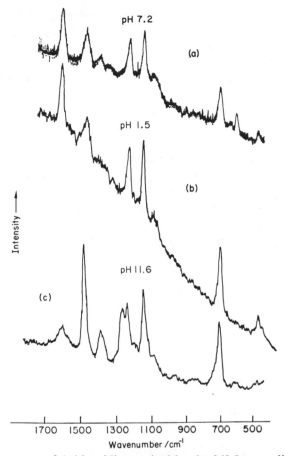

Fig. 23. Raman spectra of 4-thiouridine excited by the 363.8 nm radiation, obtained using a rotating cell. (a) In pH 7.2, (b) in pH 1.5, and (c) in pH 11.6 aqueous solutions. The concentration is 10^{-4} M.

6   RESONANCE RAMAN EFFECT OF THE CYTOSINE RESIDUE

For β-cytosine-5'-phosphoric acid (5'-CMP), which has the cytosine residue,

instead of the uracil residue in 5'-UMP, a similar series of examinations to those described in Section 5 has been made. The experimental set-up used was exactly the same as that described in Section 5.1. Some of the observed Raman spectra of 5′-CMP are shown in Fig. 24. In each of these spectra, the intensity ratio I_j/I_{st} has been determined for each Raman band (j) relative to a chosen standard band (st), the band at 980 cm^{-1} of the $[PO_3]^{2-}$ group. In Fig. 25, observed values of the relative intensity, $\phi_j(v_{exc})$, are plotted against v_{exc}, where $\phi_j(v_{exc})$ is I_j/I_{st} corrected for the v^4-factor and then normalized relative to the band excited at 647.1 nm (eqn. (36)). The continuous curves in Fig. 25 represent calculated values of $\phi_j(v_{exc})$ (eqn. (38)) for $v_{e0} - v_{g0} = 37\,300$ cm^{-1} (268 nm) ($\tilde{A} \leftarrow \tilde{X}$) and $43\,500$ cm^{-1} (230 nm) ($\tilde{B} \leftarrow \tilde{X}$). From a comparison of the observed and calculated $\phi_j(v_{exc})$ values (Fig. 25), it is shown to be probable that the Raman bands at 1296 and 1533 cm^{-1} are principally associated with the longer-wavelength absorption band at 268 nm.

A rigorous resonance Raman effect of 5′-CMP has been examined with 257.3 nm excitation. Again exactly the same experimental procedure was used as for 5′-UMP and other related compounds (Section 5.2). The result is given in Fig.

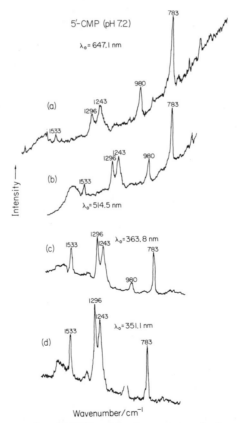

Fig. 24. Raman spectra of 5′-CMP in neutral aqueous solution. Excited by (a) 647.1 nm, (b) 514.5 nm, (c) 363.8 nm, and (d) 351.1 nm lines.

26. As is seen, six bands at 783, 1243, 1296, 1400, 1533, and *ca.* 1650 cm^{-1} show resonance Raman effects when excited within the 268 nm band. Therefore, it is evident that the 268 nm band is involved in each case. As has already been mentioned, resonance effects in the 1296 and 1533 cm^{-1} bands are considered to be associated solely with the 268 nm band. It is probable that a weaker band at 1400 cm^{-1} is also associated solely with the 268 nm band. The 783, 1243, and *ca.* 1650 cm^{-1} Raman bands, on the other hand, are considered to derive their intensities only partly from the 268 nm band; in the pre-resonance condition, they derive their intensities partly from 230 nm or longer-wavelength electronic transitions (see Fig. 25).

The 783 cm^{-1} band is assignable to the ring breathing vibration.[4,5] The Raman band at 1296 cm^{-1} is considered to correspond to the UrV vibration of

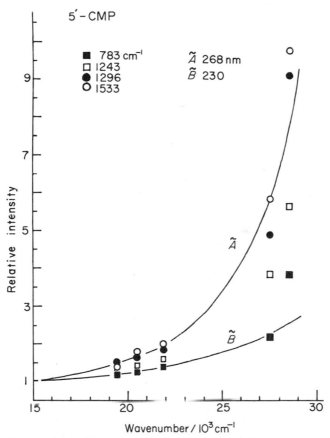

Fig. 25. The Raman intensities of 5′-CMP as a function of the wavenumber, $\tilde{\nu}_{exc}$, of the exciting light. Observed values of $\phi_j(\nu_{exc})_{obs}$ (see eqn. (36)) are plotted for the j = 783, 1243, 1296, and 1533 cm^{-1} Raman bands. Continuous lines indicate $\phi_j(\nu_{exc})_{calc}$ (see eqn. (38)) for electronic excited states $\tilde{A}$ (268 nm) and $\tilde{B}$ (230 nm).

the uracil residue. In Section 5.3.1, it was shown that deprotonation at the position-3 nitrogen of the uracil residue causes a high-frequency shift of the UrV vibration and at the same time an appearance of two satellite bands in the 1240 cm^{-1} region. The 1243 cm^{-1} band of the cytosine residue is considered to correspond to such a satellite band; the neutral cytosine residue has no hydrogen

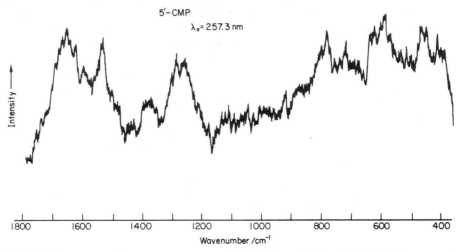

Fig. 26. Resonance Raman spectrum of 5′-CMP at 10^{-4} M (0.004%) in neutral aqueous solution, with 257.3 nm excitation.

atom at the position-3 nitrogen. When the position-3 nitrogen of the cytosine residue is protonated, this satellite band disappears and at the same time the UrV-like Raman band shifts down to 1255 cm^{-1} (see Fig. 27).

The 1400 and 1533 cm^{-1} bands are considered to correspond to the UrIV and UrIII vibrations of the uracil residue, respectively. It is understandable that the benzene-e_{2g}-like stretching vibration appears at 1533 cm^{-1}, i.e. at higher frequency than that of the uracil residue (1482 cm^{-1}), because the cytosine residue has no $C^4{=}O$ and therefore no vibrational coupling between the $C^4{=}O$ and $C^5{=}C^6$ stretching modes. Also, the vibrational coupling between the carbonyl stretching and e_{2g}-type stretching modes mentioned in Sections 4.2 and 5.5 would be weak. The band at *ca.* 1650 cm^{-1} probably is assignable to the $C^5{=}C^6$ stretching mode rather than to the $C^2{=}O$ stretching vibration. As in the case of the uracil residue, the $C^2{=}O$ stretching vibration does not seem to give a strong Raman band, although it does give a strong infrared band (at about 1670 cm^{-1} for solid 1-methyl cytosine).[5] Unfortunately, however, the evidence for this is not yet as sufficient as it is in the case of the uracil or the 4-thiouracil residue. On the other hand, such an absence of the $C^2{=}O$ stretching band in the resonance Raman spectrum (if it is established) is consistent with the idea that the $C^2{=}O$ group is not greatly involved in the electronic excitation at 268 nm.[57,58]

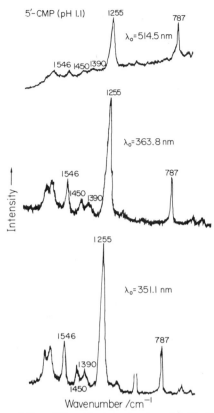

Fig. 27. Raman spectra of β-cytidine-5′-phosphoric acid (5′-CMP) in acidic (pH 1.1) aqueous solution. Excited by (a) 514.5 nm, (b) 363.8 nm, and (c) 351.1 nm lines.

It would be interesting to see the Raman spectrum of the cytosine residue when it is involved in a homopolymer, polyribocytidylic acid. As may be seen in Fig. 28, the relative intensities of the 1296 and 1533 cm^{-1} bands increase, not only when the exciting line is brought close to the 268 nm band, but also when the temperature of the solution is elevated from 27 to 75 °C. This is understandable, because on increasing the temperature the intensity of the absorption band at 268 nm itself increases (cf. Section 3.3, rule (e)).

7. RESONANCE RAMAN EFFECT OF THE ADENINE RESIDUE

7.1 Three Raman Bands in Resonance with the 276 nm Absorption Band

Figure 29 shows a typical Raman spectrum of the adenine residue. The result of an examination of a pre-resonance Raman effect of this residue has already been reported in detail.[60]

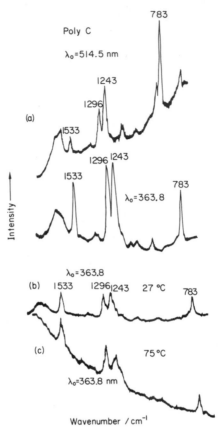

Fig. 28. Raman spectra of polyribocytidylic acid in neutral aqueous solution. Excited by (a) 514.5 and 363.8 nm radiation at room temperature, (b) 363.8 nm radiation at 27 °C, and (c) 363.8 nm radiation at 75 °C.

Concerning the electronic energy levels of the adenine residue, there are still some ambiguities. It is generally believed, however, that there are three excited electronic states corresponding to the 276, 260, and 210 nm absorption bands in the near ultraviolet region. Let us designate these three as $\tilde{A}$, $\tilde{B}$, and $\tilde{C}$ states. By a pre-resonance Raman spectroscopic study, it was shown that the bands at 1580 and 1484 cm^{-1} are associated principally with the longest-wavelength absorption band at 276 nm. The Raman band at 730 cm^{-1} (ring-breathing vibration) seems to be associated principally with the shortest-wavelength band at 210 nm.

Support for this conclusion is obtained by an examination of the effect of temperature on the intensities of the Raman bands of the adenine residue in poly(rA–rU).[19] Poly(rA–rU) is a copolymer containing riboadenylate and ribouridylate residues in alternating sequence, and this is known to form a base-paired double-helical structure [poly(rA–rU).poly(rA–rU)] in aqueous solution at temperatures below 45 °C (in 0.005 M phosphate buffer). The ultraviolet absorption spectrum of this copolymer in its aqueous solution shows a marked change on raising the temperature from 29 to 81 °C. The absorption intensities of the 260 and 210 nm bands both increase by a factor of 1.6. However, a longer wavelength band around 280 nm shifts towards shorter wavelength on heating, but does not seem to increase its intensity. On the other hand, the Raman band

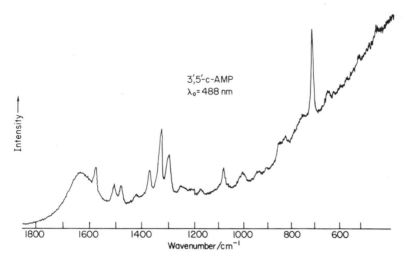

Fig. 29. Raman spectrum of 3′,5′-cyclic AMP in neutral aqueous solution. 488.0 nm excitation.

at 726 cm^{-1} of the adenine residue shows a marked increase (by a factor of 1.9) on being heated, whereas the Raman bands at 1580 and 1480 cm^{-1} do not. This fact may be taken as indicating that the 1580 and 1480 cm^{-1} bands are not caused mainly by the excited electronic states corresponding to the 260 and 210 nm bands, and that the excited electronic state of the adenine residue at 276 nm is responsible for these two Raman bands.

The Raman band at 1340 cm^{-1} is the strongest one of the adenine residue (see Fig. 29). Its intensity increases with the exciting frequency, and the steepness of this excitation profile is just equal to what is expected for a Raman band which is caused solely by the excited state $\tilde{B}$ at 260 nm. On the basis of the absence of any effect of temperature on the intensity of this Raman band[19] (see also Section 2), however, it cannot be associated with the 260 nm absorption band ($\tilde{B} \leftarrow \tilde{X}$). It is probable that this 1340 cm^{-1} band is caused partly by the lowest excited state ($\tilde{A}$) (corresponding to the 276 nm band) and partly by a higher state.

As has been stated in Section 3.3, rule (e), the values of pertinent Franck-Condon overlap integrals must be large in order to cause resonance Raman scattering. For the adenine residue, the Franck-Condon overlap integrals for the 1340, 1484, and 1580 cm^{-1} vibrations between the ground and $\tilde{A}$ (276 nm) electronic states must have appreciable values. The values of such Franck-Condon integrals, on the other hand, should be reflected in the fluorescence spectrum. Guéron et al.[61] observed the fluorescence spectrum of 5'-AMP at 80 K in an ethyleneglycol–water (1:1) glass. It shows a vibrational progression with a spacing of about 1480 cm^{-1}, and its shortest-wavelength peak (which is probably assignable to the 0—0 band) is found at 287 nm. These facts suggest that the fluorescence comes from the lowest singlet excited state ($\tilde{A}$), and that $\tilde{A}$–$\tilde{X}$ Franck-Condon overlap integrals $\langle 0|0 \rangle$, $\langle 0|1 \rangle$, . . . are large for a vibration whose ground-state mode wavenumber is 1480 cm^{-1}. From this, it is further suggested that in this $\tilde{A}$ state the equilibrium conformation is appreciably distorted along the normal coordinate corresponding to the 1480 cm^{-1} vibration.

It is worthwhile mentioning here the phosphorescence spectrum of 5'-AMP, which was observed also by Guéron et al.[61] This shows a vibrational progression with a spacing of about 1300 cm^{-1}. Therefore, in the lowest-triplet electronic state ($\tilde{a}$), the equilibrium conformation of the adenine residue must be distorted from the ground state along the normal coordinate corresponding to the 1340 cm^{-1} vibration. The lowest triplet state is considered to be similar to the lowest singlet excited state ($\tilde{A}$) as far as the orbital configuration, and therefore the geometrical structure, is concerned. Thus it is suggested that the lowest singlet excited state ($\tilde{A}$) is responsible, not only for the 1484 cm^{-1} and 1580 cm^{-1} Raman bands, but also for a part of the intensity of the Raman band at 1340 cm^{-1}.

A rigorous resonance Raman study of the adenine residue was first carried out by the use of 257.3 nm excitation.[62] Later, with a tunable ultraviolet laser, i.e. with a Chromatix CMX-4 pulsed dye laser, which was frequency doubled into the ultraviolet, a resonance Raman excitation profile for 5'-AMP was obtained.[6] It has been confirmed that the 1484 and 1580 cm^{-1} Raman bands derive their intensity from an excited state at 276 nm. It was also confirmed that the 1340 cm^{-1} band cannot be taken as being associated *solely* with the 276 nm excited state. Blazej and Peticolas[6] suggested that a vibronic coupling through this vibration (1340 cm^{-1}) between the 276 nm state and a higher electronic state may possibly occur (cf. Section 3.3.2). However, the excitation profile indicates that a considerable amount of the 1340 cm^{-1} Raman band intensity is due to the association with the 276 nm absorption band.

7.2 Normal Modes and Excited State Geometry

It is now evident that, in the adenine residue, on going from the ground state $\tilde{X}$ to the excited state $\tilde{A}$, an appreciable change in the geometrical structure takes place along the normal coordinates corresponding to the vibrations at 1580, 1484, and 1340 cm^{-1}. Therefore we now need to examine the normal modes of these vibrations.

First, it should be pointed out that all three vibrations are insensitive to the

N-deuteration of the adenine residue.[5] Therefore, they all must be primarily skeletal vibrations of the adenine ring. On the basis of our normal coordinate analysis[5] it is likely that in the 1580 cm^{-1} mode of vibration the C^4—C^5 stretching mode is predominant. In the 1484 cm^{-1} mode, on the other hand, C^4—N^9 stretching is dominant, and in the 1340 cm^{-1} mode C^5—N^7 stretching is dominant. In each of these normal vibrations, changes in many other bond lengths are also involved, but their vibrational amplitudes all are small. It may be mentioned, in addition, that most of these movements take place $180°$ out-of-phase with those of the adjacent bonds.

Finally, we consider a possible electronic structure of the excited state $\tilde{A}$ at 276 nm. A semiempirical Pariser-Parr-Pople calculation, as mentioned in Section 5.6, also was made for the adenine residue by Nagata et al.[57] They assumed that the position-6 NH_2 group provides two π-electrons to the conjugated double-bond system, and regarded the problem as that of a 10-orbital 12-electron system. They assigned the 276 nm band to an electron transfer from their 'orbital No. 6' to 'orbital No. 8'. This should bring the C^4—N^9 bond from *bonding* to *antibonding*, the C^4—C^5 bond also from *bonding* to *antibonding*, but the C^5—N^7 bond from *antibonding* to *bonding*. According to this calculation, the changes in the bond orders of other bonds are mostly much smaller than those mentioned above. It is therefore suggested that, on going from the equilibrium conformation in the $\tilde{X}$ state to that in the $\tilde{A}$ state, an appreciable stretching of the C^4—N^9 and C^4—C^5 bonds and a contraction of C^5—N^7 may take place.

8 RESONANCE RAMAN EFFECT OF THE GUANINE RESIDUE

The guanine residue has two absorption bands in the near ultraviolet region, at 276 ($\tilde{A} \leftarrow \tilde{X}$) and at 250 nm ($\tilde{B} \leftarrow \tilde{X}$). In Fig. 30, some of the observed Raman spectra of β-guanosine-5'-phosphoric acid in neutral aqueous solution excited at various wavelengths are shown. In Fig. 31, observed values $\phi_j(\nu_{exc})_{obs}$ from relative intensities of a few Raman bands are plotted against the exciting frequency ν_{exc}. In the same figure, the calculated excitation profile ($\phi_j(\nu_{exc})_{calc}$ versus ν_{exc}) is given on the assumption that the Raman band is associated solely with the excited electronic state $\tilde{A}$; also shown is the calculated profile for $\tilde{B}$. From a comparison of the observed and calculated $\phi_j(\nu_{exc})$ values, it is evident that the three Raman bands of the guanine residue at 1578, 1488, and 1322 cm^{-1} derive their intensities from the 276 nm ($\tilde{A} \leftarrow \tilde{X}$) band. Thus, the pre-resonance Raman effect for the guanine residue bears a close similarity to that of the adenine residue, where the 1580, 1484, and 1340 cm^{-1} Raman bands are associated with the 276 nm band (Section 7.1).

A more detailed inspection of Fig. 31 shows that observed excitation profiles of the three Raman bands are all slightly less steep than expected on the basis that their intensities are associated *solely* with the 276 nm band. This fact suggests that their intensities are derived partly from shorter-wavelength absorption bands. It should be remembered, however, that the three corresponding Raman bands (at 1580, 1484, and 1340 cm^{-1}) of the adenine residue cannot be associated with the second-longest-wavelength band ($\tilde{B} \leftarrow \tilde{X}$) at 260 nm. Therefore, the three Raman bands of the guanine residue probably should not be associated with the second-longest-wavelength band ($\tilde{B} \leftarrow \tilde{X}$) at 250 nm.

A rigorous resonance Raman spectrum is shown in Fig. 32 where the 257.3 nm laser beam was used for excitation (Section 5.2). The spectrum was observed with the 5'-GMP solution as dilute as 10^{-4} M. Therefore, what is observed is certainly a rigorous resonance Raman effect. The three Raman bands appeared clearly at 1578, 1488, and 1322 cm^{-1}. This fact does not contradict the idea that these bands are associated primarily with the 276 rather than the 250 nm band.

9 SOME POSSIBLE APPLICATIONS

Thus far our attention has been concentrated upon experimental results of

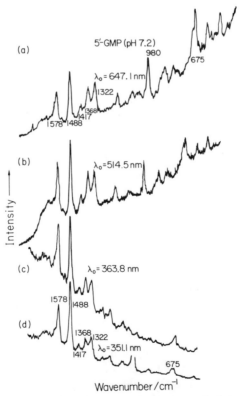

Fig. 30. Raman spectra of 5'-GMP in neutral aqueous solution. Excited by (a) 647.1 nm, (b) 514.5 nm, (c) 363.8 nm, and (d) 351.1 nm radiation.

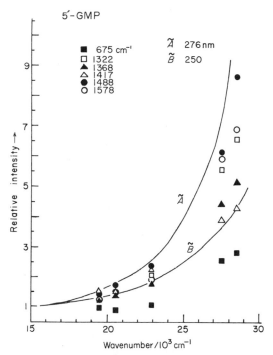

Fig. 31. The Raman intensities of 5′-GMP as a function of the wavenumber, $\tilde{\nu}_{exc}$, of the exciting radiation. Observed values of $\phi_j(\nu_{exc})_{obs}$ (see eqn. (36)) are plotted for the $j = 675, 1322, 1368, 1417, 1488,$ and 1578 cm^{-1} Raman bands. Continuous curves indicate $\phi_j(\nu_{exc})_{calc}$ (see eqn. (38)) for excited electronic states $\tilde{A}$ (276 nm) and $\tilde{B}$ (250 nm).

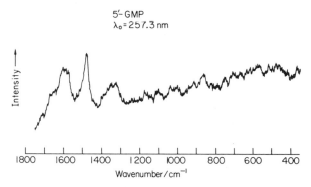

Fig. 32. Resonance Raman spectrum of 5′-GMP at 10^{-4} M (0.004%) in neutral aqueous solution with 257.3 nm excitation.

resonance Raman spectroscopy of the nucleic-acid base residues themselves, and on interpretations of such results. In this last section a question is raised as to how resonance Raman spectroscopy can be useful in understanding the physics, chemistry, and biology of nucleic acids.

9.1 General Aspects

It is obvious from the foregoing discussion that resonance Raman spectroscopy is a new tool for examining excited electronic states of the nucleic-acid base residues. Details of the excitation profile of Raman scattered intensity can provide new and extremely valuable information if the profile covers the whole range of an absorption band, and especially if this band has vibrational structure. An examination of the excitation profile by the use of a tunable ultraviolet laser may also be used to detect a weak absorption band, for example an $\pi^* \leftarrow n$ band of a base residue, if it is located sufficiently far away from other strong absorption bands.

Resonance Raman spectroscopy may certainly be useful for biochemical studies of nucleic acids and in future even for biological studies of intact living systems involving nucleic acids.

First, this technique provides a non-destructive analytical tool for nucleic acid biochemistry. The sample concentration needed is as low as that required for ultraviolet absorbance measurements but the spectra are more detailed and characteristic.

Second, we can obtain some information on the state and molecular environment of each base residue from a resonance Raman spectrum. If a residue is protonated or deprotonated rather than being in its usual neutral form this is detectable because the residue gives Raman bands at different frequencies from those of the neutral form. The base–base vertical-stacking interaction may affect the intensity of each Raman band. If this stacking causes an intensity decrease of an absorption band, and if a Raman band is in resonance with this absorption band, then the stacking should cause a decrease also in the intensity of the Raman band. The decrease in the intensity of the Raman band here should be much more pronounced than that of the absorption band; the absorption intensity is proportional to the square of the transition moment, while the Raman intensity is proportional to the fourth power of the transition moment (Section 3.3).

If such a resonance Raman spectrum of a nucleic acid is observed at various pHs and temperatures, with and without Mg^{2+}, and in D_2O as well as in H_2O, the amount and quality of information may be greatly improved. The resonance Raman spectrum of a nucleic acid in co-existence with a molecule which has an interaction with the nucleic acid molecule (for example, actinomycin D or histone H1 for DNA) can also be observed. Sometimes observation of resonance Raman spectra with several different exciting frequencies may provide yet additional information. Many of the Raman bands of nucleic acid bases overlap one another. For example, the 1233 cm^{-1} Raman band of uracil and 1243 cm^{-1} band of cytosine often fuse into a single band in a resonance Raman spectrum of an amino-acid transfer RNA (tRNA). It is probable, however, that the excitation profile of the 1233 cm^{-1} band has a peak (*ca.* 260 nm) at different wavelength from that (*ca.* 268 nm) of the 1243 cm^{-1} band. This may cause different band shapes for different exciting frequencies.

9.2 Designs for Monitoring Specific Molecular Environment

One of the shortcomings of Raman spectroscopy in the study of nucleic acids comes from the fact that the vibrational frequencies of the base residues are not sensitive to the molecular environment at which they are placed. The 1233 cm^{-1} peak (or a shoulder) in the Raman spectrum of *E. coli f*Met tRNA (see Fig. 3) is assignable to the uracil residue. However, all of the eight uracil residues are contributing to this Raman band. It is not easy, therefore, to know the molecular environment of a particular uracil residue, e.g. the position-37 uracil residue (in the anticodon).

The rate of the hydrogen–deuterium exchange reaction on a base residue is, however, extremely sensitive to the molecular environment, and can be examined by resonance-Raman measurements. When a nucleic acid in ^1H_2O is rapidly mixed with ^2H_2O, position-3 N^1H of the uracil residue is replaced by N^2H, and this should cause a time-dependent decrease in the intensity of the 1233 cm^{-1} Raman band (see Fig. 12, for example). Such a deuteration rate can also be followed by stopped-flow ultraviolet absorption spectroscopy, because deuteration of the uracil residue causes a slight change in the absorption intensity at 285 nm. This latter experiment indicates that the exchange rate constant is about 100 s^{-1} (at 23 °C) for uridine, while it is only 0.7 s^{-1} (at 23 °C) for the uracil residue involved in double-helical poly(rA).poly(rU). In general, the deuteration effect on a Raman spectrum is more pronounced than that on an ultraviolet absorption spectrum. In addition, the selection of the frequency suitable for monitoring the deuteration of each base residue is more easily done by Raman spectroscopy. The amount of sample required is not greatly different from that needed for ultraviolet absorption spectroscopy, if resonance or pre-resonance Raman spectroscopy is used. By 'stopped-flow resonance-Raman spectroscopy' we may be able to classify, for example, the eight uracil residues in *E. coli f*Met tRNA on the basis of their accessibility to the solvent (^2H_2O).

Another possible means for an effective analysis of the molecular environment is to combine chemical modification and resonance Raman spectroscopy. It has been shown, for example, that the reactivity of the adenine residue with chloroacetaldehyde depends greatly upon the molecular environment of the residue.[63] If the product of such a reaction has an absorption band at a greatly different wavelength from that of the common base residues, the Raman bands of this product can be observed without any interference from the Raman bands of common bases by the use of appropriate excitation light.

In biochemistry the adenine residue is a center of attention, not only because it is a constituent of DNA and RNA, but also because adenosine triphosphate (ATP) plays an important role in a number of systems. Suppose, for example, that we wish to monitor the molecular environment of ATP in a muscle system. In such a case, the 257.3 nm beam is not good for exciting the Raman effect, because it is completely absorbed by proteins. It has recently been found that 6-mercaptoadenosine triphosphate, which has an absorption band at 320 instead of 260 nm, can act the role of ATP. Rabbit heavy meromyosin, for example, can hydrolyse this ATP analogue with a release of free energy.[64] By the use of 351.1 nm excitation a resonance Raman spectrum of this ATP analogue has been observed (Nakanishi, Tsuboi, and others, to be published). The spectrum could be obtained with a 6SH-ATP concentration of 10^{-4} M. The important point here is that we would not see any Raman bands of proteins at all at their appropriate concentrations.

Finally, a brief description is given of an application of resonance Raman spectroscopy in examining the molecular environment of the 4-thiouracil residue in bacterial tRNAs. This is a modified base residue that occurs naturally. It is located at position 8 in the tRNA sequence. When the tRNA has, in addition, the cytosine residue at position 13, an irradiation with near-ultraviolet light (300 to 380 nm) results in the specific and quantitative cross-linking (8 to 13) of the two residues.[65] It has been found, on the other hand, that by the use of 351.1 or 363.8 nm excitation, either a resonance Raman spectrum of the intact 4-thiouridine residue or that of the photochemical product (8–13 cross linked) is observed, depending upon whether or not the tRNA under examination has the cytosine residue at position 13.[66]

Figure 33 shows a Raman spectrum of a tRNA (fMet tRNA from a thermophilic bacterium[67]) excited by 363.8 nm radiation. In comparing this with Fig. 3, it is noticeable that the spectral features of these two are completely different from each other. None of the observed bands in Fig. 33 has the same Raman frequency as those of the common base residues (Fig. 3). In addition, none of the Raman bands in question has the Raman frequencies of 4-thiouracil residue itself (see Fig. 23 and Table 1). The Raman bands observed here are all attributed to the 4-thiouracil residue (at position 8) subjected to photochemical modification caused by the laser beam used for Raman excitation. On exciting with the 363.8 nm or 351.1 nm lines, a similar spectrum is observed for E. coli fMet tRNA, and also for E. coli Gly tRNA. Both of these tRNAs have the position-8 4-thiouracil and position-13 cytosine. On the other hand, E. coli tyrosine tRNA(2), which has 4-thiouracil residues (two at positions 8 and 9) but no cytosine residue[68] at position 13, shows the Raman bands of 4-thiouracil itself. E. coli glutamic acid tRNA(2), which has no 4-thiouracil residue,[69] has been found to give no resonance Raman effect.

An interesting observation is made when a bulk tRNA sample of E. coli is placed in a rotating cell. Most of the tRNA molecules here should have the position-8 4-thiouracil and position-13 cytosine residues. Nevertheless, the

Raman bands of the 4-thiouracil residue appear. When the rotating cell is used, the chance of the laser photon hitting the intact tRNA molecule increases, so that the Raman bands of a 4-thiouracil residue free from the cross-linkage appear. After a few scans with ultraviolet excitation, however, these Raman bands are gradually replaced by those of the photochemical product. When the rotation is stopped, on the other hand, all the Raman bands of 4-thiouracil

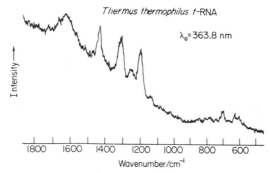

Fig. 33. Raman spectrum of formyl-methionine transfer RNA from *Thermus thermophilus* (an extremely thermophilic bacterium), excited by 363.8 nm radiation. Concentration, 0.3%; solvent, 10^{-1} M $NaCl + 10^{-3}$ M $MgCl_2 + 10^{-2}$ M Na-cacodylate (pH 7.2).

immediately disappear and are totally replaced by the Raman bands of the photochemical product. These facts in combination indicate that the photochemical process (forming the cross-link) is a rather slow one. The rate of rotation is about 2000 r.p.m., and the sample solution passes the laser focus (let us assume that its diameter is 50 μm) at the velocity of 500 cm s^{-1}. Therefore, the rate constant of the photochemical reaction is estimated to be lower than 10^5 s^{-1} (if it were equal to or higher than this value, the rotation would not cause any lowering of the amount of the photochemical product).

REFERENCES

(1) T. G. Spiro and T. M. Loehr, in *Advances in Infrared and Raman Spectroscopy*, Vol. 1 (R. J. H. Clark and R. E. Hester, eds.), Heyden, London, 1975, p. 98.
(2) H. Susi and J. S. Ard, *Spectrochim. Acta* **27A**, 1549 (1971).
(3) H. Susi, J. S. Ard and J. M. Purcell, *Spectrochim. Acta* **29A**, 725 (1973).
(4) M. Tsuboi, in *XXIIIrd International Congress of Pure and Applied Chemistry*, Vol. 7, Butterworth, London, 1971, p. 145.
(5) M. Tsuboi, S. Takahashi and I. Harada, in *Physico-chemical Properties of Nucleic Acids*, Vol. 2 (J. Duchesne, ed.), Academic Press, London, New York, 1973, p. 91.
(6) D. C. Blazej and W. L. Peticolas, *Proc. Nat. Acad. Sci. USA* **74**, 2639 (1977).
(7) A. Y. Hirakawa and M. Tsuboi, *Science* **188**, 359 (1975).
(8) M. Tsuboi, *J. Am. Chem. Soc.* **79**, 1351 (1957).

(9) G. B. B. M. Sutherland and M. Tsuboi, *Proc. R. Soc.* (*London*), A239, 446 (1957).
(10) T. Shimanouchi, M. Tsuboi and Y. Kyogoku, in *Advances in Chemical Physics*, Vol. VII (J. Duchesne, ed.), London, Interscience, 1964, p. 435.
(11) L. Lafleur, J. Rice and G. J. Thomas, *Biopolymers* 11, 2423 (1972).
(12) M. Tsuboi, S. Takahashi, S. Muraishi, T. Kajiura and S. Nishimura, *Science* 174, 1142 (1971).
(13) S. C. Erfurth, E. J. Kiser and W. L. Peticolas, *Proc. Nat. Acad. Sci. USA* 69, 938 (1972).
(14) G. J. Thomas, *Biochim. Biophys. Acta* 213, 417 (1970).
(15) G. C. Medeiros and G. J. Thomas, *Biochim. Biophys. Acta* 247, 449 (1971).
(16) G. J. Thomas, G. C. Medeiros and K. A. Hartman, *Biochim. Biophys. Acta* 277, 71 (1972).
(17) K. G. Brown, E. J. Kiser and W. L. Peticolas, *Biopolymers* 11, 1855 (1972).
(18) S. C. Erfurth, P. J. Bond and W. L. Peticolas, *Biopolymers* 14, 247, 1259 (1975).
(19) K. Morikawa, M. Tsuboi, S. Takahashi, Y. Kyogoku, Y. Mitsui, Y. Iitaka and G. J. Thomas, *Biopolymers* 12, 790 (1973).
(20) Y. Nishimura, K. Morikawa and M. Tsuboi, *Bull. Chem. Soc. Jpn* 47, 1043 (1974).
(21) G. J. Thomas and K. A. Hartman, *Biochim. Biophys. Acta* 312, 311 (1973).
(22) G. J. Thomas, M. C. Chen and K. A. Hartman, *Biochim. Biophys. Acta* 324, 37 (1973).
(23) M. C. Chen and G. J. Thomas, *Biopolymers* 13, 615 (1974).
(24) B. L. Tomlinson and W. L. Peticolas, *J. Chem. Phys.* 52, 2154 (1970).
(25) B. Prescott, R. Gamache, J. Livramento and G. J. Thomas, *Biopolymers* 13, 1821 (1974).
(26) E. W. Small and W. L. Peticolas, *Biopolymers* 10, 69 (1971); 10, 1377 (1971).
(27) Y. Nishimura, Doctoral Thesis, University of Tokyo, 1976.
(28) K. A. Hartman, N. Clayton and G. J. Thomas, *Biochem. Biophys. Res. Comm.* 50, 942 (1973).
(29) G. J. Thomas and P. Murphy, *Science* 188, 1205 (1975).
(30) T. A. Turano, K. A. Hartman and G. J. Thomas, *J. Phys. Chem.* 80, 1157 (1976).
(31) S. Mansy, S. K. Engtrom and W. L. Peticolas, *Biochem. Biophys. Res. Commun.* 68, 1242 (1976).
(32) G. J. Thomas, B. Prescott, P. E. McDonald-Ordzie and K. A. Hartman, *J. Mol. Biol.* 102, 103 (1976).
(33) G. Placzek, in *Handbuch der Radiolagie*, Vol. 2 (E. Marx, ed.), Akademische Verlagsgesellschaft, Leipzig, 1934, p. 209.
(34) B. B. Johnson and W. L. Peticolas, *Ann. Rev. Phys. Chem.* 27, 465 (1976).
(35) H. A. Kramers and W. Heisenberg, *Z. Phys.* 31, 681 (1925).
(36) C. J. Ballhausen and A. E. Hansen, *Ann. Rev. Phys. Chem.* 23, 15 (1972).
(37) A. C. Albrecht, *J. Chem. Phys.* 34, 1476 (1961).
(38) J. Tang and A. C. Albrecht, *J. Chem. Phys.* 49, 1144 (1968).
(39) J. Tang and A. C. Albrecht, in *Raman Spectroscopy*, Vol. 2 (H. A. Szymanski, ed.), Plenum, New York, 1970, p. 33.
(40) C. H. Ting, *Spectrochim. Acta* 24A, 1177 (1968).
(41) M. Tasumi, F. Inagaki and T. Miyazawa, *Chem. Phys. Lett.* 22, 515 (1973).
(42) M. Tsuboi, A. Y. Hirakawa and S. Muraishi, *J. Mol. Spectrosc.* 56, 146 (1975).
(43) M. Tsuboi and A. Y. Hirakawa, *J. Raman Spectrosc.* 5, 75 (1976).
(44) A. Y. Hirakawa and M. Tsuboi, in *Proceedings of Molecular Structure Symposium*, Chemical Society of Japan, Osaka, 1975, p. 355.
(45) F. Duschinsky, *Acta Physicochim. USSR* 1, 551 (1937).
(46) G. J. Small, *J. Chem. Phys.* 54, 3300 (1971).
(47) M. Tsuboi, *J. Mol. Spectrosc.* 19, 4 (1966).
(48) A. Y. Hirakawa, M. Tsuboi and T. Shimanouchi, *J. Chem. Phys.* 57, 1236 (1972).

(49) T. Miyazawa, *J. Mol. Spectrosc.* **13**, 321 (1964).
(50) Y. Nishimura, A. Y. Hirakawa and M. Tsuboi, *Chem. Lett.* (*Tokyo*) **1977**, 907.
(51) W. Kiefer and H. J. Bernstein, *J. Appl. Spectrosc.* **25**, 500 (1971); R. J. H. Clark, in *Advances in Infrared and Raman Spectroscopy*, Vol. 1 (R. J. H. Clark and R. E. Hester, eds.), Heyden, London, 1975, p. 58; W. Kiefer, *ibid.*, Vol. 3, 1977, p. 1.
(52) H. T. Miles, *Proc. Nat. Acad. Sci. USA* **51**, 1104 (1964).
(53) M. Tsuboi, Y. Kyogoku and T. Shimanouchi, *Biochim. Biophys. Acta* **55**, 1 (1962).
(54) S. Califano and B. Crawford, *Spectrochim. Acta* **16**, 889 (1960).
(55) J. R. Scherer and J. Overend, *Spectrochim. Acta* **17**, 719 (1961).
(56) T. Shimanouchi, *Computer Programs for Normal Coordinate Treatment of Polyatomic Molecules*, Department of Chemistry, University of Tokyo.
(57) C. Nagata, A. Imamura and H. Fujita, in *Advances in Biophysics*, Vol. 4 (M. Kotani, ed.), University of Tokyo Press, Tokyo, 1973, p. 1.
(58) W. Hug and I. Tinoco, *J. Am. Chem. Soc.* **95**, 2803 (1973).
(59) J. C. D. Brand and W. G. Williamson, *Discuss. Faraday Soc.* **35**, 184 (1963).
(60) M. Tsuboi, A. Y. Hirakawa, Y. Nishimura and I. Harada, *J. Raman Spectrosc.* **2**, 609 (1974).
(61) M. Guéron, J. Eisinger and R. G. Shulman, *J. Chem. Phys.* **47**, 4077 (1967).
(62) M. Pézolet, T. J. Yu and W. L. Peticolas, *J. Raman Spectrosc.* **3**, 55 (1975).
(63) K. Kimura, M. Nakanishi, T. Yamamoto and M. Tsuboi, *J. Biochem.* (*Tokyo*) **81**, 1699 (1977).
(64) A. J. Murphy and M. F. Morales, *Biochemistry* **9**, 1528 (1970).
(65) A. Favre, M. Yaniv and A. M. Michelson, *Biochem. Biophys. Res. Commun.* **37**, 266 (1969).
(66) Y. Nishimura, A. Y. Hirakawa, M. Tsuboi and S. Nishimura, *Nature* **260**, 173 (1976).
(67) T. Oshima, Y. Sakaki, N. Wakayama, K. Watanabe, Z. Ohashi and S. Nishimura, *Experientia, Suppl.* **26**, 317 (1976).
(68) H. M. Goodman, J. N. Abelson, A. Landy, S. Zadregil and J. D. Smith, *Eur. J. Biochem.* **13**, 461 (1970).
(69) Z. Ohashi, F. Harada and S. Nishimura, *FEBS Lett.* **20**, 239 (1972).

Chapter 5

RECENT ADVANCES IN MICROWAVE SPECTROSCOPY

J. Sheridan

School of Physical and Molecular Sciences, University College of North Wales, Bangor, U.K.

1 INTRODUCTION

Spectroscopy at the highest frequencies accessible to radio methods has long overlapped in range the extreme of the far infrared region, and hence there is no absolutely sharp distinction between the study of molecular phenomena by infrared techniques on the one hand and microwave techniques on the other. Microwave (m.w.) spectroscopy, here always taken to deal with gases at low pressures, is the spectroscopy of the whole molecule which employs radio methods, and it is well known that it normally leads to molecular information through the phenomena of changes in molecular rotational energy. It has become increasingly obvious, however, that knowledge of molecular force fields is now among the results of almost every m.w. study. Increased sophistication of techniques has greatly enhanced our ability to study species or states of molecules which are in various ways energetically less favoured, for example structurally, configurationally or vibrationally, than the abundant stable ground states which preoccupied early workers in the field. In particular, the interaction between m.w. spectroscopy and vibrational spectroscopy is now very extensive.

Within the past few years the area known as time-dependent m.w. spectroscopy has been rapidly developed, to add greatly to the precision of our knowledge of energy transfer processes in gases. This is an advance which interacts over a wide general area, and cannot be systematically considered here.

This review is mainly concerned with recent work leading to information on the structures and energetics of molecules. In a field where some 400 papers appear each year, it has been necessary to make a subjective choice of examples and areas for emphasis. After consideration of experimental developments which have contributed to the increasing power of m.w. methods, results are illustrated in terms of the different types of information obtained. Aspects which are covered in several general texts[1-3] have been mentioned only as background, and detail has also been omitted in several special areas where recent reviews are available. More comprehensive results can be found elsewhere.[4,5]

It should be noted that several related techniques which are normally considered separately from basic m.w. spectroscopy are inseparable from it in the discussion of the present state of our knowledge of molecules, since these techniques can yield the same types of information. Cases include gas-phase electron paramagnetic resonance[6] and molecular-beam work either in its most direct form of maser spectroscopy[7,8] or as electric resonance studies in which the frequencies reach the m.w. range. Laser spectroscopies[9] also yield data directly comparable with findings of m.w. spectroscopy. While use is made of results of such methods, details belong to reviews of the types indicated.

2 EXPERIMENTAL METHODS

2.1 Basic Methods

'Conventional' m.w. spectrometers, through which study of a molecule is normally opened up, have a well-documented general construction. Their range of frequency, commonly some 8 to 40 GHz, is now quite often extended to higher ranges with the development of the klystrons or, increasingly, backward-wave oscillators, used as swept sources. The cells, employing Stark-effect modulation at frequencies around 10 to 100 kHz with peak fields of 2000 V cm^{-1} or more, are usually conventional waveguides, although parallel-plate and other constructions are not uncommon for specialized studies. Cells can usually be cooled and many heatable cells have been described for work on molecules of low volatility. Standard techniques of phase sensitive detection of the signals allow, when necessary, detection of lines with absorption coefficients as low as *ca.* 10^{-9} cm^{-1}.† Such a system is well exemplified in the best-known commercial spectrometer,[10] in which the value of cell-construction for low loss and for homogeneity of Stark-effect field is particularly clear.

For millimetric and sub-millimetric wavelengths, where work with Stark-effect modulation is not usually practicable, well known alternative techniques have been in use for a long time, harmonic generators being employed as sources and source modulation as the means to sensitive detection. The group at Duke University has consistently held the lead in this area and has tested several types of detector, including the so-called Putley detector which employs indium antimonide at low temperatures and has been particularly successful in recent work.[11] Mention should also be made of the remarkable work by Krupnov and

---

† Intensities, or absorption coefficients, in microwave spectroscopy are conventionally quoted as the fraction of the radiation power absorbed per unit track-length, normally per centimetre.

colleagues using special backward-wave oscillator sources at millimetre and sub-millimetre wavelengths, in conjunction with so-called acoustic detectors.[12] With the equipment available to them, these workers have shown how wide ranges of this difficult region can be swept with high spectroscopic sensitivity.

Conventional instruments are capable of measuring the relative intensities of strong absorptions to within a few percent by well established methods and perhaps the commonest use of this facility is in estimating relative populations of vibrational or conformational states of molecules. More sophisticated work has been done on the problems raised by the complexity of the factors involved in accurate intensity studies, especially in the development of commercial spectrometers.[13] The bases of chemical analysis by m.w. spectroscopy are well established[14] and deserve more interest than they have received from the industrial side. Several laboratories have made many mechanistic studies of reactions, particularly through isotopic distribution data, by m.w. intensity methods, and the more sophisticated procedures are able to convert the intensity data into thermodynamic terms, such as those governing the equilibria among N_2O_3, water and the *cis* and *trans* isomers of nitrous acid.[15] Studies of concentrations, especially of geometric isomers in equilibrium, are also common in the general subject of 'low resolution' m.w. spectroscopy which has grown from the development of sources with wide sweeping ranges and of consistently wide-banded overall spectrometer performance, particularly in commercial instruments.[10] Use of low resolution does not, of course, increase the absolute powers of the method but, provided certain conditions of molecular shape and polarity are satisfied, low resolution m.w. spectra provide a usefully concise indication of some general features of molecular conformations present[16] and the relative intensities of spectra can be used to find free energies of conformational changes.[17]

Thus it may be said that the basic experimental techniques of m.w. spectroscopy are already very diverse, sophisticated, and of great power in the search for molecular information. It is clear, however, that while a large number of studies remain to be done or extended by such methods, many of the most interesting developments in the field are now made through special extensions of the powers of the instrumentation. An indication of some main areas of such extensions is given in the following sub-sections.

2.2   Methods of Raising Sensitivity

Inevitably, all studies are limited by the capacity available to observe weaker and weaker spectra and, for special cases, remarkable extensions of sensitivity have been achieved. The most straightforward means is the established one of computerized accumulation and averaging of the signals received over sufficiently long time intervals. In dealing with short-lived species, this has an obvious importance in the necessary integration of many fast scans of the spectrum, but attainment of special sensitivities in such ways has also been important for stable substances. As examples we may note the use of a computer-controlled spectro-meter[18] to measure spectra of the ion CO^{+}[19] in a discharge, and more recently of the ions HCO^{+}[20] and HN_2^{+},[21] and also the use of long absorption paths and signal accumulation in the study of the distortion-rotation lines of methane[22] which have intensities going as low as 2×10^{-11} cm^{-1}. High sensitivities are clearly necessary for the work on other transitions which become allowed only through centrifugal distortion or vibration and also on spectra of molecules which have only the very small polarities induced by isotopic substitution through its effect on zero point vibrations. Such work, for example that on ethane,[23] where the isotopically induced moment in CH_3CD_3 is only some 0.01 D (1D = 3.3356×10^{-30} C m), is among the most striking in the search for m.w. data on 'non-polar' molecules and commonly makes use of digital averaging to attain the required sensitivity. Several laboratories have constructed spectro-meter systems with extensive computer control and data accumulation and it is likely that such measures will become more common in the future as the search for elusive information is extended.

For specific absorptions, sensitivity can be raised by use of resonant cells with very long effective pathlengths; for example, it is claimed that a Stark-effect cell, tuned to resonance for analytical detection of formaldehyde and similar substances, can detect lines with an absorption coefficient as low as 6×10^{-13} cm^{-1}.[24]

Poor sensitivities are often partly the result of difficulties in modulation, the Stark-effect procedure being at a disadvantage for weakly polar cases and, for example, for linear or diatomic molecules in higher J-states. A modulation, which shares the advantages of Stark effects in operating through the molecular states only, is saturation-effect modulation,[25] which allows high sensitivities to be reached independently of the rotational states concerned and has proved especially fruitful in studies of heavy diatomic and linear molecules.

Many cases of special sensitivity in m.w. experiments involve double radiation methods and consequent departures from Boltzmann distributions of state-populations. An early example is the detection of $\Delta J = 3$ transitions in ethyl iodide.[26] Transitions of this type, weakly allowed here through the presence of quadrupole interaction of the iodine nucleus, have absorption coefficients not greatly in excess of 10^{-11} cm^{-1}. However, they are readily observable when the appropriate frequencies are 'pumped' with high-power radiation and the effect of this on state populations is observed through normal, permitted transitions involving one of the pumped levels. By use of such pumping processes in an on–off fashion as a modulation of level-populations, the methods of double-resonance modulation m.w. spectroscopy have been evolved. With attention to attainment of adequate pump-power density, this method has proved able to detect numerous very weak transitions, with the additional advantage (Section 2.4) of the specificity of double resonance methods for dealing with dense and complex spectra. A notable case of structural importance is that in which spectra of deuterated species of isoxazole were measured in their minute natural concentrations (0.015%).[27] Several recent publications[28–30] give details of the use of these methods as standard procedures which have considerable potential for the future.

A related aspect is that in which it is necessary to increase sensitivity in order to study states of molecules which are only very weakly populated at thermal equilibrium under normal cell conditions. A very direct example is the selective enrichment of molecules in specific excited vibrational states by energy transfer from suitable collision partners. Thus, active nitrogen, which has an energy, in vibrational terms, 2331 cm^{-1} above that of normal nitrogen, is found to enhance populations of the first excited states of the asymmetric stretching vibrations of OCS,[31] and N_2O[32] to extents which allow ready observation of rotational spectra of these states. A reasonably close matching of the excitation energy, here 2062 cm^{-1} for OCS and 2223 cm^{-1} for N_2O, is necessary but other such cases will be important where excitations are well above thermal energies. Most selective excitation of molecules to higher states, however, has been through use of suitable optical radiation from lasers and allows the powerful methods of m.w.-optical double resonance to be employed. For vibrational excitations, lines from the N_2O or CO_2 lasers are commonly used, exact coincidences with transitions linked to m.w. transitions being sometimes obtained by small tuning adjustments of the laser. Thus Stark-effect tuning of the $R(30)$ N_2O laser line gives[33] coincidence with a component of the $v_2 = 0 \rightarrow v_2 = 1$ excitation of ammonia. In another example, a Zeeman-tuned He–Ne laser was employed[34] to obtain i.r.-m.w. double resonances involving the excitation of the CH stretching mode in formic acid at no less than 2940 cm^{-1}. With untuned laser frequencies, however, coincidences involving excitations linked to m.w. transitions are readily found provided the molecule has a vibrational mode in the laser region with a dense array of sub-levels in each vibrational state, although the nature of the coincidences is, of course, a matter of chance and analysis of the effects may not be simple.[35,36] Many types of information have proved accessible in such experiments, however, including many precise vibrational data. More automation of the methods is proving possible, especially where the m.w. radiation can be swept and detection carried out at the optical frequency.[37] A number of reviews (e.g. Shimoda[38]) and general considerations of fundamental aspects (e.g. Takami[39]) of such work are available. Basically similar methods involving optical radiation of higher frequencies have allowed studies of electronically excited states of simple molecules, notably metal oxides[40] and NO_2.[41]

2.3   Methods of Increased Resolving Power

Many of the standard techniques and methods of high sensitivity make some sacrifice of resolution to obtain otherwise favourable experimental performance. The resolving powers remain very high, but factors such as the contributions of collisions and modulation effects to the linewidths are considerably more than is desirable for many refinements and well above the Doppler widths for randomly moving molecules under the given conditions. It is now commonplace for cells of large cross-section and low modulation frequencies to be used to reduce the linewidths to close to the limiting Doppler value in what may be called high-resolution conventional spectrometers. Their features have proved valuable in measuring close hyperfine structures, such as multiplets in nuclear-quadrupole splittings and especially the Zeeman-effect splittings observed when the cell of such an instrument is placed virtually entirely in a strong magnetic field. Linewidths at half maximum intensity can be typically 40 kHz or less in such conditions. Details of instruments of this type for Zeeman work are included in a recent review.[42]

Fourier transform methods, with pulsed operation of a m.w. spectrometer, have been shown[43] capable of high sensitivity and also, with the absence of modulation and power broadening, of high resolution. The cells are 'empty' sections of waveguide of large cross-section. Testing of this method, however, is at present limited to selected spectra at rather low frequencies.

By far the most striking improvements in resolution have been achieved by use of molecular-beam spectrometers, in which the Doppler widths of lines are largely eliminated. In the simplest type, the beams of molecules replace the randomly moving ones in an otherwise essentially conventional system. Recent work on methyl bromide by these means, for instance, showed linewidths at half intensity of only some 3 kHz.[44] Rather more work at such resolving powers is now done with beam-maser spectrometers, the scope of which has been extended remarkably, with results obtained for molecules as heavy as, for example, furan.[45] Details can be found in reviews already mentioned.[7,8] Beam-maser spectroscopy can now be employed at frequencies as high as the sub-millimetre region.[46] The results of beam studies naturally take precedence, when available, over the less accurate investigations of molecular constants. Recent refinements in a two-cavity beam-maser spectrometer with use of a double-resonance technique[47] have produced linewidths at half maximum intensity as low as 1 kHz.

2.4 Increasing the Selectivity of the Spectra Observed

The m.w. spectra of most systems now investigated are of considerable complexity and their assignment is much eased if conditions can be found under which only certain signals, of particular properties, are detected. A few procedures are very simple, and usually based on the Stark effect. Thus, the Stark spectrum, normally observed alongside the normal field-free spectrum, although in phase reversal, can be suppressed by 'smearing' the Stark-modulation field in the 'field-on' half of the modulation cycle. Similarly any lines which have especially large Stark-effect splittings at low fields can be selectively modulated and presented in the absence of lines which are hard to modulate. Nearly all the most powerful means of simplifying spectra in selective ways to ease assignment, however, are double-resonance techniques.

Double resonance in which both pump and signal frequencies are in the m.w. range has been mentioned in Section 2.2. In the particular case of double-resonance modulation, signals only arise when more than two levels of the molecular energy (normally three levels) are interrelated by the two known radiation frequencies, and hence the spectra are highly selectively linked to the molecular constants. Double-resonance maps[28] allow concise presentation of the predictions or findings in the two 'dimensions' of pump and signal frequencies. The shapes of the double-resonance signals fall into different types which suffice to distinguish different relative positions of the three interlinked energy levels.[29,30]

Wide use is now also made of radiofrequency-m.w. double resonance, in which a selected radiofrequency is introduced, usually via the Stark-effect electrode in a conventional instrument. Recent design refinements[48] have allowed this 'rf' pump frequency to become as high as 4 GHz and hence this method is merging with the m.w.-m.w. double-resonance methods. Attention to cell and field geometries can also allow special details of spectra to be selectively presented. Assignments assisted in such ways are regularly reported and the method also allows transitions at very low frequencies to be studied through their effects on the second transition at much greater frequency.

2.5   Techniques for Time-dependent Studies

Various spectrometer systems have been described which allow m.w. studies in the time domain, rather than the frequency domain. One of these instruments has been mentioned in Section 2.3[43] in connexion with the Fourier transformation of transient emission signals. General design considerations for experiments in the time domain are discussed in a paper[49] describing an instrument which employs a Fabry-Perot resonator external to the gas cell. No attempt can be made here to give details of the background of time-dependent studies, which are largely independent of the methods aiming at molecular structural information. A summary of the recent rapid growth of the time-dependent investigations and their relationship to the broad general subject of molecular relaxation processes has been given in reviews already mentioned.[4,5]

3   DERIVATION OF MOLECULAR CONSTANTS FROM SPECTRA

The theory of molecular rotational levels, including centrifugal distortion, and the selection rules in terms of molecular dipole-moment components, have long been described in standard works. Nearly all molecules now studied are asymmetric rotors and it is common practice for established computer procedures to be used in the prediction of spectra from molecular models and, once assignments of transitions are made, in the refinement of the rotational and centrifugal-distortion constants to give an accurate overall fit to numerous measured transition frequencies. A number of well known procedures have been described which speed the initial assignments of lines to particular transitions, Stark-effect observations being commonly used in conjunction with frequency fitting. Where necessary, and especially where any lines are appreciably displaced from the positions which they would occupy for a straightforward distortable-rotor treatment, the methods of double resonance already mentioned (Sections 2.2 and 2.4) are frequently brought to bear with advantage.

The ease of assigning a spectrum, even when no lines depart abnormally from the near-rigid-rotor pattern, varies considerably from case to case. Not surprisingly, computer programs have been evolved for near-rigid molecules which allow searches to be made among numerous measured lines for convincing assignments of transitions (e.g. up to 200 in one case),[50] provided some guidelines appropriate to the molecule concerned are introduced. No extensive use of these methods as yet appears usual, but such procedures could assume more importance as the complexity of molecules studied continues to increase, and where a family of measured lines may contain rotational information on more than one state or isotopic form of the molecule. The interesting cases where near-rigid rotor behaviour is not adhered to will normally need more special treatment.

Normally the fitting of a spectrum is finally adjusted by a computerized least-squares adjustment of an adequate number of measured frequencies to the rotational constants A, B and C of the given molecular state and its centrifugal distortion constants. Before this can be done, however, any fine or hyperfine structures are separately analysed to give the unperturbed line-frequencies. In more complex cases, computer programs are used in assignment of fine structures, coupled where appropriate with matching of shapes of incompletely resolved multiplets to synthesized spectra for given hyperfine constants and line-contours; a typical example is the fitting of nuclear quadrupole fine structure for molecules containing two or more non-equivalent quadrupolar nuclei.[51] Similarly, established computer procedures are widely used to analyse internal rotational splittings in molecules containing such groups as CH_3 or SiH_3.[52-54] Extensions of such procedures for rarer cases are found and it is sometimes necessary to involve large vibration-rotation interaction constants as part of the overall least-squares reduction process. Aspects of spectral assignment which involve procedures not normally met in dealing with near-rigid molecules will be mentioned when specific cases are considered.

4 TYPES OF MOLECULAR INFORMATION OBTAINED

The division of such information into the different classes enumerated in this section, while necessary in a descriptive sense, is artificial in that no one category of information is independent of any other category. In particular, what may rather loosely be called the molecular geometry and electron distribution in the ground state of a molecule cannot be separated from knowledge of the force field unless zero-point energy effects are allowed for. Many details of molecular geometries and electron distributions found from m.w. spectra, however, are important independent of any detailed simultaneous considerations of force fields, and these classes of information are therefore considered first in their own right, note being taken of refinements which are possible, in practice or in principle, when the non-rigidity of molecules is taken into account. In many interesting cases, force field information is a dominant objective of m.w. spectroscopy, and its details may take precedence over the more directly approachable findings of geometry or electronic structure.

4.1 Molecular Geometry

In m.w. spectroscopy, geometries are derived primarily from the averaged inverse moments of inertia represented by the rotational constants A, B and C. For any long-lived vibrational level of the molecule, these inverse moments, and hence the geometry derived from them, are averages which are dependent on the force field and on isotopic substitutions, as indeed are the different forms of average geometric parameters obtained from different techniques, such as electron diffraction. In very simple molecules the effects of the zero point vibrations on the ground state constants A_0, B_0 and C_0 can be allowed for and the so-called equilibrium moments of inertia obtained; these in turn may be converted to equilibrium geometric parameters, provided independent equilibrium moments are measured, using isotopic mass changes (if necessary) in at least equal number to the parameters defining the structure.

Diatomic molecules are, of course, a particularly straightforward case, since rotational constants are usually obtained in excited states of the molecular vibration as well as for the ground state. Extrapolation to allow for removal of the zero point half quantum to derive equilibrium properties is thus a simple matter. Among the many diatomic molecules investigated in recent years we may note much work on metal–non-metal diatomics at high-temperatures; examples include monosulphides of such elements as Ba, Ge, Pb,[55–57] monohalides of bismuth[58–60] and the cuprous halides.[61–63] Among the remarkable arrays of data derived for these and many other diatomic molecules, we find many isotopically independent equilibrium bond lengths.

Equilibrium structures for simple molecules containing three or four atoms have been evaluated in a few cases, most of the findings being available in standard works (e.g. Ref. 1). It is clearly necessary to find the effects of the vibrational modes on the rotational constants in sufficient number to solve for all the geometric parameters. Sometimes isotopic substitution is necessary, as with nitrogen trifluoride, where B_e is evaluated using $^{14}NF_3$ and $^{15}NF_3$.[64]

The poor Boltzmann factors for the excitation of molecules to the higher frequency modes makes such work difficult, though in some cases the vibrational dependence of rotational constants can be found from i.r. data. The recently developed methods (Section 2.2) of artificially increasing the populations of vibrational levels well above those at thermal energies, by means of energy transfer or laser irradiation, hold promise of an increase in the number of m.w. measurements of vibrational dependence of rotational constants and so in the number of equilibrium structures evaluated. Thus, recently, the method of energy transfer from active nitrogen has been used to obtain the dependence of B on the vibration v_3 in ClCN, BrCN and ICN[65,66] and so permit equilibrium bond lengths to be derived from m.w. data. There is still a good deal of scope for refinements in such studies of simple polyatomic molecules in order that the equilibrium geometries can be compared with the various types of 'averaged' geometry which are more easily found.

In nearly all cases, the geometry must be found by less elaborate procedures than are involved in obtaining the equilibrium structure. A comparison of the possible procedures will be found in standard works[1,3] and in a review by Lide.[67] The 'direct' average values of structure parameters, usually called r_z or $\langle r \rangle$ parameters, can be obtained in simple cases from m.w. data by removal of the harmonic part of the vibrational dependence of A, B and C.[67] The r_z parameters, unlike r_e parameters, are dependent on the isotopic combinations involved. As an example, the average geometry of the radical NF_2 has recently been derived.[68] An important property of r_z structures is that they are more strictly comparable with structures determined by electron diffraction than the other types of average structure to be considered. In the specially fundamental case of the C—C bond in ethane,[23] a preliminary r_z value of 153.1 pm is obtained, which is indeed close to the best electron diffraction value.

The more usual structures determined from m.w. data are well known and are characterized as r_0-structures (sometimes called effective structures, since they are fitted to A_0, B_0 and C_0 values) and as r_s-structures (substitution structures). For all normal purposes, r_s-structures are the preferred ones, with the well known proviso that the placing of atoms with a small coordinate in the principal axis system is not accurate. Recently a refinement of the substitution method has been proposed,[69] the so-called mass-dependence method, in which it is shown that an approximation to the equilibrium moment of inertia of a molecule is given by

$$I_e \simeq 2I_s - I_0 = I_m$$

where I_s is the moment corresponding to the substitution structure. If the r_s structure is known, the array of I_m values can be used in the usual way to derive the r_m structure. The r_m parameters for several simple molecules are close to the rigorously derived r_e values, but the method is not considered valid for the accurate placement of hydrogen atoms, which restricts its use considerably. In what follows, we normally take r_s parameters to be the most satisfactory approximation to the equilibrium geometry of the average case, allowance being made for the small coordinate restriction. If only one atom is not isotopically locatable, it may be placed from the knowledge of all other atom positions and of the mass-centre coordinates, but if two or more atoms, either through small coordinates or the lack of an isotopic substitution, remain unplaced, then assumptions of selected parameters will be necessary. Because this situation is very common, means have been sought to optimize the use of all the inertial data which are to hand for a molecule. In one such computerized procedure,[70] all ground state rotational constants and their isotopic changes, if necessary with adjusted weighting, are used in a best-fit procedure. This at least offers a standard routine to make the best use of the accessible data. Where such difficulties are met, and provided the differences in the way parameters are averaged by different experimental procedures are allowed for, the combination of m.w. and electron diffraction measurements can be a valuable way of determining structures more accurately than either method alone.[67]

The geometries of a large number of molecules are determined, either fully or in part, by m.w. methods every year. The examples now given are some of the recent cases where detailed geometry has been among the more important findings.

Among linear molecules, hydrogen isocyanide, HNC, is an outstanding example. This substance can be made in a variety of ways, one method being the reaction of active nitrogen with methyl bromide or iodide. The spectrum of HNC proved that this molecule is responsible for the emission from space at 90 663 MHz known as U90.663. Eight isotopic forms of HNC have now been studied[71,72] and the r_s structure can be calculated in eight ways, each isotopic form in turn being taken as the 'parent' molecule. Two r_s structures can be calculated using entirely different sets of I_0 values. The internal consistency of these r_s structures is very high, as shown by the final values of the lengths NH = 98.61(1) pm and NC = 117.17(2) pm. No doubt equilibrium distances will be found soon; they have already been estimated from *ab initio* calculations of the force field. Equal interest attaches to the distances in the linear ions HCO^+[20] and HN_2^+,[21] also present in space and under detailed study in the laboratory.

Also linear are most of a striking family of van der Waals molecules studied by molecular-beam techniques at m.w. frequencies. For example, the following geometries, although easily distorted, have been established: Ar $\cdots$ H—Cl;[73,74] Ar $\cdots$ H—F;[75] Ar $\cdots$ Cl—F;[76] Kr $\cdots$ Cl—F.[77] The order of the atoms, particularly in the ClF complexes, with the larger atom next to the noble gas, is especially interesting and not expected on the simplest model of van der Waals forces. The complex between argon and OCS[78] has the general geometry with the argon on the side of a roughly linear OCS chain, the Ar $\cdot\cdot$ C and Ar $\cdot\cdot$ O distances being nearly equal (358 and 360 pm, respectively) and the Ar $\cdot\cdot$ S distance greater (410 pm). Van der Waals radii do not predict the distances well and it is proposed that the interaction resembles that between a Lewis acid and a Lewis base, the highest molecular orbital of the donor (noble gas) interacting with the lowest unfilled one of the acceptor. If the acceptor orbital is a σ-antibonding orbital the complex is linear, while if it is a π-orbital the structure is non-linear. New studies by the same methods of the complex[79]

in which the heavy atoms are collinear, with the FH bond at some 50 ° to the FClF line, reinforce these ideas.

Knowledge of hydrogen-bonded systems has been obtained from a number of m.w. studies, both conventional and using beams. Thus $H-C\equiv N \cdots H-F$[80] is linear with $N \cdots F$ about 280 pm, while $H_2O \cdots H-F$[81] has either C_{2v} symmetry about the OHF line or C_s symmetry with easy inversion of the $H_2O \cdots H$ pyramid geometry. The $O \cdots F$ distance is about 268 pm. The water dimer has been studied in detail by molecular beam electric resonance.[82,83] Proton tunnelling transitions occur as well as rotational transitions, but the results show a structure

in which the $O \cdots H-O$ is linear, the bonds to the three-coordinate oxygen pyramidally arranged and the right-hand water molecule in the symmetry plane in the 'trans' conformation as indicated. The distance $O \cdots O$ is about 298 pm. Further work to give more detail of such hydrogen-bonded systems is clearly of great interest and importance.

The above-mentioned systems are of low stability and a considerable proportion of other recent examples of structure determination concern unstable or short-lived species. Thus the radicals NF_2,[68] HO_2,[84,85] and HCO[86,87] have been studied. The many details for NF_2 include accurate geometry, and the precision of the determination of rotational constants for HO_2 and HCO is increasing. Similarly, evidence of changes in geometry of NO_2 in the $^2B_2$ electronically excited state compared with that of the ground state is obtained from m.w.-optical double-resonance work.[88] Several other recent studies of detailed geometry of unstable substances are those of S_2O,[89] formyl chloride, $HCOCl$,[90] thioacetaldehyde, CH_3CSH,[91] sulphine CH_2SO[92] and methyleneimine CH_2NH.[93] The last-named molecule may be taken to contain the prototype of the $C=N$ linkage, for which an r_s length of 127.3 pm is found; this paper gives discussion of procedures in the rather common case where, as here, certain atoms are too close to the principal a-axis of the structure for straightforward substitution procedures to reach their more customary accuracy.

Notable among recent studies of substances which are unfamiliar on account of instability is the work on monothioformic acid,[94-96] which emphasizes also that one of the largest general contributions of m.w. work to our knowledge of molecular geometry is the proof of many cases of rotational and geometric isomerism about which there has often been little previous evidence. Monothioformic acid, $H \cdot CO \cdot SH$, consists of comparable proportions of the geometric isomers in which the SH bond is *cis* or *trans*, respectively, to the CH-direction (see Fig. 1). Great detail of both isomers has been obtained. Although isotopic substitutions have still to be studied at the C and O positions, the data for the parent and D- and S-substituted forms allow a comparison of the bond lengths in these two planar molecules. Thus the SH bond is somewhat longer (135.1 pm) when *trans* to the CH than when it is *cis* to it (133.6 pm). The CO bond is also slightly longer in the *trans* species (121.8 pm) than in the *cis*-form (121.0 pm). On the other hand, the C—S bond is shorter in the *trans* form (176.3 pm) than in the *cis* case (177.1 pm). These changes accompanying a simple rotation of SH are understandable if the contribution of $^{\ominus}O$—C=$S \neq H^{\oplus}$ is more in the *trans* isomer, which allows the formal changes to be in closer proximity, while other small changes are not unexpected on steric arguments.

It has also been shown by m.w. methods that formic acid itself, normally the well-studied *trans* form, also contains a small proportion of the *cis* isomer[97] (Fig. 1), detailed information about which is being obtained. The comparisons between such pairs of isomers and the knowledge of their interconversion form a most interesting contribution to new structural knowledge.

Somewhat reminiscent of such considerations is the r_s structure found from ten isotopic species of formic anhydride[98] in which two formyl groups are attached to an oxygen atom with the general planar geometry:

Distinct differences are found in the CO lengths in the two formyl groups: in that on the left C=O is 118.4 pm while in that on the right it is 119.5 pm; the C—O distance on the left is 139 pm as against 136 pm on the right. There are also differences in the corresponding angles. A comparably thorough substitution study has recently been described[99] for pyruvic acid, $CH_3CO \cdot CO_2H$, in which the conformation of the OH is such as to give a hydrogen-bonded type of interaction with the oxygen of the CO adjacent to the methyl group.

Most examples of conformational isomerism are best mentioned when considering force fields (Section 4.3) and the substances are often too complex for any great proportion of the structure to be measured easily by r_s methods without many isotopic enrichments. Geometries of several quite extensive structures in this category have, however, been accurately determined, examples being propionic acid,[100,101] ethane thiol (both *trans*[102] and *gauche*[103] rotamers) and diethyl ether.[104]

Cyclic molecules continue to provide some of the best examples of geometric studies by the m.w. method. Many structures containing three-membered rings have been accurately determined. In cyclopropyl cyanide[105] the C_1—C_2 and C_1—C_3 bonds (153 pm) are longer than in the parent cyclopropane (151 pm),

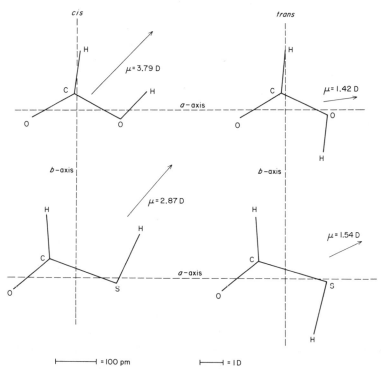

Fig. 1. Planar geometries and dipole moments of *cis* and *trans* forms of formic and monothioformic acids (redrawn from Hocking and Winnewisser, Ref. 96 and Hocking, Ref. 97). The dipole vectors in this figure point in the direction of the positive ends of the dipoles.

while the C_2—C_3 bond is shorter (150 pm), effects which are even more marked in cyclopropane-1,1-dicarbonitrile.[106] Opposite effects occur in 1,1-difluoro-cyclopropane[107] the C_1—C_2 and C_1—C_3 bonds being now only 146.4(2) pm long while the C_2—C_3 length is much larger, 155.3(1) pm. Such effects, including a wider range of data[108] are to some extent, but not entirely, in accord with theoretical expectations.

The structure of the interesting symmetric-top molecule, *cis*-1,2,3-trifluoro-cyclopropane, in which all the fluorine atoms are one side of the ring plane, has been completely determined.[109]

The bonds in cyclopropene[110] show interesting lengths; the 'single' C—C bonds (150.9(1) pm) are almost the same length as the ring bonds in cyclopropane, but the ring 'double' bond is very short, only 129.59(4) pm. When two fluorine atoms are introduced in 3,3-difluorocyclopropene,[111] the ring 'double' bond lengthens to 132.1(1) pm, while the ring 'single' bonds are shortened to 143.8(7) pm, effects parallel to those observed when cyclopropane is compared with its 1,1-difluoro derivative.

Work on four-membered rings has concerned force fields more than geometry, but the distances in trimethylene sulphide (thietane), $\overset{\frown}{C}H_2$—CH_2—CH_2—$\overset{\frown}{S}$, have been established accurately by a combination of m.w. and electron diffraction data.[112] Both CS and CC distances are, not unexpectedly, somewhat longer than in non-cyclic molecules.

The planar five-membered rings with aromatic character have provided many examples for detailed m.w. study. Substitution location of all, or almost all, the atoms has been possible in many cases, a summary of work up to 1974 being available.[113] Recent examples have included isoxazole,[27] 1,2,3-thiadiazole[114] and 1,2,4-thiadiazole.[115] In these studies, species containing carbon-13, nitrogen-15 or oxygen-18 in their small natural abundances were routinely assigned by the double-resonance modulation technique. Although some care has to be exercised on account of small coordinates of certain atoms in a number of molecules of this type, an impressive array of geometric knowledge for planar five-membered rings has been amassed, and comparisons between related structures have been made.[113] The ability to locate hydrogen atoms well is important here. The lengths of CH bonds in these molecules are all close to 108 pm, but the angular locations of these bonds depends on their ring positions. If the CH is flanked by two other CH groups in the ring (or by two hetero-atoms), its direction lies close to the bisector of the ring angle at the carbon concerned, but when one of its neighbours is a hetero-atom in the ring the CH bond is noticeably displaced from this bisector towards the hetero-atom, often by several degrees of arc. In cyclopentadiene,[116] there is a small similar tilting of CH bonds towards the adjacent methylene group, but the effect is clearly greatest when hetero-atoms are present.

Several studies of molecules in which a halogen or cyanide group is attached to these planar five-membered rings have recently appeared and there are indications that substituent effects on the ring geometry are occurring which will repay detailed study in the ways which have proved fruitful for derivatives of atomatic six-membered rings.

Among work on saturated five-membered rings, that on ethylene ozonide (1,2,4-trioxolane) and its derivatives is conspicuous. A very large array of isotopic forms of the parent molecule

$$CH_2—O—O—CH_2—O$$
$$\rule{6cm}{0.4pt}$$

has been used to obtain the r_s structure and ring configuration.[117,118] Work on derived structures, such as 3-fluoro-1,2,4-trioxolane[119] has provided interesting data on conformations and, with isotopic labelling, has cast light on the mechanisms by which such structures are formed from complex reaction mixtures.

There has been much work on benzene derivatives and other six-membered aromatic heterocycles, giving accurate geometries and indications of the influence of substituents on bond lengths. A recent example is the determination of the complete structure of 2,6-difluoropyridine,[120] which shows clear differences in certain bond lengths compared with those in pyridine itself. A full evaluation of the structure of aniline,[121] employing thirteen isotopic forms, has been made. In this case the ring geometry differs little from that of benzene, but detail is also established of the pyramidal C—NH$_2$ group structure.

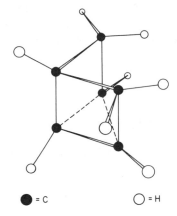

● = C   ○ = H

Fig. 2. Tricyclo[2,2,0,0^{2,6}]hexane, C$_6$H$_8$ (redrawn from Suenram, Ref. 122).

A wide variety of molecules containing larger rings and fused ring systems has been studied. Often conformations have been the main findings, but some precise structures have also emerged. A particularly striking example is found in the tricyclic hydrocarbon, tricyclo[2,2,0,0^{2,6}] hexane (Fig. 2) which has been studied in eleven isotopic forms to give a complete r_s structure.[122] The C—C bonds range in length from 151.3(5) pm to 158.4(5) pm in ways which accord with their locations. Among complex cyclic structures revealed in detail by the m.w. method, mention must be made of the remarkable series of studies of carboranes by Beaudet and co-workers. Different geometries and distances in these cage-like structures occur in fascinating variety; details can be found through the reviews mentioned.[4,5]

The subject of geometric studies cannot be left without mention of recent work on symmetric-top molecules which has overcome some of the limitations due to the normal inability to obtain, by m.w. methods, the moments of inertia about the figure axes in such cases. One advance is the success in the measurement and assignment of b-type transitions in partially deuterated simple methyl or silyl derivatives, such as CH_2DI,[123] CH_2DF[124] or SiH_2DF,[125] despite the low values of the b-components of the dipole moments. This allows accurate A_0 values to be derived and used in structure calculations. The second development is the observation of forbidden transitions in molecules such as PH_3[126,127] and AsH_3[126] or OPF_3.[128] These transitions are allowed through centrifugal distortion and yield values of the constants C_0 (or A_0) for improved structure calculations.

An advantage of the microwave method is that, even when isotopic substitutions are insufficient to give the whole structure with r_s accuracy, certain interatomic distances are, nonetheless, determined with this precision from the isotopic data. Thus bonds of particular interest may be measured. Simple cases are the CC distance in ethane already mentioned[23] ($r_s = 152.6(1)$ pm), the r_s (SiSi) length in SiH_3SiF_3[129] of 231.9(5) pm and the BC length in vinyl difluoroborane[130] ($r_s = 153.3(8)$ pm). Many other examples could be cited. The combined use of m.w. and electron diffraction data, already mentioned, is especially valuable when the m.w. method is hampered by lack of isotopes, for example, in compounds of fluorine or iodine. Molecules studied recently by these combined methods include acetyl fluoride and acetyl iodide,[131] IOF_5[132] and SF_5Cl.[133] Many molecules have, of course, been independently investigated by electron diffraction and by m.w. spectroscopy, and it is not difficult to find disagreements among the differently determined parameters which exceed the expected errors. In general, especially for those parts of larger structures which can be studied by isotopic substitution, the m.w. method can probably claim superiority.

4.2   Electron Distributions in Molecules

Several types of measurement in m.w. spectroscopy can provide important evidence of electronic structure. The experimental side here is much more dependent on quality of resolution than is the determination of geometry, since electronic properties are derived from fine structures and the effects of electric and magnetic fields on spectra.

4.2.1   Electric dipole moments

Since Stark effects are normally resolved in the detection of spectra, the measurement of molecular dipoles, which these effects allow through well established procedures, is a general part of the majority of m.w. studies. Hence many data on dipole moments by this method are published annually. In the general case of asymmetric rotors, the analysis yields the squared components of the dipole in the principal inertial axis system of the particular isotopic form of the molecule. Like other electronic properties, these components are averaged over the molecular state which is normally, but not exclusively, the ground state. Since the signs of the components themselves are not calculable from such information, the data for a single isotopic form of the molecule do not define uniquely the line of action of the moment unless this is defined by the symmetry properties of the molecule. Although cases where the dipole has components in all three inertial axes are not uncommon, very many of the cases studied have symmetry planes, which clearly limits the number of non-zero dipole components to those in the two axes in the symmetry plane, while those molecules with axes of symmetry have only one dipole component. Thus, for example, for the common case of planar molecules with no symmetry axes, μ_c is zero and μ_a^2 and μ_b^2 are generally determinable from the spectrum. The total moment is then easily derived, but two possible lines of action of this total dipole are then compatible with the data, according to the sign combination of μ_a with μ_b. In principle, a similar measurement on a new isotopic form of the molecule which has different inertial axes in the nuclear framework will yield new components $(\mu_a')^2$ and $(\mu_b')^2$ which conform with only one of the lines of action allowed by the original results for μ_a^2 and μ_b^2 and so this line of action, which is independent of the isotopic structure, is defined. In many cases the movement of axes with isotopic substitution is small and these extensions have not been made with the accuracy needed to define the line of action of the moment uniquely, but frequently only one of the possible lines of action of the moment is reasonable on general chemical grounds. A number of lines of action of dipole moments have been determined, however, entirely from m.w. Stark effects, especially when the inertial properties allow an isotopic substitution which appreciably swings the principal axes. In near-oblate rotors with no symmetry axes, such as cyclic molecules containing only first-row atoms in their unsubstituted rings (pyrazole, oxazole, etc.), very large axial swings accompany isotopic substitution, and the relative values of μ_a and μ_b often are changed dramatically, allowing accurate location of the line of action of the moment.

It is well known that the m.w. Stark-effect method of determining dipole moments is generally very accurate, especially with careful attention to cell construction for homogeneity of the Stark field, but the overall precision depends on the particular case. Small components of the dipole in particular axes are not always derived with high precision and sometimes one component has remained undetermined for long periods.

Because errors are inherent more in the measurement of the Stark splittings than in the fields necessary to produce them, the m.w. method can accurately determine total dipole moments which are too low for very precise treatment by the usual dielectric constant methods. Moments around 0.2 D present no great difficulty, examples being bromoacetylene[134] (0.23(1) D), NF_2[68] (0.136(10) D) and CF_3NO[136] (0.18(1) D). A number of extensive m.w. studies are now being made on weakly polar substances, such as various hydrocarbon structures. Thus tricyclo[2,2,0,0^{2,6}] hexane[122] (Fig. 2) has a moment of only 0.222(10) D, while 'Dewar benzene' (bicyclo[2,2,0]hexa-2,5-diene) has been studied[136] despite its moment of only 0.044 D. The even smaller moment of CH_3CD_3[23,137] could be measured, through the first-order Stark effects in this symmetric top, as

0.01078(9) D, with a very small but detectable variation with the isotopic masses of the carbon atoms. The moment of CH_2D_2,[138] although now measured by comparison of the intensity of the spectrum with a line of known intensity rather than by Stark effects, is shown to be similar to that for CH_3CD_3.

The majority of the dipole data established by m.w. spectroscopy are in general accord with expectations from the other knowledge of the structures. The lines of action of moments are established experimentally only in a relatively small proportion of cases, but the axial components are generally in agreement with the remaining evidence. Sometimes the findings can be used to discriminate between alternative interpretations of structural data. Thus the moment of the van der Waals complex[79] HF $\cdots$ ClF (see Section 4.1) is found to be 2.30 D, which agrees with a vector combination of the known moments of HF and ClF separately, with allowance for induced moments in the complex, provided the ClF moment has the 'sign' indicated by $+ClF-$. Were this sign reversed, the complex would show little polarity. Confirmatory evidence of this sign is mentioned below. Dipole moments have been found for several others of the van der Waals molecules mentioned earlier (Section 4.1). Often the complex has a higher moment than the summed moment vectors of the associated molecules, for example in HCN $\cdots$ HF[80] and $H_2O \cdots$ HF;[81] this result is not entirely unexpected. The magnitude of the effect could not, however, invalidate the argument just given about the sign of the moment in ClF.

Several interesting findings for dipole moments concern cases where internal rotation of asymmetric groups is involved. Propargyl mercaptan, $HC \equiv C—CH_2SH$, is a molecule with dipole components in all three inertial axes, but the c-component is associated with the internal rotation or tunnelling of SH about the C—S bond. All three components have been determined[139] from Stark effects. In t-butyl mercaptan, $(CH_3)_3CSH$, the two components of the moment are found,[140] and an unusual feature is here brought about by the internal rotation of SH about the CS bond. A term appears in the Stark effect analysis which contains the signed product of the two dipole components and this allows the line of action of the moment to be stated unambiguously; it makes an angle of some 25° with the C—S direction, away from the side taken by the SH bond.

When two or more rotamers are possible for a molecule, the dipole properties of each can usually be compared. For the cis and $trans$ isomers of both formic and thioformic acids,[94–97] the cis forms are considerably more polar. Their dipole magnitudes and directions are indicated in Fig. 1 and accord with reasonable expectations from group moments. It is suggested[97] that the direction of the moment in ordinary ($trans$) formic acid is not conclusively proved by the earlier work on isotopic dependence of the axial components, and the assumption has been made here that the small B-component (only 0.26 D) for this form has the orientation shown.

The accuracy of m.w. dipole moment determination has allowed many cases of isotopic variation in the dipole moment of a molecule to be detected. These effects, which are summarized to a considerable extent in standard works (e.g. Ref. 1) are naturally greatest for deuterium substitution. Noticeable effects of centrifugal distortion on the dipole moments of certain molecules are also well established,[1] particularly where the geometry is very dependent on the distribution of angular momentum in the molecule, as in such near-linear arrangements as HNCO and NH_3.

Dipole moments so far discussed, and as normally obtained, are averaged over the molecular ground vibrational state. A number of measurements of moments averaged over low-lying vibrational states of molecules have been made, and many more are accessible by these methods. Such work has obvious importance in relation to the effects of vibration on polarity, and thus to the field of infrared spectroscopy. With more recent techniques leading, as already mentioned, to increasing knowledge of vibrational states of molecules well above the ground state, we may expect an increase in the rate of acquisition of such data. For example in a recent study of fluoroacetylene[141] in which laser-m.w. double resonance was employed in the presence of Stark fields, the dipole moments of the molecule were obtained for the first excited levels of three of the modes (v_3, v_4 and v_5) as well as two of their combinations. The ground state moment of 0.7207(3) D is raised to almost equal extents in the $v_3 = 1$ and $v_5 = 1$ states (0.7447(3) D and 0.7441(3) D respectively) while in the $v_4 = 1$ state the moment falls to 0.6557(3) D. The changes are seen to be well above the uncertainties in the findings.

Much interest attaches to the 'signs' of dipole moments, by which is meant the location of the centres of positive and negative charge with respect to the molecular framework. Unlike the line of action of the moment, the sign does not emerge from analysis of Stark effects, but can be found in favourable cases from Zeeman studies through the isotopic dependence of the molecular g-factors. Originally applied to the classic case of carbon monoxide,[1] these methods have now been applied to upwards of a dozen molecules through the development of Zeeman-effect m.w. spectroscopy at high-resolution.[42] Summaries of this and other types of information on electron distributions to be derived from Zeeman studies will be found in several reviews.[42,142,143] Some of the more interesting dipole signs found are: $+ClCN-$; $-ClCCH+$; $+H_3CCCH-$; $-H_3SiCH_3+$ and $+HBS-$. The method is critically dependent on the attainment of high resolution in the Zeeman splittings, and has failed to give conclusive results for some chemically interesting cases. Thus the sign of the small moment of furan (0.66 D) could not be established.[144] The same situation exists for pyridine,[145] although there can be no doubt regarding the sign of the large moment in this case. It is noted[143] that the effects of vibrations on the Zeeman parameters should not be neglected in seeking to establish signs of moments, especially if substitution of H by D has been used. Allowing for such effects by Zeeman studies of vibrationally excited states will, however, be very time-consuming. The limitations of resolution for the determination of the sign of the dipole have been well illustrated by the case of ClF, where high resolution work with normal gas cells suggested[146] a sign of $-ClF+$. The development of beam work with much increased resolution now has allowed Zeeman studies under more favourable conditions and has led to improved precision for several types of quantity derived from such measurements. In the case of ClF, a Zeeman beam study[147] leaves no doubt that the sign of the dipole is $+ClF-$, as indicated by less direct evidence, such as the work on HF $\cdots$ ClF referred to above. Although beam methods are necessarily less simple and less generally applicable than gas-cell techniques, we may expect further examples of the advantages of beam methods in circumstances such as existed here.

4.2.2 Electronic properties derivable from the m.w. Zeeman effect

The use of Zeeman effects to determine signs of dipole moments has already been mentioned. In this, the molecular g-factors referred to the principal axes, g_{aa}, g_{bb} and g_{cc}, are obtained for two or more isotopic forms of the molecules from measurements of the first-order Zeeman effects. Other important electronic information has been derived for many molecules by measurement of second-order Zeeman effects to give the so-called anisotropies of the molecular magnetic susceptibility.[142,143] In particular, the second-order Zeeman effects, combined with the g-factors and, where appropriate, the inertial constants, the nuclear geometry and the bulk magnetic susceptibility of the substance, allow derivation of the elements of the molecular quadrupole-moment tensor (Q_{aa}, Q_{bb} and Q_{cc}) and the so-called 'second moments' of the electron distribution with respect to the inertial axes, and the anisotropies of these second moments. The determination, for numerous molecules, of these elusive types of information must rank as a major advance in the face of experimental difficulties and it is not surprising to find that some of the proportionate errors in derived constants can be large, and can be influenced by special effects. Thus, it has recently been pointed out[148] that the forces experienced by electric charges moving in magnetic fields (the Lorentz forces) cannot always be neglected in Zeeman studies of polar molecules at thermal velocities. This translational Zeeman contribution is equivalent in effect to a virtual electric field which reaches a few volts per centimetre at thermal molecular speeds; hence the effects are not negligible in cases where Stark effects on transitions are of the first-order, as in most transitions of symmetric rotors or certain transitions of other molecules. For these reasons, the phenomenon is often called the translational Stark effect. For a number of symmetric rotor molecules, etc. some re-evaluation of Zeeman measurements will have to be made, taking account of the translational effects, in order that g-factors and other properties such as quadrupole moments can be derived with the desired accuracies.

Overall, however, the array of new data from such methods is impressive. The measurements are steadily being extended and compared with those for other molecules. Thus, in a recent example, the constants derived from Zeeman work on the linear molecule HBS[149] are found to resemble the corresponding constants for the isoelectronic HCP, but not those of the equally isoelectronic

CS. Such comparisons are here dependent on the dispositions of excited electronic states of molecules. In spite of complexities, however, the information exemplified by quadrupole moments and second moments of charge distribution is of an unusual type and relates particularly to regions of the molecule well removed from the nuclei. Hence these data afford checks on, for example, *ab initio* calculations of quadrupole moments. Empirical procedures have been valuable in correlating the evidence of Zeeman studies. Thus the second moments of the electron distribution along the *c*-axis direction in planar or near-planar molecules can be fitted to a simple set of rules, which can then be used to predict, and also, for example, to select the correct absolute values of the *g*-factors, which are determined from the Zeeman effect in relative sign only. Perhaps the most striking of the chemically important findings refers to the susceptibility anisotropies of cyclic compounds in comparison with those predicted from 'group anisotropies' evaluated from an array of data for non-cyclic cases. The five- or six-membered rings with aromatic character show anisotropies reflecting large non-local diamagnetic contributions for fields impressed in a direction perpendicular to the ring planes, and these contributions are a useful measure of relative aromatic character. Similar but smaller departures from the predictions from group anisotropies occur in three-membered rings, but cannot have the same explanation in terms of ring currents. In contrast, four-membered rings show an increased paramagnetism with respect to the axes perpendicular to the ring planes, a result ascribed to the availability, in these cases, of low-lying excited electronic levels. This anti-aromatic property persists, for example, for the ring in methylene cyclobutenone,[150] even though the ring is planar and the molecule strongly conjugated.

4.2.3 Nuclear-quadrupole coupling effects

The information derivable here is primarily about the immediate electronic environments of certain nuclei, rather than the electron distributions obtained from Stark and Zeeman effects. The basis of the nuclear-quadrupole interaction and the derivation of the coupling constants with respect to the axes of inertia of a given state and isotopic form of the molecule are well known. These constants for the abundant species are normally reported in all m.w. investigations of new molecules which contain quadrupole nuclei, commonly ^{14}N, ^{35}Cl, ^{37}Cl, ^{79}Br, ^{81}Br, ^{127}I and less frequently such cases as ^{10}B, ^{11}B, ^{27}Al, ^{33}S, ^{17}O, ^{73}Ge, ^{75}As and a few others. The main structural objective is to obtain the complete nuclear-quadrupole coupling tensor, and the directions of its principal axes in the molecular frame. This information is then interpreted in terms of the asymmetry of the electron distribution in the vicinity of the nucleus.

Only when a molecule has an axis of symmetry passing through the given quadrupole nucleus can the principal axes of the coupling tensor be identified with the directions of the inertial axes, and so be obtained directly from the spectrum. When only a plane of symmetry is present, the coupling constant with respect to the inertial axis perpendicular to this plane is also a principal value for this axis in the coupling tensor, but the remaining inertial axes do not cor-respond to the remaining axes of the coupling tensor. In molecules with no symmetry, none of the coupling constants with respect to an inertial axis is a principal value of the coupling tensor, unless accidentally. Accordingly, the location of coupling tensor axes and principal coupling constants resembles the location of lines of action of dipole moments in the molecular framework.

Problems of locating tensor axes do not, of course, arise in simple symmetric molecules, examples of which will be considered first. In diatomics, the data and theoretical interpretations are already extensive.[1] Recent interesting cases have included the measurement of the couplings of chlorine, bromine and iodine nuclei in the cuprous halides.[61–63] When these findings are related in the established ways to the ionic characters of the molecules, it is found that these accord with an electronegativity of 1.7 for monovalent copper. Recently, refined measurements on $CuI^{[151]}$ have increased the precision of our knowledge of the ^{127}I coupling constant ($-938.07(20)$ MHz) and given a value for the ^{63}Cu coupling constant ca. 8.14(20) MHz. The constant for ^{63}Cu is, not unexpectedly, much less than the value 21.95(10) MHz in $CuF.^{[152]}$ Couplings for both atoms show clearly the effects of covalency in these molecules; the iodine coupling in CuI is ten times as great as in KI. New work on the bismuth monohalides, also in heated cells, is quite similar, although the only halogen coupling established is for Cl in $BiCl.^{[58]}$ In this substance the Cl coupling corresponds to 69% ionic character and an electronegativity of 1.8 for monovalent bismuth. The coupling constant of ^{209}Bi is $-1027(12)$ MHz in BiCl and $-1150.28(12)$ MHz in $BiF,^{[153]}$ the latter being expected to be largely ionic. These bismuth coupling constants largely accord with the bonding suggested by the other data.

Some small coupling constants are important in simple molecules. The constants for ^{14}N at both locations in N_2O have been remeasured with a beam-maser spectrometer[154] as $-0.7767(10)$ MHz for the terminal nitrogen and $-0.2694(18)$ MHz for the central nitrogen atom; the improved precision over conventional measurements is striking here. Other nitrogen couplings in linear molecules have, in two cases, been found with best accuracy to date from the highly resolved spectra detected in radiotelescopes. For HN_2^+, the coupling constants are[155] $-5.666(12)$ MHz for the terminal ^{14}N and $-1.426(21)$ MHz for the central ^{14}N atom. We may compare the well established coupling constant of the terminal ^{14}N atom in HCN, which is $-4.709(1)$ MHz. In HNC the ^{14}N coupling constant[156] is -0.40 MHz from astronomical data. Nuclear-quadrupole coupling constants for deuterium have now been determined for numerous molecules, especially from beam-maser work, which gives these small constants with good precision. The results, and their relation to molecular structures, are discussed in a review by Kukolich.[157]

Nuclear-coupling tensors for ^{14}N are also important in heterocyclic systems. In the simple cases where large swings of the inertial axes can be produced by isotopic substitution, the tensor axes can be located by methods analogous to the location of lines of action of dipole moments. More than one nitrogen nucleus may be present in the molecule, a good example being pyrazole,[158] and the methods have been extended to the three nitrogen atoms in 1,2,4-triazole[159] and 1,2,3-triazole.[160] The coupling tensors show clear relations with the electron distributions.[113] Particularly when the coupling tensor axes are determined by symmetry, such measurements are extended to yield information about the effects of substituents on the electron distribution at a ring nitrogen atom, such as that in 2,6-difluoropyridine.[120]

The coupling tensors for chlorine, bromine and iodine have played important roles in the study of many structures. The determination of tensor axes in asymmetric molecules by the isotopic axial-rotation method is not often easy, although a favourable situation for axial rotation in the near-oblate rotor $CSCl_2$[161] has recently, for example, allowed tensor axes to be located by this means. As in many cases, a principal axis of the tensor is close to the bond direction joining the coupling nucleus to its neighbour, and the tensor has an asymmetry associated with the different electron distributions at chlorine with respect to the other axes, this asymmetry, as in many similar examples, relating to double-bond character in the CCl linkages.

For bromine and iodine, where coupling effects are much larger than for chlorine, the axes of the coupling tensor can often be found more directly from the analysis of the second-order effects which are apparent in the splitting patterns of spectra when these atoms are present. When second-order effects are analysed, we obtain not only the coupling constants in the inertial axes (designated eQq_{aa}, eQq_{bb} and eQq_{cc}) but also the off-diagonal constants such as eQq_{ab}, from which the directions of the principal tensor axes in the inertial axial system can be derived. If, as is by no means always the case except in an approximate sense, the bond joining the quadrupole nucleus to its neighbour is located in the principal inertial axis system, the angle between the bonding direction and a principal axis of the coupling tensor can be found. Usually this angle is very small. For example, in CH_2Br_2,[162] the angle is less than the uncertainty in its value of about 1°. In this case, the tensor is nearly symmetric about the bond direction and the same is also true of the bromine tensor in 2-bromo-thiophen.[163] In 2- and 4-bromopyridine[164] and 2- and 4-iodopyridine[165] the slight asymmetries of the nuclear-quadrupole tensors about the carbon-halogen bond direction correspond to a few percent double-bond character in these linkages, somewhat more than in the corresponding bonds in bromobenzene or iodobenzene, especially for the halogens at the 2-position in pyridine.

The knowledge of types of quadrupole-coupling tensor associated with given groupings is sometimes useful in assigning molecular conformations. Thus the ^{14}N quadrupole tensors in the various rotamers of allyl amine, $H_2C=CH \cdot CH_2 \cdot NH_2$[166,167] have proved valuable, in conjunction with dipole data, in indicating the relative orientations of the nitrogen lone-pair.

The dependence of quadrupole-coupling constants on vibrational state is clearly accessible by m.w. methods, but relatively few data are so far to hand except for some diatomic molecules, particularly those containing halogens. A good example is the determination of the vibrational dependence of the quadrupole-coupling constants for both nuclei in each of the molecules IBr,[168] InBr[169] and RbBr.[170] As with the vibrational dependence of dipole moments, such information casts light on the changes of electron distribution with distortion of the nuclear framework. The increasing capacity to study vibrationally excited molecules with greater sensitivities will no doubt yield more information on vibrational dependence of couplings. Thus the iodine coupling constant in the first excited level of the symmetric stretching mode, v_1 of CF_3I, at 1075 cm^{-1}, is evaluated[35] from i.r.-m.w. double resonance as $-2150(10)$ MHz, very close to the constant for the ground state.

In beam instruments, the accuracies allow effects of centrifugal distortion on quadrupole-coupling constants to be detected. Thus for methyl iodide[44] small constants were evaluated, expressing the dependence of the iodine coupling on J and K, respectively, while the dependence of the bromine coupling on J in methyl bromide has also been measured.[171] The field asymmetry appears to increase as the carbon–halogen bond is stretched.

4.2.4 Electronic information from other hyperfine interactions

Spin–rotation and spin–spin coupling effects have been measured in the m.w. spectra of numerous molecules. When the molecule is paramagnetic, interactions of the electron spin are present, and a number of interesting studies have concerned such cases. The general theory is contained in standard works. Among recent examples we find work on HCO[87,172] and on NF_2.[68] In the latter case, where considerable difficulties in experiment and in analysis of data were overcome, the spin coupling constants for ^{14}N and ^{19}F accord with a π-radical structure, with the spin density largely on the nitrogen atom; the results confirm the state of the radical to be $^2B_1$.

The increasing amount of work at highest resolution is allowing a proportionate increase in the determinations of hyperfine effects leading to spin–rotation constants in diamagnetic molecules. Thus such constants are reported in the work with beams already mentioned in several connexions, and in many similar studies.[8] Special interest attaches to obtaining the components of the nuclear magnetic shielding tensor of a given atom; the tensor is related to the corresponding spin–rotation tensor, since both express the magnetic effects of electron motions at the particular nucleus. Simple fluorine compounds have been studied, for example, to obtain these tensors for fluorine, a recent example being 1,1-difluoroethylene, $CH_2 \cdot CF_2$.[173] The elements of the fluorine spin–rotation tensor are evaluated and employed to derive the paramagnetic contributions to the fluorine chemical shift tensor. The total magnetic shielding tensor can then be arrived at by combining these results with the reasonably reliable calculated diamagnetic contributions. It is now becoming possible to compare shielding tensors and their relation to bond directions in a few related structures. The work just mentioned[173] summarizes information on the averaged r^{-3} factors in the charge distributions around H or F atoms in several simple molecules. Large variations in this factor with changes of structure are apparent. The elements of the bromine nuclear magnetic shielding tensor in methyl bromide have been similarly determined from the spin–rotation effects in the beam work already mentioned.[171]

Nuclear spin–rotational constants are closely related to the general study of magnetic interactions in molecules and summaries will be found in reviews already cited in connexion with Zeeman measurements,[142,143] where the obvious connexions between this area of the field and n.m.r. studies are also summarized.

The study of the hyperfine interactions mentioned in this section is largely confined to very simple molecules and the limits of molecular complexity for success here seem at present exemplified by the work on furan[45] which yields the spin–rotation constants for the different H atoms, and on pyrrole.[8] Conceivably, however, it will be possible to extend these methods to other ring systems such as pyridine or simple benzene derivatives. An interesting feature of such an advance would be the gain in accuracy, over conventional methods, in evaluating the small quadrupole-coupling constants of ^{14}N, an important factor in the discussion of such systems.

4.3 Molecular Force Field Information

Even a casual survey of the thousand or so papers published in m.w. spectroscopy in the past three years shows at once that force field information is the predominant endproduct. The findings are so varied and at times complex, and merging into the general areas of vibration–rotation spectroscopy, that a full survey would require a separate review. An attempt has been made instead to indicate the main areas of activity and their significance for those interested in the internal mechanics of molecules in a general way.

It is convenient to treat separately what have become known as cases of large-amplitude internal motions. These are usually associated with highly anharmonic potential energy functions with more than one easily accessible minimum. Some of the most important and interesting contributions of m.w. spectroscopy are those concerned with such motions. Firstly, however, cases where normal vibrations only are important are considered. The types of information which emerge in these simpler cases are, of course, accessible also for cases of large amplitude motion, but only with greater difficulty. Accordingly the effects of large amplitude motion, where present, often dominate the state of knowledge.

4.3.1 Molecules without internal motions of large amplitude

In classifying a molecule here, the formal possibilities of inversion motions, e.g. of such pyramidal molecules as NCl_3 or $AsBr_3$, can be ignored if such possibilities have no influence on the measurements. Molecules of this class exemplify several general ways in which force field information is derived from m.w. data.

4.3.1.1 CENTRIFUGAL DISTORTION EFFECTS FOR A GIVEN MOLECULAR STATE

The basis of the derivation of centrifugal distortion constants to first- and higher orders is given in standard works. For linear or symmetric top molecules, very refined studies have been possible for some time. In the general case of asymmetric rotors, it is increasingly possible to analyse arrays of data to include distortion constants, usually in the formulation of Watson.[174] Such analyses may have importance for various reasons. Sometimes the best possible accuracy in rotational constants is necessary for structural calculations. On other occasions, the accurate prediction of new lines is important, an activity recently stimulated by the searches for new molecular lines in astrophysical studies over restricted frequency ranges. The precision which can be placed on a given distortion constant depends on the individual case and the nature of the lines measured, and in a relative sense the accuracy can be poor for some very small constants. To maximize accuracy, as many lines as are assignable should be used, from as many types of transition as possible. Unless they show any perturbations due to special effects, such as large amplitude motions, lines with considerable centrifugal frequency corrections naturally help the accuracy. In spite of difficulties sometimes met in obtaining centrifugal constants free from ambiguities, it is common for large proportions of the measured spectrum of a molecule to be completely assigned by such means.

In general, discussion of the values of the distortion constants themselves, in correlation with structures, is not usual. In fact, distortion constants depend more on rotational constants[175] than on details of structure and can be predicted in order of magnitude from rotational constants, particularly if some account is also taken of the vibrational modes of the molecule. More comparisons between distortion constants for different molecules may be made when more attention has been given to the relations[176] between constants obtained from different mathematical reductions of the data.

With the development of theoretical background, the growth of measurements and increased computational facilities, higher order treatments of centrifugal distortion have become common. Thus, Aliev and Watson[177] review sextic centrifugal-distortion effects in molecules of several types of symmetry. At an elementary level, it is often clear that some molecules will show more than average sensitivity to centrifugal effects in their effective rotational constants, and hence in their spectra. Where angular momenta can reach high values, extensive procedures may be needed to fit the data; thus, in the near-linear case of isocyanic acid, HNCO, terms up to the twelfth power of angular momenta were required.[178] High-order distortion effects in spectra of methane and similar non-polar substances have been the subject of many papers in connexion with the observation[22] of m.w. absorptions due to distortional dipole moments.[179,180] These effects can arise in molecules of various symmetries.[181] Measurements have recently been extended to silane[182,183] and germane.[184]

Centrifugal distortion constants are, of course, of vital value in the overall evaluation of force fields for simple molecules. A review has been given by Kirchhoff.[185] Many examples are found of the use of such constants in this way in conjunction with vibrational data. Some of the most complete studies of this type relate to water[186] and hydrogen sulphide.[187] The relation of the sextic constants to the cubic potentials[177] is important, a recent case treated being that of ozone.[188] The correlation of the force field and centrifugal-distortion constants in OCS has been considered in detail by Whiffen.[189]

Centrifugal distortion has given the key to interesting features of the weak bonding in the van der Waals complexes of inert gases.[74] The force constant of the van der Waals bond can be estimated, and its isotopic dependence in ArHCl shows that the strength of this bond is changed by the bending of the atom chain. This illustrates an unusual situation in which important structural information of a general type is directly obtained from distortion effects.

4.3.1.2 ROTATIONAL SPECTRA OF VIBRATIONALLY EXCITED MOLECULES

Rotational lines of many vibrationally excited states are continually being measured. For diatomic molecules these data often form part of the details of the total analysis and this is increasingly the position with simple polyatomic molecules. Certain types of vibration have received particular attention, such as the degenerate bending modes of linear or symmetric-top molecules.[1] More recently, the rotational spectra in various excited vibrational states of many structures have been analysed to give new vibrational information. The separation of the concepts of vibration and rotation is clearly only a convenient first step. Its inadequacy has been obvious for a long time, usually in connexion with large amplitude motions, and a number of very well known m.w. spectra are more accurately described as arising from vibrational rather than from rotational transitions. Recently this has been re-emphasized by the measurement,[190] in the m.w. range, of what is clearly properly called a vibrational band in as simple a molecule as dideutero-acetylene, C_2D_2. Lines in the $v'_5-v'_4$ difference band, predicted some time ago to be in the m.w. range, have been identified with the aid of refined i.r. data and eight P-branch lines assigned between 47 GHz and 104 GHz. The vibrational dipole moment is found from Stark effects to be 0.0358(20) D. Cases where refinements such as this can be made are, of course, very dependent on the availability of sufficiently precise vibrational information for prediction of the relevant m.w. search range.

Recent studies on vibrations of linear molecules have included particularly detailed work on OCS[191] and N_2O,[192] while such information on the new case of HNC, and perhaps the even less stable HCO^+ and HN_2^+, will be of great interest. There is an even larger current activity on vibrational states of symmetric-top molecules. Interactions among degenerate vibrational states of C_{3v} cases, particularly CH_3CN and CH_3NC, have been the subject of exhaustive studies by French workers,[193–195] who have developed the theoretical background in great detail to include high-order terms. As in other work of this type, much is owed to the use of millimetre wave techniques. Other examples include OPF_3,[196] SPF_3[197] and CF_3H.[198] An instance of how such work can refine knowledge of vibrational levels is found in silyl fluoride, SiH_3F and SiD_3F,[125,199] where the first excited levels of ν_2 and ν_5 are very close and, again, elaborate computations were needed to deal with the Coriolis interactions. The C_{4v} symmetric rotor BrF_5 has illustrated[200] several special features of this type of molecule, notably the predicted extra doubling of the $kl = -1$ levels in the singly excited state of the degenerate vibration ν_9, in addition to the usual doubling of the $kl = +1$ levels. Much vibrational information about the $\nu_5 = 1$ and $\nu_9 = 1$ states was derived, including the first accurate estimate of ν_5 as 233 cm^{-1}.

Microwave methods have also cast light on the vibrational assignments of many other molecules. Recent cases have included SF_4[201] where Coriolis effects allow a decision between two vibrational assignments, and CD_2F_2[202] where as many as eight vibrationally excited states were studied. In this latter example, six of the nine fundamentals are within the range 900 to 1200 cm^{-1} and information on their disposition is derived from the m.w. measurements, which again had to be analysed by special theoretical procedures taking account of Coriolis effects. The three-membered ring structures ethylene oxide[203] and ethylene sulphide[204] are other recent examples studied in vibrationally excited states; the position regarding the vibrational assignments in such cases, where there are still gaps in our knowledge, illustrates well the present interaction of m.w. and vibrational spectroscopy. For larger molecules still, it is also common for rotational constants to be derived for numerous vibrationally excited states. For example, in isoxazole, the high sensitivity methods used to determine the geometry[27] also yielded constants for molecules excited in all eleven distortion modes. Relative intensities of such vibrational satellite spectra, while not measurable with great accuracy in normal work, can nonetheless provide checks on vibrational assignments, while the changes in rotational constants caused by excitation can often be related with some confidence to the symmetries of vibrations.

4.3.2 Cases involving large-amplitude motions

Just as the division between large and small amplitude cases is not precise, the classification of large amplitude effects into different categories is largely for descriptive convenience and much of the basic aspects of the subject apply to all cases. It is, however, helpful to distinguish cases where the potential minima occur at structurally equivalent nuclear geometries from those where this is not true.

4.3.2.1 CASES WITH ONLY SPECTROSCOPICALLY EQUIVALENT EQUILIBRIUM NUCLEAR CONFIGURATIONS

Such equivalent configurations can arise in several ways. The double-minimum property in the bending of certain atom-chains which might formally be expected to be linear has dominated the spectroscopy of rare but interesting cases of quasi-linearity in what might otherwise be classified as linear or symmetric-top structures. The inversion motions of pyramidal molecules, notably ammonia and its simple derivatives, have been important in m.w. spectroscopy since its beginning. Similar to such inversions are the flexing motions of some simple rings in which the conformations are equivalent. Finally there is a very large range of studies of internal rotation among equivalent positions, usually among three-fold torsional energy minima, although two-fold and six-fold minima are also commonly exemplified. In cases of ring flexing and internal rotation, substitutions in the structures can readily destroy the equivalence of energy minima and move the situation into that considered in Section 4.3.2.2. In addition, where three configurations are possible, two are often equivalent.

4.3.2.1.1 *Quasi-linearity*

Quasi-linear structures fall between the normal cases where a linear set of atoms has a single potential minimum and bent arrangements of atoms in which the energy has a deep minimum at a given angular deviation from the linear geometry. The best studied case is fulminic acid, HCNO, where as a result of many detailed m.w. and i.r. studies[205-8] the potential function for the bending mode, v_5, is derived; it shows a weak but unquestionable double-minimum property. A similar case, this time in a molecule approximating in other respects to a symmetric rotor, is silyl isocyanate, H_3SiNCO,[209] where equally unusual features emerge for the SiNC bending mode. The theoretical treatment of these cases is coincident with that for more formally bent structures like H_2O or HNCO[210-212] and much progress has been made in accounting for many spectroscopic details. The transition, within families of molecules, between the strictly linear case (harmonic bending vibration) and limiting bent case (nearly harmonic flapping vibration) has been admirably illustrated by Yamada and Winnewisser,[213] who introduce a dimensionless quasi-linearity parameter dependent on the relative energies needed to bend or to rotate the molecule. A large group of molecules are classified from available data, mostly as either near the bent limit or strictly linear. However, HNCO and HNCS, for example, though generally treated as bent, show the beginnings of quasi-linearity, while carbon suboxide and fulminic acid are very clear cases where a description in terms of either extreme is too simple. The monothio analogue of carbon suboxide, OCCCS, which might have been expected to lean towards quasi-linearity, shows a normal linear behaviour.[214] A number of other molecules which show unusual vibration–rotation interactions may be compared with these; examples include alkali-metal hydroxides,[215] potassium cyanide,[216] and the van der Waals complexes such as ArHCl.[73-77]

4.3.2.1.2 *Inversion motions*

Work on ammonia now largely concerns rotation–vibration interactions and may be exemplified by recent theoretical work[217] which parallels development of the theory of bending vibrations in H_2O. Inversion in simple monosubstituted ammonias has been considerably studied in the past, particularly in simple amides. A recent extension of such work is that on cyanamide, H_2NCN, at frequencies up to 120 GHz,[218] which reveals more interactions between the rotational levels in the different inversion states and allows a new evaluation of the lowest inversion splitting in this parent isotopic form as 49.2(1.0) cm^{-1}. Cyanamide has been detected in space and great interest obviously attaches to the possible presence in the galaxy of another amide, urea. The spectrum of this substance has been assigned[219] and accurate constants obtained, but more work is needed to decide questions of planarity or otherwise of the CNH_2 groupings and any inversion splittings.

The unstable vinyl amine,[220] $CH_2{=}CH{-}NH_2$, is a basic structure which may well show interesting properties of inversion at the CNH_2 group and for which more data are awaited. In the well known analogous case of aniline,[121] non-planarity of the CNH_2 section is well established, and geometries and barriers to inversion among substituted anilines,[221] amino derivatives of pyridine[222,223] and 2-aminopyrimidine[224] have been compared by m.w. methods. The effects of substituents on the availability of the nitrogen lone-pair at that atom are clearly related to the mechanics of inversion in a classically chemical way and, today, via the more sophisticated paths of molecular-orbital treatments.

Inversion, in this case about a pyramidally coordinated oxygen atom, may well be involved in the hydrogen-bonded complex $H_2O \cdots HF$[81] and certainly also in the water dimer.[82] Inversions in methylamine, which are coupled with the internal torsion, are mentioned below.

4.3.2.1.3 *Ring flexing*

Flexing motions of simple rings between equivalent equilibrium geometries, such as in trimethylene oxide and trimethylene sulphide, have been extensively studied by m.w. methods in the past. The double-minimum property of the potential function for ring flexing gives rise to such well known features as the zig-zag dependence of constants on the vibrational quantum number for the flexing motion. Refined work[225,226] on trimethylene oxide in several isotopic forms extends such studies to distortion constants for various states. In much recent work on such systems, substituents are present which either destroy the equivalence of the alternative equilibrium geometry (Section 4.3.2.2) or lead to loss of the double-minimum property in the ring-distortion potential function. It should be emphasized, however, that the treatment of force fields in such cases is not to be distinguished in principle by the presence or absence of a double-minimum property. The many contributions, from vibrational spectroscopy as well as m.w. methods, to our knowledge of these and similar systems have been summarized in several reviews,[113,227] of which the most recent is that by Gwinn and Gaylord[228] These studies are among the most impressive contributions of high-resolution spectroscopy to our knowledge of details of elusive potential functions.

4.3.2.1.4 *Internal rotation of symmetric groups*

In most cases, the rotating groups are of the three-fold symmetric type, XY_3, most commonly methyl groups. If the 'frame' against which the group rotates has a plane of symmetry, as in acetaldehyde or propene, there are three equivalent equilibrium values of the torsional dihedral angle, as is also the case if the 'frame' itself has three-fold symmetry, as in CF_3CH_3. When the frame has a two-fold symmetry axis, as in CH_3NO_2 or toluene, there are six equivalent equilibrium positions per torsional revolution.

A very large number of cases where the barrier to internal rotation is three-fold have now been studied by m.w. methods, use being made of the well worked-out theoretical and computational background.[1,231] Nearly always the findings are expressed as the barrier height V_3, and indeed the evaluation of the much smaller next term, V_6, in the Fourier expansion of the torsional potential function is only possible in the simplest and best studied cases, such as acetaldehyde,[230] and then not without the use of a large array of data for more than one torsional vibrational state. Cases where molecules contain two or more equivalent three-fold tops are also now dealt with in similar ways in numerous examples. Findings for many V_3 barrier heights are summarized in standard works and in various reviews.[229,231] Data are being added and refined for many molecules each year. While many V_3 values fall into line with expectations based on data for similar molecules, large variations can occur, as is not unexpected in parameters determined by subtle balance among non-bonded forces. Sometimes, as with substituted propenes,[232] qualitative reasons for variations in V_3 with non-bonded effects of substituents are apparent, but prediction of variations in V_3 often remains a highly empirical process. Some recently measured barriers to XY_3 rotation include thioacetaldehyde,[91] CH_3CHS, (1572(30) cal mol^{-1}, i.e. 6.58(0.13) kJ mol^{-1}) and thioacetone,[233] $CH_3 \cdot CS \cdot CH_3$, (1300(50) cal mol^{-1}, i.e. 5.44(0.21) kJ mol^{-1}); in both cases the barriers are higher than in the oxygen analogues. In peroxyacetic acid,[234] $CH_3 \cdot CO \cdot OOH$, in which there is a hydrogen bond between the peroxide hydrogen atom and the carbonyl oxygen atom, the barrier to methyl rotation is very low (219(1.3) cal mol^{-1}, i.e. 916(5.4) J mol^{-1}). This distinguishes it from other molecules of the series $CH_3CO \cdot X$ which have barriers of at least 480 cal mol^{-1} (2.01 kJ mol^{-1}) and usually much more, apart from methyl acetate (X − OCH_3) where the acetyl methyl barrier is only 285(1) cal mol^{-1} (1.19 kJ mol^{-1}).[235] The reasons why exceptionally low barriers occur in the isoelectronic molecules $CH_3CO \cdot OOH$ and $CH_3CO \cdot OCH_3$ are not clear. There has been an increase recently in the number of barriers known in derivatives of germane. For methyl germane a V_3 value of 1240 cal mol^{-1} (5.19 kJ mol^{-1}) has been known for some time.[1] In CH_2FGeH_3[236] the barrier is somewhat higher (1390(40) cal mol^{-1}, i.e. 5.82(0.17) kJ mol^{-1}), but in CF_3GeH_3[237] the barrier (1280(150) cal mol^{-1}, i.e. 5.36(0.63) kJ mol^{-1}) is essentially the same as in the parent molecule. In CH_2ClGeH_3,[238] the barrier is distinctly higher (1740(30) cal mol^{-1}, i.e. 7.28(0.13) kJ mol^{-1}) than in methyl germane. In contrast, when a fluorine is substituted in the GeH_3 group, the barrier is lowered, being 941(20) cal mol^{-1} (3.94(0.08) kJ mol^{-1}) for CH_3GeH_2F.[239,240] This situation resembles that found earlier in derivatives of methyl silane. The behaviour of the higher barriers in substituted ethanes is somewhat different; for successive Cl or Br substitution on the same carbon, the barriers increase in height but, for fluorine substitution, CH_3CH_2F has the highest barrier.[241] Internal rotation barriers for methyl groups attached to planar five-membered rings also show a wide range of variation.[113] In methyl furans the V_3 values are near 1100 cal mol^{-1} (4.60 kJ mol^{-1}), in methyl thiophens not much more than half that figure. Recent determinations include barriers in the methyl isoxazoles (3-methyl, 961(2) cal mol^{-1} (4.02(0.01) kJ mol^{-1});[242] 4-methyl, 715(2) cal mol^{-1} (2.99(0.01) kJ mol^{-1});[242] and 5-methyl, 783(2) cal mol^{-1} (3.27(0.01) kJ mol^{-1})[242,243]) and methyl pyrazoles[244] (3-methyl, 429(2) cal mol^{-1} (1.79(0.01) kJ mol^{-1}), 5-methyl, 333(2) cal mol^{-1} (1.39(0.01) kJ mol^{-1}). The lower barriers seem correlated with higher degrees of aromatic character in the rings, which is not in disagreement with the requirement that V_3 be zero in toluene on symmetry grounds.

Work has continued on the measurement of the very low six-fold barriers in molecules such as CH_3NO_2,[245] or phenyl silane.[246,247] Because such barriers are low, torsional effects for quite heavy internal tops show in the spectral frequencies and the appropriate theory has been worked out[248] and applied to SiF_3BV_2[249] ($V_6 = 1.9(8)$ cal mol^{-1}, i.e. 7.9(3.3) J mol^{-1}) and benzotrifluoride $C_6H_5 \cdot CF_3$[250] ($V_6 = 10.2(3)$ cal mol^{-1}, i.e. 42.6(12) J mol^{-1}). There are also, of course, important cases in which V_3 terms are added to V_6 by substituents in toluene or other methyl derivatives of aromatic systems, o-fluorotoluene being an example recently studied in great detail.[251]

Less common cases show two equivalent equilibrium geometries per torsional revolution, examples including phenol,[252] ($V_2 = 3450$ cal mol^{-1}, i.e. 14.43 kJ mol^{-1}), and molecules with rotatable NO_2 groups or BF_2 groups, such as vinyl difluoroborane $CH_2{=}CH{-}BF_2$[253] ($V_2 = 4420$ cal mol^{-1}, i.e. 18.49 kJ mol^{-1}).

A number of examples naturally contain more than one structurally distinct possibility of large amplitude motion between equivalent geometries. Several molecules with structurally distinguishable XY_3 groups have been studied, notably N-methylethylidenimine $CH_3CH{=}NCH_3$[254] and silyl methyl ether, SiH_3OCH_3.[255] The computational methods for such cases, allowing both barrier heights to be evaluated, have been developed.[256] Examples are easily found for future study. In other instances, an internal top is combined with an inverting group, as in methylamine. The effects of large amplitude motions in the partially deuterated form $CH_2D \cdot NH_2$ have been described in detail.[257,258] In t-butyl mercaptan, $(CH_3)_3CSH$,[140] the methyl torsions are less interesting than the tunnelling of the SH proton among its three equivalent energy minima, the barrier (V_3) to torsion about the CS bond being 1742 cal mol^{-1} (7.29 kJ mol^{-1}).

There has been much work in recent years on the interaction of large amplitude motions, particularly internal rotation, with other vibrations in the molecule. Typical cases are found in methyl thiocyanate,[259] CH_3SCN, and ethyl cyanide[260] and a number of theoretical studies have been made.[261-264] Such papers indicate factors limiting the significance of the details of much current work on barriers, where simplified molecular models have of necessity to be used.

4.3.2.2 MOLECULES WITH MORE THAN ONE STRUCTURALLY DISTINCT EQUILIBRIUM CONFORMATION

Numerous studies are now made of substances which exhibit geometric or rotational isomerism. Each isomer can be studied as a molecule in its own right, but much interest also attaches to the large amplitude motions by which isomers are interconverted. We can distinguish two main types of circumstance in which these possibilities arise. In one type, two or more asymmetric groups can rotate about the axis (or axes) linking them while, in the other, two or more non-equivalent conformations of ring systems can occur. In some cases, not all the possible geometries have yet been detected and studied, but experience shows that this often temporary situation should be ignored in classifying examples. Naturally, many examples also contain groups such as CH_3 which, while undergoing large amplitude motion, do not add to the number of possible isomers.

4.3.2.2.1 *Molecules formed by joining groups which are asymmetric with respect to internal rotation*

When the groups are both planar, we usually obtain examples of *cis–trans* isomerism such as we have already met in formic acid[97] and monothioformic acid.[94-96] Similar cases of *cis–trans* isomerism also arise when an asymmetric group such as X—C=O is attached to a vinyl group, acrylic acid[265] and vinyl azide[266] being examples. There is also a growing number of examples of *cis–trans* possibilities where a group such as X—C=O, or vinyl, is attached to a planar asymmetric ring as in furfural.

In such cases, the study, through m.w. intensities, of the relative populations of torsionally excited states of the *cis* and *trans* forms, of the relative energies of the rotamers, and of the vibrational dependence of the inertial defects, allows construction of an approximate potential function for the *cis–trans* interconversion.

When some simple planar groups are concerned we do not necessarily obtain the simple two-minima situation of *cis–trans* isomerism, as is clear from the elementary case of hydrogen peroxide. Vinyl alcohol[267] is characterized in a planar *syn* form as is also vinyl mercaptan,[268,269] but in the latter case a second rotamer has a skew conformation and allows the possibility of torsional movement of the SH between two equivalent non-planar geometries. The behaviour of a planar group in respect of forming *cis–trans* isomers thus depends on its electronic structure (see below).

When basically three-fold groups, but with asymmetric substituents, are involved, such as CH_2X, CHX_2, $CXYZ$ etc. we normally expect three energy minima for each internal rotation. If the groups are of the type XYZ_2, two of these minima will be equivalent. Thus we find microwave studies of many cases of *trans–gauche* rotational isomerism where substituted methyl or silyl groups are joined to other asymmetric groups with local symmetry-planes. Basically the same situation arises if the groups contain lone-pairs as well as substituents, for example PF_2, NCl_2 etc. or even OCl, OH, SH etc.; the role of lone-pairs in replacing substituents doubtless enters the case of vinyl mercaptan mentioned above. Among the many examples of *trans–gauche* rotational isomerism studied by m.w. methods we find recent work on ethyl mercaptan,[102,103,270] isopropyl mercaptan,[271] propanal,[272] propionic acid,[100,101,272] isobutyraldehyde,[273] isobutyryl fluoride,[273] ethyl chlorosilane,[274] ethyl fluorosilane,[275] n-propyl isocyanide[276] and many others, although in a good proportion of these other cases only one rotamer has been characterized to date. Derivatives of propene, such as the allyl halides and various fluorinated propenes,[277,278] have received detailed study, as have various further derivatives of acetaldehyde. In some of these, such as fluoracetyl fluoride[279] and chloroacetaldehyde,[280,281] the forms found are not *trans* and *gauche*, respectively, but rather *trans* and *cis* with respect to the relative orientations of the planar group and the symmetry plane of the three-fold group. This again illustrates the delicate balance between the factors deciding the number of energy minima, since the presence of two or three minima per internal rotation depends only on the relative magnitudes of the various Fourier components of the shape of the potential function. In chloracetaldehyde, for example, the two-fold component (V_2) is large enough to compel the *cis–trans* type of isomerism, but it is not surprising to find[281] that the minimum for the *symmetrical–trans* form appears to be broad and probably shows a very weak double-minimum property which is structurally reflected only in refined details of the measurements. A further family of examples where groups of the X—C=O type assume *cis–trans* geometry, rather than *gauche* structures, is met when these groups are attached to three-membered rings.

The object of many investigations has been the detailed elucidation of the form of the potential function for internal rotation between non-equivalent energy minima. The task is difficult and has therefore been limited to cases where there are only two minima, or where two of the three minima are equivalent, at the *gauche* conformations. For fullest information, also, it is necessary to use all possible data from vibrational studies as well as m.w. measurements; the need for non-microwave information may reach extreme proportions if, for example, a rotamer is weakly polar (or perhaps even non-polar) while being an important, if not dominant, species in the equilibrium mixture.[278] The Fourier components of the potential function are built up from information so derived about the curvatures of the function at the various minima and about the relative stabilities of rotamers. Many of these studies have involved long accumulations of exacting measurements and careful interpretation, but have been rewarded by the acquisition of an elusive type of structural information.[272,276–281] The early work of Stiefvater and Wilson[282] on propionyl fluoride, CH_3CH_2COF, remains an excellent illustration of some of the methods.

A feature of certain molecules in which a light group, usually OH or SH, is involved in internal rotation between two equivalent minima is that the energetics of the situation may allow direct observation, as a major contribution to the m.w. quantum, of vibrational transitions in the torsional mode. In accordance with the symmetry of the molecule, rotational transitions due to one dipole component must connect states of opposite parity in the torsional motion between the equivalent minima, in exact parallel with the situation in certain inverting molecules. Thus in the *gauche* forms of ethyl mercaptan,[270] CH_3CH_2SH, hydroxyacetonitrile,[283] and propargyl mercaptan,[284,285] $HCC \cdot CH_2SH$, the rotational μ_c-transitions must connect the vibrationally different states, while in the *gauche* forms of isopropanol,[286] $(CH_3)_2CHOH$, the μ_a-transitions are subject to this restriction. In isopropyl mercaptan,[271] $(CH_3)CHSH$, the different inertial properties here cause the μ_b-transitions to connect torsional states of opposite parity. Each transition of the types listed for these molecules consists of two lines separated in frequency by twice the separation of the two lowest levels of the OH or SH torsion. In the absence of other data, such lines are hard to assign since their separation is unknown and their frequencies differ greatly from those predicted from inertial constants. When assigned, however, often with the aid of double resonance, these transitions yield a precise vibrational-level separation. In hydroxyacetonitrile and propargyl mercaptan, close bands of lines also appear which represent predominantly transitions between torsional levels, with little rotational contribution. A molecule showing similar spectral properties is cyclopropanol,[287]

$$CH_2CH_2CHOH,$$

where much of the spectrum (μ_b-lines) suffers from large torsional splitting. Such direct m.w.-determinations of torsional-energy changes can clearly be of value in the derivation of the potential functions for the internal rotation.

Cases are not uncommon where, although rotational–vibrational transitions of the type just discussed may not fall in the m.w. range, certain energy levels of the same J in different low lying vibrational states are close to each other and become strongly perturbed by rotation–vibrational interaction. The frequencies of transitions involving such levels are then significantly different from those expected on a rigid-rotor model, and also the selection rules for such transitions may become changed. Early examples are found in work on molecules with ring flexing vibrations,[228] and such perturbations are present in spectra of molecules mentioned in the last paragraph. The analysis of these effects is another useful contribution to knowledge of the potential functions.

Molecules in which there is more than one bond about which rotational isomerism can be generated have been the subject of many studies. There are, in general, several possible configurations. Where the spectra are analysed successfully, there is usually a strong preference for one or two of these configurations. Sometimes the reasons for this seem apparent from a feature of the preferred geometry, such as some degree of hydrogen bonding between parts of the structure, examples of this being met in 3-butyn-l-ol,[288] $HOCH_2CH_2C\equiv CH$, and earlier work on halogenated ethanols, $HO \cdot CH_2 \cdot CH_2X$. Allyl amine[166,167] already mentioned, is a case where several rotameric forms have proved capable of investigation. Not surprisingly, work on these more complex systems has not normally been extended to a detailed study of the force field.

4.3.2.2.2 *Isomerism in cyclic molecules*

The cause of geometric isomerism in ring structures is, of course, essentially due to the same balance of non-bonded interactions as in the cases considered in the previous section. The methods of securing knowledge of the dynamics of ring systems are basically similar to those outlined for the simpler examples of rotational isomerism through internal rotation.[228] In the area of rings, vibrational spectroscopic studies have played a large role. The following are some main areas in which direct evidence has come from m.w. measurements.

Equilibrium in substituted four-membered rings between axial and equatorial conformations is a simple example of the type of isomerism concerned. The m.w. evidence shows that the equatorial forms are preferred in a number of cases. A specially detailed study has been made of trimethylene sulphoxide,[289]

$$CH_2-CH_2-CH_2-S{=}O,$$

where the $S{=}O$ linkage is equatorial. This paper gives a valuable account of the details of the internal distortion motions of such a ring, as well as the accurate location of all the atoms, which reflects various tilting and twisting effects in the CH_2 groups.

Most m.w. studies of molecules with five-membered rings are cases where there is a distinct preference for one of the two classical forms of these rings, the 'envelope' (or bent) form and the 'half-chair' (or twisted) form, although some five-membered rings without aromatic character are found to be planar, for example 2-oxazoline,[290]

$$CH_2-CH_2-N{=}CH-O.$$

In other cases when there is one endocyclic double bond, there is a not unexpected preference for the envelope form in which the doubly bonded atoms tend to act as if rigidly joined. Many saturated five-membered rings are found to have the half-chair form and their preference for particular atoms defining the C_2 axis is indicated by various barriers opposing pseudorotation. Thus ethylene ozonide,[117,118]

$$CH_2—O—CH_2—O—O,$$

has this configuration with the C_2 axis passing through the ether-like oxygen atom (atom 4); pseudorotation, which is relatively easy in some analogues with fewer oxygen atoms in the ring, is impeded by a barrier of about 1500 cal mol^{-1} (6.28 kJ mol^{-1}). Similar restriction of pseudorotation occurs in several related structures such as those in which one CH_2 in cyclopentane is replaced by CO, S, Se, SiH_2 or GeH_2[113,291–293] where we find again the half-chair C_2-configurations have lowest energy. A useful summary of many of the findings regarding potential functions for four- and five-membered rings will be found in the review by Gwinn and Gaylord.[228]

In non-aromatic six-membered rings, m.w. studies are largely conformational rather than dealing with detailed energetics of interconversion of different geometries. In saturated rings of this type, the chair-configuration is most commonly found to be dominant, and the m.w. evidence is not always simply confined to the moments of inertia. Thus in thiane,[294]

$$S—(CH_2)_4—CH_2$$

the confirmatory evidence of the dipole moment components was valuable. When there is one double bond within such rings, there is a not unexpected resemblance to certain five-membered rings, twisted (or half-chair) conformations often being preferred. In 1,2,3,6-tetrahydropyridine,

$$HN—CH_2—CH_2—CH_2—CH=CH,$$

for example,[295] this form is adopted, with two isomers showing respectively axial and equatorial N—H bonds; the equatorial form is some 150 cal mol^{-1} (628 J mol^{-1}) more stable than the axial arrangement. With the inversion from equatorial to axial geometry, the nuclear coupling tensor of ^{14}N and the dipole moment reorient dramatically in the expected ways.

There is much work on more complex ring systems, mostly on fused-ring structures. Usually conformations, and in favourable cases accurate structures, are the main findings rather than the effects of large amplitude motions, not least because the fused rings are often locked in rigid geometry. Sometimes, however, the joining of rings constrains them to adopt a form in which large-amplitude motion is encouraged. A well known case is the cage-type of structure exemplified in quinuclidine (1-azabicyclo[2.2.2.]octane), $N(CH_2CH_2)_3CH.$[296] The symmetric fusion of the piperidine rings at the common groups N and CH constrains these rings to adopt the boat form, and a balance between ring-strain and the tendency of the methylene groups to twist out of the eclipse geometry leads to a large amplitude motion with a very weak double-minimum property. A more complicated case is bullvalene,[297] the $(CH)_{10}$ hydrocarbon in which three cycloheptatriene rings are similarly formed into a cage with a cyclopropane ring as base and a CH group at the apex. The internal movements of atoms in this structure are related to rearrangements involving 'fluxional' carbon–carbon bonds.

5   CONCLUSION

Reviewers in chemistry or chemical physics have reached the point where it is impossible to follow any but a highly subjective course between the numerous original publications and the complete but uncritical records of literature such as *Chemical Titles*. Hence here, several large areas of the subject have been deliberately omitted in concentrating on aspects which most fit the general purpose. Even within the aspects retained, however, we see that increasingly powerful means of unravelling molecular detail are always coming to hand, and that what has become known is little compared with new findings and refinements which will pass within the scope of m.w. spectroscopy. In this review an attempt has been made to convey something of the present balance of m.w. activity in the study of structures of free molecules, but also to show that this activity is now inevitably related to, and co-operative with, work which involves other techniques.

REFERENCES

(1) W. Gordy and R. L. Cook, in *Technique of Organic Chemistry*, Vol. 9 (A. Weissberger, ed.), 2nd edn, Wiley-Interscience, New York, 1970.
(2) J. E. Wollrab, *Rotational Spectra and Molecular Structure*, Academic Press, New York, 1970.
(3) H. W. Kroto, *Molecular Rotation Spectra*, Wiley, London, 1975.
(4) A. C. Legon and D. J. Millen, in *Specialist Periodical Reports, Molecular Spectroscopy*, The Chemical Society, London: Vol. 1, 1973, p. 1; Vol. 2, 1974, p. 1; Vol. 3, 1975, p. 1.
(5) J. N. Macdonald and J. Sheridan, in *Specialist Periodical Reports, Molecular Spectroscopy*, The Chemical Society, London, Vol. 4, 1976, p. 1; Vol. 5, 1977, p. 1.
(6) A. Carrington, *Microwave Spectroscopy of Free Radicals*, Academic Press, New York, 1974.
(7) D. C. Lainé, *Adv. Electron. Electron Phys.* **39**, 183 (1975).
(8) A. Dymanus, in *M.T.P. International Review of Science, Physical Chemistry*, Series 2, Vol. 3 (A. D. Buckingham, ed.), Butterworth, London, 1975, p. 127
(9) H. Walther, ed., *Laser Spectroscopy of Atoms and Molecules*, Vol. 2, Springer, Berlin, 1975.
(10) H. W. Harrington, J. R. Hearn and R. F. Rauskolb, *Hewlett-Packard Journal*, **22**, 2 (1971).

(11) F. C. De Lucia, in *Molecular Spectroscopy: Modern Research*, Vol. 2 (K. N. Rao, ed.), Academic Press, New York, 1976, p. 69.

(12) A. F. Krupnov and A. V. Burenin, in *Molecular Spectroscopy: Modern Research*, Vol. 2 (K. N. Rao, ed.), Academic Press, New York, 1976, p. 93.

(13) H. W. Harrington, *J. Chem. Phys.* **46**, 3698 (1967); **49**, 3023 (1968).

(14) J. Sheridan, in *M.T.P. International Review of Science, Physical Chemistry*, Series 1, Vol. 12, *Analytical Chemistry*, Part 1 (T. S. West, ed.), Butterworth, London, 1973, p. 251.

(15) R. Varma and R. F. Curl, *J. Phys. Chem.* **80**, 402 (1976).

(16) W. E. Steinmetz, *J. Am. Chem. Soc.* **96**, 685 (1974).

(17) E. M. Bellott and E. B. Wilson, *J. Mol. Spectrosc.* **66**, 41 (1977).

(18) R. C. Woods and T. A. Dixon, *Rev. Sci. Instrum.* **45**, 1122 (1974).

(19) T. A. Dixon and R. C. Woods, *Phys. Rev. Lett.* **34**, 61 (1975).

(20) R. C. Woods, T. A. Dixon, R. J. Saykally and P. G. Szanto, *Phys. Rev. Lett.* **35**, 1629 (1975).

(21) R. J. Saykally, T. A. Dixon, T. G. Anderson, P. G. Szanto and R. C. Woods, *Astrophys. J.* **205**, L101 (1976); Paper TS5, Symposium on Molecular Spectroscopy, Columbus, Ohio, 1976.

(22) C. W. Holt, M. C. L. Gerry and I. Ozier, *Can. J. Phys.* **53**, 1791 (1975).

(23) E. Hirota, K. Matsumura, M. Imachi, M. Fujio, Y. Tsuno and C. Matsumura, *J. Chem. Phys.* **66**, 2660 (1977).

(24) H. Uehara and Y. Ijuuin, *Chem. Phys. Lett.* **28**, 597 (1974).

(25) T. Törring, *J. Mol. Spectrosc.* **48**, 148 (1973).

(26) T. Oka, *J. Chem. Phys.* **45**, 752 (1966).

(27) O. L. Stiefvater, *J. Chem. Phys.* **63**, 2560 (1975).

(28) O. L. Stiefvater, *Z. Naturforsch.* **30a**, 1742 (1975).

(29) O. L. Stiefvater, *Z. Naturforsch.* **30a**, 1756 (1975).

(30) J. Ekkers, A. Bauder and H. H. Günthard, *J. Phys. E* **8**, 819, (1975).

(31) M. Bogey, A. Bauer and S. Maes, *Chem. Phys. Lett.* **24**, 1 (1974).

(32) M. Bogey, *J. Phys. B* **8**, 1934 (1975).

(33) M. Fourrier and M. Redon, *J. Appl. Phys.* **45**, 1910 (1974).

(34) M. Takami and K. Shimoda, *Jpn J. Appl. Phys.* **13**, 1699 (1974).

(35) H. Jones and F. Kohler, *J. Mol. Spectrosc.* **58**, 125 (1975).

(36) H. Jones, F. Kohler and H. D. Rudolph, *J. Mol. Spectrosc.* **63**, 205 (1976).

(37) H. Jones, *Appl. Phys.* **14**, 169 (1977).

(38) K. Shimoda, in *Laser Spectroscopy* (R. G. Brewer and A. Mooradian, eds.), Plenum, New York, 1975.

(39) M. Takami, *Jpn J. Appl. Phys.* **15**, 1063, 1889 (1976).

(40) D. O. Harris, R. W. Field and H. P. Broida, *Ber. Bunsenges. Phys. Chem.* **78**, 146 (1974).

(41) T. Tanaka and D. O. Harris, *J. Mol. Spectrosc.* **59**, 413 (1976).

(42) D. H. Sutter and W. H. Flygare, *Topics Current Chem., Bonding and Structure* **63**, 89 (1976).

(43) J. Ekkers and W. H. Flygare, *Rev. Sci. Instrum.* **47**, 448 (1976).

(44) J. Burie, D. Boucher, J. Demaison and A. Dubrulle, *Mol. Phys.* **32**, 289 (1976).

(45) G. R. Tomasevitch, K. D. Tucker and P. Thaddeus, *J. Chem. Phys.* **59**, 131 (1973).

(46) R. M. Garvey and F. C. De Lucia, *Can. J. Phys.* **55**, 1115 (1977).

(47) S. G. Kukolich, *J. Chem. Phys.* **66**, 4345 (1977).

(48) M. Suzuki, A. Guarnieri and H. Dreizler, *Z. Naturforsch.* **31a**, 1181 (1976).

(49) R. M. Somers, T. O. Poehler and P. E. Wagner, *Rev. Sci. Instrum.* **46**, 719 (1975).

(50) A. B. Delfino and K. R. Ramaprasad, *J. Mol. Struct.* **25**, 293 (1975).

(51) G. L. Blackman, K. Bolton, R. D. Brown, F. R. Burden and A. Mishra, *J. Mol. Spectrosc.* **47**, 57 (1973).

(52) R. C. Woods, *J. Mol. Spectrosc.* **21**, 4 (1966).
(53) R. C. Woods, *J. Mol. Spectrosc.* **22**, 49 (1967).
(54) D. Coffey, C. O. Britt and J. E. Boggs, *J. Chem. Phys.* **49**, 591 (1968).
(55) E. Tiemann, Ch. Ryzlewicz and T. Törring, *Z. Naturforsch.* **31a**, 128 (1976).
(56) W. U. Stieda, E. Tiemann, T. Törring and J. Hoeft, *Z. Naturforsch.* **31a**, 374 (1976).
(57) E. Tiemann, W. U. Stieda, T. Törring and J. Hoeft, *Z. Naturforsch.* **30a**, 1606 (1975).
(58) P. Kuijpers, T. Törring and A. Dymanus, *Chem. Phys.* **12**, 401 (1976).
(59) P. Kuijpers and A. Dymanus, *Chem. Phys. Lett.* **39**, 217 (1976).
(60) P. Kuijpers, T. Törring and A. Dymanus, *Chem. Phys.* **12**, 309 (1976).
(61) E. L. Manson, F. C. De Lucia and W. Gordy, *J. Chem. Phys.* **62**, 1040 (1975).
(62) E. L. Manson, F. C. De Lucia and W. Gordy, *J. Chem. Phys.* **62**, 4796 (1975).
(63) E. L. Manson, F. C. De Lucia and W. Gordy, *J. Chem. Phys.* **63**, 2724 (1975).
(64) M. Otake, C. Matsumura and Y. Morino, *J. Mol. Spectrosc.* **28**, 316 (1968).
(65) G. Cazzoli, P. G. Favero and C. Degli Esposti, *Chem. Phys. Lett.* **50**, 336 (1978).
(66) G. Cazzoli, C. Degli Esposti and P. G. Favero, to be published.
(67) D. R. Lide, in *M.T.P. International Review of Science, Physical Chemistry*, Series 2, Vol. 2 (A. D. Buckingham, ed.), Butterworth, London, 1975, p. 1.
(68) R. D. Brown, F. R. Burden, P. D. Godfrey and I. R. Gillard, *J. Mol. Spectrosc.* **52**, 301 (1974).
(69) J. K. G. Watson, *J. Mol. Spectrosc.* **48**, 479 (1973).
(70) P. Nösberger, A. Bauder and H. H. Günthard, *Chem. Phys.* **1**, 418 (1973).
(71) R. A. Creswell, E. F. Pearson, M. Winnewisser and G. Winnewisser, *Z. Naturforsch.* **31a**, 221 (1976).
(72) E. F. Pearson, R. A. Creswell, M. Winnewisser and G. Winnewisser, *Z. Naturforsh.* **31a**, 1394 (1976).
(73) S. E. Novick, P. Davies, S. J. Harris and W. Klemperer, *J. Chem. Phys.* **59**, 2273 (1973).
(74) S. E. Novick, K. C. Janda, S. L. Holmgren, M. Waldman and W. Klemperer, *J. Chem. Phys.* **65**, 1114 (1976).
(75) S. J. Harris, S. E. Novick and W. Klemperer, *J. Chem. Phys.* **60**, 3208 (1974).
(76) S. J. Harris, S. E. Novick, W. Klemperer and W. E. Falconer, *J. Chem. Phys.* **61**, 193 (1974).
(77) S. E. Novick, S. J. Harris, K. C. Janda and W. Klemperer, *Can. J. Phys.* **53**, 2007 (1975).
(78) S. J. Harris, K. C. Janda, S. E. Novick and W. Klemperer, *J. Chem. Phys.* **63**, 881 (1975).
(79) S. E. Novick, K. C. Janda and W. Klemperer, *J. Chem. Phys.* **65**, 5115 (1976).
(80) A. C. Legon, D. J. Millen and S. C. Rogers, *Chem. Phys. Lett.* **41**, 137 (1976).
(81) J. W. Bevan, A. C. Legon, D. J. Millen and S. C. Rogers, *J. Chem. Soc., Chem. Commun.* 341 (1975).
(82) T. R. Dyke, K. M. Mack and J. S. Muenter, *J. Chem. Phys.* **66**, 498 (1977).
(83) T. R. Dyke, *J. Chem. Phys.* **66**, 492 (1977).
(84) Y. Beers and C. J. Howard, *J. Chem. Phys.* **63**, 4212 (1975); **64**, 1541 (1976).
(85) S. Saito, *J. Mol. Spectrosc.* **65**, 229 (1977).
(86) J. M. Cook, K. M. Evenson, C. J. Howard and R. F. Curl, *J. Chem. Phys.* **64**, 1381 (1976).
(87) B. J. Boland, J. M. Brown and A. Carrington, *Mol. Phys.* **34**, 453 (1977).
(88) T. Tanaka, R. W. Field and D. O. Harris, *J. Mol. Spectrosc.* **56**, 188 (1975).
(89) E. Tiemann, J. Hoeft, F. J. Lovas and D. R. Johnson, *J. Chem. Phys.* **60**, 5000 (1974).
(90) H. Takeo and C. Matsumura, *J. Chem. Phys.* **64**, 4536 (1976).
(91) H. W. Kroto and B. M. Landsberg, *J. Mol. Spectrosc.* **62**, 21 (1976).

(92) R. E. Penn and R. J. Olsen, *J. Mol. Spectrosc.* **61**, 21 (1976).
(93) R. Pearson and F. J. Lovas, *J. Chem. Phys.* **66**, 4149 (1977).
(94) W. H. Hocking and G. Winnewisser, *Z. Naturforsch.* **31a**, 422 (1976).
(95) W. H. Hocking and G. Winnewisser, *Z. Naturforsch.* **31a**, 438 (1976).
(96) W. H. Hocking and G. Winnewisser, *Z. Naturforsch.* **31a**, 995 (1976).
(97) W. H. Hocking, *Z. Naturforsch.* **31a**, 1113 (1976).
(98) S. Vaccani, V. Roos, A. Bauder and H. H. Günthard, *Chem. Phys.* **19**, 51 (1977).
(99) C. E. Dyllick-Brenzinger, A. Bauder and H. H. Günthard, *Chem. Phys.* **23**, 195 (1977).
(100) O. L. Stiefvater, *J. Chem. Phys.* **62**, 233 (1975).
(101) O. L. Stiefvater, *J. Chem. Phys.* **62**, 244 (1975).
(102) M. Hayashi, H. Imaishi and K. Kuwada, *Bull. Chem. Soc. Jpn* **47**, 2382 (1974).
(103) J. Nakagawa, K. Kuwada and M. Hayashi, *Bull. Chem. Soc. Jpn* **49**, 3420 (1976).
(104) M. Hayashi and K. Kuwada, *Bull. Chem. Soc. Jpn* **47**, 3006 (1974).
(105) R. Pearson, A. Choplin and V. W. Laurie, *J. Chem. Phys.* **62**, 4859 (1975).
(106) R. Pearson, A. Choplin, V. W. Laurie and J. Schwartz, *J. Chem. Phys.* **62**, 2949 (1975).
(107) A. T. Perretta and V. W. Laurie, *J. Chem. Phys.* **62**, 2469 (1975).
(108) R. E. Penn and J. E. Boggs, *J. Chem. Soc., Chem. Commun.* 666 (1972).
(109) C. W. Gillies, *J. Mol. Spectrosc.* **59**, 482 (1976).
(110) W. M. Stigliani, V. W. Laurie and J. C. Li, *J. Chem. Phys.* **62**, 1890 (1975).
(111) K. R. Ramaprasad and V. W. Laurie, *J. Chem. Phys.* **64**, 4832 (1976).
(112) K. Karakida and K. Kuchitsu, *Bull. Chem. Soc. Jpn* **48**, 1691 (1975).
(113) J. Sheridan, in *Physical Methods in Heterocyclic Chemistry*, Vol. 6 (A. R. Katritzky, ed.), Academic Press, New York, 1974, p. 53.
(114) O. L. Stiefvater, *Chem. Phys.* **13**, 73 (1976).
(115) O. L. Stiefvater, *Z. Naturforsch.* **31a**, 1681 (1976).
(116) D. Damiani, L. Ferretti and E. Gallinella, *Chem. Phys. Lett.* **37**, 265 (1976).
(117) R. L. Kuczkowski, C. W. Gillies and K. L. Gallaher, *J. Mol. Spectrosc.* **60**, 361 (1976).
(118) U. Mazur and R. L. Kuczkowski, *J. Mol. Spectrosc.* **65**, 84 (1977).
(119) R. P. Lattimer, U. Mazur and R. L. Kuczkowski, *J. Am. Chem. Soc.* **98**, 4012 (1976).
(120) O. L. Stiefvater, S. Lui and J. A. Ladd, *Z. Naturforsch.* **31a**, 53 (1976); **30a**, 1765 (1975).
(121) D. G. Lister, J. K. Tyler, J. H. Høg and N. W. Larsen, *J. Mol. Struct.* **23**, 253 (1974).
(122) R. D. Suenram, *J. Am. Chem. Soc.* **97**, 4869 (1975).
(123) P. D. Mallinson, *J. Mol. Spectrosc.* **55**, 94 (1975); **68**, 68 (1977).
(124) W. W. Clark and F. C. De Lucia, *J. Mol. Struct.* **32**, 29 (1976).
(125) A. G. Robiette, C. Georghiou and J. G. Baker, *J. Mol. Spectrosc.* **63**, 391 (1976).
(126) F. Y. Chu and T. Oka, *J. Chem. Phys.* **60**, 4612 (1974).
(127) D. A. Helms and W. Gordy, *J. Mol. Spectrosc.* **66**, 206 (1977).
(128) R. H. Kagann, I. Ozier and M. C. L. Gerry, *Chem. Phys. Lett.* **47**, 572 (1977).
(129) J. Pasinski, S. A. McMahon and R. A. Beaudet, *J. Mol. Spectrosc.* **55**, 88 (1975).
(130) J. R. Durig, L. W. Hall, R. O. Carter, C. J. Wainey, V. F. Kalasinsky and J. D. Odum, *J. Phys. Chem.* **80**, 1188 (1976).
(131) S. Tsuchiya, *J. Mol. Struct.* **22**, 77 (1974).
(132) L. S. Bartell, F. B. Clippard and E. J. Jacob, *Inorg. Chem.* **15**, 3009 (1976).
(133) C. J. Marsden and L. S. Bartell, *Inorg. Chem.* **15**, 3004 (1976).
(134) H. Jones, J. Sheridan and O. L. Stiefvater, *Z. Naturforsch.* **32a**, 866 (1977).
(135) R. H. Turner and A. P. Cox, *Chem. Phys. Lett.* **39**, 585 (1976).
(136) D. W. T. Griffith and J. E. Kent, *Chem. Phys. Lett.* **25**, 290 (1974).

(137) E. Hirota and C. Matsumura, *J. Chem. Phys.* **55**, 981 (1971).
(138) E. Hirota and M. Imachi, *Can. J. Phys.* **53**, 2023 (1975).
(139) A. M. Mirri, F. Scappini and H. Mäder, *J. Mol. Spectrosc.* **57**, 264 (1975).
(140) E. A. Valenzuela and R. C. Woods, *J. Chem. Phys.* **61**, 4119 (1974).
(141) T. Tanaka, C. Yamada and E. Hirota, *J. Mol. Spectrosc.* **63**, 142 (1976).
(142) W. H. Flygare, in *Critical Evaluation of Chemical and Physical Structural Information* (D. R. Lide and M. A. Paul, eds), National Academy of Sciences, Washington, D.C., 1974, p. 449.
(143) W. H. Flygare, *Chem. Rev.* **74**, 653 (1974).
(144) B. Bak, E. Hamer, D. H. Sutter and H. Dreizler, *Z. Naturforsch.* **27a**, 705 (1972).
(145) E. Hamer and D. H. Sutter, *Z. Naturforsch.* **31a**, 265 (1976).
(146) J. McGurk, C. L. Norris, H. L. Tigelaar and W. H. Flygare, *J. Chem. Phys.* **58**, 3118 (1973).
(147) B. Fabricant and J. S. Muenter, *J. Chem. Phys.* **66**, 5274 (1977).
(148) L. Englebrecht and D. H. Sutter, *Z. Naturforsch.* **30a**, 1265 (1975).
(149) E. F. Pearson, C. L. Norris and W. H. Flygare, *J. Chem. Phys.* **60**, 1761 (1974).
(150) W. Czieslik and D. H. Sutter, *Z. Naturforsch.* **29a**, 1820 (1974).
(151) K. P. R. Nair, E. Tiemann and J. Hoeft, *Z. Naturforsch.* **32a**, 1053 (1977).
(152) J. Hoeft, F. J. Lovas, E. Tiemann and T. Törring, *Z. Naturforsch.* **25a**, 35 (1970).
(153) P. Kuijpers and A. Dymanus, *Chem. Phys.* **24**, 97 (1977).
(154) K. H. Casleton and S. G. Kukolich, *J. Chem. Phys.* **62**, 2696 (1975).
(155) P. Thaddeus and B. E. Turner, *Astrophys. J.* **201**, L25 (1975).
(156) L. E. Snyder, J. M. Hollis and D. Buhl, *Astrophys. J.* **215**, L87 (1977).
(157) S. G. Kukolich, *Mol. Phys.* **29**, 249 (1975).
(158) L. Nygaard, D. Christen, J. T. Nielsen, E. J. Pedersen, O. Snerling, E. Vestergaard and G. O. Sørensen, *J. Mol. Struct.* **22**, 401 (1974).
(159) G. L. Blackman, R. D. Brown, F. R. Burden and A. Mishra, *J. Mol. Spectrosc.* **57**, 294 (1975).
(160) G. L. Blackman, R. D. Brown, F. R. Burden and W. Garland, *J. Mol. Spectrosc.* **65**, 313 (1977).
(161) J. H. Carpenter, D. F. Rimmer, J. G. Smith and D. H. Whiffen, *J. Chem. Soc. Faraday Trans.* 2, **71**, 1752 (1975).
(162) D. Chadwick and D. J. Millen, *Trans. Faraday Soc.* **67**, 1539, 1551 (1971).
(163) P. J. Mjoberg, W. M. Ralowski and S. O. Ljunggren, *Z. Naturforsch.* **30a**, 541 (1975).
(164) W. Caminati and P. Forti, *Chem. Phys. Lett.* **15**, 343 (1972).
(165) W. Caminati and P. Forti, *Chem. Phys. Lett.* **29**, 239 (1974).
(166) I. Botskor, H. D. Rudolph and G. Roussy, *J. Mol. Spectrosc.* **52**, 457 (1974).
(167) I. Botskor, H. D. Rudolph and G. Roussy, *J. Mol. Spectrosc.* **53**, 15 (1974).
(168) E. Tiemann and T. Möller, *Z. Naturforsch.* **30a**, 986 (1975).
(169) E. Tiemann, U. Kohler and J. Hoeft, *Z. Naturforsch.* **32a**, 6 (1977).
(170) E. Tiemann, B. Hölzer and J. Hoeft, *Z. Naturforsch.* **32a**, 123 (1977).
(171) J. Demaison, A. Dubrulle, D. Boucher and J. Burie, *J. Chem. Phys.* **67**, 254 (1977).
(172) J. A. Austin, D. H. Levy, C. A. Gottlieb and H. E. Radford, *J. Chem. Phys.* **60**, 207 (1974).
(173) K. H. Casleton, T. D. Gierke, J. H.-S. Wang and S. G. Kukolich, *J. Chem. Phys.* **64**, 471 (1976).
(174) J. K. G. Watson, *J. Chem. Phys.* **46**, 1935 (1967); **48**, 181 (1968), **48**, 4517 (1968).
(175) J. Demaison, *J. Mol. Struct.* **31**, 233 (1976).
(176) K. Yamada and M. Winnewisser, *Z. Naturforsch.* **31a**, 131 (1976).
(177) M. R. Aliev and J. K. G. Watson, *J. Mol. Spectrosc.* **61**, 29 (1976).
(178) W. H. Hocking, M. C. L. Gerry and G. Winnewisser, *Can. J. Phys.* **53**, 1869 (1975).

(179) I. Ozier, *J. Mol. Spectrosc.* **53**, 336 (1974).
(180) I. Ozier, A. Rosenberg and D. B. Litvin, *J. Mol. Spectrosc.* **58**, 39 (1975).
(181) M. R. Aliev and V. M. Mikhailov, *Opt. Spektrosk.* **35**, 251 (1973).
(182) W. A. Kreiner and T. Oka, *Can. J. Phys.* **53**, 2000 (1975).
(183) I. Ozier, R. M. Lees and M. C. L. Gerry, *Can. J. Phys.* **54**, 1094 (1976).
(184) W. A. Kreiner, U. Andresen and T. Oka, *J. Chem. Phys.* **66**, 4662 (1977).
(185) W. H. Kirchhoff, in *Critical Evaluation of Chemical and Physical Structural Information* (D. R. Lide and M. A. Paul, eds), National Academy of Sciences, Washington, D.C., 1974, p. 312.
(186) R. L. Cook, F. C. De Lucia and P. Helminger, *J. Mol. Spectrosc.* **53**, 62 (1974).
(187) R. L. Cook, F. C. De Lucia and P. Helminger, *J. Mol. Struct.* **28**, 237 (1975).
(188) M. Y. Chan and P. M. Parker, *J. Mol. Spectrosc.* **65**, 190 (1977).
(189) D. H. Whiffen, *Mol. Phys.* **31**, 989 (1976).
(190) W. J. Lafferty, R. D. Suenram and D. R. Johnson, *J. Mol. Spectrosc.* **64**, 147 (1977).
(191) J. G. Smith, *J. Chem. Soc., Faraday Trans.* 2 **72**, 2298 (1976).
(192) B. A. Andreev, A. V. Burenin, E. N. Karyakin, A. F. Krupnov and S. M. Shapin, *J. Mol. Spectrosc.* **62**, 125 (1976).
(193) A. Bauer and M. Godon, *Can. J. Phys.* **53**, 1154 (1975).
(194) A. Bauer, G. Tarrago and A. Remy, *J. Mol. Spectrosc.* **58**, 111 (1975).
(195) A. Bauer, M. Godon and S. Maes, *J. Mol. Spectrosc.* **59**, 421 (1976).
(196) J. G. Smith, *Mol. Phys.* **32**, 621 (1976).
(197) J. G. Smith and I. Thompson, *Mol. Phys.* **32**, 1247 (1976).
(198) Y. Kawashima and A. P. Cox, *J. Mol. Spectrosc.* **61**, 435 (1976).
(199) C. Georghiou, J. G. Baker and S. R. Jones, *J. Mol. Spectrosc.* **63**, 89 (1976).
(200) P. N. Brier, S. R. Jones and J. G. Baker, *J. Mol. Spectrosc.* **60**, 18 (1976).
(201) H. Inove, A. Naruse and E. Hirota, *Bull. Chem. Soc. Jpn* **49**, 1260 (1976).
(202) E. Hirota and M. Sahara, *J. Mol. Spectrosc.* **56**, 21 (1975).
(203) N. Yoshimizu, C. Hirose and S. Maeda, *Bull. Chem. Soc. Jpn* **48**, 3529 (1975).
(204) C. Hirose, K. Okiye and S. Maeda, *Bull. Chem. Soc. Jpn* **49**, 916 (1976).
(205) B. P. Winnewisser, M. Winnewisser and F. Winther, *J. Mol. Spectrosc.* **51**, 65 (1974).
(206) M. Winnewisser and B. P. Winnewisser, *Z. Naturforsch.* **29a**, 633 (1974).
(207) B. P. Winnewisser and M. Winnewisser, *J. Mol. Spectrosc.* **56**, 471 (1975).
(208) K. Yamada, B. P. Winnewisser and M. Winnewisser, *J. Mol. Spectrosc.* **56**, 449 (1975).
(209) J. A. Duckett, A. G. Robiette and I. M. Mills, *J. Mol. Spectrosc.* **62**, 34 (1976).
(210) A. R. Hoy and P. R. Bunker, *J. Mol. Spectrosc.* **52**, 439 (1974).
(211) J. M. R. Stone, *J. Mol. Spectrosc.* **54**, 1 (1975).
(212) J. A. Duckett, A. G. Robiette and I. M. Mills, *J. Mol. Spectrosc.* **62**, 19 (1976).
(213) K. Yamada and M. Winnewisser, *Z. Naturforsch.* **31a**, 139 (1976).
(214) M. Winnewisser and J. J. Christiansen, *Chem. Phys. Lett.* **37**, 270 (1976).
(215) P. Kuijpers, T. Törring and A. Dymanus, *Chem. Phys.* **15**, 457 (1976).
(216) P. Kuijpers, T. Törring and A. Dymanus, *Chem. Phys. Lett.* **42**, 423 (1976).
(217) V. Špirko, J. M. R. Stone and D. Papousek, *J. Mol. Spectrosc.* **60**, 159 (1976).
(218) D. R. Johnson, R. D. Suenram and W. J. Lafferty, *Astrophys. J.* **208**, 245 (1976).
(219) R. D. Brown, P. D. Godfrey and J. Storey, *J. Mol. Spectrosc.* **58**, 445 (1975).
(220) F. J. Lovas, F. O. Clark and E. Tiemann, *J. Chem. Phys.* **62**, 1925 (1975).
(221) G. Cazzoli, D. Damiani and D. G. Lister, *J. Chem. Soc. Faraday Trans.* 2 **69**, 119 (1973).
(222) D. Christen, D. Norbury, D. G. Lister and P. Palmieri, *J. Chem. Soc., Faraday Trans.* 2 **71**, 438 (1975).
(223) R. A. Kydd and I. M. Mills, *J. Mol. Spectrosc.* **42**, 320 (1972).

(224) D. G. Lister, S. E. Lowe and P. Palmieri, *J. Chem. Soc. Faraday Trans.* 2 **72**, 920 (1976).
(225) R. A. Creswell and I. M. Mills, *J. Mol. Spectrosc.* **52**, 392 (1974).
(226) P. D. Mallinson and A. G. Robiette, *J. Mol. Spectrosc.* **52**, 413 (1974).
(227) V. W. Laurie, *Acc. Chem. Res.* **3**, 331 (1970).
(228) W. D. Gwinn and A. S. Gaylord, in *M.T.P. International Review of Science, Physical Chemistry*, Series 2, Vol. 3 (A. D. Buckingham, ed.), Butterworth, London, 1975, p. 205.
(229) N. L. Owen, in *Internal Rotation in Molecules* (W. J. Orville-Thomas, ed.), Wiley, London, 1974, p. 157.
(230) A. Bauder and H. H. Günthard, *J. Mol. Spectrosc.* **60**, 290 (1976).
(231) H. Dreizler, *Fortschr. Chem. Forsch.* **10**, 59 (1968).
(232) R. A. Beaudet, *J. Chem. Phys.* **40**, 2705 (1964).
(233) H. W. Kroto, B. M. Landsberg, R. J. Suffolk and A. Vodden, *Chem. Phys. Lett.* **29**, 265 (1974).
(234) J. A. Cugley, W. Bossert, A. Bauder and H. H. Günthard, *Chem. Phys.* **16**, 229 (1976).
(235) A. Bauder, W. Bossert and J. Sheridan, to be published.
(236) L. C. Krisher, W. A. Watson and J. A. Morrison, *J. Chem. Phys.* **60**, 3417 (1974).
(237) L. C. Krisher, W. A. Watson and J. A. Morrison, *J. Chem. Phys.* **61**, 3429 (1974).
(238) J. Nakagawa and M. Hayashi, *Bull. Chem. Soc. Jpn* **49**, 3441 (1976).
(239) L. C. Krisher and J. A. Morrison, *J. Chem. Phys.* **64**, 3556 (1976).
(240) R. F. Roberts, R. Varma and J. F. Nelson, *J. Chem. Phys.* **64**, 5035 (1976).
(241) J. R. Durig, W. E. Bucy and C. J. Wurrey, *J. Chem. Phys.* **63**, 5498 (1975).
(242) S. L. Srivastava, C. Walls, J. N. Macdonald and J. Sheridan, to be published.
(243) P. J. Mjöberg, W. M. Ralowski and S. O. Ljunggren, *Z. Naturforsch.* **30a**, 1279 (1975).
(244) S. L. Srivastava and J. Sheridan, to be published.
(245) F. Rohart, *J. Mol. Spectrosc.* **57**, 301 (1975).
(246) W. Caminati, G. Cazzoli and A. M. Mirri, *Chem. Phys. Lett.* **35**, 475 (1975).
(247) W. Caminati and G. Cazzoli, *Chem. Phys. Lett.* **38**, 218 (1976).
(248) T. Ogata, *J. Mol. Spectrosc.* **54**, 275 (1975).
(249) T. Ogata, A. P. Cox, D. L. Smith and P. L. Timms, *Chem. Phys. Lett.* **26**, 186 (1974).
(250) T. Ogata and A. P. Cox, *J. Mol. Spectrosc.* **61**, 265 (1976).
(251) D. Schwoch and H. D. Rudolph, *J. Mol. Spectrosc.* **57**, 47 (1975).
(252) E. Mathier, D. Welti, A. Bauder and H. H. Günthard, *J. Mol. Spectrosc.* **37**, 63 (1971).
(253) J. R. Durig, L. W. Hall, R. O. Carter, C. J. Wurrey, V. F. Kalasinsky and J. D. Odom, *J. Phys. Chem.* **80**, 1188 (1976).
(254) J. Meier, A. Bauder and H. H. Günthard, *J. Chem. Phys.* **57**, 1219 (1972).
(255) C. D. Le Croix, R. F. Curl, P. M. McKinney and R. J. Myers, *J. Mol. Spectrosc.* **53**, 250 (1974).
(256) W. Bossert, Paper E5, Third European Microwave Spectroscopy Conference, Venice, 1974.
(257) K. Tamagake and M. Tsuboi, *J. Mol. Spectrosc.* **53**, 189 (1974).
(258) K. Tamagake and M. Tsuboi, *J. Mol. Spectrosc.* **53**, 204 (1974).
(259) U. Andresen and H. Dreizler, *Z. Naturforsch.* **29a**, 797 (1974).
(260) H. M. Heise, H. Mäder and H. Dreizler, *Z. Naturforsch.* **31a**, 1228 (1976).
(261) B. Kirtman, W. E. Palke and C. S. Ewig, *J. Chem. Phys.* **64**, 1883 (1976).
(262) C. R. Quade, *J. Chem. Phys.* **65**, 700 (1976).
(263) H. Dreizler, in *Molecular Spectroscopy: Modern Research*, Vol. 1 (K. N. Rao and C. W. Mathews, eds), Academic Press, New York, 1972, p. 59.

(264) A. Bauder, R. Meyer and H. H. Günthard, *Mol. Phys.* **28**, 1305 (1974).
(265) K. Bolton, D. G. Lister and J. Sheridan, *J. Chem. Soc., Faraday Trans.* 2 **70**, 113 (1974).
(266) R. G. Ford, *J. Mol. Spectrosc.* **65**, 273 (1977).
(267) S. Saito, *Chem. Phys. Lett.* **42**, 399 (1976).
(268) V. Almond, S. W. Charles, J. N. Macdonald and N. L. Owen, *J. Chem. Soc., Chem. Commun.* 483 (1977).
(269) M. Tanimoto, V. Almond, S. W. Charles, J. N. Macdonald and N. L. Owen, unpublished work.
(270) R. E. Schmidt and C. R. Quade, *J. Chem. Phys.* **62**, 3864 (1975).
(271) J. H. Griffiths and J. E. Boggs, *J. Mol. Spectrosc.* **56**, 257 (1975).
(272) H. M. Pickett and D. G. Scroggin, *J. Chem. Phys.* **61**, 3954 (1974).
(273) O. L. Stiefvater, Paper W.A.2, Sixth Symposium on Gas Phase Molecular Structure, Austin, Texas, 1976.
(274) V. Typke, M. Dakkouri and W. Zeil, *Z. Naturforsch.* **29a**, 1081 (1974).
(275) M. Hayashi, H. Hikino and M. Imachi, *Chem. Lett.* (1976).
(276) M. W. Fuller and E. B. Wilson, *J. Mol. Spectrosc.* **58**, 414 (1975).
(277) I. Botskor and E. Hirota, *J. Mol. Spectrosc.* **61**, 79 (1976).
(278) A. D. English, L. H. Scharpen, K. M. Ewool, H. L. Strauss and D. O. Harris, *J. Mol. Spectrosc.* **60**, 210 (1976).
(279) E. Saegebarth and E. B. Wilson, *J. Chem. Phys.* **46**, 3088 (1967).
(280) R. G. Ford, *J. Chem. Phys.* **65**, 354 (1976).
(281) T. B. Malloy and L. A. Carreira, *J. Chem. Phys.* **66**, 4246 (1977).
(282) O. L. Stiefvater and E. B. Wilson, *J. Chem. Phys.* **50**, 5385 (1969).
(283) G. Cazzoli, D. G. Lister and A. M. Mirri, *J. Chem. Soc., Faraday Trans.* 2 **69**, 569 (1973).
(284) K. Bolton and J. Sheridan, *Spectrochim. Acta, Part A* **26**, 1001 (1970).
(285) A. M. Mirri, F. Scappini, R. Cervellati and P. G. Favero, *J. Mol. Spectrosc.* **63**, 509 (1976).
(286) S. Kondo and E. Hirota, *J. Mol. Spectrosc.* **34**, 97 (1970).
(287) J. N. Macdonald, D. Norbury and J. Sheridan, to be published.
(288) L. B. Szalanski and R. G. Ford, *J. Mol. Spectrosc.* **54**, 148 (1975).
(289) J. W. Bevan, A. C. Legon and D. J. Millen, *Proc. R. Soc. London, Series A* **354**, 491 (1977).
(290) J. R. Durig, S. Riethmiller and Y. S. Li, *J. Chem. Phys.* **61**, 253 (1974).
(291) H. Kim and W. D. Gwinn, *J. Chem. Phys.* **51**, 1815 (1969).
(292) A. H. Mamleev, N. M. Pozdeev and N. N. Magdesieva, *J. Mol. Struct.* **33**, 211 (1976).
(293) J. R. Durig, W. J. Lafferty and V. F. Kalasinsky, *J. Phys. Chem.* **80**, 1199 (1976).
(294) R. W. Kitchin, T. B. Malloy and R. L. Cook, *J. Mol. Spectrosc.* **57**, 179 (1975).
(295) S. Chao, T. K. Avirah, R. L. Cook and T. B. Malloy, *J. Phys. Chem.* **80**, 1141 (1976).
(296) E. Hirota and S. Suenaga, *J. Mol. Spectrosc.* **42**, 127 (1972).
(297) W. M. Stigliani and V. W. Laurie, *J. Mol. Spectrosc.* **60**, 188 (1976).

Chapter 6

MEAN AMPLITUDES OF VIBRATION FOR ORGANIC MOLECULES

S. J. Cyvin and B. N. Cyvin

Division of Physical Chemistry, The University of Trondheim, N-7034 Trondheim-NTH, Norway

J. C. Whitmer

Department of Chemistry, Western Washington State University, Bellingham, Washington 98225, U.S.A.

1 INTRODUCTION

The theory of mean amplitudes of vibration (l or u values)† was developed principally by Morino *et al.*[1,2] although it was considerably extended and broadly applied in the monograph by Cyvin.[3] The l values are of great interest in modern electron diffraction studies of gases[4] and are obtainable from vibrational spectroscopic data if the normal coordinate analyses can be accomplished. In fact, for the two major techniques for determining molecular structure—diffraction and spectroscopy—the l values are one of the strongest interconnecting links. Cyvin's book[3] lays emphasis on the calculation of l values and related quantities from spectroscopic data, but also includes a survey of references to mean amplitudes and selected numerical values for individual molecules quoted both from spectroscopic and electron diffraction work.

The major part of this chapter consists of a survey of mean amplitudes for selected organic molecules and classes of organic molecules. In the first two sections, however, some theoretical aspects of the computations of mean amplitudes are discussed briefly. At the end of this chapter some theoretical implications of the mean amplitudes are considered, and recent developments in this area are reviewed briefly.

---

† The mean amplitudes of vibration are defined as the r.m.s. values according to the equation

$$l_{ij} = \langle (r_{ij} - r_{ij}{}^e)^2 \rangle^{1/2}$$

where r_{ij} is the instantaneous internuclear distance and $r_{ij}{}^e$ is the corresponding equilibrium distance.

2 MEAN AMPLITUDES: AN APPROACH CONVENIENT FOR COMPUTER SOLUTION

We briefly outline here the principles for calculating mean-square amplitudes (l^2) in a form that is especially convenient for computer solution in conjunction with normal coordinate analysis[5] based on internal coordinates. This theory represents a modification of the calculations of l which is not contained in Cyvin's book.[3] Only a short description is found elsewhere.[6] Stølevik et al.[7] recently have presented a more extensive treatment, including computations of perpendicular amplitude-correction coefficients, or K values.[3,8] They referred to Gwinn's program,[9] which solves the problem of normal coordinate analysis in terms of cartesian displacement coordinates. Cyvin has discussed the general theoretical aspects (which are independent of the type of coordinates used in the analysis) of this new, practical method of computing l[10] and K.[10,11] By this method the K values are obtained without explicit computation of the inherent mean-square perpendicular amplitudes.[3,8,12] The K values are of great interest in electron-diffraction analysis,[4,8] although they are not as important as the l values. The K values are not included in the subsequent parts of this chapter.

Consider an arbitrary interatomic distance deviation (bonded or non-bonded), d_{ij}, between atoms i and j, the mean amplitude of which we wish to compute. It can be shown[10] that d_{ij}, in terms of the cartesian displacement coordinates $(x_1, y_1, z_1, \ldots, x_N, y_N, z_N)$, is given by

$$d_{ij} = \ell^x_{ij}(x_i - x_j) + \ell^y_{ij}(y_i - y_j) + \ell^z_{ij}(z_i - z_j) \tag{1}$$

The components of the unit vector from atom j to atom i, ℓ_{ij}, are given by

$$\ell^x_{ij} = (X^e_i - X^e_j)/R^e_{ij}, \text{ etc.} \tag{2}$$

where $X^e_i, \ldots, Z^e_j$ are the cartesian coordinates of the equilibrium positions of atoms i and j, and R^e_{ij} is the interatomic distance,

$$R^e_{ij} = [(X^e_i - X^e_j)^2 + (Y^e_i - Y^e_j)^2 + (Z^e_i - Z^e_j)^2]^{\frac{1}{2}} \tag{3}$$

We now wish to express d_{ij} in terms of the normal coordinates, Q_k,

$$d_{ij} = \sum_k \gamma_{(ij)k} Q_k \tag{4}$$

which is then easily related to the mean-square amplitude of vibration (l^2_{ij}) by

$$l^2_{ij} = \langle d^2_{ij} \rangle = \sum_k \gamma^2_{(ij)k} \langle Q^2_k \rangle \tag{5}$$

where

$$\langle Q^2_k \rangle = (h/8\pi^2 c\omega_k) \coth(hc\omega_k/2kT) \tag{6}$$

is the well-known temperature-dependent frequency parameter (δ_k).[3]

The computation of the coefficients, γ, of eqn. (4) are most compactly described in matrix notation and in this form easily carried out by computer in conjunction with normal coordinate analysis. We define d as a column matrix containing the arbitrary number of interatomic distance deviations, d_{ij}, for which we wish to compute the mean amplitudes. The matrix expression of eqn. (1) then becomes

$$d = \ell \mathbf{x} \tag{7}$$

where $\mathbf{x}$ is a column matrix of the cartesian displacement coordinates of all atoms in the molecule and the rows of ℓ contain the appropriate elements ℓ_{ij} from eqn. (1). Suppose the coordinates used for carrying out the normal coordinate analysis are internal (valence or symmetry) ones and are designated by the column matrix $\mathbf{S}$. We can express d in terms of $\mathbf{S}$ with the equation first derived by Crawford and Fletcher,[13]

$$\mathbf{x} = \mathbf{AS}, \qquad \mathbf{A} = \mathbf{m}^{-1}\tilde{\mathbf{B}}\mathbf{G}^{-1} \tag{8}$$

in the notation of Cyvin.[3] Thus we have

$$d = \ell \mathbf{m}^{-1}\tilde{\mathbf{B}}\mathbf{G}^{-1}\mathbf{S}, \qquad \mathbf{S} = \mathbf{LQ} \tag{9}$$

and consequently

$$d = \ell \mathbf{m}^{-1}\tilde{\mathbf{B}}\mathbf{G}^{-1}\mathbf{LQ} \tag{10}$$

Thus the coefficients, γ, of eqn. (4) are the elements in a row of the matrix obtained by the multiplication series $\ell \mathbf{m}^{-1}\tilde{\mathbf{B}}\mathbf{G}^{-1}\mathbf{L}$. Defining Γ as a matrix formed from the *squares* of the elements of this matrix, one has the mean-square amplitudes in the form of a column matrix, $[\mathbf{l}^2]$:

$$[\mathbf{l}^2] = \Gamma[\delta_k] \tag{11}$$

where $[\delta_k]$ is a column matrix of the frequency parameters defined by eqn. (6).

3   COMPLEX NUMBERS IN THE NORMAL COORDINATE ANALYSIS

The occurrence of complex numbers in character tables of symmetry groups[5,14] is relatively rare in the molecular context, but not negligible. The method outlined below has been applied to some inorganic molecules of C_{3h} symmetry, viz. boric acid[15,16] and methyl borate,[17] to a C_{4h} model of the copper tetrammine ion,[18] and to cyclic hydrogen fluoride hexamer[19] of symmetry C_{6h}. Among organic compounds the method would be appropriate to an analysis of the triphenylmethyl radical according to the non-planar model of C_3 symmetry.[20] Fragments of the theory are contained in several of these papers.[15,16,19]

The complex numbers in the character table give rise to complex symmetry coordinates,

$$\mathbf{S} = \mathbf{U}\mathbf{R} \tag{12}$$

where the transformation matrix $\mathbf{U}$ is unitary rather than orthogonal. For the normal coordinate transformation matrix ($\mathbf{L}$) one has the usual relations[3,5]

$$\mathbf{S} = \mathbf{L}\mathbf{Q}, \quad \mathbf{G}\mathbf{F}\mathbf{L} = \mathbf{L}\lambda \tag{13}$$

where $\mathbf{L}$ is in this case complex. Hence the familiar relations for the $\mathbf{G}$ and $\mathbf{F}$ matrices must be written

$$\mathbf{G} = \mathbf{L}\mathbf{L}^\dagger, \quad \mathbf{F} = (\mathbf{L}^{-1})^\dagger\lambda\mathbf{L}^{-1} \tag{14}$$

where $\mathbf{L}^\dagger$ is the associate matrix of $\mathbf{L}$ and not only its transpose. The λ matrix is, as usual, a diagonal matrix of real numbers.

The complex numbers always pertain to a degenerate species. When the a and b sets of degenerate symmetry coordinates are properly constructed, the respective two blocks of the block-diagonal $\mathbf{L}$ matrix, viz. $\mathbf{L}_a$ and $\mathbf{L}_b$, have the property

$$\mathbf{L}_b = \mathbf{L}_a^* \tag{15}$$

where * denotes a complex conjugate.

Consequently the $\mathbf{G}$ and $\mathbf{F}$ matrices for the degenerate coordinates have the same block structure, where the a and b blocks are complex conjugate to each other:

$$\mathbf{G} = \begin{bmatrix} \mathbf{G}_a & \mathbf{O} \\ \mathbf{O} & \mathbf{G}_a^* \end{bmatrix}, \quad \mathbf{F} = \begin{bmatrix} \mathbf{F}_a & \mathbf{O} \\ \mathbf{O} & \mathbf{F}_a^* \end{bmatrix} \tag{16}$$

In the presence of complex symmetry coordinates, the $\mathbf{F}$ and $\mathbf{G}$ matrices, as well as the $\mathbf{F}_a$ and $\mathbf{G}_a$ blocks, are Hermitian rather than symmetric. In the two-dimensional case, for instance, one has the form:

$$\mathbf{G} = \begin{bmatrix} A_1 & B+iC & 0 & 0 \\ B-iC & A_2 & 0 & 0 \\ 0 & 0 & A_1 & B-iC \\ 0 & 0 & B+iC & A_2 \end{bmatrix} \tag{17}$$

and similarly for $\mathbf{F}$.

From the complex symmetry coordinates it is possible to construct real coordinates ($\mathscr{S}$) by means of the unitary transformation

$$\mathscr{S} = \mathbf{W}\mathbf{S} \tag{18}$$

where

$$\mathbf{W} = \frac{1}{\sqrt{2}} \begin{bmatrix} \mathbf{E} & \mathbf{E} \\ -\mathbf{I} & \mathbf{I} \end{bmatrix} \tag{19}$$

In the two-dimensional case, for instance, the submatrices are:

$$\mathbf{E} = \begin{bmatrix} 1 & 0 \\ 0 & 1 \end{bmatrix}, \quad \mathbf{I} = \begin{bmatrix} i & 0 \\ 0 & i \end{bmatrix} \tag{20}$$

The $\mathscr{G}$ and $\mathscr{F}$ matrices in terms of the real coordinates are then obtained by

$$\mathscr{G} = \mathbf{WGW}^\dagger, \quad \mathscr{F} = \mathbf{WFW}^\dagger \tag{21}$$

Using $\mathbf{W}$ from eqn. (19) and the form of $\mathbf{G}$ shown in eqn. (16), one obtains

$$\mathscr{G} = \tfrac{1}{2} \begin{bmatrix} \mathbf{G}_a + \mathbf{G}_a^* & -i(\mathbf{G}_a - \mathbf{G}_a^*) \\ i(\mathbf{G}_a - \mathbf{G}_a^*) & \mathbf{G}_a + \mathbf{G}_a^* \end{bmatrix} = \begin{bmatrix} \mathrm{Re}(\mathbf{G}_a) & \mathrm{Im}(\mathbf{G}_a) \\ -\mathrm{Im}(\mathbf{G}_a) & \mathrm{Re}(\mathbf{G}_a) \end{bmatrix} \tag{22}$$

Referring to the special case of eqn. (17), the corresponding real matrix becomes

$$\mathscr{G} = \begin{bmatrix} A_1 & B & 0 & C \\ B & A_2 & -C & 0 \\ 0 & -C & A_1 & B \\ C & 0 & B & A_2 \end{bmatrix} \tag{23}$$

In general the $\mathscr{G}$ matrix is real and has the form

$$\mathscr{G} = \begin{bmatrix} \mathbf{A} & \mathbf{B} \\ -\mathbf{B} & \mathbf{A} \end{bmatrix} \tag{24}$$

where the submatrix $\mathbf{A}$ is symmetric while $\mathbf{B}$ is skew-symmetric. As a whole $\mathscr{G}$ is symmetric. The evaluation of the real $\mathscr{F}$ matrix of eqn. (21) follows exactly the same pattern as $\mathscr{G}$, and results in the same form as eqn. (24).

The problem of normal coordinate analysis is soluble in terms of the real coordinates according to

$$\mathscr{S} = \mathscr{L}\mathbf{Q}, \quad \mathscr{G}\mathscr{F}\mathscr{L} = \mathscr{L}\lambda \tag{25}$$

Here all the matrices are real. The solution results in a normal-coordinate transformation matrix ($\mathscr{L}$) of the same form as $\mathscr{G}$ and $\mathscr{F}$; cf. eqn. (24). The diagonal λ matrix of frequency parameters is basically the same as in eqn. (13). Since both the a and b blocks are contained in the $\mathscr{G}$ and $\mathscr{F}$ matrices, every frequency will occur twice in the λ matrix.

An example of constructing the complex symmetry coordinates is furnished by the case of trigonal symmetry appropriate for C_3 and C_{3h}. A typical pair of degenerate symmetry coordinates has the form

$$S_a = \frac{1}{\sqrt{3}}(a_1 + \epsilon a_2 + \epsilon^* a_3), \quad S_b = \frac{1}{\sqrt{3}}(a_1 + \epsilon^* a_2 + \epsilon a_3) \tag{26}$$

where

$$\epsilon = e^{2\pi i/3} \tag{27}$$

The transformation to real coordinates in this case results in

$$\mathscr{S}_a = \frac{1}{\sqrt{6}}(2a_1 - a_2 - a_3), \qquad \mathscr{S}_b = \frac{1}{\sqrt{2}}(a_2 - a_3) \qquad (28)$$

which is the familiar form of symmetry coordinates pertaining to the symmetry groups C_{3v} or D_{3h}.

From a mathematical standpoint it is interesting to notice that the present method is equivalent to a well-known treatment of complex matrices.[21] Any complex $n \times n$ matrix of the form

$$\mathbf{G} = \mathbf{A} + i\mathbf{B} \qquad (29)$$

is isomorphous with the $2n \times 2n$ real matrix of the form in eqn. (24).

In summary, the method of solving the vibrational problem for a model of a symmetry group with complex characters is straightforward. Complex symmetry coordinates are replaced by real coordinates for a molecular model of higher symmetry. Then the a and b blocks of degenerate coordinates must be taken together when the secular equation is solved. The method has a great advantage because of its simplicity. On the other hand, it requires the solution of a secular equation of twice the usual size, and all frequency values are computed twice. In the case of the triphenylmethyl radical,[20] $(C_6H_5)_3C$ (C_3 symmetry; $32a + 32e$) the degenerate-block dimension would be sixty four.

4   PREVIOUS REVIEWS AND INTRODUCTION TO THE SURVEY OF ORGANIC MOLECULES

The number of mean amplitudes of vibration reported both from electron diffraction and spectroscopic studies has increased greatly since Cyvin's monograph[3] was published. In a series of supplements to Chapters 12 and 15, the mean amplitudes and Bastiansen-Morino shrinkage effects[3,22-24] for individual molecules were again reviewed.[25-27] This material was arranged according to increasing number of atoms in the molecules treated, or classes of molecules represented by given molecular models. However, the majority of these molecules are inorganic compounds. In another supplement,[28] organic molecules with a carbonyl group were reviewed.

The present chapter is intended to give a comprehensive survey of mean amplitudes of vibration for organic molecules. Much of the data has not been published previously. This survey treats the molecules in a systematic way, as far as is possible; it does not seem expedient to adhere strictly to a classification of the molecules according to the number of atoms, but rather to follow other structural characteristics and conventional classifications of organic chemistry. From this material it should easily be possible to extract characteristic values of mean amplitudes for different types of bonds, and to some extent also for non-bonded atom pairs. Thus the material should be useful not only for studies of the molecules listed here, but also for estimating mean amplitudes in related molecules.

In the present chapter extensive use is made of a schematic representation of the mean amplitudes by means of figures. This form was first used by Cyvin et al.[29] and referred to as a 'condensed representation'. For a number of molecules mentioned, the mean amplitudes of vibration are not quoted; however, references are given to the appropriate papers where such data may be found. It is not intended to present complete reviews of references; such material is found in Chapter 2 of Ref. 3 and supplemented in Chapter 22 of Ref. 8. In the present citations, preference is given to work in which the spectroscopic mean amplitudes are considered fairly reliable, if no special comments to the contrary are made. In the subsequent sections, the IUPAC names of organic compounds are given in parentheses.

5   CONDENSED VALUES FOR SOME SIMPLE MOLECULES

The schematic ('condensed') representation of mean amplitudes of vibration is illustrated by Fig. 1 for several simple molecules. The values on these drawings comprise the mean amplitudes (in 10^{-3} Å units = 0.1 pm) at the temperature of 298 K for formaldehyde (methanal), formaldehyde-d_2 (dideuteromethanal),

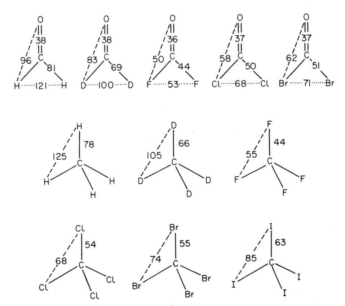

Fig. 1. Mean amplitudes of vibration/10^{-3} Å for light and heavy formaldehyde, carbonyl halides, light and heavy methane, and carbon tetrahalides. All data relate to 298 K.

and carbonyl halides (difluoro-, dichloro- and dibromo-methanal) taken from Müller et al.[30] and for carbon tetrahalides (tetrafluoro-, tetrachloro-, tetrabromo- and tetraiodo-methane) from Müller et al.[31] These data are very well in agreement with the values from previous calculations quoted in Ref. 3: Bakken,[32] Rajalakshmi et al.,[33] and Cyvin et al.[34] For methane and methane-d_4 the values in Fig. 1 were taken from Ref. 3. Among the more recent work on these molecules we wish to mention that of Kato et al.[35] on formaldehyde, which includes both electron diffraction and spectroscopic studies.

6 ACETYLENE AND MOLECULES WITH CONJUGATED TRIPLE BONDS

6.1 Acetylene and Its Linear Derivatives

Figure 2 shows the mean amplitudes of vibration for acetylene (ethyne) and acetylene-d_2 (dideuteroethyne); cf. Ref. 32. Values of shrinkage effects[3] for acetylene from Meisingseth et al.[36] are included in parentheses. These quantities follow the definition[3]

$$-\delta_{1N} = R^g_{1N} - (R^g_{12} + R^g_{23} + \cdots + R^g_{(N-1)N}) \tag{30}$$

In the same figure are given the corresponding data for cyanoacetylene (propynenitrile) according to Cyvin et al.[37] The values for cyanoacetylene reported here are not in agreement with the calculations by Ramaswamy et al.,[38] which are believed to be less reliable.

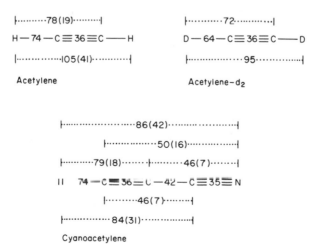

Fig. 2. Mean amplitudes of vibration/10^{-3} Å and shrinkage effects (parenthesized) for acetylene, acetylene-d_2 and cyanoacetylene at 298 K.

Venkateswarlu *et al.*[39] have given the mean amplitudes and shrinkage effects for some monohalo-acetylenes and their deutero- compounds, but not all of their results seem reliable when compared with characteristic values for similar atom-pairs in related molecules. More recent data on mean amplitudes and shrinkage effects from spectroscopic calculations for the four monohalo-acety-lenes (fluoro-, chloro-, bromo- and iodo-ethyne) are furnished by Rogstad *et al.*[40] Figure 3 gives a representation of the mean amplitudes and shrinkage effects for halo-cyanoacetylenes (chloro-, bromo- and iodo-propynenitrile) according to Klæboe *et al.*[41]

For dicyanoacetylene (butynedinitrile), *cf.* Fig. 4, the mean amplitudes and shrinkage effects were recalculated by Cyvin.[42] He confirmed the calculated data of Venkateswarlu *et al.*[43] for the same molecule, but concluded that the values of Nagarajan *et al.*[44] are in error. The latter ones are regrettably quoted in Ref. 3.

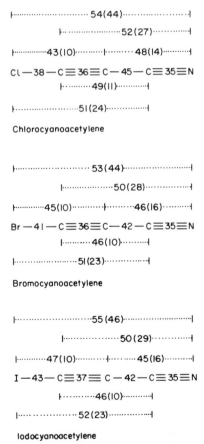

Fig. 3. Mean amplitudes of vibration/10^{-3} Å and shrinkage effects (parenthesized) for halo-cyanoacetylenes at 298 K.

6.2   Diacetylene and Its Linear Derivatives

The previously published mean amplitudes[45] and mean-square amplitudes[46] for diacetylene are not at all compatible with each other, and the same is the case for the reported shrinkage effects for this molecule. The results of present calculations of mean amplitudes and shrinkage effects for diacetylene and diacetylene-d_2 (butadiyne and dideuterobutadiyne) are presented in Fig. 4. For a definition of the shrinkages, see eqn. (30). These results basically confirm the calculations of Venkateswarlu et al.[46] except for their $l^2(C_1 \cdots C_3) = 0.001241$ Å^2 (at 300 K), which evidently is too small. The present values (Fig. 4) agree very well with more recent calculations by Tanimoto et al.[47] who have reported also their results from a significant electron-diffraction investigation. Mean amplitudes of vibration and shrinkage effects for monohalo-diacetylenes (chloro-, bromo- and iodo-butadiyne) have been calculated by Klæboe et al.[41] and by Minasso et al.[48]

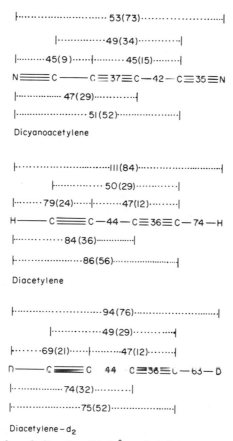

Fig. 4. Mean amplitudes of vibration/10^{-3} Å and shrinkage effects (parenthesized) for dicyanoacetylene, diacetylene and diacetylene-d_2 at 298 K.

6.3 Other Acetylene Derivatives

Devarajan et al.[49] have performed spectroscopic calculations of mean amplitudes and linear shrinkages for methylacetylene (propyne) with some of its deuterated compounds (1-deutero-, 3,3,3-trideutero- and tetradeutero-propyne) and some halo substituents (1-chloro-, 1-chloro-3,3,3-trideutero-, 1-bromo- and 1-iodo-propyne). Similar data exist for CF_3CCH and CF_3CCD (3,3,3-trifluoro- and 1-deutero-3,3,3-trifluoro-propyne)[50-52] and some completely halogenated methylacetylenes (1-chloro-, 1-bromo- and 1-iodo-3,3,3-trifluoropropyne).[53] Dimethylacetylene (2-butyne) was studied by electron diffraction in conjunction with spectroscopic calculations by Tanimoto et al.[54] The spectroscopic analysis of the corresponding perfluorinated compound (hexafluoro-2-butyne) by Elvebredd[55] includes the framework mean amplitudes.[56-60] Electron diffraction investigations of this molecule are also available.[61,62]

Mean amplitudes and linear shrinkage effects from spectroscopic data for methyldiacetylene (pentadiyne) and some of its halo substituents (1-chloro-, 1-bromo- and 1-iodo-pentadiyne) have been reported by Rogstad et al.[63]

In this connection some interesting work on systems with a conjugated triple and double bond are worth mentioning. Fukuyama et al.[64] have studied vinylacetylene (butenyne) by electron diffraction and spectroscopic analysis. Their mean amplitudes are given in Table 1; there is very good agreement between observed and calculated mean amplitudes. Similar studies have been

TABLE 1
Mean amplitudes of vibration/Å for vinylacetylene[a]

Distance	Observed[b]	Calculated
C—C	0.048 ± 0.006	0.0473
C=C	$0.043_9 \pm 0.004$	0.0439
C≡C	0.038 ± 0.005	0.0367
C—H_v[c]	0.074 ± 0.006	0.0775
$C_1 \cdots C_3$[d]	$0.059_4 \pm 0.002$	0.0635
$C_2 \cdots C_4$	$0.053_9 \pm 0.003$	0.0520
$C_1 \cdots C_4$	0.084 ± 0.005	0.0867

[a] From Ref. 64.

[b] From electron diffraction studies of gases.

[c] All the vinyl C—H amplitudes were assumed to be equal. Mean amplitudes for C—H_e were varied with a fixed difference from those for C—H_v: $l(C—H_v) - l(C—H_e) = 0.0033$ Å. H_v is a vinyl hydrogen atom, H_e is the end hydrogen atom of the acetylenic part of the molecule.

[d] Numbering of carbon atoms: $C_1=C_2—C_3≡C_4$.

reported for a series of chlorinated vinylacetylenes: *cis-* and *trans*-1-chloro-butenyne,[65] 2-chloro-butenyne[66] and 4-chlorobutenyne.[67]

7 ETHYLENE AND SUBSTITUTED ETHYLENES

7.1 Ethylene with Its Deutero- and Halo-Derivatives

Figure 5 shows the mean amplitudes of vibration for ethylene (ethene), ethylene-d$_4$ (tetradeuteroethene) and halogenated ethylenes (tetrafluoro-, tetrachloro- and tetrabromo-ethene). The values for ethylene and ethylene-d$_4$ are taken from Ref. 3 and, in particular, those for ethylene are in excellent agreement with more recent calculations.[68] Extremal values of mean amplitudes for ethylene have been studied by Fogarasi *et al.*[69] and by Török *et al.*[8] Schmidling[70] has, in an interesting work, reported the mean amplitudes for ethylene obtained by MINDO/2 calculations. He concludes that the method

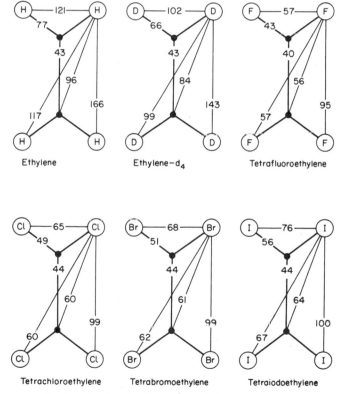

Fig. 5. Mean amplitudes of vibration/10⁻³ Å at 298 K for ethylene, ethylene-d$_4$ and tetrahaloethylenes.

(applied to ethylene and benzene) gives mean amplitudes in good agreement with spectroscopic results (average deviation about 4%); there is a tendency for the mean amplitudes for bonded atom pairs to be too low and for non-bonded atom pairs to be too high. For the halogenated ethylenes Cyvin[3] has quoted several mean amplitudes with partially differing magnitudes. The recalculated quantities (see Fig. 5) according to Cyvin[71] basically confirm the calculations for C_2F_4, C_2Cl_4 and C_2Br_4 of de Alti et al.[72] The l values from Venkateswarlu et al.[73] for the X $\cdots$ X(trans) distances, where X = F, Cl or Br, and which show the largest deviations from the results of the other authors, seem clearly to be in

TABLE 2
Mean amplitudes of vibration/Å from electron diffraction studies on halogenated ethylenes

C_2X_4	$C_2F_4{}^a$	$C_2Cl_4{}^b$	$C_2Br_4{}^b$	$C_2I_4{}^b$
C—X	0.045 (0.003)	0.048 (0.001)	0.043 (0.004)	0.074 (0.007)
C=C	0.041 (0.004)	—	—	—
C$\cdots$X	0.060 (0.003)	0.058 (0.002)	0.045 (0.006)	0.071 (0.010)
X$\cdots$X (com)^c	0.057 (0.004)	0.064 (0.001)	0.074 (0.002)	0.090 (0.002)
X$\cdots$X (trans)	0.067 (0.006)	0.064 (0.002)	0.070 (0.002)	0.081 (0.002)
X$\cdots$X (cis)	0.091 (0.009)	0.096 (0.002)	0.107 (0.003)	0.144 (0.009)

^{a} From Ref. 78. Parenthesized figures are three times the standard deviations.

^{b} Ref. 79. Standard deviations in parentheses. Reported nozzle temperatures: 50, 85 and 170 °C for the Cl, Br and I compounds, respectively. Cyvin[71], has reported the calculated mean amplitudes also at these temperatures.

^{c} com = attached to a common carbon atom.

error. For C_2F_4 the results of Cyvin[71] are remarkably close to the early values of Morino et al.[1] Cyvin[74] has used C_2Cl_4 to illustrate the method of specific imposition of potential parameters on non-bonded distances in the course of refining calculated mean amplitudes. Extremal values of mean amplitudes for C_2F_4, C_2Cl_4 and C_2Br_4 have been studied by Fogarasi.[75]

Electron diffraction values of mean amplitudes for ethylene (ethene) and ethylene-d_4 (tetradeuteroethene) are fully reviewed by Cyvin.[3] The same is the case for the early results for C_2F_4 (tetrafluoroethene)[76] and C_2Cl_4 (tetrachloroethene).[77] Table 2 shows the more recent electron diffraction values for C_2F_4,[78] C_2Cl_4,[79] C_2Br_4 (tetrabromoethene)[79,80] and C_2I_4 (tetraiodoethene).[79]

Carlos et al.[78] have investigated all the fluorinated ethylenes (fluoro-, cis-1,2-difluoro-, trans-1,2-difluoro-, 1,1-difluoro-, trifluoro- and tetrafluoroethene) by electron diffraction on the gases. Mean amplitudes from electron diffraction for two of these gaseous compounds (cis-1,2-difluoro and trans-1,2-difluoroethene) are also reported by van Schaick et al.[81] Similar reports by Davis et al. exist for cis-1,2-dichloroethene[82] and cis-1,2-dibromoethene.[83]

Vinyl chloride (chloroethene) was studied by Ivey *et al.*[84] A spectroscopic study by Lie *et al.*[85] produced the calculated mean amplitudes for *trans*-1,2-dichloro-1,2-diiodoethene.

7.2 Cyanoethylenes

Tetracyanoethylene (ethenetetracarbonitrile) has been investigated by electron diffraction in work by Hope,[86] but the reported mean amplitudes are inaccurate; *cf.* Table 3. Vibrational assignments and normal coordinate analyses without calculated mean amplitudes are available for this molecule.[87-90] The mean amplitudes were calculated from spectroscopic data for the first time by Hagen, but are unpublished. He applied experimental frequencies from two of the works cited above[89,90] in a re-assigned version. Hagen's results of mean amplitudes are included in Table 3 and show satisfactory agreement with the electron diffraction values.

It would also be feasible to calculate reliable mean amplitudes from existing spectroscopic data for other cyanoethylenes: acrylonitrile (propenenitrile),[90,91] fumaronitrile (*trans*-butenedinitrile),[87,89-91] maleic nitrile (*cis*-butenedinitrile),[87,89-91] vinylidene cyanide (ethene-1,1-dicarbonitrile),[90] and tri-

TABLE 3
**Mean amplitudes/Å for tetracyano-
ethylene at 298 K from spectroscopic
calculations and electron diffraction**

Distance[a]	Calculated[b]	Observed[c]
$C \equiv N$ (1.162)	0.034_6	0.035
$C = C$ (1.357)	0.042_9	0.046
$C-C$ (1.435)	0.047_0	0.047
$C \cdots C$ (2.432)	0.059	0.060
$C \cdots C$ (2.457)	0.076	0.090
$C \cdots C$ (2.839)	0.100	0.097
$C \cdots C$ (3.755)	0.062	0.074
$C \cdots N$ (2.597)	0.050	0.060
$C \cdots N$ (3.497)	0.076	0.120
$C \cdots N$ (3.504)	0.097	0.120
$C \cdots N$ (3.581)	0.149	0.120
$C \cdots N$ (4.873)	0.070	0.089
$N \cdots N$ (4.040)	0.223	0.192
$N \cdots N$ (4.447)	0.139	0.144
$N \cdots N$ (6.008)	0.072	0.096

[a] Parenthesized values are interatomic separations/Å consistent with the equilibrium structure parameters used in the spectroscopic analysis.
[b] Personal communication from G. Hagen.
[c] Gas electron diffraction.[86]

cyanoethylene (ethenetricarbonitrile).[90,91] Calculated mean amplitudes for dichloro-, dibromo-, and diiodo-fumaronitrile (*trans*-1,2-dichloro-, *trans*-1,2-dibromo- and *trans*-1,2-diiodo-butenedinitrile) have been reported by Lie *et al*.[92] and likewise for tribromo- and triiodo-acrylonitrile (tribromo- and triiodo-propenenitrile).[93]

7.3 Propylene

Propylene (propene) may be considered as a substituted ethylene with a methyl group. The structural investigation of propene and 3,3,3-trifluoropropene by Tokue *et al*.[94] contains both calculated and observed mean amplitudes. It is an example of an excellent structural analysis of gases by electron diffraction combined with microwave data on rotational constants.

8   HYDROCARBONS WITH CUMULATED C=C BONDS

The mean amplitudes of vibration for allene (propadiene) with isotopic substitutions have been calculated several times. Figure 6 shows the values for allene and allene-d_4 (tetradeuteropropadiene) at 298 K taken from Andersen *et al*.[95] The symmetry group is D_{2d}. The linear shrinkage effects, defined in eqn. (30), are given in parentheses. The cited paper[95] includes the calculated mean amplitudes and shrinkage effects also for C_3T_4 and all partially deuterated allenes. The values for C_3H_4 are in very good agreement with more recent calculations.[68] In the present work a recalculation of mean amplitudes for allene and allene-d_4 was performed, utilizing the most recent force constants for the *e* species obtained with the aid of observed Coriolis constants.[96] These recalculations showed barely significant effects on the mean amplitudes.

Figure 6 also shows the mean amplitudes and linear shrinkage effects of butatriene and tetradeuterobutatriene (symmetry D_{2h}). The data were taken from the paper of Cyvin *et al*.,[68] which also contains the corresponding calculations for C_4T_4 and all partially deuterated butatrienes. The existing electron diffraction data on mean amplitudes for allene[97] and butatriene[98] are quoted elsewhere.[3]

Divinyl allene (1,3,4,6-heptatetraene) is an interesting molecule with both cumulated and conjugated C=C bonds. The symmetry group is C_2. Unpublished results of some of the calculated mean amplitudes of vibration from the normal coordinate analysis of Phongsatha *et al*.[99] are shown in Table 4. These values are compatible with previous calculations[100] for similar systems, vinylallene (1,2,4-pentatriene) and biallenyl (1,2,4,5-hexatetraene). It means that the calculated mean amplitudes for corresponding distances in all three molecules have similar values. An electron diffraction investigation for one of these molecules, viz. biallenyl, is available.[101]

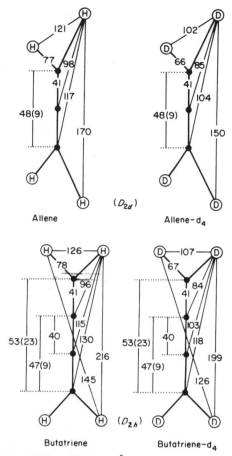

Fig. 6. Mean amplitudes of vibration/10⁻³ Å and shrinkage effects (parenthesized) for light and heavy allene and butatriene at 298 K.

TABLE 4
Calculated mean amplitudes/Å for the CC distances at 298 K in divinyl allene:
$C_1{=}C_2{-}C_3{=}C_4{=}C_5{-}C_6{=}C_7$

Distance	Mean amplitude	Distance	Mean amplitude
$C_1{=}C_2$	0.042	$C_1{\cdots}C_4$	0.071
$C_2{-}C_3$	0.046	$C_2{\cdots}C_5$	0.100
$C_3{=}C_4$	0.040	$C_1{\cdots}C_5$	0.087
$C_1{\cdots}C_3$	0.071	$C_2{\cdots}C_6$	0.142
$C_2{\cdots}C_4$	0.071	$C_1{\cdots}C_6$	0.152
$C_3{\cdots}C_5$	0.046	$C_1{\cdots}C_7$	0.152

9 CYCLIC HYDROCARBONS WITH ONE C=C BOND

Mean amplitudes of vibration along with perpendicular amplitude correction coefficients[3,8] have been calculated for cyclopropene, 1,2-dideuterocyclopropene, 3,3-dideuterocyclopropene and tetradeuterocyclopropene.[102] The paper also includes the calculated atomic vibration mean-square amplitudes[8] for C_3H_4 and C_3D_4. In Fig. 7 the mean amplitudes for cyclopropene are shown. The molecule is the smallest cyclic hydrocarbon and contains one CC double bond. Two independent electron diffraction investigations with observed mean amplitudes exist for gaseous tetrachlorocyclopropene.[103,104]

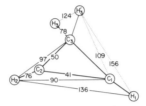

Fig. 7. Mean amplitudes of vibration/10^{-3} Å for cyclopropene at 298 K.

For other cyclic hydrocarbons with one CC double bond very few spectroscopic calculations of mean amplitudes have been completed. No such data exist for comparison with electron diffraction data for cyclobutene[105] and its halogen substituents.[106,107] The same is the case for bicyclo[2.1.0]pentene (C_5H_6),[108] benzvalene (tricyclo[3.1.0^{2,6}]hexa-3-ene, C_6H_6),[109] cyclopentene (C_5H_8),[110] bicyclo[2.1.1]-hexa-2-ene (C_6H_8),[111] Δ^6-bicyclo[3.2.0]heptene (C_7H_{10}),[112] and bicyclo[4.1.0]hept-2-ene (C_7H_{10}).[113] For cyclooctene (C_8H_{14})[114,115] a few calculated mean amplitudes have been reported.[115] Cyclohexene (C_6H_{10}) is the molecule within this category for which the most extensive spectroscopic calculations have been performed. Table 5 shows the calculated[116] and experimentally determined[117] CC mean amplitudes for this molecule.

10 HYDROCARBONS WITH CONJUGATED C=C BONDS AND SOME OF THEIR SUBSTITUENTS

10.1 Acyclic Compounds

The calculated mean amplitudes of vibration for 1,3-butadiene[118] agree satisfactorily with electron diffraction values.[119–122] Figure 8 shows a reproduction of the mean amplitudes from the spectroscopic work of Trætteberg et al.,[118] which also includes the corresponding data for hexadeutero-1,3-butadiene and 2-deutero-1,3-butadiene. The most recent calculations of mean

TABLE 5
Calculated mean amplitudes/Å for the CC distances in cyclohexene at 298 K along with electron diffraction values

Distance	Calculated[a]	Observed[b]
$C_1{=}C_2$	0.0480	0.048 ± 0.002
$C_2{-}C_3$	0.0471	0.063 ± 0.010
$C_3{-}C_4$	0.0476	0.057 ± 0.010
$C_4{-}C_5$	0.0427	0.049 ± 0.006
$C_1{\cdots}C_3$	0.0551	(0.061)
$C_2{\cdots}C_4$	0.0619	(0.085)
$C_3{\cdots}C_5$	0.0781	(0.070)
$C_1{\cdots}C_4$	0.0706	(0.085)
$C_3{\cdots}C_6$	0.0659	(0.080)

[a] Ref. 116.
[b] Gas electron diffraction.[117] Values in parentheses are assumed ones.

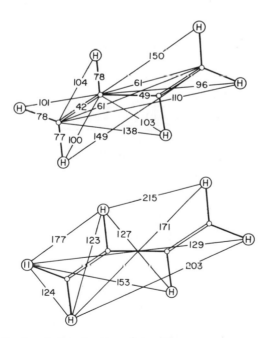

Fig. 8. Mean amplitudes of vibration/10^{-3} Å for 1,3-butadiene at 298 K. Above: CC and CH distances. Below: HH distances.

amplitudes for 1,3-butadiene are due to Panchenko.[123] Observed mean amplitudes from electron diffraction also exist for hexafluoro-1,3-butadiene[62] and hexachloro-1,3-butadiene.[124]

Mean amplitudes from electron diffraction have been produced for trans-1,3,5-hexatriene[120,125] and cis-1,3,5-hexatriene.[126] A spectroscopic analysis of the same molecules with calculations of mean amplitudes is also available.[127] Electron diffraction investigations including measurements of mean amplitudes exist for 2-methyl-1,3-butadiene[128] and 2,3-dimethyl-1,3-butadiene.[129,130]

10.2   Cyclic Compounds

Cyclic (non-aromatic) hydrocarbons with conjugated $C=C$ bonds have been studied extensively by electron diffraction.

TABLE 6
Calculated mean amplitudes/Å for the CC distances at 298 K in 1,3-cyclohexadiene and electron diffraction values

Distance	Calculated[a]	Observed[b]
$C_1=C_2$	0.0427	0.046 ± 0.001
C_2-C_3	0.0484	0.052 ± 0.002
C_4-C_5	0.0478	0.048 ± 0.001
C_5-C_6	0.0482	0.053 ± 0.002
$C_1 \cdots C_3$	0.0580	0.065
$C_3 \cdots C_5$	0.0570	0.065
$C_4 \cdots C_6$	0.0633	0.065
$C_1 \cdots C_4$	0.0635	0.070
$C_2 \cdots C_5$	0.0719	0.070

  [a] Ref. 131.
  [b] Gas electron diffraction.[132]

Table 6 shows the calculated[131] and observed[132] mean amplitudes of CC distances in 1,3-cyclohexadiene. Additional electron diffraction work on the same molecule has been reported.[133,134]

Several molecules belonging to this category have been investigated by electron diffraction, but not followed up by spectroscopic calculations of mean amplitudes, e.g. hexachlorocyclopentadiene,[135] 1,3-cycloheptadiene,[112,136] spiro[2,4]-hepta-4,6-diene,[137] 1,3,5-cycloheptatriene[138] and 1,3-cyclooctadiene.[139]

1,3,5,7-Cyclooctatetraene has been reinvestigated by Haugen et al. in Andersen et al. (Ref. 121) after previous electron diffraction studies.[140,141] The values in Fig. 9 are taken from the spectroscopic results for C_8H_8 by Trætteberg et al.[142] This work also contains the calculated mean amplitude values for C_8D_8 (octadeutero-1,3,5,7-cyclooctatetraene).

Aromatic hydrocarbons are treated in a subsequent section.

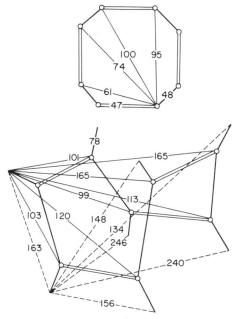

Fig. 9. Mean amplitudes of vibration/10^{-3} Å for 1,3,5,7-cyclooctatetraene at 298 K. Above: CC distances. Below: CH and HH distances, indicated with solid and broken lines, respectively.

11 MOLECULES WITH THE CARBONYL (C=O) GROUP

Figure 1 includes the mean amplitudes of vibration for formaldehyde and some carbonyl halides. Additional small molecules with the carbonyl bond are found in Fig. 10, viz. (c) ketene,[6] (d) formic acid (methanoic acid)[143] and (e) glyoxal (ethanedial).[144] The mean amplitudes for (a) carbon dioxide[3] and (b) carbon suboxide[145] are included in Fig. 10 for comparison.

Mean amplitudes of organic molecules with the carbonyl group are given in a paper by Cyvin et al.[28] More recent results are included in the present survey.

An electron diffraction investigation of formaldehyde (methanal), acetaldehyde (ethanal) and acetone (2-propanone) is available;[35] additional references are given[146,147] for acetaldehyde. In one of these papers[147] a theory for vibrational effects in a molecule containing a symmetrical internal rotor is applied to acetaldehyde. In Ref. 28 some of the spectroscopic mean amplitudes for acetaldehyde due to Hagen[148] are quoted. This work also contains the

calculated mean amplitudes for fluoral, chloral and bromal (trifluoro-, trichloro-
and tribromo-ethanal) with that for several deuterated species of the molecule in
question. Electron diffraction investigations, including mean amplitudes from
spectroscopic calculations, are available also for all acetyl (ethanoyl-) halides:
the fluoride,[149] chloride,[150] bromide[150] and iodide.[149] In the previous
review[28] the electron diffraction mean amplitudes of acetone[35] are compared
with original spectroscopic calculations. The paper[28] gives also the calculated
atomic-vibration mean-square amplitudes[8] of acetone for the first time.
Another significant structural analysis of this molecule is due to Iijima.[151]
Some electron diffraction investigations of halogenated acetones also are
available, viz. trifluoroacetone (1,1,1-trifluoro-2-propanone),[152] hexafluoro-
acetone (hexafluoro-2-propanone)[153] and hexachloroacetone (hexachloro-
2-propanone).[154] Biacetyl (*trans*-2,3-butanedione) has been investigated by
electron diffraction.[155] Another electron diffraction work which includes

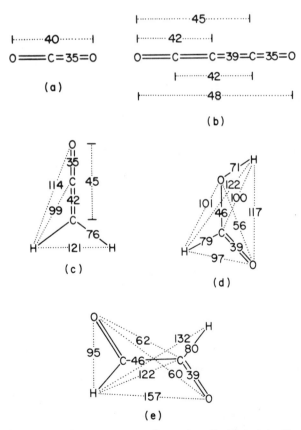

Fig. 10. Mean amplitudes of vibration/10^{-3} Å at 298 K for (a) carbon dioxide, (b) carbon
suboxide, (c) ketene, (d) formic acid and (e) glyoxal.

spectroscopic mean amplitudes deals with fumaraldehyde (*trans*-2-butene-dial).[156] Acrolein (propenal) was included in the previous review.[28]

Data for ketene are shown in Fig. 10. Spectroscopic calculations of mean amplitudes are also available for methylketene,[6,157] its deuterated species, and dimethylketene.[6]

Electron diffraction data are available for formic acid (methanoic acid) monomer[8,158] and dimer,[158] oxalic acid (ethanedioic acid)[159] and acetic acid (ethanoic acid) monomer and dimer.[160] Fluoroacetic acid[161] and chloroacetic acid[162] (fluoro- and chloro-ethanoic acid) have been studied by combined electron diffraction and microwave data. Furthermore, two conformers of difluoroacetic acid (difluoroethanoic acid)[163] have been detected by electron diffraction. No mean amplitudes are reported from the electron diffraction work on propionic acid (propanoic acid).[164] Extensive spectroscopic analyses are published in a series of four papers dealing with formic acid monomer,[143] acetic acid monomer,[165] oxalic acid[166] and formic acid dimer.[167]

12 MOLECULES WITH THE CYANO (C≡N) GROUP

Organic molecules with the cyano group have not previously been reviewed as extensively as those with the carbonyl group (*cf.* Section 11). Cyanoacetylene and its halogen substituents are found in Figs 2 and 3; dicyanoacetylene in Fig. 4. Cyanoethylenes are treated in Section 7.2; see Table 3 for tetracyanoethylene.

Acetonitrile, CH_3CN (ethanenitrile) has been studied by several workers. The first calculations of mean amplitudes for this molecule were unreliable, but recalculated values have been published[168] and later confirmed by independent spectroscopic calculations in connection with electron diffraction work;[169] *cf.* Table 7. Tetracyanomethane (methanetetracarbonitrile) is an interesting

TABLE 7
Observed and calculated mean amplitudes/Å for acetonitrile (methyl cyanide)

Distance	Obs.[a]	Calc.[a]	Calc.[b]
C—C	0.048 ± 0.003	0.0483	0.0476
C≡N	0.036 ± 0.003	0.0342	0.0343
C—H	0.075 ± 0.009	0.0780	0.0779
C···N	0.055 ± 0.005	0.0505	0.0504
C···H	$(0.102)^c$	0.1020	0.104_5
N···H	$(0.120)^c$	0.1196	0.118_4
H···H	$(0.126)^c$	0.1260	0.126_8

[a] Reference 169.
[b] Reference 168; values at 298 K.
[c] Fixed on calculated values (calc. *a*).

molecule of T_d symmetry, which has been subjected to electron diffraction studies by Oberhammer.[170] The observed mean amplitudes are in good agreement with results from spectroscopic calculations given here for the first time, cf. Table 8.

TABLE 8
Observed and calculated mean amplitudes/Å for tetracyanomethane

Distance	Observed[a]	Calculated[b]
C—C	0.054 (2)	0.049
C≡N	0.039 (1)	0.034
C···C	0.069 (3)	0.071
C···N (linear)	0.058 (3)	0.053
C···N (non-lin.)	0.120 (3)	0.095
N···N	0.179(12)	0.143

[a] Reference 170.
[b] Unpublished results at 398 K, which is the reported nozzle temperature for the electron diffraction experiment.[170]

Müller et al.[8] have stated that the mean amplitude of vibration for the C≡N bond is characteristic, as expected from the fact that the corresponding normal frequency and force constant also are characteristic. The numerical value is actually between 0.034 and 0.035 Å, with negligible temperature variation between 0 and 300 K. For HCN the value of 0.03417 Å has been reported.[3,8]

13   AROMATIC HYDROCARBONS AND SOME OF THEIR SUBSTITUTED ANALOGUES

13.1 Benzene and Substituted Benzenes

Mean amplitudes of vibration for benzene have been investigated several times both by electron diffraction and spectroscopy.[3] Values[3] for C_6H_6 (benzene) and C_6D_6 (hexadeuterobenzene) are given in Fig. 11. The same values were used in the first schematic representation of mean amplitudes.[29] The same force field for benzene, which is consistent with the mean amplitudes of Fig. 11, was used to calculate the atomic-vibration mean-square amplitudes[8] with the results given in Table 9. These quantities are supposed to be of great interest in precise crystal structure studies by X-ray and neutron diffraction. More recent developments in the force field for benzene[171,172] seem to be minor refinements, which do not warrant a recalculation of the mean amplitudes and related

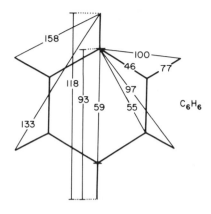

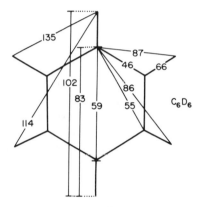

Fig. 11. Mean amplitudes of vibration/10^{-3} Å for benzene (above) and benzene-d_6 (below) at 298 K.

TABLE 9
Atomic vibration mean-square amplitudes/$Å^2$ for benzene

Atom	Temp./ K	$\langle \Delta x^2 \rangle$ radial	$\langle \Delta y^2 \rangle$ tangential	$\langle \Delta z^2 \rangle$ out-of-plane
C	0	0.00123	0.00083	0.00143
	298	0.00129	0.00086	0.00174
H	0	0.00643	0.01331	0.02027
	298	0.00650	0.01345	0.02232

quantities. Schmidling[70] used benzene as an example for calculating mean amplitudes and shrinkage effects by the MINDO/2 method. He reported a tendency for the mean amplitudes for bonded atom-pairs to be too low and for non-bonded atom-pairs to be too high, but the agreement with the spectroscopic values is still good (typical differences in mean amplitudes around 0.001 Å). Recently calculated mean amplitudes of benzene are also reported by Yokozeki et al.[173] Probably the most recent work on the structure of benzene is due to Tamagawa et al.,[174] who applied moments of inertia from infrared spectroscopic data in combination with new electron diffraction measurements.

Halogenated benzenes have been extensively investigated by electron diffraction; viz. perhalogenated molecules: hexafluorobenzene,[175,176] hexachlorobenzene[177] and hexabromobenzene[80,178]; partially halogenated molecules: 1,3-difluorobenzene,[179] 1,3,5-trifluorobenzene,[176] 1,2,4,5-tetrachlorobenzene[177] and 1,2-dibromobenzene.[178]

13.2 Condensed Aromatics

Electron diffraction studies have been performed on naphthalene ($C_{10}H_8$), anthracene ($C_{14}H_{10}$) and coronene ($C_{24}H_{12}$).[180] No mean amplitudes of vibration were reported from these investigations. Several years later the mean amplitudes were calculated from spectroscopic data for two of these comparatively large molecules. The first calculations for naphthalene[29,181] have been revised in some respects.[182,183] This revision mainly affected the mean amplitude for the C_2—C_3 distance. The results from the revised calculations for $C_{10}H_8$ at 298 K are reproduced in the schematic form in Figs 12 and 13. The corresponding data for $C_{14}H_{10}$ are shown in Figs 14, 15 and 16 for the CC, CH and HH distances, respectively. Atomic-vibration mean-square amplitudes of naphthalene and naphthalene-d_8 have been calculated.[8]

Perylene ($C_{20}H_{12}$)[184,185] has been studied by electron diffraction. The recent electron diffraction work on biphenylene ($C_{12}H_8$)[173] contains both observed and calculated mean amplitudes of vibration. Another independent calculation of mean amplitudes from spectroscopic data for the same molecule has been reported.[186]

A systematic approach to spectroscopic analysis of condensed aromatics with calculations of mean amplitudes has been taken up again recently, and the first report has been published.[187] In this work a seven-parameter force field was developed and proved to be applicable to a number of condensed aromatics. The seven parameters are four in-plane and three out-of-plane valence force constants. One of these parameters, viz. the CC stretching force constant, was modified according to the bond order ($0 \leqslant P \leqslant 1$) from the simple Hückel molecular orbital theory.[188] The following semi-empirical formula was produced for this force constant:[187]

$$f/\text{mdyn Å}^{-1} = 1.793[(0.235\,P+0.765)/(0.00916\,P+0.6548)]^3 \qquad (31)$$

The approach makes it a matter of routine to calculate the mean amplitudes for

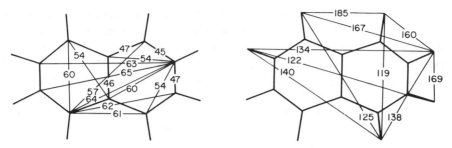

Fig. 12. Mean amplitudes of vibration/10⁻³ Å for naphthalene at 298 K : CC (left) and HH (right) distances.

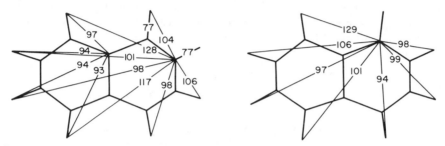

Fig. 13. Mean amplitudes of vibration/10⁻³ Å for naphthalene at 298 K : CH distances.

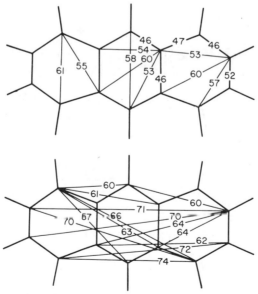

Fig. 14. Mean amplitudes of vibration/10⁻³ Å for anthracene at 298 K : CC distances.

condensed aromatics, inasmuch as no experimental frequencies are needed in the computation. The usefulness of this method, although based on a very simple force-field approximation, was proved by checking the calculated mean amplitudes for naphthalene, anthracene and biphenylene against the more accurate previous calculations.[183,186] Original results of calculated mean amplitudes were produced for perylene[187] and so-far-unpublished values for coronene and chrysene ($C_{18}H_{12}$). Figure 17 shows the more-or-less characteristic values of mean amplitudes obtained for the different types of non-bonded CC distances in perylene; see Fig. 18 for the numbering of atoms in this molecule. The corresponding mean amplitudes for the other condensed aromatics studied in the same way (see above) were mostly found within the same ranges. The calculated mean amplitudes for practically all of the bonded CC distances were found in the narrow range of $0.047 < l < 0.049$ Å. As expected this l value has a tendency to increase with decreasing bond order, but this increase is not exactly uniform; cf. Table 10.

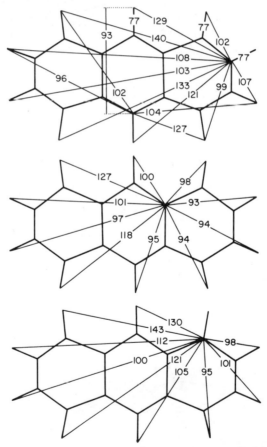

Fig. 15. Mean amplitudes of vibration/10^{-3} Å for anthracene at 298 K: CH distances.

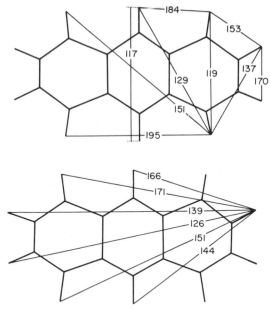

Fig. 16. Mean amplitudes of vibration/10⁻³ Å for anthracene at 298 K: HH distances.

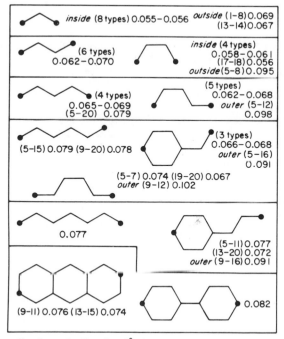

Fig. 17. Mean amplitudes of vibration/Å for the different types of non-bonded CC distances in perylene at 298 K.

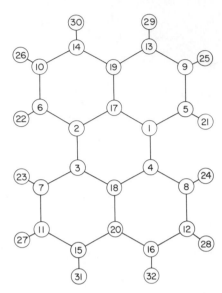

Fig. 18. Numbering of atoms in the perylene molecular model.

TABLE 10
Bond orders (in falling sequence) and mean amplitudes/Å for conjugated CC bonds in some condensed aromatic molecules

Bond order	Mean amplitude	Molecule	Bond order	Mean amplitude	Molecule
0.754	0.0469	Chrysene	0.568	0.0480	Chrysene
0.745	0.0469	Coronene	0.565	0.0473	Biphenylene
0.737	0.0470	Anthracene	0.555	0.0481	Naphthalene
0.725	0.0471	Naphthalene	0.552	0.0482	Perylene
0.712	0.0472	Chrysene	0.538	0.0474	Coronene
0.707	0.0473	Chrysene	0.538	0.0483	Coronene
0.707	0.0472	Perylene	0.538	0.0483	Chrysene
0.691	0.0474	Biphenylene	0.535	0.0481	Chrysene
0.683	0.0470	Biphenylene	0.535	0.0483	Anthracene
0.644	0.0474	Perylene	0.529	0.0475	Perylene
0.629	0.0479	Perylene	0.526	0.0475	Perylene
0.621	0.0480	Biphenylene	0.522	0.0465	Coronene
0.617	0.0480	Chrysene	0.521	0.0484	Chrysene
0.606	0.0477	Anthracene	0.518	0.0482	Naphthalene
0.603	0.0481	Naphthalene	0.485	0.0485	Anthracene
0.586	0.0483	Anthracene	0.476	0.0484	Chrysene
0.583	0.0479	Chrysene	0.414	0.0489	Perylene
0.573	0.0478	Chrysene	0.263	0.0491	Biphenylene

14   HETEROCYCLIC FIVE-MEMBERED RING MOLECULES

There are not many spectroscopic calculations of mean amplitudes available for heterocyclic organic molecules. Here we shall only refer to the results for a number of five-membered ring molecules:[189] 1,2,5-thia-, oxa- and selena-diazole, 1,3,4- thia- and oxa-diazole, thiophene, thiophene-d_4, furan (1,4-epoxy-1,3-butadiene) and furan-d_4. Some of the results of mean amplitudes are represented in Figs 19–21.

15   ALICYCLIC HYDROCARBONS AND THEIR SUBSTITUENTS

A recalculation of the mean amplitudes of vibration for cyclopropane[102] has confirmed the calculations reviewed previously.[3] The work mentioned[102] includes a calculation of the atomic-vibration mean-square amplitudes.[8] Mean amplitudes of vibration from electron diffraction work are available for hexa-

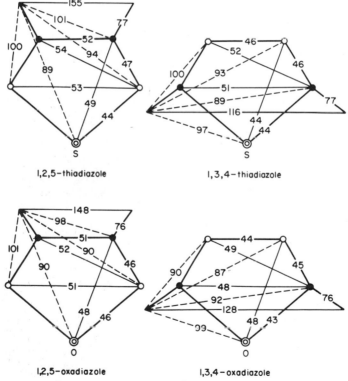

Fig. 19. Mean amplitudes of vibration/10^{-3} Å for thia- and oxa-diazoles at 298 K. Black circles: C atoms. White circles: N atoms. Broken lines indicate X $\cdots$ H distances (X = C, N, S or O).

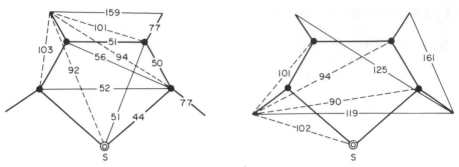

Fig. 20. Mean amplitudes of vibration/10^{-3} Å for thiophene at 298 K. Broken lines indicate C$\cdots$H and S$\cdots$H distances.

fluorocyclopropane,[190] hexachlorocyclopropane[191] and 1,1-dichlorocyclo-propane.[192] For the latter molecule the mean amplitudes determined from spectroscopic calculations have been published.[193]

Cyclobutane was investigated early by electron diffraction,[194] but very little information on mean amplitudes was deduced. Later, the complete set was obtained from spectroscopic calculations.[195] The electron diffraction work cited[194] includes cyclopentane, which was investigated later.[196]

For cyclohexane the 'chair' form has been proved to be the dominant conformation by extensive electron diffraction studies.[197–199] In two of the early papers[198,199] some observed mean amplitudes of vibration were reported. Several re-investigations[200–202] furnished more accurate structural parameters and mean amplitudes. The mean amplitudes of the CC distances are quoted in Table 11. In two of the recent works[201,202] the results of mean amplitudes from spectroscopic calculations were also reported. The most recent[202] contains the observed and calculated mean amplitudes for dodecadeutero-cyclohexane. Other substituted cyclohexanes which have been investigated by

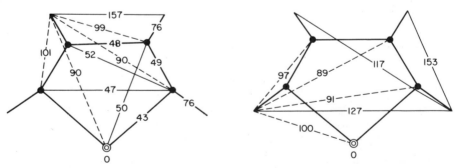

Fig. 21. Mean amplitudes of vibration/10^{-3} Å for furan at 298 K. Broken lines indicate C$\cdots$H and O$\cdots$H distances.

electron diffraction, are: dodecafluorocyclohexane,[203] monofluorocyclo-
hexane,[204] monochlorocyclohexane,[205] cis-1,4-chlorobromocyclohexane[206]
and 1,1-dimethylcyclohexane.[207]

Some larger cycloalkanes have been studied by electron diffraction, viz.
cyclooctane[208] and cyclodecane.[209]

TABLE 11
Mean amplitudes of vibration/Å for the CC
distances in cyclohexane from electron diffraction

$C_1—C_2$	$C_1 \cdots C_3$	$C_1 \cdots C_4$	Reference
0.055	0.078	—	(198)
0.048	0.062	0.070	(199)
0.054	0.071	0.070	(200)
0.050 ± 0.002	0.068 ± 0.003	0.077 ± 0.004	(201)
0.051 ± 0.002	0.069 ± 0.003	0.077 ± 0.003	(201)
0.049 ± 0.002	0.067 ± 0.003	0.076 ± 0.007	(202)

16 OTHER GROUPS OF ALIPHATIC MOLECULES

In the present review a complete survey of all groups of organic molecules is
not attempted. However, there exists a great number of polycyclic saturated
hydrocarbons which have been subjected to extensive electron diffraction
studies, in many cases accompanied by spectroscopic calculations of mean
amplitudes. One interesting example is norbornane (C_7H_{12}, bicyclo-[2.2.1]-
heptane), which has been studied by several groups of workers.[210–213]

16.1 Alcohols and their Substituents

The complete set of mean amplitudes of vibration for methanol[214] and some
of its deuterated species have been calculated from spectroscopic data. Some of
these results are shown in Table 12, where calculated values for CH_3OH (not
including the $H \cdots H$ distances) are compared with early electron diffraction
data.[215] Structural investigations of ethanol by electron diffraction are
unknown, but some of its halogen substituents have been so studied: viz.
ethylene fluorohydrin (2-fluoroethanol),[216] ethylene chlorohydrin (2-chloro-
ethanol)[217] and 2,2,2-trifluoroethanol.[218] n-Propyl alcohol (1-propanol)[219]
and isopropyl alcohol (2-propanol)[220] have been investigated by electron
diffraction, but no mean amplitudes were reported. Calculated mean amplitudes
from spectroscopic data are available for 1,1,1,3,3,3-hexafluoro-2-propanol.[221]

16.2   Alkanes and their Substituents

The largest alkane studied by electron diffraction is n-heptane (C_7H_{16}, heptane) in work[222,223] also dealing with other n-alkanes viz. C_6H_{14} hexane and C_5H_{12} pentane. Neopentane or tetramethylmethane (C_5H_{12}, 2,2-dimethyl-propane) has been studied by electron diffraction,[224–226] and a complete set of calculated mean amplitudes from spectroscopic data has been produced for this molecule.[227] Excellent electron diffraction studies along with both observed and calculated mean amplitudes for different chlorinated neopentanes have been furnished by Stølevik[228–230] in his systematic conformational analysis. Electron diffraction studies are also available for C_4H_{10}, and for both n-butane (butane)[223,231,232] and isobutane (2-methylpropane).[233] Iijima[234] has investigated the structure of propane, C_3H_8, using electron diffraction combined with microwave data. Spectroscopic vibrational analyses have been reported for propane[235] and some halogenated propanes.[236,237] Halogenated propanes were included in the extensive conformational analysis by Stølevik et al.[238–244] and others.[245–247] For ethane, C_2H_6, we only give two references[248,249] to supplement previous reviews.[3,8] Hexachloroethane has been fully reviewed previously,[3,8] while recent work on hexafluoroethane[250] and hexabromoethane[251] has been reported.

Finally, this review brings us back to methane, CH_4, for which the reader is referred to Fig. 1 and Section 5.

TABLE 12
Calculated and observed mean amplitudes/Å for methanol (H···H distances not included)

Distance	Calculated[a]		Observed[b]
	$T=0$ K	298 K	
O—H	0.0695	0.0695	0.073 ± 0.015
C—H	0.0791	0.0791 ⎫	0.080 ± 0.010
C—H	0.0785	0.0785 ⎭	
C—O	0.0453	0.0455	0.049 ± 0.005
C···H	0.1013	0.1015	0.110
O···H	0.1008	0.1011 ⎫	0.090 ± 0.01
O···H	0.1024	0.1027 ⎭	

    [a] Ref. 214.
    [b] Ref. 215.

17   BROADER OUTLOOK ON MEAN AMPLITUDES AND CONCLUSION

17.1   The Mean-Square Amplitude Matrix

The mean amplitudes of vibration (l) are closely connected with the mean-square amplitude matrix, Σ, which is obtainable from a normal coordinate analysis by

$$\Sigma = L\, \delta L^{\dagger} \tag{32}$$

For the L matrix; see eqns. (9) and (13). δ is the diagonal matrix of the frequency parameters δ_k given in eqn. (6). The connection between Σ and the mean amplitudes is realized by deducing the latter quantities from an approach somewhat different from the one described in Section 2. The mean-square amplitudes (l^2) may be obtained as linear combinations of the Σ-matrix elements. For methane, for instance, it has been found that

$$l_{CH}^2 = \tfrac{1}{4}[\Sigma(a_1) + 3\Sigma_{11}(t_2)] \tag{33}$$

$$\begin{aligned} l_{HH}^2 = \tfrac{1}{3}[2\Sigma(a_1) + \tfrac{1}{3}\Sigma(e) \\ + 2\Sigma_{11}(t_2) - 2\Sigma_{12}(t_2) + \tfrac{1}{2}\Sigma_{22}(t_2)] \end{aligned} \tag{34}$$

where the Σ elements are based on a set of conventional symmetry coordinates.[3]

17.2   Fundamental Properties of Σ

The fundamental role of the mean-square amplitude matrix in the theory of molecular vibrations is apparent from the secular equation[3]

$$\Sigma G^{-1} L = L\, \delta \tag{35}$$

It may be compared with the well-known secular equation (13) containing the F-matrix.

Another significant contribution to the theory of Σ is based on the studies of the classical limit of mean-square amplitudes due to Decius.[252,253] In the formulation of Cyvin[3] one has

$$\Sigma^{cl} = kTN, \qquad \Sigma_{ij}^{cl} = \lim_{T \to \infty} \Sigma_{ij} = kTN_{ij} \tag{36}$$

Here N is the compliance matrix,[3,253] and N_{ij} represents its elements. The compliance matrix appears in the first term of a power-series expansion[3,253] of Σ based on the expansion of the hyperbolic cotangent, cf. eqn. (6), or actually $x \coth(x)$. The result may be formulated as[8]

$$\Sigma = kT\left[N + \sum_{m=0}^{\infty} \left(\frac{h}{2\pi kT}\right)^{2m+2} \frac{B_{2m+2}}{(2m+2)!} (GF)^m G \right] \tag{37}$$

where B_{2m+2} are Bernoulli numbers. The deficiency of this power-series expansion has clearly been pointed out by Ra.[8] It converges (and often slowly) only for temperatures above a certain critical value, which depends on the highest normal frequency. At room temperature convergence occurs only when all wavenumbers are below ca. 1300 cm^{-1}.

17.3   Recent Developments in the Theory of Σ

Ra in Ref. 8 has commented on the more refined approaches to expansions of Σ based on empirical functions which should fit $\coth(x)$ within certain ranges of x.[3] He has made it clear that a point-by-point fit to $\coth(x)$, for the x values corresponding to the actual normal frequencies and a given temperature, is essential, rather than an overall fit. This feature has been exploited[254] in a new approach to the calculation of mean-square amplitudes. This involves an explicit equation for Σ in the two-dimensional case (two normal frequencies, ω_1, ω_2). Especially for Σ at $T = 0$ K, this equation reads

$$\Sigma(T = 0) = [h/(\omega_1+\omega_2)][\tfrac{1}{2}c\omega_1\omega_2\mathbf{N}+(1/8\pi^2 c)\mathbf{G}] \tag{38}$$

The formula may be applied to simple molecular models. Thus for the mean-square amplitude of the bond distance in methane, cf. eqn. (33), we find the following new result:

$$l_{CH}^2(T = 0) = \tfrac{3}{8}hc\omega_3\omega_4(\omega_3+\omega_4)^{-1}N_{11}(t_2)$$
$$+ (h/32\pi^2 c)[\mu_H\omega_1^{-1}+(3\mu_H+4\mu_C)(\omega_3+\omega_4)^{-1}] \tag{39}$$

Here μ_H and μ_C denote the inverse masses of the respective atoms.

The most profound contribution to the theory of Σ is probably that given by Ra, in Ref. 8. Ra established the connection between Σ and the compliance matrix, regarded as a collection of double-time Green's functions of amplitudes:[255]

$$\mathbf{N}(z) = -(z^2\mathbf{G}^{-1}-\mathbf{F})^{-1} \tag{40}$$

Since the ordinary compliance matrix ($\mathbf{N} = \mathbf{F}^{-1}$) is obtained as $\mathbf{N}(z = 0)$, it may be referred to $\mathbf{N}(z)$ as the generalized compliants. When starting from the elegant formulation in terms of a Cauchy integral,

$$\Sigma = -\frac{h}{4\pi^2 i} \oint [2\Phi(z)+1]\mathbf{N}(z)\,dz \tag{41}$$

Ra succeeded in expanding Σ in residue matrices or generalized compliants on the imaginary frequency axis. The integral is taken over a counterclockwise contour encircling all the normal frequencies without enclosing any of the poles, $\omega_n = iy_n = 4\pi^2 inkT/h$, of the function

$$\Phi(z) = (e^{hz/2\pi kT} - 1)^{-1} \tag{42}$$

By virtue of the Cauchy theorem, and considering the residue of $\Phi(z)$, one obtains

$$\Sigma = kT\left[\mathbf{N}+2\sum_{n=1}^{\infty}\mathbf{N}(\omega_n)\right] \tag{43}$$

This equation may also be regarded as a relation between Σ and the set of finite-temperature propagator matrices.[255] By invoking conformal-mapping techniques, Ra in Ref. 8 subsequently arrived at Σ as the classical limit augmented with Tchebycheff polynomials in **GF**. The resulting power-expansion of Σ proved to have considerably superior convergence properties compared with those of eqn. (37). Further improvements were achieved[256] by changing the contour of integration in eqn. (41).

17.4 Practical Applications of Mean Amplitudes

The theoretical aspects of mean amplitudes (l) and the Σ matrix described above would hardly be enough to justify the calculation of l values for hundreds of molecules and the systematic compilation of these for organic molecules. In this final section we attempt to provide a justification with other reasons.

The use of calculated mean amplitudes in the interpretation of gas-phase electron diffraction measurements[4,8,257] is still the most widely applied excuse for publishing long lists of such data. This feature is mentioned in the Introduction (Section 1), and reference is made to much electron diffraction work throughout the present review.

Much work has also been done in the attempts to proceed along the reverse path, namely, to utilize mean amplitudes deduced from electron diffraction measurements as constraints in normal coordinate analysis. The Jacobian elements of Σ with respect to the force constants are relevant in this connection. It has been found[8,25] that

$$\frac{\partial \Sigma_{ij}}{\partial F_{kl}} = \sum_r L_{ir}L_{jr}\frac{\partial \delta_r}{\partial F_{kl}} + \left(1 - \frac{\delta_{kl}}{2}\right)\sum_{r<s}\sum (L_{ir}L_{js}+L_{is}L_{jr})(L_{kr}L_{ls}+L_{ks}L_{lr})\frac{\delta_r - \delta_s}{\lambda_r - \lambda_s} \quad (44)$$

where δ_{kl} is the Kronecker delta: $\delta_{kl} = 0$ for $k \neq l$, $\delta_{kk} = 1$; this should not be confused with the frequency parameter δ_r. The Jacobians of this frequency parameter are obtained from differentiation of eqn. (6) and the well-known expression for the Jacobians of $\lambda_r = 4\pi^2 c^2 \omega_r^2$:[8,259,260]

$$\frac{\partial \lambda_r}{\partial F_{ij}} = (2 - \delta_{ij})L_{ir}L_{jr} \quad (45)$$

Both theoretical considerations and practical experience have led to the conclusion that the mean amplitudes usually cannot be observed with sufficient accuracy to be an efficient tool in determinations of force constants (see, for example, Ref. 121). In general the situation is more favourable for Coriolis coupling constants, centrifugal distortion constants and isotopic frequency shifts.[3,121,259] The calculated mean amplitudes may be decisive, however, when choosing between substantially different sets of force constants or gross trends in vibrational frequency assignments. Observed Bastiansen-Morino shrinkage effects[3] from electron diffraction may in some cases be useful too. The situation becomes more favourable when the electron diffraction experiments are performed at high temperatures and preferably for molecules with extremely low frequencies. Among the successful results in this area we wish to mention the work on some simple inorganic molecules, $MnCl_2$,[261] $CoCl_2$[262] and $NiBr_2$,[263] for which the Bastiansen-Morino shrinkage effects were used in a non-spectroscopic determination of the low bending frequencies. Among the organic molecules, we may refer to the halogenated propanes and neopentanes studied by Stølevik et al.[228-230,238-244] at temperatures moderately above ambient (up to ca. 100 °C). In this work special attention was paid to the torsional-sensitive mean amplitudes. Their determination from electron diffraction data has allowed fairly accurate determinations of the torsional force constants and frequencies.

Mayants[264-267] has contributed to the theory of Σ, including the determination of partial derivatives of its elements. Among his results is a link between mean-square amplitudes and the vibrational free energy, F_{vib}. Let F_{vib} be defined with the zero-point energy included, viz.

$$F_{vib} = \sum_k [(hc\omega_k/2) + kT\ln(1 - e^{-hc\omega_k/kT})] \tag{46}$$

Then, a slight generalization of the remarkable relation of Mayants,[264,265] reads

$$\Sigma_{ij} = (1 + \delta_{ij}) \frac{\partial F_{vib}}{\partial F_{ij}} \tag{47}$$

This relation has not yet found practical application.

In general terms the mean amplitudes of vibration characterize, vaguely stated, the looseness or rigidity of a molecule or part of a molecule. Large mean amplitudes occur for loosely bonded atoms while small mean amplitudes indicate rigid structures. Force constants are often assumed to describe the same characteristics for interatomic bonds, but it should be remembered that the definition of individual force constants is obscured by their lack of invariance properties with respect to the selection of coordinates.[3,5,253] Compliants do possess these invariance properties in common with the mean-square amplitudes. This is not the place to discuss the merits and demerits of compliants versus force constants. It should rather be stressed that the mean amplitudes of vibration for the bonded as well as non-bonded interatomic distances are physical quantities which, in principle, are accessible by experimental measurements. They are independent of the vibrational coordinates used in the normal coordinate analysis. The mean amplitudes are recognized as important parameters, in addition to the bond distances and interbond angles, of a vibrating molecule.

ACKNOWLEDGMENT

Financial support to BNC from The Norwegian Research Council for Science and the Humanities is gratefully acknowledged.

REFERENCES

(1) Y. Morino, K. Kuchitsu and T. Shimanouchi, *J. Chem. Phys.* **20**, 726 (1952).
(2) Y. Morino, K. Kuchitsu, A. Takahashi and K. Maeda, *J. Chem. Phys.* **21**, 1927 (1953).
(3) S. J. Cyvin, *Molecular Vibrations and Mean Square Amplitudes*, Universitets-forlaget, Oslo, and Elsevier, Amsterdam, 1968.
(4) K. Kuchitsu, in *M.T.P. International Review of Science, Physical Chemistry*, Series One, Vol. 2, *Molecular Structure and Properties* (G. Allen, ed.), Butterworth, 1972.
(5) E. B. Wilson, J. C. Decius and P. C. Cross, *Molecular Vibrations*, McGraw-Hill, New York, 1955.
(6) S. J. Cyvin and I. Alfheim, *Indian J. Pure Appl. Phys.* **8**, 629 (1970).
(7) R. Stølevik, H. M. Seip and S. J. Cyvin, *Chem. Phys. Lett.* **15**, 263 (1972).
(8) S. J. Cyvin, ed. *Molecular Structures and Vibrations*, Elsevier, Amsterdam, 1972.
(9) W. D. Gwinn, *J. Chem. Phys.* **55**, 477 (1971).
(10) S. J. Cyvin, *J. Mol. Struct.* **15**, 189 (1973).
(11) S. J. Cyvin, *Chem. Phys. Lett.* **18**, 150 (1973).
(12) Y. Morino and E. Hirota, *J. Chem. Phys.* **23**, 737 (1955).
(13) B. L. Crawford and W. H. Fletcher, *J. Chem. Phys.* **19**, 141 (1951).
(14) F. A. Cotton, *Chemical Applications of Group Theory*, 2nd ed., Wiley-Interscience, New York, 1971.
(15) R. W. Mooney, S. J. Cyvin, J. Brunvoll and L. A. Kristiansen, *J. Chem. Phys.* **42**, 3741 (1965).
(16) S. J. Cyvin, R. W. Mooney, J. Brunvoll and L. A. Kristiansen, *Acta Chem. Scand.* **19**, 1031 (1965).
(17) A. Rogstad, B. N. Cyvin, S. J. Cyvin and J. Brunvoll, *J. Mol. Struct.* **35**, 121 (1976).
(18) B. N. Cyvin, S. J. Cyvin, K. H. Schmidt, W. Wiegeler, A. Müller and J. Brunvoll, *J. Mol. Struct.* **30**, 315 (1976).
(19) S. J. Cyvin, V. Devarajan, J. Brunvoll and Ø. Ra, *Z. Naturforsch.* **28a**, 1787 (1973).
(20) P. Andersen, *Acta Chem. Scand.* **19**, 629 (1965).
(21) E. Bodewig, *Matrix Calculus*, North-Holland, Amsterdam, 1959.
(22) O. Bastiansen and M. Trætteberg, *Acta Crystallogr.* **13**, 1108 (1960).
(23) Y. Morino, *Acta Crystallogr.* **13**, 1107 (1960).
(24) Y. Morino, S. J. Cyvin, K. Kuchitsu and T. Iijima, *J. Chem. Phys.* **36**, 1109 (1962).
(25) S. J. Cyvin, *Kgl. Norske Videnskab. Selskabs Skrifter*, No. 1 (1969).
(26) S. J. Cyvin, *Kgl. Norske Videnskab. Selskabs Skrifter*, No. 7 (1971).
(27) S. J. Cyvin, *Z. Anorg. Allg. Chem.* **378**, 117 (1970).
(28) S. J. Cyvin and B. Vizi, *Acta Chim. Acad. Sci. Hung.* **70**, 55 (1971).
(29) B. N. Cyvin, S. J. Cyvin and G. Hagen, *Chem. Phys. Lett.* **1**, 211 (1967).
(30) A. Müller, B. Krebs, A. Fadini, O. Glemser, S. J. Cyvin, J. Brunvoll, B. N. Cyvin, I. Elvebredd, G. Hagen and B. Vizi, *Z. Naturforsch.* **23a**, 1656 (1968).
(31) A. Müller and S. J. Cyvin, *J. Mol. Spectrosc.* **26**, 315 (1968).
(32) J. Bakken, *Acta Chem. Scand.* **12**, 594 (1958).
(33) K. V. Rajalakshmi and S. J. Cyvin, *Acta Chem. Scand.* **20**, 2611 (1966).
(34) S. J. Cyvin, J. Brunvoll, B. N. Cyvin and E. Meisingseth, *Bull. Soc. Chim. Belg.* **73**, 5 (1964).
(35) C. Kato, S. Konaka, T. Iijima and M. Kimura, *Bull. Chem. Soc. Jpn* **42**, 2148 (1969).
(36) E. Meisingseth and S. J. Cyvin, *Acta Chem. Scand.* **15**, 2021 (1961).

(37) S. J. Cyvin and P. Klæboe, *Acta Chem. Scand.* **19**, 697 (1965).
(38) K. Ramaswamy and K. Srinivasan, *Aust. J. Chem.* **21**, 575 (1968).
(39) K. Venkateswarlu and M. P. Mathew, *Z. Naturforsch.* **23b**, 1296 (1968).
(40) A. Rogstad and S. J. Cyvin, *J. Mol. Struct.* **20**, 373 (1974).
(41) P. Klæboe, E. Kloster-Jensen and S. J. Cyvin, *Spectrochim. Acta, Part A* **23**, 2733 (1967).
(42) S. J. Cyvin, *J. Mol. Struct.* **3**, 520 (1969).
(43) K. Venkateswarlu, M. P. Mathew and V. Malathy Devi, *J. Mol. Struct.* **3**, 119 (1969).
(44) G. Nagarajan, E. R. Lippincott and J. M. Stutman, *Z. Naturforsch.* **20a**, 786 (1965).
(45) G. Nagarajan, *Acta Physiol. Pol.* **30**, 743 (1966).
(46) K. Venkateswarlu, S. Mariam and Y. Anantarama Sarma, *Opt. Spektrosk.* **22**, 210 (1967).
(47) M. Tanimoto, K. Kuchitsu and Y. Morino, *Bull. Chem. Soc. Jpn* **44**, 386 (1971).
(48) B. Minasso and G. Zerbi, *J. Mol. Struct.* **7**, 59 (1971).
(49) V. Devarajan and S. J. Cyvin, *Aust. J. Chem.* **25**, 1387 (1972).
(50) M. G. Krishna Pillai, K. Ramaswamy and A. Perumal, *Indian J. Pure Appl. Phys.* **3**, 276 (1965).
(51) V. Galasso and A. Bigotto, *Spectrochim. Acta* **21**, 2085 (1965).
(52) K. Venkateswarlu and M. P. Mathew, *Curr. Sci.* **35**, 562 (1966).
(53) E. Augdahl, E. Kloster-Jensen, V. Devarajan and S. J. Cyvin, *Aust. J. Chem.* **26**, 269 (1973).
(54) M. Tanimoto, K. Kuchitsu and Y. Morino, *Bull. Chem. Soc. Jpn* **42**, 2519 (1969).
(55) I. Elvebredd, *Acta Chem. Scand.* **22**, 1606 (1968).
(56) R. E. Knudsen, C. F. George and J. Karle, *J. Chem. Phys.* **44**, 2334 (1966).
(57) J. Karle, *J. Chem. Phys.* **45**, 4149 (1966).
(58) S. J. Cyvin, I. Elvebredd, B. N. Cyvin, J. Brunvoll and G. Hagen, *Acta Chem. Scand.* **21**, 2405 (1967).
(59) S. J. Cyvin and J. Brunvoll, *Acta Chem. Scand.* **22**, 2718 (1968).
(60) S. J. Cyvin, I. Elvebredd, G. Hagen and J. Brunvoll, *J. Chem. Phys.* **49**, 3561 (1968).
(61) K. Kveseth, H. M. Seip and R. Stølevik, *Acta Chem. Scand.* **25**, 2975 (1971).
(62) C. H. Chang, A. L. Andreassen and S. H. Bauer, *J. Org. Chem.* **36**, 920 (1971).
(63) A. Rogstad, L. Benestad and S. J. Cyvin, *J. Mol. Struct.* **23**, 265 (1974).
(64) T. Fukuyama, K. Kuchitsu and Y. Morino, *Bull. Chem. Soc. Jpn* **42**, 379 (1969).
(65) A. Almenningen, G. Gundersen, A. Borg, M. Granberg and F. Karlsson, *Acta Chem. Scand.* **A29**, 545 (1975).
(66) A. Almenningen, G. Gundersen, M. Granberg and F. Karlsson, *Acta Chem. Scand., Ser. A*, **29**, 725 (1975).
(67) A. Almenningen, G. Gundersen, M. Granberg and F. Karlsson, *Acta Chem. Scand., Ser. A* **29**, 731 (1975).
(68) S. J. Cyvin and G. Hagen, *Acta Chem. Scand.* **23**, 2037 (1969).
(69) G. Fogarasi and P. Mezey, *Acta Chim. Acad. Sci. Hung.* **63**, 167 (1970).
(70) D. G. Schmidling, *J. Mol. Struct.* **25**, 313 (1975).
(71) S. J. Cyvin, *Czech. J. Phys.* **B20**, 464 (1970).
(72) G. de Alti, V. Galasso and G. Costa, *Spectrochim. Acta* **21**, 649 (1965).
(73) K. Venkateswarlu and S. Mariam, *Czech. J. Phys.* **B16**, 290 (1966).
(74) S. J. Cyvin, *J. Chem. Phys.* **59**, 1365 (1973).
(75) G. Fogarasi, *Acta Chim. Acad. Sci. Hung.* **66**, 87 (1970).
(76) I. L. Karle and J. Karle, *J. Chem. Phys.* **18**, 963 (1950).
(77) I. L. Karle and J. Karle, *J. Chem. Phys.* **20**, 63 (1952).

(78) J. L. Carlos, R. R. Karl and S. H. Bauer, *J. Chem. Soc., Faraday Trans. 2* **70**, 177 (1974).
(79) T. G. Strand, *Acta Chem. Scand.* **21**, 2111 (1967).
(80) T. G. Strand, *Acta Chem. Scand.* **21**, 1033 (1967).
(81) E. J. M. van Schaick, F. C. Mijlhoff, G. Renes and H. J. Geise, *J. Mol. Struct.* **21**, 17 (1974).
(82) M. I. Davis and H. P. Hanson, *J. Phys. Chem.* **69**, 4091 (1965).
(83) M. I. Davis, H. A. Kappler and D. J. Cowan, *J. Phys. Chem.* **68**, 2005 (1964).
(84) R. C. Ivey and M. I. Davis, *J. Chem. Phys.* **57**, 1909 (1972).
(85) S. B. Lie, P. Klæboe, D. H. Christensen and G. Hagen, *J. Cryst. Mol. Struct.* **1**, 33 (1971).
(86) H. Hope, *Acta Chem. Scand.* **22**, 1057 (1968).
(87) D. A. Long and W. O. George, *Spectrochim. Acta* **19**, 1717 (1963).
(88) T. Takenaka and S. Hayashi, *Bull. Chem. Soc. Jpn* **37**, 1216 (1964).
(89) F. A. Miller, O. Sala, P. Devlin, J. Overend, E. Lippert, W. Lüder, H. Moser and J. Varchmin, *Spectrochim. Acta* **20**, 1233 (1964).
(90) A. Rosenberg and J. P. Devlin, *Spectrochim. Acta* **21**, 1613 (1965).
(91) P. Devlin, J. Overend and B. Crawford, *Spectrochim. Acta* **20**, 23 (1964).
(92) S. B. Lie, P. Klæboe, D. H. Christensen and G. Hagen, *Spectrochim. Acta, Part A* **26**, 1861 (1970).
(93) S. B. Lie, P. Klæboe, E. Kloster-Jensen, G. Hagen and D. H. Christensen, *Spectrochim. Acta, Part A* **26**, 2077 (1970).
(94) I. Tokue, T. Fukuyama and K. Kuchitsu, *J. Mol. Struct.* **17**, 207 (1973).
(95) B. Andersen, R. Stølevik, J. Brunvoll, S. J. Cyvin and G. Hagen, *Acta Chem. Scand.* **21**, 1759 (1967).
(96) L. Nemes, J. L. Duncan and I. M. Mills, *Spectrochim. Acta, Part A* **23**, 1803 (1967).
(97) A. Almenningen, O. Bastiansen and M. Trætteberg, *Acta Chem. Scand.* **13**, 1699 (1959).
(98) A. Almenningen, O. Bastiansen and M. Trætteberg, *Acta Chem. Scand.* **15**, 1557 (1961).
(99) A. Phongsatha, P. Klæboe, H. Hopf, B. N. Cyvin and S. J. Cyvin, *Spectrochim. Acta*, in press.
(100) A. Eriksson, G. Hagen and S. J. Cyvin, *Chem. Phys. Lett.* **24**, 571 (1974).
(101) M. Trætteberg, G. Paulen and H. Hopf, *Acta Chem. Scand.* **27**, 2227 (1973).
(102) S. J. Cyvin and G. Hagen, *Z. Naturforsch.* **25b**, 350 (1970).
(103) P. P. Barzdain, N. V. Alekseev, V. I. Sokolov and I. A. Ronova, *Dokl. Akad. Nauk SSSR* **192**, 801 (1970).
(104) H. J. Mair and S. H. Bauer, *J. Phys. Chem.* **75**, 1681 (1971).
(105) E. Goldish, K. Hedberg and V. Schomaker, *J. Am. Chem. Soc.* **78**, 2714 (1956).
(106) O. Bastiansen and J. L. Derissen, *Acta Chem. Scand.* **20**, 1089 (1966).
(107) C. H. Chang, R. F. Porter and S. H. Bauer, *J. Mol. Struct.* **7**, 89 (1971).
(108) J. F. Chiang, M. T. Kratus, A. L. Andreassen and S. H. Bauer, *J. Chem. Soc., Faraday Trans. 2* **68**, 1274 (1972).
(109) R. R. Karl and S. H. Bauer, *J. Mol. Struct.* **25**, 1 (1975).
(110) M. I. Davis and T. W. Muecke, *J. Phys. Chem.* **74**, 1104 (1970).
(111) D. L. Zebelman, S. H. Bauer and J. F. Chiang, *Tetrahedron* **28**, 2727 (1972).
(112) J. F. Chiang and S. H. Bauer, *J. Am. Chem. Soc.* **88**, 420 (1966).
(113) K. Hagen and M. Trætteberg, *Acta Chem. Scand.* **26**, 3636 (1972).
(114) R. M. Gavin and Z. F. Wang, *J. Am. Chem. Soc.* **95**, 1425 (1973).
(115) M. Trætteberg, *Acta Chem. Scand., Ser. B* **29**, 29 (1975).
(116) S. J. Cyvin and O. Gebhardt, *Monatsh. Chem.* **105**, 1374 (1974).
(117) J. F. Chiang and S. H. Bauer, *J. Am. Chem. Soc.* **91**, 1898 (1969).

(118) M. Trætteberg, G. Hagen and S. J. Cyvin, *Acta Chem. Scand.* **23**, 74 (1969).
(119) A. Almenningen, O. Bastiansen and M. Trætteberg, *Acta Chem. Scand.* **12**, 1221 (1958).
(120) W. Haugen and M. Trætteberg, *Acta Chem. Scand.* **20**, 1726 (1966).
(121) *Selected Topics in Structure Chemistry* (P. Andersen, O. Bastiansen and S. Furberg, eds), Universitetsforlaget, Oslo, 1967.
(122) K. Kuchitsu, T. Fukuyama and Y. Morino, *J. Mol. Struct.* **1**, 463 (1967–68).
(123) Yu. N. Panchenko, *Spectrochim. Acta, Part A* **31**, 1201 (1975).
(124) G. Gundersen, *J. Am. Chem. Soc.* **97**, 6342 (1975).
(125) M. Trætteberg, *Acta Chem. Scand.* **22**, 628 (1968).
(126) M. Trætteberg, *Acta Chem. Scand.* **22**, 2294 (1968).
(127) S. J. Cyvin, G. Hagen and M. Trætteberg, *Acta Chem. Scand.* **23**, 3285 (1969).
(128) L. V. Vilkov and N. I. Sadova, *Zh. Strukt. Khim.* **8**, 398 (1967).
(129) J. Donohue and A. Caron, *J. Phys. Chem.* **70**, 603 (1966).
(130) C. F. Aten, L. Hedberg and K. Hedberg, *J. Am. Chem. Soc.* **90**, 2463 (1968).
(131) S. J. Cyvin and O. Gebhardt, *J. Mol. Struct.* **27**, 435 (1975).
(132) M. Trætteberg, *Acta Chem. Scand.* **22**, 2305 (1968).
(133) G. Dallinga and L. H. Toneman, *J. Mol. Struct.* **1**, 11 (1967–68).
(134) H. Oberhammer and S. H. Bauer, *J. Am. Chem. Soc.* **91**, 10 (1969).
(135) C. H. Chang and S. H. Bauer, *J. Chem. Phys.* **75**, 1685 (1971).
(136) K. Hagen and M. Trætteberg, *Acta Chem. Scand.* **26**, 3643 (1972).
(137) J. F. Chiang and C. F. Wilcox, *J. Am. Chem. Soc.* **95**, 2885 (1973).
(138) M. Trætteberg, *J. Am. Chem. Soc.* **86**, 4265 (1964).
(139) M. Trætteberg, *Acta Chem. Scand.* **24**, 2285 (1970).
(140) I. L. Karle, *J. Chem. Phys.* **20**, 65 (1952).
(141) O. Bastiansen, L. Hedberg and K. Hedberg, *J. Chem. Phys.* **27**, 1311 (1957).
(142) M. Trætteberg, G. Hagen and S. J. Cyvin, *Z. Naturforsch.* **25b**, 134 (1970).
(143) S. J. Cyvin, I. Alfheim and G. Hagen, *Acta Chem. Scand.* **24**, 3038 (1970).
(144) H. H. Jensen, G. Hagen and S. J. Cyvin, *J. Mol. Struct.* **4**, 51 (1969).
(145) J. Brunvoll, S. J. Cyvin, I. Elvebredd and G. Hagen, *Chem. Phys. Lett.* **1**, 566 (1968).
(146) T. Iijima and M. Kimura, *Bull. Chem. Soc. Jpn* **42**, 2159 (1969).
(147) T. Iijima and S. Tsuchiya, *J. Mol. Spectrosc.* **44**, 88 (1972).
(148) G. Hagen, *Acta Chem. Scand.* **25**, 813 (1971).
(149) S. Tsuchiya, *J. Mol. Struct.* **22**, 77 (1974).
(150) S. Tsuchiya and M. Kimura, *Bull. Chem. Soc. Jpn* **45**, 736 (1972).
(151) T. Iijima, *Bull. Chem. Soc. Jpn* **45**, 3526 (1972).
(152) A. L. Andreassen and S. H. Bauer, *J. Mol. Struct.* **12**, 381 (1972).
(153) R. L. Hilderbrandt, A. L. Andreassen and S. H. Bauer, *J. Phys. Chem.* **74**, 1586 (1970).
(154) P. Andersen, E. E. Astrup and A. Borgan, *Acta Chem. Scand., Ser. A* **28**, 239 (1974).
(155) K. Hagen and K. Hedberg, *J. Am. Chem. Soc.* **95**, 8266 (1973).
(156) G. Paulen and M. Trætteberg, *Acta Chem. Scand., Ser. A* **28**, 1155 (1974).
(157) S. J. Cyvin, D. H. Christensen and F. Nicolaisen, *Chem. Phys. Lett.* **5**, 597; **6**, 552 (1970).
(158) A. Almenningen, O. Bastiansen and T. Motzfeldt, *Acta Chem. Scand.* **23**, 2848 (1969).
(159) Z. Náhlovská, B. Náhlovský and T. G. Strand, *Acta Chem. Scand.* **24**, 2617 (1970).
(160) J. L. Derissen, *J. Mol. Struct.* **7**, 67 (1971).
(161) B. P. van Eijck, G. van der Plaats and P. H. van Roon, *J. Mol. Struct.* **11**, 67 (1972).

(162) J. L. Derissen and J. M. J. M. Bijen, *J. Mol. Struct.* **29**, 153 (1975).
(163) J. M. J. M. Bijen and J. L. Derissen, *J. Mol. Struct.* **27**, 233 (1975).
(164) J. L. Derissen, *J. Mol. Struct.* **7**, 81 (1971).
(165) I. Alfheim and S. J. Cyvin, *Acta Chem. Scand.* **24**, 3043 (1970).
(166) S. J. Cyvin and I. Alfheim, *Acta Chem. Scand.* **24**, 2648 (1970).
(167) I. Alfheim, G. Hagen and S. J. Cyvin, *J. Mol. Struct.* **8**, 159 (1971).
(168) S. J. Cyvin and V. Devarajan, *J. Mol. Struct.* **10**, 393 (1971).
(169) K. Karakida, T. Fukuyama and K. Kuchitsu, *Bull. Chem. Soc. Jpn* **47**, 299 (1974).
(170) H. Oberhammer, *Z. Naturforsch.* **26a**, 2043 (1971).
(171) J. C. Duinker and I. M. Mills, *Spectrochim. Acta, Part A* **24**, 417 (1968).
(172) P. C. Painter and J. L. Koenig, *Spectrochim. Acta, Part A* **33**, 1019 (1977).
(173) A. Yokozeki, C. F. Wilcox and S. H. Bauer, *J. Am. Chem. Soc.* **96**, 1026 (1974).
(174) K. Tamagawa, T. Iijima and M. Kimura, *J. Mol. Struct.* **30**, 243 (1976).
(175) A. Almenningen, O. Bastiansen, R. Seip and H. M. Seip, *Acta Chem. Scand.* **18**, 2115 (1964).
(176) *Structural Chemistry and Molecular Biology* (A. Rich and N. Davidson, eds), Freeman, San Francisco, 1968.
(177) T. G. Strand and H. L. Cox, *J. Chem. Phys.* **44**, 2426 (1966).
(178) T. G. Strand, *J. Chem. Phys.* **44**, 1611 (1966).
(179) E. J. M. van Schaick, H. J. Geise, F. C. Mijlhoff and G. Renes, *J. Mol. Struct.* **16**, 389 (1973).
(180) A. Almenningen, O. Bastiansen and F. Dyvik, *Acta Crystallogr.* **14**, 1056 (1961).
(181) G. Hagen and S. J. Cyvin, *J. Phys. Chem.* **72**, 1446 (1968).
(182) S. J. Cyvin, B. N. Cyvin and G. Hagen, *Chem. Phys. Lett.* **2**, 341 (1968).
(183) B. N. Cyvin and S. J. Cyvin, *J. Phys. Chem.* **73**, 1430 (1969).
(184) M. Trætteberg, *Proc. R. Soc. London, Ser. A* **283**, 557 (1964).
(185) G. Dallinga, L. H. Toneman and M. Trætteberg, *Rec. Trav. Chim. Pays-Bas* **86**, 795 (1967).
(186) B. N. Cyvin and S. J. Cyvin, *Monatsh. Chem.* **105**, 1077 (1974).
(187) J. C. Whitmer, S. J. Cyvin and B. N. Cyvin, *Z. Naturforsch.* **33a**, 45 (1978).
(188) E. Heilbronner and H. Bock, *The HMO Model and its Application*, Wiley-Interscience, London, 1976.
(189) S. J. Cyvin, B. N. Cyvin, G. Hagen and P. Markov, *Acta Chem. Scand.* **23**, 3407 (1969).
(190) J. F. Chiang and W. A. Bernett, *Tetrahedron* **27**, 975 (1971).
(191) P. P. Barzdain, N. I. Gracheva and N. V. Alekseev, *Zh. Strukt. Khim.* **13**, 717 (1972).
(192) N. V. Alekseev, P. P. Barzdain and V. M. Shostakovskii, *Zh. Strukt. Khim.* **13**, 512 (1972).
(193) K. C. Cole and D. F. R. Gilson, *J. Mol. Struct.* **28**, 385 (1975).
(194) A. Almenningen, O. Bastiansen and P. N. Skancke, *Acta Chem. Scand.* **15**, 711 (1961).
(195) O. Gebhardt and B. N. Cyvin, *Monatsh. Chem.* **105**, 1050 (1974).
(196) W. J. Adams, H. J. Geise and L. S. Bartell, *J. Am. Chem. Soc.* **92**, 5013 (1970).
(197) M. Davis and O. Hassel, *Acta Chem. Scand.* **17**, 1181 (1963).
(198) N. V. Alekseev and A. I. Kitaigorodskii, *Zh. Strukt. Khim.* **4**, 163 (1963).
(199) M. I. Davis and O. Hassel, *Acta Chem. Scand.* **18**, 813 (1964).
(200) H. J. Geise, H. R. Buys and F. C. Mijlhoff, *J. Mol. Struct.* **9**, 447 (1971).
(201) O. Bastiansen, L. Fernholt, H. M. Seip, H. Kambara and K. Kuchitsu, *J. Mol. Struct.* **18**, 163 (1973).
(202) J. D. Ewbank, G. Kirsch and L. Schäfer, *J. Mol. Struct.* **31**, 39 (1976).
(203) K. E. Hjortaas and K. O. Strømme, *Acta Chem. Scand.* **22**, 2965 (1968).
(204) P. Andersen, *Acta Chem. Scand.* **16**, 2337 (1962).

(205) V. Atkinson, *Acta Chem. Scand.* **15**, 599 (1961).
(206) V. A. Atkinson and K. Lunde, *Acta Chem. Scand.* **14**, 2139 (1960).
(207) H. J. Geise, F. C. Mijlhoff and C. Altona, *J. Mol. Struct.* **13**, 211 (1972).
(208) A. Almenningen, O. Bastiansen and H. Jensen, *Acta Chem. Scand.* **20**, 2689 (1966).
(209) R. L. Hilderbrandt, J. D. Wieser and L. K. Montgomery, *J. Am. Chem. Soc.* **95**, 8598 (1973).
(210) Y. Morino, K. Kuchitsu and A. Yokozeki, *Bull. Chem. Soc. Jpn* **40**, 1552 (1967).
(211) G. Dallinga and L. H. Toneman, *Rec. Trav. Chim. Pays-Bas* **87**, 795 (1968).
(212) J. F. Chiang, C. F. Wilcox and S. H. Bauer, *J. Am. Chem. Soc.* **90**, 3149 (1968).
(213) A. Yokozeki and K. Kuchitsu, *Bull. Chem. Soc. Jpn* **44**, 2356 (1971).
(214) O. Gebhardt, S. J. Cyvin and J. Brunvoll, *Acta Chem. Scand.* **25**, 3373 (1971).
(215) K. Kimura and M. Kubo, *J. Chem. Phys.* **30**, 151 (1959).
(216) K. Hagen and K. Hedberg, *J. Am. Chem. Soc.* **95**, 8263 (1973).
(217) A. Almenningen, O. Bastiansen, L. Fernholt and K. Hedberg, *Acta Chem. Scand.* **25**, 1946 (1971).
(218) R. L. Livingston and G. Vaughan, *J. Am. Chem. Soc.* **78**, 2711 (1956).
(219) N. E. D. A. Aziz and F. Rogowski, *Z. Naturforsch.* **21b**, 1102 (1966).
(220) N. E. D. A. Aziz and F. Rogowski, *Z. Naturforsch.* **21b**, 996 (1966).
(221) S. J. Cyvin, J. Brunvoll and M. Perttilä, *J. Mol. Struct.* **17**, 17 (1973).
(222) R. A. Bonham, L. S. Bartell and D. A. Kohl, *J. Am. Chem. Soc.* **81**, 4765 (1959).
(223) L. S. Bartell and D. A. Kohl, *J. Chem. Phys.* **39**, 3097 (1963).
(224) R. L. Livingston, C. Lurie and C. N. R. Rao, *Nature* (*London*) **185**, 458 (1960).
(225) W. Zeil, J. Haase and M. Dakkouri, *Z. Naturforsch.* **22a**, 1644 (1967).
(226) B. Beagley, D. P. Brown and J. J. Monaghan, *J. Mol. Struct.* **4**, 233 (1969).
(227) S. J. Cyvin, *Indian J. Pure Appl. Phys.* **9**, 1027 (1971).
(228) R. Stølevik, *Acta Chem. Scand., Ser. A* **28**, 327 (1974).
(229) R. Stølevik, *Acta Chem. Scand., Ser. A* **28**, 455 (1974).
(230) R. Stølevik, *Acta Chem. Scand., Ser. A* **28**, 612 (1974).
(231) K. Kuchitsu, *Bull. Chem. Soc. Jpn* **32**, 748 (1959).
(232) R. A. Bonham and L. S. Bartell, *J. Am. Chem. Soc.* **81**, 3491 (1959).
(233) R. L. Hilderbrandt and J. D. Wieser, *J. Mol. Struct.* **15**, 27 (1973).
(234) T. Iijima, *Bull. Chem. Soc. Jpn* **45**, 1291 (1972).
(235) S. J. Cyvin and B. Vizi, *Acta Chim. Acad. Sci. Hung.* **64**, 357 (1970).
(236) I. L. Andresen, S. J. Cyvin, B. Larsen and O. Tørset, *Acta Chem. Scand.* **25**, 473 (1971).
(237) B. N. Cyvin and S. J. Cyvin, *Acta Chem. Scand.* **27**, 1740 (1973).
(238) R. Stølevik, *Acta Chem. Scand., Ser. A* **28**, 299 (1974).
(239) P. E. Farup and R. Stølevik, *Acta Chem. Scand., Ser. A* **28**, 680 (1974).
(240) P. E. Farup and R. Stølevik, *Acta Chem. Scand., Ser. A* **28**, 871 (1974).
(241) L. Fernholt and R. Stølevik, *Acta Chem. Scand., Ser. A* **28**, 963 (1974).
(242) J. P. Johnsen and R. Stølevik, *Acta Chem. Scand., Ser. A* **29**, 201 (1975).
(243) J. P. Johnsen and R. Stølevik, *Acta Chem. Scand., Ser. A* **29**, 457 (1975).
(244) L. Fernholt and R. Stølevik, *Acta Chem. Scand., Ser. A* **29**, 651 (1975).
(245) Y. Morino and K. Kuchitsu, *J. Chem. Phys.* **28**, 175 (1958).
(246) A. L. Andreassen and S. H. Bauer, *J. Chem. Phys.* **56**, 3802 (1972).
(247) H. Kakubari, T. Iijima and M. Kimura, *Bull. Chem. Soc. Jpn* **48**, 1984 (1975).
(248) T. Iijima, *Bull. Chem. Soc. Jpn* **46**, 2311 (1973).
(249) L. S. Bartell, S. Fitzwater and W. J. Hehre, *J. Chem. Phys.* **63**, 3042 (1975).
(250) K. L. Gallaher, A. Yokozeki and S. H. Bauer, *J. Phys. Chem.* **78**, 2389 (1974).
(251) R. C. Ivey, P. D. Schulze, T. L. Leggett and D. A. Kohl, *J. Chem. Phys.* **60**, 3174 (1974).
(252) J. C. Decius, *J. Chem. Phys.* **21**, 1121 (1953).

(253) J. C. Decius, *J. Chem. Phys.* **38**, 241 (1963).
(254) S. J. Cyvin, *Spectrosc. Lett.* **8**, 399 (1975).
(255) J. Linderberg and Y. Öhrn, *Propagators in Quantum Chemistry*, Academic Press, London and New York, 1973.
(256) Ø. Ra, *J. Mol. Struct.* **12**, 471 (1972).
(257) M. I. Davis, *Electron Diffraction in Gases*, Dekker, New York, 1971.
(258) V. S. Kukina, *Opt. Spectrosk.* **26**, 111 (1969).
(259) I. M. Mills, *J. Mol. Spectrosc.* **5**, 334 (1960).
(260) T. Miyazawa and J. Overend, *Bull. Chem. Soc. Jpn* **39**, 1410 (1966).
(261) I. Hargittai, J. Tremmel and Gy. Schultz, *J. Mol. Struct.* **26**, 116 (1975).
(262) J. Tremmel, A. A. Ivanov, Gy. Schultz, I. Hargittai, S. J. Cyvin and A. Eriksson, *Chem. Phys. Lett.* **23**, 533 (1973).
(263) Zs. Molnár, Gy. Schultz, J. Tremmel and I. Hargittai, *Acta Chim. Acad. Sci. Hung.* **86**, 223 (1975).
(264) L. S. Mayants, *Dokl. Akad. Nauk SSSR* **151**, 624 (1963).
(265) L. S. Mayants, *Zh. Fiz. Khim.* **38**, 623 (1964).
(266) L. S. Mayants, *Dokl. Akad. Nauk SSSR* **202**, 124 (1972).
(267) L. S. Mayants and S. J. Cyvin, *J. Mol. Struct.* **17**, 1 (1973).

AUTHOR INDEX

A

Abbas, M. M., 32 (205, 206); *62*
Abelson, J. N., 272 (68); *275*
Abhivantanaporn, P., 124 (161); 125 (161); *148*
Abrams, R. L., 10 (40, 41, 43); 30 (40); 32 (40); 39 (40); 55 (341); *58*; *66*
Adams, D. M., 133 (176); 138 (176); *148*; 209 (158); 210 (158); *216*
Adams, W. J., 352 (196); *363*
Aggarwal, R. L., 12 (65); 13 (67); 14 (67); 19 (115); 20 (115, 124, 125); 21 (124, 125); 23 (145); *58*; *60*
Ahmed, S. A., 38 (235); *63*
Ahrens, H., 2 (11); *57*
Albano, V. G., 73 (28); 82 (28); *145*
Albrecht, A. C., 226 (39); 227 (37, 38, 39); 228 (39); 239 (39); *274*
Alcock, A. J., 10 (45); *58*
Aldridge, J. P., 30 (187); 35 (231); 37 (260); 38 (239, 248); 39 (254, 257, 260); 40 (276); 41 (231); 43 (276); *62*; *63*; *64*
Alekseev, N. V., 338 (103); 352 (191, 192, 198); 353 (198); *361*; *363*
Alfheim, I., 323 (6); 341 (143); 343 (6, 143, 165, 166, 167); *359*, *362*; *363*
Aliev, M. R., 302 (177); 303 (177, 181); *318*; *319*
Allariv, F., 9 (35); 41 (35); 55 (342); *58*; *66*
Allen, M. C., 88 (74); 91 (74); 115 (74); 117 (74); 119 (74); 120 (74); 121 (74); 122 (74); 139 (74); *146*
Allwood, R. L., 15 (82, 83); *59*
Almenningen, A., 333 (65, 66, 67); 336 (97, 98); 338 (119); 343 (158); 346 (175, 180); 352 (194); 353 (208, 217); *360*; *361*; *362*; *363*; *364*
Almond, V., 309 (268, 269); *321*
Alti, G. de, 334 (72); *360*

Altona, C., 353 (207); *364*
Ambartsumyan, R. V., 15 (85); 17 (99); *59*
Amberg, C. H., 115 (133); 117 (133); *147*
Amiot, C., 29 (174); *61*
Anantarama Sarma, Y., 331 (46); *360*
Andersen, B., 336 (95); *361*
Andersen, P., 324 (20); 327 (20); 338 (121); 340 (121); 342 (154); 353 (204); 357 (121); *359*, *362*; *363*
Anderson, J. R., 70 (24); 76 (24); *145*
Anderson, T. G., 279 (21); 286 (21); *315*
Andersson, S., 69 (23); 86 (23, 59); 87 (23, 59); 89 (23, 59); 95 (23, 59); 141 (23); 142 (23); *145*, *146*
Andreassen, A. L., 332 (62); 338 (108); 340 (62); 342 (152); 354 (246); *360*; *361*; *362*; *364*
Andreev, B. A., 303 (192); *319*
Andresen, I. L., 354 (236); *364*
Andresen, U., 303 (184); 309 (259); *319*; *320*
Ansorge, J., 88 (78); *146*
Antcliffe, G. A., 5 (19); 31 (19, 194); 40 (19, 271); 41 (194); 45 (271); *57*; *62*; *64*
Antipov, B. A., 11 (54); 38 (54); *58*
Apatin, V. M., 17 (99); *59*
Appt, W., 16 (92); *59*
Ard, J. S., 218 (2, 3); 232 (2, 3); *273*
Argano, E. S., 108 (107); 110 (107); 130 (107); *147*
Arié, E., 10 (39); *58*
Arimondo, E., 36 (234); *63*
Aronson, J. R., 39 (252, 253); *63*
Asprey, L. B., 23 (144); *60*
Astrup, E. E., 342 (154); *362*
Aten, C. F., 340 (130); *362*
Atkins, P. W., 171 (100); *215*
Atkinson, V., 353 (205, 206); *364*
Atwood, J. G., 32 (200); *62*

McClatchey, R. A., 26 (156); 39 (266); 55 (266, 341); *61*; *64*; *66*

McClellan, A. L., 149 (2); 152 (2); 153 (2); 154 (2); *213*

McCoy, E. F., 90 (69); 132 (69); *146*

McCubbin, T. K., 28 (173); *61*

McDonald, D. G., 27 (160); 43 (160); *61*

Macdonald, J. N., 277 (5); 282 (5); 291 (5); 308 (242); 309 (268, 269); 311 (287); *314*; *320*; *321*

McDonald-Ordzie, P. E., 222 (32); *274*

McDowell, R. S., 2 (13, 15); 3 (13); 23 (144); 35 (231); 38 (239, 241, 247, 248); 40 (13, 247, 273, 274, 275, 276, 277, 278); 41 (231); 42 (247); 43 (13, 15, 273, 274, 276, 277, 278); 44 (273, 274, 275, 278); 50 (278); *57*; *60*; *63*; *64*

McElroy, J. H., 34 (210); *62*

McGraw, R., 159 (62); *214*

McGurk, J., 296 (146); *318*

McGurk, J. C., 35 (230); 39 (230); 40 (230); 41 (230); *63*

Mack, K. M., 287 (82); 306 (82); *316*

McKeown, D., 35 (230); 39 (230); 40 (230); 41 (230); *63*

McKinney, P. M., 308 (255); *320*

McLaren, R. A., 34 (213, 214, 215, 216); *62*

McLean, M., 116 (140); *147*

McMahon, S. A., 292 (129); *317*

McManus, J. C., 88 (68); 90 (68); 97 (68); 98 (68); 108 (68, 109); 109 (68, 109); 119 (68); 120 (68); 121 (68); 122 (68); 123 (68); 124 (68); 125 (68); 126 (68); 127 (68); 129 (68); 132 (68); *146*; *147*

McNeish, A., 39 (262); 40 (262); *64*

Mackrodt, P., 88 (77); 90 (77); 94 (77); 130 (77); *146*

Madden, W. G., 159 (62); *214*

Mäder, H., 294 (139); 309 (260); *318*; *320*

Madey, J. M. J., 23 (151, 152); *61*

Maeda, K., 322 (2); *359*

Maeda, S., 150 (28); 191 (28); *214*; 304 (203, 204); *319*

Maes, S., 280 (31); 304 (195); *315*; *319*

Magdesieva, N. N., 313 (292); *321*

Magnusson, L. B., 171 (97, 98); 176 (97, 98); *215*

Magyar, J. A., 53 (327); *65*

Maier, H., 7 (27); *57*

Mair, H. J., 338 (104); *361*

Maker, P. D., 39 (259); 40 (269); 46 (269); *64*

Malathy Devi, V., 330 (43); *360*

Mallinson, P. D., 292 (123); 306 (226); *317*; *320*

Malloy, T. B., 310 (281); 311 (281); 313 (294, 295); *321*

Mamleev, A. H., 313 (292); *321*

Mann, B., 170 (90); *215*

Manson, E. L., 284 (61, 62, 63); 298 (61, 62, 63); *316*

Mansy, S., 222 (31); *274*

Maremnikov, S. I., 23 (148); *61*

Margolis, J. S., 39 (261); 45 (261); 56 (261); *64*

Mariam, S., 331 (46); 334 (73); *360*

Markov, P., 351 (189); *363*

Marsden, C. J., 292 (133); *317*

Martin, G. A., 77 (36); 79 (36); 80 (48); 81 (36, 48); 82 (36, 48); 84 (36); 88 (36, 48, 78, 81); 90 (48); 91 (36, 78, 81); 92 (36); 93 (36); 94 (81); 101 (36); 129 (48); 130 (81); 133 (36); 136 (36); 137 (36); 138 (36); 142 (36); *145*; *146*

Martin, J. M., 21 (134); 22 (134); 39 (134); 48 (134); *60*

Martin, R., 108 (116); 111 (116); 130 (116); 131 (116); *147*

Marx, G., 88 (77); 90 (77); 94 (77); 130 (77); *146*

Mason, R., 74 (32); 75 (32); *145*

Matarrese, L. M., 29 (178); *61*

Mathew, M. P., 330 (39, 43); 332 (52); *360*

Mathier, E., 308 (252); *320*

Mathieu, J. P., 99 (90); 101 (90); 133 (90); 136 (90); *146*

Mathieu, M. V., 80 (45); 82 (51); 90 (51); 97 (51); 98 (51); 108 (51, 112, 116); 109 (51); 111 (51, 112, 116); 120 (51); 122 (51); 123 (51); 124 (51); 130 (51); 131 (51, 116); 132 (51); *145*; *147*

Matsumura, C., 279 (23); 284 (64); 285 (23); 287 (90); 292 (23); 293 (23, 137); *315*; *316*; *318*

Matsumura, K., 279 (23); 285 (23); 292 (23); 293 (23); *315*

Maurel, R., 108 (118); 111 (118); 127 (118); 128 (118); *147*

Mayants, L. S., 358 (264, 265, 266, 267); *365*

Max, E., 56 (351); *66*

Mazur, U., 290 (118); 291 (119); 313 (118); *317*

Mecke, R., 172 (103); 176 (103); 178 (103); *215*

Welti, D., 308 (252); *320*
Weston, R. E., 202 (141); 209 (141); *216*
Whalley, E., 149 (26, 27); 159 (61, 63, 64); 176 (61); 188 (126, 127); 189 (26, 132); 192 (26, 61, 126); 193 (63); 195 (26); 196 (64); 205 (26); *214*; *216*
Wharton, L., 35 (227); *63*
Wherrett, B. S., 12 (59); 15 (82); *58*; *59*
Whiffen, D. H., 299 (161); 303 (189); *318*; *319*
Whitford, B. G., 28 (167); *61*
Whitmer, J. C., 346 (187); 348 (187); *363*
Whitney, W. T., 10 (47); 11 (48); *58*
Wiegeler, W., 324 (18); *359*
Wiesendanger, E., 33 (208); *62*
Wieser, J. D., 353 (209); 354 (233); *364*
Wilcox, C. F., 340 (137); *362*; 353 (212); *364*
Williams, D., 149 (25); *213*
Williamson, W. G., 256 (59); *275*
Willis, R. F., 127 (167); 128 (167); 129 (167); *148*
Wilson, E. B., 167 (84); *215*; 278 (17); 310 (276, 279); 311 (276, 279, 282); *315*; *321*; 323 (5); 324 (5); 325 (5); 358 (5); *359*
Winnewisser, B. P., 305 (205, 206, 207, 208); *319*
Winnewisser, G., 286 (71, 72); 288 (94, 95, 96); 289 (96); 294 (94, 95, 96); 309 (94, 95, 96); *316*; *317*
Winnewisser, M., 286 (71, 72); 302 (176, 178); 305 (205, 206, 207, 208, 213, 214); *316*; *318*; *319*
Winther, F., 305 (205); *319*
Wojtczak, J., 120 (156); 122 (156); 123 (156); 124 (156); 131 (156); *148*
Wolga, G. J., 35 (233); 39 (233); 40 (233); *63*
Wollrab, J. E., 277 (2); *314*
Wong, P. T. T., 159 (61, 64); 176 (61); 192 (61); 193 (64); *214*
Wood, R. A., 12 (59); 15 (82); 39 (262); 40 (262, 270); *58*; *59*; *64*
Woods, P. T., 29 (177); *61*
Woods, R. C., 279 (18, 19, 20, 21); 283 (52, 53); 286 (20, 21); 294 (140); 308 (140); *315*; *316*; *318*

Wright, N., 157 (56); *214*
Wrobel, J. S., 31 (194); 41 (194); *62*
Wurrey, C. J., 308 (241, 253); *320*
Wyatt, R., 16 (96, 97); 20 (120); *59*; *60*
Wynne, J. J., 22 (137, 138); *60*
Wyss, H. R., 201 (136); 208 (144); 209 (136); *216*

Y

Yajima, T., 20 (111); *60*
Yamada, C., 295 (141); *318*
Yamada, K., 302 (176); 305 (208, 213); *318*; *319*
Yamamoto, T., 271 (63); *275*
Yang, A. C., 123 (159); 124 (159); 137 (159); *148*
Yang, K. H., 20 (123); 21 (123); *60*
Yarborough, J. M., 16 (88, 89); *59*
Yaniv, M., 272 (65); *275*
Yariv, A., 17 (105); 18 (105); *59*
Yates, D. J. C., 88 (71); 90 (71); 91 (71); 92 (72); 94 (71); 118 (144); 119 (144); 133 (71); 136 (71); 138 (144); *146*; *148*
Yates, J. T., 88 (70); 91 (70); 92 (70); 94 (70); 127 (168); 128 (168); 129 (168); 130 (70); 131 (168); 136 (70); *146*; *148*
Yeung, K. F., 40 (269); 46 (269); *64*
Yokozeki, A., 353 (210, 213); 354 (250); *364*
Yoshimizu, N., 304 (203); *319*
Young, J. F., 18 (107); *59*
Young, R. P., 132 (174); *148*
Yu, T. J., 262 (62); *275*
Yusek, R., 53 (331); *66*

Z

Zadregil, S., 272 (68); *275*
Zare, R. N., 35 (226); *63*
Zebelman, D. L., 338 (111); *361*
Zeil, W., 310 (274); *321*; 354 (225); *364*
Zerbi, G., 331 (48); *360*
Zernike, F., 20 (116); *60*
Zuev, V. E., 11 (54); 38 (54); *58*
Zumbrunn, R., 39 (258); 54 (258); *64*

FORMULA INDEX

SUBJECT INDEX

A

Acetaldehyde, 310, 341
Acetic acid, 343
Acetone, 175, 341
Acetonitrile, 172, 175, 177, 182, 303, 343
Acetophenone, 175
Acetylene, 329–333
Acetyl fluoride, 292
Acetyl iodide, 292
Acoustic detector, 278
Acrolein, 249, 256
Acrylic acid, 309
Acrylonitrile, 335, 336
Actinomycin D, 270
Adenine, 219, 222, 263–267
β-Adenosine-5′-phosphoric acid, 219
Adenosine triphosphate, 272
Adenylic acid, 220
Adiabatic expansion, 35
ADP, 219, 240
Adsorption, 70–77, 83–131, 104, 106
Albrecht term, 226, 227, 239
Allene, 336, 337
Alloy, 80, 129
Allylamine, 299, 312
Alumina, 67, 68, 90, 94, 99, 100, 109, 110, 112, 116–134
Aluminium, 89
Amine, 80, 130
2-Aminopyrimidine, 306
Ammonia, 14, 15, 29, 34, 40, 46, 47, 55, 56, 119, 130, 305
Ammonium dihydrogen phosphate (ADP), 219, 240
3′-5′-c-AMP, 265
5′-AMP, 266
t-Amyl alcohol, 177
Anharmonicity, 149, 154–156, 173, 177, 212

Aniline, 229, 306
Anisole, 175
Anthracene, 346–349, 350
Anticodon, 271
Argon, 21, 54, 119, 122, 170, 173, 174
Asymmetric rotor, 292
Atmospheric studies, 54–56
Auger spectroscopy, 131

B

Band, analysis, 36–44
Band, shape, 164
Band fitting, 163
Bandwidth, 185–187, 194–196
Barium, 16
Barium monosulphide, 284
Barrier height, 307
Base residue, 218, 219
Bastiansen–Morino shrinkage effect, 327, 357, 358
Benzaldehyde, 175
Benzene, 130, 172, 174, 232–235, 249, 251, 262, 291, 301, 334, 344–346
Benzonitrile, 175
Benzotrifluoride, 308
Benzvalene, 338
Biallenyl, 336
Bicycloheptene, 338
Bicyclo[2,2,0]hexa-2,5-diene, 293
Bicyclo[2,1,0]-pentene, 338
Biphenylene, 346, 348, 350
Bismuth monohalides, 284
Boltzmann distribution, 279
Boltzmann factor, 164, 285
Boric acid, 324
Born-Oppenheimer adiabatic approximation, 225
Bremsstrahlung radiation, 23